I0802665

SHADOW BEFORE THE FLAME

SHADOW BEFORE THE FLAME

THE *HINDENBURG* DISASTER AND THE PRELUDE TO WAR

CATHERINE GRACE KATZ

VIKING

VIKING
An imprint of Penguin Random House LLC
1745 Broadway, New York, NY 10019
penguinrandomhouse.com

Grateful acknowledgment is made for permission to print excerpts of letters by Burtis J. Dolan from the collection of the Dolan family.

Image credits may be found on pages 467–68.

Designed by Christina Nguyen

LIBRARY OF CONGRESS CONTROL NUMBER PERMALINK:
https://lccn.loc.gov/2026006339

ISBN 9780593832189 (hardcover)
ISBN 9780593832196 (ebook)

Printed in the United States of America
1st Printing

The authorized representative in the EU for product safety and compliance is Penguin Random House Ireland, Morrison Chambers, 32 Nassau Street, Dublin D02 YH68, Ireland, https://eu-contact.penguin.ie.

For my family, and for all the families who have so generously shared their stories with me

It is easy for us to assume that as the result of modern science "we have conquered nature," that nature is now confined to beaches for children and to national parks where the few remaining grizzly bears have been shot with tranquilizers and removed to above the timberline, supposedly for their safety and our own. But we should be prepared for the possibility . . . that the terror of the universe has not yet fossilized and the universe has not run out of blowups.

—NORMAN MACLEAN, *YOUNG MEN AND FIRE* (1992)

CONTENTS

1936

1937

1938

AFTER

1936

CHAPTER 1

Berlin, Germany: April 16, 1936

In the vast dining room of the American ambassador's residence in Berlin, William Shirer sat down to lunch. Crimson tapestries from a bygone era hung down from the dining room walls, serving as a reminder that it was not so long ago that giant red banners had been nothing more than decoration the wealthy used to illustrate their fortunes. These luxurious fabrics long had the effect of dampening the sound of whispered conversations in shadowy corners, whether those of timeless love affairs or, more recently, of political dissent, which had grown more dangerous with every passing month.

Since moving to Berlin as a correspondent for William Randolph Hearst's syndicated Universal Service in 1934, Shirer had observed that this house had increasingly become a haven for those who sought to speak freely in Hitler's nation. Shortly after Shirer arrived in Berlin, the Nazi Party had declared it illegal to make derogatory statements about its leaders in public. But in the ambassador's dining room, where visitors were shielded by the American eagle staring out from its plaque on the iron fence surrounding the property, subversive sentiments found a welcome audience, as Shirer was once again witnessing that afternoon.

Compared with the grand affairs of state, the day's luncheon was a humble affair. At thirty-two, Shirer was perhaps the least distinguished and youngest guest at the table, though his prematurely balding head and partial blindness might have suggested otherwise. (There was little Shirer could do about the baldness, but the blindness was his own fault, a result of misadventure on an Austrian ski slope.) Still, for a young man from the American Midwest who had worked his way across the ocean to Paris on a cattle boat, the luncheon was sufficiently cosmopolitan. Alongside Shirer, those at the table included the American ambassador, William Dodd, one of his deputies, and several other American journalists, among them fellow Hearst correspondent Karl von Wiegand, a veteran reporter of the Great War. Von Wiegand had been the first foreign correspondent to take Hitler seriously over a decade earlier, introducing him to American readers as the "German Mussolini" a year before his failed coup in the 1923 Beer Hall Putsch. "Hitler has the earmarks of a leader," von Wiegand had written. "Whether it will be a band or a great movement, only the future will reveal. . . . There is fear that Hitler may someday proclaim himself dictator of Bavaria." If only that were all he had desired.

The lunch was a send-off of sorts for the day's guest of honor, Dr. Hugo Eckener, a sixty-seven-year-old, white-haired German man thickened by middle age, the long, rectangular shape of his face accentuated by a goatee. Though he looked the part of a philosophy professor, Eckener was actually the most daring, experienced, and successful airship captain on the planet, and he was about to embark upon the first transatlantic flight to North America aboard Germany's brand-new zeppelin, the *LZ-129 Hindenburg*.

The man at the helm of the zeppelin enterprise was as unique as the great machines he flew. Originally from the city of Flensburg, on the Danish border, Eckener had stumbled into the nascent airship industry as a sometime journalist himself just after the turn of the century. He had earned his PhD in the innovative field of behavioral psychology from the University of Leipzig, after which he moved to Friedrichshafen, a city in southwestern Germany situated on a glassy lake called the Bodensee, in pursuit of peaceful tranquility for his writing and studies. In Friedrichshafen, he contributed pieces to the *Frankfurter Zeitung*, including stories about early airship demonstration flights back when the inventor of rigid airships, Count (or *Graf* in German) Ferdinand von Zeppelin, flew his rudimentary contraptions over the Bodensee. Though Eckener was not initially impressed with the slow, sausage-like dirigibles, by 1909 he had been recruited to work for Zeppelin's company as a publicist, using his understanding of the connection between aesthetics and social psychology to sell airships to both the German and the international public. In time, Eckener trained as an airship captain, eventually becoming even more skilled at the controls than the old count himself. After Zeppelin died in 1917, Eckener took over as head of the Luftschiffbau Zeppelin company.

Though Germany had used zeppelins to bomb cities like London and Paris during the Great War, rapid advancements in the capabilities of heavier-than-air craft, or airplanes, quickly rendered their lighter-than-air cousins obsolete as weapons. By war's end, it was clear that the airship's future lay in the domain of civilian and scientific aviation. While anti-German sentiment still ran high in places like Britain and the United States in the 1920s, Eckener believed the postwar zeppelins could help "[attain] a moral and political success for the half-ostracized German people which . . . was perhaps more important than the aeronautical benefits" of which they were capable. Suddenly, the behemoths of the sky that had briefly terrified Germany's enemies with the threat of aerial bombardment became the defeated nation's best advertisement.

In a world not far removed from the days of Shirer's youth, when he used to run out of his Chicago home to catch a rare glimpse of an automobile driving by, Eckener's zeppelins seemed the stuff of science fiction. As commander of the *LZ-127 Graf Zeppelin*, the pride of the German airship fleet, which took to the skies starting in 1928, Eckener became internationally renowned for record-setting flights across Europe, to the United States, to South America, and beyond. In August 1929, just two years after Charles Lindbergh achieved the unprecedented—and nearly suicidal—feat of flying an airplane across the Atlantic Ocean from New York to Paris, Eckener and the *Graf Zeppelin* circumnavigated the globe with a full complement of passengers and journalists on board. During its voyage, the *Graf Zeppelin* flew northeast across Europe and Asia, where passengers and crew looked down at desolate stretches of Siberia never before seen by man.

Though the U.S. stock market crashed less than two months later, triggering a global economic depression, the great silver airship symbolized the promise of a more hopeful, technologically endowed future as it flew over London's Wembley Stadium and appeared with cinematic flourish at sunset over San Francisco. In 1931, the *Graf Zeppelin* showcased its potential yet again as it commenced regular passenger service to South America and conducted a scientific expedition to the Arctic. With an international team of scientists on board to survey uncharted stretches near the North Pole, the *Graf Zeppelin* helped transform cartographic understanding of the region. Whole islands that had long appeared on maps were found to be nonexistent, while others were newly discovered.

Most remarkable of all was the fact that over the course of so many miles covered on all of these groundbreaking journeys, as well as hundreds of other commercial flights within Germany and overseas, the *Graf Zeppelin* flew with an unblemished safety record. In fact, no passenger had even been injured on a German airship since the end of the war. Meanwhile, genuine transatlantic passenger flight in an airplane remained a distant dream. Many people even saw local and domestic flights as excessively risky. In the last two years alone, airplane crashes had killed more than eight hundred people in the United States.

After proving zeppelins' capabilities time and again, Eckener was now due to return to the air at the helm of the *LZ-129 Hindenburg*, the largest aircraft ever built, in three weeks' time to establish yet another aviation first: regular commercial passenger service between Europe and the United States. In part thanks to William Randolph Hearst's sponsorship of the 1929 round-the-world flight as a publicity stunt to sell newspapers, zeppelins had become wildly popular among Americans. Eckener had even received invitations from Presidents Coolidge, Hoover, and Roosevelt to visit the White House. May 6, 1936, would mark the first of the *Hindenburg*'s ten scheduled round-trip flights between either Friedrichshafen or Frankfurt, Germany, and the Naval Air Station in Lakehurst, New Jersey, not far from New York City.

As admired as Eckener was, not just among Americans but around the world, Bill Shirer knew that, as of late, the airship captain seated at the ambassador's table had gained a more controversial reputation in his home nation, having inadvertently found himself at odds with the Nazi regime. The trouble had started four years earlier after Eckener, a political centrist, had rather innocuously spoken on a radio program in support of aging incumbent President Paul von Hindenburg. During the segment, Eckener urged Germans to set aside their postwar discontent, particularly with Germany's acute financial and economic crisis, and unite behind the president to lead them through the chaos. These comments caught the rising Nazi Party's attention, indicating to them that Eckener was inimical to their interests. Later that summer, as party officials were looking for a location to stage a massive demonstration in support of Hitler, they asked Luftschiffbau Zeppelin for use of the gigantic airship hangar in Friedrichshafen where the company built its dirigibles. Eckener had refused the request, preferring to keep his zeppelins above the overtly political fray. Unfortunately, others were insistent upon inserting the famous zeppelin captain with an international profile into the partisan arena. In 1933, a German tabloid ran a front-page spread with the inflammatory headline DANGER FOR HITLER? . . . WILL HINDENBURG BE FOLLOWED BY HITLER OR DR. ECKENER? Eckener had no intention of entering politics, but the headline propelled him further into the crosshairs of Nazi hostility as Hitler consolidated power following President Hindenburg's death in August 1934.

Though the Nazis may not have liked him, Eckener believed he faced no real danger under the new regime. His zeppelins were immensely popular, and there was no one else who could rival his technical expertise in the field. Still, it was best not to court trouble, and he had agreed to give a three-minute radio address alongside scores of other prominent Germans in a show of support for Hitler becoming president of Germany in a so-called election in August 1934. Eckener's occasional cooperation aside, Shirer still thought the airship captain was one of the "2 or 3 men—out of jail at least—with guts in this country" who had yet to totally acquiesce to the regime.

That afternoon, secure within the walls of the American ambassador's residence, Eckener held nothing back as he shared his true feelings about Germany's ruling party. He cracked one joke after another about Nazi leadership, particularly Hitler's propaganda minister, Dr. Joseph Goebbels, for whom he held "nothing but contempt." With Goebbels's sparrowlike head that seemed too large for his body, there was much to mock about the diminutive man who ran all aspects of the Reich's media empire. However, to make such statements publicly could result in the death penalty.

With the group keen to hear Eckener's insubordinate opinions, the conversation soon turned to recent political developments and the very public part the Nazis had decided the new *Hindenburg* should play in their increasingly dangerous machinations. After taking power, Hitler had pledged to respect Germany's postwar treaties and its commitment to peace in Europe after the bloodshed of the Great War. However, since March, the führer had been singing a much more bellicose tune.

The events of the last six weeks had transpired in a seemingly compressed acceleration of time. During the first week of March, the "wildest rumors" about Hitler's designs on the Rhineland, a strip of territory on Germany's border with France, began to sweep through the correspondent corps. Under the postwar peace treaties, Germany had agreed to completely demilitarize this industrial region long at the center of its clashes with France (and, ironically, as Shirer noted later, his ancestors' homeland, from which they had emigrated to the United States to "seek freedom" in the 1840s, back when the family name was *Scheurer*). However, many speculated that Hitler planned to march troops into the Rhineland after pointing to a new mutual-assistance pact between France and the Soviet Union as evidence that hostile powers intended to encircle Germany. Shirer had called his contact at the German Foreign Office to press him on the rumor of military action across the French border. His contact had categorically denied it, scoffing at the suggestion. A clash with the 400,000-man French army was a dismal prospect.

And yet, on March 7, Shirer found himself among fifty other correspondents in the press gallery at a meeting of the Reichstag, the German parliament, watching as Hitler completely upended the fragile postwar order. A "hysterical 'parliamentary' mob" leaped to their feet with rabid enthusiasm. Shirer saw hundreds of "little men with big bodies and bulging necks and cropped hair and pouched bellies" turn into "automatons," chanting "*Heil!*" nearly thirty times with their right arms outstretched, their eyes "burning with fanaticism" before their "Messiah" as Hitler announced that at that very moment, German troops were crossing into the Rhineland. To Shirer, the audience in their brown uniforms and boots seemed like "little men of clay" in Hitler's hands, their shouts almost like a perverted "college yell" on a football Saturday.

Shirer was by now all too familiar with scenes like this. He was ashamed to admit that even he had once been taken in, not by Nazism but by Hitler's oratorical power. Shortly after arriving in Berlin two years earlier, he had covered the annual Nuremberg Party Congress, then in its sixth installment. After listening to hours and hours of rousing speeches that captivated the crowd, Shirer came away assured that the führer really did want peace in Europe—so long as certain postwar grievances, some of which even reasonable people felt were legitimate, were rectified.

At that point, Shirer was, fortunately, immune to his earlier, naive misjudgments, but the parliamentary mob had lapped up the führer's every word. "Now, more than ever, we shall strive for an understanding between European peoples," Hitler insisted. "We have no territorial demands to make in Europe! . . . Germany will never break the peace." The audience erupted once more as if under a "magic spell."

When the crowd finally dispersed, Shirer and another journalist were in such a state of shock at what they had just witnessed that all they could do was stumble in dumbstruck silence to the foreign press corps's favorite watering hole, at the Hotel Adlon. However, underneath the Reichstag members' ringing cheers, Shirer thought he might have detected just a hint of "nervousness" about those 400,000 French soldiers. Evidently, those troops were also on the mind of the Wehrmacht's commander in chief, General Werner von Blomberg, who, as Shirer described, had "swung the army over to Hitler" when he became chancellor in 1933. Shirer spotted him nervously walking his two dogs that afternoon with an ashen face, fully aware that Hitler was taking an enormous gamble.

But the next morning, Shirer awoke to the realization that everyone except the führer had sorely miscalculated. "Hitler has got away with it!" the journalist wrote with shock and horror in the notes he kept as a sort of diary. "France is not marching. Instead it is appealing to the League!" The League of Nations had been President Woodrow Wilson's grand attempt to guarantee postwar peace in Europe through collective security agreements, whereby member states would intervene in the event of the threat of war. When finally faced with such a threat, however, the league simply sat on its hands for fear of further provocation, thus allowing Hitler to effectively tear up the postwar peace agreements in the blink of an eye.

It was then that Eckener and his zeppelins were thrust squarely into the center of what was potentially the most destructive geopolitical controversy that had occurred since the end of the war. To give the aggressive maneuver in the Rhineland a gloss of democratic legality, Hitler ordered new elections across Germany and a national referendum of the entire German people asking whether they approved of the military action. The Propaganda Ministry also "request[ed]" that a number of prominent Germans publicly "declare their support" and praise Hitler's cleverness. This time, when the party asked Eckener to offer an enthusiastic statement, he cheekily informed Goebbels that he was "not capable of judging [the] significance" of Hitler's actions. Unsatisfied with this response, Goebbels then instructed Eckener to take both the *Graf Zeppelin* and the just-completed *Hindenburg* up in a series of propaganda flights in support of the elections and referendum. As Shirer quickly learned, Eckener had refused. The *Hindenburg*'s engines were not fully tested and needed a full range of safety trials before its first transatlantic test voyage to Brazil four days later. More important, Eckener considered this use of his majestic airships "in bad taste" and "a sort of sacrilege."

Hitler had reportedly thrown a fit, ranting and raving that Eckener should immediately be dismissed. But Goebbels, who Shirer knew was also "howling mad," realized that with Eckener's popularity abroad, it was unwise to immediately replace him. Goebbels found a temporary solution to the problem. If Eckener would not fly the *Hindenburg*, Captain Ernst Lehmann, Eckener's second-in-command and heir apparent, would do it. Lehmann had captained hundreds of zeppelin flights over the course of more than twenty years, including one of the first aerial bombardments of a civilian area in history during a mission over Antwerp in the early days of the Great War. The forty-nine-year-old veteran had not joined the Nazi Party, but he was happy to have the new regime's support for the zeppelin program. Still, Goebbels needed to punish Eckener. As the zeppelin captain explained to his lunch companions, Goebbels had declared him persona non grata in Germany. Under no circumstances was Eckener's name to appear in the German press. American papers were even reporting that a Berlin street was being renamed from Hugo-Eckener-Allee to Adolf-Hitler-Strasse.

Despite Goebbels's gag order on all things Eckener, Hitler's propaganda chief was able to claim only a hollow victory. On the day of the referendum, high winds picked up around the airship hangar at Friedrichshafen. Surrendering to the pressure of Goebbels's directive, Lehmann allowed the crew to ignore safety protocols and begin removing the *Hindenburg* from the hangar. As the crew eased the sleek airship from its home, a great gust blew the giant dirigible sharply out of their control. The *Hindenburg*'s stern smashed into the ground, the force of the impact damaging the delicate lower fin. Technicians jumped into action and after about two hours it was airworthy once more, but it was hardly an auspicious start to the working life of the greatest zeppelin ever built.

While this debacle unfolded, Shirer was reporting on the elections and referendum, and it was becoming clear to him how skilled the Nazis were at maximizing the propaganda value of the tools at their disposal. He had recently been in Friedrichshafen and had seen the brand-new zeppelin up close. With its shimmering silver cover, which stretched over a frame more than 800 feet long and 130 feet high, Shirer had to admit that the *Hindenburg* truly was a modern "marvel of German engineering genius." Just a few days later, on March 28, he saw the new zeppelin again during the *Hindenburg* and the *Graf Zeppelin*'s seventy-four-hour cruise over Germany. Around 5:00 p.m., the two zeppelins appeared in the sky over Berlin. From the ambassador's residence, Dodd and his family watched as pieces of paper floated down toward amassed crowds, asking them to vote unanimously for "liberty, equality and peace" in support of the referendum that would bring an end to Germany's postwar humiliation. The *Hindenburg* then turned east and sailed silently and "gracefully" over Shirer's office at Dorotheenstrasse 29.

Hitler must have been pleased with the results of the referendum, which he claimed returned a vote of 99 percent approval. On the *Hindenburg*, a ballot had been taken among the crew while flying over the Rhineland. The results were even better than those on the ground.

"Goebbels hung up a new record," Eckener cracked to his lunchmates. "There were forty persons on the *Hindenburg*. Forty-two *Ja* votes were counted." The results were so good, he figured, that "next time we have an election on the ship, the vote will be 110%" in Hitler's favor.

"The sheep!" Shirer thought to himself with exasperation. How far a once-proud population had fallen.

Unfortunately, the propaganda flights were not the end of Eckener's troubles. Though Luftschiffbau Zeppelin's engineers had managed to quickly repair the *Hindenburg*'s damaged tail, small problems with the new airship had persisted in the weeks since. As Eckener explained to Ambassador Dodd, Shirer, and the others, as the zeppelin was crossing Gibraltar on its way home from its test flight to Rio de Janeiro, it had run into engine trouble. It was not so severe as to require an emergency landing—an all but impossible feat on the water—but upon arrival, he immediately sent the engines back to Daimler-Benz in Stuttgart for a full inspection. This meant the inaugural North Atlantic flight to Lakehurst, scheduled for May 6, might have to be slightly postponed. The Propaganda Ministry would be furious, but so be it. Though not usually superstitious, Eckener could not help but feel that by insisting the *Hindenburg* be used in the political charade of the Rhineland referendum, Goebbels had, "like a wicked fairy . . . conferred on her as a present in the cradle" a "bad omen" from which the ship had only narrowly escaped on the flight to South America.

Still, however tempting it was to blame all of the *Hindenburg*'s problems on Goebbels and his "bad omen," there remained one other key problem that was somewhat overshadowing this official launch of the new airship. If Eckener were to be completely honest, this problem had little to do with the Nazi regime's meddling in operations. There was a fundamental issue with the *Hindenburg*'s design—and the design of all of Germany's zeppelins that had preceded it since the turn of the century. It was a design flaw that Eckener and his engineers knew exactly how to fix and yet could do nothing about, save grounding the zeppelins entirely, which they would never do. The zeppelins were Germany's pride and joy and the technology upon which Eckener and his men had staked their entire careers.

There were only two gases that could lift a dirigible as large as the *Hin-*

denburg: hydrogen and helium. Hydrogen, the lightest gas with the greatest lifting capacity, was cheap and widely available, and it had been used in zeppelins since the very beginning despite being extremely flammable. Helium, meanwhile, was heavier and thus had less lifting capacity but was not flammable. The two gases' relative degrees of flammability clearly made helium the more attractive option, but it was not as simple as that. While helium was abundant in the atmosphere, it was a scarce resource on earth and thus inordinately expensive. The United States also had a near monopoly on helium. A sizable helium deposit had been discovered underground in the American Southwest, where it was captured as a by-product of natural gas extraction, and practically nowhere else. Even if Germany was willing and able to pay for the helium, which itself was questionable, Congress's Helium Act of 1925, which declared helium a vital natural resource and thus essential to national security, prohibited the United States from exporting any of it. This forced Germany to use flammable hydrogen as the only available alternative.

The German zeppelin men were well aware of the risks of using hydrogen, but they believed they had taken every precaution to make its use safe. For example, they had engineered the dirigibles' frames using essential properties of chemistry and physics to ensure that lightning strikes would not harm the airship, carefully used less-conductive materials to minimize the risk of sparks inside, and replaced petrol-powered engines with diesel engines. They even confiscated cigarettes, matches, and lighters on board so that no accidents could occur. Time and again, they assured passengers that their precautions had made it perfectly safe to fly on a hydrogen-filled airship.

Over the last decade, it seemed that Eckener and his men had indeed perfected the safe use of hydrogen on airships. And yet they were walking a delicate line, one that he would not address head-on, not even within the walls of the American embassy. There was a fundamental difference between taking precautions to make hydrogen as safe as possible and using a gas that simply was not flammable. Eckener and his team earnestly believed he had done everything he could to make hydrogen safe. And yet, despite the gas ostensibly being perfectly safe, Eckener was still trying to secure helium from the United States.

Talking somewhat around the crux of the issue, Eckener told Shirer and the others that, between the arrival and departure legs of the *Hindenburg's* first round-trip flight to Lakehurst, he planned to make a quick trip down to Washington. He had arranged a meeting at the White House in hopes of persuading Roosevelt to work with Congress to grant Germany an exception to the Helium Act. Eckener knew that Roosevelt had a soft spot for airships and a long-held personal interest in the technology. As assistant secretary of the navy in 1918, Roosevelt had traveled to the war front in western France, where the French operated airships on scouting missions. While he was there, they offered Roosevelt a ride on one of their small airships. For half an hour, he had flown between five hundred and one thousand feet in the air, a sensation he described as "distinctly curious," and even had a go at operating the steering and elevating mechanisms. The experience had left such a striking impression that in the early 1920s, he and several friends formed a company to advance civilian airship development. The enterprise soon fizzled, but not before Roosevelt was "horrified" to discover that his mother had flown from London to Paris in a flimsy airplane in the summer of 1921. "Wait until my dirigibles are running," he told a friend, "and then you will be able to take a form of transportation that is absolutely safe."

Eckener had his work cut out for him. Thanks to the separation of powers, Roosevelt's personal enthusiasm for airships did not mean he could snap his fingers and change Congress's law. The American helium embargo was turning into a yearslong source of frustration. However, Eckener did make it clear to the Americans around the table that while he would ideally like to secure helium, his quarrel was not with Roosevelt. It was entirely with Goebbels and the Nazi Party, whose recent hostile actions were making it even harder to convince the United States to look upon Germany with favor.

As Eckener was explaining his plans to discuss the helium issue with Roosevelt, the normally reserved Ambassador Dodd, a former University of Chicago history professor, abruptly chimed in to the conversation, "Well are you bringing Dr. Goebbels along to America?"

A look of amazement passed over Eckener as everyone paused, suspended. Dodd was a career academic, not a charming, trained diplomat, and he had a unique way of conducting business. It was obvious to Shirer, who knew Dodd well, that the ambassador was making an "awkward" and "indiscreet" crack of his own at Goebbels, but the others were clearly unsure. After an uncomfortable silence, they finally realized Dodd was attempting his own subversive joke and erupted in laughter.

All jokes aside, Eckener continued, he was perfectly willing to call the Nazis' bluff. Unless Goebbels stopped interfering and thus endangering the whole zeppelin enterprise, "there would be no flight this year across the dangerous North Atlantic."

1937

CHAPTER 2

Frankfurt, Germany: April 1937

It was a shame that politics had been the impetus for Ernst Lehmann's recent promotion to director of flight operations for the zeppelin company, for it detracted from both his real qualifications as an airshipman and his lifelong infatuation with the sleek silver giants of the sky. By the spring of 1937, he had been commanding airships for almost twenty-five years and knew all of their idiosyncrasies by heart. He was an aviator down to his core.

Like his longtime superior, Hugo Eckener, Lehmann had devoted nearly his entire adult life to the airships, joining Count Zeppelin's flourishing enterprise as a twenty-six-year-old naval engineer in 1912. He became a qualified airship pilot a year later, flying passengers aboard the old *LZ-17 Sachsen*. During the war, he commanded five different airships in raids over Britain, Belgium, and France. He even chased the enemy across Russia in hot pursuit of Grand Duke Nicholas of Russia, the czar's cousin and commander in chief of the Imperial Russian Army, whose military headquarters were on a luxurious train. Lehmann and his men had tracked the generalissimo like a "hunter trailing a wolf." When they caught up with his train, their bombs fell directly on target, but the grand duke either survived the attack or was not on board at the time, as he later appeared very much alive.

Small and svelte with an impish smile and nearly unaccented English,

Lehmann had quickly risen through the zeppelin company after the war, both as a captain and in its international business operations, solidifying his position as Eckener's second-in-command. In fact, in recent months, he had spent many more hours at the controls than Eckener, who was still part of the company but, thanks to his disagreements with the Nazi Party, had been promoted to the largely symbolic role of chairman and out of day-to-day functions. Even before these leadership changes, it was the charming Lehmann whom the company often trotted out to speak with important passengers and the international media. He had also beaten Eckener to write and publish a memoir about his lifetime of thrilling experiences aboard the zeppelins. The book, *Auf Luftpatrouille und Weltfahrt: Erlebnisse eines Zeppelinführers in Krieg und Frieden* (On air patrol and world travel: Experiences of a zeppelin leader in war and peace), which he had written with his longtime friend, author and journalist Leonhard Adelt, had come out a year earlier. It was so popular that an American publisher had already commissioned an English-language translation, though under a more benign title, *Zeppelin: The Story of Lighter-Than-Air Craft*. Lehmann and Adelt had a meeting in New York the following week to discuss business with that publisher, Longmans, Green & Co., and to present them with a copy of the manuscript for translation.

On that trip to New York the following week, Lehmann would mark a quarter century as an airshipman, and the *Hindenburg* would officially commence its second full season of passenger service between Germany and the United States. As with the ten successful round-trip flights the year before, the *Hindenburg* would fly to the Naval Air Station in Lakehurst, New Jersey, only this time, all of the trips would depart from the growing airport in Frankfurt for the sake of passenger convenience and more favorable elevation, rather than from Friedrichshafen in the South, where the zeppelins were built. Despite this move, only about half the passenger tickets for this first flight of the year had been sold. Surely there would be some last-minute bookings. Still, how any tickets were ever left unsold was perplexing. Yes, tickets were expensive, but among those who could afford them, who would not want to fly on a zeppelin, even just for the thrill?

Zeppelins and their future possibilities occupied practically every space in Lehmann's brain. As another longtime friend and colleague, American naval airship commander Charles Rosendahl, described, Lehmann had a "progressive vision . . . wandering far ahead, reflecting on the part which his beloved airships were to play in man's romantic conquest of atmospheric oceans." Lehmann's "whole existence was bound up in a great ideal—the perfection of the Zeppelin principle of airships for the commercial transportation of the peoples of the world." To fellow German airship captain Hans von Schiller, who had served with Lehmann since the war and now commanded the *Graf Zeppelin*, Lehmann was "a true artist," his mind "bubbling over" with ideas. Von Schiller found sketches of airship designs everywhere Lehmann had been, on nautical charts and in the margins of books, each design tried in myriad alternatives until he found his ideal concept.

For Lehmann, airships were not simply a means of transporting people from place to place. As he wrote in his memoir, there was something magical about how, on westbound journeys to South America, zeppelins "defrauded nature" as they "flew out of the autumn and into the spring," challenging the steady forward march of time as the crew set their onboard clocks back as they ventured across the Atlantic. Remarkable as that was, zeppelins represented something even more important than the next step in man's quest to conquer nature and time. To Hugo Eckener, zeppelins may have been born in Germany and perfected by German engineering, but he considered them part of a new international world order in which technology and invention rose above national origin to serve humanity at large. But to Ernst Lehmann, there was no separating zeppelins from their German roots.

Writing a memoir had allowed Lehmann to reflect on the remarkable place zeppelins had secured in history, and on his own part in their story. After years of condemnation and humiliation on the world stage following the Great War, the global popularity of zeppelins represented the first international embrace of something entirely German since 1914, though postwar peace agreements had nearly clipped their metaphorical wings. Following the armistice, the Treaty of Versailles had temporarily barred

Germany from building airships. Their zeppelins were given to the war's victors as reparation payments, and their hangars were put to use as soundstages for the country's nascent motion picture industry.

In the meantime, other countries tried to copy German airship technology and surge ahead. In 1919, the British dirigible *R.34* made the world's very first transatlantic flight in an airship, a remarkable voyage between Scotland and Long Island that nearly ended in disaster several times. Though the Brits had beaten the Germans to a long-sought milestone, their design was almost an exact replica of a German zeppelin shot down over Britain during the war. Meanwhile, the U.S. Navy started its own airship program and, in 1923, launched the USS *Shenandoah*, also modeled after a German airship but filled with helium from American domestic reserves unavailable to other nations. However, the U.S. Navy quickly recognized Germany's superior engineering and contracted with Luftschiffbau Zeppelin to form a joint venture with the Goodyear Tire & Rubber Company in Akron, Ohio, which had been constructing nonrigid pressure airships out of rubberized material since 1911. Under the new agreement, Luftschiffbau Zeppelin would help the United States manufacture two naval airships, the USS *Akron* and the USS *Macon*. Luftschiffbau Zeppelin soon found other ways around the armistice's ban on building airships. They negotiated with the United States to build a new zeppelin, the *LZ-126*, to be given to the United States as a reparation payment. When it was finished in October 1924, Eckener and his men flew it across the Atlantic to deliver it, with Lehmann serving as Eckener's deputy.

Thinking back, Lehmann recognized that something profoundly changed the moment the *LZ-126* moored at the Naval Air Station in Lakehurst on that fall day over a decade earlier. Lehmann heard "such shouting and hurrahing that [he] couldn't hear [himself] talking." Congratulations poured in from across the country. President Coolidge lauded the significance of the delivery of the *LZ-126*, rechristened the USS *Los Angeles*, as a "brilliant feat" that had "reaffirmed" relations between the two countries. Journalist Karl von Wiegand went even further: With the USS *Los Angeles*, Germany had "rehabilitated herself in the eyes of the world."

Four years later, on October 15, 1928, the *Graf Zeppelin* completed the world's first scheduled commercial passenger flight across the Atlantic

Ocean and inspired a different level of enthusiasm altogether. By then, postwar zeppelin construction restrictions had been lifted, and the American people were in the throes of aviation mania thanks to Charles Lindbergh's solo, nonstop New York–to–Paris flight the prior May. Over 111 hours and 44 minutes, Eckener and Lehmann steered the airship through storms that raged across the ocean, arriving safely in New Jersey before an uproarious American public. If the delivery of the USS *Los Angeles* was about German rehabilitation, this flight was pure celebration. The age of transatlantic passenger flight had truly arrived. Decorated automobiles drove the crew up Broadway to New York's city hall, and crowds greeted them with "spontaneous enthusiasm" wherever they went. As Lehmann could still remember, "factory sirens were blowing, locomotive and steamer whistles shrilled out; the automobiles blew their horns, and a veritable storm of confetti and paper streamers fell from the windows of skyscrapers."

Wherever the *Graf Zeppelin* went, breaking new ground with practically every flight, it was met with rabid excitement. When the silver giant arrived in Tokyo during its 1929 round-the-world journey, zeppelin fever gripped the Japanese even more fiercely than it had the Americans, as the Japanese associated anything German with the zenith of technological achievement. They used German scientific advancements as a yardstick against which to measure their own progress, whether in shipbuilding, aviation, or the pharmaceutical industry, where certain unscrupulous merchants would label Japanese drugs as German to increase sales. During their four days in Tokyo, Lehmann felt that a genuine "bridge of sympathy" had formed between "Germans and the sons of the Far East."

Thrilling as it was to hear foreign crowds' adulation, it could not touch what Lehmann knew the airships meant to the German people and to their sense of honor. As German President Paul von Hindenburg had proclaimed, "The heart of all Germany beat proudly for the airship." Whenever it appeared in the sky above German towns and cities, cheers would erupt, the gathered masses drowning out the *Graf Zeppelin*'s motors. Across the country, zeppelin-themed merchandise filled shops: zeppelin-shaped piggy banks and cocktail shakers, pocket knives and pens, even mudguard ornaments for bicycles.

By the early 1930s, as German zeppelins soared, other nations' airships had met with spectacularly public disasters. British airships had jumped out to a short-lived lead, inspiring hopes of connecting the far-flung reaches of the British Empire by air. But in 1921, a British naval airship, the *R.38*, broke apart mid-flight, killing forty-four, while Britain's glamorous passenger airship, the *R.101*, crashed in France in 1930 en route to Karachi, killing forty-eight. In both instances, the accidents were due to inherent design flaws, poor operational decisions, and weather conditions. In 1923, the French-operated airship *Dixmude*, originally a German zeppelin given to the French in reparations, exploded off the coast of Sicily, killing all fifty-two on board. The lack of survivors made it impossible to explain the cause of the accident. In 1926, the Italian airship *Norge* became the first aircraft verified to have reached the North Pole, but two years later, its sister ship, *Italia*, fatally crashed on a subsequent Arctic expedition after encountering severe weather conditions, killing half the crew. The two American-built, helium-filled naval airships were felled by storms, the USS *Akron* in 1933, killing seventy-three, and the USS *Macon* two years later, though the death toll was far lower at just two. To be sure, Germany's early airship records were far from perfect, and several zeppelins were lost during the war, but since the armistice, Germany's zeppelins had performed flawlessly. No passenger had suffered so much as a scratch. "Of what other means of transportation could the same be said?" Lehmann had queried in his book. Post-war Germany seemed to have engineered the perfect airship.

Though the German zeppelins' engineering was second to none, that came with a steep price tag that Lehmann now had to confront in his new role as director of flight operations. Despite its immense size, the *Graf Zeppelin* could carry just twenty passengers, and profitability remained heavily dependent on transatlantic airmail contracts. The Weimar government had also failed to sufficiently invest in zeppelins' future technological development, citing Germany's bleak economic conditions. Lehmann frustratedly felt this justification was pretextual for a lack of foresight. Valuable time had been lost in airship development and construction, which threatened Germany's edge in the field, and Luftschiffbau Zeppelin could not afford to build a new, state-of-the-art airship without government support.

Fortunately for the zeppelin company, Hitler's new government came to power just in time to provide the financing necessary to complete the new, larger *LZ-129 Hindenburg*. Of course, this came with strings attached. In March 1935, Luftschiffbau Zeppelin agreed to the formation of a new entity called Deutsche Zeppelin-Reederei (DZR). Technically, Luftschiffbau Zeppelin was DZR's majority shareholder and would continue to build the airships, but its entire stake in the venture was the value of its aircraft, the *Graf Zeppelin* and the not-yet-complete *Hindenburg*. They had no liquid assets and were completely reliant on the cash that Hermann Göring's Ministry of Aviation and the state airline, Deutsche Lufthansa, put up to finance operations and finish the *Hindenburg*.

When the *Hindenburg* was finally completed in 1936, it had more than two and a half times the lift capacity of the *Graf Zeppelin* and triple the passenger load. Thanks to the "empire of Adolf Hitler, who gave German aviation the strength and means to flourish," as a DZR report touted, German aviation was finally on solid footing. The industry to which Lehmann had devoted his life was finally back on track. The Nazis, it seemed, truly understood the "importance of Zeppelin airships for Germany's global reputation," as DZR's annual report announced. One publicity article even effused that "the German airship, the heritage of German creative genius, German technology, and German craftsmanship" would represent "one of Germany's best ambassadors abroad," bringing the "spirit of the new Germany to distant lands and build[ing] bridges between people." Under Göring's direction, the *Hindenburg* would be the first in a fleet of airships to operate on "highways of the air."

While the regime liked to promote its vital support for zeppelins, Lehmann and anyone else in DZR management knew that its investment in lighter-than-air aviation actually paled in comparison to the money it was pouring into heavier-than-air aviation and a fleet of modern airplanes. Göring, who had scored numerous victories as a Fokker D.VII pilot during the war, vastly preferred airplanes over airships, the latter of which he derisively referred to as "Eckener's flying sausages." (This was actually a cleverer joke than it appeared on its face. Not only did the first zeppelins look like white Bavarian sausages, but the gas cells in early airships were made of "goldbeater's skin," a material largely made up of processed animal intestine membranes.) As Reich minister of aviation, Göring instigated a rapid expansion in aircraft manufacture. Between 1933 and April 1937, Germany produced over 10,000 airplanes, compared with a single zeppelin. While more than half of these were trainers, this figure also included over 1,000 fighter planes and roughly 1,800 bombers. Throughout the spring of 1937, the Luftwaffe had been experimenting with new Heinkel He 111s and Messerschmitt Bf 109s in Spain. That very week, on April 26, the Luftwaffe's Condor Legion had bombed the town of Guernica with 100,000 pounds of ordnance. Though the number of Spanish Republican soldiers and civilians killed was disputed, ranging from the low hundreds to several thousand, the bombers had completely flattened the town, giving Göring key insights into future aerial bombing capabilities.

Overall, Lehmann took a utilitarian view toward the new government-controlled airship entity and the regime's relative investment in airships compared with airplanes. The two technologies could serve complementary purposes. Politically, Lehmann was not a critic of the new regime like Eckener, nor was he a signed-up party man like his friend and colleague Captain von Schiller, who was either a true believer or a pragmatist who saw party membership as a path to career advancement. Von Schiller had been a Nazi Party member as early as 1922, had served as leader of a local Friedrichshafen Sturmabteilung paramilitary group, known as the SA or the Brownshirts, since 1932, and made speeches on the party's behalf during a lecture tour through South America. (Von Schiller's party membership had somehow lapsed in the intervening period, and he had been rather embarrassingly rejected from full reinstatement after the party instituted a membership ban in 1933 following a surge of applications from ambitious, self-interested individuals. In his reapplication, von Schiller had obviously thought an exception to the rule would be appropriate for a zeppelin captain. He was mistaken. As the party official who returned his application and ancestry certificate informed him, no exceptions were permitted, "even by express order of the Führer.")

Aside from von Schiller, a handful of the zeppelin crew members had joined the Nazi Party. Some, like navigator Eduard Boëtius, had to join in order to take technical accreditation exams. Two of Lehmann's longtime colleagues, Captains Max Pruss and Anton Wittemann, had also joined, though their level of ideological commitment was less clear. Most of the crew had mixed feelings about the zeppelin flights to promote the 1936 referendum. They generally did not want to become propaganda instruments of the state, but on the other hand, they were glad to have the new government's financial support. The one vocal party member among the crew was the chief engineer, Rudolf Sauter, but even he was first and foremost loyal to Eckener. Sauter had a high-ranking position in the Brownshirts, and some said that when Eckener could not get what he wanted from the Reich Ministry of Aviation, he would dispatch Sauter to Berlin to use his connections to secure it for him. Overall, national politics were hardly a contentious issue within the brotherhood of airshipmen. If there was any rivalry, it was of a friendly, regional nature, with the crew's Southerners mocking the Northerners for their affinity for "smelly old fish" and the Northerners teasing the Southerners for their love of "stodge" like pasta or spaetzle.

Lehmann could not deny that Hitler's government used the zeppelins to enhance its public image. The swastika had been clearly emblazoned on the airships' tails since 1933, when aerial identification laws required that the standard of the new regime replace the old colors of imperial Germany. Even the Zeppelinfeld in Nuremberg, named for the old count after he landed one of his early airships on the vast plain outside the city, was now the site of the annual party rallies. From a brand-new grandstand designed by the führer's favorite architect, Albert Speer, and topped with a massive limestone swastika, Hitler and other party leaders addressed crowds of thousands as searchlights projected their beams straight up into the night sky, creating a magical "Cathedral of Light."

Still, for Lehmann and most of the crew, this mattered less than the tangible results the new government could deliver, both to the zeppelin company and to Germany writ large. Gone were the days of hyperinflation, when a zeppelin mechanic became a paper millionaire on payday. After years of flying over dark German factories, whose poverty the twinkling lights of nearby Rotterdam seemed to ridicule, it was satisfying to see the "endless forest of foundries and smelteries" in the industrial northern cities over which they flew—Essen, Dortmund, Bochum, and Witten—smoking once more. By the spring of 1937, with additional funding from the Reich Ministry of Aviation, two more *Hindenburg*-class airships were already in the works: the *LZ-130*, on which construction had begun, and the *LZ-131*, scheduled for completion in the fall of 1938. DZR was also discussing building a new revolving hangar so that the zeppelins would no longer be dependent on the wind blowing in the right direction at departure.

After one successful year of transatlantic operations, 1937 would be crucial for the zeppelins to cement their place in the modern sky. To prove the *Hindenburg*'s successful 1936 performance was no fluke, DZR had planned an ambitious schedule of eighteen round-trip flights, eight more than the year before, with quick turnarounds between the west- and east-bound crossings. On these eighteen voyages, Lehmann and his men would demonstrate that zeppelins were no relic of a short-lived era, even as German airplane manufacturers made great strides toward larger, faster, safer machines. Zeppelins were undoubtedly the fastest and safest means of crossing the ocean and would remain so for years to come.

As director of DZR, it was ultimately Lehmann's responsibility that the *Hindenburg* start the year on a strong note, with the captains and crews beginning as they meant to go on. Even after the last decade of sensational, record-breaking feats, it felt as though mounting pressure from rapidly improving heavier-than-air technology meant that the zeppelins had to continually justify their place in the sky. Unfortunately, for this first flight, such a start was largely out of Lehmann's hands. He would be on board the *Hindenburg*'s first flight of 1937, but not as the man at the controls.

CHAPTER 3

Nice, France: Late April 1937

For those who grew up in Chicago at the turn of the century, it was easy to assume that humanity had become invincible in the face of nature. Looking at the city, one could almost believe that man's grit, determination, and industrial ingenuity had permanently triumphed over the vast plains, transforming the landscape from one of "fatiguing monotony," as one visitor had described in 1823, into the "lightning city," as another wrote less than fifty years later. The back half of the 1800s was proof of this manifest destiny. Over just six years in the 1850s, one railroad line turned into a spiderweb of ten lines with three thousand miles of track feeding into the city. In the next decade, a billion and a half feet of wood were sold in a single year as homes and wooden sidewalks sprawled over marshland south, north, and west of Lake Michigan. By the time Chicago hosted the World's Columbian Exposition in 1893, the population had more than tripled since the city was incorporated in 1837, swelling to over a million people.

Outpacing the city's growth was the scale of its imagination, not the kind that dwelled on fantasy but rather the kind that applied practicality and pragmatism to the seemingly insurmountable challenges of scale in the proving ground of industrial dreams. Starting in the 1850s, the grade of the city was gradually raised plot by plot some four to six feet to allow sewers to be dug beneath buildings to flush away wastewater that bred disease. Engineers sometimes lifted buildings covering whole city blocks at a time, jacking up entire rows of stores and hotels off their foundations as business continued as usual with patrons and guests still inside. After several decades, they realized the sewer system was sweeping wastewater into the Chicago River and out to Lake Michigan, polluting the city's invaluable source of fresh water. In response, engineers devised a canal that reversed the course of the river, bringing fresh water not only to Chicago but also to downstream cities like St. Louis.

Of course, this rapid growth was not without setbacks and tragedy. The Great Chicago Fire of 1871 left 100,000 people homeless, killed at least 250, and wiped out the city's entire business section across four square miles. This might have served as a reminder that nature had not quite had its final say, but Chicagoans paid little heed. The opportunity to rebuild the city in the wake of the inferno allowed it to become a laboratory of urban planning. Small wooden buildings were outlawed to prevent future conflagrations, and steel-and-iron skyscrapers soon sprang from the ashes. As Louis Sullivan, the innovative architect who crafted much of the modern skyline, acknowledged about the booming Midwest, "Here . . . was power, naked power, naked as the prairies, greater than the mountains . . . greater than the lake and the prairie below, but not greater than man in his power."

Perhaps Chicago's greatest example of man's brute strength and organizational capacity prevailing over nature was its radical transformation of the levers of national consumption, particularly of meat. Though the livestock trade was once a localized industry dominated by small to midsize cattle ranches and butchers, the rapidly expanding railroad networks intersecting with Chicago created a Midwestern meatpacking metropolis. In 1863 alone, all the hogs slaughtered in Chicago would have reached from the shores of Lake Michigan to New York City if arranged in a line from tail to snout. By the turn of the century, the city had become, as Carl Sandburg wrote in his iconic poem "Chicago," the "Hog Butcher for the World," with fortunes to be made for those who could stomach it. If Indigenous tribes like the Ojibwe, Odawa, and Potawatomi, who once occupied the land where the stockyards now stood, used every part of an animal they killed out of respect for its sacrifice, the slaughterhouses made a macabre mockery of this practice. No scrap of cattle or hog was wasted where profits could be found. As Upton Sinclair famously described in *The Jungle*, packers found a use for "everything about the hog but the squeal." Hair became brushes, bones turned to buttons, blood to fertilizer, and cartilage to glue. Even spoiled meat was mixed with flour and spices and rebranded as bologna.

Three families quickly dominated the Chicago packing industry. For four decades spanning the turn of the century, they collectively butchered no fewer than thirteen million head of livestock every year. Describing the concentration of the industry in the hands of so few in his 1905 exposé, *The Greatest Trust in the World*, Charles Edward Russell wrote that the kings of meatpacking held "such a power as no other man has ever had; for who has ever controlled the food supplies of one hundred million people?" These three families were the Armours, Swifts, and Morrises, and the tall, dark, and dashing Nelson Swift Morris was a descendant of two of them.

Coming from such a world, it was little wonder that Nelson, the forty-six-year-old grandson of two of the world's greatest industrialists, had always been "attracted by new technology, inventions, experiments, explorations, adventure, perhaps even danger," as his sister would describe. Nelson was born in 1891 and raised in the Prairie Avenue neighborhood of Chicago's South Side, then the choicest part of the city where its wealthiest residents, like department store magnate Marshall Field and railcar tycoon George Pullman, built their mansions. Nelson and his three younger siblings, Edward, Ruth, and Muriel, were raised in an imposing "castle-like house of brown granite" with stables and an enormous play yard. Later, the family built an even larger Tudor mansion, this time adding a tennis court, the full spread of their property consuming half a city block. They might have lived in the American heartland, but the Morrises were far from provincial. Throughout Nelson's childhood, the family made regular ocean crossings to Europe via steamship. During these voyages, he liked to entertain his siblings or perform at elegant onboard gatherings with a series of magic tricks he had mastered, always ending his performance with the traditional act of conjuring a white rabbit from a silk top hat.

From a young age, Nelson and his siblings were well aware they were rich, but they were not necessarily spoiled. Their parents came from stern families where ethics, hard work, discipline, and obedience were prized above all, as those qualities had paid dividends on the American dream. Nelson's paternal grandfather, also called Nelson Morris, though it was not the name with which he had started in life, was the embodiment of the rags-to-riches story that characterized Chicago's nineteenth-century millionaires. The erstwhile Moritz Beisinger was a Jew from a small town on the German side of the Black Forest–shrouded foothills of the Swiss Alps, where his family raised and traded cattle until their land was confiscated in the revolutions that swept across Europe in 1848. Young Moritz was sent to America with the classic dollar in his pocket to live with an uncle who worked as a peddler. He soon ran away, changed his name to the more American "Nelson Morris," and found work as a coal miner and on a canal boat, eventually working his way west to Chicago, where he took a job as a stockyard watchman. No matter how far from his family's farm he had flown, cattle trading seemed to run in his blood. Just over a decade after arriving in America, Nelson Morris used his savings to become a cattle trader for the Union army when the Civil War broke out in 1861. With lucrative contracts initially paid on credit, he bought his own stockyard and processing plant and soon helped lead the development of the Union Stockyards. Less than ten years later, his annual sales reached $11 million. By the time he died in 1907, this figure had soared to $100 million.

On the other side of the family, the younger Nelson's maternal grandfather, Gustavus Swift, had similarly risen from nothing to become American Gilded Age royalty. While Morris led meat processing consolidation with the Union Stockyards, Swift revolutionized the broader meatpacking supply chain, driving profits skyward for every packer who could afford to keep pace. Through the mid-nineteenth century, the processed-meat industry faced a crucial limitation: spoilage. Consumers were understandably skeptical of meat that had been slaughtered far away and then sent in hot railcars across the country. Swift and his engineers solved this problem by developing the first practicable refrigerated railcar. Swift also recognized the importance of presentation. Realizing consumers would be more likely to overcome an aversion to distantly butchered beef if it looked appetizing, he directed his agents to cut and package the meat, particularly the less desirable cuts, in small pieces and display them in a visually appealing manner, rather than hack off pieces from carcasses suspended in butchers' shops one order at a time.

In 1890, Morris's son Edward married Swift's daughter Helen, but the Morris and Swift packing companies remained independent. Edward Morris had learned the business of Morris & Company from the ground up, starting in the stockyards as a teenager. He took over the company after Nelson the patriarch's death in 1907, though he ran it for a mere six years before succumbing to a kidney ailment known as Bright's disease in 1913 at the age of forty-seven. This coincided with his son Nelson's senior year at Harvard. At the time of Edward's death, Morris & Company, famous for the black-and-yellow labels on its "Supreme" cuts of meat, was estimated to be worth $40 million. While his sisters went off to Wellesley, Nelson refused to finish college, instead insisting on joining with his younger brother to manage the business. With help from their mother, Nelson and his brother Edward avoided the common pitfall of a third generation losing the fortune the first built and the second sustained. In 1923, they negotiated the merger of Morris & Company with their rival, Armour & Company, creating a packing conglomerate worth $550 million.

Nelson looked the part of a dashing young millionaire with his dark brown eyes, Clark Gable mustache, and Brylcreemed black hair perfectly coiffed on his high forehead. However, while certainly capable, Nelson was not the hard-driving businessman at the reins of a gory industry that his grandfather and father had been. Beneath the dinner jackets and charming white smile, Nelson had a compassionate and tender soul. He felt a particular attachment to his sisters, especially Muriel, who was ten years his junior and to whom he had always been, as she described, "a person of rare kindness and generosity."

Though Nelson remained an executive with his family's packing company now entirely trading under the Armour name, he gave up his involvement in the day-to-day business. Instead, he used his fortune to invest in other companies that interested him. One such investment was in Parisian couturier Lucien Lelong, specifically Lelong's international perfume business, which had offices in both Paris and Chicago. Perhaps a lifetime spent surrounded by the stench of the blood-soaked stockyards had pushed him to seek out their antithesis. Nor was it any accident that he decided to pursue businesses in Paris, which had long since left its own days of blood-soaked streets behind. France had captivated him since he was a young man during the Great War, and it was France that had provided him with the two greatest loves of his life.

In 1917, almost exactly one month after the United States declared war on Germany, Nelson, like so many other young American men, had registered for the draft. He initially volunteered his services as an expert in refrigeration in Washington, taking up a civilian post with a salary of one dollar per year, but the army took that as indication he was dispensable to his business in Chicago, so he was drafted as a sergeant alongside the farmers, rail operators, and factory workers his family employed. He remained in a billet overseeing refrigeration as part of the Quartermaster Corps—a job that sometimes included serving soft drinks at the regimental canteen, as *The New York Times* was so generous to point out—and was eventually shipped off to France with the American Expeditionary Force. He arrived in late September 1918, less than two months before the end of the war.

The end of the action meant that Nelson had had to find his own excitement in France. Well before the Wright brothers made their famous flight, Nelson's grandfather and namesake had predicted that his children would live to see "people flying through the air." Nelson did not just want to see people flying through the air. He decided to join them as he waited for a troop ship to take him back home.

To Americans, the sandy stretch of shore on the Outer Banks of Kitty Hawk, North Carolina, represented the birthplace of aviation, thanks to the Wright brothers' historic twelve-second flight in 1903, but France was the true historic home of aviation, thanks to another pair of brothers, paper manufacturers and amateur scientists Joseph-Michel and Jacques-Étienne

Montgolfier. In 1783 the Montgolfiers invented the *globe aérostatique*, the first hot-air balloon capable of human-piloted flight, which they demonstrated for the first time before King Louis XVI, Marie Antoinette, and a crowd of 100,000 at Versailles by sending a sheep, a duck, and a rooster into the air in a basket suspended from the balloon. A few weeks later, chemist and physicist Jean-François Pilâtre de Rozier and soldier François Laurent, Marquis d'Arlannes, made the world's first untethered, manned flight in a balloon, creating a marriage between the realms of civilian and military in the development of aviation.

Over the next two hundred years, aviation slowly advanced in a give-and-take between civilian sport and military utility and between the old world and the new. Ballooning became a popular nineteenth-century European pastime, while in the United States the Union army established a Balloon Corps during the American Civil War, using nonsteerable hot-air balloons to conduct reconnaissance on Confederate army movements. Meanwhile, on the Continent, the French had added motors to their balloons, which became known as "dirigibles," after the French word *diriger*, or "to steer."

The next great technological leap forward came not from France but from Germany. Count Ferdinand von Zeppelin embodied this tug-of-war between military and civilian motivations driving the development of aviation. As a young officer in the army of the Kingdom of Württemberg, he spent time as an observer with the Union army during the American Civil War. He also traveled through the Midwest to St. Paul, Minnesota, where he met John Steiner, a former army balloonist, with whom he made a tethered aerial ascent. In 1890, after a controversy over Zeppelin's handling of a cavalry brigade resulted in his dismissal from the army, he devoted himself to airships, machines he envisioned as "destined to erase the advantages or disadvantages of the geography of nations." Rather than attach a basket or gondola to a single fully inflatable balloon envelope—a type of aircraft colloquially known as a "blimp"—Zeppelin's great innovation was to create lift by attaching smaller individual gasbags to the inside of a metal frame, the basis for the world's first rigid airship.

But Zeppelin's ambitions were loftier than simply improving lighter-than-air technology. First and foremost, he saw his airships as having the potential to be "splendid instruments of war" that he trusted would "harm only the weapons of our enemies and not the unwarlike citizenry." More important for Germany, he saw his airships as "assur[ing] her military domination," which would in turn foster "a complete revolution in commerce and transportation" to further his nation's advantage in the civilian sphere.

By the end of the nineteenth century, heavier-than-air experiments had also begun in earnest, with prototypes advancing from birdlike winged gliders to box kite–inspired biplanes and ultimately to the more sophisticated Wright Flyer, the first manned, controlled aircraft propelled with a gasoline engine that was capable of sustained flight. Above all, it was the Great War that propelled both lighter-than-air and heavier-than-air aviation to a point of practical utility. Hydrogen-filled German zeppelins, now several hundred feet long, became the menacing instruments of war that Count Zeppelin had predicted, though they were soon carrying out air raids on civilian targets, contrary to the old count's perhaps naive vision. In the skies above France, fixed-wing airplanes began as reconnaissance tools, until the British Vickers company designed the first fighter aircraft with a mounted machine gun, a concept later perfected in Germany by Dutchman Anthony Fokker, whose innovative synchronization gear allowed machine guns to fire through an airplane's propeller without striking its blade. Early dogfights turned ace pilots like American Eddie Rickenbacker, Frenchman Roland Garros, and German Baron Manfred von Richthofen, known as the "Red Baron," into national heroes.

With the end of the war, military aviation gave way once more to sport and leisure as the rich and the reckless took to the skies with either a death wish or a sense of invincibility, having survived the "War to End All Wars." Nelson Morris was among the first wave of Americans abroad to take flying lessons and quickly earned his pilot's license, though it was good only in France. More pressing matters occupied his time once back in Chicago, including his work with Armour, his other investments, and his position as a colonel in the Illinois National Guard (an upgrade from his wartime service as a sergeant, and a position he publicly embraced with gusto), so he never earned his American pilot's license. However, he was early among executives to embrace air travel for business and was especially enamored with zeppelins, the only means of airborne transatlantic passenger travel for the foreseeable future.

Nelson had twice flown across the Atlantic on the *Graf Zeppelin*. On his first trip, in 1928, passenger accommodations were sold out, but he had managed to convince the zeppelin company to let him share a German captain's rudimentary quarters in the airship's keel. This had given him the run of the inner workings of the zeppelin, an experience he found utterly captivating. The second time, in 1929, he had been traveling in Europe and had run into his uncle Ira Nelson Morris, formerly the U.S. ambassador to Sweden, who was set to return home by steamship. Nelson bet his uncle he could beat him back to their respective desks in Chicago if he flew home on the zeppelin. Nelson flew from Friedrichshafen to Lakehurst, New Jersey, in three days, then caught the train from New York to Chicago's Union Station, and finally hailed a taxi to his office, where he was met by a "squad" of reporters who had heard about the race between uncle and nephew. Silencing the hubbub around him, he called in a stenographer and dictated a simple radiogram to his uncle: "I win." Then he settled back in his desk chair to wait for Ira with a "satisfied smile."

In the midst of his bet with his uncle, Nelson was grappling with the other great passion his time in France had thrown his way: French actresses. He had fallen in love with Jeanne Aubert, a slim blond with a Cupid's bow mouth, who had appeared in a 1929 silent film called *La possession*. Jeanne was performing in a play in Paris, where Nelson was happily vacationing. Deciding he was possessed with love, he went to the theater to see her onstage not just once but fifty nights straight, anonymously sending her expensive baskets of gifts and flowers. When the actress finally met the mustachioed millionaire installed in the front row, Nelson proposed to her on the spot, though it took some convincing—jewelry, a château in Le Véstinet, a promised honeymoon in Morocco—before Jeanne finally accepted.

Unfortunately, shortly after moving to Chicago with Nelson, Jeanne realized she loved the stage more than her husband. She had worked hard for her career, starting as an understudy during the dark days of the war when German zeppelin bombing raids on Paris had threatened to close her very first show, and she was determined not to give it up. She fled to Paris and filed for divorce, while Nelson sent a fleet of lawyers after her to bring her home by filing injunction after injunction to keep her from performing, which, apparently, a husband could still do in Europe. News of the wife on the run quickly made it back to the United States, thanks to frequent updates from *The New York Times*. The story was so sensational that it even made the news all the way out in Helena, Montana, where the *Independent Record* published a full account of Nelson's romantic woes. No doubt the cattle farmers so integral to his family business's supply chain had a good laugh at his expense.

But Nelson lived by the adage "The world is a wheel, and it will all come round right," a saying he had had incorporated into bookplates for his library when he was sixteen years old. Finally accepting that Jeanne did not want him, he agreed to a divorce—and then promptly fell in love again with another slim, blond, French actress, Blanche Bilbao, who starred at the Comédie-Française, Paris's historic state theater. They married in October 1933, five months after his divorce from Jeanne was finalized.

By the spring of 1937, Nelson and Blanche had been happily married for three and a half years. They had sailed through the Depression, feeling few of its effects, and had even recently constructed a new home, a sprawling Spanish colonial in the growing suburb of Homewood, Illinois. Nelson had also kept up his travels. Apparently confident that Blanche would not try to leave him to return to the French stage, that April he brought her back to her home country, first for a week in Paris and then on to Nice for some Mediterranean sunshine. While in Paris, they spent the week with Nelson's mother and younger sister, Muriel, who had brought her six-year-old daughter with her to visit from Vienna, where Muriel studied and practiced psychiatry in Freud's circle.

As April wound to a close, Nelson said goodbye to his mother, sister, and niece and traveled south with Blanche to the French Riviera. While he had anticipated a relaxing stay at the Nice seaside, his holiday was abruptly cut short by urgent business concerns that required him to return to Chicago. Nelson was keen to address his business and resume his vacation as swiftly as possible, but the standard modes of transit were maddeningly slow. A steamer from Cherbourg would take a minimum of five days to reach New York, followed by a flight or a train to Chicago. Add on the time needed to sort out his business, plus another week for the trip back to France, and there was little point in returning to his holiday at all. There was, however, one other option. It would be expensive, but Nelson had cash to burn.

It had been eight years since Nelson had last flown on a zeppelin, and in that time the Germans had constructed a brand-new airship, the *Hindenburg*, a craft so modern it made luxurious steamships look dated and dowdy. With publicity photos touting its art deco aluminum-and-chrome interiors, the *Hindenburg* was a testament to the era to which it belonged. It had been in passenger service for a year, but Nelson had yet to see it for himself. Fortuitously, the first trip of the airship's 1937 season was scheduled to depart several days later from Frankfurt on the evening of May 3. It was a quick train trip from Nice to Paris and then to Frankfurt, and nearly as fast—a mere two and a half days—from Germany to the United States on the zeppelin. If he booked a round-trip ticket, returning to Europe on the *Hindenburg*'s second scheduled eastbound trip on May 17, he could make it back to his wife in time to continue their holiday.

Blanche, however, was less convinced about the idea of flying and made her protestations known. As it did many people, flying clearly made her nervous. But Nelson brushed off her concerns. Besides, shortly after arriving in Nice, he had run into his close friend and business associate from Chicago, Burtis Dolan, whom he had persuaded to join him for the trip.

Burtis Dolan, known as Bert, was vice president of the American subsidiary of the Lucien Lelong Importing Company and had been friends and colleagues with Nelson since before the war. Bert had been in London and Paris on business since January. It had been a long and exhausting spring, and he was eagerly looking forward to returning home to his wife and four children via the SS *Hamburg* the first week of May. Why not, Nelson had suggested, return on the "Zep" with him instead? Not only would it be pleasant to have a friend along, but it would be good publicity for the perfume business, as the names and businesses of the several dozen passengers on board always received wide circulation in the press.

Bert was a successful businessman, but a $450 one-way ticket on the *Hindenburg*—half the annual salary of one of the mechanics who had built the airship—was beyond even his means. Nelson was a generous man, but knowing that Bert's pride would keep him from accepting the ticket for nothing, he had cajoled his friend into a deal. Nelson would cover the ticket if Bert would pick up their combined bar tab on the flight to Lakehurst (though, judging by the amount of bootleg liquor that went up the back stairs of the Dolan household during Prohibition—and none of it "medicinal" Jeppson's Malört—Nelson might have had the better end of the bargain).

Ever persistent, Nelson had added one last inducement to persuade his friend to come along. If Bert flew on the *Hindenburg*, he would make it home to his wife, Mildred, and their four children in time for Mother's Day. They would arrive at Lakehurst the morning of Thursday, May 6, catch an American Airlines DC-3 to Newark Metropolitan Airport, and then hopefully one of the airline's "Skysleepers" to Chicago that night. In the worst-case scenario, they would stay overnight in New York and catch the first flight to Chicago Friday morning.

At first, Bert had politely refused. He had already written to Mildred to expect him on the *Hamburg* and had arranged to send his trunks on the ship. Nelson had a plan for that, too. Bert's trunks could stay on the *Hamburg*. They would simply be forwarded on to him in Chicago. He and Bert would not tell Mildred about the change of plans and let it be a terrific Mother's Day surprise when he walked through the door days earlier than expected.

Finally persuaded, Bert had accepted the offer. They would arrange the ticket with the Hamburg-America Line office in Paris, and as it was nonrefundable, there would be no backing out. With plans to meet again in advance of the westward journey, Bert returned to his business in Paris, leaving Nelson to enjoy a few more days with his wife in the Riviera sunshine.

CHAPTER 4

Berlin, Germany: April 24, 1937

It had been a quiet, gray spring in the Berlin bureau of Universal Service, where Bill Shirer had been holding down the fort alone. April had nearly come and gone in the Mitte neighborhood in the center of Berlin, where his office was situated, and the city remained eerily calm compared with the same time last year, when it had been roiling in the wake of the Rhineland remilitarization and the referendum. Shirer had come to Europe for a front-row seat to world affairs. However, while Berlin was certainly the epicenter of activity and excitement, on a gray spring day, it was not so different from the world he had left behind. Mark Twain had once called Berlin "the Chicago of Europe" after visiting in 1892. Both cities were bathed in an aura of newness, with wide streets that seemed to Twain to "stretch out to prodigious distances . . . as straight as a ray of light." Bill Shirer knew Chicago. It was the city of his birth, where his father had worked his way up from an Iowa farming family to become a federal prosecutor. Respect for Twain notwithstanding, Berlin in early spring was not Chicago. It was Kansas City, "cold, misty, and ugly," with "something in the air that takes the lead out of your behind."

As Berliners began to let their guard down and believe that winter was well and truly behind them, Shirer felt he could almost relax. The Spree River ran cold and clear several blocks to the east, and full green leaves appeared on the branches of the eponymous trees that lined Unter den

Linden, one of Berlin's main thoroughfares, a block to the south. Over the last few weeks, Shirer had found his thoughts drifting to the old sailboat he had recently purchased for four hundred marks from a retired boxer who was short on cash. It had a cabin and two bunks, making it perfect for weekending down the Wannsee with his Viennese wife, Tess. He might even get to use it soon, because, for the first time in several years, it appeared that there would truly be no springtime "Hitler surprise."

The so-called springtime surprises had begun in 1933, shortly after Hitler took power. They started with the Reichstag Fire Decree, when Hitler suspended constitutional protections. This was followed the next spring by the purge of those Hitler viewed as a threat to his consolidation of political power. During the bloody Night of the Long Knives, the Brownshirts' leader, Ernst Röhm; former Chancellor Kurt von Schleicher; the leader of the left-wing faction of the Nazi Party, Gregor Strasser; and others were brutally murdered by the Gestapo and the Schutzstaffel, or SS. In 1935, Hitler turned his attention outward and announced Germany would rearm, in flagrant violation of the Treaty of Versailles, a move the treaty signatories failed to challenge, thus emboldening him to take the Rhineland the following spring. After calling France and Britain's bluff in a high-stakes game of chicken, it appeared to Shirer that Hitler now needed time to strengthen his armed forces and build upon his blossoming relationship with the Italian Prime Minister Benito Mussolini.

Though Hitler had long admired the Italian fascist's rise to power, Mussolini had initially been suspicious of Hitler and his designs on historically Austrian territories that now comprised portions of northern Italy. Mussolini had set his qualms aside after Hitler supported Italy's imperialist invasion of Abyssinia in 1935, against the admonitions of the wholly ineffectual League of Nations. Both countries had then come to the aid of Francisco Franco's nationalist, fascist-leaning forces fighting against the Republicans in Spain in 1936, paving the way for a new Berlin-Rome Axis announced that October.

Shirer was skeptical the alliance was anything more than a facade for an unequal partnership. More than anything, he thought Hitler needed to give the "nerves of the German people a little rest." Hitler himself had declared during a speech in January that the "so-called period of surprises has come to an end." For once, he appeared to be keeping his word.

Amid the relative tranquility, the führer still enjoyed flaunting his success. He had declared his birthday, April 20, a national holiday, prompting "sickening adulation from all the party hacks" and "a great military parade," as Shirer recorded. Heavy artillery and tanks rolled through the city in style, with Hitler, happy as a boy playing with his tin soldiers, saluting every one that filed past his reviewing stand.

It seemed to Shirer that the man became "more and more like a Caesar" with every passing day. How easy it would have been, he and his fellow correspondents had mused during his first visit to the annual Nuremburg rally in September 1934, for someone to have thrown a bomb into Hitler's car during one of those rallies and escaped into the fanatical crowds. Shirer even had an obituary ready to go. Like most news outlets, Universal Service kept obituaries on hand for prominent figures, lest it be caught flat-footed if a world leader keeled over unexpectedly. He had been tasked with writing the 1935 version for Hitler: "No figure in postwar Europe leaped from such obscurity to such heights of power. . . . In the days just before the war, an unknown house-painter, struggling to become an artist, or at least an architect. Fifteen years after the war, chancellor of the German Reich and virtual dictator." Shame the opportunity to run it had not yet arisen.

The shrill of the telephone interrupted the contemplative solitude of the near-empty bureau. Shirer lifted the receiver and answered. It was the DZR press agent calling again. He had called the day before, quite unexpectedly, to make Shirer an unbelievable offer: free passage to the United States on the first voyage of the *Hindenburg*'s 1937 season, departing in ten days' time. Apparently, there were a handful of tickets they had been unable to sell, so the press office was willing to provide an American correspondent with a free trip home, no doubt in exchange for some positive publicity.

For a journalist with minimal savings, the offer had real appeal. And, like so many others, Shirer had somewhat succumbed to *Hindenburg* hysteria when the airship made its maiden transatlantic voyage to Lakehurst the year before. While the limited number of passenger tickets were out of reach for all but the wealthiest segments of society, many people, including Shirer, had sent air mail to friends and family in the United States on the new zeppelin for the valuable novelty of a *Hindenburg* cancellation stamp on the envelope. Shirer had sent letters to everyone from his sister, Josie, to his first editor, Verne Marshall of *The Cedar Rapids Gazette*, the latter of whom had published excerpts of his letter so the Cedar Rapids community could share in the wonder of modern technology.

There had also been a moment exactly a year earlier when Shirer thought he might have a chance to fly on the *Hindenburg* for a reporting assignment. Americans were obsessed with all things enormous—longer bridges, taller skyscrapers—and the *Hindenburg* was by far the largest thing ever to appear in the sky. He had written a popular four-article syndicated series on the zeppelins for American readers in advance of the *Hindenburg*'s first flight to New Jersey, and for a few weeks, there was a slim chance of writing a follow-up piece from firsthand, onboard experience. In the end, the opportunity never materialized. Nor had any other opportunity to take a brief trip home in the interim.

It had now been a year and a half since Shirer had been able to take a real break from the "bloody, hysterical land" that was Germany, and while he was privately desperate for a reprieve, unfortunately, as he explained to the press agent, it was "impossible" for him to leave Berlin, as he was "holding down the office alone." The New York bureau had promised him an assistant, but the man had yet to materialize. Enticing as the offer was, his bosses would be anxious if he left Berlin unattended. After all, as his old editor Verne Marshall had puffed about his former employee to Cedar Rapids readers, Berlin was a city "where almost anything can happen almost any minute, to affect not only the powder magazine that is Europe, but the rest of the world as well." Shirer had no choice but to tell DZR they had better offer the ticket to someone else.

Shockingly, after twenty-four hours, they had yet to find a journalist to take it, so the press agent was calling back with a different proposal. If Shirer could not get away, would his wife, Tess, like to go instead?

Tess was a slim, fair, and fashionable Austrian woman, and though just twenty-seven, she was a person of staggering composure, wisdom, and intelligence. She was both artistic and athletic, a voracious reader, an accomplished photographer, and became fluent in any language practically overnight. At fourteen, she had written to a London newspaper offering to work as their Vienna theater critic because she wanted free tickets. They had hired her, never realizing Fraülein Theresa Stiberitz was, in fact, a child. By her late teens, Tess was working as a translator for journalists in Vienna, which was how she had met Shirer when she was just nineteen and he was twenty-five and stationed in Vienna with the *Chicago Tribune*. Shirer had been struck by the "brilliant mind" of this young woman who brought clarity and order to the ideas that pinballed in his brain. After six years of marriage, Tess still helped him with his articles by conducting interviews for him and taking photographs. The prior February, she had assisted with a substantial amount of research for his zeppelin article series. Apparently the DZR man was well aware of Tess's contributions. Perhaps she would like to take a ride on the airship she had come to know so intimately on the page?

It was an intriguing offer, albeit a little unusual, and one that, for some inarticulable reason, gave Shirer pause. There were plenty of points Shirer could have mustered to explain why accepting such an offer on Tess's behalf was a poor idea. If DZR wanted an article full of platitudes, they clearly did not know Tess. Alongside her many accomplishments, the subject on which she was most passionate was her hatred for anything related to the Nazis. She was a proud Viennese woman who steadfastly believed in her country's uniquely elegant and creative culture, which the Nazis were trying to subjugate with their own interpretation of what it meant to be German. Tess's family had also suffered terribly during and after the war. Her father had served in the Austrian army and was captured by the Russians on the Eastern Front. No one had heard from him for years, until he turned up one day after walking all the way back to Vienna through the hinterlands of the erstwhile Russian Empire. Not long after the family was reunited, food shortages and rampant inflation in Austria forced her mother to send Tess and her younger brother for two and a half years to Denmark, where the siblings were separated. Her family's story was one shared by millions of Europeans after the Great War, and the possibility of the Nazis driving Europe back to the brink of destruction was anathema. Now the airships had come under Nazi control and had forty-five-foot-long Nazi flags with ugly, black hooked crosses on their tail fins, and the idea of providing positive publicity for the new regime in exchange for a free trip likely would have made Tess's stomach churn.

Existential geopolitical concerns aside, Shirer selfishly would have hated to lose Tess's presence during this rare period of calm. They had been looking forward to taking out that new sailboat as soon as they could manage a work-free weekend—if he ever learned to sail it properly. He had taken it for a test run two weekends prior using diagrammed instructions a German colleague had scrawled on the back of an envelope. Shirer had quickly learned he needed to work on his docking skills; otherwise he would soon be out more than the five marks he had spent to pay off the dock's owner, who had raised an "awful howl" about his rough landing.

Shirer could not honestly say he had an overtly bad feeling about the idea of Tess traveling on the *Hindenburg*, but for reasons beyond conscious thought, something about it did not feel right. Thanks to the time he had spent with Eckener's crews at Friedrichshafen while researching his article series, Shirer knew that the zeppelin engineers had studied the structural weaknesses of other nations' failed airships and their resulting crashes. The postwar German zeppelins were thus the soundest airships in the world, having flown over a million miles in passenger service without any serious mishaps. He had even quoted Eckener saying that the new *Hindenburg* would be "as safe as anything else that men travel in nowadays," if not safer.

Perhaps the source of his unease was a fragment of a memory following his lunch with Eckener and Dodd the prior April. Eckener had gone to America in part to ask Roosevelt for helium specifically because of the *Hindenburg*'s novel gas-cell design. Its engineers had intended the *Hindenburg* to have sixteen large gas cells filled with helium lining the frame of the airship. Inside each gas cell would be a smaller, hydrogen-filled cell to balance increased safety with both lift and cost concerns. Helium had less lifting power and was considerably more expensive than hydrogen, so by maintaining some hydrogen safely nested within the outer helium cells, the airships would remain lighter and zeppelin crews could valve off gas from the inner hydrogen cells to adjust the airship's altitude without worrying about releasing precious helium into the air. After interviewing the engineers at Friedrichshafen, Shirer had assured readers "that there virtually is no danger of fire or explosion" with the hydrogen so well insulated. Unfortunately, when Eckener arrived in Washington, he was rebuffed by the secretary of the interior, Harold Ickes, who was responsible for the country's export of natural resources and was a staunch anti-Nazi. Roosevelt might have been willing to lobby Congress to amend the 1925 Helium Act on Germany's behalf, but Ickes was not, and Roosevelt was ultimately disinclined to expend political capital over such a minor issue. In the end, with no helium, Eckener had had to abandon the dual-pocket gas-cell design and revert to the traditional hydrogen cells instead.

Shirer articulated none of these musings out loud to the DZR press agent, but before he hung up the phone, he promised that he would talk the offer over with his wife. However, after taking the U-Bahn to his Tempelhof neighborhood and settling in for the evening, he never mentioned it to Tess. It could hardly have slipped his mind. Simply living in his flat would have made him think about aviation. Coincidentally, the Shirers had leased the stately third-floor unit from Hermann Köhl, the Great War German flying ace. Köhl had been the first man to make the headwind-riddled east-to-west journey across the Atlantic in a fixed-wing aircraft, which he had done less than a year after Lindbergh's historic flight from west to east with the benefit of a tailwind. Now, almost exactly nine years later, Köhl had become something of a tragic figure. While Lindbergh had been promoted into the rarefied air of global celebrity, Köhl, a devout Catholic, had been fired from Lufthansa, as Shirer understood, for refusing to "curry Nazi favor." More likely his termination was a result of the ultranationalist Nazi government's bias against Catholics, whom they viewed as insufficiently loyal to Germany due to their supposed allegiance to the pope in the Vatican. Rather than cling to his fading fame, Köhl now preferred to spend his days in obscurity on a farm in southern Germany.

The night came and went in the aviator's apartment, and still Shirer did not mention his telephone conversation to Tess. When he returned to the Universal Service office the next day, he called the DZR man back, as promised, and "politely declined" the offer on Tess's behalf without her ever knowing about it at all. Then he hung up the receiver, got back to work, and promptly forgot about the whole thing.

CHAPTER 5

Paris, France: Late April 1937

At the end of a cold, damp winter, Bert Dolan could not have asked for a better time to be in Europe than the late spring of 1937. London and Paris were decked out in their finest glory. The British capital was readying itself for King George VI and Queen Elizabeth's coronation, while France's jewel prepared to welcome visitors from far and wide for its world exposition, set to open at the end of May. Between the new king and queen and their charming young daughters making up the image of a happy family and the exposition in Paris profiling the art and technology of modern life, there was more optimism in Europe than there had been for quite some time. After three years of German belligerence following Adolf Hitler's rise to power, it seemed that a period of crisis had cooled. Frayed nerves had settled, and Europeans were ready to celebrate.

Bert seemed to have a knack for arriving in France just as a crisis ended. During the war, he had served as a lieutenant and the most junior staff officer in the 332nd Field Artillery Regiment of the 86th "Blackhawk" Division, eventually rising to the rank of major. Having completed a year of intensive training, he had arrived in Bordeaux a mere six weeks before the armistice and thus was "denied the Great Adventure," as his commanding officer had said. Instead of serving in the "greatest destructive force" in modern warfare, the 332nd's regimental history explained, Bert's unit took courses in math, history, law, and hygiene, played football and baseball, and went on "wine caravans." He was, of course, lucky to have been spared the misery of trench warfare and the horrors of the Somme and Verdun. Thus far, it seemed that the men of the next generation would avoid the tragic fate that his own had suffered—unless the Germans and Soviets came to blows at the exposition, with their pavilions located directly across from each other.

Despite the spirit of relieved jubilation in the air, Bert was struggling to join in. Though only forty-six and known for his jovial personality that lit up a room, he was exhausted after weeks of grueling work on the back of a particularly difficult time for his family. Just before Christmas, his younger brother, Leslie, had fallen ill, and he had died on Christmas Eve at age forty-two. The day after Christmas, they had buried him in the family plot of the Calvary Cemetery overlooking Lake Michigan on a day that felt more like spring. Three weeks later, on January 16, Bert's wife and four children had seen him off at Chicago's Union Station, from which he would travel on to New York to board a steamship bound for England for a four-month business trip. A prolonged absence would have broken his heart at any time, but that January, it also meant leaving Mildred and the children with his grieving mother so soon after the unexpected loss of one of her two sons.

Bert was an executive with Lelong Importing, a subsidiary of the eponymously named Parisian haute couture fashion house Lucien Lelong. Like Coco Chanel, Lelong believed scent was an essential element of style. The designer began a perfume line in 1924, with the evocatively named fragrances Mon Image, Indiscreet, Tailspin, and Balalaika. Lelong soon opened international offices to meet global demand, including in Chicago, the second-largest city in the United States. Harmonizing the various operations of an international business presented challenges, and Bert had been dispatched first to London to hold a series of meetings to reorganize that office, and then to confer with Lucien Lelong and other executives at the home office in Paris.

Once Bert arrived in London, which he told his wife was as "gloomy as ever," he found himself working practically every minute of the day. The London office urgently needed new management. "We can do business here if properly organized but we must have a British organization and that is hard to locate," he told Mildred in early February. Their local employee, a Mrs. Wood, had "tried hard—has done well, but the task is too much for her." However, he remained optimistic about the business. "I find my thoughts crystallizing into definite plans and I feel certain of the results," he wrote, perhaps simply to reassure himself, as he knew "it may take a year to show a profit."

After three weeks in London, he had identified some viable prospects, but matters were not quite settled before he left for meetings in Paris. "We are making some progress on perfumes and bottles but it is awfully slow," he told Mildred two weeks later, "and there is always the conflict between the idea of the Paris and Chicago offices." Both sides had "temperamental" personalities, including Lelong himself, who kept a keen eye on everything that bore his name. Caught in the middle, Bert had to delicately cajole them back on track.

Despite the personality clash, Bert had to admit he "like[d] Lelong better all the time," admiring him for both his designs and the business he had built. He visited the atelier, where Lelong put out about one hundred looks a year across his handmade couture "Collection," as well as the machine-sewn, ready-to-wear "Edition" designs, a concept he had helped pioneer during the Depression, when few could afford couture. "You and the girls would have a picnic if you were here," he told Mildred, or "Angel mine," as he liked to call her. "I never saw so many dresses." His French colleagues were kind, showering praise on the photographs of his beautiful family, saying Mildred looked young and pretty enough to be the sister of her daughters. Their thirteen-year-old, Mary Alice, was the image of her father; ten-year-old Mildred, nicknamed "Babs," "should be in the Louvre"; and four-year-old Jimmy could be the "future President of France." (Amusingly, they had no comment about his older son, eleven-year-old Burtis Jr., or "Bud," who he supposed was of the age that the French would simply ship their sons off school.)

However, the long hours wore on Bert, not least because of a lack of urgency in any decision-making, especially over drawn-out meals: "They are moving too slow and I find it difficult getting them up to speed. . . . It's strange how long they take here to eat. Two hours is not too long for lunch and more for dinner and then your day is gone." His colleague Sprague, on the other hand, was enjoying the Continental lifestyle and fancied himself a "gourmand" who knew "the best and famous restaurants. One noon, it's the famous tripe place. The next suckling pig—the next some famous pâté and so on." He had been eating too much rich food, and the "present rebellion" in his stomach was to be expected after suffering such abuse. Bert tried to break away whenever he could, whether to Mass on Sundays, the odd hour at a museum, or to visit a "smart shop," where he purchased a gray cashmere coat that he was pleased needed no alterations and he knew Mildred would like. She had suggested gray, after all, to go with his gray hat. He also tried to practice his French at every opportunity, though he found "everyone talks English and I get little chance." He was "planning some little way to bring about more conversation" so the opportunity was not entirely wasted.

But by the end of April, Bert was not merely exhausted; he was also in a bit of personal turmoil, albeit of his own making. Nelson Morris had not meant to land him in hot water when he offered to have Bert fly home with him on the *Hindenburg*. After all, it had been Bert's choice to accept, and, as ever, Nelson had only meant to be kind.

Bert Dolan and Nelson Morris were unlikely friends and business partners. Bert was the son of first-generation Irish Americans and had grown up on Chicago's heavily Irish North Side. His family were among the 1.5 million who had flocked to the United States from Ireland to find work as laborers, salesmen, and domestics in the second half of the nineteenth century. In Chicago, the Irish found backbreaking work in the steel mills; digging the ambitious ninety-six-mile Illinois & Michigan Canal with little more than shovels, wheelbarrows, and explosives; and, of course, in the Morris, Swift, and Armour families' stockyards.

Though none of Bert's family had been stockyard laborers, he found himself working for the packers nonetheless. Like many in the growing middle class, Bert was the first in his family to attend college, enrolling initially at the University of Illinois, where he pledged Psi Upsilon fraternity in the fall of 1911, before transferring to DePaul University, just down the street from where he had grown up, to study law. Rather than sit for the bar exam, Bert was instead drawn to business, particularly sales, where his outgoing nature quickly won him friends and a job with Morris & Company. He landed in the banking department under a hard-driving Scotsman but made time for friends who had a similarly impish sense of humor, especially at lunchtime, when he and a buddy made it a daily ritual to slip away to the cafeteria of nearby competitor Swift & Company, where the food was considerably better.

It was around this time that Nelson Morris took notice of Bert. The two men were only a year apart in age but entirely different in looks and demeanor. Where the slightly younger Nelson was classically tall, dark, and handsome, Bert was small, solid, and fair. Though only a compact five foot seven and 140 pounds, he played basketball and baseball with great skill, at one point even securing a tryout for third base with the Chicago Cubs. As an adult, he added golf to his repertoire and became friends with champion golfer Chick Evans, a fellow member of the Edgewater Golf Club. People could not help but be drawn to Bert's gregarious personality and athletic prowess, and he and Nelson became fast friends. Bert was soon promoted to serve as Nelson's personal secretary, handling his confidential meetings with clients and foreign importers. After the interruption of the war, the two friends reunited, with Bert and Nelson joining the same Illinois National Guard unit. Meanwhile, Bert briefly took a job as an executive at a sign and advertising company. Before long, he rejoined Morris & Company, and he remained after the 1923 merger with Armour and through the Depression, until Nelson recommended him for the Lelong job in 1936.

Throughout his career, it had served Bert remarkably well to join Nelson whenever the opportunity arose. Working with Nelson had elevated him beyond his middle-class upbringing and allowed him to buy a house on Kennesaw Terrace in Lakeview, a quiet enclave of early prairie-style single-family homes where they were more likely to hear cheers from Wrigley Field than catch a whiff of the slaughterhouses over ten miles away, unless there was a strong southern breeze blowing on a particularly hot summer's day. It had also allowed him to afford to keep that house during the Depression so his children could continue to play football in the street, play baseball in the open lot next door, and walk across Lake

Shore Drive to swim in Lake Michigan. On their way they might catch young Father Dempsey from the neighborhood parish, Saint Mary of the Lake, where Mildred attended Mass every day. If they were lucky, the soft-spoken and reserved priest would pull out his wallet to buy everyone a hot dog from the Greek vendor on the corner. Bert loved that neighborhood. He loved it so much that when the city renamed Kennesaw Terrace, honoring the famous Civil War battle of Kennesaw Mountain, to the bland West Hutchinson Street after a prominent Chicago businessman and philanthropist, he retrieved the old sign from the rubbish heap, removed the new sign, and put KENNESAW TERRACE back up.

Joining his friend on a flight home would mean getting back to his beloved home and family several days sooner, so it was surprising that the decision was causing so much mental anguish. Most people would have been thrilled to fly on the *Hindenburg* for the price of a bar tab.

But Bert had a very good reason. When Mildred embraced him goodbye at Union Station back in January, she had pressed a rosary into his hand before he boarded the train and asked him to promise he would keep it with him always until he returned home. She also made him promise that, while his business in Europe would require him to travel back and forth between Britain and France, he would not fly while he was away. Flying made Mildred nervous, and she wanted him to stick to the reliable trains and ships with his feet firmly beneath him. He loved his wife dearly, so he had agreed before he bade his family farewell.

By the time Nelson made his offer when they crossed paths in Nice, Bert was so anxious to get home that his promise had flown right out of his head. But as the days passed, the idea of breaking his word began to weigh on him, even if Mildred's reasons for not wanting him to fly lay somewhere between excessive caution and superstition. Bert did not like being at odds with his wife. Their relationship was precious to him, not least because of how long it had taken for them to finally be together. They had met in 1913 when Bert was twenty-two and Mildred seventeen. She had been orphaned at a young age and raised by an unmarried aunt in a Lincoln Park mansion that had belonged to Mildred's grandfather, Irish immigrant Thomas "Black Tom" Mackin. Black Tom had made, lost, and recovered a substantial fortune after securing a monopoly on the sand mixed into concrete and cement building materials following the Great Chicago Fire (or so went the family lore). The somewhat dubious nature of the family fortune aside, Mildred's aunt had imagined a smart match for her niece. A middle-class college student apparently was not that, and she made every effort to break up their courtship by sending Mildred away to boarding school and then to college at Saint Mary-of-the-Woods, near Terre Haute, Indiana. But Bert persisted, and in 1922, after a romance that spanned his army service, Mildred's cousin, the Reverend Thomas J. Mackin, arranged for them to elope at St. Joseph's church in the far northern Chicago suburb of Waukegan. Mildred was nervous about sneaking off to be married, but Father Mackin, with droll Irish cheek, emphatically informed his cousin, "This man has been doting on you for nine years, so I'm marrying you today!"

Bert had tried to rationalize that flying on the *Hindenburg* would drum up business for Lelong, and the idea of surprising Mildred on Mother's Day was a happy coincidence, but the simple truth was that he was desperate to get home. He had put up pictures of his wife and children in his room at the Hotel la Pérouse, situated on a quiet Parisian street just a few minutes from the Arc de Triomphe. He cherished the letters he received from his children, whom he lovingly called "the Bunnies" even though they were getting older. He sent letters back to them, realizing too late that he had forgotten to send a special message in time to reach Bud for his twelfth birthday. He was devastated that he could not simply pick up the telephone and call. Telephoning from overseas was a luxury, and he was missing the precious milestones in his family's life. "Monday is our anniversary," he wrote to Mildred. "I planned to phone but it is terribly expensive and I am not sure to catch you in. Consequently, I plan to cable although I would love to hear your voices. Maybe I will take the chance and call although I realize how little we can afford to be extravagant." They had weathered the Depression, but they still had to be sensible. As a consolation, he told his family, he kissed their pictures, though he "sure wish[ed] you all were here. All write often because I am really awfully lonesome." Even in his lonely state, he tried to keep up his trademark sense of humor. "Give grandmere a hug and tell her not to get married again," he wrote jokingly of his widowed mother.

When Bert returned to Paris from Nice, he found a letter from Mildred waiting at his hotel. He had put off telling her that he planned to fly home, instead allowing her to continue to believe he would be on the steamship *Hamburg*. But after reading her most recent letter, his guilt over having accepted Nelson's offer must have weighed on him like a bag of Black Tom's construction-grade sand. As if reading his mind from four thousand miles away, Mildred had written reminding him of his promise not to fly.

Uncharacteristically, he put off writing to Mildred for the rest of that week. Her letter had spooked him, and he did not know what to do. The ticket was already booked and the money spent. The only thing he could do was back out entirely and at great cost to Nelson, which seemed both ungrateful and perhaps a bit cowardly when his only reason for wanting to cancel was his wife's superstition.

April rolled into May, and still he had not told her as he clung to the idea that he would spoil her Mother's Day surprise. Just before he left Paris to meet Nelson in Frankfurt, he could no longer stand it, so he took a blank piece of hotel stationery from the desk in his suite and began to write Mildred a letter, unburdening himself of the anxiety building inside.

"Dearest One," he wrote. "For the past week I have just been distracted and here is the reason why. When I was at Nice, Nelse suggested I return on the Zep with him and offered to pay the additional expense. Without thinking I accepted and it now occurred to me that you might object. . . . Your letter came and startled me terribly and ever since, I have been so unhappy."

CHAPTER 6

Frankfurt, Germany: May 3, 1937

From the window of the airplane that circled the skies above Frankfurt airport as it came in for a landing, Margaret Mather could see the great silver airship *Hindenburg* tethered beside its giant hangar, surrounded at a distance by a lush forest. The gentle rain landing on the airship's delicate exterior made it glisten in the overcast morning light. Its cotton canvas skin, made up of 28,000 square meters of fabric stitched together by more than thirty tailors and sailmakers, was covered in an aluminum powder mixture called "dope," which had been painted on by workers standing atop ladders forty-five meters high, giving the airship its silvery hue. While the paint-like glue's purpose was to help the canvas remain taut as it was pulled across the airship's frame, the result was so well suited for the omnipresent chrome aesthetic that had swept across Europe and the United States in the last decade that it was little wonder the public had become transfixed by this giant flying machine that seemed the very embodiment of the era.

It had long been Margaret's dream to fly across the gray and stormy Atlantic Ocean. Though she was an otherwise unremarkable-looking woman of middle age with sympathetic eyes, a long face, and a graceful bearing that suggested a comfort with the world, her appearance belied a zeal for travel and adventure and a desire to keep pace with the world's progress. She had flown over the sparkling blue Mediterranean and Ionian Seas, the Gulf of Corinth and Greek islands, the Dolomites, and the golden deserts of Africa. She had even looked down from above at the "high secrets" of the once impassible Accursed Mountains of Albania, with rugged peaks made fierce and wild by the tectonic collisions of Europe and Africa and punctuated by steep glacial valleys. Margaret's travels had taken her as far as North Africa, where a public official in Tunis had once invited her to attend a noontime hanging (an invitation she had politely declined). But when it came to the relatively pedestrian activity of crossing the Atlantic, Margaret had long resigned herself to the far more limited view of a toilet bowl on a steamship, its luxurious comforts and entertainments meaning nothing to a "seasick wretch" like her.

The *Hindenburg* seemed like a sudden answer to both her troubles and her dreams. It was departing exactly when she wanted to leave, places remained available on board, and if she paid half the fare in reichsmarks, the favorable exchange rate set it within her means. Why, then, was it that Margaret, who loved the air, was suddenly seized by a strange reluctance about this trip to which she had long looked forward? It wasn't fear, she told herself. She had so desired to be one of the lucky passengers on one of the *Hindenburg*'s regular trips to New Jersey the previous summer. Margaret decided she must be tired, as her flight to Frankfurt had departed early that morning. She told herself to let it go at that.

Margaret was bound for Princeton, New Jersey, to visit her eldest brother, Frank. She and her seven siblings had grown up in Morristown, New Jersey, where her father had a successful legal practice, but she had not been home in several years—if she could even consider New Jersey home after having lived in Rome for the last three decades. Frank was a professor of postclassical art and archaeology and director of the Princeton University Art Museum, a position he had obtained thanks to their family's time abroad. Margaret, Frank, their parents, and two younger siblings had moved to Italy seeking the rejuvenating Italian air to improve the poor health of several members of the family. They lived first in Naples, then Florence, and finally Rome, taking in both the natural and the artistic beauty of the country. Through the expat community, Frank, who was an art critic and journalist, met the founder of Princeton's Department of Art and Archaeology, who offered him a job. The Mather family had a distinguished academic pedigree. They were descendants of Puritan ministers who had fled England for the Massachusetts Bay Colony in pursuit of religious freedom three hundred years earlier. Increase Mather had served as president of the fledgling Harvard College for nearly two decades at the end of the seventeenth century. His controversial son, Cotton Mather—known both for his forward-thinking advocacy of inoculation against smallpox and for his less-enlightened support for the Salem witch trials, during which nineteen people were hanged—had vied to succeed him. After he failed to gain the Harvard post, he convinced a Boston-born British merchant, Elihu Yale, who had made a fortune in diamonds, to leave his money to a small university in Connecticut that supposedly maintained truer Puritan values.

Frank took the job and moved home while the rest of the family remained in Italy, their Mather forefathers no doubt turning in their graves to see them back in Europe—and surrounded by papists to boot. Somehow, thirty years had come and gone. Frank had recently retired from the university, but he and his wife still lived in Princeton. It was strange to think that in those almost thirty years Margaret and her brother had lived across the ocean from each other, he had seen an entire career to completion.

Meanwhile, in those thirty years, Margaret had experienced the life cycle of a nation. First came the devolution of a great European kingdom into a reluctant junior partner of the Triple Entente—the United Kingdom, France, and Russia—during the Great War, in exchange for territory meant to have been carved from the former Ottoman Empire and Austria-Hungary. After the war, Italy declined further into a state filled with bitterness and resentment after the loss of over half a million men and the denial of territorial promises. Margaret watched as labor unrest and anger over economic upheaval found voice in the leader of the National Fascist Party, Benito Mussolini. In the last years of his life, Margaret's father had looked at Mussolini with hope for Italy's future after a decade of turmoil. "Mussolini is certainly a wonderful man and has put a new breath of life into the Italian nation," her father, Frank Sr., who was certainly no fascist, had written in a memoir-like reflection on his life in 1924. "I do not think in the history of the nation more has been accomplished in the interests of high civilization than in the last few years under the inspiration and direction of Mussolini." But the following year, Mussolini had dismantled parliamentary democracy and formed a dictatorship.

By the time Frank Sr. died in 1929, Mussolini was forming plans to strike out on expansionist conquests. In Abyssinia, he sought to rebuild both Italy's East African empire and its standing as a formidable world power. The League of Nations, led by Britain and France, responded by imposing sanctions on Italy but otherwise did nothing to stop it from invading a sovereign neighbor, thus exposing the league's feebleness, of which Hitler took note. Such territorial conquests, while wildly popular domestically, were also costly for both the country's relationships and its finances. Italy had regained some of its imperial foothold and access to dearly needed natural resources in East Africa but at the price of worsening relations with Britain and France and increasing economic dependence on Germany.

Margaret's father had had such high hopes for Italian culture and civilization but a more tempered wish for Germany as it licked its self-inflicted wounds following the Great War. "I hope," he wrote, "Germany will experience a decided, lasting reformation." Germany was certainly going through a reformation. Whether it would ultimately be the kind Frank Sr. had imagined remained to be seen.

Margaret's flight touched down under the gray sky that hung over Frankfurt, and all the passengers disembarked. Collecting her luggage, she asked an attendant if she could leave it at the airport, as she would be returning for the *Hindenburg* departure that evening. No, they told her, she would have to take it into the city to the Frankfurter Hof, the hotel that served as the departure point for the trip. It did not seem to be a prime example of German orderly efficiency. But then again, perhaps they had so mastered efficient processes that there really was some sensible reason to lug it all the way to the city and back.

The bus to Frankfurt was not scheduled to depart for some time, so Margaret took a taxi. The ten-kilometer drive wound through the peaceful beech forest she had seen from the air, and Margaret found the trees with their "young green leaves" of spring simply "enchanting."

What a beautiful farewell to earth, she thought to herself.

The Frankfurter Hof was an elegant Beaux Arts structure in the middle of Frankfurt's historic downtown, just five minutes' walk from the home where Goethe had once lived, the Main River, and the medieval Römer Rathaus, Frankfurt's city hall for six hundred years. In front of the hotel, an enormous fountain bubbled in the Kaiserplatz. The hotel itself was perfectly symmetrical, with two wings built from sandy stone that stood six stories high. In front was a curved, cloister-like passageway separating its elegant courtyard from the noise and hubbub of the street, all nicely situated and respectable for a rainy afternoon's wait.

Passengers who were not already staying at the Frankfurter Hof had arrived with their boxes, bags, packages, and trunks in tow, turning the elegant hotel's understated foyer into a miniature version of the waiting rooms at Grand Central Station. People milled about among armchairs covered in printed fabrics and trod softly on Oriental rugs, quietly waiting for something to happen as the time to departure ticked by. Despite the rain, the day was surprisingly hot, and a palpable humidity hung in the air, adding to the "silent tension" that languished in the room. This group of strangers would spend the next three days in close quarters, and by the end of the trip they would no doubt declare themselves intimate friends, but there seemed to be an unwritten rule that the process of converting strangers into friends could commence only with the beginning of the journey itself. The silence had clearly become too uncomfortable for one man, who felt compelled to jump the starting gun. "We sit here together like convicts," he joked to the group. But no one answered and the joke fell flat.

There were thirty-six passengers in all, a mix of Americans and Europeans, businessmen and pleasure-seekers, the old, the young, and everyone in between. There were two Swedes—a journalist and a worldly businessman of military bearing—and a retired Dane. Several guests of DZR: a proper Brit, a middle-aged American couple, and a German husband-and-wife pair of journalists. There were expats like Margaret, including a German pharmaceutical executive who was treating his wife and three of their five children to a thrilling trip home to Mexico City, where they had lived for many years. Their youngest child was just eight years old. German and Austrian manufacturers, brokers, and wholesalers represented industries from paint and varnish to the seed trade to cotton and wire. One of the Germans owned a company called Teekanne and employed the engineer who had invented the tea bag–packing machine and preportioned tea bags.

The American passengers had similarly built successful careers, and some of them eye-popping fortunes, making the stuff essential to everyday life. They included a surprisingly sizable contingent from Chicago, whose businesses reflected the heartland that fueled the rest of the country: coal and coke, farm equipment, and meatpacking. Two of the Chicagoans, the meatpacker and a man in imports, were traveling together. There were also a handful of unique characters among the Americans. There was a successful Italian American clothing designer, as well as a handsome young Yale graduate and son of a wealthy Washington, DC, diplomat on his way home from a year spent studying in Paris. Perhaps most excited for the voyage was a Jewish food-canning executive from San Francisco who had emigrated to the United States from Prussia shortly before the turn of the century and who had had special postcards made up for family and friends to mark his first flight on the *Hindenburg*. All together, the passengers were like the cast of characters in one of Agatha Christie's popular mysteries.

Margaret soon understood why she had not been allowed to leave her luggage at the airport, as DZR officials descended on the hotel to organize the passengers for the journey ahead. They promptly asked for everyone's tickets and passports. Then the luggage examination began. Each of the passengers had to open his or her belongings for inspection to ensure that neither restricted exports nor dangerous objects would be aboard the ship. All cigarettes, matches, and lighters were collected by the crew and placed into small bags illustrated with a grinning carnival mask and a warning: "*Sehr wichtig!* . . . Smoking on the *Hindenburg* is only permitted in the specially insulated smoking room. Smoking is strictly prohibited in all other areas!" Crucially, there was a space at the top for the passenger's name and cabin number. These little bags were a new addition to the flight protocol after an incident the year before when the crew had somehow lost a valuable lighter belonging to automobile tycoon Walter Chrysler's son-in-law, much to the company's embarrassment. Once on board, passengers' cameras would also be confiscated, albeit briefly, while flying over Germany's border with the Netherlands as they made their way west. As DZR reminded passengers in its advertising pamphlet, this was merely to honor "existing air-navigation laws of most countries," which prohibited aerial photographs within three miles of their national borders. Flying over France would have been a more direct route to the Atlantic than over the Netherlands, but France rarely allowed zeppelins to fly over its territory, and only with French airplanes escorting them. It seemed that centuries-old suspicion between hostile neighbors remained alive and well on the Continent.

Margaret found the DZR employees' search "courteous," if she could be so generous, but it was extremely thorough, as if they suspected everyone of carrying contraband. "Every inch" of Margaret's luggage "was searched, every box opened." Inevitably, it was not long before someone discovered an infraction. Margaret's luggage was over the stipulated weight limit of sixty-six pounds, approximately thirty kilograms. Any excess weight was supposed to have been sent ahead on a fast mail steamship, as arranged by Hamburg-America Line booking agents. The employee informed Margaret that she was required to pay for the fifteen extra kilos at a rate of two reichsmarks per pound.

But this was ridiculous, she tried to argue the point with the DZR representative. "I weigh twenty kilos less than the average man." If anything, between her luggage and herself, she was *under* her weight allotment. Surely DZR could see her logic.

"It is the rule," she was told.

The matter was closed. The official moved on to the next person.

While the passengers had their luggage checked in downtown Frankfurt, the *Hindenburg* crew made its final preparations for the transatlantic journey at the airfield. Alongside the decision to move the departure point for Atlantic crossings from Friedrichshafen to Frankfurt, that April, DZR had also laid the cornerstone for a prefabricated company town called Zeppelinheim, which stood just beyond the trees on the edge of the Frankfurt airport. This was where the zeppelin crews would live to facilitate smoother, more efficient operations.

As the evening's departure drew near, the gas cells, diesel stores, and ballast tanks were topped off and provisions were loaded onto the airship in preparation for a final weighing off to bring the 242-ton airship into balance. It was incredible that, when empty of passengers, provisions, and fuel, an airship with a volume of over seven million cubic feet weighed about the same as a locomotive. When its sixteen gas cells were fully inflated, the *Hindenburg* had a lift capacity of over half a million pounds, all of it held together by a frame made of a superlight aluminum-and-copper alloy called duralumin and covered in doped canvas.

Though the *Hindenburg*'s total volume was utterly enormous, the casual observer would have been surprised to learn how little of it was dedicated to passenger and crew space. The nerve center of the airship was actually contained in a windowed gondola affixed to its exterior about one quarter of the way down the body, moving from nose to tail. This was where the officers controlled the primary functions of steering, altitude, and navigation. Just above the control gondola were two small rooms divided by a narrow walkway, the radio room and the mail room. Almost directly behind this was the passenger area, which comprised two decks built directly on top of each other—A and B decks—nestled into the keel of the airship. This area was only about fifty feet long on each deck, or one sixteenth of the entire length of the *Hindenburg*, but it spanned the width of the keel, which itself was only about eighty feet across at this level. On the upper A deck were long, windowed promenades bordering the portside dining room and starboard-side lounge and writing room, with twenty-five double-occupancy passenger cabins in between. Downstairs on B deck were the bar and smoking lounge, as well as more passenger cabins, toilets, and a shower. Beside the passenger quarters on B deck were the crew's mess, officers' mess, and kitchen, while farther down along the keel were the majority of the crew's bunks, with a few scattered aft, closer to the tail, for those who worked toward the rear, behind the space for cargo. All this meant was that the overwhelming majority of the *Hindenburg*'s interior volume was taken up by the behemoth gas cells.

The hydrogen that filled the gas cells was piped in from a nearby IG Farben chemical plant directly to the airfield.

With only thirty-six passengers booked on this flight out of a possible seventy-two, the *Hindenburg* would be traveling lighter than usual and could carry some additional men for training and observation, making for a total of sixty-one crew members. The commanding officer for the journey was Captain Max Pruss, a forty-six-year-old East Prussian with graying hair, who was a veteran airship captain with over twenty years of experience. Pruss had worked his way up from a lowly trainee before the war to become one of the zeppelin company's elite commanders. He had served as commanding officer on the *Graf Zeppelin* on nearly three dozen flights since 1934 and had been placed at the helm of the *Hindenburg* midway through the 1936 season as Eckener was promoted to the role of figurehead and Lehmann's time became increasingly occupied with company operations. Though Pruss had a soldierly tone, his eyes were like those of a sailor, which one crew member described as being able to see both into the distance and into people.

Under Pruss were three watch officers, the highly experienced Captain Albert Sammt and two younger captains, Heinrich Bauer and Walter Ziegler, as well Anton Wittemann, who usually served on the *Graf Zeppelin* but had joined the flight as an observer. Alongside the captains were four navigators: Max Zabel (who doubled as postmaster), Franz Herzog, Eduard Boëtius, and Christian Nielsen. These officers served in the control gondola affixed to the airship's keel in groups of three on four-hour shifts. Joining them were three elevator men, whose exacting work keeping the airship perfectly in balance in all weather and pressure conditions was so precise and demanding that they would alternate in two- or three-hour watches. Just as on an airplane, by adjusting the flat, horizontal panels on the airship's tail, the elevator men could pitch its nose up or down to dynamically adjust its altitude without having to valve gas. Captain Hans von Schiller, who was piloting the *Graf Zeppelin* on a flight from Brazil while the *Hindenburg* made its way to Lakehurst, said that the touch of the elevator man was so sensitive and unique to a person that an experienced airship traveler could recognize who was on duty when lying in bed in his cabin simply from the way the ship moved in gusts of wind.

The elevator men were also responsible for loading freight into the cargo hold in the belly of the airship. As the quickest way to send cargo across the ocean, both the *Hindenburg* and *Graf Zeppelin* had on past journeys featured some unique freight on board: gorillas and chimpanzees, bees, rare birds, prize racehorses and purebred dogs, exotic orchids, medicines, and films. On its next round-trip journey from Europe, the *Hindenburg* was supposed to carry films from the upcoming May 12 coronation of King George VI to America, just as it had ferried photographs to be developed from the Berlin Olympics to the United States the prior summer. Freight sometimes included other means of transportation, from cars to airplanes with their wings detached inside the cargo hold. In 1936, the *Hindenburg* had carried a 2,500-pound Beechcraft Staggerwing biplane, whose pilot had reassembled the wings upon landing in Frankfurt and had immediately flown off. DZR did, however, draw the line when an Indian maharaja asked to fly an elephant on board to present as a gift to the British monarch.

Rounding out the crew in the control gondola were a rotating team of three helmsmen responsible for the rudder and for physically steering the airship, as well as four radio operators in the radio room, located just above. But the work was not confined to this tiny portion of the airship. Affixed to the outside of the airship aft of the control gondola and passenger area were four Daimler-Benz sixteen-cylinder diesel-powered engines in separate, relatively spacious gondolas—called nacelles—which could run at 1,320 horsepower on takeoff and continuously at 900 horsepower during flight. These engines were so quiet that they were almost imperceptible to guests sitting in their cabins or in the lounge. If a New York subway train rattling down its track generated eighty-two to one hundred decibels of noise, and airplane engines and Pullman cars roared at sixty-five to eighty decibels, the *Hindenburg* was the quietest form of transport available, with engines creating a mere forty to sixty-one decibels, which was further dampened as the gas cells absorbed the sound. Four engineers oversaw groups of three to four mechanics specifically dedicated to each engine. Inside the engine gondolas, the mechanics and engineers had sufficient space to work in teams and, in the event of engine trouble, could shut down an engine, strip the power plant, and rebuild it mid-flight.

Thirty-two 660-gallon duralumin tanks filled with diesel fuel powered the engines. Beside the fuel tanks, smaller cisterns stored water for ballast, cooking, drinking, and bathing in the onboard shower. Farther aft, three riggers operated the tail fin while three electricians roved across the airship's catwalks checking for issues with fuel pumps, gas valves, the switch room, or the fully equipped all-electric kitchen.

In the kitchen beside the passenger quarters, twenty-five-year-old head chef Xaver Maier, a pastry chef, and three assistants oversaw the loading of provisions. While the journey would last just two and a half days, they carried sufficient food for four days in case of delays or problems landing. Maier was responsible for 5,500 total pounds of food and other mealtime essentials, including 440 pounds of meat and poultry, 220 pounds of fish, 330 pounds of cold cuts and sausages, 440 pounds each of vegetables and potatoes, 440 pounds of canned goods, 220 pounds of butter, cheese, and other spreads, and 40 gallons of milk. The kitchen was connected by dumbwaiter to a serving pantry above, the door to which was to remain closed as much as possible so that no unpleasant food smells could waft through the airship and disturb the travelers.

The bar steward, Max Schulze, perhaps the most popular member of the crew among the passengers, ensured sufficient libations were aboard. The crew stocked no fewer than 250 bottles of German wine and champagne, along with sherry, port, gin, vermouth, whiskey, and rum. Despite its central place in German culture, beer was carried only in small quantities, as it was considerably heavier per serving than wine or spirits. When passengers purchased drinks or other small souvenirs, like postcards, from the stewards on board, no physical currency was exchanged. Instead, the airship's doctor, Kurt Rüdiger, who doubled as purser, kept track of the passengers' bills, which they settled by check with the chief steward at the end of the journey.

As the last of the gas, fuel, water, and provisions were loaded, six stewards readied the passenger cabins. Clad in fresh white jackets and dark slacks, the stewards were the crew members with whom the passengers primarily interacted. They served as waiters, housekeepers, and tour guides, attending to passengers' needs at any hour of the day. They were led by a chief steward, forty-nine-year-old Heinrich Kubis, who had begun his career at the Frankfurter Hof in 1902 and went on to work in hotels in London, Paris, and Cairo. Below him were forty-three-year-old Max Henneberg and four younger men in their mid-twenties, Fritz Deeg, Severin Klein, Eugen Nunnenmacher, and Wilhelm Balla, who had varying backgrounds as waiters, stewards, and butlers in smaller German hotels.

Alongside these men, the sole female member of the crew, forty-seven-year-old stewardess Emilie Imhof, was making her maiden flight as the first woman to work aboard a zeppelin. More women and children were traveling by air than ever before, so the company thought it wise to employ some female attendants. (Some also thought it advantageous to have female staff on airships because they weighed less on average than their male counterparts, an important consideration, as total weight had to be carefully managed.) Over the winter, DZR had hired Imhof, who had previously worked as an ocean liner stewardess and hotel proprietor.

One of the younger stewards, Wilhelm Balla, had one additional, special charge. He was responsible for the final member of the crew, the fourteen-year-old cabin boy, Werner Franz. Franz had joined the crew in 1936 after his older brother, who was a waiter at the Frankfurter Hof, used the hotel's connection with DZR to persuade Chief Steward Kubis to hire the boy on a trial basis, as their father, a telephone operator, was ill and the family desperately needed additional income. Kubis had agreed and put the boy to work washing dishes, setting the table in the crew's mess, and serving coffee for the officers on a flight to South America. Balla, who was the oldest child in a family of fourteen, was instructed to look after Franz. Franz passed his trial and was hired as a permanent member of the crew for 1937 with a handsome salary of sixty reichsmarks per month. While Balla and the other stewards made the passengers' beds and placed fresh flowers on the dining room tables in preparation for departure, Werner Franz, dressed in a white jacket and black tie that his mother had bought for him, made up the beds for the crew, the same sort of task with which he had helped his mother at home.

At seven o'clock, Margaret Mather and the other passengers were ushered onto three large buses waiting outside the Frankfurter Hof to begin their drive out to Frankfurt airport. It was strange to think that in just over an hour, they would have left the ground behind. They had been joined in the meantime by three officers from the German Luftwaffe who were making the trip as observers to learn about navigation practices. Though one might have thought the addition of crisply uniformed officers would have brought order to the traveling party, the return trip to the airfield through the beech woods was hardly the serene affair Margaret had experienced that morning. As they wound their way through the forest, one of the American passengers, who had apparently celebrated the voyage with one too many of Germany's national beverages, burst out in song, serenading the others at full volume. Perhaps this man actually had the right attitude. The fact that they would soon be transported across the ocean by a tangle of aluminum girders held in the air by a series of balloons was a remarkable feat worth celebrating.

Sunset was still an hour off as they emerged from the forest, but even though it was drizzling and overcast, there remained plenty of light to appreciate the spectacle that had transformed the airfield from a dreary place of function into something akin to a pier before the launch of a great ocean liner of the Gilded Age. The moment the airfield came into view, the feeling of apprehension that had nagged at Margaret earlier that day immediately dissolved, replaced by a wave of pure joy that suddenly swept over her. Gone were the feelings of reluctance and doubt. Here was the sense of pleasure and elation she had hoped she would feel, for there it was, tethered to the ground beside the hangar, the zeppelin Margaret had so long admired.

The *Hindenburg* stood 804 feet long and 135 feet high, larger than the entire United States Capitol building, longer than the Roman Colosseum, and more than half the height of the Empire State Building if balanced on its nose. Its name was painted on its belly above the control gondola in red Gothic lettering with its official classification, *D-LZ129*, painted farther toward the stern. In between were the Olympic rings, a reminder of the part it had played in the 1936 Olympics as it floated above crowds of thousands at the Berlin stadium. And on the tail fins, both top and bottom, was the Nazi flag, painted deep red with a white circle, the black, crooked swastika at the center, a blaze of color offset against the silver airship and the gray, stormy sky.

In the face of such an impressive display, it was little wonder that so many spectators had braved the rain to see it depart, even though the *Hindenburg* had now been in transatlantic service for a year. It was the physical manifestation of the new Germany's national pride. The enthusiastic crowd was kept back from the ship and allowed to observe it only from afar. On the zeppelin's port side, a brass band had assembled to treat the audience to triumphant, martial tunes. The musicians were dressed all in yellow and blue and had decorated their instruments with streamers of the same. In the middle was a funny instrument Margaret could not name that looked like an enormous lute with bells instead of strings, one blue and one yellow horsetail fluttering at either side. Most excited were the children who had come to see the launch, a scurrying mass of Hitler Youth boys in their tan jackets and red armbands, and the only spectators DZR officials allowed to come up close to examine the giant machine. No doubt their dreams would be filled with airships that night—flying on airships, captaining airships, even imagining they *were* airships—if their parents could manage to settle them down to sleep.

As Margaret was ushered into the hangar to wait for yet another passport inspection, she was struck by how, for such a mammoth airship, there really were so few passengers on board. Among both the passengers and crew, it also occurred to her that there were only a few women. On this trip, only seven of the thirty-six passengers happened to be female: Margaret and a German lady a bit older than she were the only women traveling alone. Then there were the mother and daughter from the German family on their way to Mexico City, the middle-aged wife of the German seed trader, a slightly younger American woman with her husband who worked with DZR in the United States, and the much younger wife of the German journalist.

While the passengers finished their final passport check, the crew loaded the last of seventeen thousand pieces of mail into the cargo hold for delivery in the United States. One bag was separated from the rest and brought forward to the mail room. En route to the Atlantic, the *Hindenburg* would make a mail drop. A batch of letters was supposed to have been delivered as part of a May Day flight over a Hitler Youth parade at the Olympic Stadium in Berlin earlier that week, but the flight had been canceled due to poor weather, so the *Hindenburg* would deposit it in the lower Rhine River city of Cologne to be forwarded to Berlin as it made its way west.

As Captain Pruss oversaw the final weighing off of the airship, Margaret and the others were taken from the hangar up the narrow gangway into the belly of the zeppelin to finally board. They entered on B deck, the smaller of the two levels of the passenger area, in the very bottom of the keel. The first area the passengers reached was the stairwell, where two staircases on either side of the hall led upstairs to A deck and then converged. Decorating the upper landing was a bust of the airship's namesake, Paul von Hindenburg, the Great War field marshal and president of the German Weimar Republic from 1925 until his death in 1933, after which Chancellor Hitler had declared himself both chancellor and president.

At the bottom of the stairs, one could turn right down a corridor toward the bar and smoking lounge as well as several passenger toilets. Turning left toward the stern, there were eight double passenger cabins and one larger room with four berths for a family traveling together. These rooms were exactly the same as those on A deck, except they had been constructed along the exterior part of the zeppelin's frame and had their own windows. Fortunately, because the airship was only half full, everyone who so desired had a cabin to him- or herself.

A steward politely showed Margaret to her B deck cabin. She slid open the light foam door to reveal a small, tidy room just five feet wide and six and a quarter feet long that, much like a sleeper berth on a train car, was efficiently constructed to maximize limited space. Inside, the walls were covered in pearl-gray linen, and there were two narrow bunks with soft pillows and blankets, the upper of which could be accessed by a five-step aluminum ladder with holes in the sides designed to cut down on weight. A small desk flipped down from the wall in front of a folding stool, and there was a curtain-covered closet large enough to hold a half dozen dresses or suits, and finally a white plastic washbasin with hot and cold taps. Luggage would be stowed beneath the lower bunk. It was "very tiny but complete," and with the sloping plexiglass window, it offered everything she had never been able to enjoy on an ocean liner.

There was scarcely time to look around before the captain announced "*Schiff hoch!*"—"Up ship!"—so Margaret left her belongings in her room and dashed out to the hall, up the stairs, and past the bust of President Hindenburg to find a place from which to watch the ship cast off. More open plexiglass windows lined the entire fifty-foot promenades. With their forty-five-degree slant closely matching the angle of the airship's exterior, they offered the perfect means to watch the ground shrink below. The signal went out from Captain Pruss to the ground crew to loosen the mooring ropes and detach the sandbags that kept the airship on the ground, and the *Hindenburg* began to rise ever so subtly as the ropes slackened in the crew's hands.

At that instant, an order rang out to halt and a voice called over a loudspeaker asking for a woman to come forward. It seemed most unusual that after keeping the onlookers far away, someone should be plucked out to come near. There was a senior Luftwaffe officer on board, Colonel Fritz Erdmann, commander of an air intelligence school at Halle, who was traveling as an observer. Apparently, he needed to say something to his wife. Someone announced her name, and she was brought from the crowd to meet him at the airship. There was no explanation for this irregularity, not from Erdmann or any member of the staff, only a general assumption that the colonel's rank was sufficient to halt the takeoff because he wanted to give his wife one last farewell. After a minute, they said a final goodbye, and Frau Erdmann retreated back into the crowd.

For a second time, the order was given to release the mooring ropes. As the ship broke loose, it began to drift to port as a slight wind pushed it toward the assembled band. They paused their song, marched back several yards, and were about to begin again when the ship drifted farther, forcing them to beat a hasty retreat. After a day of rain, Frankfurters no doubt appreciated having a good, strong breeze to blow the humidity away, but it was posing an added challenge for the crew. This dance between the wind, the zeppelin, and the band happened several times more, each time just as the bandleader lifted his baton to give the signal to play on. Eventually the ship began to rise once more and the band launched into its powerful send-off, a hymn by Martin Luther, "Ein feste Burg ist unser Gott"—"A mighty fortress is our God."

As they gained altitude, Margaret sensed an almost "indescribable feeling of lightness and buoyancy—a lift and pull upward, quite unlike the takeoff of an airplane." She leaned out the open window to watch the "receding earth" below. The Hitler Youth boys scrambled over the airfield with overwhelming excitement, their blond and brown heads growing smaller and smaller until they were specks against the ground.

Suddenly, Margaret's sense of serene weightlessness was punctuated by "short, jerky exclamations" of someone nearby sputtering the words "*Mein Gott! Mein Gott!*"

She turned and saw an older, red-faced man. It was the man from the bus who had turned the drive from the city into a cabaret. Margaret found his wave of emotion "so intense that he seemed quite alone in it"—possessed, even—that "it surrounded him like an aura, and isolated him."

He must have felt Margaret's gaze upon him, for suddenly he snapped out of his reverie and cried, "*Herrlich, nicht wahr?*"

"I don't speak German," Margaret replied, perhaps thinking it would be most prudent to withdraw before she could be pulled into too deep a conversation with someone with whom she quite easily could become stuck for the next three days.

"My God! Are you an American?" he exclaimed. "So am I!" And before Margaret could react, he "threw an enraptured arm" around her, overcome by the thrill of it all.

CHAPTER 7

Frankfurt, Germany, to the North Sea: May 3, 1937

For Gertrud Adelt, it was the feeling of the air on her hand as she stood reaching out the observation window and into the night sky that made the reality of the day begin to slip away. The silent tension of the salon at the Frankfurter Hof in the afternoon juxtaposed against the American's songs of parting on the drive to the airfield "reced[ed] into a kind of dream state from which images emerge[d] in fragments, seemingly torn out of context." As she stood at the window, those fragments of reality became "inextricably linked" to the feeling of one's hand in a cloud.

As they turned into the northwest sky, the rolling Taunus mountains above Frankfurt quickly disappeared into the distance in the dusky blue twilight. They were soon replaced by "glittering rows of lights" that "accompanied the darkening Rhine," which the *Hindenburg* followed northward as it made its way gently and silently toward the Netherlands and eventually the Atlantic Ocean. Gertrud was traveling to New York with her husband, Leonhard. They were both journalists and had received complimentary tickets on the *Hindenburg* courtesy of DZR, specifically thanks to the company's director, Ernst Lehmann, who was Leonhard's longtime friend and whom Leonhard had helped to write, edit, and now translate his memoir about his career in the airship industry. Not only did Lehmann and Leonhard have a meeting with their publisher in New

York, but Leonhard was also exploring the possibility of securing some onboard footage for a related project, a feature film about Count Zeppelin. He had other ideas for films, and while in the United States he was hoping to establish contacts with American film companies. Perhaps there would even be a chance to stay in the United States and pursue opportunities in Hollywood?

For Gertrud's husband, the trip also had great personal significance. Two of his brothers had immigrated to America as young men, had become American citizens, and now lived in Mays Landing, New Jersey, near Atlantic City. They planned to meet Leonhard and Gertrud at Lakehurst for their long-awaited reunion. Leonhard had not seen either of them for thirty years—almost as long as Gertrud had been alive.

Gertrud had met Leonhard several years earlier while she was working part-time for a newspaper and finishing her PhD at the University of Münster. Leonhard, a tall, blue-eyed man with light blond hair very much fitting the image of the ideal Aryan the Nazis so prized, was in his early fifties. He was divorced from his first wife and had a son from that marriage. Meanwhile, Gertrud was in her early thirties, just a few years older than Leonhard's son. Though small in stature with unremarkable medium-blond hair, Gertrud had a distinguished bearing that bordered on intimidating. Always proper and tidy in both appearance and mind, she held high standards for herself and what she wanted to accomplish, and in Leonhard she found a partner willing to support that. They married in 1935, and in 1936 Gertrud both gave birth to a son, Christian, and earned her doctorate in art history. When her husband mentioned her in his own writing, he referred to his thirty-four-year-old wife as "the editor, Dr. Gertrud Stolte-Adelt." She was proud of her PhD, and the title in front of her name mattered a great deal to her.

The lights below, which bordered the Rhine like a jeweled collar, were scarcely one hundred miles southwest of the rural roads surrounding Münster that she had cycled, camera around her neck, while conducting her dissertation research on Baroque *Volkskunst*, or folk art. While folk art was often dismissed in favor of that of a supposedly higher standard, art, she believed, should suit its purpose. There was perhaps no better example of art suiting its purpose than the interior of the airship. Beside the observation windows was the dining room. This was filled with aluminum chairs so light a child could lift them with one hand and tables that could be rearranged to accommodate couples, families, or twenty-some passengers together as if at a banquet. Most eye-catching of all were the walls made of silk that had been painted by German graphic artist Otto Arpke, whose designs ranged from advertisements for Hamburg-America Line cruises to movie posters for the Weimar era's famous silent expressionist horror film, *Das Cabinet des Dr. Caligari*. Arpke's art, which decorated the walls of not just the dining room but also the passenger lounge, writing room, and smoking room, evoked the history of travel and aviation. The theme of the dining room was a zeppelin flight to South America, and each panel portrayed the sights a traveler would experience along the way: the Spanish coast, the Canary Islands, Cabo Verde, the open ocean, and finally Brazil's Sugarloaf Mountain. By painting directly on the silk walls, the airship designers had achieved a practical yet artful balance in the ambiance—providing something tasteful but not too bland, while also minimizing the weight of decorations and purely aesthetic touches. Nearly everything about the *Hindenburg* married form and function. Pound for pound, the heaviest item on board was the champagne bucket.

If Gertrud was practical, Leonhard was the romantic dreamer, a side to his personality that was not immediately evident. The one great love of Leonhard's life was flight. Alongside his journalism and work as a translator, Leonhard was a novelist and had pioneered a genre of literature in Germany before the Great War. After taking flying lessons in Leipzig in rudimentary aircraft, in 1913 he published a novel called *Der Flieger*, or *The Aviator*, a story about a young man from a small farm who becomes transfixed by the idea of flight and the secrets of science that will unlock the heavens for man's exploration. "Since I learned how man harnesses all the forces of nature and how no goal seems unattainable," he wrote in the voice of one his characters, "it has never occurred to me that the kingdom of air should be denied to us." Even Leonhard's bookplates, which depicted a winged man chained to the ground, certainly revealed his fixation on the skies as liberation from the bondage of life on earth.

Gertrud leaned over the downward-slanted windows to watch as flashing beacons guided the airship from hill to hill. Currents of air passed over her hand as it dangled out the window. It was just as the celebrated German writer Hermann Hesse had observed over a quarter of a century earlier when he had flown on one of Count Zeppelin's early airships: "In the cabin . . . there was hardly a trace of draft to be noticed, but as soon as you stuck your head or hands out of the window, the air rushed past like a heavy gale." Gertrud was beginning to feel a sense of the dreamlike fantasy that had so long captivated her husband. Though Leonhard was nowhere near as famous as Hesse, his words came to life before Gertrud's eyes and captured the sensation of floating in the air in a way that even the great German writer and poet could not. "The world ran beneath us, patterned and divided," Leonhard had written, "with flat mountains, combed fields, colorful forests and farms that were neatly laid out. We were the still point in the drifting universe. . . . And the shadow of our ship, like Schlemihl's"—the man in a German fable who sells his shadow to the devil in exchange for riches—"had become detached from the physical. He scurried sideways across the field and rushed forward; we turned, he stalled and also turned; we rose—he uncertainly struck a bow: a dog jumping around his master questioningly."

A succession of villages and hamlets were linked to larger towns below by the ribbon of the autobahn. Before long, a great mass of lights appeared in the distance, growing close and spreading wide before them. It was Cologne, the last major city the *Hindenburg* would pass until it reached Boston in two days' time. Beyond the rows of city lights, Leonhard noticed a silhouette leaping high above the shadows. The famous Cologne cathedral's twin spires reached up as if to meet the airship in the night sky.

As they approached the city, something fluttered from the zeppelin and quickly fell from view as it descended toward the Cologne airfield below them. A small package attached to a parachute had dropped from the control gondola and floated silently through the darkness to the ground. It was the Berlin-bound package of mail. The onboard mail room was technically a suboffice of the Frankfurt post office, but letters carried on the *Hindenburg* received their own special markings in pink reading "Luftschiff Hindenburg: Deutschlandfahrt," with an image of the airship and the German eagle holding a swastika-adorned wreath. Down below, the specially stamped mail would be collected and put on a Berlin-bound flight, slightly delayed, but that was of little consequence to the many stamp collectors who simply wanted a unique souvenir for a small price, which added up to a tidy sum for the zeppelin company.

By about 9:15 p.m., the *Hindenburg* had passed over the German-Dutch border. After clearing the three-mile mark, the stewards returned passengers' cameras. In the darkness, such a precaution seemed quite unnecessary, but rules were rules. As the clock struck ten, the chief steward, Heinrich Kubis, announced that a light supper of salad and cold meats was served. Gertrud and the others tore themselves away from the sights below as the airship continued west over Holland and the small city of Bergen op Zoom, completing its detour around France. Typically, the passengers would change before dinner as if on a steamship, a practice that divided passengers' opinions, as their trip was so short and their baggage allotment so small, but as it was already late, there was no reason to bother. The stewards had arranged the dining room, which was separated from the observation gallery by a railing, with a long table set for twenty in the middle of the room and a collection of smaller tables along the interior wall. Solo travelers would sit together at the communal table, while the side tables were reserved for married couples and families, or, in this instance, the one family on board, the Doehners. Parents Hermann and Matilde sat together with their three youngest children, fourteen-year-old daughter Irene and two blond sons, ten-year-old Walter and eight-year-old Werner. (Two older sons had remained in Darmstadt and Mexico City.)

Aside from Gertrud and Leonhard, there were only two other couples traveling together. There was an older German husband and wife, Otto and Elsa Ernst, and an American couple, John and Emma Pannes, who were Leonhard's age. Otto Ernst was an executive for his family's seed business in Hamburg, and he and his wife had been flying for more than two decades. Meanwhile, John Pannes was a manager for the New York office of the Hamburg-America Line, the *Hindenburg*'s booking agency, and typically would be in Lakehurst to greet the airships for all arrivals and departures. Like the Adelts, the Panneses were traveling as DZR's guests.

Typically, Captain Lehmann would be seated at the head of the long table as the man helming the ship, but for this flight, he was slated on the manifest only as an observer and company director. As commander of the flight, Max Pruss was entitled to the head of the table, and Lehmann thus would be sitting with his friends the Adelts instead. Of course, from time to time, Lehmann could not help but wander down to the familiar control gondola, where his longtime colleagues were running the airship, but he had no official duties on board. He was even staying in one of the passenger cabins, not the captain's quarters.

Whether it was difficult for Lehmann to sit beside Gertrud and Leonhard rather than instinctively take the still-empty seat at the head of the table where Pruss was yet to appear, Lehmann did not say, but this was hardly surprising. He was too courteous and well-mannered. Though he was quite small, much closer to Gertrud's own height than to someone like Hugo Eckener, who towered over him in photographs, his quietly forceful personality commanded attention. To his crew members he gave clear and determined orders, never needing to raise his voice to anything more than a conversational level. His appearance was always "dapper, polished, suave," as his friend Commander Charles Rosendahl described. Lehmann wore his hair carefully slicked back off his tan forehead, preferred a bow tie while in uniform, and could be found in a fur-lined leather coat with an upturned collar that partially hid his face. He was a fundamentally studious man who put on his glasses to peer at navigational charts, but when he smiled, his eyes were warm with a hint of mirth, especially when he had a pipe tucked happily in the corner of his mouth.

At last, Captain Pruss appeared in the dining room and strode over to the empty seat at the head of the long table. As the only unmarried female passenger traveling alone, Margaret Mather was seated next to him. Before Pruss sat down, he shook hands with her, as well as with several of the men nearby. Pruss appeared polite and cordial but was clearly in a hurry to eat and return to his post.

Though the late meal was a relatively simple picnic compared with the luxurious, multicourse meals the *Hindenburg*'s chef would be preparing with his electric stove and range for the remainder of the journey, the table was set as impeccably as one might find on any Cunard steamship or in a fine European hotel. Each place setting was anchored by a porcelain charger plate with gold-and-blue trim around the edge and the DZR crest at the top. The words *Deutsche Zeppelin-Reederei* encircled a blue globe with gold parallels of latitude and meridians of longitude and an airship floating in the center. It was the same insignia that appeared on the caps and uniform pins of the crew. All of the dishes on the *Hindenburg*—bread plates, bowls, tea and coffee cups and demitasses, serving platters and dishes, soup tureens, even vases for flowers in the middle of the table—used this same china pattern. The globe emblem on each dish was similarly engraved on each fork, knife, and spoon and etched into the water and wine glasses. This was actually a new pattern that had been introduced for the 1936 travel season. The old dishes on the *Graf Zeppelin* had had a thicker gold-white-and-blue design circling each plate with an art deco rendering of the letters *LZ* for *Luftschiffbau Zeppelin.* When the reich's Ministry of Aviation had formed DZR in 1935, the older design schemes had been discarded. Perhaps the most notable difference was on the new patches embroidered on each crew member's hat. Beneath the globe-and-zeppelin insignia was a silver swastika, and on top of each globe was an eagle that looked like it was holding the world in its talons.

The only curious factor clearly distinguishing a meal on an airship from that in a fine hotel was that each passenger was presented with an individually labeled paper envelope with a scalloped edge containing a crisp white napkin. It was embroidered with the same design as the dishes in a contrasting shade of pearl. In an effort to cut down on weight, each passenger was to keep this napkin for the duration of the flight, replacing it inside the envelope he or she had been given at the conclusion of each meal. Completing each place setting was a menu. By the end of every flight, the white-gloved stewards had come to expect that not a single paper menu would remain on board and that a fair number of spoons and demitasses would have gone missing, as the small objects could be well concealed inside the pocket or handbag of even the most well-heeled travelers looking for souvenirs. In a single season, roughly four hundred spoons and cups had disappeared—never mind that *Property of the Deutsche Zeppelin-Reederei* was stamped on the underside of each item.

The stewards poured glasses of wine and mineral water for each of the passengers. In addition to the many technical and safety experiments the zeppelin company had conducted, it had also tested the maximum pitch the airship could sustain before bottles would tumble off the tables. It found they would start to slide when the airship tilted ten degrees either up or down. Out of an abundance of caution, the airship was never supposed to be tilted more than five degrees. On airships predating the *Hindenburg*, empty bottles also had a second purpose. Early altimeters were highly sensitive to the weather, and it was difficult for the captain and navigator to ascertain whether the altitude that the instruments displayed was accurate. Rather than disturb passengers by using a gunshot as a sonic altimeter, the crew would drop empty mineral water bottles into the ocean, timing their fall to establish the airship's height and recalibrate their instruments. Fortunately, by the time the *Hindenburg* was constructed, sonar was sufficiently advanced to make such crude methods unnecessary.

As the passengers settled in for their meal, they began to chat with their neighbors at the table. It promised to be an exciting week in current events. That day, Margaret Mitchell's epic Civil War novel, *Gone with the Wind*, had been awarded the Pulitzer Prize. On Saturday, the nation's fastest three-year-old thoroughbreds would race to wear a blanket of roses at the Kentucky Derby. Meanwhile, the most salacious gossip was that that very morning a British court had finally granted a divorce decree to Wallis Simpson, the American woman who had so enraptured King Edward VIII that he had renounced the throne for her the previous December. During the monthslong legal saga that had ensued following his abdication, Wallis and Edward had been living apart to maintain an air of respectability. Wallis had taken up residence in a château south of Tours, France; meanwhile, Edward had been living free and easy at the Hotel Appesbach in St. Wolfgang am Wolfgangsee in the Austrian Alps. The American press had received a tip that Wallis had been keeping busy with Parisian couture atelier Schiaparelli, which had made her a new wardrobe for her impending marriage. Reportedly, she had seventeen new ensembles, which had cost five thousand dollars.

Knowing that the divorce court was scheduled to make its ruling and that Edward would soon be departing, the local merchants in St. Wolfgang had hosted a send-off for him the night before. Apparently, during the festivities, a group of Austrian Nazis on the opposite shore of the lake had set fire to an enormous wooden swastika, reportedly prompting Edward to retort, "Why must politics try to spoil everything?" Once the British courts had made Wallis's divorce from her second husband, Ernest Simpson, official that morning, Edward promptly left Austria, speeding across Germany toward Paris by train to reach his lover (and apparently leaving behind two cases of his luggage in his rush to join her). Had the *Hindenburg* departed from Friedrichshafen rather than Frankfurt, perhaps it might have passed over his train as it cut across Germany toward France.

With the dramatic ordeal of Wallis and Edward now firmly out of the way, the coronation of Edward's brother, George VI, could take place without being overshadowed by the couple, who could not bring themselves to eschew the limelight. It was vital that the *Hindenburg* remain on schedule, as its return flight to Europe was fully booked by Americans making the crossing for the special occasion on May 12. Unfortunately, the present flight was barely underway, and already they were falling behind. While the passengers were enjoying their meal with the sound of silverware cheerfully clinking against the blue-and-white porcelain, a storm had begun to gather over the English Channel, forcing Max Pruss, who had eaten just one course before disappearing back down to the control gondola, to steer in a more northerly arc over the North Sea before cutting west across the channel.

As dinner concluded and the stewards cleared the tables, many of the group said their good nights and departed for their narrow but comfortable bunks. Small groups formed among those who lingered, who, like Gertrud, Leonhard, and Captain Lehmann, were not quite ready to turn in. They left the dining room for the lounge or the bar and smoking room, where they could continue drinking and talking as long as they wished.

Despite the storm, the airship's flight remained remarkably smooth, even as lightning played in the clouds. Gertrud had taken notice of one of the younger men among the night owls who had settled into a fabric-covered aluminum chair in the lounge. He had dark hair, was close to her age, and was even smaller than Lehmann. He had a "quiet, swaying step" and a German accent, though he spoke fluent English. His name was Benny Spah, and he was an acrobat, comedian, and performer who was on his way home to his wife and children on Long Island after a months-long tour performing in a variety show across Europe. Normally, he liked to take his family with him, but the duration of this tour had made it impractical to travel with three children under six, and he was eager to return to them. He was supposed to have traveled home by steamer but had changed his plans at the last minute when an opportunity to open at Radio City had come up, prompting him to speed back to New York. He had cabled his wife, Vera, from the airship that night to let her know he had made it on board.

Benny Spah, who apparently had some apprehension about the lightning licking the clouds outside the windows of the promenade, noticed Lehmann. He asked the captain whether "there was any chance of the ship being struck."

Lehmann was well aware that imaginations could run wild with fears of mid-ocean emergencies. For those less familiar with the technical aspects of airships, it was a fair concern, especially if they knew of the French airship, the *Dixmude*, that had exploded and crashed during a thunderstorm off Sicily. Though the cause of the accident would never be known, Lehmann suspected that the *Dixmude*'s crew had become disoriented during the storm and had hit the Sicilian volcanic mountain range, which ultimately brought the airship down. For an experienced airman, however, it was "almost impossible to conceive of an accident which would force an airship to come down upon an undesired spot, such as the middle of the Atlantic Ocean," which he had proudly explained in his book.

It was not so much that the airship could not be struck by lightning. It certainly could, and Lehmann had seen tiny singe marks left in one airship's outer covering after a particularly violent storm. However, due to the zeppelins' design, a lightning strike posed no danger. As a young captain during the Great War, Lehmann had experienced a phenomenon called Saint Elmo's fire, in which a luminous corona forms around an object in an atmospheric electrical field. During a storm that had surrounded his airship, the *LZ-98*, "from all directions," one of his crew, who had climbed to the top to serve as a lookout, had reported to him that "a bolt of lightning had struck the nose of the ship" and "tongues of fire [were] licking around the muzzles of [his] machine guns, and around

[his] head, too." When the man spread out his hands before him, tiny flames seemed to spurt from his fingertips. "To the non-expert, it may seem well-nigh unbelievable that an airship filled with inflammable gas was not destroyed in such a storm," Lehmann explained in his book. But lightning, too, "obeys the laws of nature." An airship was essentially an enormous Faraday cage, a simple, mesh-like enclosure made up of conductive material that distributes external electric charges, such as lightning, in a current around the *exterior* of the cage but never the *interior*. It was a scientific concept understood for a hundred years. As long as no gas seeped out and collected between the cells and the outer canvas covering the frame, none of the charge would pass through the space within the structure.

Rather than provide the entire scientific explanation, Lehmann simply answered, "*Nein*," and assured Benny Spah and the others who were listening that the lightning posed no danger. Zeppelins could fly right through a storm. Even if the lightning struck the airship, its charge would simply be directed outward and safely away. The passengers seemed to accept him at his word and settled back into their chairs in the lounge, where they resumed their writing, talking, and drinking.

Leonhard Adelt, who had gone up in airships many other times, was less than impressed with the poor visibility over the North Atlantic, which it appeared they would "barely glimpse" before crossing it. He briefly visited the smoking salon, where he had found its occupants "discussing Germany's problems," before deciding to turn in for the night.

For an experienced flier like Leonhard, the trip might thus far have been mundane, but for Gertrud, it remained anything but. She would soon return to her cabin, but sleep seemed out of the question, for fear she would miss something "irretrievable." Black storm clouds surrounded them, but still the airship sailed on as if it were a "calm, moonlit night." The startled barks of farm dogs in Dutch fields, the last sounds they would hear of Europe, had long since faded into the distance. Instead, she sat up, listening to the silence that seemed to reverberate, with her "hand out the window" in the middle of the black cloud, and "felt the storm going on outside."

CHAPTER 8

Over the North Sea: May 3, 1937

In the quiet of night, sleep often evaded Ernst Lehmann. His nocturnal hours were so pronounced that the young crew members who served under him would remark on how little he slept. But it was in the darkness that the most remarkable sights revealed themselves to those who had harnessed the power to transcend the earth and observe it from above. On a clear night when the full moon shone, a halo would form around the shadow of the airship below as it passed over the water, creating a rainbowlike ring one hundred meters across. Or, when it was pitch black, a certain light would glow from within the ocean itself as millions of tiny phosphorescent creatures illuminated the waves below. If fortune had not blessed him with an airman's life, he would have wanted nothing more than to be a passenger and to "devote [him]self entirely to the observation of the thousand-fold play of colours and forms which Nature contrives out of nothing more than air and water."

That evening, the most ethereal sights man could experience were stolen from view by the surrounding clouds, but Lehmann had been on airships so long that he could feel the "eternal difference and change in the seeming monotony" of sailing through the dark sky as the engines propelled the *Hindenburg* westward. After decades of flying, his brain was so finely attuned to the infinitesimally small changes in temperature or pressure, currents of air, and how they combined to affect an airship's speed, elevation, pitch, roll, and yaw that he could give his crew instinctive commands like a great conductor managing the Berliner Philharmoniker.

As Lehmann's friends and crewmates knew, he was wonderfully musical. American Commander Charles Rosendahl, who was waiting for the *Hindenburg*'s arrival at Lakehurst, and fellow zeppelin captain Hans von Schiller had spent countless hours with Lehmann at his home on the Bodensee near Friedrichshafen. There he had entertained his friends for hours on the cello, piano, and accordion, or, as von Schiller called them, Lehmann's "three favorite companions in his leisure hours." During the *Hindenburg*'s inaugural season, there had been a piano on board. It was an aluminum baby grand covered in yellow pigskin and weighing just 397 pounds that the Blüthner piano company had specially designed for the airship's lounge. After dinner, Lehmann had liked to sit and play classical concerts for the passengers. Even more remarkable was his skill with his "seaman's piano"—the accordion—which he reserved for quieter moments among friends and colleagues, such as when he would play old German folk tunes for his fellow officers in the mess.

But his favorite place to play was in a small, secluded space in the prow of an airship, where the handling ropes were stored before they were thrown down to the landing crew. There was a small opening in the hull that looked out over the miles and miles of land and sea, and it was there that he went to be alone. There was no sound other than a soft swishing of air passing over the airship's canvas skin, until Lehmann coaxed his instrument to life, transforming the accordion into something transcendent. When he played Bach fugues, von Schiller remarked, the accordion became "an organ," and he could conjure the "most wonderful fantasies," like "Beethoven's magical symphonies" or excerpts from Wagner's four-and-a-half-hour opera, *Die Meistersinger von Nürnberg.*

Sometimes, when the young crewmen climbed into the prow to take in the view before or after a shift, they would find Lehmann there, at peace with his music. As much as he cherished his quiet hours, he was generous with his solitude, especially with the young men in his charge whose souls beat for the airship, just like his own. One of the stewards, Wilhelm Balla, had been so keen to secure a place on the *Hindenburg* that he had visited Lehmann's father at his home in Munich. Balla had no technical skills, he told the older man, but he would happily wash dishes for a chance to fly, if only Herr Lehmann could put in a good word with his son. A week later, Balla received a letter instructing him to report to Friedrichshafen. On his first trip to North America, he had come upon Captain Lehmann at 3:00 a.m., and the captain had invited him to sit down for a chat. Lehmann and the junior steward spent the next two hours in wide-ranging conversation, Lehmann's mind too active for sleep. In those wee hours, it made him happy to share in the quiet wonders of the airship with an apprentice who appreciated its enchantment.

But on this flight, there would be no music. Over the winter, the piano had been removed from the lounge, and Lehmann had left his accordion at home. Nor did he have command of the baton to conduct the orchestra of finely tuned pieces that constituted the *Hindenburg* and its crew. On this flight, the baton was in Pruss's capable hands, while Lehmann, for once in his life, was learning what it was to be just a passenger. There was nothing to accompany him in the loneliness of those wee hours, a loneliness that had only grown in recent weeks.

It was true that the new regime's dynamism of the last few years had reinvigorated the airship industry, and the Nazis' investment in the zeppelins seemed to be providing Lehmann with everything he had ever wanted, both for his beloved zeppelins and for his own role at the helm of the company. But progress inevitably meant change. However much he looked forward to a more secure and prosperous future for zeppelins, there was much that the veteran captain wished could have remained frozen in time.

The last three years had marked a unique time for Lehmann, in which he had found a quiet happiness that was, to him, "almost the most desirable thing" in the world. In June 1934, Lehmann's first marriage had ended in divorce with no children. He had soon remarried to a woman named Marie. Marie had several grown children, but as he was then fifty and Marie forty-three, there was little expectation of any more, particularly a son of his own to whom he could pass on his love of the sky. In hopes of starting anew with a sense of peace between his trips on the zeppelins, which he found he had lately been missing, he and his new wife had rented a small house with a garden and boat shed from a kindly landlady in the town of Kressbronn, on the Bodensee between Friedrichshafen and Lindau. Soon afterward, his stepdaughter became engaged to one of the younger airship officers, whom Lehmann was proud to consider one of his protégés. Best and most surprising of all, in that haven of domestic tranquility in 1936, Lehmann and his wife were blessed with the unexpected gift of a baby, Otto Luv, named after Lehmann's brother Otto, who had died during the war.

In the beautiful little house in Kressbronn, their baby boy with curly blond hair and blue eyes had slept, toddled, and teethed. But such goodness was fleeting. Little Otto became seriously ill, so Lehmann and his wife had to send him away to be nursed in the alpine town of Garmisch-Partenkirchen, where they hoped the clean mountain air would help him recover. The worried parents could see their poor little boy only for a short visit during Christmas.

The growing success of the zeppelins under DZR also meant that Lehmann's idyllic days in Kressbronn came to an end far too soon. The company had decided it was more efficient to house the captains and crews in Frankfurt, from which the airships departed, rather than Friedrichshafen, where they were constructed. "Zeppelinheim" was tucked into the forest on the edge of the Frankfurt airport and had a town hall, a post office, a school, and approximately sixty homes built in several different types and sizes, leased to each permanent crew member by rank and seniority. It was so quiet and secluded among the lush trees that anyone who stumbled out of the woods and onto neatly arranged streets named for the great figures in the history of airships—Dr.-Eckener-Platz, Ludwig-Dürr-Strasse (after the zeppelins' chief designer and engineer), Kapitän-Strasser-Strasse (named for famed early airship captain Peter Strasser, who had died during the Great War)—might have felt they had fallen into a utopian workers' village. As director of the company, Lehmann was expected to move to Zeppelinheim, where, naturally, he would have one of the largest houses, but he made the move with a "bleeding heart." He was devastated to leave his little slice of heaven on the Bodensee. As he told his landlady when he wrote to give up the lease, that little house was where "everything good" had started for his family. To him, it would always be home. He had improved the living room heater and the garage; fixed up the bedroom vanity here and the kitchen seating there. Most important, it was where his "sunny little boy grew up." In December, after halfheartedly handing over the keys, he and his wife moved north to Frankfurt. Then, at Easter, news came that the worst had happened. His sunny little boy had died. With his boy went an entire, unwritten chapter of his life, one that must have seemed even more like a fleeting and elusive dream than moments spent flying through the night sky above a phosphorescent ocean set aglow by a moonbeam.

The passengers on board the flight that evening who did not know Ernst Lehmann might have thought him somewhat subdued. They knew him not as the charming, cosmopolitan performer with his crisp English and warmhearted smile. Outside of his fellow officers down in the control gondola, only his friends the Adelts knew he was grieving. It was good of DZR to allow him this time to go to New York with Leonhard and distract himself with another project, and where his only responsibility on board this flight was to generally represent the company. And yet, while having the Adelts on this trip was a comfort in some ways, it was also a cruel irony. When Lehmann looked at Leonhard Adelt, it must have felt like looking at an alternate version of his own future.

Alongside their mutual and lifelong love affair with aviation and apparent need to take up the pen, life had set fifty-five-year-old Leonhard and fifty-one-year-old Lehmann on similar courses. After unsuccessful first marriages, each man had remarried and had been given a second opportunity at fatherhood. The Adelts' one-year-old baby boy, Christian, was healthy, safe, and sound in the quiet Berlin neighborhood of Zehlendorf with his nanny, Wawa. Meanwhile, Lehmann, whose life had been so happily and unexpectedly changed with the arrival of a child, was now left with just a picture of his son in a locket and a few handwritten pages in a dark-bound book on which he memorialized his son's short life.

In the early days of Lehmann's friendship with Leonhard Adelt, back when both men were young, Adelt had posed a question in his book about the idealistic young man intent on conquering the skies: "We are all absorbed in the idea that captivates us," the father of the young aviator in his story had observed when the boy informed him that he wished to leave the family farm in pursuit of his dream. Fine, the father told the lad, "You want to go your own way—are you strong enough for loneliness?"

For years, the sky had offered a welcome kind of loneliness for Lehmann. In the air, he was surrounded by a crew that became a family, but one that he could hold at a respectful distance and steal away from to be alone with his thoughts in a tranquil silence unlike anything man could find on earth. But on this voyage, his crew was not even his own.

Was there ever anything lonelier than a man surrounded by that which was usually under his command but where he was now without charge or responsibility? Perhaps a man without his music and without his child, whose greatest love in life was a machine that could never love him back, floating ever farther away from his earthbound fellow men and off into the night sky over the "blue Atlantic," where the "heavens curved off into infinity."

CHAPTER 9

Berlin, Germany: May 3, 1937

Before Bill Shirer left his office on Dorotheenstrasse for the night, he fired off a cable to New York as a news flash, something simple to the effect of "Airship Hindenburg departs Frankfurt en route to Lakehurst." The New York office did not ask him to elaborate further. Just as Shirer had asserted in his December "Review of the Year" article for Universal Service for 1936, zeppelins had "for a time gripped people's imagination," and to a large extent they still did, but now they were simply "too regular and ordinary and safe" to warrant front-page coverage.

With nothing else to report on the zeppelin front until it reached American shores, Shirer closed up shop for the night and set off down Unter den Linden to meet Gordon Young of Reuters for a nightcap at the American bar at the Hotel Adlon to see what interesting sources they might dig up at Berlin's famous watering hole.

CHAPTER 10

Chicago, Illinois, USA: May 4, 1937

Over four thousand miles away in Chicago's Near West Side, situated almost equidistant between Nelson Morris's childhood home to the south and Bert Dolan's neighborhood to the north, stood a relatively unremarkable three-story building at 1230 West Washington Street. Like many others nearby, it was simply constructed from red brick and graced the neighborhood with a practical, unadorned presence, save for a few art deco stone embellishments and a radio broadcast antenna protruding from the roof. The Near West Side had once been a thriving, if somewhat malodorous, neighborhood where urban and rural collided. Massive warehouses and cold storage facilities where packers had once staged their products for cross-country rail distribution stood behind the old Fulton Street wholesale meat market. Two blocks south, produce-filled stalls had lined West Randolph Street. In the intervening years, the neighborhood's tangible signs of failure to keep pace with the times, which were then compounded by the Depression, became impossible to ignore. The warehouses were now abandoned, the produce stalls derelict. In place of horse-drawn carts on the cobbled neighborhood streets, refrigerated trucks rumbled down paved roads, which had allowed packers to move their operations out of the city and establish new facilities where land was cheap.

The building at 1230 West Washington had been constructed in 1928, right before the economy came crashing down, for *Prairie Farmer*, a regional newspaper with roots dating back to the mid-nineteenth century. The paper was just one of roughly 6,400 weekly publications circulating in the United States when it moved into the neighborhood; its audience were the farmers whose livestock and produce once filled the surrounding blocks. Midwestern publications proudly competed with the coasts' best. The *Chicago Tribune* was second only to the *New York Daily News* in circulation, with its Sunday edition passing one million subscriptions in 1936. While the *Tribune*'s circulation extended far beyond the city limits, farmers' concerns were unique and specialized. For nearly one hundred years, publications like *Prairie Farmer*, "devoted to western agriculture, mechanics, and education," as its original masthead read, helped fulfill this demand. Still, much of the rural market remained untapped, especially for entertainment.

Radio broadcasting was a relatively new endeavor that had exploded as a commercial enterprise thanks to Guglielmo Marconi's development of practical, long-distance wireless telegraphy at the turn of the century. Radio was initially adopted by shipping companies and navies, which realized the lifesaving potential of being able to call for help in emergencies at sea. It was radio that allowed the RMS *Carpathia* to save seven hundred souls from frigid waters after receiving the Marconi operator's distress call from the RMS *Titanic* after the ocean liner struck an iceberg in 1912. However, it was radio's entertainment potential that launched a multimillion-dollar industry.

Unlike in Britain, where radio was operated by the state British Broadcasting Corporation (BBC), in the United States, the early days of radio were a more fragmented affair. The U.S. Navy controlled radio frequencies during the war, but they were returned to private entities in 1919. The British Marconi company wanted to buy access to high-powered American frequencies, but the U.S. government opposed having a majority foreign-owned entity controlling a vital communication channel. Instead, the navy persuaded General Electric, which manufactured radio transmitters, to buy out the American Marconi subsidiary and create a new company called Radio Corporation of America (RCA). RCA became the first national wireless juggernaut. Its objective was to sell radio equipment, and American families would be more likely to purchase radio receiver sets for their homes if RCA also offered entertaining content for them to hear.

In the meantime, hundreds of small, local stations had popped up across the country. These stations, run by schools, churches, and even stores, provided entertainment, but their reach was limited by the strength of the frequencies on which they operated. RCA, however, had access to AT&T's telephone and Western Union's telegraph lines, which allowed it to broadcast to listeners across the nation. In 1926, RCA created a new company, the National Broadcasting Company, or NBC, to deliver content from coast to coast. NBC also struck deals with small-time stations to serve as local affiliates, paying them to broadcast sponsored commercial entertainment programs. Meanwhile, affiliates paid NBC to air enriching cultural and educational content, which was in turn financed by local sponsors who wanted to advertise to a targeted, regional audience. The following year a rival nationwide broadcasting company, Columbia Broadcasting Service, or CBS, emerged, and in 1934, Mutual Broadcasting System joined them on the air. During the Depression, radio was an industry that actually grew. By 1937, 74 percent of American homes had at least one radio, and the average household listened to over four and a half hours of radio programming per day.

Around the same time *Prairie Farmer* built its office on the Near West Side, it acquired a radio station from Sears, Roebuck and Company, the Chicago-based mail-order retailer. Sears had started a radio station in the 1920s. With specialized content relevant to a rural audience, including its marquee Saturday evening show called *National Barn Dance*, it hoped farmers would purchase radios from its catalog. Sears had given the station the call sign WLS, an acronym for the self-proclaimed "World's Largest Store," which *Prairie Farmer* kept when it acquired the station.

While the neighborhood around WLS had suffered an abrupt reversal of fortune, the little radio station headquartered at 1230 West Washington quickly became known as the "50,000-Watt Blowtorch out of the Midwest." Innovative owner Burridge D. Butler created an entertainment network that reached seven million people across the Mississippi River Valley. With NBC as its national affiliate partner, WLS's *National Farm and Home* program became one of the most popular programs NBC carried. WLS hired up-and-coming personalities like "Singing Cowboy" Gene Autry, who started at the station in 1930 for thirty-five dollars per week and by 1937 was a bona fide movie star. It also broadcast daily variety programs like the *Swift Roundup*, sponsored by Swift & Company packers. Butler even arranged for the station to air directly from the 1933 Chicago World's Fair.

By 1937, WLS was a legitimate broadcast powerhouse. As the station puffed in an advertisement, it was the "greatest single radio service in America," broadcasting "for all classes all of the time." Whether a new champion was being crowned or the president was delivering a message to the people, WLS was "on its toes—ready." Even "when disaster strikes," the station proclaimed, "WLS and its legion listeners take to the air in a plea for humanity, and humanity always answers."

But for all WLS's bluster and supposed commitment to being "on its toes," ready to transport listeners to the most exciting and momentous events of the day, one of WLS's announcers, Herbert Morrison, knew this simply was not true. WLS was severely hampered by outdated regulations and a backward approach to technology that prevented it from being able to take listeners practically anywhere of interest, and Morrison had weeks of wasted research about zeppelins and the men who flew them sitting on his desk to prove it.

Though only thirty-one years old, Herbert Morrison was a radio veteran. Black-haired and deeply blue-eyed, he had grown up in Scottdale, Pennsylvania, a town in the southwest corner of the state not far from the West Virginia border. His father had left when he was a toddler, so his mother, who raised him in his grandmother's boardinghouse, took odd jobs to make ends meet.

Something about machines and inventions that made the world feel a little smaller had always captured Morrison's attention. His first experience with radio had come when he was in high school, when he had played the banjo live on air for the local station with his school's band. After graduating from high school in 1923, he became a cadet at the

United States Military Academy at West Point, where he took up fencing and continued with the banjo in the cadet orchestra, occasionally performing on the radio and even in the background of a motion picture called *Classmates* that was filmed on campus. Unfortunately, like forty-two other members of his class, he was deemed too "deficient" in math to continue in West Point's math-intensive curriculum, by far the biggest source of dismissals, and returned to Scottdale, where his mother had taken up work as a technician repairing radios.

Morrison worked various jobs in Scottdale until June 1930, less than eight months after the crash of the New York Stock Exchange, when he applied to the radio station WMMN in nearby Fairmont, West Virginia, with an idea of working on the technical end of the booming radio industry. The station did not need a radio operator, but it did need an announcer, so the station manager asked him to audition for the job. The audition consisted of the manager calling up his friends and asking how they liked the sound of Morrison's voice on air that night. They must have liked it well enough, because WMMN hired him to start the next week. From there Morrison followed opportunities with stations across the country—Gary, Indiana; Waukegan, Illinois; Milwaukee; Pittsburgh; even a stint at the superpowerful AM station just over the border from Del Rio, Texas—before ultimately landing in Chicago in 1936, inspired by the allure of the Chicago World's Fair and its tagline, "A Century of Progress."

From the very beginning of broadcasting, well before Morrison began working in radio, there was a universal expectation that everything on the air—every voice, sound effect, and musical note—would be broadcast live. This had been NBC's official policy since its founding and, by extension, the policy of all its affiliates. This was partly due to listener preference, as many felt that live radio was more authentic and reliable. Stations were also concerned that recorded broadcasts would confuse or deceive listeners in some way. But the primary reason for the live-only mandate was an agreement the original national networks had made with the Department of Commerce to gain access to the best radio frequencies.

Frequencies were not unlimited, and the airwaves had become so crowded there were not enough frequencies to satisfy demand. Many stations were forced to share, with time slots allocated to multiple groups over the course of a day. In the 1920s, the Department of Commerce under then-Secretary Herbert Hoover brought order to the chaos. The Commerce Department granted a class of broadcast licenses for the clearest frequencies with the best reach to a group of approved broadcasters with widely appealing, high-quality content. They were initially called "Class A" licenses, but Hoover renamed them "Class B" so as not to give the impression they were better than any other (though they most certainly were). In exchange for better frequencies, the large networks promised not to play "mechanical music" or "phonographs" and to broadcast only actual "talent." Recorded "talent" did not count. Ultimately, this licensing scheme was short-lived, but the live-only policy remained within national broadcasting companies like NBC and CBS largely due to technical constraints.

In the early years of radio, live broadcasting sounded far superior to recorded material, as the technology available to make a recording produced poor sound quality. This remained the case until 1934, when the Presto Recording Corporation developed a lacquer-covered aluminum disc and a heavy, fifteen-pound turntable that enabled consistent rotational speed, which finally allowed for recordings with top-notch sound transcription. Starting in 1935, NBC began making simultaneous recordings of live broadcasts of special events, such as high-profile concerts, World Series games, or historic presidential addresses, but it did not air them on its network.

In Morrison's opinion, this now largely arbitrary, archaic policy was holding back both WLS and the entire radio and mass-media industry. On the technical side, reporting live from anywhere but a studio was cumbersome and awkward. Broadcasters had to connect with their stations via short-distance microwave transmission or call in over a telephone for which other reporters would undoubtedly be competing for time. This was hindering radio's ability to physically take listeners to the day's action, as WLS's advertisement had promised. To make a recording, however, particularly with the new, high-quality equipment, all one needed was a connection to AC electrical current. It took the pressure off limited transmission resources and gave broadcasters nearly free range.

More important was the potential impact of recorded content on programming. Sure, radio shows were becoming more creative in their use of sound effects or inventive ways to subliminally transfer the American marketplace from brick-and-mortar stores into the homes of listeners from coast to coast. However, at its core, radio was no different in 1937 than it had been back when Morrison was a high school kid playing the banjo on the local station in Scottdale. Stations were missing out on the most important and exciting dramas unfolding every day in the real world. Unfortunately, the real world rarely cooperated with producers' preset weekly schedules. But with new recording technology, networks like NBC would not have to cut away from popular programs like *Amos 'n' Andy*. As soon as it was over, they could simply play a recording of whatever exciting event had transpired while the famous sitcom was airing. Morrison was eager to show his bosses why his vision for radio was the way of the future, and he believed he had the perfect test scenario to prove it.

Herb Morrison could not take all the credit for the idea of recording a broadcast of the arrival of the *Hindenburg* on its first flight to the United States in 1937. In large part, credit belonged to the creative minds at a fledgling aviation company, American Airlines, with whom Morrison had first come in contact several months earlier in the wake of a monumental disaster. When Morrison joined WLS in October 1936, he had primarily been hired as an announcer for the station's popular staples, like its Sunday-morning show *Everybody's Hour*, but he was eager to do more. His first opportunity to prove himself came that winter in the wake of devastating floods that had swept across the Midwest. From Pittsburgh to southern Illinois, torrential rains poured down for over two weeks in January, dumping 165 billion tons of water into the Ohio and Mississippi River Basin. Seventy percent of the Louisville area was underwater, while in Cincinnati, the Ohio River crested at nearly eighty feet. Even though the worst of the Depression had passed, these farming communities continued to struggle due to low crop prices, and most farmers in the region earned less than two hundred dollars per year. Suddenly, 200,000 square miles were covered in an average of eleven inches of water as more than

350 people were killed and 1 million left homeless. It was by far the worst flood in the nation's history. Morrison later told a colleague, "You have no idea and it cannot be exaggerated. . . . This flood catastrophe" was, without a doubt, "the worst thing I ever saw in my life."

It was almost impossible to adequately describe the scale of the disaster from the ground, not least because the floodwaters had cut power to telephone lines and local radio stations across the area. Without the means to communicate, relief efforts remained significantly handicapped. The up-and-coming commercial airline had an idea. American Airlines was a conglomeration of a number of smaller carriers that had sprung up in the postwar aviation boom. By 1934, under its colorful and forward-thinking CEO, C. R. Smith, American Airlines had become the first airline to turn a profit carrying only passengers, rather than mail, in its brand-new airplane, the DC-3, which was both comfortable and economical to operate.

Motivated somewhat by humanitarian concerns but perhaps a bit more by the opportunity for some creative advertising, for which he was known in the industry, Smith sent a flight crew with one of the new airplanes to ferry a team of photographers, newspapermen, and local radio correspondents, including from WLS, to assist first responders. WLS tapped Morrison for the job. As local radio stations, which could have helped direct victims to safety and emergency crews to devastated areas, had been washed away, Morrison and his colleagues took their place from the sky. That February, he and six other print journalists and photographers logged over 1,400 miles in the air. From their bird's-eye view, newspaper reporters and photographers were able to introduce the broader American public to the extent of the human suffering on the ground. Meanwhile, the radiomen helped to direct victims to food and lodging, transmitted messages for agencies managing disaster relief, and dispatched fundraising appeals to aid the suffering. In the process, Morrison and his fellow announcers broke new ground. Never before had radio so immediately, collaboratively, and comprehensively responded to a domestic crisis in real time, and in a manner that brought a widespread disaster into the homes of listeners. The impact on listeners was immediate and tangible. One person was so moved he made an anonymous twenty-thousand-dollar donation to flood-relief efforts that WLS had helped to organize.

For Morrison, assisting with the flood disaster was the perfect assignment, as it married his interests in both radio and aviation. Since his days in Scottdale, he had been scraping together whatever extra money he could from odd jobs—ranging from shoe salesman to Boy Scout fencing instructor to airplane assembly plant worker—to supplement his income to be able to afford flying lessons. As the years went by, he kept up his hobby whenever possible, and he hoped to someday earn his pilot's license. Unsurprisingly, he hit it off with the American Airlines representatives, who liked this forward-thinking young radioman who had suddenly become very popular with WLS listeners and management.

With his angular jaw and black hair carefully slicked back off his high forehead, Morrison was as appealing in front of a camera as his rich, baritone voice was on the air. Alongside the radio station, *Prairie Farmer* published a small magazine called *Stand By*, in which it profiled the voices listeners heard on WLS. After his part in the flood coverage, *Stand By* made Morrison the cover star of its February 13, 1937, issue. Alongside advertisements for Jolly Time Pop Corn, pygmy water lilies, and insurance policies, the magazine informed readers and listeners that the correspondent with the handsome voice helping flood victims was an unmarried "available bachelor" standing five feet eight inches tall and weighing 142 pounds, "16 of which he had gained since he came to Chicago." (However, if you asked Morrison's radio engineer, Charlie Nehlsen, those sixteen pounds were a figment of the editor's imagination—as were three to four extra inches in height.) Morrison was an ambitious rising star, and American Airlines wanted to further its relationship with him.

While Herb Morrison was eager to advance radio, American Airlines wanted to be known as the airline service that was fast, safe, and reliable at a time when many Americans saw airplanes as excessively dangerous. The young radio announcer was perfectly placed to help. The American public was understandably nervous about flying on airplanes, as headlines announcing small-plane crashes appeared with regularity. In reality, private pilots for whom flying was a hobby were giving regulated aviation a bad reputation. Commercial carrier–operated flight was statistically safer than driving a car and had been for years. The fatal-accident rate for commercial air transport was, in fact, lower than those of all other forms of motorized land and water transport (railroads, streetcars, automobiles, and boats) except for motorcycles, with which it was approximately tied. For non-carrier-operated flights in 1936, there were 1,674 accidents, 155 of which were fatal and resulted in 261 fatalities, for a rate of 602,000 plane miles flown per fatal accident. By comparison, for scheduled, carrier-operated flights, there were a mere sixty-five accidents, and only eight were fatal. In those eight accidents, forty-four people died in total, making for a rate of over 8.04 million plane miles flown per fatal accident. Statistics, unfortunately, could only move people so far. What airlines needed were appeals to positive emotions. The public needed to believe that flying was both stable and joyful, and American Airlines knew just the thing that could evoke that reaction: zeppelins.

In nearly a decade of transatlantic commercial service, the wildly popular German airships *Graf Zeppelin* and *Hindenburg* had maintained an impeccable safety record as passengers traveling on the glamorous, chrome-like zeppelins enjoyed three-course meals accompanied by the gentle strains of classical music played on an aluminum piano in the background. The bright minds at American Airlines had an idea: If members of the American public were to shed their fear of flying and embrace airplanes as the future of commercial aviation, it was essential that they view lighter- and heavier-than-air craft as a unified form of transportation. If the general public associated words like *safe*, *comfortable*, and *luxurious* with zeppelins, C. R. Smith wanted Americans to similarly think of those words when they saw his DC-3s. The DC-3's sleek design and Smith's deliberate use of nautical associations in his branding, such as referring to pilots as "captains" and "first officers," were in perfect harmony with both luxurious ocean liners and the futuristic ships of the sky. Smith went even further, naming his novel VIP members' organization for frequent fliers the "Admirals Club" and directing first officers to mount four-star pennants outside their windows before takeoff and after landing. In a 1936 issue of the *Official Aviation Guide*, the airline even ran an ad with an illustration of a passenger beside an American Airlines DC-3 exclaiming, "Say! These new Flagships look like the 'Hindenburg' with wings!"

The airline needed to tie the safety of airships and the speed of airplanes together as one big air transport service in the minds of the American public, but print advertising could only take them so far. The best way to reach the greatest number of people in a way that would move them to *feel* the wondrous splendor and security of air travel was over the radio, and Herb Morrison was just the man to help them.

The upcoming start of the *Hindenburg*'s 1937 season offered the perfect opportunity for American Airlines and the young WLS radioman to advance their parallel ambitions, particularly Morrison's with his vision for an experiment with recorded content. It was just the kind of dramatic, real-life event he had in mind. On its first arrival on American shores a year earlier, the *Hindenburg* had drawn 100,000 spectators to Lakehurst. Traffic had stopped as drivers gawked at the silver giant passing over Boston and New York, and newspapers had sent cameramen to snap images of the airship flying over the Manhattan skyline. The Lakehurst Naval Air Station expected a similarly enthusiastic turnout for 1937 and had even decided to allow up to 1,500 cars to park directly beside the landing field, rather than make everyone take a bus from far-off parking areas miles away. The variability of weather over a multiday journey also meant no one could predict the exact minute the *Hindenburg* would arrive in Lakehurst, so a live broadcast spot could not be assigned in advance with any certainty. Thus, a recording of the arrival was the only feasible solution, as it could simply air later that day at a convenient time in the schedule. The Presto Recording Corporation was even offering state-of-the-art recording equipment to assist in the scheme in exchange for Morrison including its name during his broadcast. At the same time, it was a fairly safe type of event with which to experiment. As it was the start of the second year of operations, the *Hindenburg*'s arrival was no longer headline news in the eyes of newsroom editors, who were unlikely to dispatch their top reporters to cover it. This just meant there would be less media competition surrounding the event, and newspapers would be less upset than if an upstart radio station tried to scoop them for some really big breaking news. Perhaps most important of all, in the event the recording did not work or Morrison made a mistake operating the new equipment, he would not have blown his chance to capture a truly historic event.

Once Morrison and American Airlines hatched their plan, Morrison spent his spare time over the next few weeks researching whatever he could find on the *Hindenburg* and the zeppelin program to make his pitch to WLS as compelling as possible. He read about the *Hindenburg*'s technical specifications, meteorological conditions on its flight path, the impressive facilities and personnel advancing American aviation at Lakehurst, and two of Germany's most famous airship captains, Ernst Lehmann and Max Pruss, who would be responsible for the *Hindenburg*'s continued success in this new year of transatlantic service. Once WLS approved it, he would prepare some opening remarks, highlighting all of these details while making sure to mention American Airlines' brand-new twenty-one-passenger Flagships connecting travelers from Lakehurst to Newark and beyond—the only airline to do so. Morrison even secured permission from the head of the Naval Air Station, Commander Charles Rosendahl, to record the landing. Every piece was falling into place.

But when he presented the idea to station management, WLS immediately balked. Faced with the idea of breaking NBC's live-only broadcast policy, the station turned squeamish. A partnership with just one of many nascent airlines with questionable future profitability did not offer sufficient clout to induce management to risk the wrath of the higher-ups at the national network. It likely also did not help that the story had so little to do with the station's agrarian roots and listenership, though excitement about the zeppelins was certainly not limited to the urban East Coast if Midwestern and Western newspaper coverage of the *Hindenburg*'s 1936 Atlantic crossings were any indication.

Undeterred, Morrison tried to approach the pitch from a technical angle. Presto was offering the station several hundred pounds of brand-new technology for free. Surely this was the perfect opportunity to test it.

The answer was still no.

But it would be a real human-interest story for Chicago, he offered, having learned that several passengers from the city would be on board. In fact, Chicago would be the most represented American city on the airship.

The station was unmoved.

What if, Morrison suggested as April turned to May and the day of the *Hindenburg*'s arrival crept ever closer, he made the recording on his day off? American Airlines would fly him there and back, and he would do the work for free. The experiment would not cost WLS a dime.

But still WLS refused. As far as the station was concerned, Morrison should just go back to announcing his usual programs, a job he had held for less than a year and perhaps should have felt lucky to have at such an impressive station in the first place.

With each day that passed, Morrison could feel his chance slipping further away. On the morning of May 4, short articles of just one or two paragraphs from the wire services' German bureaus appeared in the papers across the country announcing the *Hindenburg*'s departure from Frankfurt. How could the station not see that this was a prime opportunity to do something exciting and unique?

And yet his bosses continued to suffer from an utter lack of imagination as the hours ticked by. Minute by minute, the *Hindenburg* drew ever closer to American shores, and Morrison's golden opportunity faded further and further into the realm of unfulfilled dreams.

CHAPTER 11

Over the Atlantic Ocean: May 4, 1937

Though rotating shifts of the *Hindenburg*'s officers and crew manned the airship at full strength around the clock, one could mark the beginning of a new day on board at 6:00 a.m., when fourteen-year-old cabin boy Werner Franz rubbed the sleep from his eyes in his upper bunk in the keel. The overnight crew was just coming off their watch, and Franz had to vacate his bunk for the night steward, Wilhelm Balla. Hot bunking was not ideal but had been standard practice for centuries on ships where space was limited, usually among the junior crew members. The roughly dozen senior officers on the *Hindenburg* each received their own berth, as did the chief steward and the sole female stewardess, but the rest of the men, typically another thirty to fifty per flight, had to rotate among the remaining thirty-four bunks depending on their numbers.

Balla had taken Franz under his wing like one of his half dozen little brothers. Looking after him had included making sure he received the airshipman's rite of passage, the "equatorial baptism." On the return leg of Franz's first trip to South America, as they were approaching the point where they would cross the equator from the Southern to the Northern Hemisphere, one of the cooks told the cabin boy to grab a bucket and a scrubber and hurry down to the control gondola to "wash off the equator line." It did not make any sense. *Wash off the equator line?* But Franz was eager to make a good impression and hustled down, bucket and scrubber in tow. When he arrived at the control gondola, the watch officer asked what he wanted, so he repeated the cook's message. "Right," said the officer. They were not quite at the equator line yet, so he would have to come back with his bucket a bit later. As Franz was walking back to the kitchen, a sudden shower of cold water splashed down on his head. When he looked up, the cook was standing in a nook just above him, empty pot in hand, having a good chuckle along with a few other crew members as the skinny boy stood dripping in the corridor. But it was all in good fun, and a sign that the others had welcomed him into their ranks. They handed him a ceremonial certificate with his name written on an illustration drawn by Dr. Eckener's brother depicting Neptune, god of water, greeting an airship as it flew overhead to officially mark Franz's first trip crossing the equator. In the control car, the elevator man adjusted the pitch of the airship so it momentarily bowed its nose in homage to Neptune, the zeppelin crew's variation on a centuries-old custom of honoring the god of the sea.

Werner Franz's days aboard the airship always began and ended with coffee. It was the first thing he delivered to the new crew that had taken over the watch in the early hours of the morning and last thing he delivered to the officers on duty in the gondola before he went to bed at night. As he brewed a fresh pot on the electric stove in the airship's efficient kitchen, he washed the cups and saucers left over from the previous night's coffee delivery, put them away, and set the table for the officers' breakfast in the narrow mess.

While the stewards looked after the passengers, Franz did the same for the officers. Along with bringing them coffee and serving and clearing their meals, he brushed their suits, cleaned their shoes, and made their beds. The twelve officers' bunks were located just forward of the control gondola, separate from those of the deck force responsible for the airship's operations and maintenance, who slept just aft of B deck in the keel. The captain, of course, had a separate stateroom, which Franz also tidied.

There was a clear hierarchy to the rank and duties of those who worked on board the airship to keep everything running in smooth and orderly fashion. This was true even among the smaller groups of crew members who performed unique, technical tasks and worked in distinctly separate parts of the zeppelin far from the commanding officers. Overall, though, the crew felt quite like a found family. Most groups within the crew—stewards, mechanics, riggers, helmsmen, and more—comprised an older, senior man with a team of younger but highly capable junior crew members under him, with Franz, of course, the most junior of them all. Airship veterans with over twenty years of experience welcomed newer faces with warmth and patience as their young apprentices learned special trades, such as swiftly making fifty beds in narrow spaces, or the numerous crucial tasks that the passengers would never see, like repairing a damaged rudder while cruising over open ocean or safely scaling the internal scaffolding to check for leaks in the gas cells. There were no internal divisions between those who came to airships from a background at sea and those from more traditional civilian trades, many of whom, like Franz and Balla, had found their way to the zeppelin company in desperate need of a job during troubled economic times.

Even the stewardess, Emilie Imhof, had found a new beginning among a crew entirely made up of men after long years of trial and strife. Back in the early 1920s, Imhof and her husband owned and ran a small hotel. When he died of a heart attack, without a will, in 1923, his mother and his nine siblings had each claimed a share of his estate, which plunged her into debt. She tried to continue with the hotel for several years but was eventually forced to sell. She still had outstanding debts, including to her brother-in-law, a grocer, so she went to work for Norddeutscher Lloyd as a steamship stewardess before being hired by DZR. She spoke five languages and was immensely qualified, and as a widow in her early forties, she was perhaps less daunted by any challenges others might find overwhelming, especially those occurring several hundred feet in the sky.

Franz set out clean cups and saucers and a pot of fresh coffee on the tray. After taking a quick sip himself before picking up his precious cargo, he made his way forward up a slightly inclining corridor toward the control gondola, never having to worry that turbulence might upset his balance and send the coffee splashing to the floor. The ride was so smooth he might have carried the tray on his head with little trouble.

The crew accessed the control gondola below the radio and mail rooms via a narrow duralumin ladder, which let down into a small cabin with a slim, leather-covered bench and seats that folded down from the wall, where the officers could relax or confer. Just in front of the lounge was the navigation room, where the airship's navigators charted the *Hindenburg*'s progress and any weather reports radioed by passing ships or stations on either side of the Atlantic. Finally, in the very front was the control room—the bridge—where the captains managed the airship's heading with a ship's wheel that controlled the rudder, adjusted its pitch and elevation with the elevator wheel, and monitored the ballast and gas cells on two light boards mounted to the wall that indicated the volume in each ballast tank and the pressure in each gas cell. They could valve the gas cells or ballast tanks individually or across the entire ship simultaneously to adjust its buoyancy. Though not a large space, there could be half a dozen officers or more in the control gondola at any one time, and sweeping windows offered a 360-degree view that made it feel spacious.

Franz handed the coffee down to the officers waiting below. It was something of a treat for the cabin boy to visit this unique part of the airship with its normally spectacular views, as there were few windows where he performed most of the rest of his duties. Unfortunately, that morning, there was little to see, as the gray storms from the night before had yet to pass.

While Franz was sleeping, one of the four navigators had marked the airship's last European land-based bearing between Beachy Head, the chalk sea cliff on the English Channel in East Sussex, and St. Catherine's Point on the Isle of Wight, at 2:00 a.m. Their most recent coordinates, taken at 4:45 a.m., were 49.52″ N, 3.35″ W, over the English Channel. By now, they would have just about pulled level longitudinally with Land's End in Cornwall, England, and Pointe de Corsen in Brittany, France, the westernmost points of the two countries' mainlands. From there, as they continued their westerly course, they would be surrounded by nothing but open ocean until they reached Newfoundland's Cape Race, typically in the afternoon of the second full day. However, after the delay from steering around the storm the previous night, they would be lucky if they reached Cape Race before dark. If Captain Pruss could find more favorable winds at a higher elevation, perhaps they could make up some time.

The delay concerned Werner Franz only insofar as whether the darkness would veil his first glimpse of North America. Delays might worry those at the top who had business operations to consider, but the fourteen-year-old would have been happy enough to continue cruising among the clouds forever.

CHAPTER 12

Over the Atlantic Ocean: May 4, 1937

It was really rather a nuisance that passengers could go back into the cargo area only accompanied by a steward, because Benny Spah had a high-maintenance dog to feed. She was temperamental about other people tending to her, and he was already tired of having to wait for a steward to take him to the freight room, where she was being kenneled in a large basket near the rest of his luggage, including three oil paintings he had acquired in Germany. The dog, Ulla, was a prize-winning two-year-old Alsatian, or German shepherd, whose pedigree paperwork he kept tucked inside his wallet alongside his (expired) driver's license, a boxing club membership card, and his U.S. Volunteer Air Service identification. He had purchased Ulla on the final leg of his eight-month vaudeville show's European tour as a surprise for his three young children, five-year-old Gilbert, two-year-old Marilyn, and the baby, Richard. As an Alsatian himself, having been born in the sometimes German, sometimes French city of Strassburg (or Strasbourg, depending on who was in charge at the time), in the Alsace region, no other breed would have been as appropriate. DZR had even let him take the dog on board for free. They wanted to publicize her arrival with him in New York to show that the zeppelins were so safe that passengers could take their household pets along.

Benny's wife, however, was less enthusiastic about his special cargo. In April, Benny had written to Vera to tell her about his "new pal," for which he had paid a whopping $250. While Vera wrote that she was "getting so thrilled inside" that her husband was coming home, she was far less thrilled about the dog. "I hope she is all you say she is," she wrote, like many a wife since the dawn of time surprised by a husband's well-intentioned impulse purchase. "I am not so keen on having a female dog. You know they are very messy at times & hard to watch. But I guess you knew what you were doing." Fortunately, she missed him too much to keep him in the doghouse for long. "I love you & need you," she signed off with a flourish. "I am yours forever." And she covered the bottom of the letter with twenty kisses from herself and their children.

Benny Spah had been one of the last to book his ticket on the *Hindenburg* after his agent had contacted him in Munich with that last-minute offer to open at Radio City. Initially, Benny thought he would have to decline, as no ship could get him there in time, but then he had run into an old friend, fellow vaudevillian performer and trick bicycle rider Joe Jackson, who told Benny that he planned to return to New York on the *Hindenburg* to drum up publicity for his popular show. Luck seemed to follow Benny wherever he went. At the Hamburg-America Line office in Munich, he discovered that *Hindenburg* tickets were still available, so he booked his place—expensive as it was. He did not, however, tell his friend he was coming along for the ride. "Oh, wait until Joe Jackson sees me on the Hindenburg," he thought to himself, eager to put one over on his friend, who had played many a practical joke on him over the years. Unfortunately, when he arrived, Jackson was not there. In the meantime, Jackson had accepted a coronation gig at London's famous Dorchester Hotel and canceled his passage home. Perhaps, Benny thought, it was his friend's cabin the travel company had just sold him.

It was entirely reasonable that the zeppelin crew did not want the average passenger wandering around the operational area of the *Hindenburg* unaccompanied, lest they slip and, as the night steward, Wilhelm Balla, quipped, take an "aerial journey into the depths" of the airship (or perhaps drop straight through the cover in areas where it had less reinforcement). For Benny, however, such a concern was a little ridiculous considering what he did for a living. Benny Spah was famous for an act called the "Convivial Inebriate," a vaudeville routine of the kind popular across the

United States since the turn of the century. Until the advent of the "talking picture" in the late 1920s, vaudeville was the single most popular form of entertainment in America. From small towns to big cities, vaudeville revues would go on for hours, featuring dozens of acts, from musicians and dancers to ventriloquists and magicians, jugglers, trick cyclists, comedians, and contortionists. The acts ran the gamut from the odd to the most remarkable of talents, from a man with an unusually strong stomach named Frank Richards taking a cannonball shot from a compressed air gun to the gut, to the athleticism and rhythmic genius of brothers Fayard and Harold Nicholas, whose acrobatic tap dancing eventually made them movie stars. Even Charlie Chaplin got his start in vaudeville.

Benny Spah combined the physical and comedic in traditional vaudevillian style. In his act, he dressed up in a top hat and disheveled tails and wobbled along the stage as if returning home late from a party. As he artfully pretended to stumble along the streetscape set, he would pause under a lamppost and take out a cigarette, only to realize he had no matches with which to light it. Glancing up at the streetlamp beside him, he would suddenly be seized with an idea. If he could just reach the gas flame at the top, he could light his cigarette. With feigned intoxicated overconfidence, he would shinny up the narrow lamppost in a series of acrobatic maneuvers as gracefully as a trained gymnast, eventually standing on the very top in triumph. Sitting down on the top of the post, he would then bend over to light the cigarette, when, all of a sudden, the lamppost would start to sway, gently at first and then violently back and forth as he pretended to hang on for dear life, though with his firm grip, developed over years spent performing, his security was never in doubt. Throwing in some additional tricks, he would dangle from the lamppost with one arm as the springs at the base of the contraption he had built himself whipsawed him from side to side. Night after night, Benny would elegantly flip himself around on the lamppost, giving audiences a thrill.

Only once had his routine gone awry. In 1932, his agent had called with an offer to do a special stunt performance for two hundred dollars. The money was good, especially near the peak of the Depression, so he had agreed. The idea was to film the lamppost routine on top of a fifty-six-story Manhattan skyscraper, with the lamppost positioned on the edge of the building so that when it swung over to the side, he would be dangling over the edge some 650 feet above the ground. Or at least, that was how it was supposed to look. With clever camera work, they positioned his lamppost where audiences could not see there was a lower surface about ten feet below that would catch him should he fall. Sill, a ten-foot drop was considerable, and there was not much room for error. Off he went as the cameras rolled, shinnying up the lamppost and rocking it from side to side until it swung out over the roof—and got stuck. Benny had to hang on for dear life, pulling himself back up hand over hand on the extended lamppost until he reached the edge of the roof. On the drive home, he was so exhausted from the slightly terrifying ordeal that his hands cramped around the steering wheel and refused to let go.

The next night, he was performing for an audience in New York. When he climbed up the lamppost, the top went sailing off and clattered to the stage. If that had happened on top of the skyscraper, he easily could have slipped and been thrown clear on his own aerial journey down to the sidewalk below.

Everywhere he went, audiences loved the Convivial Inebriate. His routine was so popular that he had been performing it across the United States and Europe since 1925, just a few years after he had moved to New York. Thanks to the popularity of that routine, he had achieved the American dream. He had married a beautiful American girl named Evelyn "Vera" Franke, a talented dancer in one of the revues in which he performed. Together they had three happy, healthy children. He owned a charming Tudor-style house in Douglaston on Long Island with a pool and diving board in the backyard, an enormous player piano, and a brand-new blue Ford station wagon, which his wife would drive to Lakehurst with their children in two days' time for their long-awaited reunion.

It was a remarkable turn of events for a man who had become an entertainer quite by accident. Benny was born not as Benny or Benjamin but as Joseph Spah, or von Späh (pronounced similarly to "Speh"), as the family had previously called themselves, in 1905 in that war-torn strip that seemed to change hands between Germany and France every other generation. For several hundred years, France and Germany, and the smaller German-speaking kingdoms that predated a unified Germany, had fought over the Alsace–Lorraine region on their border. Germany had annexed it from France during the Franco-Prussian War in 1871. The region remained German until after the Great War, when it was returned to France under the Treaty of Versailles in 1919, when Benny was fourteen.

Like so many families in Alsace, the Spah family blended French and German heritage. Benny was the fourth of six children born to a French mother and German father who toiled as poor farmers and sausage makers. The Spah family was Catholic, and as a child, Benny frequently served as an altar boy at their local parish. He was also clever—and hungry. As an altar boy, he was privy to information about when special Masses would be said at the church, including for funerals. With growling stomachs drowning out any moral qualms about the Lord and his good opinion, Benny and his hungry friends would hang around the church and pretend to be among the mourners so they could sneak in and grab a few bites of food from the receptions.

When Benny was eight, his parents sent him to sell their vegetables in town. He would put on his best clothes and slick back his hair and stand on the corner with a basket of produce. There he would see soldiers marching through the streets. Imitating the way they would swing their legs, he paraded up and down the sidewalk, mocking them. His flair for physical comedy proved more lucrative than the vegetables. Passersby would toss him coins as he made a charade of the soldiers who, in all likelihood, were probably only a few years older than he was, and who no doubt took themselves very seriously.

By eleven, he was still small, and fortunately too young to be drafted into the Imperial German Army once the Great War broke out, but he discovered he had a talent for gymnastics and acrobatics, wining prizes in local gymnastics competitions. At fourteen, he briefly ran away to join the circus. His father managed to get him back and apprenticed him to a master tailor. His contract was supposed to last three and a half years, but by then, the war was ending, leaving behind thousands of American soldiers waiting for transit ships home. Benny and a fellow named Bernt put together an acrobatic routine to perform for the American soldiers, passing the hat as they went. The routine did well, but he became even more successful as a small-time gambler. The soldiers who had taught him to play cards no doubt regretted it.

By the time he was sixteen, in 1922, he and Bernt had decided to try their luck in America. He broke his contract with the tailor and set sail for New York. For a boy from war-torn Alsace, America was a shock. He found himself genuinely perplexed by the way Americans seemed to go around chewing like cows, moving their jaws back and forth and round and round without ever swallowing. They were, of course, chomping on chewing gum. He had never heard of it.

Benny was not just coordinated. He also had remarkable flexibility, and soon after moving to New York, he added contortionist elements to his *Kautschuk Gymnastiker* (literally "rubber gymnastics") routine, which prompted a booking agent to rechristen him with the stage name "Ben Dover." Initially, his English was too poor to understand why hotel clerks laughed when he signed the register under his stage name, but eventually he got the joke and added his own flourish, dropping the "er" at the end to become "Ben Dova." Soon he began to go by the more American "Benny," rather than Joseph, not just onstage but all the time as part of his fresh start. He would go by that name for the rest of his life.

Benny and Bernt parted ways, and Benny struck out as a solo act. In an effort to improve himself, he also took night classes at Jamaica High School in Queens and earned his high school degree. By early 1925, he had decided to stay in New York. On his permanent-residence application, he listed himself as nineteen years old, with brown hair and brown eyes, standing five foot four and weighing 122 pounds, though he was probably closer to five foot two. On the form, he had to attest, "It is my bona fide intention to renounce forever all allegiance and fidelity to any foreign prince, potentate, state, or sovereignty, and particularly to The French Republic and (or) The German Empire, of whom I am now a subject." If the two countries could not resolve hundreds of years of territorial claims, the U.S. government would cover both, just to be safe.

For Benny Spah, new skills came naturally. He enjoyed amateur filmmaking and took hundreds of home movies of distinctly high cinematographic quality. He even dabbled as a scratch golfer, a sport he taught himself out of a book after purchasing a snappy roadster that had a special indentation and straps on the side for golf clubs, which he figured he needed to complete the car. One other hobby he quickly took up was aviation. Shortly after he arrived in New York, he started hanging around airports, where he scraped together lessons in old Jennys, the rickety planes of the barnstorming days. To earn extra money, he took on jobs like testing parachutes for seventy-five dollars, a tidy sum for a kid who, less than a decade earlier, had been selling vegetables on a street corner. Still, seventy-five dollars was nothing considering he was risking his life, for testing parachutes meant jumping out of planes, hoping that the fabric and strings strapped to his back were structurally sound. Once again, luck was on Benny's side. Within a year, he had his pilot's license and joined the U.S. Volunteer Air Service, for which he received a pair of gold wings.

Like so many young men, he could not resist using his newfound skills to try to woo young ladies. Before he met Vera, he decided to show off for another girl he liked by flying over her house and dropping a box of candy. Unfortunately, he failed to account for a glass-roofed greenhouse in the garden, through which the candy landed with a smash. The girl's parents were undoubtedly unimpressed.

The candy incident was not the only aviation-related scrape in which he had landed. Benny had also survived three separate crashes. In the first, he landed in a Long Island potato field, which cost him several teeth and thirty-nine dollars for the crops he had ruined. In the second, he nearly lost his head after landing on an East River dock on the Fourth of July, earning himself a fractured skull and concussion. The third time he came down, his wife helped him see sense and give up flying.

Though he was perhaps foolhardy as a young man and had certainly honed the part of a fool onstage to great effect, Benny Spah was nobody's fool, especially not when it came to his country of origin. Though he would always retain a heavy German accent as a remnant of his childhood, he had little sympathy for the political turn his homeland had taken since he had emigrated. He visited Germany intermittently as he toured with vaudeville shows over the next decade and a half, and each time he returned, enough time had elapsed to make the changes starkly evident.

Benny returned to Germany with his act in the spring of 1934, a little over a year after Hitler became chancellor. While he was performing in Düsseldorf, a letter arrived from a local official addressed to "Herr Ben Dova!" The official said that the prior evening he had seen Benny's performance, which had received rapturous applause. While the official thought the show was excellent, he had one suggestion for how Benny could improve it. During the applause at the end of the performance, he thought perhaps Benny could add a special acknowledgment for his home country and proposed he say something to the effect of "As I say goodbye to you today, ladies and gentlemen, and go back to America, I would like to express my very special joy at how beneficial it has been for me over the last six months to see my German fatherland again in this wonderful and changed form since 1919. This time I am leaving my fatherland Germany under this joyful impression and will proudly say over in America our Germany has found itself again." The official also suggested that "it would be good if you raised your right hand in the national-socialist greeting at the end. All of this will certainly recruit you friends for your next guest performance."

Benny, of course, did not take either of his suggestions.

Politics aside, he felt no ill will toward the German people, and if he had qualms about flying on a German airship, he did not express them. Though it was impossible to ignore the enormous flag of the new Germany when looking at the airship from the outside, once inside, one could almost forget Germany's ugly political turn entirely. Inside, there were no symbols of the new establishment, save the swastikas now incorporated into the patches on the officers' uniform caps, and the officers themselves kept their political opinions quiet. In fact, Benny quite liked Ernst Lehmann, whom he had found polite and courteous during their brief exchange about whether lightning could hurt the airship the previous evening. Benny had run into Lehmann again that day while taking care of a few onboard errands, like feeding Ulla and sending fourteen postcards that a German theater friend had entrusted to him to mail on board to get that souvenir zeppelin stamp.

It would have surprised many to learn that in his private life, the onstage comedian was quite a serious person. He was disciplined, strict with his children, and a devout Catholic (his earlier transgressions as a boy nicking food from funerals notwithstanding). But he was not above a bit of friendly ribbing now and then. Perhaps to prove he really was not afraid of flying after expressing concern about the lightning, he told Lehmann, stopping the senior captain as he passed, that he was something of a "flying jinx." One might even call him a "Jonah," he said, referring to the biblical story of the man swallowed by a whale, a harbinger of bad luck to superstitious sailors for centuries.

It might not have been the best time to raise the subject of his teenage flying accidents, seeing as they were out over the Atlantic Ocean. But Lehmann, calm as ever, simply waved him off with a laugh, refusing to take the bait. "You don't need to worry, my friend," he said. "Zeppelins never have accidents."

CHAPTER 13

Over the Atlantic Ocean: May 4, 1937

Ernst Lehmann had transported some interesting creatures in his time as a zeppelin captain—prize Trakehner horses from Prussia; gorillas, chimpanzees, and monkeys used in scientific research; guinea pigs; canaries; carrier pigeons; even queen bees—but perhaps the species that made itself the biggest nuisance for the crew was dogs. Dogs always seemed to come along with American entertainer owners who were apparently unable to travel without them. The year before, the silent film actor Douglas Fairbanks, star of swashbuckling hits like *The Mark of Zorro*, *Robin Hood*, and *The Three Musketeers*, was traveling home from Europe with his new bride, the former Lady Sylvia Ashley, and their six-month-old Scottie named Bobby Burns. While in flight, Mrs. Fairbanks had allowed little Bobby Burns off his leash so he could avail himself of the facilities. As the first animal aboard the new airship, he decided to mark his territory, leaving, as steward Wilhelm Balla quipped, his "business cards everywhere" while Mrs. Fairbanks worked on a jigsaw puzzle.

Passengers' casual disregard for the sheer wonder of flight, or just how quickly they became bored and defaulted to their mindless earthly activities, never ceased to amaze Lehmann. On the *Graf Zeppelin*'s very first flight over Germany in 1928, he had passed through the dining room and found two passengers who had already grown tired of looking out the window and were instead sitting quietly playing a game of chess. "How quickly men become accustomed to the unusual!" he had remarked with disdain. Man had dreamed of flying for centuries. "What was a miracle yesterday, becomes a habit today," he had harrumphed in his memoir. Lehmann's was a complaint shared by many groundbreaking aviators, of the heavier- and lighter-than-air varieties alike. Even Charles Lindbergh agreed. "In developing aviation, in making it a form of commerce, in replacing the wild freedom of danger with the civilized bonds of safety," he mused, "must we give up this miracle of air?"

It could not have been lost upon Lehmann that this first trip of the *Hindenburg*'s 1937 season had commenced a mere eighteen days shy of the tenth anniversary of Lindbergh's own "miracle of air." While Lindbergh's achievement was remarkable, many seemed to forget that he had only accomplished what airships had been proving possible since the British beat the Germans to transatlantic zeppelin flight in 1919. The rivalry between airships and airplanes aside, the brotherhood of aviators had witnessed some remarkable sights in the first three decades of the twentieth century. Only an airman knew that when flying over London, the lights along the Thames looked like the Milky Way, and only from an aircraft could the "benumbing" and "monstrous" vastness of the swamps, forests, and streams of Siberia be appreciated in their endless expanse. So uncharted was their route on the round-the-world flight that when planning their journey over the Stanovoy mountains in the Russian Far East, the crew could find almost no information about the height of the range aside from one report that suggested the section in question was 3,500 feet high. As a precaution, Eckener added an extra 2,000 feet of clearance as they groped their way through fog and clouds. Just before they reached the Sea of Okhotsk, the clouds finally dispersed, and only then did the crew realize they had cleared the mountain ridge by a mere three hundred feet. After Siberia's wild, hostile nature, it was a "refreshing" relief when they reached the island of Hokkaido the next morning and could look down to see "neatly divided . . . rice fields, gardens, and clean houses."

On a zeppelin, as a DZR marketing pamphlet exclaimed, "the prophetic vision of Jules Verne has been realized." Passengers could experience for themselves the stuff of science fiction novels. In describing this balance between wonder and commerce, DZR might have done a bit too much to convince nervous fliers that riding on a zeppelin was as easy as sitting in their own living rooms. In the passenger lounge, where card games and jigsaw puzzles always began to appear midway through the first full day of the crossing, some passengers seemed oblivious to the fact they were airborne at all.

Perhaps Lehmann's frustration with the passengers was unfairly placed and actually had more to do with the demands of his job, which had changed considerably since he had been promoted. Lehmann now had to be bothered with all the nonflying aspects of the zeppelin business, in which he had little interest but which made a great impression on the passengers. Things like advertising, marketing, and the minutiae of internal operations now took up a great deal of his time. Over the last year, DZR had been making a series of investments in its future operations to ensure that its international clientele saw zeppelins as the height of comfort, convenience, safety, and glamour in travel. It had been aggressively expanding advertising abroad, including a targeted effort to promote airship service to Europe for the coronation and the Paris Exposition. DZR had also offered some of its business associates free flights in exchange for a report with their general impressions and suggestions for improvement. One of them, a Brit named George Grant, who was an assistant manager at the firm that handled zeppelin bookings in London, had joined this flight. Grant seemed to be enjoying his paid vacation. So far, he had neglected his report, aside from noting that linen covers should be placed at the heads of the beds in the cabins to prevent grease marks marring the cabins' fabric-covered walls, and went about touring the airship with the stewards instead.

While DZR actively courted such feedback from its own associates, the general public sometimes took it upon themselves to write in with unsolicited advice. DZR had recently received a letter from a man named Hinrich Schröder, a children's toilet seat manufacturer. He had noticed a newspaper article about DZR having hired a stewardess, from which he concluded there would be increasingly more children traveling on board. Therefore, he concluded, the zeppelins required sanitary facilities for these "little guests." He wrote that he hoped to receive an order from DZR for his toilet seats, which attached to the main seat and could be folded up so that adults need not be bothered and children would not have to use a pot. Herr Schröder would, unfortunately, be disappointed.

DZR's biggest effort by far, which had taken up considerable amounts of Ernst Lehmann's time over the last few months, was a push to capture the attention and the business of wealthy American travelers, who, attracted by the time savings of zeppelin travel, made up 70 to 80 percent of its paying customer base by 1937.

"Our century has been called the technical age. It has also been called the age of abbreviation," Lehmann wrote in his memoir with an air of disdain. "Time is money, the American says; to decrease time means to save money." This deliberate shift toward the American market had begun in earnest the prior October with the *Hindenburg*'s "Millionaires Flight," where over seventy mostly wealthy and high-profile American passengers took a ten-and-a-half-hour cruise over the Eastern Seaboard. They included Wall Street financiers like Nelson Rockefeller and Winthrop Aldrich, aviation leaders like Great War ace and Eastern Airlines General Manager Eddie Rickenbacker, Pan Am founder Juan Trippe, and Goodyear's Paul Litchfield. All together, the passengers' net worth was over a billion dollars.

By the beginning of 1937, it appeared that overtures to American passengers were proving successful. It was only May, and three quarters of the *Hindenburg*'s 1937 bookings were for Americans. If the numerous American passengers relaxing in the smoking lounge with drinks in hand or inscribing postcards in the writing room were any indication, DZR seemed to be attracting exactly the kind of well-heeled executives it sought to entice.

American packer Nelson Morris was by far the wealthiest passenger on board, and both the speed of travel and the allure of flight clearly appealed to him. Better yet, he had purchased a second ticket for his friend Bert Dolan. Fortunately, Morris was the antithesis of unimpressed passengers who so rankled Lehmann. He clearly fancied himself a fellow airman and was already seeking out the steward for a tour of the *Hindenburg*'s vast structure.

Also keen was passenger Peter Belin, the young Yale graduate on his way home to Washington, DC, after a year in Paris. Belin was related to the Du Pont family of gunpowder-industry millionaires, but his presence also showed that DZR was making inroads with the influential Washington set. His father, F. Lammot Belin, had left private business to become a diplomat, serving as one of the State Department's earliest chief protocol officers and then as ambassador to Poland from 1932 to 1933. Peter Belin planned to have a similar career and already had that inherent cosmopolitan ease about him. As with Morris, he enjoyed the technical aspect of flight. Alongside being a member of the undefeated Yale soccer team, the Alpha Delta Phi fraternity, and the Book and Snake secret society, Belin had also taken flying lessons at New Haven Municipal Airport and received his pilot's license from the Boeing Aeronautical School. Throughout the day, the square-jawed, dark-haired young man with a broad smile would take out a pen and a folded paper map of the Western Hemisphere and smooth it out on one of the small writing tables. Checking the airship's coordinates, which the crew posted along with news bulletins in the reading room, he would draw a dot to mark their position and connect it back to the previous dot, charting their progress since their Frankfurt departure.

Fantastically wealthy passengers like Nelson Morris and Peter Belin had easily been sold on air travel as fellow, albeit not terribly experienced, airmen, but San Francisco canning executive Moritz Feibusch was part of the next tier of lower-profile but highly successful Americans whom DZR was courting and who had been drawn in by the promise of adventure. Feibusch was a German Jewish immigrant originally from Rogasen, or Rogoźno, a now Polish town that, like Alsace, had traded hands at various times in its history. Feibusch, a slender, gray-haired, bespectacled fifty-seven-year-old of average height, seemed utterly delighted by his good fortune in life and was determined to make the most of it. As a young man, he had moved to San Francisco, where he got a job working for Prager's Department Store. He became a merchandise broker and within a few years had built his own canned foods company, which sold products like Pebble Beach Tuna Flakes and Sardines and Calbear Fruit Salad. He owned a home on the edge of Golden Gate Park, and he and his wife, a violinist and composer, had traveled extensively throughout Britain, Italy, Turkey, Czechoslovakia, Egypt, Syria, the British Mandate of Palestine, and, of course, back to Germany and Poland to visit his large family. He had even managed to bring three of his brothers, their wives, and three nephews over from Germany—its climate increasingly hostile to Jews—to live in San Francisco and was in the process of adopting one of his nephews. After his wife died in 1935, he took several extended trips, including to Paris, where he began a new travel tradition. He had a set of custom postcards designed with the words "*Souvenir de mon ascension*" and a cartoon of himself as a giant wearing a boater hat and spats standing jauntily on the Eiffel Tower, which he sent to business contacts, family, and friends.

Feibusch was on his way home from his annual business trip to Europe. His manager and secretary had returned by steamship, but Feibusch had decided to treat himself to a few additional weeks abroad with an airship journey as a climactic conclusion. This adventure had clearly been on his mind for some time, as he had previously sent souvenir mail to his brother in Berlin on the 1929 round-the-world flight of the *Graf Zeppelin*. Once again he had a set of two hundred custom postcards printed, this time a compilation of his passport photo and an image of the zeppelin flying above. (Interestingly, despite being Jewish, he opted for authenticity and included the *Hindenburg*'s very visible swastikas on the artistic rendering.)

Though enthusiastic travelers were more likely to proselytize zeppelin travel to family and friends, DZR was happy to sell a ticket to anyone willing to pay. Philip Mangone, for example, who had thus far put in little appearance in the public rooms and largely kept to his cabin, was a sturdy fifty-two-year-old Italian American and a dispassionate traveler. This was just one more transatlantic crossing to add to an impressive tally over nearly half a century after having immigrated to New York from Calabria with his family as a child. He was a seventh-generation tailor with an eighth-grade education who started his career as a fitter at the B. Altman department store on Fifth Avenue in Manhattan and had gone on to become one of the era's chicest designers, specializing in women's tailored looks, particularly suits and reversible capes. He was best known for having developed the swagger coat and topper. Back in 1915, twenty-two years earlier almost to the day, he had been booked to travel on board the *Lusitania* but had canceled at the last minute, narrowly escaping disaster.

On that very voyage, the *Lusitania* was torpedoed and sunk by a U-boat off the coast of Ireland. Such a near miss with fate apparently left Mangone unfazed. His booking on the *Hindenburg* was purely practical in nature. True to American form in this age of abbreviation, he had decided to fly simply to save four extra days to stay on schedule with his fall collection.

The reality was that as the novelty of the technology wore off and airship journeys became as commonplace as crossing the Atlantic on an ocean liner, no doubt there would be more and more travelers with Mangone's attitude than with that of Morris, Belin, and Feibusch. Lehmann really should not complain, because those time savers were the difference between a profitable enterprise and his beloved airships becoming an odd relic of a short-lived era.

DZR had recently implemented a number of changes for the 1937 season to ensure that the onboard experience met with these Americans' approval. There was a sense of irony to this, as the zeppelin company was facing an increasingly split reality. On the one hand, the outward image of the zeppelins was becoming progressively more associated with the Nazi regime. Meanwhile, *inside* the airships and in DZR's commercial practices, everything was becoming more and more American every day.

Over the winter, Willy von Meister, DZR's representative in the United States, had written Lehmann a twenty-page letter filled with suggestions for improvement. Von Meister, a tall and imposing six foot six (compared with Lehmann's approximate five foot two), was culturally well placed to make these suggestions. Through his German father, the former governor of the state of Hesse, von Meister was a godson of the last kaiser, Wilhelm II, but his mother was an American raised in London. He had lived in the United States for over a decade.

First and foremost, von Meister instructed Lehmann, the stewards must provide carafes of ice water on the tables in the lounge and dining room: "Americans should not have to give up the habit of drinking ice water on board." Menus and news posted on the reading room blackboard should be posted in both German and English, and on all trips to Germany, the chief steward should announce which golf club Americans could use while in Frankfurt. Von Meister also emphasized the need to provide additional entertainment on board, no doubt much to Lehmann's chagrin, as it carried the implication that zeppelin travel was, well, rather boring. As it took most of the first day of a two-day trip for passengers to get to know each other sufficiently to gather for games of bridge and skat, the stewards should supply more games for two people, such as chess and backgammon, both very popular in the United States. They should also provide other physically lightweight entertainments, like Ping-Pong balls and paddles for play on the longer dining tables between meals and jigsaw puzzles with pleasant scenes (though none so large that they could not be finished by the end of the short trip).

It was also essential to have a doctor on board. Thus far, DZR had been lucky that no passenger had fallen seriously ill while in the air, but it was only a matter of time until their luck ran out. "It is very easy to imagine that a German doctor who doesn't have a private practice or is not a particularly good doctor, or has too little interest in private practice" would be interested in such a unique (and generally unchallenging) occupation, wrote von Meister. "I am convinced that the extra weight and the additional cost of one such man would pay off in spades," he concluded, not least because a small number of American passengers tended to show up drunk and could cause themselves small injuries. When his medical services were not required, the doctor could conduct airship tours or organize bridge games as a sort of entertainment czar. As doctors were generally good with people, his thinking went, the doctor could also serve as a guest relations go-between for American passengers and German crew. Passengers had complained on several occasions that the stewards could be a bit overbearing in suggesting they change out of their relaxed daytime traveling suits and into proper dinner attire. DZR had accepted von Meister's suggestion and hired twenty-seven-year-old Dr. Kurt Rüdiger for the 1937 season.

Another point of contention between passengers and crew was the meals themselves, particularly special requests the kitchen was unenthusiastic about accommodating. "The kitchen," von Meister instructed Lehmann, "is generally described as 'difficult.' A large percentage of Americans either have spoiled stomachs or an 'idiosyncrasy' that means they can't eat this or that." Each morning, the crew should put out the full day's menu (in English) at breakfast so that passengers could communicate which foods they could not tolerate. The bar steward, Max Schulze, also needed to be "more courteous in his dealings with the guests," whose egress to and from the smoking room he patrolled to ensure no one brought anything flammable out from behind the air-lock door. As a previous passenger who had flown to Rio the year before had quipped, so tight was the security around anything flammable leaving the smoking lounge that "one felt like a boy having a fag behind the greenhouse. I always imagined that Dr. Eckener was waiting for me outside with a birch and mortarboard and gown." Schulze also needed to "drink less himself and avoid ingratiating himself too much with the passengers." It was essential that the bar never run out of liquor, especially rye or bourbon whiskey, necessary ingredients in the popular Manhattan cocktail. The bar should also provide a souvenir. "I will send you a small metal 'skewer' that is served with the cocktails in the Hotel Waldorf-Astoria," von Meister offered.

Finally, DZR needed to concede to Americans where their preferences related to cleanliness and comfort differed. In the four B deck lavatories, DZR needed to supply either a basket of small, single-use hand towels or disposable paper napkins for drying hands, rather than one large communal towel, which "according to American custom" was "very undesirable." "The American has a need for freshness" and did not want to "participate in a communal towel." Nor did Americans like the bedding offered. Rather than one single, fluffy duvet, DZR should switch to the American style of bedding with a sheet and several wool blankets, even though the duvet was far easier for the stewards to shake out and refold in tight cabins. Though it was not the German way, von Meister felt strongly that "these things don't cost much and are amenities that improve the overall impression of the service."

Von Meister did have one other suggestion at large, and that was to expand the fire-protection measures in the passenger compartments. "I'm thinking about the possibility of rapid-fire extinguishing systems, with compressed carbonic acid, [and] smoke detectors, as used on seagoing ships. . . . It could happen that a drunk passenger starts smoking and is careless," assuming he got past Max Schulze at the bar. Of course, such equipment, he recognized, could "only be of use in the early stages of a fire."

None of von Meister's suggestions were meant to directly criticize Lehmann or any other individual and their work. They were merely a reflection of the reality that "we are dealing with a very spoiled public in the North Atlantic service" who would "only be prepared to use the airship if the entire journey is smooth, comfortable and without unpleasant incidents."

That such mundane minutiae should frustrate Lehmann was no surprise. He was not a businessman who enjoyed tinkering with inputs to maximize the bottom line. He was a true airman in his heart and soul. Nor was he alone in his frustration over the direction in which his beloved industry had turned. Reflecting on how attitudes toward air travel had changed in the short amount of time since he had first crossed the Atlantic, compared with the millennia that men had spent yearning for the freedom of birds and control over the air above, Charles Lindbergh mused, "Will men fly through the sky in the future without seeing what I have seen, without feeling what I have felt? Is that true of all things we call human progress—do the gods retire as commerce and science advance?"

Since the allegorical days of Icarus, countless men had lost their lives in failed experiments as they strove to achieve the miracle of flight. Now, thanks to the airship and its perfection in the hands of German engineers, Lehmann could proudly say, "The fight to conquer the air has ended in the defeat of the elemental forces of Nature." And yet, just as quickly as the fight had been won, the beneficiaries of such a triumph of human engineering went back to their newspapers, their card games, and their cheap jigsaw puzzles, their tricky stomachs and their nuisance pets, and had the nerve to be bored.

CHAPTER 14

Over the Atlantic Ocean: May 4, 1937

Nelson Morris was keen to take in all the details of the Germans' latest airborne masterpiece—beyond the smoking room, with which he had already acquainted himself. It was one of the design innovations in this new class of zeppelins for which Nelson, as a chain-smoker, was no doubt most grateful. His ever-industrious friend Bert Dolan had gotten an early start writing postcards to neighbors, friends, and some of Lelong's clients who would appreciate the goodwill gesture of a *Hindenburg* souvenir, but Nelson had evidently persuaded Bert to leave his correspondence aside for the time being. The two men set off in search of the chief steward to take them back into the depths of the leviathan.

The environment on the *Hindenburg* was clearly more regimented than what Nelson had experienced on the *Graf Zeppelin* a decade earlier. Back then, Eckener had indulged Nelson's curiosity by allowing him to spend a good deal of time in the control gondola, where the officers had kindly instructed him on their activity as they rode across the ocean. This time, none of the travelers were allowed to wander beyond the passenger decks unaccompanied, but the stewards would take them in groups of no more than five as far forward as the control gondola and as far aft as the engineer's control cabin on the starboard side of the airship. Though that left the vast majority of the airship's interior to the passengers' imaginations, it was certainly enough of a demonstration for them to fully appreciate the precise engineering at a mammoth scale that held them aloft as they made their way out over the ocean.

Few in the airship business could offer a better tour of the *Hindenburg* than Chief Steward Heinrich Kubis. Kubis, who was about Nelson and Bert's age, had been flying on airships about as long as Captain Lehmann. After beginning his career as a waiter at the Frankfurter Hof hotel at fourteen, he had worked at some of Europe's finest hotels before being hired as a waiter on Luftschiffbau Zeppelin's most successful prewar airships. He had served on a total of seven hundred airship flights, had crossed the ocean by air 168 times, and had covered two million kilometers in the sky, including taking part in the 1929 round-the-world trip and the 1931 polar expedition.

By a quirk of design, the belly of the airship was accessed through the chief steward's cabin, next to the air-lock door to the smoking lounge and the bar, where Nelson was already putting Bert's offer to pay their combined bar tab to good use. Once inside the crew area, Nelson, Bert, and anyone else taking a tour could see into the tiny kitchen across the narrow hall, which somehow managed to fit the chef and his four subordinates, who were making three multicourse meals a day for ninety-seven passengers and crew, plus afternoon tea and snacks, using only three electric burners and three small electric ovens. Their pots, pans, and utensils were cleverly stacked and hung using every available inch of space.

Compared with the compact efficiency of the passenger decks and mess area, stepping into the vast expanse of the structure of the *Hindenburg* was like falling through the looking glass. "It is false to imagine the inside of the airship as crammed with swollen gas-cells," Captain Lehmann had written in his memoir. The large gas cells were, of course, visible, but the interior was so much more sophisticated than a cavernous space bulging with gas bags. As Lehmann described, "One can see a great part of the frame-work, which is covered with a steel-blue protective coat of paint. With its ribs and struts it seems like a cathedral"—one that was "speeding along 3,000 feet over the sea." Had their journey spanned a Sunday, perhaps the experience would have been sufficiently holy for the devoutly Catholic Bert Dolan to feel he had kept his weekly sacrament.

The enormous scale of it all was almost too much to comprehend for passengers gazing at the giant duralumin rings that made up the main skeleton of the structure. The two friends were standing well within the fifteen main rings in the middle of the airship that surrounded the largest gas cells, each one of which held more hydrogen than the entire capacity of the first zeppelin the old count had constructed almost forty years earlier. The rings resembled bicycle wheels, a design that had hardly changed since it was first developed by Luftschiffbau Zeppelin in 1915. Each ring was composed of eighteen diamond-shaped trusses, which were further supported by a crosswork of intermediate frames and steel wire bracing cables. Thirty-six longitudinal girders reduced the load. All together, the frame of the *Graf Zeppelin* would have stretched ten miles if laid out end to end. The *Hindenburg*'s frame would have stretched miles longer.

Looking up, passengers on their tours could see that the engineers had painted the inside of the top half of the canvas cover with a layer of iron oxide. Exposure to intense heat would have caused the cells to expand and become more porous, so this precaution, along with the reflective aluminum powder mixed into the dope painted on the outside of the cover to deflect ultraviolet and infrared radiation, helped to shield them from the sun beating down from above. Notably, the cover that enveloped the *Hindenburg* did not actually sit directly on top the frame. Instead, panels of the cover were tied to the frame with twine, leaving a small gap between fabric and metal. These gaps were sealed with additional strips of doped canvas, which were in turn held just off the frame by narrow wooden dowels. This was yet another safety feature. If the outer skin of the airship became charged by the outside atmosphere, the charge would not pass to the frame of the airship, as the twine and wooden dowels were poorly conductive material, meaning there was no cover-to-frame electrical connection.

Remarkably, if the outer canvas cover became damaged, a man could be sent out to repair it mid-flight. This occurred on the *Graf Zeppelin* in 1928 during the first passenger-carrying transatlantic flight, a voyage that was too important to the future of lighter-than-air aviation to fail. Halfway across the Atlantic, the *Graf Zeppelin* was caught in a squall, which tore the cover on the left tail stabilizer. With the airship more than

1,500 feet above the white, foamy waves, Dr. Eckener's twenty-six-year-old son, Knut, a skilled elevator man crewing the flight, and three other crew members climbed out to the tail and repaired it while clinging to the skeleton of the airship with nothing but a rope to protect them should they slip and plunge toward the sea. Their quick work saved the airship from a devastating elevator jam, without which it would have been all but impossible to adjust altitude, and prevented what would have been an utterly calamitous blow to the entire enterprise.

Knut Eckener's heroics outside the airship were all the more impressive considering that even the interior of the structure was not an easy place to maneuver. One had to be sure-footed on the narrow catwalks and ladders. For a compact natural athlete like Bert Dolan, or the trim and energetic Nelson Morris, it was no trouble, but for some of the older, portlier, or generally less agile passengers, Kubis could hardly have been an enthusiastic guide, for fear they might put a foot wrong and tumble into the keel below.

In the keel area directly beneath Nelson and Bert were one set of the crew's quarters and eight freight rooms, which contained a complete spare Daimler-Benz engine and could accommodate heavy cargo like automobiles. On this trip, there was nothing too unusual in the hold. The most interesting cargo in the freight room was two dogs, one of which belonged to Benny Spah. The other was being sent to its owner in America. Also distributed along the sturdy keel were tanks containing ballast water and fuel, a light oil that was more stable and required a much higher temperature to produce combustible vapors than gasoline, and therefore was far less flammable. Crews working in the engine nacelles, which resembled "baby whales swimming beneath their mother," as Lehmann described, accessed their posts via four lateral passages that led to catwalks extending out to the engines, which could be closed to form a single aerodynamic bar. The engines each weighed 4,410 pounds. Telephone lines ran throughout the ship connecting the crew located in fourteen different posts, from the control gondola to the engine nacelles to just inside the tail. Out of an abundance of caution, engineers had decided not to install any electrical equipment that could possibly serve as a fire hazard in proximity to the gas cells. Old-fashioned speaking tubes were used to transmit orders to riggers making hourly maintenance checks of the gas cells along the axial walkway above. Here, the catwalks were made of a light wood, and riggers wore rubber- or straw-soled shoes and workman's jumpsuits without buttons so as not to risk snagging the fabric of the cells.

The gas cells themselves, which loomed above the walkway, threw down giant shadows that appeared almost like "giant mushrooms in a prehistoric landscape," as Captain Lehmann described in his memoir. On average, each gas cell contained approximately 400,000 cubic feet of hydrogen, though the volume of each cell was not uniform and depended where along the elliptical shape of the airship it was located. There was so much gas contained in the older *Graf Zeppelin* that Lehmann estimated that had it been used to light a watchman's gas lamp as in days gone by, it still would have been burning in the year 2400. The *Hindenburg* contained twice as much hydrogen. One of the greatest challenges for the engineers was how to keep gas from seeping out of the fabric cells, as no fabric was entirely impermeable. For decades, gas cells had been made out of goldbeater's skin, largely the outer membrane of cow intestines, a product that would have been familiar to anyone at Morris & Company. In the last decade, American engineers at Goodyear in Akron, Ohio, had developed a material called filmstoff, in which coats of gelatinized latex were brushed onto cotton. It had a permeability rate of less than one liter per square meter in twenty-four hours, far less than any other material discovered to date. The filmstoff was somewhat translucent, and when the gas cells were hung partially inflated from the airship frame, they looked like jellyfish with umbrellalike bells from which wavy arms and tentacles appeared to spill as if suspended in water.

Though the gas cells in the *Hindenburg* had initially been designed differently than those used in the past, as the German engineers had assumed they would acquire helium from the United States by the time they finished constructing it, they never intended to use helium alone to lift the *Hindenburg*. Valving off helium to adjust altitude over the course of a flight would be an enormous waste of a precious resource, so the Germans had to find a way to preserve as much of it as possible.

While zeppelins often flew at several thousand feet over mountains or cities, to rise above a storm, or to find the most favorable winds, they typically cruised somewhere between 575 and 820 feet above the earth's surface, roughly the height of many Manhattan skyscrapers. Airships had to constantly adjust altitude and buoyancy in response to environmental factors. Colder night air made gas denser and decreased its lifting capacity, while warmer air during the day made the gas less dense and the airship more buoyant. Rain could also change the weight of the airship quite dramatically. A light rain could add 660 to 880 pounds across the surface area of the airship, while a heavy rain could add as much as 2,200 to 3,300 pounds. Ice was even worse, adding 4,400 to 6,600 pounds. It was possible to counteract several thousand pounds of water or ice by applying dynamic pressure using the elevators to fly the airship at a continuously inclined position of several degrees. When the airship was slightly too heavy, the weight could be offset by pointing the nose up. When the airship was slightly too light, the nose could be pointed down. However, there was no way around the reality that eventually either ballast water or gas would have to be released to make the airship lighter or heavier. This was especially important as fuel was consumed during the flight. Sometimes as much as one third of the original volume of gas would have to be released to keep the airship from becoming progressively more buoyant and thus rising to a higher elevation as the engines burned fuel over the course of the journey.

Luftschiffbau Zeppelin had experimented with several innovative designs, including a water ballast recovery system using silica gel to absorb moisture from the air to minimize the need to valve helium. Their eventual, proposed solution was to have helium-filled outer gas cells and smaller, inner cells with 35 percent of the larger cells' volume that would be filled with hydrogen and could be valved directly and inexpensively using valves and vents to take the hydrogen up to the spine of airship and out into the ambient atmosphere.

Though Luftschiffbau Zeppelin had tested this design, there remained some questions as to whether it would have ever actually been implemented. Even if American helium was available, the Germans were not exactly champing at the bit to use it. First, they had an excellent safety record using hydrogen. In the late fall of 1936, the zeppelin company's representative in the United States was trying to arrange to have American airshipmen train on the German zeppelins in exchange for increased lobbying efforts to amend the Helium Control Act. In response, Captain Lehmann had retorted, "That is really no inducement; we have been operating our commercial service with hydrogen very successfully for years." Second, for a transportation system that could barely turn a profit, the loss of 10 percent of lifting capacity when using the heavier helium gas also meant transporting fewer passengers and cargo. This concern was top of mind for Dr. Eckener and the chief engineer, Ludwig Dürr, especially once they learned the weight of the fully constructed *Hindenburg* was going to exceed estimates. In the event the Americans were willing to sell Eckener helium and his engineers could find a way to cut some weight to operate profitably, it was not clear how DZR would be able to pay for it. The Nazis instituted tight controls over foreign exchange to prevent reichsmarks from leaving the country, going so far as to check passengers for any currency in their possession that they had not exchanged, as passengers like Margaret Mather had experienced at the Frankfurter Hof.

If helium proved unobtainable, the zeppelin crew was confident they could continue to operate safely using the highly flammable hydrogen. Even if a gas cell developed a small leak, it was not necessarily a problem, provided there was a current of air that quickly dispersed the gas. While the airship was in motion, there was enough air to sweep it away while a rigger located and patched the leak. It was only when hydrogen was able to build up in a concentrated pocket that the potential for danger quickly escalated. One particularly dangerous scenario could occur during valving, when a substantial stream of hydrogen was released from the ship into the surrounding air at one time. Under normal conditions, this was not a problem, but it could become dangerous during a storm.

It was a matter of basic physics. Usually, electric charges between objects in the natural environment are fairly balanced, and when they become unbalanced, they try to equalize. Thunderstorms are one such instance when environmental factors such as pressure, wind, and humidity drive positive and negative charges apart, creating starkly different electric potentials. Clouds build up different electric charges at varying elevation levels within the cloud: Lighter ice crystals at the top of a cloud carry a positive charge, which separates from negatively charged, heavier water droplets at the bottom. Meanwhile the ground is always positively charged. As clouds pass near the ground, a large differential between the negatively charged bottom of the cloud and the positively charged ground leads to an electrical discharge as the charge differential seeks to equalize. Negative charges in the cloud begin to jump toward the ground in a formation called a stepped leader, like a downward-facing branch. At the same time, an upward leader of positive charges rises from the ground, usually from the tallest object in the vicinity, such as a tree or telephone pole. These streams of charges jumping toward each other meet and produce an electric current, manifested as light and heat. The light produces a bolt of lightning, while the heat, which causes air to suddenly expand, creates a clap of sound, or thunder. Charges can also jump from the more negatively charged bottom parts of clouds to the positively charged upper parts of other clouds nearby, creating lightning between cloud formations. This, of course, carried implications for airships.

As Dr. Eckener had instructed his crews in one of his early operating manuals, "experience indicates that the ship will very quickly assume the potential of the surrounding air masses." When an airship was flying through cloud formations or close to the ground, distinct electrical differentials between clouds or between clouds and the ground could seek to equalize through the airship as a bridge for the current. So long as the equalization did not happen too abruptly, as Captain Lehmann had tried to explain in layman's terms to Benny Spah the night before, it would not pose a problem. The charge would be absorbed by the metal frame serving as a Faraday cage beneath the canvas and redirected back outward away from the airship. However, Eckener warned, "if one quickly changes altitude, the adaptation of the ship would not take place so promptly and one could easily come in contact with electrically charged clouds with considerable potential differences from the ship." Most important, Eckener warned, while in environments with large electrical potential differentials, "one will particularly do everything in one's power to avoid . . . the ship valving gas!" This was crucial. A valved concentration of hydrogen gas suddenly exposed to the heat and light of an electric current between clouds could cause a spark. Eckener took care to emphasize to his crew, "Every equalizing spark between ship and cloud, which does not always have to take the form of real lightning, can, if the ship is valving gas, easily discharge into a layer of explosive gas and lead to ignition. Also the possibility cannot be excluded that lightning leaping from cloud to cloud may accidentally strike through the stream of valved gas and so set it afire."

Nelson Morris may have had little recollection of such principles of electric charges from high school or college science courses, but he was all too aware of fire's capacity for destruction under a set of unlikely but deadly conditions. At 4:00 a.m. on December 22, 1910—Nelson's nineteenth birthday—a fire had broken out in warehouse 7 of Nelson Morris & Company at the Union Stockyards. Warehouse 7 was a cold storage facility filled with processed hogs preserved in saltpeter, a core component of gunpowder. When a faulty electrical socket malfunctioned, a spark quickly ignited the chemicals and spread to the grease-soaked wooden walls and floors. Immediately, the warehouse went up in flames. As the heat from the fire expanded the cold air inside the building, pressure built up dangerously quickly. Firefighters could reach the blaze with their hoses only by climbing to the top of a covered loading dock closed off from behind by railroad boxcars. As the heat and smoke intensified the rapidly expanding pressure in the building, an explosion occurred and the warehouse collapsed, sending six stories of bricks down on the firemen. Twenty-one were killed, including the beloved Irish American fire chief, James "Big Jim" Horan. The Chicago Union Stockyards fire left nineteen women widowed and thirty-five children fatherless just days before Christmas. Twenty-seven years later, it remained the single greatest loss of life among firefighters in American history.

Dr. Eckener and the zeppelin company engineers had taken every conceivable precaution to ensure that safe practices were followed when flying with flammable hydrogen, and their track record suggested they had succeeded. Still, it would have surprised many to learn that, despite the new regime's increasing investment in the zeppelin program, the one person who could not be convinced of their safety, regardless of what precautions engineers implemented, was Adolf Hitler. As Hitler quipped to one of his generals, Walter Dornberger, an engineer overseeing Germany's developing rocket capabilities, "The whole thing always seems to me like an inventor who claims to have discovered a cheap new kind of floor covering which looks marvelous, shines forever, and never wears out. But he adds that there is one disadvantage. It must not be walked on with nailed shoes and nothing hard must ever be dropped on it because, unfortunately, it's made of high explosive." "No," Hitler concluded to Dornberger, "I shall never get into an airship."

Hitler's enormous fear of flying on a zeppelin notwithstanding, there remained rumors that he had wanted the newest airship to be named after him and that Eckener had refused in yet another snub to the führer. Eckener had reportedly declared to German journalist Bella Fromm, "I couldn't think of going to the United States with '*Adolf Hitler*' painted on the ship." In reality, no one from DZR's leadership had proposed naming the *LZ-129* "Hitler." Initially, they suggested two names, either "Hindenburg" after Paul von Hindenburg, the Great War leader of the imperial army and president of Germany, or "Germania" as a nod to the German people at large. Company executives favored "Germania," which they believed preferable for "linguistic reasons" abroad, and "particularly suitable for the promotion of the German cause in South America," where the *Graf Zeppelin* continued its regular flights to Brazil. DZR had communicated this preference to the Reich's minister of aviation, Hermann Göring, in July 1935. Ultimately, Hitler decided to honor the deceased German president instead. The name was painted on the *Hindenburg*'s belly in a vibrant shade of vermillion in the angular script lettering called Fraktur, which the Nazis believed most authentically German. Each letter was deliberately written in lower case, as heavy Fraktur capitals were more difficult to read from a distance. Laden with symbolism, the *Hindenburg* would boldly announce itself as it appeared over the horizon, its chrome body and red detailing flashing brilliantly in the sunlight.

As Nelson Morris toured the airship, perhaps the thought crossed his mind that here he was, the grandson of a German Jew, now flying as the wealthiest passenger aboard the pride of the Nazi lighter-than-air fleet. If it did, he never said. Nor did he dwell on the fact that had his grandfather not emigrated from Germany, his family would have been subject to the laws that now limited Jews' participation in German public life, stripped them of their property and businesses, and denied their German citizenship, even for those who had converted to Christianity.

Had Nelson's sister Muriel continued from Paris with him in place of Bert Dolan, no doubt she would have had something choice to say on the subject. Like Nelson's other sister, Ruth, a noted pediatrician at New York University Medical School, Muriel had graduated from Wellesley College. She later studied at Oxford before moving to Vienna to pursue psychoanalysis and medicine. In 1932, Muriel had enrolled in the University of Vienna's medical school, where she was greatly disturbed to find anti-Semitic ideology surrounding her. Her anatomy classes were divided into two sections in two separate wings of the building: one for Christians and other non-Jews and the other for Jews and socialists. (Technically, under this Nazi-inspired view of the world, Muriel herself should have been placed in the Jewish wing, as she had one Jewish grandparent.) Non-Jewish students sometimes attempted to raid the Jewish section, and clashes occasionally turned violent. At least once, Jewish students were thrown out of windows.

Muriel had thought she would transfer to an American medical school after her second year, but in 1934, following an outbreak of violence in Vienna when the Austrian army and police forces under Chancellor Engelbert Dollfuss brutally crushed an uprising of the leftist Social Democratic Workers' Party, she had a change of heart. She resolved to stay in Vienna and do what she could to fight back against the violent, right-wing political ideology taking Europe by storm. Though she had a three-year-old daughter from a short-lived marriage, Muriel began taking strangers, mostly socialists, into her apartment when their work in the resistance movement placed them in danger. She took on the code name "Mary" and was soon hiding members of the underground in her cottage in the Austrian countryside. One of those she housed was a man named Joseph Buttinger, a leader in the socialist movement who was coordinating the various factions of the Austrian underground. Amid the thrill of danger, Muriel and Buttinger fell in love.

By the time Nelson saw his sister in Paris in April, Muriel had established herself as an important member of the Austrian underground resistance movement and was deeply in love with Buttinger, though she told her family about neither her work nor her lover. She was hardly the little girl Nelson used to entertain with magic tricks anymore.

From their respective positions, Muriel and Nelson Morris saw two different currents sweeping across the world, currents that thus far had run parallel to each other. Muriel undoubtedly would have hated traveling on the glamorous Nazi airship. It represented the antithesis of every political, economic, and moral instinct she held dear as she watched with alarm as the contagion of political violence sweeping across Europe threatened to spread to the rest of the world. Nelson, by contrast, likely looked with optimism at the technological progress man had achieved over the course of his lifetime and saw something like the *Hindenburg* as the next great innovation that would pave the way for a better, brighter, more connected future. At that moment in time, it was possible for each of them to feel completely assured that their view of the future was destined to win out. However, it was only inevitable that those two currents would eventually converge, likely to destructive effect.

Whatever the future held, Nelson's outlook as a forty-five-year-old man was likely not so different from that of his sixteen-year-old self, a boy who embraced the mantra that he pasted into his books. In Nelson's world, everything had a habit of working itself out. Even if Muriel was correct in the near term, surely man's drive toward creation, innovation, and industry would ultimately prevail. And until the day came that those two great global currents came to a head, Nelson Morris was going to enjoy every minute he could in the *Hindenburg*'s smoking lounge with a drink in hand, courtesy of his friend's bar tab.

CHAPTER 15

Berlin, Germany: May 4, 1937

It was just about midnight when Bill Shirer arrived at the Hotel Adlon the previous evening to meet his friend Gordon Young from Reuters for a nightcap and late-night scoops. Midnight was still early for the journalists who gathered for their ritual *Stammtisch* at the popular watering hole. Only in the wee hours did the real tongue wagging begin, when sources and journalists could be frank with one another about the strange world in which they found themselves. There was a closeness among the journalists in Berlin that he had not felt with his colleagues and competitors in prior postings. "The foreign correspondents are a nice lot and inclined to hang together more than Paris," he wrote to a friend six months after arriving in Germany. "In Naziland you feel the need of it."

When Shirer and Young walked into the Adlon lobby, they almost immediately ran into someone they both recognized: Philip Kerr, 11th Marquess of Lothian, who had come to Berlin from London. As one of Lord Lothian's contemporaries described him, he was "handsome into middle age" and had an "oratorical temperament" that suggested he had "done the thinking and solved the difficulties for you." He also tended to be "influenced by the country and the company he had most recently visited."

Though not presently active in government aside from his seat in the House of Lords, Lothian had once wielded considerable influence over British foreign policy as private secretary and, as some said, gatekeeper to

Prime Minister David Lloyd George during and after the Great War. Initially a staunch supporter of imposing stiff reparations on Germany for the sake of the British wounded and widowed, in the intervening years he had quite dramatically changed his mind. As time went by, he came to believe that Germany had been treated far too harshly under the peace terms of the Treaty of Versailles.

Gordon Young asked Lothian why he had come to Berlin, apparently quite suddenly, the day before. "Oh, Göring asked me to," he told the two journalists. Lothian also planned to write an article in a British magazine after he returned home about how Germany was not unreasonable in its desire for increased rights for German-speaking minorities in Czechoslovakia and some sort of unification with Austria. No doubt Shirer had to restrain himself from shaking his head. In his opinion, Lothian was "probably the most intelligent of the Tories taken in by Hitler, Göring, and Ribbentrop," a frightening trend he had noticed over the last few years. Ambassador Dodd, who would be seeing Lothian two days later at a dinner in honor of the newly appointed German ambassador to the United States, Hans-Heinrich Dieckhoff, simply thought Lothian was a fascist.

It was alarming just how deeply such thinking had penetrated elite British society. Shirer's close friend John Gunther, a fellow journalist for the *Chicago Daily News* and author of the bestselling book *Inside Europe*, which detailed disturbing trends on the European continent, had recently had a revealing exchange with the Czech ambassador to Britain, Jan Masaryk. The two men had been discussing how much more destructive such opinions could have been had the reign of King Edward VIII not been cut short by his abdication. Edward was, in Masaryk's opinion, "a most especially undisciplined" person who had a habit of doing "astoundingly unconstitutional things" and to whom "the slow and boring ways of democracy were especially distasteful." On top of such predispositions, his romance with Mrs. Simpson (though, as Masaryk suggested, "the word 'romance' is not the right name for this affair") only made the middle-class Britons who had once "adored" him have a visceral change of heart. They had even "boo[ed]" his picture in cinemas on the evening of his abdication.

There was no reason to believe Edward was anything but loyal to Britain, but his personal shortcomings certainly left him vulnerable to negative influences. While Masaryk believed the rumors that Wallis Simpson was a German spy were "utter nonsense," he conceded that the "Germans did make a terrific fuss over her," including at a dinner hosted at the German embassy in London. "Politically speaking," Masaryk concluded, "I am convinced that [the abdication] is all to the good. The present gentleman," Edward's brother, King George VI, "will be an ideal constitutional servant." This, to Masaryk, was vitally important. "If democracy is to mean something in the future . . . the constitutionalism of the British régime is one of its most substantial pillars. . . . With Bolshevism on one side and Fascism on the other, democracy could easily be ground up between the two unless we make a stand."

In Gunther's opinion, however, the risks to European democracy were not even as ideologically driven as all that. As he was drafting *Inside Europe*, which sold over a million copies, Gunther had written that the Nazis were simply "gangsters," which made them "cold-minded and desperate at the same time" as well as "irrational" and thus "unpredictable." More than any ideology, that was what made them so dangerous.

Shirer and his wife, Tess, experienced the fear that came with that unpredictable type of violence that increasingly flared in hot spots across Europe, whether instigated by the Nazis, by other authoritarian leaders, or by their opponents in response. Three years earlier in Tess's native Vienna, as Social Democrats clashed with the Austrian army and police, news reached Berlin that a nineteen-year-old student had been hanged as the state tried to quell the agitators. As Shirer wrote to Gunther, he and Tess had had a few anxious days: "Tess's brother is a 19 year old student, and we felt pretty bad until we had got a wire that the family had survived intact." Though the odds of it having been Tess's brother were infinitesimally small, there was a palpable sense that violence could reach out and touch anyone at random, anywhere, anytime.

The rising Nazi threat on the Continent was obvious to journalists like Shirer or Gunther or any of their colleagues like H. R. Knickerbocker or Dorothy Thompson, both of whom had been expelled from Germany for reporting the truth (Thompson, coincidentally, on the very day Shirer arrived in Berlin in August 1934). However, it was galling to see that even their own publications back home failed to see the danger the Nazis posed. Shirer knew Gunther had been particularly frustrated, as he had taken personal risks to report on such important issues, only to then discover his editors had left his articles on the *Chicago Daily News*'s cutting-room floor. "I was pretty heartbroken returning last week from Czechoslovakia to find a big bunch of *Daily Newses* with five of my recent stories not printed or shortened to a paragraph," he wrote to his boss. His paper, however, paid little heed to his complaints and instead asked Gunther for a "more diversified report." "The whole paper has been loaded with anti-Hitler copy for two weeks," his editor explained when similar cuts occurred again three months later, following a spate of alarming Nazi legislation, including the repeal of German citizenship for recently naturalized German Jews and mandated sterilization for people with certain physical and mental disabilities. "It was just one of those things that happen now and then and through no desire on our part to advocate the cause of minority elements in Germany or otherwise change our established practice of reporting events without injecting editorial prejudice. It seemed to me the time [has] come to write about something else besides the infringement of personal liberty. We can't play one note through the whole symphony concert." Otherwise, the editor warned, the paper might be slapped with the "charge of bias."

As Shirer looked around and saw the "hooked-cross boys," as he called them, gaining in strength and power with every passing year, he could imagine little opposition coming from any corner in the near future. "One of the important things to remember about national-socialism," Shirer wrote to a friend, "is that it does seem to approximate what the majority of Germans want. Or to put it negatively, they don't mind having it." For the average German, there was no doubt they were economically much better off than they had been just a short time ago. In less than a decade, they had experienced economic whiplash, starting with hyperinflation that spiraled out of control in 1923. At its peak, Germans faced a monthly inflation rate of nearly 30,000 percent, in which prices doubled every three to four days and sent the cost of bread to 200 billion reichsmarks. From the mid-1920s, the German economy had steadied thanks to loans from the United States, but as a result, Germany became deeply dependent on American credit. In late 1929, those loans were called as the American economy buckled and sank into the Great Depression, sending the German economy into a parallel free fall. Layoffs and business closures triggered unemployment rates that peaked at 24 percent of the labor force by the time Hitler became chancellor in January 1933. Within a year, the Nazi government had halved that figure.

Under Hitler, not only were people able to return to work, but certain luxuries that had previously been out of reach for the average German quickly became affordable. The *Volkswagen* (or "people's car") gave families mobility. The *Volkskühlschrank* ("people's refrigerator") transformed the drudgery of daily meal preparation for millions of German women. Perhaps the item that brought the most widespread excitement was the *Volksempfänger* ("people's radio"). Made of Bakelite, cardboard, and cloth, with a little embellishment of an eagle and swastika beside the tuner, these small radios cost just seventy-six reichsmarks and soon filled 65 percent of German households. They listened to great German classical composers like Wagner and Beethoven, light dance music, folk songs, and patriotic tunes, but especially the führer's political speeches. "Those who do not possess a radio apparatus will listen to it through public loudspeakers in every town and village of Germany," Shirer had written in a Universal Service dispatch in March 1935 as Hitler announced his plans to reconstruct the German army and institute conscription. "There must not be a single person in Germany who is not a witness by means of the radio of this historic mass meeting."

The rapid advance of technology and its availability to the common man made Shirer and his colleagues pause and consider their own position. Shirer had wanted to work as a foreign correspondent more than anything, as it gave him the chance to "report at first hand from day to day the events that were making the history of our time." But as another journalist friend mused to him, with such innovations transforming media, "where are we to belong in that high and faroff but oncoming time when we are to be told that we are not 'fast' enough for the new news system . . . ?"

Alarmist as it may have sounded to some, it was not such a stretch to imagine a world in which newspapermen might soon be put out to pasture. As of the mid-1930s, there really was no such thing as a radio journalist. The public received its news from newspapers, while radio was for entertainment and perhaps a bit of cultural enrichment. The news made up less than 10 percent of national broadcasting time. Radio announcers occasionally provided a few incidental comments on relevant matters of local or global importance between program introductions and sponsorship messages. NBC ran a news hour with Lowell Thomas, who essentially reported the day's headlines just before *Amos 'n' Andy*. Occasionally, stations would broadcast live special-interest features from presidential nominating conventions or outside of sensational courtroom events, like the 1925 Scopes monkey and 1932 Lindbergh baby kidnapping trials. However, no one from the radio was setting out into the field, press badge tucked into the band of a fedora, like reporters dispatched from an actual newsroom.

The reason for this was twofold. First, companies paying great sums to advertise products with sponsored programming liked to control what was attached to their names. Some, like consumer goods powerhouse Procter & Gamble, wanted so much control they had even taken to producing their own programs, colloquially known as "soap" operas, through in-house creative studios. By contrast, the nature of breaking news was that it was entirely beyond anyone's control, and advertisers liked associating with comedic programs, talented singers, and gripping thrillers interwoven with moral lessons, not grisly unsolved murders or fascists bombing civilians an ocean away. Second, there was a resource-allocation issue. Station managers, whose role was more akin to vaudeville variety show producers than newsroom editors, would have had difficulty dispatching reporters to cover breaking stories and then slotting them in amid live, lucrative sponsored programming with a preset schedule.

Challenges aside, Shirer could see the media landscape just beginning to shift. CBS had copied NBC and introduced a news hour with Boake Carter, and journalists were occasionally asked to comment during live coverage of special events. That trend was likely to continue. Technology would only improve, making it easier to send instantaneous dispatches from anywhere in the world, and Shirer and his colleagues would have to find new ways to keep up.

Thankfully, the media revolution was still some time away. Even more important, some of the Nazis' recent schemes showed that even they, adept with radio as they were, had yet to completely master mass communication. Elements of the Nazi menace still felt comically unserious. As part of the campaign to drive up enthusiasm for the Reichstag elections the year before, Goebbels's propaganda ministry had sent a three-man team on the *Hindenburg* as it flew over Germany to inspire voters to do their patriotic duty. Along with the thousands of slips of paper with the slogan "Say YES to Hitler" loaded on board to be dropped over German cities, loudspeakers had also been affixed to the airship, from which election jingles and patriotic music were to be broadcast to the ground. Early one morning, the *Hindenburg* reached the industrial Ruhr Valley, where Hitler wanted a particularly strong showing. The propaganda men had overslept, so the zeppelin crew woke them up. Realizing their mistake, Goebbels's minions shot out of bed, ran to their speakers, and began blaring the "Badenweiler March" and shouting to the ground without a hint of irony, "You late risers down there, get up, do your duty to vote." It was only then they realized they were flying over the middle of a large cemetery. The *Hindenburg* crew could not help but burst out laughing.

Beneath the Nazis' regular bouts of buffoonery, the threat of what still could come lingered palpably over the correspondent corps. Small but obvious signs were everywhere. For example, Hitler's Four-Year Plan, announced in 1936, included a provision for increased production of synthetic fabrics, such as *Zellwolle*, literally "cellulose wool," by chemical companies like IG Farben. Germany produced no cotton and very little wool, and in an effort both to reduce reliance on imports from nations with which relations were quickly souring and to continue diverting massive funds to its military buildup, Germany had no choice but to make synthetic fibers as cheaply as possible. "As its official name implies, it is made from wood," Shirer wrote. Despite an attempted rebranding with the chic-sounding name "Vistral," the fabric still had a distinctly paperlike feeling. If Germans were willing to accept clothes made of paper so they could have their guns and tanks, Shirer concluded to a friend, "I say then: let them have it. Only—when the terrific energy that is being generated here . . . hits the rest of Europe, that will be another story and maybe a very sad one."

It was perplexing that people back home were not more alarmed by such blatantly obvious facts that showed Germany was clearly on a warlike path. Still, for every figure like Lord Lothian who intellectualized their way to supporting Hitler's regime, the naively optimistic worried Shirer, Gunther, and the other correspondents even more. Gunther's friend Jan Masaryk was one of these people. For all his talk about the ill winds threatening democracy, Masaryk had also written to Gunther, "I don't believe for a moment that Germany is going to attack my country—not yet anyway. Things are improving economically in Europe: the Xmas shopping in Prague this year was as good as in 1928." Of course, the moment one assumed a certain outcome could never come to pass was often precisely when it did.

If Bill Shirer's father had still been alive, he would have been shocked to see that the world had become significantly more dangerous over the past two decades. Men of Seward Shirer's generation had had a firm belief in the inevitability of progress as the "eternal law of life." Shirer's father, the grandson of German immigrants, was a federal prosecutor but also keenly interested in labor and social reform. He counted Clarence Darrow among his friends, and every Christmas he would take his children to deliver baskets to the poor, largely immigrant Chicago Union Stockyards workers living in slums not far from the Shirers' leafy Woodlawn neighborhood. As Bill would later describe, Seward Shirer was confident that "despite a few flaws in society the human race was moving inexorably along a splendid road that led toward a promised land where everyone would be free, happy and even well-off." Perhaps nothing better captured his outlook on the world than his 1893 college oration, titled "The World Citizen." "Throughout the world there is a cry on human lips against war," he wrote. "The art of bloodshed belongs to a past age. It is at variance with all modern enterprise and industry, and inconsistent with the enlightened idea of moral obligation." Less than a year after Seward Shirer died of appendicitis in 1913, a global war had nearly torn humanity apart. Perhaps it was best that he had not lived to see what had transpired—and would once again if Hitler was allowed to have his way.

The world outside Germany found it difficult to understand that the reports Shirer, Gunther, and the others sent back were not hyperbole written by the postwar generation for whom pessimism had replaced the idealism of their fathers. In large part, this was because the Nazis were forever "outdoing themselves to create a favorable impression on foreign visitors." They dazzled American tourists with their "magnificent" stadium built for 100,000 spectators for the Olympics in August 1936. Here they orchestrated an opening ceremony "on a lavish scale never before experienced," even including features like an Olympic torch relay from Athens to Berlin, designed to suggest that Germany was the natural Aryan descendant of ancient Greece. It was a masterful way to link past, present, and future, particularly once the *Hindenburg* appeared above the stadium, sailing silently and majestically overhead.

It was just a more spectacular follow-up to the well-mannered smoothness with which they had run the 1936 Winter Olympics that February in the alpine ski town of Garmisch-Partenkirchen. In the run-up to the Games, Shirer had written an article series in which he stated the Nazis had "pulled down all the signs saying that Jews were unwanted," which were typical all over Germany. This had resulted in a call from the fanatical head of foreign press at the Reich Ministry of Public Enlightenment and Propaganda, who accused him of writing a "fake story about the Jews." The ministry followed this up with a searing personal attack on the radio suggesting that Shirer himself was "a dirty Jew and was trying to torpedo the winter Olympic Games." It also threatened to expel him from Germany.

Whenever influential foreigners came to Germany, whether for the Olympics or otherwise, Shirer and his fellow foreign correspondents tried to "enlighten" them to the reality the Nazis went to such lengths to conceal. In August 1936, Shirer had organized a lunch for visiting businessmen with the "best-informed man on Germany" he could find at the American embassy, but instead, the businessmen "told *him* what things were like" and he "scarcely got a word in." In another instance, a group of Americans who had recently spoken with Göring told Shirer and Ralph Barnes of the *New York Herald Tribune* that the "American correspondents were unfair to the Nazis."

"Did [Göring] tell you about Nazi suppression, say, of churches?" Shirer had asked them.

"He did," one of them replied, "and he assured us there was no truth in what you fellows write about persecution of religion here."

But for Shirer, there was one American visitor who disappointed him most of all: Charles Lindbergh. Lindbergh had come to Berlin with his wife, Anne, the previous July to meet with Hermann Göring and officials from the Reich Ministry of Aviation. For all his apparent—and growing—admiration for certain aspects of the Nazi regime, the thirty-five-year-old Lindbergh first and foremost saw himself as a global ambassador for responsible aviation and wanted to use his pulpit to warn against the "temptation of scientific power" left unchecked by moral philosophy. At a luncheon at the ministry, Shirer had heard that Lindbergh "spoke out somewhat, warning that the airplane had become such a deadly instrument of destruction that unless those 'who are in aviation' face their heavy responsibilities, the world, and especially Europe [would be] in for irreparable damage." Though by no means a condemnation of the Nazi regime, Shirer did feel it was a "well-timed little thrust" that annoyed Göring, who was in the process of "building up the deadliest air force in Europe." Shirer could see that buildup for himself. Just over a year earlier, a squadron of bombers had flown over his office in tight formation. It was the first time they had been unveiled in urban skies for the general public's admiration.

After the lunch, Shirer and other correspondents had been invited to a tea party in the Lindberghs' honor at the Tempelhof airfield hosted by the German state airline, Lufthansa. For fear that the Lindberghs would object to having press present after a media circus had so cruelly exploited their grief following the kidnapping and murder of their twenty-month-old baby just five years earlier, the Germans had not told them that Shirer and the others would be there. They showed "no enthusiasm" for the unwelcome surprise. The journalists, in this instance, did not press them. However, they did have the opportunity to go for a ride in the largest land plane in Germany's fleet, the *Field-Marshal von Hindenburg* (not to be confused with the airship). "Somewhere over the Wannsee," Shirer wrote in his diary, "Lindbergh took the controls himself and treated us to some very steep banks, considering the size of the plane, and other little manoeuvres, which terrified most of the passengers," despite Lindbergh being one of the most experienced and capable pilots in the world.

For Shirer, the opportunity to see Lindbergh up close was particularly revealing. It was the first time he had seen the famous aviator in almost exactly ten years, back when Shirer had covered his world-changing New York–to–Paris flight in 1927. Shirer was surprised at how, on the surface, there was so little about Lindbergh that seemed altered since he was twenty-five-years old, except perhaps an increase in confidence that came with life experience. But it was also disheartening to see that he and his wife had been so "favourably impressed by what the Nazis [had] shown them," not least since Shirer's personal history with Lindbergh had had such a "shining beginning."

In many ways, Shirer had Lindbergh to thank for his career as a foreign correspondent, as the aviator's flight in the *Spirit of St. Louis* had given Shirer his big break back when he was a twenty-three-year-old cub reporter for the *Chicago Tribune* in Paris. Shirer was then working for the local Paris edition of the *Tribune* with aspirations of becoming a full-fledged foreign correspondent for the home edition of the paper. Unfortunately, instead of covering lofty and important matters of foreign affairs, Shirer found himself filling in as a sports reporter, particularly covering the French Championships tennis tournament on the clay courts at the Stade Français.

The biggest talk of Paris that May was whether the lithe and crafty Frenchman René "Le Crocodile" Lacoste could upset American Bill Tilden, known for his "cannon-ball" serve. Meanwhile, Charles Lindbergh was considered an unserious afterthought in the world of aviation. Back in 1919, hotelier and businessman Raymond Orteig had sponsored a prize, one of several of the era meant to reward the bold pursuit of scientific progress, that promised $25,000 to the first man to fly from New York to Paris, or vice versa, in a nonstop flight across the Atlantic Ocean. To date, the most successful transatlantic effort had been that by John Alcock and Arthur Brown, who had flown nonstop from Newfoundland to Ireland in

June 1919, but that was little more than half the distance between New York and continental Europe. New York–to–Paris attempts had already claimed the lives of several more famous pilots with sophisticated planes and crews of two or more. Meanwhile, this unknown Midwestern airmail pilot whom the press dubbed "Lucky Lindy" or the "Flying Fool" had assembled a group of private backers from St. Louis to commission a small plane from an obscure California aviation outfit. Furthermore, he planned to fly approximately thirty-six hours across the stormy North Atlantic all on his own.

Shirer had been keen on aviation since he was a boy playing with rubber band–powered toy propeller planes with his friends in the streets of the South Side of Chicago, before his father's death had prompted the family to return to Iowa. The Wright brothers had made their first flight the year before his birth, and Shirer would never forget the day he spent with his father in Grant Park along Lake Michigan when he was just seven years old, watching a "half-dozen sputtering little biplanes [fly] back and forth" at an air show staged for an aviation-crazy public. Young Shirer thought the air show "the most wonderful thing [he] had ever seen."

In early May 1927, two experienced French pilots, Charles Nungesser and François Coli, decided to fly from Paris to New York, and Shirer's editor had sent him out to the Paris airfield, Le Bourget, to get a quote about their decision to fly east to west against the North Atlantic headwinds. Shirer was there when they took off on May 8. Several hours later, they were spotted flying over Ireland and out to sea, but the plane was never seen again.

On May 20, Shirer was back at the Stade Français covering the tennis when news broke that this young Lindbergh fellow had taken off from Roosevelt Field in New York. Earlier in the day, Shirer had stopped at the International League of Aviators headquarters to collect a few quotes about Lindbergh's chances, all of which were resoundingly pessimistic. As soon as the semifinals were over for the day, Shirer had raced back to the office to make plans for someone, hopefully himself, to cover the Lindbergh flight. Shirer's editor was similarly unenthusiastic about Lindbergh and told Shirer to turn his notes over to a colleague who could perhaps use them in a wrap-up story about yet another foolhardy transatlantic attempt. The next day, Shirer asked if he could go to Le Bourget to cover Lindbergh's arrival. His editor told him he could—on the outside chance Lindbergh even made it—but only after he finished covering the tennis. Shirer stayed awake late that night studying up on Lindbergh, just in case.

Partway through the third set of the marquee doubles match on May 21, Shirer noticed people stirring in the American ambassador's box. Reports claimed Lindbergh's plane had been spotted over Ireland. Once he was sighted again over Plymouth, England, there seemed no doubt he would make it all the way to Paris. Shirer and two other reporters jumped in a taxi, but before they had even reached the outskirts of the city, they ran into traffic the likes of which Shirer had never seen. "Every motor vehicle in town of whatever sort seemed to have converged on the road to Le Bourget," he remembered, so he and his colleagues decided to hoof it the remaining two miles. When they reached the airfield, the crowd surrounding the terminal was the largest he had ever witnessed and growing by the minute, from 100,000 to half a million people.

By 10:00 p.m., there was still no sign of Lindbergh. Spirits began to drop. Perhaps the earlier reports had been false. But twenty minutes later, they heard a plane overhead. A searchlight flashed into the sky above, and there it was: the *Spirit of St. Louis.* A wave of fevered enthusiasm swept over the crowd as utter "bedlam" broke out, the masses surging forward to meet the plane as it landed. Shirer worried for a moment that they were moving too close and that someone would be shredded by the propeller before Lindbergh could cut the motor. Thankfully, they stopped short just in time. A sandy head emerged from the cockpit and there was Lindbergh, grinning from ear to ear—until he realized the mob had climbed onto his plane and was tearing fabric from the wings for souvenirs. The French air force soon led Lindbergh away for his own safety, and Shirer raced back to the office to file his story. His editor had initially assigned the write-up to a different man, but he was nowhere to be found. "I guess it's your story," the editor harrumphed. "But don't make it too long."

By 4:00 a.m., Shirer and a colleague, veteran reporter Harry Wales, filed a firsthand tale of Lindbergh's arrival. A cable soon arrived confirming their copy had hit the presses in Chicago even before the usually quicker wire services. As Shirer and Wales sat in an all-night café munching on some well-deserved croissants, Wales said to Shirer, "Not bad . . . In fact, damn good. I think maybe you got what it takes. . . . Maybe"—he hesitated—"maybe I can find room for you." The very next day, Wales did just that, making Shirer a foreign correspondent.

In the days that followed, Shirer was struck by how Lindbergh "remained simple and modest, full of poise" despite becoming the most famous person in the world literally overnight. In New York City, four million people attended his ticker-tape parade. *The New York Times* received over two thousand poems from his admiring fans. Souvenir seekers ransacked his house in Little Falls, Minnesota, and souvenir makers rushed to cash in on the national hero. The U.S. Patent Office received hundreds of applications for knickknacks modeled after or inspired by the *Spirit of St. Louis*. There were, of course, Lindbergh figurines and models of his famous plane, but also busts and bookends, china services, clocks, coin banks, jewelry, cosmetic cases, chocolate molds, nail files, poker chips, even oddities like Lindy Hand Cleanser, "the first hand cleanser to make dirt fly," and a line of perfume called "Lucky Lindy," designed to give the wearer the "Essence of Luck." By the end of his ninety-five-day, eighty-two-city barnstorming tour across the country, where he gave speeches promoting the future of safe, responsible, and innovative aviation, some thirty million Americans had seen him in the flesh—a full quarter of the U.S. population. Shirer had "never seen a man, let alone one so young, bear such fantastic adulation with such good grace and modesty."

But in the intervening years, something inside Lindbergh changed. When Shirer saw him again at Tempelhof that day in July, he was still tall and lanky with sandy hair and a modest disposition, but he was a different, darker man inside. Part of that, of course, was his grief over his child and the highly politicized trial of the kidnapper, German immigrant Bruno Richard Hauptmann, that had ensued. Along with that came further deprivation of privacy, the inevitable curse of becoming, in Shirer's mind, the nation's "one authentic hero." After being hounded by a sensational press and surrounded by the rich and powerful, Shirer could see that a "conservative and sometimes reactionary and even anti-democratic view of the world appeared to gradually rub off on him." It was a view that found fertile soil. Lindbergh's father, Charles August Lindbergh, a congressman from Minnesota with a strong isolationist outlook, had been a staunch opponent of American entry into the Great War. As far as Shirer could gather, "the fantastic adulation of [Lindbergh's] fellow-countrymen" brought "disillusionment, bitterness, tragedy, deep sorrow . . . and a confusion about life and politics and war and peace." The siren call of fame "tempted him to use this immense following for political ends, both foreign and domestic, a course that once embarked upon finally, after . . . years of being worshipped as a nonpartisan hero, would prove disastrous." As another commentator similarly described, Lindbergh wanted nothing more than to "bestow upon his countrymen the boon of safe and easy flight, but his countrymen demanded of him other gifts which it was not in his nature, or in the nature of mortal man, to bestow."

To Shirer, the greatest tragedy was that Lindbergh seemed to have become "shockingly admiring of a mindless, bloody, barbarian dictatorship" that deprived human beings of the "very freedoms which the famous flyer proclaimed he valued," the same freedoms that lay at the core of the earthly liberation of flight itself.

Perhaps such an outcome was only inevitable for the world's most famous aviator because of something inherent in the nature of aviation itself, something that seemed to corrupt men who flew close to the sun, until nature struck back against those who had taken too many gifts of the sky for themselves. "Is aviation too arrogant?" Lindbergh himself would later go on to wonder. "I don't know. Sometimes, flying feels too godlike to be attained by man. Sometimes, the world from above seems too beautiful, too wonderful, too distant for human eyes to see, like a vision at the end of life forming a bridge to death. Can that be why so many pilots lose their lives? Is man encroaching on a forbidden realm? Is aviation dangerous because the sky was never meant for him? When one obtains too great a vision is there some power that draws one from mortal life forever?"

CHAPTER 16

Over the Atlantic Ocean: May 4, 1937

Margaret Mather slept comfortably in her "charming" pearl-gray cabin, cozily tucked under linen sheets and soft blankets. Throughout the night, they had flown "high above the storm" as the *Hindenburg* was "buffeted" by a headwind that had further delayed their progress. To Margaret, the wind whipping against the airship's canvas cover "sounded like surf, but the ship sailed calmly through it," and her sleep was undisturbed.

Margaret spent most of the first full day on board in her cabin, where she was glad to take in all that she had missed during previous ocean crossings. As she looked down through her "sloping window," she could see the "angry waves, whitening the sea so far below." She had imagined the wind would rock what was essentially a giant assemblage of balloons to and fro, but if she "looked attentively at the horizon," only the "slightest variation from the horizontal was perceptible" and "there was no feeling of unsteadiness."

There was something restorative about sailing above the water, a sense of energy and tranquility to be gathered in one's soul. Margaret had derived this indefinable sense of rejuvenation from the water since she was just an infant, when her parents had taken her to the shore at Sea Girt, New Jersey, to help her recover from a serious illness. They had engaged a nursemaid, but Margaret's father had taken to caring for her himself. As he recalled in the manuscript he wrote later in life, he and his wife had had five sons before Margaret came along, and they were "most anxious to save this one girl." The wife of the landlord from whom they rented a seaside cottage observed him nervously pushing his baby girl in a carriage on the veranda. "I see Mr. Mather you are anxious about that child," she said to him. "If you wheel her right down on the tideway, following the tide and receding when it turns, you will derive much greater benefit for your child." Frank Mather Sr. did what the woman prescribed, always "keeping within a few feet of the water," and found his daughter's health soon began to improve. As a descendant of two of the most famous men of the cloth ever to preach on American shores, he was a deeply religious man, but even so, he felt there was a sort of mystical power coming from the sea, "a positive electric force in an ocean surf, as it throws itself on the land and is shattered by the impetus." Day after day, he wheeled Margaret up and down the seashore, and before long, she was well. Those days by the water in Margaret's infancy had also created a special bond between father and daughter. In later years, after her father lost two of his sons, a younger daughter, and his wife, Margaret "devot[ed] herself with untiring affection and loyalty" to him during those painful days when his grief left him bereft, just as he had devoted himself to her, wheeling her back and forth beside the sea.

Margaret's father had died eight years earlier at the age of ninety-four. Toward the end of his life, he reflected on all the changes he had seen over the course of nearly a century. He had witnessed marvelous creations: the invention of the telegraph and telephone, which linked the country of his birth with the continent he had adopted via undersea cables running across the ocean floor. He could drive through tunnels that connected New York with New Jersey beneath the Hudson River, and over the newly constructed Brooklyn Bridge. He had also seen the invention of forces of destruction. In his "wildest dreams," he wrote, he "never expected to see submarines bring down the large warships and least of all that battles should be fought in the air." And never did he anticipate that "aircraft should be built in such numbers and such size and convenience, and should carry passengers, mails and light freight from continent to continent." When the guns fell silent, even these forces of destruction could be the harbingers of a more prosperous future. As he observed, "The aeroplanes and dirigibles seem to bid fair to be serious commercial rivals to the railways and [s]teamers." If only he could have seen Margaret living out that very prediction.

Much like Margaret, a plain-looking woman who few could have guessed had seen the brilliant magnitudes of stars spangling the tropical skies above Jamaica or the azure and sandstone jewel that was Tunis, her father was an unexpected global adventurer. Though pious and often sickly as an adult, in his youth, Margaret's father had been just that. When he was a boy, his older half brother, Samuel Mather, was a young and distinguished sea captain. In 1853, when Samuel was just twenty-nine, he was given command of a clipper ship called the *Nightingale*. Back then, it took ninety days on average to sail to Australia from the United States, and seventy days by steamer. But the *Nightingale* was an extreme clipper, a new type of sailing vessel built not to carry maximum cargo but to cut across oceans at maximum speed. Extreme clippers did carry some passengers in a rush to set out for far-flung places like California and Australia, where gold had been discovered, but they were primarily intended for the tea and silk trade and carried goods from Australia, Java, and China back to Britain and the United States. They were also the fastest form of mail transport in the world.

Captain Mather was not only in command of the world's swiftest ship. He was also willing to try a new method of navigation, which at first glance seemed counterintuitive but had the potential to cut weeks off a voyage from one hemisphere to another. This new navigational theory was pioneered by Lieutenant Matthew Maury of the U.S. Navy, who led the Depot of Charts and Instruments in Washington, DC. Maury was a student of meteorology, astronomy, and navigation, and especially of winds and currents. After scrutinizing data from thousands of captains' logbooks, Maury believed ships looking to cut time on a voyage between Europe or the United States and Asia and the South Pacific should not hug the Cape of Good Hope but should instead sail much farther south to the 57th southern parallel. There, captains would find more favorable winds that would propel them across the ocean at such a rate that they would discover the "longest way round was the shortest way there." When the Australian Pioneer Line chartered the *Nightingale* to carry mail, freight, and passengers from New York to Melbourne and then on to Java, Shanghai, and Hong Kong to retrieve tea and silk, Maury approached Captain Mather about his new method. Mather, whose ship's reputation was entirely based on its speed, was game to try. Mather also invited his eighteen-year-old brother, Frank, to come along.

On May 19, 1853, Frank set out from New York Harbor with his brother, 120 other passengers, and a ship full of commodities of every kind. As Maury had instructed, the ship sailed at once directly for the 57th parallel, and though they were "seriously delayed by calms and baffling winds" en route along the equator, by the time they reached the 45th parallel, the winds had picked up from the west. By the 55th parallel, "unseen hands were pushing [the *Nightingale*] from behind," and on the Fourth of July, Frank wore a heavy coat and boots and watched as a foot of snow fell on deck. "Our speed was terrific," Frank recalled. The ship was "more like a bird in the air than a craft afloat," making over sixteen knots, or a statute mile every three minutes. By the 57th parallel, the wind was so strong it seemed the topgallant sail would blow away entirely as storms raged. Surrounded by a starless sky and "steel-gray air," Frank was struck by the realization that they were in "unknown waters, on untried routes; that, in case of disaster, there is not the slightest chance for rescue."

But the *Nightingale* required no rescue. They reached Melbourne in seventy-five days, smashing the average speed for sailing ships. But for the equatorial doldrums, they would have come in well under seventy days flat. Maury's theory was proven, and Samuel Mather was hailed as one of the youngest and ablest navigators on the high seas.

Sadly, the thrilling beginnings for the *Nightingale* and Samuel Mather's adventures with his clipper were not to last. In 1860, the ship changed hands. New owners hired a new captain and engaged the *Nightingale* in the illegal transatlantic slave trade. It was soon captured by the USS *Saratoga* and purchased by the U.S. Navy from an American prize court for use as a supply ship during the Civil War. Meanwhile, Samuel Mather promptly volunteered for the Union Navy in 1861 and was placed in command of the USS *Henry Andrews*. In March 1862, while it was on a reconnaissance mission off the coast of Florida, rebels fired on the USS *Henry*

Andrews, killing Captain Mather. He was just thirty-seven years old. While Samuel Mather's life was cut short, Maury's methods of navigation he had helped to pioneer soon became standard practice, and it was the idea of harnessing the power of the prevailing winds at high latitudes—both north and south—that had made possible decades of breakthroughs in transportation at sea and in the air.

On the wall of the *Hindenburg*'s passenger lounge, Margaret had admired a painted map of the world illustrated with "soft colors, showing the history of navigation." The map depicted the "routes and the ships of the first explorers, with their billowing sails"—Christopher Columbus, Vasco da Gama, Captain Cook—and the modern German ocean liners SS *Bremen* and SS *Europa* alongside them. "Above them all," she noted, was the "beautiful, silver *Hindenburg* sailing the great circle," following the curvature of the earth to the high North Atlantic, the shortest distance point to point on a sphere between Frankfurt and Lakehurst. Her uncle's *Nightingale* and its route across the Southern Hemisphere deserved its own place among them. In the Northern Hemisphere, those prevailing winds above the 50th northern parallel had helped Lindbergh push his rickety *Spirit of St. Louis* to its limits as he traversed the great circle route across the North Atlantic. The same winds were similarly being harnessed by Juan Trippe of Pan Am, along with British Imperial Airways, to run experimental routes between Newfoundland and Ireland, initially just with mail and express packages but with plans to establish regular passenger service. And while those winds cut the *Hindenburg*'s travel time by half a day on eastbound trips across the Atlantic, they were currently beating fiercely against the nose of the zeppelin, continually setting back the timeliness of its progress until it could clear the path of the storm.

Margaret's father had been so impressed with the almost century of progress in his lifetime that the rapid advances in transportation and communication in the eight years since his death hardly would have shocked him. "It would strike me with no great surprise if it were certified that we had actually communicated with the Planet Mars," he had quipped in his memoir written for his children, "and I rather expect that it will not be long before the resources of science will be so developed as to make such communications possible. It might well be that the customs of life and the modes of civilization will be changed by such communications."

Though no one was yet in touch with Mars, elements of his prophetic prediction were already proving out. Just over a year earlier, as the *Hindenburg* was about to depart on its first trial flights, German scientists announced they had successfully tested the *Gegensehn-Fernsprechanlagen*, or the "long-distance seeing telephone," developed by engineer Dr. Georg Schubert. On March 1, 1936, the minister of posts in Berlin spoke with the burgomaster of Leipzig in the first two-way video, two-way audio closed-circuit connection, with both men seeing and hearing each other simultaneously. The video screen "flickered after the manner of old prewar motion pictures," as a newspaper report described, but the Germans were confident the video quality would improve over time. Though Margaret's father's projections of interplanetary communication might have been overly ambitious, he could be forgiven for such a stretch of the imagination, as the rate of technical innovation he had witnessed gave little evidence of limitation.

The only thing that might have given Margaret's father pause as the world became ever more interconnected was that so many of these innovations had been achieved by the Germans. As much as he celebrated the past century of achievements, toward the end of his life, as he surveyed the world following the Great War, he became somewhat pessimistic in his outlook on man's future. His primary concern was not that another global conflict would finish the world as he knew it. Instead, and unsurprisingly for a descendant of Increase and Cotton Mather, he worried about a decline in religious life and moral conduct that was slowly degrading humanity. He largely attributed this to the rising influence of the new Germany: "My quarrel with the Germans, is not merely the immense loss of life they have occasioned, though that is awful; not the barbarities and cruelties inflicted upon the living; not the tremendous loss of property," he wrote, "but that they have destroyed civilization." He saw the Germans as focused entirely on the outputs of labor, rather than on any kind of spiritual life or development of moral character, which was a sort of disease that he feared was spreading from Germany across the "learned" nations of the world. “I know that there are those who are hopeful for the future,” he set out on the record for posterity. “I am sorry to say that I am not one.”

Whether Margaret dwelled on what her father might have thought of her traveling on a German airship, especially one so recently used to fan the flames of the German nationalism that her father scorned, she did not say. However, as a religious man, her father also believed in redemption. As he had concluded, “I hope Germany will experience a decided, lasting reformation.” Otherwise, to paraphrase his Mather ancestors, perhaps it would be a future of fire and brimstone after all.

CHAPTER 17

Over the Atlantic Ocean: May 4, 1937

By morning, Gertrud Adelt's excitement from the first few hours on board the *Hindenburg* had yet to subside. She had barely closed her eyes in the cabin she shared with her husband for fear of missing something, and when she awoke the next morning before sunrise, she immediately returned to her position at the window. The storm clouds had briefly cleared, and she could see that the ocean below her "lay like molten silver in the invisible rising light." Dolphins played in the surf, and the shadow of the airship "wandered along in infinity." Between the impressions of the sea and the sensation of the "fluffy, light floating of the ship," Gertrud was transfixed. Leonhard, on the other hand, was still apparently unimpressed by the poor visibility that would largely obscure the North Atlantic below for the better part of the day.

With the return of cloud cover, there was little to see, so Gertrud followed the lead of many of her fellow passengers and took a tour of the airship. While most were awestruck by the colossal expanse of the main body of the *Hindenburg*, Gertrud was instead intrigued by the men guiding the airship forward across the ocean. On her tour, she was able to visit the operational center of the zeppelin, including the control gondola, the onboard post office, and the radio room. Both the post office and radio room were tight spaces, large enough only for one man to maneuver comfortably. In the mail room, postmaster Max Zabel already had a stack of mail to stamp with his rubber cancellation marker, which he had rotated forward to the day's date, May 4. The mail room was connected to the passenger area by pneumatic tubes in the reading and writing room. Letter writers could drop their notes and postcards into a slot to be whisked directly forward to the post office. That day, Zabel stamped the stack of postcards Benny Spah had put into the post for his friend. Bert Dolan would soon be adding a few of his own, including a note to a buyer at Bullock's Wilshire department store in Los Angeles and another to a neighbor on Kennesaw Terrace (which he continued to write on his correspondence).

Across the narrow hallway, the chief radio operator, a friendly Rhinelander named Willy Speck, manned the radio room. This was where the *Hindenburg* communicated with passing ships and shore-based stations. Both the long- and shortwave radios were battery powered to minimize the risk of sparks in electrical wiring. If either of those radios or their batteries malfunctioned, there was an emergency radio installed in the bow of the airship that could be powered by a crew member pedaling a stationary bicycle attached to a generator.

Willy Speck was a longtime airship crew member who had been with the zeppelin company for two decades. At sixteen, he told his parents he intended to fly on airships and left his hometown of Cologne for Friedrichshafen, where he presented himself to old Count Zeppelin, who was then still at the helm of the company, and asked for a job. Count Zeppelin admired Speck's youthful enthusiasm and hired him on the spot. Speck was now forty-six and more heavyset than he had once been. Despite having lived away from his home region for many years—a region recently roiling with tension following Hitler's remilitarization the previous spring—he still had a classic Rhinelander personality with his gregarious manner, spirited storytelling, and affinity for a good prank.

But today, Gertrud observed, Speck seemed rather downcast. When someone asked what was the matter, he replied that he was thinking about his son. Several weeks earlier, the boy and his friends had been playing a game of "Indians," perhaps inspired by American spaghetti western films popular in Germany that Goebbels tried to replicate in domestic productions. Speck's son was taken "captive" by his companions and tied to a tree. In an effort to make the game more realistic, they lit something on fire. It must have gotten out of control, as Speck's son had been "miserably burned due to the ignorance of his comrades" while still tied to the tree. The boy had later died of his injuries. As the mother of a young son and the friend of another man already mourning the death of a child, Gertrud was deeply affected by this story, and it stayed with her long after.

For two of the small number of officers on board to have so recently lost their young sons was a cruel irony, especially considering that they must have felt a sense of relief having made it through to the sunlight meadows of relatively tranquil middle age, having survived years of warfare and economic tumult in their youth. Speck was a bit younger than Gertrud's husband, Leonhard, but he was still of the generation of German men who, like Leonhard, had served during the Great War. Ten of the *Hindenburg*'s crew had served: Speck; Captains Lehmann, Pruss, Sammt, and Wittemann; Chief Steward Kubis; helmsman Kurt Schönherr; chief rigger Ludwig Knorr; room steward Max Henneberg; and chief electrician Philipp Lenz, some on zeppelins but others in more traditional military billets. Gertrud's husband was thirty-two when the war started, a bit older than the average age of men conscripted to serve, and had been in the prime of his career. For that generation of German men, the devastation of war, defeat, and economic ruin that followed left deep, invisible scars beyond the very visible ones that many who survived carried with them the rest of their lives. As Leonhard's friend and famous Austrian writer Stefan Zweig remarked to another in their circle after a visit with Leonhard over a decade after the end of the war, "Our whole generation is strange." Leonhard in particular was "surprisingly young and at the same time tired: the War years are weighing on all of us. Despite our physical wellbeing, our trust in the world has been shaken once too severely."

There was a certain strangeness about Gertrud's husband, but whether it had been brought on by the war or had been there all along Gertrud did not know. There was a deep exhaustion in Leonhard Adelt's soul, and not just because his trust in the world had been shaken by the war and its aftermath. The formative years of his career and his time for youthful optimism had been filled with compounding disappointments, which, oddly, he seemed to seek out, both in his pursuits and in his choice of friends who tended to remind him of his failures by their sheer existence. Since he was a teenager, Leonhard had wanted to be a novelist. At seventeen, he published his first novel, one considered very racy at the time, which must have seemed to him like a bright beginning writing boundary-pushing literature. A few years later, he moved from Dortmund, where he was raised, to Vienna, where he fell in with a circle of writers, including Stefan Zweig, who was about his age and from an upper-middle-class Jewish Viennese family. In the early days of their friendship, both men were similarly idealistic, though Zweig's interests tended toward the historical, while Leonhard's were focused on the future. Leonhard worked as a journalist while mulling over ideas for other novels, while Zweig had the luxury of writing fiction, sometimes publishing more than one novel a year.

After several years in Vienna, Leonhard moved south to the Bodensee and immersed himself in the excitement surrounding Count Zeppelin and the airships he was testing out of his floating hangar on the lake. This was also where Leonhard likely first met Captain Lehmann. Flying filled Leonhard's consciousness. He studied Count Zeppelin's airships and took flying lessons in heavier-than-air craft. Soon he began working on a novel about a young farm boy with dreams of becoming an aviator.

By 1909, Zweig had firmly established himself as a writer, while Leonhard, who had bounced from a newspaper in Vienna to another in Hamburg, found his attention divided. He wrote to Zweig presenting a plan for an airship company he wanted to create, despite having no technical background in aviation or any experience in business. Clearly, he was looking to wealthier friends to invest. Unsurprisingly, Zweig declined and called his friend a "fantasist." "Today an airship business is still a sport, never a matter of profit," he chided Leonhard. "Whoever buys one has to own a piece of land, build a hangar, and employ a large crew. And only 50 private individuals in the whole of Europe can afford such luxury. Of these 50, 45 are not interested in it at all, and the last 5 buy airplanes." Zweig could feel his friend was distracted by this pipe dream. "How your novella is doing," he added, "is the most important thing for me: make sure it does not become an airship." Leonhard took this encouragement to focus on his novel as a reprimand. He wrote back angrily, furious at being pigeonholed into only one role and one dream. "After you once pinned me down to one species 10 years ago—your preconceived opinion prevents you from making a correction which alone could have saved our friendship on your part from a continued disappointment which would gradually turn into indifference." Leonhard and Zweig did not speak for two years.

But Leonhard must have known that Zweig was right. When his novella, *Der Flieger*, was published in 1913, there was something of Zweig's admonishment in it and a recognition that the enterprise into which he had invested so much time and thought, if not funds, was already obsolete. In the book, his young aspiring aviator speaks with an inventor who builds rigid airships, surely a stand-in for Count Zeppelin.

"So does the airship have a future?" the inventor quizzes his would-be protégé.

"A near future, yes," the young man responds. "What a person has once conquered, he no longer lets go. The air route is predetermined for us as the final form of transport for human cultural community: and that is why we will stick to the motorballoon—as long as we have nothing better."

"And what would that be?" asks the inventor, looking at the young man fixedly.

"The flying machine," the young man replies. The reason for the longevity of the balloon and the airships that followed in the century and a half since the Montgolfier brothers' invention took to the sky was that there was no engine both light and strong enough to keep a heavier-than-air craft in flight. Light, strong engines now existed that could propel rigid airships forward, meaning that mankind was on the cusp of developing similar engines that could propel the flying machine. The very thing that "makes the airship possible," the young aviator explains, "also makes it unnecessary." With that final step on the inevitable path toward heavier-than-air flight so close at hand, the airship's short heyday would promptly come to a close. "The airship," Leonhard wrote in the voice of his character, "will later be given no historical significance than that it was a provisional device before our transition to the balloon-free flying ship. . . . The time of the flying machine has come." He was effectively killing off his own dream.

It was a future already predicted by Jules Verne almost three decades earlier in his 1886 novel *Robur the Conqueror*, in which a mysterious stranger presents a heavier-than-air flying machine called the *Albatross* to a crowd of committed dirigible enthusiasts and proves its dominance in the sky. It was a view shared by Hiram Maxim, inventor of the automatic machine gun, who had also experimented with engine-powered flying machines and had written in 1891, "It is quite as impossible to propel a balloon with any considerable degree of velocity through the air as it is for a jellyfish to travel through the water at a high rate of speed. . . . In all nature we do not find any bird or insect which navigates the air after the manner of a balloon."

Leonhard had wanted to build airships, but what he had actually created with his distinctively poetic and impressionistic novella was a new genre of popular fiction in Germany: the aviation novel. And yet, despite the success of his novel and his own character's predictions about airships' future, Leonhard persisted in trying to make airships succeed in the real world. The very same year he published *Der Flieger*, he participated in an unsuccessful test flight in Düsseldorf of a semirigid steel airship that he had helped to design.

When the war broke out in 1914, Leonard was assigned to the war press headquarters in Vienna. As a pilot himself, he had the unique role of serving as a flying reporter from time to time. He also continued writing and translating aviation novels. While he found moderate success, by 1919 Adelt was crushed financially by hyperinflation. He was once again on speaking terms with Zweig, and his friend sympathized with him in a letter, acknowledging that only "swindlers and profiteers" were making out well in the postwar world.

Throughout the 1920s and early 1930s, Zweig's literary star continued to rise, making him one of the most popular and most translated German-language writers of the era. Leonhard, meanwhile, continued both his journalism and his creative writing, including a play in 1930, albeit one that he knew was "never much more than a theatrical tearjerker." By 1933, Austria had become increasingly hostile to Jews. Zweig, along with other Jewish and non-Jewish writers and thinkers whose work the Nazis deemed "degenerate," from Erich Maria Remarque to Thomas Mann, Sigmund

Freud, and Albert Einstein, had his books burned on a pyre in front of Berlin's Humboldt University. In 1934, Zweig moved to London, while Leonhard had since moved to Berlin. He still had not given up on his quixotic dreams of airships, as he embarked upon a project assisting his friend Ernst Lehmann as a ghostwriter for his memoir and laid plans for a film about Count Zeppelin, for which he had lofty aspirations that his ideas would be snapped up by Hollywood.

Strangest of all for a man so transfixed by airships, once on board the *Hindenburg*, he seemed entirely indifferent to the experience. It was a far cry from the exuberant romanticism with which he had once written in the genre for which he was known. If he pretended not to care for the very things he wanted most, perhaps he could protect himself from his own awareness that he would never be a great writer or a great airman, especially when faced with the harsh reality that two of his closest friends had already succeeded in ways he knew he never would.

Though a rational person could see that the airship was obsolete practically from the day Count Zeppelin's first "flying sausage" had taken flight, on the *Hindenburg*, Gertrud could perhaps fully and finally understand her husband's lifelong obsession. The writing may have been on the wall for the zeppelins long before the *Hindenburg* ever took to the sky, but there was something heady and intoxicating about the feeling of riding on a cloud that even the most logical and rational among them could not deny.

CHAPTER 18

Over the Atlantic Ocean: May 4, 1937

On the *Hindenburg*, lunch was the main formal meal of the day. It was a multicourse affair for which the stewards had arranged the dining room with one long table so that all of the passengers could eat together. Once again the blue, white, and gold DZR porcelain had been laid out, and each individual's napkin in its special folder had been set at his or her assigned place.

When the appointed lunch hour arrived, Margaret Mather left her cabin to join her fellow passengers with whom she had begun to become acquainted the night before. She particularly enjoyed a kindly older German couple, Elsa Ernst and her husband, Otto, the seed merchant from Hamburg, who told Margaret that they had been flying for twenty-five years. They were so fond of the air that they were traveling to the United States for a week so that they could return on the *Hindenburg*'s next eastbound journey. Margaret could entirely understand their enthusiasm.

The Ernsts were one of only four couples on the flight, including Mr. and Mrs. Doehner with their children. The majority of the passengers Margaret met were men who were traveling alone. A sizable contingent were rather young and had been in Europe for a variety of reasons, whether for work, study, or pleasure. Others were a good bit older, like sixty-three-year-old George Grant, the only Brit on the flight, who was traveling on zeppelin company business and had a neatly clipped mustache. Fortunately,

Margaret had thus far been able to avoid the drunken man from the night before. His name was William Leuchtenberg, and he was a German immigrant to the United States who lived in New York and worked as president of a manufacturing company.

The only other solo female traveler, Marie Kleemann, was just a few years older than Margaret and lived in Nuremberg and Bad Homburg, a spa town rich in mineral waters just north of Frankfurt. Her daughter, who had moved with her husband and two children to Andover, Massachusetts, had recently had an operation, and Frau Kleemann was flying over to be with her during her convalescence. Frau Kleemann's son-in-law was president of a company that manufactured rubber products and had plants in Lawrence, Massachusetts, and Nuremberg. She was very proud to see that the stewards were, in fact, using rubber-based trays that her son-in-law's company had produced. He and his wife had traveled on the *Hindenburg*'s first flight from the United States to Germany in 1936 and on the *Graf Zeppelin* before that, and they had suggested that Frau Kleemann try the new airship rather than take a steamer.

As the bulk of zeppelin passengers were typically business travelers, it was not surprising that the majority were men, though it was certainly not a novelty to have women flying alone on either airplanes or airships. While women made up a mere 10 percent of passengers on American commercial airlines in 1930, by 1936 that proportion had jumped to 34 percent. In their projections for 1937, airlines in the United States anticipated carrying a whopping 250,000 female passengers. Solo dirigible travel in particular had the stamp of approval of socially distinguished women like the quintessentially British and aristocratically styled Lady Hay Drummond-Hay, who, after the death of her much older husband, worked as a journalist for William Randolph Hearst. As the only woman on board the 1928 maiden transatlantic voyage of the *Graf Zeppelin*, she had reported on the groundbreaking journey from the sky. The next year, she became the first woman to circumnavigate the globe as the only female passenger on the *Graf Zeppelin*'s round-the-world flight.

Alongside Lady Hay Drummond-Hay, an American woman named Clara Adams had made history as the first ticketed female passenger aboard the *Graf Zeppelin* on its first 1928 return flight from Lakehurst to

Germany. Like Margaret Mather, Clara Adams appeared respectable and demure, which disguised the fact that she had a thrill-seeking nature. After becoming the first woman to travel on both lighter- and heavier-than-air craft on first flights from New York to Bermuda, New York to Rio, San Francisco to New Zealand, and more, she became known as the "Maiden of Maiden Flight." Lady Hay Drummond-Hay and Clara Adams had even traveled together a year earlier as the only women aboard the *Hindenburg*'s first North Atlantic crossing. To mark the occasion, Lady Hay Drummond-Hay had written a souvenir letter to Adams while en route, telling her, "I cannot tell you how happy I was to find you on board the *Hindenburg* as one of the passengers on her first flight from Germany to America. I hope we will meet again as 'companions in adventure' when the next Zeppelin is completed, and that once more we will pioneer a path through the air together."

Not only were women flying as passengers, but in the heavier-than-air domain, nearly eight hundred American women had pilot's licenses by 1937. That March, famed aviatrix Amelia Earhart had made her first attempt at a planned round-the-world flight with a three-man crew in a Lockheed Electra. She had flown from Oakland to Honolulu, but after a problem with the forward landing gear caused the plane's propellers to hit the ground and the plane to skid on a failed takeoff to Howland Island, the Electra was in need of significant repairs, setting back the attempt by several months.

Aside from Earhart, many other female pilots had reached celebrity status. Charles Lindbergh's wife, Anne Morrow Lindbergh, had become a fixture of the skies in her own right. Early in their marriage, Lindbergh had taught his wife to fly and to serve as his radio operator, including on a daring trip made to the Far East by crossing north over the Arctic Circle en route to Siberia, over the Kuril Islands, onward to Japan, and finally to China, which she had chronicled. In 1933, in the wake of the heartbreak and loss they experienced after the death of their son, they embarked on another epic series of flights together, battling the winds and the doldrums south of the equator as they crossed the Atlantic between Africa and South America. "'Hurtling across the skies anywhere . . . That is no longer a fairy tale. That is almost everyday life!'" she had written in an imagined conversation in her book *North to the Orient*, which had won the inaugural National Book Award for nonfiction in 1935. "Yesterday's fairy tale is today's fact."

At the long lunch table, Margaret's status as a woman traveling unaccompanied had its perks, as she was again seated in a place of honor beside Captain Pruss, who had reemerged from the control gondola. On her other side was one of the young American men traveling home from Europe. Twenty-eight-year-old Herbert O'Laughlin from River Forest, Illinois, was one of the four men from the Chicago area on board, along with Nelson Morris and Burtis Dolan, seated somewhere farther down the table, and a man named Clifford Osbun, a thirty-nine-year-old sales manager for Oliver Farm Equipment Co. O'Laughlin was on his way home from a three-week European vacation.

Margaret turned to ask her younger neighbor about his travels across the Continent during his break from the executive office of his family's coal and coke business. "Which country," she wondered, did "he [like] best?"

"U.S.A.," he replied, "where you can drink plain water and there's no bother about passports." Clearly, he was not destined to follow Margaret's example and live abroad.

Picking up her conversation with Captain Pruss from dinner the previous evening, Margaret told him "how much [she] was enjoying the trip," especially given "what a wretched sailor [she] was on the sea." Pruss replied that he was very pleased to hear it but remarked that this stormy crossing was actually "one of the worst trips he had made." This would have surprised many of the passengers. While they were aware the headwinds were causing delays, none would have been the wiser about the condition of the crossing, given the smoothness of the airship in the storm. As before, Margaret found Pruss "courteous and genial" as they chatted, though always a consummate professional. As at dinner the previous evening, he did not touch the wine or beer on the table.

The same could not be said for the "merry young man" on the other side of Herbert O'Laughlin, whose name Margaret did not catch but who seemed to be enjoying himself and the *Hindenburg*'s wine cellar immensely. Even if the captain was not imbibing, he chided her, how could she be drinking only water while they were passing over so much water at that very instant? "At least, have a dash of wine in it," he urged her. When she finally accepted, he leaned over and sloshed a generous "dash" from the bottle in front of him into her glass, which he would continue to do at every meal henceforth, waving off her protests by assuring her that she was "saving him from a drunkard's grave."

Conversation at the table turned to the airship tours that many passengers had taken that day. Heinrich Kubis had been kept busy running groups back and forth, from pairs like Nelson Morris and Bert Dolan to larger groups of five like the one George Grant had joined.

Down the table, where Gertrud Adelt sat with her husband and Captain Lehmann, Gertrud's ears perked up as one of the tourists relayed an anecdote. One of the groups had been allowed to climb up to the long axial walkway between the gas cells. The axial walkway was much like a catwalk, which at first had a railing alongside it but farther down had nothing for balance as it ran through the "dim, airy vault." "One misstep," the storyteller relayed, "and you fell almost into the bottomless space." Apparently, one of the handful of female passengers, though the narrator did not reveal who, had been leading the way. Concerned more for her propriety than for her balance, she had walked upright along the catwalk rather than crawl and risk allowing any of the men to catch a glimpse up her skirt. The men in the group were evidently not as brave and had opted to stay behind.

When the woman walked as far as she could and turned back to face the rest of the group, she suddenly turned quite pale as a delayed sense of vertigo washed over her. Hearing this, others at the table started teasing the unnamed woman for suddenly becoming nervous.

Just then, a soft but decidedly serious voice interjected, quieting the joshing. It was Captain Lehmann. "Oh," he remarked in his light German accent, his voice sounding rather tired, "not to be afraid and to be courageous, that's not great art. But to be afraid and yet dare—that's probably the hardest thing."

That brought the teasing to an end.

CHAPTER 19

Chicago, Illinois, USA: May 4, 1937

By the late afternoon of May 4, with the *Hindenburg* halfway across the Atlantic Ocean, Herb Morrison had practically given up all hope that the plan he had hatched with American Airlines would ever come to fruition. All that day, he heard nothing further that suggested WLS leadership would have a change of heart. It was all but too late now. Morrison would have to grudgingly accept that his chance was gone, as were whatever future opportunities to collaborate with American Airlines that might have followed.

Since he was apparently not going to New Jersey the next day, he left the office that evening to keep a date with a young woman. The date was unremarkable, or at least unremarkable compared with the utterly unexpected message he received when he returned home.

"OK," his editor finally acquiesced. Morrison could go. The editor did not elaborate but simply told his younger colleague he could go to Lakehurst and make the recording. Morrison could take the new Presto recording equipment and also his sound engineer, Charlie Nehlsen, with him to man the recording device. They could both fly out with American Airlines the next morning. The addition of Charlie Nehlsen was perhaps more than he might have dared hope. If there was any more literal interpretation of changing plans at the eleventh hour, Morrison certainly could not have come up with one.

However, there remained one key sticking point. WLS was allowing Morrison to go and make this recording on American Airlines' dime, but it made no promise to actually *air* the recording when he brought it home. He was welcome to test the equipment and further the station's relationship with the fledgling airline, potentially a good source of future advertising revenue, but in all likelihood, the recording would just go into storage for posterity along with the concerts, presidential addresses, and World Series games no one would ever hear on the airwaves again.

CHAPTER 20

Over the Atlantic Ocean: May 5, 1937

In the late afternoon of May 5, the fog and clouds that had surrounded the *Hindenburg* for the better part of two days began to clear. Passengers looking out the observation windows along the promenade started to see great ice fields in the shape of horseshoes bobbing along the surface of the water. Typically, the zeppelin reached this point some hours earlier in its westward journey, but as Peter Belin, the handsome young Yale graduate, had marked on his map charting their progress, Captain Pruss had steered the zeppelin in a more northerly direction than the *Hindenburg*'s usual route to avoid the storms over the Atlantic. Finally, after nearly two full days, the floating fields of ice signaled that land was near, the ice having broken off from solid formations along the Canadian coast and drifted out to sea.

Margaret Mather had been relaxing in the passenger lounge and chatting over cups of hot coffee with the lovely American couple, Emma Pannes and her husband, John, who worked for the Hamburg-America Line in New York. While John Pannes was in his sixties, the two women were about the same age and had been knitting and writing letters together while amusedly watching the Doehner children playing in the lounge. Margaret was impressed by how well-behaved they were and was glad to see how much they seemed to be enjoying the experience with their parents.

Around five o'clock, this charmingly domestic scene was interrupted when a group of passengers suddenly flocked toward the starboard windows as large white dots punctuated the horizon along the approaching Newfoundland coastline. As the *Hindenburg* drew closer, those white dots revealed themselves to be three large icebergs extending sharply out of the sea. The passengers crowded around the long, slanted plexiglass windows, some of them even leaning out the open windows to get a clearer view of the great white formations ahead. Several had put on their coats as brisk sea air filled the promenade, and Benny Spah nearly lost his flat cap when it practically blew off his head as he leaned out to take a better look. He secured it back on with the brim facing backward, which also made it easier to film the remarkable nature below.

Over the last two days, Benny had been using his Bell & Howell motion picture camera to document the journey, attempting to record anything his wife and children would find interesting or exciting. As they had drawn closer to North America, large sailing ships and steamships had begun to appear in the water below. He had leaned out the open window with his camera to capture them as they crossed the airship's path. His best shots yet were those of the airship's shadow racing along on the glistening surface of the sea toward the United States, ferrying him ever farther away from his German homeland but closer to his family and the home and life he had chosen.

Benny stepped back from the windows and put the viewfinder to his eye and recorded a few moments of footage of the passengers crowding around the windows, enraptured by the sights below. Through the lens, he could see fashion designer Philip Mangone leaning intently over the windowsill. The Dresden tea merchant, Ernst Rudolf Anders, crouched down to peer out with binoculars while the German Jewish expat, Moritz Feibusch, observed the wondrous scene from over his shoulder. Beside them, one of the Luftwaffe men, Oberleutnant Claus Hinkelbein, similarly looked on. After dozens of crossings, the ocean's magic still had not worn off for Ernst Lehmann, whom Benny captured taking a turn with some binoculars. Even the cabin boy, Werner Franz, paused his chores long enough to take a peek.

Captain Pruss ordered the ship to slow its engines and descend so that the passengers could get a better view of the wonders of nature. The airship flew low and steered directly toward the giant icebergs. One of the younger men, a thirty-five-year-old half-German, half-American cotton broker named George Hirschfeld, estimated these "fantastic" giant formations stretched about eighty meters high out of the water and three hundred meters in length, making them twice as tall as the *Hindenburg* and fifty meters longer. In more expressive terms, as Marie Kleemann observed, the icebergs were like "swimming castles" that climbed up out of the water, and, as Margaret Mather noted, they shone "white against the stone-gray sea." Gertrud and Leonhard Adelt had also joined at the window. To Gertrud, the icebergs also appeared to "[rise] from the depths like crystal castles and domes." Even the reticent Leonhard thought they looked like "magic marble statue[s]."

Suddenly, the sun came out from behind a cloud and a ray of light hit the water and the icebergs below. A double rainbow appeared around the zeppelin, turning the giant iceberg into, as Leonhard described, "a monument of sparkling brilliants." "Rainbows sprang from everywhere," Margaret noticed with wonder as she "watched one grow and grow till it completed a perfect circle beneath the ship." It was a sight unlike anything they could have witnessed from the ground. Any feelings of monotony, comfortable normality, or even boredom they had experienced over the last two days were washed away by the awesome panoramas Captain Lehmann had so wished to share with those who had never seen the world from the privileged heights of an airship.

Tempting as it was to keep one's eyes on the shimmering play of light on ice as colors separated as though passing through a prism, Margaret's gaze was drawn down below the waterline, where the vast bases of the icebergs lurked. Beneath the surface, the gleaming ice formations turned the water into striking "pools of vivid green in their depths . . . under the pale water." Gertrud, too, was struck by what lay beneath the surface like "glassy, bottle-green foundations that floated treacherously under the water." As she looked down, it occurred to her that twenty-five years earlier, the "*Titanic* fell victim not far from here," just about four hundred miles due south of their position off the Newfoundland coast. It now lay in a barnacle- and silt-covered wreck, its "unsinkable" mass a watery grave for hundreds of souls.

Gertrud was not the only passenger on board the *Hindenburg* with reason to think of the *Titanic* and other disasters at sea. Peter Belin's father had booked passage on the *Titanic* in April 1912 to return home after contracting typhoid while on his honeymoon in Europe, but for reasons not entirely clear to his son, he had canceled his booking at the last minute. As Philip Mangone leaned out the window looking down, perhaps he thought about his near brush with catastrophe after canceling his passage on the *Lusitania*, torpedoed by German U-boats on May 7, 1915, almost exactly twenty-two years earlier to the day.

As his camera rolled, Benny Spah, too, reflected on the *Titanic*. "How dangerous it must be on the ocean," he thought to himself, feeling oddly relieved to be many hundreds of feet in the air above the icebergs, especially after having captured those ships with his camera as they traversed the icy North Atlantic below.

Though he had only a high school education, Benny Spah had a serious and inquiring mind. He always read prodigiously in both German and English, especially histories and novels, from popular modern works like Erich Maria Remarque's postwar writings to Shakespeare's masterpieces. On his travels, he carried with him a pocket-size edition of *The Taming of the Shrew*. Benny was also a romantic at heart, composing love letters to his wife, Vera, when they were apart, even early in their courtship when he felt "ashamed" that he had not the English "words big enough to tell [her] what [she] mean[t]" to him. Perhaps his romantic soul would have appreciated a poem by the English novelist and poet Thomas Hardy of *Tess of the d'Urbervilles* and *Far from the Madding Crowd* fame. Ten days after the loss of the *Titanic*, Hardy had written "Convergence of the Twain," a poem memorializing the tragedy in rhyming tercets to help raise money for the Titanic Disaster Fund.

In his poem, Hardy recounted a tale of hubris and foreboding, where, "in a solitude of the sea / Deep from human vanity / . . . The Immanent Will that stirs and urges everything / Prepared a sinister mate / For her—so gaily great." After alluding to the opulence and riches that adorned man's greatest seaborne creation, Hardy marched the ship and the iceberg toward one another, their intertwined fates racing toward collision:

Alien they seemed to be;
No mortal eye could see
The intimate welding of their later history.

Or sign that they were bent
By paths coincident
On being anon twin halves of one august event,

Till the Spinner of the Years
Said "Now!" And each one hears,
And consummation comes, and jars two hemispheres.

Twin halves, two hemispheres colliding. East and west, man and nature, land and sea, each pole set on a path toward collision, but one that was not inevitable—until the moment when it was.

After quietly lingering in the background to capture the delight and amazement of the passengers as they crowded around the windows like schoolchildren at a variety show, Benny returned to his position at the plexiglass window and trained his viewfinder back down toward the sea below. Just at that moment, the shadow of the airship passed from the water over one of the icebergs, the starkness of the brilliant white ice contrasting sharply against the *Hindenburg*'s dark silhouette. In that moment of transition from water to ice, just as Benny was thinking of the *Titanic* colliding with its fate, it appeared to him almost as if the zeppelin were "ramming the iceberg" or "crashing" into its solid form. Of all the shots the amateur cinematographer had captured on the journey thus far, this was the one of which he was proudest, and one he knew would stay with him long after the journey was over.

CHAPTER 21

Chicago, Illinois, to Newark, New Jersey, USA: May 5, 1937

Herb Morrison and his sound engineer, Charlie Nehlsen, set out from Chicago, each with what felt like one hundred pounds of equipment in tow. They had lugged their new sixteen-inch portable Presto recording device and a half dozen blank lacquer-coated discs out to Chicago Municipal Airport that morning to catch American Airlines' noon flight to New York. By the spring of 1937, American Airlines was running nine daily flights between the two cities, up from six the year before. Most of the routes hopped from Chicago to Detroit to Buffalo, and then on to Newark, the closest airport to New York City, but the airline had booked Morrison and Nehlsen on its "Eagle" nonstop service, one of two such routes per day. It cut about an hour off the trip, making the leap from one metropolis to the other in three hours, fifty-five minutes flat, a point Morrison would be sure to note in his recording the next day. He also needed to make it very clear that American Airlines was the only carrier providing connections with the *Hindenburg*, quickly and comfortably whisking passengers over the traffic between Newark and Lakehurst to catch the airship's evening departure and returning with those who had just crossed the ocean.

Morrison had, of course, flown in one of the airline's new DC-3s just a few months earlier, but this was quite a different experience compared with the last time, when he and half a dozen other radio- and newspapermen had been anxiously trying to assist with disaster relief. Now he could sit back and relax, make his notes for his introductory remarks for the next morning's recording, and enjoy a hot meal served on porcelain dishes painted with the airline's crest, an eagle with wings aloft nestled between two capital *A*'s.

While he was most "anxious to see the *Hindenburg* land" the next day, there was no denying that even this first leg of the journey was quite a perk for someone like Morrison, who was born a year and a half after the Wright brothers' first flight and had grown up in a boardinghouse. And now here he was, the guest of an airline in a gleaming, polished aluminum monoplane on his way to see the greatest aircraft ever constructed.

If this adventure was a stroke of good fortune for Herb Morrison, it was a greater turnup for Charlie Nehlsen, whose background was even more modest than Morrison's. Native Chicagoan Charlie Nehlsen, or "Nelly" to his friends, was thirty-five, just three years older than Morrison. He was a touch taller at five feet seven inches, with dark hair and a round face, but he had a good forty to fifty pounds on his slight colleague. Like Morrison, Nehlsen was a bachelor, but he was a quieter man, describing himself as "not much of a mixer." He lived with his father, liked to bowl in winter and golf in summer, but otherwise enjoyed solitary activities like stamp collecting and landscape photography.

Over the years, Charlie Nehlsen had had to learn to keep his own company and look after himself, relying on his wits while he tried to land on his feet. He had been with WLS for twelve years but had worked in radio and communication in various capacities since he was a teenager, at least when there was radio work to be had. In his younger years, he spent some time with Western Union and Western Electric in Chicago but also worked in machine shops in Chicago and Cleveland and, when that dried up, as a stevedore and dishwasher in Cleveland and then New York. When he first arrived in New York City, he spent three weeks looking for a job as a radio operator. He had no money for a place to stay, so he spent those three weeks sleeping on park benches, until an acquaintance who worked for the Post Office allowed him to sleep at New York's main branch building, where Nehlsen would lay out newspaper on the floor and try to catch whatever sleep he could. Occasionally, his friend would slip him a coffee and a roll, but most of the time in those weeks he had nothing to eat. He finally found a job as a radio operator, not in the city but on a ship, an itinerant employment he maintained for the next five years. When he collected his first paycheck from the shipping company, he sent his friend at the Post Office ten dollars to pay him back for his kindness.

Both Morrison and Nehlsen had grown up alongside aviation in America, the two men and the industry coming of age together in the postwar world over the last decade. As they had matured from little more than boys into men, American aviation had similarly left behind its fitful adolescence seemingly overnight.

It was hard to overstate the degree to which Charles Lindbergh's heroic flight had inspired aviation-obsessed Americans to flock to the air in record numbers. In 1927, there were 1,572 licensed pilots in the United States. By the end of 1928, there were 4,887. In that time, the number of civil aircraft in operation almost doubled, as did miles flown for both scheduled commercial and private flights. Nearly two hundred new airports were built, and existing airports improved their facilities by adding lights and paved runways.

However, the aviation boom was not entirely down to the young national hero. Thanks to both public and private investment in the nascent industry, Lindbergh mania occurred at almost the exact moment that the country was finally primed with the resources and structures necessary to incubate a technological explosion that would ultimately send more than a million Americans into the skies in a single year just a decade later. In 1926, the U.S. Congress passed a sweeping new piece of legislation, the Air Commerce Act, which took a haphazard community of barnstormers and chancers who staved off perpetually imminent bankruptcy with air mail contracts and turned it into a well-regulated industry attractive to mature investors and serious scientific study. The Air Commerce Act made flying considerably safer. It transferred jurisdiction over aviation from the Post Office to the Commerce Department and established safety oversight mechanisms. Crucially, the act also created accident investigation protocols, mandated licensing and certification, and accredited flying schools.

At the same time, philanthropist Daniel Guggenheim endowed the generous $3 million Daniel Guggenheim Fund for the Promotion of Aeronautics. Within three years, this endowment funded 575 new aeronautical schools and financed research and development that allowed for a rapid shift from biplanes made of fabric and wood to metal-clad monoplanes. These studies advanced propeller, flap, and wing design, created retractable landing gear, and helped develop new engines designed by the Wright Company and Pratt & Whitney. Guggenheim also funded Lindbergh's national barnstorming tour to spread the gospel of heavier-than-air flight and "blind flying," or instrument navigation. Writing off the gutsy, instinct-based flying of the barnstorming old guard, Lindbergh demonstrated how navigational tools were considerably safer and more reliable than a pilot's own senses.

While the 1929 stock market crash left many up-and-coming aviation companies bankrupt, for those that survived, Congress fundamentally altered the economics of the aviation industry. Recognizing that short-term air mail contracts were unlikely to spur necessary long-term investment in a technology that could soon allow airlines to transport passengers at scale, the McNary–Watres Act of 1930 offered airlines bonuses for improvements in passenger transport.

Still, even though flying was materially safer than it had been a decade earlier, especially for commercial carriers, the occasional sensational accident caused outsize reputational damage for the industry. Just that February, on a clear and calm night, a United Airlines DC-3 approaching a runway in San Francisco had suddenly gone into a steep dive and crashed into the bay, killing all eleven people on board. The crash had nothing to do with the plane's fundamental design. An investigation revealed that the copilot's radio microphone had become wedged into a small space at the foot of the yoke in the cockpit, completely jamming the pilot's controls. It was the definition of a freak accident, and the airline quickly implemented changes to ensure it could not happen again, but nonetheless it spooked the public.

American Airlines CEO C. R. Smith liked to point out that someone would have to "fly around the world 425 times—or make approximately 14,165 flights back and forth between New York and Chicago—before you would be liable to meet with an accident," but he recognized that cold, hard statistics would not persuade people to overcome their fear. Changing hearts and minds required a creative, multipronged approach.

As businessmen made up the majority of commercial airline customers, there was a general impression among the airlines that if they could persuade businessmen's wives that flying was safe, the wives would be less likely to insist their husbands remain grounded. Anecdotally, there seemed to be some truth in it, if Nelson Morris's and Bert Dolan's wives' reluctance for them to fly was indicative of a broader trend. Two of American Airlines' competitors, United and TWA, launched a promotion to "fly wives free." The campaign was an instant hit. Suddenly, men were bringing their wives on board in droves. Optimistic about the results of this gimmick, United and TWA followed up with the wives by mail, sending letters directly to their homes to ask how they had enjoyed their experience. Unfortunately, the seemingly brilliant strategy hit a snag. "WHAT FLIGHT?" a number of wives wrote back. The answer to the question was rather embarrassingly revealed when the papers delightedly reported on an incident in which a taxi careened onto the tarmac alongside a flight that was about to depart, and a rather large woman appeared from within. After marching up the steps and into the airplane's cabin, she promptly reemerged with a red-faced husband by the ear and a skinny blond just behind. (While American Airlines instituted its own version of "fly wives free," it had the good sense not to follow up with the wives after the fact.)

Still, gimmicks alone were not going to materially move public opinion. In the middle of April, as Herb Morrison was preparing his pitch to WLS on recording the upcoming *Hindenburg* landing, the airline did something truly novel that no competitor would have dared consider. On April 19, a full-page advertisement appeared in leading newspapers addressing the issue that everyone was thinking about but no one in the industry would discuss publicly. "Why dodge the question: Afraid to Fly?" the ad asked in bold letters, with C. R. Smith's picture front and center. "We know that fear keeps many people from enjoying the advantages of air transportation," the ad began. "*So why should we be silent on this subject?* Regrettable as it is, the records show there *have been* accidents and fatalities in *every* form of transportation. What we do not understand," the ad continued, "is why some people associate danger with a transport plane more than they do with a train, a boat, a motor car." Smith would readily concede that "no form of transportation . . . can guarantee its passengers absolute immunity from danger." However, as he summed up his argument in block capital letters: "PEOPLE ARE AFRAID OF THE THINGS THEY DO NOT KNOW ABOUT." In refusing to fly, travelers saved themselves no risk but merely denied themselves the "*enjoyment of the many advantages of air travel*."

Notably, nowhere in the ad did Smith mention airships directly. He had a separate marketing plan for that. The relationship between airships and airplanes was one that American Airlines saw as symbiotic rather than competitive, at least for now. In 1936, American Airlines had launched a marketing campaign offering timetables linking its routes with those of the *Hindenburg*. "Now . . . FLY TO EUROPE!" its brochures exclaimed, listing the total time and fare to fly to Germany from eight major American cities, particularly for the Summer Olympics. In 1937, it refreshed this with enticing descriptions of all that Europe had to offer that spring, like the coronation and the Paris Exposition. "Of all the years," the airline declared, "this is the year to see Europe on Parade!" It also produced special oval baggage labels with horizontal blue, white, and red stripes. "Airship Hindenburg," they read on top, and "American Airlines, Inc. Exclusive Connecting Service" on the bottom, with patriotic stars on either side of a majestically oriented DC-3 with passengers boarding in the foreground and the *Hindenburg* hovering above.

Interestingly, on the airship's tail, the baggage label's artist had drawn a rectangular flag shape with a little red dot in the middle. The airline had left a gesture to the Nazi flag but blurred out the swastika. Whether or not the airline's public relations staff mentioned anything to Herb Morrison about how to handle some of the uncomfortable details about the government that owned and operated the airships he did not say, but it was certainly not something to which it would have had any desire for him to draw attention.

While mutually beneficial for now, the relationship between airships and airplanes would inexorably become more parasitic over time as airplanes buzzed around the large, whale-like zeppelin like gnats. The heavier-than-air industry's leaders knew that airships' days were numbered, as they simply were not scalable like airplanes. They were incredibly resource intensive to build and operate and simply could not carry many more passengers than they already did because their size-to-weight ratio would become unmanageable. For Smith and other airline executives, anyone who refused to accept that airplanes were the way of the future was merely forestalling the inevitable. They were only a few short years away from reaching that inflection point, and it could not come soon enough, not least because there was a real awkwardness about the zeppelins that was getting harder and harder to ignore.

It was true that the flying silver Goliaths long predated the Nazis. They had even overcome their association with enemy bombing raids over allied cities during the Great War. But in the last year, they had become inextricably linked to regime propaganda. Blurring out the inconvenient details of Nazism seemed to be the general tendency of many Americans these days, not just American Airlines.

In both private industry and government, it was easier to simply turn a blind eye to reality and move forward than to address it head-on, especially as the Nazi threat so often seemed clownish and silly. On April 19, the same day American Airlines ran its "Afraid to Fly?" ad, a kerfuffle flared up in Hollywood and Washington. Universal Pictures was finalizing a motion picture called *The Road Back*, an adaptation of a novel by Erich Maria Remarque, a sort of sequel to his global bestseller, *All Quiet on the Western Front*. In the story, a group of German war veterans struggle to return to civilian life as the war's futility becomes increasingly evident with the passage of time. The Nazis had banned the novel in Germany for its unflattering portrayal of the country's recent history, and now they wanted to block the release of the film. James Clement Dunn, a senior State Department expert on western Europe and special assistant to the secretary of state, Cordell Hull, told Hull that the German consul in Los Angeles had sent a letter to sixty of the film's cast members. The letter informed them that "any film in which an actor has participated who has previously taken part in a film which has been declared inimical to German interests may not be granted a permit for exhibition in Germany." Rather than stand its ground and accept that it might lose the German market, Universal Pictures hastily reshot the film, making it more of a comedic story to pass German censorship. The resulting movie was completely unlike the novel and received resoundingly critical reviews when it was released in American theaters.

As silly as the controversy over *The Road Back* seemed, it was a sign that Germany was becoming progressively more emboldened in its attempts to interfere in American domestic affairs. Meanwhile, the U.S. embassy in Berlin was looking increasingly impotent of late. Diplomatic tension between the two countries had flared over the case of a young Jewish student named Helmut Hirsch, who was technically a U.S. citizen through his German father, who had become naturalized after working in the United States for some time. Hirsch had lived his whole life in Germany until being forced to attend university in Prague after Jews were barred from German educational institutions. There he became involved in resistance activities though a group called the Black Front. The Gestapo arrested Hirsch in Stuttgart in December 1936 on the charge of conspiracy to commit high treason through a bombing plot against the Reich, though no explosives were found on him. That little detail did not stop the Nazis from sentencing him to death.

Given Hirsch's American citizenship, U.S. ambassador William Dodd strenuously argued for clemency. Over several months, Hirsch's case wound its way through diplomatic channels in Washington, where Hans Luther, the imminently retiring German ambassador to the United States, was called in for a meeting with Dunn. He, too, argued for leniency, but Luther merely responded that domestic law was what it was and that "punishment for a similar crime in this country would be equally drastic and severe," referring to the case of Bruno Richard Hauptmann, the Lindbergh baby's kidnapper and a German citizen, which the German embassy had followed closely at every stage from arrest to trial to conviction and execution.

Germany's brazen attitude toward the United States was certainly encouraged by a relatively small but vocal group of American Nazi sympathizers of German descent. The German American Bund had officially formed in 1936 after earlier, similar organizations like the Friends of New Germany had been investigated by a congressional committee and disbanded. The Bund was led by a Munich-born war veteran and naturalized American citizen named Fritz Julius Kuhn, who, prior to becoming head of the German American Bund, worked in a Ford automobile factory in Detroit. The Bund established training camps for adults and children in places like Wisconsin (where the camp was called "Camp Hindenburg") and New Jersey, including several not far from Lakehurst. Bund members occasionally turned up at Lakehurst and caused trouble, such as during one *Hindenburg* landing in 1936 when they insisted on being allowed out on the field near the airship during its landing maneuvers, which was against the rules. They had complained to Nazi Party headquarters in Berlin that they were turned away. Though appearing comically blundering in their uniforms modeled after the those of the Nazi SA—the Brownshirts—and likely numbering no more than 25,000 members at its peak, the Bund was vocally anti-Semitic, held rallies where they saluted the führer, and flew the swastika alongside the American flag.

Perhaps the oddest episode in German-American relations that spring that had rankled the Nazi government as it turned its ire on American shores occurred in March and involved the mayor of New York, Fiorello La Guardia. On March 3, La Guardia was speaking at a lunch for one thousand women at the American Jewish Congress at the Hotel Astor in New York City. In his remarks, he referenced plans for the New York World's Fair, which was still two years away. La Guardia facetiously told the audience that if he were designing a building for the fair, he would include a "chamber of horrors," with the coup de grâce being a "figure of that brown-shirted fanatic who is now threatening the peace of the world." It was not the first time La Guardia, an Episcopalian with a Jewish mother and a Catholic father, had called out Hitler. In 1933, even before he was mayor, he had publicly referred to Hitler as a "perverted maniac" seeking to "complete the annihilation of the Jews in Germany." After becoming mayor the following year, he participated in a mock trial of Hitler at Madison Square Garden before 20,000 people as a so-called witness to

Hitler's "crimes against civilization" and his pursuit of the "complete extermination" of 600,000 German Jews.

While certainly antagonistic, La Guardia's remarks were far from front-page news. A reader would have had to flip all the way to page twenty-five, more than halfway through that day's *New York Times*, to find them. That did not stop the Germans from creating a big stink. Immediately following the luncheon, Ambassador Luther complained to Secretary Hull. Hull, who had been trying to negotiate a treaty for improved commercial terms between the two nations, rushed to apologize. He then issued a formal apology to the German government on March 5 amid a series of vicious Nazi government protestations demanding to know why an official American representative was allowed to speak in such a manner about a foreign power.

Ambassador Dodd did not agree with Hull's feeble acquiescence to Luther's demands. As he wrote to the secretary of state from Berlin, the "Nazi press," which was having a domestic heyday over the affair, "cannot or will not understand that freedom of speech is a constitutional right in the United States, and that any official on any given occasion may not be a national or government spokesman." Furthermore, he explained, for the Nazi regime, any clash with La Guardia was merely an "opportunity not to be overlooked to attack his ancestry and American Jewry in general."

When the subject came up in a cabinet meeting the next day, President Roosevelt inquired about the La Guardia situation. Before Hull could even reply, Roosevelt asked him, "What would you say if I should say that I agreed completely with La Guardia?" As Secretary of the Interior Harold Ickes observed, "It was plain that [Roosevelt] would like to see a gold medal pinned on La Guardia's lapel for what he had said about Hitler." Still, Roosevelt declined to become personally involved in the spat.

La Guardia's comments and the Universal Pictures film may have annoyed the German government, but the efforts to which they went to protest them merely served as a distraction from the very real and terrifying repression taking place in Germany. On April 19, the very same day as the controversy over *The Road Back*, Nazi secret police visited the homes of members of the historic Jewish benevolent society B'nai B'rith, confiscating members' passports, ostensibly, as Dodd reported to Hull, for the purpose of "uncovering possible infractions of the foreign exchange laws." They placed a general ban upon meetings of Jews, including language courses for Jews emigrating from Germany and agricultural training for those looking to move to the British Mandate of Palestine. By the end of the next week, they had shut down eighty B'nai B'rith lodges and confiscated 3.5 million reichsmarks in Jewish property.

On April 29, Dodd sent a telegram to Washington, writing, "The suppression of the B'nai B'rith appears to have been activated by the desire to retaliate against foreign anti-Nazi agitation to deliver another blow at the freedom of association of Jews and finally to carry out a profitable raid upon independent Jewish funds." As he had suspected back in March, the vituperative campaign the Nazi government launched against La Guardia, as well as its insistence on executing Helmut Hirsch, were little more than pretexts to justify actions it had already planned. He laid out his rationale to Hull: "With the termination of the so-called Olympic games truce of last year the radical Nazis now seem anxious to apply Hitler's threat delivered at the Party Congress of 1935 that he would in effect hold the Jews in Germany as hostages for the good behavior of fellow members of their race abroad."

Assessing the situation as a whole, Dodd was not optimistic about the future prospects for Jews in Germany, nor, as recent events suggested, for Jews in other countries where their own governments failed to challenge Nazi Germany's gangster tactics: "In our opinion the present action is not so much a new departure as a logical evolution of a policy of antisemitism which we consider permanent." To Dodd, it was clear that the Nazis had just ratcheted up the pressure. The U.S. government would be wise to take notice, especially as an airship emblazoned with an enormous swastika was floating closer to its shores, where it would be met by cheering, adoring crowds.

CHAPTER 22

Over the Atlantic Ocean: May 5, 1937

Over the last two days, perhaps no two passengers had made better use of the *Hindenburg*'s writing room than Moritz Feibusch and Bert Dolan. With silk walls charmingly decorated with more of Otto Arpke's illustrations—this time scenes depicting different methods of delivering the mail, from bicycle to automobile to caribou-pulled sled—the writing room was a cozy place to sit. Passengers could write letters at one of the four slim half desks along the wall or flip through a magazine in a cloth-covered aluminum armchair. There were also a handful of books on a shelf—though not too many, so as not to add unnecessary weight to the airship—which the passengers could check out from a steward and return before the end of the journey.

While Bert Dolan addressed postcards to buyers at various department stores across the country that sold Lelong perfume, Moritz Feibusch was hard at work scribbling notes on his two hundred special postcards. With enough siblings, nephews, and nieces to make a full American football roster, he needed several dozen just to cover his family members in Germany, Poland, and the United States alone.

As passengers and crew circulated through the comfortable space, someone—perhaps it was the ship's chief steward, Heinrich Kubis—stopped to look over Feibusch's shoulder at the custom postcards, particularly noting the message that was printed on the front: "Greetings on the maiden voyage of the Hindenburg, May - 1937, M. Feibusch."

But Feibusch was a year too late, the man pointed out. The maiden voyage of the *Hindenburg* had taken place a year earlier.

This was true, Feibusch responded with good humor, but it was *his* maiden voyage on the *Hindenburg*!

Even though Bert Dolan had written many postcards and letters over the last two days that had swooshed off to the mail room through the pneumatic tube, there was one letter he had kept back that was now burning a hole in his pocket. It was the one he had written to Mildred before leaving Paris. She still had no idea that he was not going to be with his luggage on the steamship *Hamburg*, as he had originally told her. Nelson had cabled his brother, Edward, from Frankfurt on Monday, May 3, before they had left for the airfield about their change of plan. As Edward was also a friend of the Dolan family, Nelson instructed him to keep Bert's surprise a secret. Other than the Morris brothers, no one else knew he was on board.

The letter in Bert's pocket still had no postage. On the front of the envelope in the lower left-hand corner, he had written and underlined the words "Strictly Personal." He had also addressed it to both himself and his wife at his office in the Pittsfield Building at 55 East Washington, perhaps hoping that if it got lost and someone kindly posted it for him, he could simply collect it there when he returned home and Mildred would be none the wiser.

While the letters Bert had written home over the last few months were full of newsy detail about his work, loving notes for his children, and amusing quips about his mother, the letter in his pocket had a different tone. It was written even more deeply from the heart, almost as a sort of confessional, like a letter from a Civil War soldier with a premonition, unburdening himself of all the words he wished he had said before heading into battle.

"Dearest One," Bert had begun his note in a swooping but clear hand just below the letterhead of the Hotel la Pérouse. "For the past week I have just been distracted and here is the reason why. When I was at Nice, Nelse suggested I return on the Zep with him and offered to pay the additional expense. Without thinking I accepted and it now occurred to me that you might object. The reservation was made, the money spent and there is no refund. Furthermore I would feel awfully silly backing out because some publicity with the new perfume might result." His diligent attention to writing postcards to clients throughout the flight was clearly his attempt to will this possibility into reality and make his subterfuge worthwhile. "So much was said" about Nelson's grand plans for their return trip that Bert feared he "would be subject to ridicule if I did not go." But then Mildred's letter had arrived, he explained, reminding him of his promise not to fly, which, he confessed, "startled me terribly and ever since, I have been so unhappy. Not that I fear in any respect the safety of the journey," he qualified. "There is less risk than ordinary flying and I have had to do some of that."

"Now," he continued, getting to the heart of his quandary, "I feel I want to back out so that I do not displease you, but I just cannot without hurting my prestige and perhaps my income." Nelson was his friend, but he was also his longtime boss and now business partner, and Bert feared looking foolish or small after many years of working to build mutual respect on a more even footing, lopsided as their financial positions would always be. So, Bert admitted, "I misled you in my letter re the *Hamburg.* I did make arrangements for my trunk to go on that ship," he explained, and it should arrive as scheduled.

Turning over the page, he finally confessed to the apprehensions that had been weighing on him since he left Nice, that had followed him to Paris, to Frankfurt, and now across the ocean:

> *Of course, precious, none of us know the Lord's will and if anything should happen to me en route, it will be too late to regret. Please don't think I was in any way forgetful of you and the bunnies. As usual, I seem to get into difficult situations and this one, in my judgment, I couldn't withdraw from. Somehow I am a little afraid because I am opposing your wishes as expressed in your letter. But sweet, I got into the whole thing carelessly and too far into it to get out without great embarrassment.*

So there is the story, angel, and if the Lord may call me, I wanted you to have my explanation.

After his confession, the letter continued simply and honestly with words of love Bert hoped Mildred would never have to read in this letter. Better for him to say them to her in person when he surprised her by walking through the door.

Bert had a naturally upbeat and gregarious personality that made him seem ten feet tall, but he was also a devout man. If God had a greater plan for him, at least he knew he had conveyed the words to his wife that were written on his heart. To do well by his family was all Bert Dolan wanted. He and Mildred had waited so long to finally be together, and now they had the family and the life that was as close to perfect as any could be. He would do anything to ensure that their lives remained so, especially after the uncertainty and upheaval of the last few years, between the Depression and his brother's death. His conscience may not have been entirely clear, but hopefully when he rang the bell at 734 Kennesaw Terrace on Sunday morning, all would be forgiven.

CHAPTER 23

Over the Eastern Seaboard, USA: May 6, 1937

On her final night aboard the *Hindenburg*, after the thrill of seeing the dazzling icebergs off the coast of Newfoundland, Margaret Mather "slept like a child and awoke in the morning with a feeling of well being and happiness such as one rarely experiences after youth has passed." The skies, which had cleared the previous afternoon, had closed in again overnight, and it was raining. There was no land in sight when she went upstairs to the dining room for breakfast, seated near the boisterous young men who got a kick out of comparing the size of their hearty appetites with hers. These unlikely new friends were jolly messmates and made the trip all the more enjoyable.

While the passengers ate breakfast, the crew began to prepare for what would need to be a very quick turnaround for the already delayed airship's departure for Frankfurt that evening. The stewards stripped the beds and collected the sheets and blankets at the ends of the bedroom corridors. Normally, if the zeppelin landed in the morning as scheduled, there would be time for the laundry to be sent out and returned for the next departure in the evening, but they would have to collect this batch on their next trip.

Benny Spah also had an extra spring in his swaying step that morning. It was funny, he thought to himself, he had not consciously felt nervous as they crossed the ocean with nothing but water below them for hundreds of miles, but that morning, he found himself rather relieved to be back over land. Wearing a pinstripe suit and playful plaid tie as he went up to breakfast, he made sure to keep his Bell & Howell camera, as well as a pair of binoculars, out of his packed luggage. He did not want these to be swept up by the stewards gathering the bags from the staterooms and assembling them in the hall near the double stairs. When they reached Lakehurst, he wanted to be able to see his family at the first possible instant, and maybe even film them waving from above.

As the passengers tidied the last of their belongings, they had to remember not to pack away their passports, as there would be customs inspections when they landed. DZR had been trying to speed up the customs process, including with a novel innovation it had hoped to implement that year but that had not entirely succeeded. The idea was that as the zeppelin approached the New England coast, a small American plane would fly up to the *Hindenburg*, slow down to match the speed of the airship, and hook itself onto the underside of the keel on a sort of trapeze-like crossbar hanging down to catch the airplane. From there, two customs officials would climb out of the plane and board the zeppelin through a hatch to process the passengers for landing during the final approach to Lakehurst. The pilot of the small plane would then pull a lever to detach the plane and fly away, taking with him express mail bound for destinations beyond New York City. Benny Spah had observed something similar on one of his return steamer crossings. A small mail plane had been launched by a catapult from the ship's deck once it was in range of the United States, to get the mail to American recipients sooner.

The idea of an airplane flying up and attaching itself to a zeppelin was not as crazy as it seemed. The hook-on technology already existed and had been implemented on the two helium-filled U.S. Navy airships that Goodyear-Zeppelin had designed, the USS *Akron* and the USS *Macon*, which had served as flying aircraft carriers before they had crashed in 1931 and 1935, respectively. Inside the cavernous bodies of both the *Akron* and the *Macon*, a novel monorail trolley-and-trapeze system could accommodate five Curtiss F9C Sparrowhawk fixed-wing fighter planes. The trolley would lower a Sparrowhawk hanging from a trapeze through a hatch in the keel and into the slipstream. With its engine running, the Sparrowhawk would release itself from the trapeze, fall away, and fly off into the sky. When it returned, the trapeze would again be lowered into the slipstream, where the Sparrowhawk would fly up from below, hook onto the crossbar, idle its engine, and shut it off as it was winched back up into the belly of the airship.

The *Hindenburg* did not have an internal trolley system, but it could accommodate an experimental trapeze so that a plane could fly up, hook on, and fly away. That spring, the *Hindenburg* had attempted a series of hook-on experiments with a German pilot, Ernst Udet, a Great War ace who, with sixty-two victories, was second in lethal prowess only to Manfred von Richthofen, the "Red Baron," who had eighty. Udet, now in charge of technical development for the Luftwaffe, had made several attempts with a training biplane in March and did manage to hook on after three or four tries. He made another series of attempts at the end of April, again hooking on successfully several times, but each time he had to pull the release lever and fly away because gusty winds made the plane swing so much that the trapeze damaged the tips of his plane's propeller. The experiments remained a work in progress, so customs clearance would have to proceed in the traditional manner until they had perfected the operation.

After breakfast, Margaret packed the rest of her things away, wrote her final postcards, and joined her new friend Emma Pannes at the observation window as they approached the city of Boston, which was still shrouded in clouds. Just as the clouds had lifted over the icebergs like the curtain on opening night at the opera, nature seemed to be helping the zeppelin show itself to its greatest advantage. In front of the city, the fog cover tore open once more and ships' horns saluted from Boston Harbor as the *Hindenburg* slid out of the mist and into view. Perhaps Margaret's infamous Puritan ancestors, who lay buried on a bluff overlooking the nearby Charles River, would have taken it as a sign of divine providence. (More likely, they would have considered the idea of man in flight akin to witchcraft and a great silver fish in the sky an apparition of the occult.) As she looked down, "great elation" washed over her. It remained gray and overcast, but she could see flowers, grass, and blooming apple trees and could hear the howls of dogs frightened by the unfamiliar sensation of the great silhouette of the airship passing over them from on high.

"It is ridiculous to feel so happy," Margaret said to Emma Pannes as she took in the sight of people below who had stopped their cars on the side of the road to look up. Her friend, who was every bit as delighted, thoroughly agreed.

The thrill of seeing the city below was infectious. Across the passenger lounge, Gertrud Adelt noticed that as soon as the clouds parted and the American coast came into view, "all conversations stopped." The passengers around her were suddenly like children, walking back and forth between the port and starboard windows, taking in the view from every vantage as the "shadow of the airship glided in the surf along the edge of the new continent."

As they sailed over the historic American city that had once served as the gateway between the old world and the new, Captain Lehmann, who was standing near Leonhard and Gertrud Adelt, found Frau Kleemann looking out the window with a wistful air. Leonhard assumed that she was thinking of her daughter, who lay recovering from surgery at her home in Andover, Massachusetts, just north of the city.

"Sorry I can't let you down here," Captain Lehmann told her sympathetically.

Her son-in-law was coming down to Newark to pick her up that evening and fly back to Boston with her by airplane, but to have passed so close to a child in need—a child of any age—and yet be so far out of reach produced a pang of longing only a parent could have known.

Herb Morrison and Charlie Nehlsen had spent the night in the American Airlines passenger lounge at Newark Metropolitan Airport. The *Hindenburg* was meant to have arrived in Lakehurst at dawn, but after additional delays due to headwinds over Newfoundland, their progress had slowed even further. With thunderstorms brewing over the Eastern Seaboard, it would still be hours before the zeppelin made its landing. From the research he had done to prepare for his broadcast, Morrison knew that even without the storms, it was best for the great zeppelins to depart and land at either dusk or dawn, when surface winds tended to be the calmest.

Morrison and Nehlsen had rested as well as they could on the relatively comfortable lounge seats, all the while keeping in touch with the airline's radiomen, who received the *Hindenburg*'s intermittent updates about its progress. In the morning, American Airlines finally received word that the *Hindenburg* was making its way south from New England. The pilots started up the engine on the waiting DC-3 to fly the two radiomen on the quick puddle jump south. As they took off, Charlie Nehlsen looked out the window and thought he could see the great airship far off in the distance, but surely it was just his imagination.

With only sixty-three miles separating Newark and Lakehurst, the airplane ferrying the two Chicagoans had barely reached the low-hanging clouds before starting its descent. Sweeping pine forests gave way to a great open clearing, and Morrison could see that the expansive field was covered in a sandy, grassy surface with nothing but a mooring mast standing in the middle a half mile between the edge of the trees and the buildings of the Naval Air Station. The top of the mooring mast, to which the zeppelin would be anchored during its brief stop, could rotate so that the airships could be wheeled around to adjust to prevailing wind conditions and thus needed a full 360 degrees of clearance. Ten years earlier, the mooring mast at Lakehurst had been the site of one of the more bizarre episodes in airship history. On August 25, 1927, the USS *Los Angeles* had been moored on the field when the wind suddenly reversed direction and a very cold draft of sea air caused the tail to rise straight up into the sky so that the airship was almost completely perpendicular to the ground, as if doing a headstand. Remarkably, the acrobatics caused almost no damage, and none of the twenty-five crew inside were hurt. Thanks to quick adjustments, they managed to bring the airship back down to an even keel. After that, the Lakehurst team installed a smaller "stub" mast to which an airship's stern would be affixed to prevent such an episode from occurring in the future.

The Naval Air Station at Lakehurst had been operating as the base of American military experimentation with lighter-than-air craft since 1921 when the navy took over what had been an army training facility during the war, but the land had served a military purpose even before that. Originally, this tract was owned by the Eddystone Ammunition Corporation, which had leased the grounds to the Imperial Russian Army during the early part of the Great War for use as a proving ground for munitions testing. "The story is told at Lakehurst," a local newspaper had reported in December 1915, "that the Russians say their defeat by the Germans this summer was caused by graft in the ordinance [*sic*] department, which resulted in their shrapnel and other shells manufactured in Russia, being loaded with sawdust instead of explosives; and that the men in charge of these inspections intend to see that they get the real thing this time." After the Russian Revolution broke out in 1917 and the new Bolshevik government began to target the aristocracy during the Red Terror, many of the Russian officers based at Lakehurst decided to stay and established a small Russian Orthodox enclave nearby.

Before their plane even touched down, Morrison could tell that the Naval Air Station was abuzz with energy in a prelude to a "great event." Charlie Nehlsen, an amateur photographer, was smart to have brought a camera along to take some personal snapshots. Spectators swarmed the airfield as navy personnel made last-minute preparations. There were almost one hundred naval officers and enlisted men in the landing crew, but the *Hindenburg* required over two hundred men to properly pull it down to the landing mast. Local men and high school boys supplemented the navy crew, the boys sometimes cutting school to earn one dollar's pay. Off in the distance towered hangar number 1, the massive structure that housed the USS *Los Angeles*, which was currently moored inside and was now relegated to testing and experiments. The hangar had been built more than fifteen years earlier, well before anyone had designed an airship as large as the *Hindenburg*, but the *Hindenburg* fit inside the cavernous space with about eighty feet of clearance on either end. In fact, the hangar was just wide enough to simultaneously accommodate both the *Hindenburg* and the *Los Angeles*, which could nestle in beside and below the giant zeppelin. When it was time to take the airships out, the hangar's massive doors, which ran on a rail system built into the ground, took a team of eight to twelve men an hour to open. Spark-resistant bricks covered the floor inside, and the windows of the structure were made of a special amber-tinted glass to keep the sun from raising the temperature in the hangar, so that the gas in the airships would not expand on a sunny day and make their tails lift up inside. Still, the space was so vast that a microclimate could develop, and clouds would form and release rain within the hangar.

Regardless of whether the atmospheric conditions would be right for such a phenomenon to occur inside the hangar that afternoon, it would be a wet day outside. Clouds hung over the landing field and it had been raining on and off, but the thousands of people who had arrived to see the *Hindenburg* land would not be deterred. Vendors had set up booths selling wrapped sandwiches, doughnuts, and coffee to the tourists, more of whom were arriving from the packed roads every minute. There were mothers with small children looking to distract their broods with an airship and a picnic, workers making the most of a local outing on a day off, and even a group of young men who had come from the pulmonary rehabilitation facility at St. Rita's House in nearby Lakewood looking for a diversion during treatment and recovery from long bouts of pneumonia. The zeppelin arrivals were especially popular with the many families of German heritage who lived in the New Jersey suburbs of New York and felt a sort of kinship with and pride in the magnificent zeppelin crews who traversed the ocean.

With the forecast showing on-and-off rain, Morrison and Nehlsen decided to set up their equipment in the office of the heavier-than-air hangar beside the massive hangar number 1. It was an ideal place to watch the landing. There was a clear view of the mooring mast through the window where Morrison could stand if it was raining. He could also string the microphone just outside to a sort of patio beside the building if it was dry. Better yet, it was the perfect location to catch passengers for an interview, as they would have to pass through the office into the next room, where customs officials had set up their operation. The office even had one of the few telephones in the vicinity, should they require it.

After Nehlsen finished connecting the recording equipment, they made a few test cuts on the sixteen-inch discs. Though more unwieldly to carry, sixteen-inch discs were preferable to the standard twelve-inch model, which recorded only seven to eight minutes per side. The sixteen-inch version allowed for fifteen minutes per side and thus gave Morrison more time to speak before Nehlsen had to interrupt him to change it.

Morrison spoke into the microphone as the needle cut into the spinning disc, and all seemed to be running smoothly until Nehlsen started to hear some cross-talk feedback on the transmitter. The base's radio connection at the field station had opened, and they were getting interference. Nehlsen ran around the office trying to find the best place to ground the equipment and filter the feedback, but then the field radio turned off and the cross talk stopped, so he could only guess at whether he had fixed the problem. Until the radio turned on again closer to the landing, they would have no way of knowing.

As expected, Morrison was the only radioman at Lakehurst that day, but there were a handful of newsreel crews from Pathé, Paramount, Movietone, and Hearst and a half dozen photographers, local newspaper reporters, and freelance "stringers" milling about. The newsreel men set up closer to the mooring mast with their cameras on top of their cars while the photographers roamed around near the office, smoking, drinking, telling stories, and generally complaining about the *Hindenburg*'s tardy arrival. Murray Becker, a twenty-eight-year-old photographer from the Associated Press, had taken a 5:00 a.m. ferry from the city to get there. This was his sixth time photographing the *Hindenburg*, and he was thoroughly bored and "all teed off" because of the wait.

With nothing to do but hang around until the airship appeared on the horizon, Morrison joined them as they lounged in the grass. One of the hardened news veterans handed him an extra flask of whiskey, welcoming him as a brother-in-arms to the boredom that defined a reporter's natural state of existence: waiting around for something to happen. Morrison appreciated the gesture and politely took the flask, but as he did not drink, he put it away in a pocket of his overcoat and settled in to wait.

As the clock struck 3:00 p.m. Eastern Daylight Time, the skyline of New York City "swam into view" before Margaret Mather as Emma Pannes pointed through the window and down to a bay off Long Island. Mrs. Pannes's house was just below, and she told Margaret that her son was somewhere on the road driving toward Lakehurst to pick up his parents that evening. As they passed over the pointed inlet of Little Neck Bay, Benny Spah, too, could almost make out his house. His wife, Vera, the three children, and Vera's sister, who was kind enough to lend a helping hand, were likely already at Lakehurst after having stopped for Mass for the Feast of the Ascension, a holy day of obligation signifying the date Catholics believe Jesus ascended into heaven, forty days after Easter Sunday. Seven hundred miles west in Chicago, Bert Dolan's wife, Mildred, had certainly begun her day in the same way at her parish church, Saint Mary of the Lake.

In a show of German efficiency, the zeppelin company liked to have everything well in hand in advance of landing. Hamburg-America Line's public relations office had already prepared an arrival notice listing the names, occupations, and national origins of passengers on board, including short biographies of anyone of note. Their records, however, were perhaps not quite as accurate as they imagined. In addition to including the names of several people who were not on board, they mistakenly wrote that Ira Nelson Morris, the former U.S. ambassador to Sweden, was one of the travelers, rather than his nephew, though the confusion was understandable.

The stewards served the passengers an early lunch so they could be free to take in the grand finale of their airborne sightseeing adventure. As they cruised over Brooklyn, they were just in time to catch a glimpse of America's pastime. Black clouds hung in the distance, but the rain had stopped before the Brooklyn Dodgers took the field against the first-place Pittsburgh Pirates. By the time the *Hindenburg* flew over Ebbets Field, Dodgers pitcher Van Lingle Mungo had no-hit the Pirates through the top of the fifth inning. Perhaps Dodger fans took the appearance of the airship as a sign of continued good fortune during a sterling game in an otherwise lackluster season.

Down in the control gondola, Captain Pruss asked the radio operator on duty to request an update from Lakehurst about the weather, especially a passing storm front near the landing field. The last communication they had received from Commander Rosendahl, chief of the Naval Air Station, was that his crew would be ready to land them at 5:00 p.m., once the weather improved and he could get enough men coming from work and school to fill out the crew. Zeppelins were capable of landing safely during thunderstorms and had on many occasions, but it was generally not advisable to valve gas—an essential part of landing—while flying through storm clouds, given the potential for an equalizing spark to ignite the gas between the airship and the clouds. The differences in the air temperature that storm fronts produced high above versus closer to the ground were also difficult to navigate, as temperature changes made gas expand and contract, and the gas needed time for its temperature to equalize with that of the surrounding air. Furthermore, coordination with the ground crew was essential. It was much more difficult for the crew to pull the ship down in muddy, wet conditions, especially when many of the ground crew were less-experienced locals. As he waited out the storm front to the south, Pruss had more than enough time to take his passengers on a tour over New York City. If the clouds in the distance did not clear soon, he might need to keep the passengers, who would by then be anxious to get on with their homeward journeys, occupied for another hour or two.

As Pruss swooped them northward along the island of Manhattan, tracking the East River all the way up to the Bronx before cutting back south over Harlem and down Fifth Avenue to Central Park, Werner Franz hurried through his chores in the mess so he could catch his first glimpse of New York City. His trial flights at the end of 1936 had all been to Brazil. For months he had been saving up pocket money in hopes of spending half a day in New York City and seeing a film in an American cinema. The newest Fred Astaire and Ginger Rogers feature, *Shall We Dance*, with music by brothers George and Ira Gershwin, was due out the next day. But with the *Hindenburg* running behind schedule, his first trip into the city would have to wait.

Looking down, he noted that the "sidewalks were swarming with people." He saw cars snaking among buses, trams, and elevated train lines, and every so often he caught a glimpse of "a subway coming out of the earth." The cacophony of the world below made for a stark contrast with the silence of the zeppelin as it sailed smoothly through the air, the hum of its engines barely perceptible. Looking down from above New York City, the inspiration for George Gershwin's Jazz Age magnum opus "Rhapsody in Blue" would have been readily apparent to the musically inclined like Captain Lehmann. The idea for the composition had come to Gershwin while on a train as it rushed in a clatter from New York to Boston, "with its steely rhythms, its rattle-ty-bang," the composer recalled, describing it as "a sort of musical kaleidoscope of America, of our vast melting pot, of our unduplicated national pep, of our metropolitan madness." The sounds of the urban symphony might have made a good background accompaniment for Lehmann had the aluminum piano still been on board in the lounge.

As the airship reached Midtown, the sun came out from behind the clouds, striking the *Hindenburg*'s glistening silver skin and illuminating the giant red-and-black flag on its tail. On the ground, the sun hit the steel and glass of skyscrapers, making them resemble glinting "needles" to Gertrud Adelt and "a board full of nails" to her husband, with the razor-sharp Empire State Building preeminent among them. Chicago may have been the birthplace of the steel-framed skyscraper, but New York had far surpassed what the Midwestern city had thus far offered. The Pittsfield Building, where Bert Dolan worked, was built in 1927 and stood 551 feet and thirty-eight stories high. For several years, it was the tallest building in Chicago. Meanwhile, the Empire State Building, built just four years later, was over twice as tall. Completed in 1931, the structure surged 102 stories into the air, replacing the Chrysler Building as the tallest in New York City. Down below on the famous eighty-sixth-floor observation deck Leonhard Adelt could see amateur photographers snapping pictures of them as they passed overhead, clearing NBC's antenna tower on top of the building with ease.

When laying plans for the Empire State Building in 1929, its investors expressed aspirations, likely just as a publicity stunt, to have a mooring mast on the very top so that airships could anchor themselves to the skyscraper. The idea was that passengers would disembark down a gangplank, descend on an elevator, and be on the ground in the heart of New York City in a mere seven minutes. At the time, Dr. Eckener had dismissed the idea as completely unworkable, given the dozens of men that landing crews required to pull airships down for a safe landing. There was also no way there would be sufficient stability in such gusty conditions that high up for passengers to exit via gangplank. In 1930, as construction was underway on the Empire State Building, a doctored photograph circulated among the press showing a U.S. Navy airship supposedly docked to a mooring mast on top of the sleek new skyscraper, leading many to think such landings had actually occurred. The following year, a small, privately owned dirigible did dock for three short minutes in a brisk wind while traffic below jammed as commuters stopped to crane their necks and look at the spectacle above. A Goodyear Blimp similarly tried to dock but failed, and soon after that, NBC began using the tower as a broadcast antenna, which brought an end to the far-fetched idea.

After soaring over Midtown, Captain Pruss steered the airship down to the Battery and over New York Harbor, where Gertrud could hear the "voice of the ports" calling up to them as ships welcomed the great German visitor to America, just like the chorus of ships' horns in Boston. In the distance, young Werner Franz could see the Statue of Liberty rising up from her pedestal with her torch over three hundred feet in the sky. From his vantage in the passenger lounge, Leonhard Adelt thought the copper-and-steel lady looked as delicate as a porcelain figure. From the slanting plexiglass window of the airship, the vastness of New York City appeared in delicate miniature. "The viaducts and highways were in relief as in a model," Leonhard observed, finally impressed with something on this voyage, "and in a filigree of steel the bridges swung across the rivers."

Finally, after about an hour spent traversing the sky above Manhattan, the captain turned back north, sailing over the city's west side. With a final flourish of fanfare, Pruss took them across Times Square and over the Upper West Side, where a group of fourteen-year-old boys playing basketball on the roof of their school suddenly froze as a massive dark shadow blocked out the sun. The airship then turned toward New Jersey, the swastikas on its tail visible to New Yorkers for miles around as the *Hindenburg* bade the city farewell.

CHAPTER 24

Lakehurst, New Jersey, USA: May 6, 1937

The road to Lakehurst was packed with cars as locals leaving work realized they still had an opportunity to see the *Hindenburg* land, now that it had been delayed a full twelve hours. As another curtain of rain swept through the Lakehurst area, Commander Rosendahl had recalled his ground crew and radioed Max Pruss, "Conditions still unsettled recommend delay landing until further word from Station." Pruss confirmed that they would wait until the weather improved and sailed straight over the Naval Air Station and out to the New Jersey shoreline.

As Dr. Eckener had maintained since writing his manual for airship crews back in 1919, it was "not necessary to execute 'fancy' landings, perhaps in daring fashion, but rather the main point is to bring the fragile ship safely and unharmed to the ground. A good normal landing is a smooth landing with the trail rope, not a show-off landing which, with the giant modern ships, results all too often in a sporting event of a decidedly risky nature." Those observing zeppelin landings at Lakehurst were accustomed to seeing the *Hindenburg* make a long, low-altitude approach where the airship would valve off gas gradually and settle gently into the hands of the ground crew, who would grab hold of the landing ropes and walk the airship to the mooring mast. In some conditions, it was better to make a high approach and a "flying mooring," with a closer, rapid descent with more active use of the airship's elevators, gas valves, and reversing of engines as a braking mechanism, which could bring an airship traveling as much as thirty-three miles per hour to a halt in about one thousand feet. Neither approach was necessarily better, so long as attention to safety remained paramount at all times.

While he cruised along the New Jersey coast, Max Pruss used the delay to send a cable from the radio room back to Germany to the Naval League, which planned to unveil a memorial the next day to those lost on German naval zeppelins shot down during the Great War. Pruss, who had been a young officer and elevator man on zeppelins during the war, had known and admired many of those comrades who had been lost. "The captain and crew of the *Hindenburg* send you best wishes in memory of our fallen heroes," he wired. Such a message and the novelty of its being sent just before the *Hindenburg* completed its first transatlantic flight of the year would no doubt be appreciated.

The revised landing time had now come and gone, and the giant airship hangar at Lakehurst had faded into the distance. Down below, Werner Franz could see boys on the beach racing their bicycles as fast as they could to keep up with the zeppelin. Curious about the detour, the cabin boy set aside the dishes he was wiping and popped his head into the kitchen to ask the cooks why they had not landed yet.

"It must have been bad weather over the field," one responded. "We have time, Pruss is very cautious, and Lehmann is also on board."

Franz paid a thought to Lehmann, who earlier that day had given him a friendly nod of thanks when he served the famed captain his coffee.

Up in the passenger lounge, Leonhard Adelt had been looking down out the window as they had flown over Lakehurst, taking in the crowds that had gathered like "a pack of hungry wolves." He knew his brothers were somewhere down there waiting for him. He had not seen them in thirty years. As Gertrud observed, the nearby "line of thunderstorms" that "leaned over the scrub forests" surrounding the airfield clearly explained why they had sailed away. After all those years, what was an hour or two more to wait for Leonhard's family reunion? Beside her husband, Gertrud took in the suburbs of New Jersey with "semicircular yellow gravel driveways" carved out in front of "white-painted bungalows [that] shone with dazzling cleanliness." These stood in stark contrast to the "desolate terrain" of the landing field she had briefly seen, which she thought looked akin to a "steppe-like expanse of the alluvial plain," where sediment from river runoff creates arid soil in which grasses struggle to take root.

With lunch now hours in the past, stewards passed out sandwiches on silver trays as a handful of small press planes buzzed along outside taking pictures of the airship. One of the stewards offered his tray to Margaret Mather. At first, she refused, thinking she would be having dinner soon enough, as they had just passed over the landing field, but after the steward told her it could be another hour or two before they were on the ground, she changed her mind. Margaret and Emma Pannes had been looking at the hangar through the driving rain. When Margaret turned back to the window from the sandwich tray, she could no longer see it and playfully chided her friend for not having kept an eye on it. They flew over sparse woods, where a startled deer jumped out of the trees, much like the dogs outside Boston caught unawares by the shadow of the airship hanging overhead in the lowering light.

As they rode along the New Jersey coast, they passed near Sea Girt, where Margaret's father once wheeled her in a pram along the shore. In the distance, Margaret saw "black and ominous" clouds. An occasional bolt of lightning flashed about sixty miles to the south.

"Not at all dangerous," she heard someone say. "A Zeppelin can cruise about indefinitely above the storms. It is not like a plane, which has to come down for fuel." Once, in November 1935, the *Graf Zeppelin* had been transporting mail between the British colony of Gambia in West Africa and Brazil when a communist revolt broke out in the Brazilian city of Recife, making it unsafe to land. The *Graf Zeppelin* had to fly along the South American coast for three days until the revolt was quelled, nearly claiming the record for the world's longest flight—almost 119 hours, set by the *Dixmude* in 1923—in the process.

If others were becoming irritable or anxious about the delay, Margaret was not one of them. Sailing along the shore and out over the ocean made her "foolish with happiness," just as she had felt when she first spied the *Hindenburg* in Frankfurt three days earlier. She was enjoying herself so much that she decided she "didn't really care how long this cruising lasted."

"How d'you do, everyone? We're greeting you now from the naval air base in Lakehurst, New Jersey, from which we are going to bring you a description of the landing of the mammoth airship *Hindenburg*, which was due here in America this morning at dawn, completing the first transatlantic crossing of the 1937 season," Herb Morrison spoke into the microphone, beginning his recorded broadcast. It was now just after 7:00 p.m. To the crowd's delight, the mighty zeppelin had returned in the sky just beyond the Naval Air Station. It seemed that this time it would indeed be landing. In a resonant baritone voice, Morrison recited the introductory script he had jotted down en route, keeping his own excitement at bay as he projected in a professional tone.

Though the darkest clouds had cleared, a light rain had started up again, so the two radiomen had retreated back inside, where Morrison was watching for the inbound airship through the office window. "Charlie Nehlsen, one of our WLS engineers, is here at my side working the controls," Morrison told listeners, grateful for Nehlsen's ability to troubleshoot the new equipment at the last minute. Just before they started the recording, Nehlsen had had to scramble to rearrange their equipment once more when customs officials descended upon them and began to set up in the office.

"We both flew down from Chicago yesterday afternoon aboard one of the giant new twenty-one-seat passenger Flagships of American Airlines," Morrison continued, making sure to emphasize all the perks that travel with their generous sponsor had to offer. "It took us only three hours, fifty-five minutes to fly nonstop from Chicago to New York. When we landed at Newark, we found another Flagship of American Airlines waiting to take us to Lakehurst with our equipment when we were ready to go. And incidentally," Morrison emphasized, delivering the crucial piece of information that formed the entire basis for his sponsor's desire to make this broadcast in the first place, "American Airlines is the only airline in the United States which makes connections with the *Hindenburg*."

Morrison then went into the background research he had been compiling since the idea for the broadcast had come about. It was just one year ago to the day that the *Hindenburg* had commenced its inaugural transatlantic journey from Germany to the United States. This flight, he explained, had departed from Frankfurt two and a half days earlier but had encountered headwinds that slowed the zeppelin's progress. He and Nehlsen had been able to track its westward journey thanks to the American Airlines team at Newark, he added, once again plugging the sponsor and the very comfortable seats in the airport lounge. Despite the rain, he said as the needle carved a groove into the green acetate disc, "winds and weather conditions have proven to be most satisfactory. In other words, nothing has been left to chance."

The *Hindenburg*'s approach to the mooring mast took a bit longer than he expected, so he found himself ad-libbing to eat up extra time, praising the Naval Air Station and its crew and describing the mooring mast's ability to swing with the airship in any direction to adjust for the wind. At last, someone gave him a signal that the zeppelin was starting its final maneuvers.

"Now, we've been told that the airship is going to make an attempted landing in the rain," he explained, "and if that is the case, we're going to have a mighty fine description of it for you." From where he stood, he said, he could see the passenger quarters in the *Hindenburg*'s keel, just about a third of the way down the airship from the nose. There were the observation windows, slanted to give the passengers a fine view of the ground below. "And no doubt," he said, speaking excitedly as the giant zeppelin flew overhead, the passengers on board were "looking down at the great mass of humanity assembled here in the field. Thousands of people have come out to witness the landing of this great airship."

The heavier rain had let up so that just a fine mist was falling. "I'm going to step out here and cover it from the outside," he narrated, signaling to Nehlsen that he wanted to string the microphone out the door, where he could get a better view, hopefully without black umbrellas and children propped on shoulders blocking him. "As I move out, we'll just stand by a second." Nehlsen lifted the needle momentarily as Morrison headed out the door.

The *Hindenburg* had flown as far south as the mouth of the Delaware River when Captain Pruss received a message from the Naval Air Station at 6:23 p.m.: "Recommend landing now." He ordered the crew to turn around and set course for Lakehurst. At 7:10 p.m., just as they were approaching the Naval Air Station, the base confirmed with a second radio message: "Conditions definitely improved recommend earliest possible landing."

In the passenger lounge, Leonhard Adelt watched as the zeppelin, "with lowered nose and high speed . . . pushed through a last rain curtain" that separated them from the landing field. It was actually the first time they had flown directly through falling rain that evening, and it left a sprinkling of precipitation on the airship's silver skin, which was already coated with a layer of salt from evaporated seawater. It was getting on toward dusk, and the light was low as the giant hangar once again came squarely into view. Beside her husband, Gertrud noticed how the "encroaching darkness of the evening combined with the shadow of murmuring clouds to form a pale twilight." There was a certain beauty to a dusky landing with the western sunset shrouded in receding clouds. Surely landing at dawn would have been just as beautiful, but there was an elegiac poignancy to concluding a journey at day's end.

Nearby, stewards were bringing out the last of the luggage and setting up a table for customs officials to come on board and ensure all passports were in order. The chief steward, Heinrich Kubis, settled the last of the passenger bills, including Peter Belin's bill for martinis, stamps, and a telegram he had sent to Princeton, as well as what was Bert Dolan's undoubtedly rather large bar tab, if the amount of time he and Nelson Morris had spent in the smoking lounge was any indication. Nearby, British passenger George Grant hastily finished typing up the report he was meant to have been writing for DZR. The result was too lacking in either detail or concrete recommendations for improvements to be of much use to his employer. He concluded with what DZR surely already believed: "AIR TRAVEL has certainly come to stay and the 'HINDENBURG' is likely to go down to posterity as a fore-runner of what may eventually become REGULAR WORLD WIDE TRAVEL by AIRSHIP. Not even the most timid or nervous person need have any qualms about Airship Travel. . . . MOTTO: TRAVEL by AIRSHIP and avoid SEA SICKNESS."

Downstairs on B deck, Werner Franz was putting the last of the clean dishes away in the cupboard while his friend and supervisor, Wilhelm Balla, passed the bar on his way up to the dining room to watch the landing. The bar steward, Max Schulze, was still tidying up. Balla asked if he wanted to come and watch, but he still had work to do and declined. As Balla made his way to A deck, he also passed the stewardess, Emilie Imhof, and inquired whether she wanted to come and see, especially as this was her first landing. She also declined, as she had to finish assisting Frau Kleemann with last-minute odds and ends in her stateroom.

Balla joined the group in the dining room on the port side behind the three Doehner children, who were standing with their mother looking out the open window as the airship began to swoop low over the field, the Olympic rings and red script lettering proclaiming the name of the zeppelin for all to see. Herr Doehner crossed to the starboard windows to take in the view from the other side. Nearby, Benny Spah was also in the cluster of about twenty passengers and crew peering out promenade windows along the dining room. He stood beside Heinrich Kubis, binoculars around his neck, camera and passport in hand, joking and exchanging addresses. He had just said goodbye to Captain Lehmann, who had left his friends the Adelts on A deck to supervise the landing from the control gondola, unable to keep himself from his traditional position. Old habits were hard to break. Benny told Lehmann he would look him up when he was next performing in Germany. They parted with smiles.

Benny put his camera's viewfinder back up to his eye and took some footage of the ground below, where the landing crew were running forward to their positions, the uniformed sailors scurrying across the wet ground like a swarm of white ants. Benny looked out the window for his family. In the distance, he saw a new blue Ford station wagon with windows so covered in finger smudges they were visible all the way from the airship. "It must be Vera and the children," he thought to himself, and pointed his camera in that direction.

Farther along the dining room windows were Margaret Mather, Emma

Pannes, and Peter Belin. Earlier that afternoon, as they were flying along the coast between Providence and New London, the proud young Yale man had told Margaret how interested he was to be flying near his alma mater. It was that glorious time in the school year when the weather finally turned warm but final exams had yet to start, and for about a week, students could lounge on one of Yale's quads casually throwing upside-down pie tins from the nearby Bridgeport Frisbie Pie Company to one another. Somewhere down there, his cousin Gaspard d'Andelot Belin, a name practically drowning under the weight of family history, was still an undergraduate and ostensibly hard at work as an editor of the *Yale Daily News*.

Emma Pannes told Margaret she was going down to fetch her coat from her cabin, leaving Margaret, who was already wearing hers, to chat with the young man. Like Benny Spah, he liked to experiment with his camera, and he told Margaret he had taken eighty snapshots during the trip. The roll of film was in his pocket, along with the map where he had traced their route over the last two and a half days. Down in the throngs of people below were his parents, who had come north from Washington and had driven over with a family friend from Princeton to retrieve him.

Margaret felt the airship make a quick turn and listened to a faint change of sound from the engines. She glanced over at Belin, a licensed pilot, for reassurance that the mysterious noises were nothing out of the ordinary.

It was now 7:15 p.m., and Max Pruss gave the order to begin the *Hindenburg*'s final approach. The conditions were right for a dynamic, high landing. As Pruss, Lehmann, and Commander Rosendahl had discussed, one of their objectives that year was to test both landing styles and determine whether one or the other was definitively superior or if there was an ideal middle ground between them.

With Pruss manning the engines and the rudder, the first officer, Captain Albert Sammt, was in charge of navigation and adjusting the altitude through a combination of maneuvering the elevators, releasing ballast, and valving gas. They brought the *Hindenburg* up from the south and passed over the hangar, the zeppelin's skin glistening after the light shower. Then they turned and banked out to the west to test the wind conditions. Slowing the engines to half power, Pruss and Sammt swung the airship around in a tight turn to reorient the zeppelin, with the bow now facing toward the mooring mast. Pruss cut the back motors and reversed them to slow the airship's speed as it began to nose forward toward the middle of the field.

With the zeppelin out beyond the buildings at the western end of the airfield, Sammt checked the trim. They were about seventy meters above the ground and needed to come down. He gave the order to valve gas across the whole airship for about twenty seconds to reduce their elevation to sixty meters.

At the elevator controls, navigator Eduard Boëtius noticed the ship was not quite in trim, meaning the bow and the stern were not balanced on the same plane. The tail was a little heavy, so Sammt ordered another fifteen seconds' worth of gas to be valved from the five cells closest to the nose while they simultaneously released about three hundred kilograms of ballast aft. As they dropped ballast water, they sailed right over the base's bachelor officers' quarters, drenching a steward who was standing out front in the process. Still, they were somewhat heavy in the tail, so Sammt repeated the order to release gas and ballast, followed by an additional round of five seconds' worth of gas from the forward cells. Even after all this, the trim was still a bit off and a little wind had picked up, so Sammt ordered six of the crew positioned in the middle of the airship to move forward toward the nose to manually shift their weight.

Now they were practically over the landing crew. Off to the edge of the sandy field, spectators waved handkerchiefs and shouted with excitement. In just minutes, the passengers would emerge from inside. As Pruss cut the engines, the airship came to a standstill, save for a light breeze pushing it from the port side.

Looking down out the window, Leonhard Adelt watched as the Manila hemp landing ropes were tossed out from the airship's bow. They unfurled down to the ground crew below like the proboscises of giant butterflies, just as he had described in a scene from his imagination in his book *Der Flieger* many years ago. They hit the ground with a thud, sending a plume of dust into the humid air on impact.

Nelson Morris and Bert Dolan were standing together at the forward window of the writing room as light rain misted the outside of the plexiglass. It was now 7:21 p.m. They were going to miss the 8:00 p.m. American Airlines flight from Newark to Chicago, but assuming customs did not take hours, they could catch the 1:00 a.m. "Night Owl" flight on one of the airline's "Skysleepers," with seats that converted to Pullman car–style sleeping berths. That would have them home just before 6:00 a.m. Looking down, they saw the ground crew quickly catch hold of one of the forward landing ropes while the other flapped momentarily. The ropes, fourteen centimeters in circumference, were heavy, thick, and braided, and they were difficult to grab as the airship moved slightly in the wind. Nelson was a bit surprised by the landing, which felt different from those he thought he remembered from his flights on the *Graf Zeppelin* with Dr. Eckener at the helm. If his memory served, they had approached much more rapidly this time, and from a higher position and a much shorter distance. They had also made a sharp turn at the end to swing off to the side of the mooring mast, rather than flying low and straight directly toward it. True, it was a much larger airship this time, and they were landing in different weather conditions, but still, he noticed.

Down in the control gondola, the bubble in the inclinometer in front of navigator Boëtius was still slightly off-center. Even after twice releasing ballast in the tail section, valving the gas in the nose three separate times, and redistributing a half dozen of the crew, the *Hindenburg* was still ever so slightly heavy in the tail.

"Well, here it comes, ladies and gentlemen," Herb Morrison narrated as the recording rolled. "We're out now, outside of the hangar, and what a great sight. It's a thrilling one. It's a marvelous sight." Thank goodness he had moved outside, even with the persistent rain. Seeing the *Hindenburg* right there down the field produced a feeling unlike any other. In its scale, proportion, and sheer majesty, there was nothing to which it could possibly compare. "It's coming down out of the sky pointed directly toward us and toward the mooring mast," he described as it drifted closer to the A-shaped structure where the navy men waited on top to winch it in. "The mighty diesel motors just roared, the propellers biting into the air and throwing it back into a gale-like whirlpool. No wonder this great floating palace can travel through the air at such a speed with these powerful motors behind."

Out to the west, the clouds parted briefly, allowing a late ray of sun to peek through just before it sank over the horizon. The effect was spectacular. "The sun is striking the windows of the observation deck on the eastward side and sparkling like glittering jewels on a background of black velvet," he illustrated. "Every now and then, the propellers are caught in the rays of the sun." The setting sun reflected off the polished blades whirring in the engines, creating little flecks of gold.

There was an older woman standing just to Morrison's left watching the approaching airship intently. Downfield, men were rushing to adjust their final positions to catch the *Hindenburg*'s mooring ropes as they tumbled down.

The moment had finally come, said Morrison, "the moment we have waited for so long. The ship is riding majestically, toward us like some great feather, riding as though it were mighty, mighty proud of the place it's playing in the world's aviation."

Orders were shouted to the crew, and passengers at the windows looked down to catch a final glimpse of the mooring mast before it was obscured by the rest of the airship. A little cross talk filtered across the radio frequency just before Morrison remembered to mention once more that the American Airlines Flagships were ready and waiting to "race into all points in the United States" as soon as the airship moored and the passengers disembarked. There were a number of important persons aboard, he continued, "and no doubt the new commander, Captain Max Pruss, is thrilled, too, for this is his great moment, the first time he's commanded the *Hindenburg*." On this point, Morrison had his facts slightly mixed up.

Pruss had commanded the *Hindenburg* on several transatlantic flights to both North and South America in 1936. Pruss was no novice, and on many previous flights, Morrison correctly stated, Pruss had "acted as the chief officer under Captain Lehmann."

"It's practically standing still now," Morrison said, a tremor of anticipation in his voice, as he watched as the crew on board threw ropes out of the nose. "It has been taken ahold of down on the field by a number of men. It's starting to rain again—the rain had, uh, slacked up a little bit. They backed the motors of the ship for just—holding it, just enough to keep it from—"

In a split second, before his eyes could properly connect with his brain, a collective primal shriek rang out across the airfield.

"It burst into flames!"

CHAPTER 25

Lakehurst, New Jersey, USA: May 6, 1937

Along the windows of the lounge, Gertrud and Leonhard Adelt were enjoying the momentary silence as the engines shut off for the last time and the world around them was washed in a "remarkable stillness" as they hung almost motionless in the air. For an instant, no commands were shouted, no calls went down to the ground crew. It felt to Leonhard as if "the whole world was holding its breath." Just then, Gertrud heard a noise, like a "faint little bang" that "emerged out of the silence." To her, it sounded like "someone hitting an inflated bag." Leonhard heard it too, but to him, it was not even that jarring, "no louder than the sound of a beer bottle being opened."

At the same instant, others around them heard what sounded like a pop or a muffled report. Depending on where they were standing, some of the passengers and crew also felt a momentary vibration. To Nelson Morris in the writing room, it was a bit louder, more like the volley of a rifle. On the port side, Margaret Mather heard a "dull muffled sound." Her eyes again quickly darted toward Peter Belin. If she was seeking reassurance after another odd sound, his expression certainly did not provide it. "A look of incredulous consternation" had clouded his face.

Down in the crew's mess on B deck, the impact of this unusual noise was slightly more severe. Werner Franz both heard and felt a "dull thud," which knocked him against the cupboard, making the dishes he had just put away start to sway. He shot his hands out, prepared to catch the cups and plates now teetering precariously.

Closer to the bow in the control gondola, the sound had been almost imperceptible. Captain Lehmann was standing at the window with Captains Sammt and Pruss, their work now complete as they waited for the ground crew to finish pulling them down, when the three men felt a small jolt. They looked at each other quizzically. "What could that be? Maybe a tether broke?" Nearby, one of the other captains, Anton Wittemann, had a similar thought and asked whether a rope had broken. But another officer shouted that no, as far as he could see, the ropes were intact.

Sammt looked out the window toward the giant hangar and its partially glazed doors. In the panes, he thought he saw something reflected, but before he could take a good look, the airship abruptly lurched.

Upstairs, Leonhard Adelt noticed something strange. The light outside took on a "delicate rose glow, as though the sun were about to rise," despite it being nearly half past seven. Just then, there was a terrific movement. The floor beneath them had "risen steeply" and all of the furniture in the lounge—aluminum chairs, tables topped with flower-filled vases—began to slide uncontrollably across the floor. "Suddenly we weren't standing at the window anymore," Gertrud realized with alarm.

Across B deck, Margaret Mather felt the floor lurch out from under her, and she was "hurled a distance of fifteen or twenty feet" and slammed into a wall. An aluminum bench crashed into her, followed by several large German men who had been thrown off their feet after her like puppets on strings whose master had grown tired of them and cast them into the corner. Their weight crushed her between the bench and the wall, the impact suffocating. The collision knocked the wind out of her and she gasped for air as the ground continued to pitch upward, the force of gravity compressing the weight against her. Nearby, Wilhelm Balla and everyone else around him were suddenly "thrown together like rubber balls," bouncing across the room and into one another with no control over their direction. Somehow, in the writing room, Nelson Morris and Bert Dolan managed to remain upright by grabbing hold of a post beside the window as the floor in front of them swelled up and chairs, books, and magazines went crashing and sliding around them until they ran into a fixed object.

Gertrud had landed in a crushed and tangled heap of arms and legs of both aluminum furniture and other passengers thrown against the back wall of the lounge, which was now practically horizontal, as if it had become the floor. From within the pile of bodies, she was able to pick her head up just enough to look out the window, where the odd, sunrise-like light her husband had seen now "bloomed" in a "yellow-red glow" outside. Even in her haze of confusion, it took Gertrud just seconds to realize: "Fire!"

It burst into flames! It burst into flames and it's falling! It's crashing!" Herb Morrison shouted as the *Hindenburg*, which had been standing still before him just a moment ago, was suddenly engulfed in fire. To some on the ground, it looked as if, for a moment, a tiny light had appeared on the *Hindenburg*'s cover just in front of the tail, like the flame from a paper match smoldering at a distance. Almost instantaneously, a neon glow ran along the nearby riblike girders. Then a burst of light appeared, which erupted into a giant inferno near the airship's tail as the crowd around Morrison let out a terrified scream. Before anyone could register what they had just seen, the entire tail section of the zeppelin was consumed in a fireball spitting tongues of flames up into the sky as if the *Hindenburg* were made of flash paper.

"Watch it, watch it—get out of the way, get out of the way!" Morrison yelled as a crush of people from downfield surged toward him, racing for their lives as the mushrooming fire reflected in his eyes. Vast portions of the cover seemed to have evaporated, leaving the *Hindenburg*'s skeleton momentarily silhouetted against the fire's searing light.

"Get this, Charlie! Get this, Charlie!" he yelled back to his sound engineer. The noise of the crowd screaming cut into the grooves of the disc as background to his own shouts, the massive throng panicking at the unbelievable sight.

Flames shot out from the spine of the silver giant as an explosion sounded. It was one or more of the main gas cells bursting. The thud of sound that hit the needle of the recorder on the turntable was so percussive that the needle jumped and overcut, scratching the record. Dust from the whitewash of the office ceiling rained down on the recording equipment as the building shook in its foundations. Charlie Nehlsen threw his body over the turntable to shield the spinning disc from falling debris. Working to clear the dust without stopping the recording, he prayed that the scratch had not irreparably damaged the record. He signaled back to Morrison that the equipment was okay, not missing a second of sound as the size of the fire grew. The flames roared louder and louder as they swallowed more hydrogen and more oxygen with every passing second.

For a brief moment, the airship hung so still and so steady in the air that it was likely no one on board or the crew directly below them on the ground even realized for a number of crucial seconds that it was on fire at all. They had no way to see what was happening on top of the stern section. In those seconds, the flames had raced fore and aft, eating the hydrogen gas and the doped cotton cover, leaving more of the zeppelin's skeletal frame completely exposed. Morrison stared in horror at the flames, which changed from a reddish color to a stomach-turning shade of pale yellow, as thousands and thousands of cubic feet of hydrogen caught fire at an exponential rate. Over the rapidly building roar of gas igniting, he heard a "terrific swish like compressed air being set free," followed by another muffled explosion as the flames reached the next set of gas cells, and then the next and the next, running a relay through the airship. From the rate at which the fire grew, it was as if a portal had opened between earth and Dante's seventh circle of hell and the infernal river Phlegethon was pouring out, its rapids boiling with fire to swallow up the defiant, demonic swastika that had been emblazoned on the *Hindenburg* to herald

Nazi Germany's arrival over the horizon. The rabid yellow flames devoured the black hooked cross on its bloodred field in an instant, leaving the image of the inferno seared over its previous form in the minds of everyone who looked upon it.

For what seemed like an age but was only a moment, the *Hindenburg* remained suspended, hanging just where it had stopped when the ground crew took the ropes in hand. While the fire engulfed the entire stern half of the airship, the midsection to the nose briefly remained untouched. But then the zeppelin's back suddenly broke and the enormous frame gave a swift jolt upward so that it was suspended at a forty-five-degree angle to the ground. The stern began to crumble apart and drag the zeppelin down, leaving a smear of fiery debris in the night sky resembling the trail of light in a time-lapse photograph. Fireworks seemed to explode from the stern, pitching the bow into the air and littering the sky like a pumpkin shot to smithereens.

"It's crashing—and it's crashing, it's crashing—terrible—" Morrison hollered into the microphone above the roar of sound, not quite sure what he was saying and barely able to find any words at all to describe the oblong fireball that towered and spread a thousand feet above the ground and across the sky. It was almost as if a spectral airship made of burning gas were hanging directly above its corporeal sister.

"Oh my—get out of the way, please!" he begged as people ran in front of him while he shouted, "It's burning, bursting into flames, and it's falling!" With all the gas instantly released from the cells lining the tail section, the bow was now significantly lighter than the stern. The still-inflated gas cells in the bow drove the nose up, up into the clouds as the flames raced toward the heavens like a chimney on fire. On the ground, the men from the landing crew sprinted away from the blaze above them in every direction as fire ripped straight up the chimney and out of the zeppelin's nose, spitting a yellow dragon's tongue straight into the sky.

"It's burning, bursting into flames and it's falling on the mooring mast and all the folks between the fence!" Morrison cried, fearing that spectators and crew had been caught beneath the flaming debris that had begun to drop. "This is the"—his voice caught—"one of the worst catastrophes in the world, ohhh! Four, five hundred feet into the sky." The frame of the tail now dragged the entire airship down toward the ground, the whole eight hundred feet of the *Hindenburg* ablaze as it collapsed upon itself.

"It's a terrific crash, ladies and gentlemen, there's smoke and there's flames, now, and the frame is crashing to the ground, not quite to the mooring mast. Oh, the humanity, and all the passengers—"

Morrison's voice broke as he gaped at the hellscape before him. The sentences coming out of this mouth were pure instinct, shouted off the top of his head and straight from the heart. While he searched for the right words, the black and twisted tail smashed directly into the sandy field. The rest of the zeppelin's stern crumpled around it in a vast pool of fire. Its nose remained pitched high above the ground, surely pinning anyone inside who was still alive against the walls that confined them, until the great airship bent at the waist, the nose now settling back toward horizontal. As the bow of the *Hindenburg* finally tilted down toward the field, several black silhouettes fell from the flames as the smoke billowed up in a great black-and-yellow plume, the aluminum-doped cover around the belly just forward of the passenger quarters the last to burn. And as the nose finally hit the field, the fire devoured those red, hooked letters that had proudly spelled out the name "Hindenburg," one by one.

The gas in the tail section had already entirely burned out by the time the nose hit the ground, and Morrison paused long enough to listen. The air feeding the flames seemed to have been sucked entirely inside the burning wreckage like a vacuum, and he was shocked at how little sound there was compared with a moment before. Where he stood, it was nearly silent now, like the silence of the zeppelin in flight. When the frame of the bow finally collapsed to the ground, it did not crash but rather settled, rising up once before its mass of twisted girders buckled and crumpled, and it gave out a sigh as it sank onto the field in its final repose. Somehow, barely more than half a minute had elapsed since the moment that the first flash had appeared. In just thirty-four seconds, the eight-hundred-foot-long pride of Germany that had traversed thousands of miles over oceans and mountains had been felled, its seven million cubic feet of hydrogen eaten alive. In the time it took to sing "Take Me Out to the Ballgame," this marvel of engineering—the great silver machine that seemed to embody the iconography of the future—had been reduced to a smoking, charred pile of rubble.

Columns of black smoke from the engines' diesel fuel towered into the night sky. Morrison choked on both tears and the char in the air, made thicker by a slight mist that continued to fall. "I—I can't talk, ladies and gentlemen, honest," he gulped. "It's just laying there a massive smoking wreckage, and everybody can hardly breathe and talk."

Since he had begun his broadcast, the older woman to his left had remained at his side. Now her knees gave out and she swayed. Morrison instinctively reached out to catch her as she fainted, quickly switching his microphone from his left hand to his right to grab her clumsily. But he could not help her. He knew he had to keep going, he had to keep speaking. Realization dawned on him that his could be the only record of what had just unfolded in real time, and he had to continue until there was nothing left to say. He set the woman down gently on the damp ground, the microphone picking up his voice apologizing to her with a tearful "Lady, I'm sorry" as the fire trucks from the Naval Air Station raced forward to the wreck to extinguish what remained of the blaze.

"Honestly, I can hardly breathe—" He broke off, swallowing hard on his words as he looked over at his colleague just inside the doorway of the building and sobbed, "Charlie, that's terrible." He had to stop again to catch his breath, his voice almost entirely gone. The winter Midwestern floods had shown him a certain kind of tragedy, vast and sweeping in scope and duration, but this? This was a horror of another kind entirely.

"This is the worst thing I've ever witnessed," he confessed into the microphone, fighting back his tears. As far as he could tell, there was "not a possible chance for anyone to be saved."

CHAPTER 26

Lakehurst, New Jersey, USA: May 6, 1937

When they thought back to the moment they realized the *Hindenburg* was on fire and was crashing to the ground, some of the passengers remembered every detail of what came next with an almost out-of-body lucidity, aware of every word they spoke, every movement they made, all seared into their memories for eternity. For others, it was as if their minds had been wiped blank. One instant they were happily gazing out the window, and the next they were strewn on the ground, watching as the ship that had ferried them across the sky poured toxic black smoke into the air. But for most of them, it was something in between, fragments of memory and motion, of screams exchanged and images flashing before their eyes as fire leaped around them.

"Come on, Mr. Pannes, jump!" shouted one of the German passengers, Karl Otto Clemens, urging the American agent for the Hamburg-America Line to save himself.

"Wait until I get my wife!" he called back, scrambling away toward the B-deck stairwell as soon as the nose of the ship began to right itself. But there was almost no time for the *Birkenhead* drill—women and children first—save for the Doehner children, whose mother was frantically grabbing for her boys, Walter and Werner, to lift them up and throw them out the window as the flaming structure started sinking toward the ground. She tried to lift her daughter, Irene, but she was too heavy, and the girl went scrambling away to find her father. Otherwise, it was every man for himself.

Benny Spah never actually saw the *Hindenburg* on fire. He just knew he had to get out. He groped his way toward the dining room window, realizing he still had his camera around his neck. Taking it off, he raised it and smashed it down on the plexiglass, breaking it fully open, just as the Italian American designer, Philip Mangone, was doing with a shoe—or maybe a chair? It was all such a blur that later Mangone could not recall with certainty. But they were still much too high, at least one hundred feet in the air. If they jumped now, they would be killed on impact by the fall. Benny knew he had to get away from the heat that was building second by second. He scrambled up to the windowsill and threw his legs over the side, gripping the ledge as hard as he could, and hung there by one arm, suspended from the side of the airship. He had hung by one arm a thousand times in his act, and now he was counting on the strength that he had built up performing night after night to save his life while he waited for the ship to get low enough for him to drop. As he dangled, the metal under his hand grew hotter and hotter until he nearly lost his grip, and he became disoriented with the curious sensation not of falling but of the earth rising up to meet him.

In the lounge, passengers were screaming as they tried to free themselves from the barricade of tables and chairs that had trapped them against the wall. Someone next to Gertrud Adelt started to pray as flames began licking toward them. All she could think was, "Quickly the end, quick!" Just then, she heard a voice cry out, "Through the window!" snapping her out of her daze just enough to propel her limbs into motion to push and slide the tables and chairs out of the way so she could free herself. She was in such a state of confusion she did not realize that the voice that had called out was that of her own husband.

Leonhard knew they had to jump if they were going to survive. For an instant, he thought of the pile of used bed linens the stewards had assembled in the bedroom corridor and of throwing it out the window to soften their fall, but there was no time. He grabbed his wife, dragging her out of the mound of rubble and toward the window where they had been standing just seconds before. At that moment, "reality ceased with one stroke" and Leonhard's mind went blank, "as though fate in its cruelty was yet compassionate enough to withdraw its victims from the consciousness of their horror."

In the writing room, Nelson Morris and Bert Dolan were still on their feet, gripping the post tightly as the tail of the airship crashed into the ground and the nose began to tip back toward horizontal. Bert somehow managed to let go long enough to reach into his pocket for the rosary Mildred had given to him before he left. He held it in his fist while he and Nelson readied themselves to leap the moment they were close enough to the ground.

At the same instant, in the portside dining room, William Leuchtenberg, the German American manufacturer who had imbibed too heavily the night they left Frankfurt, threw himself into the rail along the window, his arms and legs spread wide. "*Es ist das Ende!*" Margaret Mather heard him cry out with fear, in stark contrast to his enraptured wonder at the start of their journey. Around her, people's faces and hands were bleeding, cut by the metal furniture that had fallen against them. She felt the heat at her back rising quickly, and she believed she was going to die. "The flames blew in, long tongues of flame, bright red and very beautiful," she observed in an eerily gruesome moment of clarity. It looked to her like a "medieval picture of hell," like a painting she might have seen in an Italian museum. Holding the lapels of her coat over her face, she beat at her hat and her hair, trying to extinguish the sparks that fell upon her. She wanted to keep her eyes shielded by her coat, but she could not help but watch the "horrified faces" of her "companions as they leaped up and down."

At the window, William Leuchtenberg prepared to jump. For reasons known only to God, he first removed his false teeth from his mouth and put them in his pocket.

The ship is burning!" one of the officers cried out in the control gondola. The *Hindenburg* lurched skyward, and one of the junior captains, Heinrich Bauer, asked if they should give up ballast in the stern to try to right the ship, likely not realizing there was probably no ballast left.

"No!" Captain Sammt shouted. They needed all the weight they had. "Get down as quickly as possible!" As the nose tipped higher into the air, Sammt feared they would all "fall backwards into the embers of the stern." For the six crewmen who had been sent to the nose to trim the ship, it was undoubtedly too late.

"Everyone find a window!" Captain Lehmann called to his crew over the growing roar.

Sammt and Pruss had just managed to get themselves near the window of the navigation room on the starboard side when the bottom of the control gondola made impact with the ground. The *Hindenburg* bounced once and then sank back down again, the framework of the girders crumbling down around them.

"Everybody outside," Lehmann commanded as he went out the starboard window. Pruss, Sammt, Wittemann, and the other officers did the same. It was still about a five-meter drop, and Sammt landed on all fours. Pruss was disoriented as he landed and ran back into the raging flames, disappearing into a wall of fire as the bright-white smoke of hydrogen was quickly replaced by black clouds of burning diesel fuel.

In the crew's mess on B deck, fourteen-year-old Werner Franz found himself completely alone. After the initial thud that had pitched him into the cupboard, the world around him had tilted sharply. Cups, plates, and silverware tumbled off their shelves and out of drawers, smashing against the floor with a massive clatter. For a moment he froze. Then, as the raining dishware fell down around him, he reached forward to try to catch it.

"What happened?" he asked himself. He jumped up and ran toward the walkway connecting the crew's mess with the rest of the ship. Just then, his throat caught. A massive wave of flame was rising up from the stern and heading straight for him. Franz crouched down and began to backpedal, trembling as he looked around for someone—anyone—who could help him. Stories some of the older crew members had told him about airships catching fire during the Great War began to race to the forefront of his mind. A new jolt threw him to the floor. He grabbed the ropes on either side of the walkway and held on with both hands as his world tilted. Everything around him was bathed in an angry, red glow. The flames raged up toward him as the ship rose to an ever-steeper pitch, threatening to send him sliding down into the tongues of fire.

Suddenly, Franz felt a deluge of water crash down around him, completely soaking him from head to toe. It was reminiscent of his equatorial baptism, only this time more like a biblical flood. One of the ship's ballast tanks, containing hundreds of gallons of water, had ruptured, sending water pouring down the hall and drenching everything in its path. As the wave of water passed, the bow of the ship began to settle forward and Franz was able to regain his balance.

The cabin boy was so disoriented he was unable to tell whether his clothes were wet or burning with fire, but a single thought had seized him. The hatch. The large hatch in the keel where they loaded food provisions into the kitchen was just ahead of him. Scrambling to his feet, he rushed toward it and kicked it open. Below him, he could see the earth rising toward him. It was six, maybe seven meters away. He had to jump. With instinct taking control, he dropped through the hatch and fell toward the ground, ballast water pouring out around him like a waterfall. He hit the ground and ran for his life as the frame of the airship collapsed like faulty scaffolding, fire erupting where he had dropped to the ground just a moment ago.

All around the cabin boy, men were running. Except these men were running toward, not away from, the flames. Suddenly, a large American man appeared in front of him and grabbed him. It was an American marine who thought a "curious rascal" had run forward from the crowd of onlookers and had gotten loose on the landing field, utterly unaware of the danger he faced. The marine tried to pull him back, away from the blaze. But Franz spoke no English to try to explain. All he could do was point frantically at the airship and shout, "*Ich bin der* cabin-boy *vom Hindenburg, ich bin doch der* cabin-boy *vom Hindenburg!*" as the man pulled him away. Finally, the marine understood. It had made no sense at first that the boy had come from the fire. He did not have a scratch on him, the white uniform his mother had bought for him still gleaming, but he was inexplicably soaking wet. Taking off his jacket and putting it over Franz's shoulders, he said, "Come on, boy, there's nothing left to do here, it's over now," and led him away from the burning wreck.

Of those who jumped from the airship, preferring to take their chances rather than meet their certain fate in the flames, Benny Spah was probably the first one who hit the ground alive. When he finally had no choice but to let go of the window ledge, he felt he had been hanging on for hours. The keel of the *Hindenburg* was somewhere between twenty and forty feet off the ground when the duralumin window frame searing into his hand became too hot to hold any longer and his grip gave way. Benny plunged through the air down toward the sandy field from the height of a three- or four-story building. He landed hard on his feet and felt his ankle snap as he fell forward on his face in the sand, his elastic athleticism the only reason the impact had not been worse. His hand was bleeding and the lapel on his jacket was torn, his collar and plaid tie askew. After he had climbed out the window, someone else had climbed out after him. He did not know who it was, but they had lost their grip and clawed at him as they plunged forward, grabbing at his jacket as they fell.

Benny scrambled away as fast as his ankle would allow as the flaming wreck plunged toward him. The next thing he knew, a pair of hands grabbed him and a giant man began to haul him away from the fire while sparks lit up the night sky.

Neither Leonhard nor Gertrud Adelt knew how they leaped from the airship. Leonhard thought they must have been about twelve to fifteen feet up when they jumped out the window. Maybe they jumped holding hands, maybe they did not. Neither could say for sure. Both of their minds were blank until they felt the sand and grass beneath their feet, the smell of damp earth hitting their noses and jarring their senses. Leonhard came to just in time as an "impenetrable darkness of black oil clouds, shot through with flames enveloped" them. Hot wires and pieces of metal surrounded them like an obstacle course in a hellscape, and they bent the blackened metal apart with their bare hands, feeling no pain. "We freed ourselves and ran through a sea of fire," Leonhard remembered of those desperate seconds. "It was like a dream. Our bodies had no weight. They floated like stars through space."

Suddenly, Leonhard had the sense that his wife was no longer beside him. He turned around, the flames and toxic smoke hitting him squarely. Gertrud had fallen face down in the wet sand, and she lay there, heavy and unmoving, like something was holding her down. She felt "tired, dead tired." Leonhard felt himself float toward her as if disembodied, and he reached out to grab her and pull her upright.

Gertrud felt a hand haul her up by the collar, again unaware it was her husband. The hand gave her a push, and she "ran like a 'robot'—nothing could stop [her]." The force of the push now left Leonhard splayed out on his side, watching his wife "running again like a mechanical toy that has been wound up." As he lay on the oil-soaked ground, he felt that he was "at the goal," that "this was dying, but it was such a feeling of well-being to stretch out and await death" that he was not afraid. Then he lifted up his head to make sure Gertrud was safe, and saw through blurred eyes that she was running and running through the vapors. This gave him a new will to go on. He "sprang up as though electrified and hurled [him] self after the phantom of life." Whether "guided by a steward" or Gertrud's "guardian angel," he staggered on and emerged "like a somnambulist" through the smoke into the open field, where he once again found himself at her side. They turned and looked back from whence they had come, and Gertrud, her senses returning to her, stared wide-eyed at the "smoldering black skeleton in a bleak cloud of fire" that was all that was left of the *Hindenburg*.

Nelson Morris hit the ground, landing in a minefield of burning girders. He had to clear the metal barring his way. He had to break free. Nelson took metal rails an inch thick in his bare hands and broke them apart. It was the most remarkable sensation he ever felt in his life. Metal strong enough to carry nearly half a million pounds of airship, fuel, cargo, passengers, and crew dissolved at his touch like paper. Girder after girder crumbled in his hands, and he started running as fast as his legs and the debris would allow. But then he stopped. Bert was not there. They had jumped together. Bert had been right at Nelson's side. Bert was the athlete. If either of them should have had the easier time getting out, it was him. But now he was not there.

Nelson looked around. Black smoke poured out of the burning diesel engines, making it almost impossible to see anything or anyone. The fire in the body of the zeppelin, which had just moments earlier been raging a hundred feet skyward, was nearly out, its smoldering contained to the few pieces of flammable material within the *Hindenburg*'s twisted skeleton. Sparks flew off the warped and deflated mass of metal. But Bert was nowhere to be seen.

"Come out, lady!" Margaret Mather heard an incorporeal voice calling to her. She looked around. Emma Pannes had vanished; Margaret had not seen her since before the final landing maneuvers. Peter Belin was also gone. But the voice belonged to a man. Several men, in fact, who were on the ground beckoning to her to come out. The *Hindenburg* had gone down with Margaret pinned against the wall, but somehow she was still alive. The flames receding around her were replaced by thick, noxious smoke, but she was almost untouched. Margaret peeled herself up and, in an instinctive motion she had made a thousand times, started groping around her feet for her handbag.

"Aren't you coming?" one of the men called urgently. Margaret snapped out of it and rushed forward toward the voice, running over and across metal girders and framework that lay smoldering on the ground.

Stewards and other crew members who had gotten out had rushed back into the wreckage to help, some of their uniforms blackened with soot, others still pristine. While a group of them helped Margaret, another steward climbed over the framework to help Marie Kleemann, who was practically as unsullied as Margaret, with just some bruising on her forehead, perhaps from other passengers falling against her when the airship lurched into the air, and a slight singe to her hair. Frau Kleemann's hat was lost, but she was still clutching her gloves, which had been in her hand the whole time.

CHAPTER 27

Lakehurst, New Jersey, USA: May 6, 1937

Black smoke towered a third of a mile into the sky as intermittent flames leaped thirty to forty feet off the ground all along the *Hindenburg*'s charred and twisted frame. Herb Morrison watched as the first wave of firefighters, sailors, and civilians rushed toward the smoldering mass to extinguish the blaze but were beaten back by the heat from the burning diesel. An emergency call had gone out to nearby fire departments and hospitals to send all the fire trucks, ambulances, doctors, nurses, and first aid workers they could muster. The coast guard base at Cape May and the Philadelphia Naval Yard sent reinforcements. American Airlines also dispatched a message calling for every one of the company's stewardesses who could be located in Newark to go to Lakehurst, as they were all trained nurses.

Morrison tried to stay composed while he continued to describe the macabre horror unfolding in front of him. He had to stop and swallow several times to catch his breath and clear his throat of the smoke and smog hanging heavy in the damp air.

"Charlie, this is terrible," Morrison said to his sound engineer as he briefly paused. "It's the worst thing I ever witnessed." He was going to move closer to the crash site to see what he could learn. Nehlsen told him to "relax," if that was even possible, and not to worry about the equipment. He would keep an eye on it. They were both beginning to realize the value of what they had just recorded.

Morrison raced down toward the picket line separating the burning wreck from the spectators, the smoke thickening as he got closer. Just as he crossed the line, he saw a man walking toward him. The man was in a daze and at first could not catch his breath. Morrison grabbed hold of him and asked him his name.

"Philip Mangone," he told Morrison. Despite his glazed expression, he spoke in a plain and distinct voice. He had just come from the *Hindenburg*, he said. He was one of the passengers.

Morrison must have been bowled over. He had just watched masses of hydrogen combust in the sky. He had been so sure there was no possible way anyone could have survived.

Mangone was terribly burned on his hands and face, and the back of his coat was completely scorched. His eyebrows and all his hair had been burned off, save a Kewpie's lock on his forehead. One minute Mangone felt like a "rat in a trap," and the next he was "scrap[ing] a hole into the dirt," burrowing out of the fire "like a mole," losing the rings on his fingers in the process. And all around him was the "smell of burning flesh."

He jumped with other passengers, he told Morrison, as navy sailors rushed forward to help. He had jumped and survived.

Morrison did not press him further. All he needed was Mangone's name to identify him on the broadcast so that family and friends would know that he had been saved. Mangone spelled it out while Morrison and several navy sailors helped him into a car, careful to support him under his arms so as not pull at his burns. Boy Scout training that Morrison had likely not thought of in years sprang to mind.

Someone announced the name "Mangone" into the crowd, and two frantic and relieved women came rushing up. One was Mangone's daughter, who had been desperately searching for her father. They crawled into the car with him, and it sped off to the base field hospital.

Just then, a second man appeared. This one was younger and much shorter, and he was far less burned. He seemed to have hurt his leg and was being helped away. Morrison asked him his name. It sounded to Morrison like the man said "Spay," but he was not sure. But the man was in no mood to talk. His family was there, and he was desperate to find them.

By some miracle, more and more people were emerging from the smoke and flames. Some moved under their own power with hardly a scratch. Others' backs were black like broiled meat. Cars and ambulances raced down toward the wreck at the mooring mast to take them to the field hospital, which would not be nearly large or sophisticated enough to handle the dozens of very serious injuries. These people needed a proper hospital, but some were so badly burned it would be nearly impossible to move them.

By the time Morrison arrived back at the office where Nehlsen was guarding their equipment, the building was in a frenzy. Fifteen minutes had elapsed since the *Hindenburg* went up in flames. In the office, people were busy pulling out tables to make makeshift cots for an overflow room for those not so bad off. Everyone, from the military to Post Office employees, was pitching in as more helpers arrived every minute. The scene inside was a tableau of the same chaos unfolding across the entire base. There were people everywhere, some running, some sobbing. Others were so distraught they were simply numb. While Morrison was out collecting information, Charlie Nehlsen had seen a frightened little girl. She was crying and she wore no shoes. At first, he thought she had come from the *Hindenburg*, but he quickly realized she had been in the crowd of spectators and had become separated from her parents in the pandemonium.

Nehlsen resumed the recording, giving Morrison the all clear so he could narrate what he had just witnessed. Morrison spoke into the microphone, telling future listeners of finding Philip Mangone, of his eyebrows and hair that had been burned off, but also of his clarity of mind. Then he told them of the "Mr. Spay" he had spoken to for a moment. "It sounds like Spay. We're not sure of it," he clarified, relieved that they were still "taking people out of the wreckage" but perhaps a bit terrified of the state in which they would be found when the emergency crews reached them. The diesel fuel was "still flaming ten or fifteen feet high," he explained. "Now it is my sincere hope that as many as possible, and as many as I think, got out. I think a majority of the passengers jumped when it came close to the ground, according to what Mr. Mangone told me. He says, thank God he jumped, and we say, 'Thank God,' for him, also."

Charlie Nehlsen faded out the recording and Morrison handed over the microphone again to run back down to the eight-hundred-foot skeleton to see whether he could learn how many had been saved.

While Morrison was running down to the wreck, another young man was running through the crowd of spectators looking for his family. Peter Belin had jumped out of the *Hindenburg* alongside two stewards as soon as it was safe enough to have a chance. By sheer luck he had landed in a soft sandbank. He was practically unscathed, his receipts, map, and roll of film still safely in his pocket. Now he had to find his parents, who were probably certain he was dead. The young man let out his distinctive whistle. It was unique to him and one that his parents would know when they heard it, assuming they could hear anything above the commotion.

After about fifteen minutes of searching, he found them. They had retreated to the car, "insensate" with grief over losing their beloved son, the shock of it making them so confused and distraught that they had been about to drive away when they heard his whistle.

Belin was eager to get in the car and drive straight to their friend's home in Princeton, not just to get as far away as possible from the horror he had just experienced. He had to make a call to New Haven, specifically to the office of the *Yale Daily News*.

The university daily was nearly ready to go to print for the next day with six pages of articles and advertisements. The May 7 paper included showtimes for *Shall We Dance* and *A Star Is Born* at the Roger Sherman and College Theaters; an advertisement proclaiming, "Wanted! A few Yale men to join an expedition leaving in June for lands on the Arctic Circle"; and another for Viking Flying Boat Co. at the New Haven Municipal Airport, "Where Yale Flies." On page four was a review of a new film called *The Girl from Scotland Yard*, about an inventor with a grudge laying plans to use a "death ray" to destroy British ships, airplanes, and bridges, "not to mention His majesty, at the approaching coronation ceremony." Three minutes into the film, a plucky traveler on a steamer says to her companion, "It's all sheer nonsense! Nobody's going around breaking boats and blowing up dirigibles for no reason. It's an accident, and accidents are always happening."

Life had an eerie way of imitating art, lowbrow as the film might have been compared with the others playing that week. Peter Belin was going to give his cousin, the paper's editor, the exclusive of his life.

Someone was helping Margaret Mather into a car to take her away from the flaming wreck when a man called out to her with relief. "Thank God, you are safe," he said, limping up to assist her. It was the British passenger, George Grant. He had been standing right near Margaret when the ship had caught fire and had jumped out one of the lounge windows. Grant had landed safely, but as he was getting up to run away, another passenger jumped down and landed on him, leaving him with a broken ankle and an injured back.

The scene around the wreckage had been gruesome, and after days of the happiest tranquility she had known, all Margaret wanted was to find her family and get away from this place. Most of the fire had burned out, but it had created a ghoulish dystopia in its wake. There was a steward wandering around, his uniform immaculate, with two equally spotless packages under his arms, which he must have been holding when the airship went down. In his state of shock, he had forgotten to let go. Meanwhile, a public relations executive from Esso, the company that had provided the diesel fuel that was still smoking a mile high, was helping a young girl, Irene Doehner, into an ambulance to receive treatment. When he took her arm to assist her, she was so badly burned that her flesh disintegrated to the bone.

Some of these passengers urgently needed a doctor, but Margaret was absolutely fine. She asked the driver to let her out near the entrance to the airfield.

"Can't do it," he told her flatly. "Orders are to take everyone to the First Aid Station."

"But I am not asking you to go out of your way," she replied. "Put me down at the nearest point. I am not hurt."

He disagreed. "Look at your hands, lady."

She looked down at her flesh. Her palms were completely seared, and yet she had not felt a thing. Margaret thought she was going to be sick. She let the driver take her to the field hospital and said no more about it.

Margaret was among the first to arrive at the infirmary on the north end of the Naval Air Station. As helpers led her inside and toward a table, the shock started to wear off. Someone swabbed her hands with picric acid, an antiseptic and astringent, which made them start to feel as painful as they looked.

As she sat with stinging hands, Margaret glanced around to see who else had come in. Nearby, a terribly injured man was sitting on another table. Most of his hair and his clothes had been burned off. Someone told her discreetly that it was Captain Lehmann. With his skin ravaged and his fur-lined coat with its upturned collar gone, she had not recognized him. During the trip, he had "always looked alert but genial, with keen blue eyes." Now, as he sat stoically through what must have been excruciating pain, his face looked "grave and calm, and not a groan escaped him as he sat there, wetting his burns" with swabs of antiseptic.

More passengers and crew started to arrive in carloads from the crash site, and Margaret could hear "howling and groaning." None of those who had come in thus far were her new friend Emma Pannes, nor Emma's husband, John. The nurse who had been tending to Margaret and Captain Lehmann left the bottle of picric acid with them and went to assist those who were more gravely injured. Lehmann sat quietly and steadily with a large piece of gauze in one hand and the bottle in the other, swabbing through the agony. "His mental anguish must have been as intense as his physical pains," Margaret thought, knowing that the loss of the *Hindenburg* and his resulting injuries almost certainly meant the loss of everything he had worked toward his entire adult life, "but he gave no sign of either." When Margaret's burns became unbearable, she would reach for the bottle, and he would pass it to her with "grave courtesy, wait patiently while I wet my hands and receive it back with a murmured '*Danke schön*.'" Amid all of the chaos and the horror, it was "a strange, quiet interlude," she thought, "almost as though we were having tea together."

After some time, Margaret could no longer take the sounds of agony emanating from the victims who continued to arrive. She was well enough to move around under her own power and decided to go outside to get away from the screams of burn victims writhing in pain. But as she stood under the stoop at the entrance, where she was shielded from the rain, another ambulance pulled up. The attendants opened the doors, and inside she could see men piled up like cigarettes, blackened by the inferno. They removed the men one by one, and when the final man remained, all she could see were his legs, "burned and stiff like charred pieces of wood." Margaret again thought she was about to be sick and ran out into the rain.

Downfield, she could see the *Hindenburg* still burning, a cloud of black smoke "soar[ing] above" the skeleton. She watched it burn with "anguish" but found that the strongest feeling inside her at that moment was one of regret. Just yesterday, they had been flying over icebergs and rainbows. And now? Had one of her ancestors been at her side, they might have quoted Genesis: "For you are dust, and to dust you will return." But Margaret could not take her mind off the memory of that beauty. "Even in the midst of human suffering and death," she thought with pity, "I could not but regret the destruction of so beautiful a thing."

When Gertrud Adelt finally stopped running, she turned around and looked back to see her husband standing some yards behind, staring out at the *Hindenburg*'s skeleton, possessed by what he would later describe as a "demon-like urge of self-destruction which drives the moth into the flame." She yelled back to him urgently to snap him out of his daze, hurried to his side to take his hand in hers, and led him away, stumbling as they tripped over the body of what she thought was a member of the landing crew. An ambulance pulled up beside them, but when the door opened, a woman's voice barked out, "There is no more room here." Gertrud recognized Mrs. Doehner, who looked at her "like a tigress, clutching her three children, all of whom were very close to death."

The field hospital was swarming with people when the Adelts arrived. The chaos reminded Leonhard of a "disturbed ant heap." Gertrud looked on as "young nurses dressed in white, with terror in their eyes, rushed through the confused rooms with morphine syringes and whiskey bottles." Leonhard thought he saw an orderly with a "morphine syringe the size of a bicycle pump." Gertrud sat in a wicker chair. Someone tried to give her a shot of morphine, but she swatted them away angrily. How would anyone know to whom she belonged if she fell asleep? At her feet was a dying crewman calling out that his shoes were too tight. Gertrud bent down and took them off his coarse wool socks and broken feet as he cried alternately for his bride back home in Germany and for a priest. A priest appeared and listened as the man mumbled out a confession that Gertrud could hear was in Swabian German, a dialect spoken in a small southwestern region of the country, "which only God underst[ood]."

Meanwhile, in the next room, Leonhard found Captain Lehmann. He was sitting hunched over on a table, unclad from the waist up where the nurses had cut away what was left of his clothes. He was burned, but not as badly as some others Leonhard had seen. Leonhard approached him.

"What caused it?" he asked his old friend.

"Lightning," the captain replied.

Those were the only words the two men exchanged. What else could they have said to each other? All they could do was look one another in the eye, for now leaving all of the grief that was to come for another day.

When Leonhard could "no longer contain" himself, he went outside. Once again, he found himself staring down at the airship, which was still smoldering. Years earlier, Leonhard had written in one of his novels about the danger of flight and the risk of death, dismissing it, saying, "Only the flying poseur plays with the thought of death; the true flyer does not let it approach him." "Danger," Leonhard had written, is "not outside us," in the elements between ground and sky, but rather, it is "within."

Werner Franz stood outside the field hospital in his soaking-wet uniform. Tears were pouring down his cheeks, merging with rivulets of rain. He was still wearing the jacket of the American marine who had helped him when his friend Wilhelm Balla found him. Balla had just hobbled out from the infirmary, where he had seen many of his colleagues "writhing in their pain and crying bitterly." One, a helmsman named Ludwig Felber, even begged Balla to go and see his wife and children once he returned to Germany. Felber knew he was not going to make it back.

The Lakehurst staff was establishing a makeshift morgue in a room just inside hangar number 1, and Balla had been asked to identify his comrades. This, unfortunately, was impossible. The bodies lay beside each other, "completely disfigured, still and calm." It was too difficult to even say who was a passenger and who was crew. At least Captains Pruss and Lehmann were alive. Pruss, whom Captain Sammt had seen disappear into that curtain of fire, had miraculously walked out. Sammt had found him again a short time later, though he had not realized who it was at first. Pruss was wearing his coat, but his cap was gone, his hair burned off, and his head completely disfigured with burns.

"Pruss, is it you?" Sammt had called out.

"Yes," the figure groaned in reply.

"Oh dear, what do you look like?" Sammt said to his captain.

Somehow mustering a sense of humor in the face of agony, Pruss retorted, "Yes, you look good, too."

Pruss looked much worse than Lehmann, his face practically unrecognizable. Everything from the base of his nose up would have to be wrapped in gauze while the medical staff waited to see if he would stabilize sufficiently to allow him to be transported to a proper hospital in the city. Meanwhile, Commander Rosendahl was sitting with Lehmann and refused to leave his friend's side.

Balla limped over to Franz on his wounded leg, undoubtedly flooded with relief to find his young charge wet but unhurt. Some of the wives of Lakehurst officers, who lived nearby on the base and had come to watch the landing, came over to the two young men standing in the rain. They offered to take them into their homes to get warm and dry. One of them had a twelve-year-old son. She had a woolen sweater and pants that would fit the cabin boy.

The marine who had given Franz his jacket was still nearby. Franz went to him and returned the jacket, then got in a car with Balla to drive over to the woman's home. Once they arrived, several of the wives tried to speak to young Franz in a soothing manner, but he did not understand them and took some time to calm down. When he had, he only wanted to talk to Balla. He told his friend how he had been in the officers' mess when the fire started, and how flames had already started licking at him when the ballast tank burst and practically washed him out of the airship.

After changing into dry clothes and drinking a hot cup of coffee, all Franz could think about was his family. When the news of the disaster went out over the radio back home, how would his parents know he was alive?

"Mrs. Spah, please come to the hangar. Your husband is alive," a voice called out over a loudspeaker. Benny was sitting in a big chair when Vera appeared, children in tow. As she threw her arms around him, all his strength left him and he collapsed into her.

"Journey's end," he said, and she began to cry and pat him all over as if she could not believe he was actually in front of her. His ankle was broken, but he was otherwise in one piece. He even still had his wallet in his pocket, though his driver's license, Volunteer Air Service card, and boxing membership were badly singed.

Someone found a couch for the family to sit on together. Ignoring the pain in his ankle, he pulled little Gilbert and Marilyn onto his lap while Richard sat on Vera's lap beside him, reaching out to his father. The children's chubby toddler legs, clad in shorts and ankle socks, projected out in all directions. When a photographer came up to snap their picture, two-year-old Marilyn grinned right at the camera, her hair sticking up every which way as if someone had rubbed a latex balloon against her head.

After a little while, one of the children asked about the dog Benny had brought from Germany. Evidently, Vera had let them in on the surprise. But Benny could not bring himself to tell them the truth about Ulla's fate. There was nothing anyone could have done for the poor animal. Instead, he told them, "Ulla jumped out, and she's running around. She's gonna come." They seemed to accept the story. In a few days, maybe he could find another dog and say it was Ulla to spare them from the heartbreaking reality.

While he sat with his children clutched safely in his arms, Benny found his thoughts wandering to the Doehner children. As he had watched them play on board, they had made him think of his own children. Now he did not know if they would survive. "Oh those poor kids," he thought. "God pity them. God help them."

In downtown Chicago, Edward Morris, Nelson's younger brother, was driving in traffic when the NBC program to which he was listening in his car cut to a news bulletin from the station's New York studio. Earlier that evening, the broadcast announced, at approximately 7:25 p.m. Eastern Daylight Time, the German airship *Hindenburg* had crashed as it was coming in for a landing in Lakehurst, New Jersey, where an enormous fire ensued. The news was stunning. Both his brother Nelson and his friend Bert Dolan were on board. And Bert's wife had no idea.

Edward was the only person in Chicago who knew that both Nelson and Bert were on the *Hindenburg*, having been enlisted by Nelson to help arrange the domestic end of their travel to ensure that Mildred would be surprised. He immediately turned his car north and drove straight to the Dolan home. He had to tell Mildred her husband was in danger. He could not have her finding out when she read his name on the passenger list in the paper the next morning.

When he pulled up to the Dolans' Spanish Mission–style white stucco house, it was still light outside. The Catholic schools had been closed for the Feast of the Ascension, and the neighborhood kids, including two of Bert's children, twelve-year-old Bud and ten-year-old Babs, were still playing basketball in the empty lot beside the house. He parked his car, covered the short walk up to the door, and rang the bell. A girl opened the door. It was fourteen-year-old Mary Alice, who had been inside studying for an exam. Edward wasted no time on pleasantries and immediately asked her to find her mother.

He might have found a better way to break the news to Mildred, but instead, as she came down the stairs, he blurted out bluntly, "Brace yourself, Mildred. Bert's gone down with the *Hindenburg*."

For a moment, she stood there confused. She had no idea what he was talking about. She had not heard anything about the *Hindenburg* crashing and did not understand what it had to do with her husband. He was returning from Europe by steamer that very week. That was what he had written in his letter.

Yes, Edward explained, Bert had planned to come back on a steamer, but he had seen Nelson in Nice, and Nelson had persuaded Bert to come back on the *Hindenburg* with him. They had meant it to be a wonderful Mother's Day surprise for her after he had been away for so long. Edward did not have any other information beyond the headline he had heard on the radio. He did not know how many people had survived, or if anyone had survived at all.

Just then, there was a thump at the top of the stairs. Bert's mother, Catherine, who lived with them, had been listening from the landing. She had just buried one son at Christmas and now faced the prospect of burying the other. Fearing the worst, she had fainted.

CHAPTER 28

Berlin, Germany: May 7, 1937

It was pitch-dark when the shrill of the telephone jarred Bill Shirer from slumber in his Tempelhof apartment. He rolled over and picked up the receiver. It was Bill Hillman, chief of staff of foreign correspondents for all Hearst publications in Europe, calling from London. The words hitting Shirer's groggy, sleep-filled brain sounded like something having to do with the airship *Hindenburg*. Yes, Hillman was indeed talking about the zeppelin, which should have been landing sometime while Shirer was asleep.

Only, it seemed, it had not. The *Hindenburg*, Hillman told him urgently, had "crashed, caught on fire and blown up on landing at Lakehurst, New Jersey, with a heavy loss of life." The New York bureau wanted the German "reaction" to the disaster within the hour to make their print deadline for the next morning. Then he hung up.

Before he could even process what Hillman had just told him, Shirer turned and looked at the clock. He might have had only one good eye, but that clock definitely said it was 4:00 a.m. Who in Germany would be awake at that hour to give him a comment, or even be able to confirm what Hillman had just told him was true? Shirer climbed out of bed and dug through his papers, looking for his contacts for the article series he had written about the *Hindenburg* the year before. He found the number for Ludwig Dürr, the chief engineer and designer for Luftschiffbau Zeppelin, whom Count Zeppelin himself had hired over thirty years earlier and who had designed every zeppelin since the *LZ-2*. Remarkably, Dürr answered.

At first, the longtime engineer was unable to speak. He had not yet heard the terrible news and initially refused to believe what Shirer was telling him. It was impossible. The very idea of the *Hindenburg* having crashed left him completely "overwhelmed."

After he collected himself, he began to think like the careful, meticulous engineer that he was. "I cannot imagine [what] caused it. I must wait for the reports: for the evidence," he told Shirer. Immediately, Dürr's mind went to the second- and third-order effects of what this crash could mean for the zeppelin company and airships in general. He was all too aware of the crashes of the *Akron* and the *Macon* in the United States, the *Dixmude* in France, and Britain's *R.101*. He had heard the voices saying that hydrogen was dangerous, that airplanes were the way of the future. He was having none of it. Whatever happened, he said to Shirer, "I must tell you we will go on. We will learn from this. We have had other severe setbacks since I first joined Count Zeppelin many years ago. The new *LZ-130* will be completed on schedule. I have full confidence in it." Then he hung up the phone. No doubt the rest of his night would be sleepless.

Unsurprisingly, no one else Shirer tried answered the phone, and Eckener was away on a lecture tour in Austria. Someone there would surely track him down if they wanted a more fulsome report in the morning. Dürr's comments would have to do for New York for now. He called the London office with this "reaction" from Germany, which was all they could expect at four in the morning. Then he went back to bed and tried to sleep.

"Seven years of flying, almost a million miles, and not a mishap," he had written just over a year earlier.

As he lay there with his head on his pillow, the hands on the clock inched closer to five. But sleep would not come. His mind was racing. He could not stop thinking about how if he had accepted the offer when DZR had called with the free ticket just days earlier, either he or Tess might have been on board the *Hindenburg* that very night.

CHAPTER 29

Lakehurst, New Jersey, USA: May 6–7, 1937

Herb Morrison tried to make his way over to the field hospital to learn what he could about the survivors, but he quickly found that if he left the area around the heavier-than-air office where he and Charlie Nehlsen were set up, he would not be allowed back in again. Security had tightened in the immediate aftermath of the crash, and there were a few anxious minutes when the police tried to clear them out of the building entirely. Fortunately, someone from American Airlines had informed the police that the radiomen were with the airline in an official capacity, and they were left alone after that.

Morrison had to wait his turn for the telephone to call WLS to say that they were unhurt and, crucially, that they had captured the entire disaster on the recording, as many people kept coming through to report that certain individuals were alive or dead. Meanwhile, Nehlsen continued to stand guard over their precious discs where Morrison's reaction to what they had just seen was preserved.

As it turned out, they were perfectly placed to continue gathering information. So far, with the help of someone nearby who spoke German, Morrison had managed to interview a German passenger, Carl Otto Clemens, who had not been burned at all, as well as one of the Chicago-based passengers, Herbert O'Loughlin. O'Loughlin had been the one to first come upon Ernst Lehmann and had rushed to beat the flames off the

German captain's coat and hair, burning himself in the process. His face was somewhat blackened but otherwise he did not seem too bad off and was intent on calling his mother to tell her he was alright. Morrison had also spoken with another Chicago man, Nelson Morris, with whom local listeners would certainly be familiar. That made two of the four Chicagoans aboard the *Hindenburg* present and accounted for. Morrison had not heard anything about Clifford Osbun, nor did Nelson Morris know the fate of his business partner, Bert Dolan. The former packing executive had been searching for his friend but had not seen him since they jumped from the airship together.

As far as Morrison had gathered from one of the American Airlines stewardesses, a Miss Tyler, who had been called down to Lakehurst as a registered nurse, there were between twenty-five and thirty people who had been saved, judging by the overflowing infirmary. She was too overcome to tell him much more than that. Among the saved were three children by the name of Doehner, as well as a radio officer named Schweikard, who told Morrison he had jumped through the plexiglass window of the radio room. Remarkably, despite Morrison's initial certainty that not only had all the passengers and crew been killed but also the navy and civilian landing crew working beneath the airship, it appeared that all but one of the landing crew had managed to run clear in time. At 8:21 p.m., less than an hour after the disaster, a civilian ground crew member, Allen O. Hagaman, tragically died from third-degree burns suffered when wreckage fell on top of him.

The range of outcomes that Morrison had personally seen over the course of the last hour was staggering. There were those, like Mangone, who were clearly burned but walking and talking normally, while others were disfigured beyond recognition. As survivors worked through a state of shock, the thoughts that had fixed themselves in certain people's minds were also understandably peculiar. The chief steward and purser, Heinrich Kubis, survived the crash, only to then run back into the burning wreck to save the metal cash box in the charred remains of his office. He had brought it with him from the crash site to open in front of officials so that there could be no doubt that the full sum was still there, only to turn the key and find the paper bills inside had been "toasted to ashes." Then there were the scenes that were downright bizarre. One crew member had been burned on his hands, his arms, and the back of his neck, but strangest of all were his shoes. The force of the heat of the blast had "blown the tops of his shoes off back to the heel." As Morrison illustrated for listeners, "they were just sticking on by laces and a little bit of the felt covering the soles of the shoes still on his feet." And then there was the steward, Max Henneberg, who walked into the building entirely uninjured. "He has two paper bundles, and there's not a bit of scorching on either bundle. Now, how it happened, I couldn't begin to tell you," a perplexed Morrison explained.

All night, American Airlines had been flying in supplies, doctors, and stewardess nurses like Miss Tyler, who later updated Morrison that she now thought there were between forty and sixty survivors in various states of infirmity. The base had set up a directional beam and landing lights so airplanes could continue operations all night, though the smoking diesel fuel on the ground was certainly a clear enough signal to guide them. The airline soon began taking the survivors who were stable enough to fly back to New York for treatment.

Over the course of about two hours, Morrison recorded forty-two minutes of commentary, from his praise for American Airlines before the idyllic arrival of the *Hindenburg*, to his anguished cry of "Oh, the humanity!" the moment it went up in flames, to his interviews with survivors and descriptions of the heroic efforts of navy and civilian first responders. What Morrison and Nehlsen had captured was unlike anything that had been heard on the radio before. They had to get it back to their station immediately—and before anyone realized how valuable those seemingly innocuous green discs spinning on the recorder truly were.

It was after 9:00 p.m. by the time NBC and other stations managed to dispatch mobile units down to Lakehurst to provide a few minutes of live content via microwave transmission for additional short special updates later that evening, and they had already missed the main event. Morrison had approached the NBC crew to tell them he was from a Chicago affiliate station and was an eyewitness who could provide commentary, but they waved him off, apparently not understanding what a Midwestern announcer from a mid-market station had to do with the events at hand.

Meanwhile, CBS was preparing its regular Thursday-evening radio program, *March of Time*, a thirty-minute show that re-created the newsworthy events of the day using actors, hurriedly written scripts, sound effects, and music. In the three short hours between the disaster at the airfield and its regularly scheduled 10:30 p.m. time slot, the show's producers were hastily compiling what they had learned from news flashes from Lakehurst with a history of airship travel plus sound effects of an explosion—complete with screaming crowds, hissing flames, and the zeppelin's frame collapsing. None of the radio producers in New York had any idea that Morrison and Nehlsen actually had the real thing.

Later that night—neither Morrison nor Nehlsen really knew what time exactly—someone from American Airlines announced that its last flight was about to leave for Newark. The WLS men "hustled to knock down equipment," packed it up, and raced out to the waiting airplane south of the airship field and the wreck, which now looked rather like the mangled carcass of a whale beached on the shore for some time. Morrison took on the task of helping to haul the equipment into the baggage hold, since Nehlsen would not let the discs out of his grasp. The image of his slight colleague, who probably weighed less than all of their equipment combined, heaving the recorder into the fuselage of the plane struck Nehlsen as oddly funny despite the grim circumstances.

Nearby, photographer Murray Becker from the Associated Press, who had been grumbling earlier about having to wait around all day and who now had not secured a seat on the last plane, was begging the American Airlines press agent to take his film on the flight with her. A motorcycle courier from his office would come to meet the plane in Newark, then rush the film back to the AP in Manhattan to be developed and printed alongside stories of the disaster in the papers the next morning. The AP wire service had been initiated only two years earlier. If he got these photos off, it would be the biggest breaking news story yet that had pictures side by side with the very first report. All the press agent had to do was hand it off. Becker did not quite know what he had captured, but he was almost certain he had snapped the moment of the explosion and was afraid that someone was going to come along and confiscate his film for official purposes before he even had a chance to develop his pictures. The press agent finally agreed, so long as any other news photographers also had an opportunity to put their film on the plane. Becker did not have much choice but to trust her and handed over his negatives.

As the DC-3 taxied down the runway for takeoff with Morrison, Nehlsen, their discs, and Becker's film on board, Becker slumped down against the front of a nearby hangar and cried.

When they landed at Newark, Morrison and Nehlsen had a few hours to kill before the American Airlines "Night Owl" flight departed for Chicago via Buffalo and Detroit. The pilots, Johnny Deater and Robert Young, had been in a newsreel theater when they received a message that an accident had occurred at Lakehurst and it would be all hands for the rest of the night. The airport was now crawling with reporters and photographers trying to gather whatever information they could from those arriving from Lakehurst over the last few hours. Nehlsen hung back with the discs and let Morrison do the talking. As they still had a bit of a wait, they decided to take their precious recordings and slip away on a bus uptown to the Newark location of Childs, the restaurant chain known for its white-uniformed chefs flipping pancakes on a griddle in the front window of every location. They did not have any particular reason to think anyone was tracking them or trying to take their recording from them, but they figured it was best if they kept a low profile. They wanted their discs safely back in the WLS office in Chicago before anyone realized what they had, not least someone from the German American Bund, with its deep connections in New Jersey. Those folks would not take kindly to the prospect of a detailed description of the great Nazi airship's demise being broadcast from coast to coast.

At 2:00 a.m., Deater and Young started the engines of the waiting plane. Morrison and Nehlsen had returned and boarded, Nehlsen keeping the discs with him at his seat. As they left New Jersey and the awful night in the distance, Morrison realized that the heat from the fire had cooked his rain-soaked wool suit. Inside one of his pockets, the flask of whiskey one of the reporters had handed him remained untouched.

Just before 4:00 a.m., the Night Owl flight landed in Buffalo. Morrison got off with most of the other passengers for a few minutes to stretch his legs, while Nehlsen stayed behind with the valuable cargo. Reporters swarmed the passengers and crew as they exited the plane, catching Morrison and the pilot Johnny Deater together. The reporter asked Deater if he knew how anyone from the *Hindenburg* had survived.

Deater did not know, but from what he had gathered from colleagues who had flown down to Lakehurst, he reported, "It was probably the ship's settling ten feet above the ground that saved the lives of many."

"Some of them dropped sixty feet," Morrison interjected to clarify. "It was terrible. The big gas bag seemed to hang in the air, almost in an upright position, and then slowly crumble as the flames ravaged the structure. All the time, people kept dropping to the ground, their clothes afire, to writhe or lie still upon the ground, with the white heat of flaming gas checking efforts of rescuers to beat their way to their sides." If the reporter was stunned by the graphic description Morrison had just given him, he did not say so in his article.

Somehow, the man had caught wind that Morrison's traveling pal had remained on the plane. He was also under the mistaken impression that the two were brothers, calling Herb Morrison "Herbert Nehlsen." The reporter inquired why his "brother" had not gotten off, perhaps thinking he was injured or there was otherwise something wrong.

"Too tired" was the response. The reporter went back to peppering Deater with questions.

It took some hours, but by midnight, most of the *Hindenburg* passengers whose families had come to the airfield to greet them had been reunited with their loved ones. Gertrud and Leonhard had finally found Leonhard's brothers. It took three hours, but Karl Adelt eventually convinced someone to let him through the security cordon. It was hardly the reunion any of them could have imagined. Though Leonhard was somewhat burned and had inhaled smoke, Gertrud's injuries were quite minor, and both were allowed to go home. They got into Karl's car to make their way down to his house in Cape May, driving "with numbed senses," as Gertrud later recalled thinking, "into the new world for the first time in our lives."

Nelson Morris was lucky that his sister, Ruth, and her husband were both renowned doctors in New York City and more than capable of looking after him. Compared with some of the other passengers and many of the crew, whose burns rivaled mustard gas victims from the Great War, he was relatively unharmed, practically as unblemished as the white rabbits he used to pull out of top hats. He was only slightly singed on his face. The worst of his injuries were on his palms where he had grabbed burning metal girders and pushed them aside in his desperate search for Bert as he ran out of the flaming wreckage. Now his hands were wrapped in so much gauze it looked like he was wearing boxing gloves. By the time an ambulance had driven him to the city, there was still no sign of his friend. Nelson had not found Bert in the hellscape of the zeppelin's remains, nor elsewhere in the turmoil on the landing field in the hours that followed.

Margaret Mather still had not located her family. She had given their names to kind people offering to help locate them amid the chaos. One woman even drove her to the entrance of the Naval Air Station and walked through the crowds calling out their names while Margaret waited safely in the car. Still, she did not find them. The aid station was quieter now, with most of the victims having been transported to nearby hospitals. She saw the Englishman, George Grant, carried out on a stretcher with a bandaged leg.

Though nearly all the wound dressings had been used over the last few hours, someone found a tube of Vaseline, which they squeezed onto her hands and wrapped with a loose gauze covering. She was now one of the last people there. An ambulance was free, and the driver offered to take her to either her brother's house or a hospital. Without her address book, which was presumably reduced to ash, it would be difficult to navigate to Frank's home from memory, so she asked them to drive her to her niece's house instead. She lived just off Nassau Street, the main road that ran past the gates of Princeton University, so if the ambulance driver could just get her to the town of Princeton, she knew she could direct them the rest of the way.

Someone swaddled Margaret in a blanket and put her on a stretcher, which she did not really need, and helped her into the ambulance. Four ex-servicemen kindly offered to escort her, and as they drove off, they promptly began to regale her with the tale of the *Hindenburg* falling out of the sky in a ball of fire as they had seen it from the ground—as if she had not just lived through it on the inside. Margaret graciously overlooked their perhaps less than sensitive topic of conversation, appreciating that they were nice men who propped up her burned and aching hands as the driver tried to avoid the bumps in the road.

When lying on the stretcher became too uncomfortable, they helped her to sit up.

"Do you know that your coat is all burned?" one of them asked her as he placed a hand on her back to support her.

She had not realized it at all. Aside from her burned hands, she had thought she was as "immaculate" as the steward she had seen wandering around with his crisp white uniform looking as clean as if he were about to pass out another tray of sandwiches.

The journey seemed interminable, as the driver had to stop frequently to ask for directions to Princeton, but eventually the familiar towers of the university came into view. In a few more moments they turned onto Prospect Avenue and she spotted her niece's door. Margaret was finally safe and home.

Benny Spah had a bit farther to go. After receiving treatment for his ankle at Fitkin Memorial Hospital near Asbury Park, he was discharged and sent home. It was typically a three-hour drive from Lakehurst to

Douglaston, but he asked Vera to go very slowly. When they finally arrived at their beloved Tudor house, they found a crush of reporters waiting outside, representing outlets from the United Press syndicate to the Hearst broadsheet the *Times Union*, based in Albany. It was shocking how quickly they had figured out where he lived.

As Vera put the children to bed, Benny gamely agreed to talk to the reporters as he sat in a chair smoking a cigarette. His ankle, now in a cast, was propped up in front of him. He was still wearing the same pinstripe suit with its torn lapel and plaid tie, all of his clothes reeking of smoke and ash.

"I was literally blown into the United States," he jokingly told reporters. "I never entered this country so fast, and I didn't even need a passport." Harrowing ordeal aside, he clearly had not lost his sense of humor.

Once he had loosened up the room, he took on a more serious tone, the German accent in his English readily apparent. "I do think I am very lucky, sitting here in my own home again after this experience," he said. "I'm just happy and I guess I never really did think it ended up for me as easy as it really did. I'm sitting at home again smoking a cigarette and enjoying myself and I want as much as possible to forget I was so close to a tragedy as I ever want to come."

The United Press reporter asked him if, after this horrific experience, he would ever fly on a zeppelin again.

He flicked the ashes from his cigarette, looked up with an odd little smile, and said, "I haven't lost faith in the Zeppelins."

When the plane carrying Morrison and Nehlsen briefly landed in Detroit, Nehlsen again refused to get off. And when they finally landed in Chicago around six o'clock that morning, rumpled, unshaven, and a little worse for wear, there were more reporters there to meet them. They rushed right past the press, dove into a cab, and headed straight to the Prairie Farmer Building on West Washington Street.

Charlie Nehlsen did not relax until he had physically placed the green discs safely on his desk. From there, they would go in the station's vault for safe keeping. Still, he could not be sure of exactly what he had been guarding all night until he tried to play them. The Presto equipment they had with them allowed them only to make recordings, not to play them back. In the light of day, it was very clear that the recording needle had punctured a small hole in one of the discs, that crucial disc, when the percussive blast of the first large explosion echoed through the building where Nehlsen had set up the equipment. Either they had about forty minutes of some of the most valuable recorded content ever produced, or they had the greatest missed opportunity in the history of radio.

When the disc was settled onto the spinning platter of a record player in the studio and the tonearm positioned, a crackle sounded, followed by a familiar voice.

"How d'you do, everyone? We're greeting you now from the naval air base at Lakehurst, New Jersey, from which point we're going to bring you a description of the landing of the mammoth airship *Hindenburg*, which was due here in America this morning at dawn."

Nehlsen probably took a real breath for the first time in twelve hours. The recording was fine. He had, unfortunately, set the speed slightly too slow on the new equipment, which, when played back at the proper speed, made Herb Morrison's rich baritone voice sound slightly higher and more frantic than it actually was. That small hiccup aside, it was a remarkable record. The slightly fast speed, combined with the sound of screaming crowds in the background that filtered into Morrison's microphone, only added to the sense of urgency as the disaster unfolded. Now they had to wait to see what the studio head and NBC were going to do with it.

CHAPTER 30

Berlin, Germany: May 7, 1937

Bill Shirer had barely managed to fall back to sleep before the phone rang again. This time it was Claire Trask, who helped arrange European programs for CBS. She was asking if he would come on the air to do a special broadcast for the audience back home to share the German reaction to the disaster that had occurred while they were sleeping.

By this time, Shirer was feeling decidedly "ill-tempered" at having his slumber twice interrupted by news that had broken an ocean away. Furthermore, he was not a radio announcer. He was a journalist. He suggested a few other correspondents who would be much better men for the job. Then he hung up the phone and got himself ready for what was evidently going to be a rather busy day.

Before Shirer even had a chance to leave for the Universal Service office, cables from New York began to flood in demanding to know what local German citizens thought about the disaster as the nation came to terms with the loss of its beloved airship. Above all, New York wanted to hear from Dr. Eckener about what could have caused the traumatic inferno, images of which would be splashed across the front cover of practically every American newspaper, with newsreel soon to follow. Evidently, the American Airlines press officer had handed off Murray Becker's negatives to the courier to be developed in time for the morning papers. The moments he had captured, frozen in time on a filmstrip of cellulose acetate, were remarkable. He had managed to snap the instant flames shot out of the zeppelin's nose as the tail slammed into the ground. Just as impressive were the photographs taken by Sam Shere from Hearst's photo service. Remarkably, Shere had photographed the secondary explosion, which looked like fireworks erupting from the *Hindenburg*'s tail, with the silhouette of the mooring mast in the foreground. It was perhaps the most visually sensational story ever to hit American newsstands.

At 10:00 a.m., Claire Trask called Shirer again. She either could not reach the others he had recommended or they, too, were not interested. Trask pressed him. It did not matter that he had "never broadcast in [his] life." He had the background knowledge on the story, having written a whole series of articles on the *Hindenburg* the year before. He would have the contacts to get the reactions audiences abroad wanted to hear.

Even though the "very idea of talking into a microphone frightened [him]," and he would have to scramble to write a broadcast script alongside his dispatches, he finally relented. At least he would not go on air until evening. As he set about gathering his sources, the idea that either he or Tess could have been on board continued to haunt him.

German papers went to press around midnight, which meant that morning editions had already been printed and distributed on Berlin streets with headlines proclaiming things like NEW YORK WELCOMES THE HINDENBURG without any "hint of the catastrophe." The country's publishers had had to race to print new, special editions to replace the false jubilation with the true and tragic reality. As Germans across the country realized that a horrific accident had, in fact, occurred overnight, reactions were those of disbelief that their magnificent airship, the pride of the German skies, was no more. Flags were promptly lowered as the nation went into mourning. No doubt the Hitler Youth boys who had scrambled across the landing field in Frankfurt to watch the *Hindenburg* depart on Monday night were devastated to learn that the gigantic machine of their dreams had perished in perhaps the worst demise imaginable.

Throughout the day, cables expressing condolences for the large number of German victims arrived for the führer from foreign dignitaries. President Roosevelt was on a fishing trip aboard the USS *Potomac* off the coast of Galveston, Texas, when his secretary, Marvin McIntyre, cabled with the news and a draft public statement of sympathy and condolence. Roosevelt released the statement to Adolf Hitler early the next morning, offering "you and the German people my deepest sympathy for the tragic loss of life." Hitler responded, thanking "your excellency sincerely for the heartfelt words of sympathy which you have expressed to me and the German people." From Britain, George VI telegrammed, "I am deeply shocked by the news of the disaster which has befallen the airship *Hindenburg* and I hasten to express to you, Mr. Chancellor, my sincere condolences on this tragic event, involving as it does the loss of so many lives." Similar messages arrived from the Italian king, Victor Emmanuel III, as well as Prime Minister Benito Mussolini.

Hitler himself had just returned from a trip to Hamburg for the launch of the *Wilhelm Gustloff*, the first cruise ship built under the auspices of the German Labor Front for its "Strength Through Joy" initiative to provide German workers holidays and recreation. The United Press reported that Hitler was apparently "stunned by the news" about the *Hindenburg* but "refused formal comment." Instead, the Deutsches Nachrichtenbüro (DNB), the official German news agency, stated that the new *LZ-130*, currently under construction, would "continue to carry the German flag across the Atlantic."

Shirer's sources had told him that Hitler spent much of the day conferring privately with officials while announcing a relief fund for the families of the crew who had perished. He personally contributed a gift of thirty thousand reichsmarks. Publicly, the führer said nothing about his belief that zeppelins were dangerous. The zeppelins mattered too much to German public imagination for him to criticize them at such a moment. Germans were so attached to them that, according to the Berlin press, factory workers had already offered to work an extra hour per week and donate that pay to a fund to finance a new airship to replace the *Hindenburg*. Hundreds of German organizations had offered to help subsidize the cost. As he did his research throughout the day, it became clear to Shirer that the German people's confidence in the future of zeppelins remained unshaken. The regime really had no choice but to support the zeppelin program—at least for now.

In the meantime, one of *The New York Times*'s Berlin correspondents had tracked down Eckener in Graz, Austria, during the middle of the night. The reporter's call must have seemed like a terrible dream or some kind of prank. False reports of an airship's demise were nothing new to Eckener or the airship community. In fact, practical jokes about airships went back nearly a century. In 1844, Edgar Allan Poe even managed to publish a fake news story in *The New York Sun* about a gas balloon crossing the Atlantic Ocean, a fiasco known as "The Balloon-Hoax." The general public believed it was real, not least because it had taken the paper two full days to retract and correct the story, and only after it had been reprinted in several broadsides.

Eckener wanted to leave Graz and return to his office immediately, but he had to let his driver have some sleep. He agreed to wait until morning. By then, he had been summoned to the Ministry of Aviation in Berlin to discuss what had transpired. Göring had conveniently made a plane available to him in Vienna, just a two-hour drive from Graz in a government-provided car, complete with swastika flag attached to the front (usefully providing Eckener with a sense of the direction the winds were blowing in Austria). As he left the hotel, Ministry of Aviation minder in tow, Eckener stopped to speak with the press. He was still utterly shocked by what had happened, and with so little information at his disposal, he told the press he "could only conclude" at the present time that "an act of sabotage might be responsible" for the disaster. "I do not want to believe it," he told Shirer's Universal Service colleague in the Vienna bureau, "but nevertheless it is possible that the disaster was caused by sabotage. I have received many threats during the last few years and it is possible that some fanatic was responsible for the terrible accident." Eckener simply could not fathom how a design that he and his team had perfected over more than three decades could have had some sort of fatal flaw.

"The only thing which the accident appears to have shown clearly," Eckener stated, "is the necessity, which I have always urged, of using helium in preference to hydrogen in airships." To say he had always urged the use of helium might have been a bit of an overstatement, but he certainly had been steering the company toward what had appeared to be that inevitable direction. Perhaps this would finally convince the Americans to sell the zeppelin company the helium it had long sought.

Once in Berlin, Eckener had several hours of meetings with Göring and other top brass. Göring, like Hitler, had "never thought much of airships," an opinion he reiterated to Eckener, but now, given this public disaster, the Ministry of Aviation "had to hold out." More information had since come in, including about thunderstorms in the Lakehurst area when the *Hindenburg* was trying to land. One of the other Ministry directors suggested that Eckener should refrain from discussing sabotage and that, "on political grounds," he should publicly retract his earlier suggestion of foul play in a radio message in English for the American audience. Sabotage necessarily implied that there were those out there who did not hold Nazi Germany in high regard, and the regime certainly did not want to suggest that. Eckener did not entirely mind this directive, as he found the idea of deliberate sabotage against a zeppelin "most unpleasant," and with this information about the thunderstorm, perhaps there was some sort of atmospheric explanation he had overlooked.

All this time, the *Graf Zeppelin*, under command of Captain Hans von Schiller, was on its way back to Germany from Brazil, having departed before the disaster at Lakehurst occurred. When von Schiller's radio operator first passed him the news, he, too, thought it was a hoax. He was not convinced until they received a second transmission. Von Schiller had grown up on airships with Max Pruss. He did not yet know the fate of his friend. So as not to distract his crew from their duties, he decided not to inform them until nearly the end of their journey, nor would he tell the passengers until they landed. Once back in Germany, the *Graf Zeppelin* would remain grounded until investigators uncovered the source of the catastrophe. It was a shame to lose all that future revenue, especially with the next trip being sold out.

From his calls to DZR in Frankfurt, Luftschiffbau Zeppelin in Friedrichshafen, and the Ministry of Aviation in Berlin, Shirer learned that the German government was immediately dispatching a panel of technical experts, including Eckener and Ludwig Dürr, to America to resolve the question of what had transpired. They would fly by airplane to Cherbourg the next morning to catch up with the steamer SS *Europa*, which had already left Bremerhaven and stopped in France en route to New York. Captain Lehmann's wife would also join the ship at Cherbourg. Eckener departed so quickly he had no time to pack a suitcase, not even a clean shirt or a toothbrush.

As Shirer finished sections of his script for the special broadcast in between his dispatches to New York, he passed them on to Claire Trask, who picked them up at his office. She personally ran it over, page by page, to the censor's office twenty minutes away in the Ministry of Aviation headquarters on Wilhelmstrasse. The massive limestone structure, which had just been constructed for Göring's department of four thousand people on the site of the old Prussian War Ministry, was the largest office building on the continent. Shirer was surprised to learn that the Nazis had instituted censorship for international radio broadcasts. The stories he and many other foreign correspondents filed for their newspapers on a daily basis were far more provocative to the regime, and yet there was no censorship for the articles they wired to New York and London—at least not yet. Trask told him the censorship was a onetime measure given the sensitive nature of the broadcast, which was an exception to the typically noncontroversial light entertainment on the radio. The families of many of the crew were still waiting on news of their loved ones' fates, and it would not be right for them to first receive heartbreaking news from a radio broadcast.

Feelings about the regime and the Luftwaffe bureaucracy aside, the human side of the tragedy unfolding in Friedrichshafen was gut-wrenching. Shirer might have even shaken hands with some of the crew who had perished, during his visit to the zeppelin facility just over a year earlier. Friedrichshafen was a close-knit community in a provincial city on the Bodensee, far removed from Hitler's hate-spawning speeches. The men who had perished were no different from American boys who liked to show off for their sweethearts, pose for silly photographs, and play practical jokes on their crewmates. Most were young men who simply craved adventure. The technical explanation for the disaster would come in due course, but for Shirer, the tragedy's impact on humanity was what he decided to emphasize to the folks back home. Yes, he had deep fears about what Hitler had in store, both for Germany and for the world, but that was a continuing story whose next installment could wait until tomorrow.

"Here in Berlin flags are flying at half-mast today," he decided to begin. "People are stunned at the tragic news from Lakehurst. . . . The families of the sixty-one members of the crew of the great airship still wait anxiously, but with stoical patience, for news of husbands or fathers or sons. Whether they are alive or dead. And if alive whether they will live." It was a universal story, and one that would resonate no matter one's politics. "The zeppelin came here to be considered as safe as a streetcar. After all, no German manned dirigible had crashed since the war." Shirer highlighted the Germans' praise for the heroic efforts of the American rescuers, who had dashed into the flames with no thought for their own safety. He wrote about the donations pouring in from everyday Germans determined to see the *LZ-130* succeed, and Dürr's conviction that they would continue to build zeppelins. They would learn from the disaster and rise above it, quite literally, Eckener insisted, with helium from the United States.

But the "saddest scene" in all of Germany that day, he wrote, was in Friedrichshafen, where the families of the crew had gathered in the *Hindenburg*'s hangar for a "simple but moving mourning ceremony. Hundreds of workers and the mothers, wives and children of the crew crowded into the gaunt hall," where Dürr, before he departed for Cherbourg, called out the names of those known to have perished. If the story Shirer had written on Lindbergh's historic flight almost exactly a decade earlier represented the apex of what aviation could inspire, here was its nadir in the spirit of Icarus, a story of nature clawing back when man encroaches on the dominion of the gods.

That evening, Shirer arrived at the CBS recording studio fifteen minutes before he was supposed to go on air. Worryingly, Claire Trask was not there, nor was the approved script. With five minutes to spare, she rushed in the door with his pages. He could see that the censors had removed his references to Eckener's initial suspicion of sabotage, even though he had already cabled the same information in a story he had filed that afternoon. This was ridiculous. Eckener, the world's foremost zeppelin expert, had said it, so why couldn't he? He and Claire Trask called the Ministry of Aviation to argue about it further, but the government still refused.

As they hung up, the radio engineer was already counting down the sixty seconds to broadcast. Time waited for no one. Such was the nature of live broadcasting. As the seconds ticked ever closer to zero, Shirer began to feel like he had a frog in his throat. "What a lot of nerve-wracking commotion before you even begin a simple broadcast!" he thought, swallowing hard.

The engineer signaled he was on the air. Shirer opened his mouth to speak, his lips parched and throat dry, and a quivering sound came out. His "voice skipped up and down" as he delivered a very squeaky rendition of the information he had previously conveyed in writing with a considerably greater degree of confidence and eloquence.

After the first page, the acute anxiety passed and he began to feel that this radio broadcasting might not be *quite* so bad. At least he did not have "microphone fright," which he had heard made people completely speechless. Still, as he read through his script, he continued to struggle, perhaps not giving the words he had prepared the depth of feeling they deserved. But he persevered, struggling right on to the end until, at last, he was done.

By the time he was finished, he was exhausted and "limp." He felt relief that it was over. No doubt CBS would have second thoughts before enlisting his help again.

When he went home that night, drained from the evening's ordeal, he jotted down some thoughts in his semiregular end-of-day ritual of noting for posterity what had transpired during his days in Berlin. The tragedy at Lakehurst had at least provided one point of clarity.

"Fear I will never make a broadcaster," he concluded.

CHAPTER 31

New Jersey to Chicago, Illinois, USA: May 7, 1937

While many Germans had awakened to false hope when they opened their morning newspapers, there was no such uncertainty in the United States. As the sun rose over the charred remains of the zeppelin, newspapers landed on Americans' doorsteps across the country, proclaiming news of the disaster in banner headlines. In New Haven, Connecticut, Yale students sat down to breakfast with a unique report from the perspective of one of their own. YALE MAN LEAPS FROM HINDENBURG, the *Yale Daily News* headline proclaimed. "Peter Belin, 1936, Jumps 30 Ft. From Blazing Wreckage to Safety." The article promised a "chilling tale of men and women trapped in the blazing wreckage," thanks to an "exclusive telephoned interview from a Princeton house" where Belin had "arrived after a hair-raising escape from the doomed ship."

Thankfully, not all articles covering the disaster were filled with such purple prose. Americans wanted the facts, not least to see if they knew anyone who had been on board. Newspapers large and small announced the names of passengers who had traveled on the airship, including some extraneous names of people who had not. Perhaps several were those who had canceled their tickets and were now reading their own names and imagining a grim alternate version of reality. Though his name was not incorrectly printed on the list, Max Schmeling, the famous German heavyweight boxer, had intended to take that flight. He had just traveled on the *Hindenburg* with Douglas Fairbanks and his uncooperative dog the year before and was in New York preparing for a prospective world championship match against American boxer James J. Braddock at Madison Square Garden. "*Gott im Himmel!*" he shouted when he learned the news at his New York hotel. "How did it happen? How could it happen? . . . I had booked passage on the *Hindenburg* . . . but had to change my plans." He and his trainer had returned their tickets. "I meant to go back to Germany aboard her, too. I just can't understand it. Only yesterday I was telling some friends in New York it was safer to travel on the *Hindenburg* than by boat." Up until that day, that had been true.

The Associated Press, which circulated a correct roster (albeit with many misspellings) directly from the American office of the zeppelin company, listed sixty-three surviving passengers and crew out of a total of ninety-seven people on board. The AP also provided a list of twelve names of passengers who were either dead or as yet unaccounted for by the time the paper went to press, including Hermann Doehner, John and Emma Pannes, and Moritz Feibusch. Twenty-two crew members were presumed dead. Also listed among the missing was Bert Dolan. With Clifford Osbun now confirmed saved, Dolan was the only one of the four Chicagoans on board who had not yet been found.

Meanwhile, in Washington, bureaucrats swiftly jumped into action. Around 11:00 a.m., the U.S. Department of Commerce announced it would be conducting an investigation into the cause of the tragedy. The department appointed one of its senior attorneys, South Trimble Jr., formerly the acting secretary of commerce, to lead the investigation.

For nearly four hours after the crash, the fire and heat from the diesel engines had poured thick, black smoke into the atmosphere, thwarting immediate rescue and recovery efforts. The next morning, the fires were out, and the wreck was in the process of being secured so that no curious tourists or morbid souvenir hunters could gain access until after an investigation had been completed. Still, that did not stop certain opportunists from taking silverware and setting it on fire in trash cans to sell as "authentic" disaster souvenirs.

Alongside doctors, nurses, and military personnel, undertakers had also been called to the scene to assist. They came from as far as Newark, including a sixteen-year-old named Francis Xavier Fahey, who worked at a Newark funeral home as his after-school job and was sent to the disaster site to help clean up. Crews combing through the wreckage started to compile lists of personal effects gathered from the airship's remains. They found binoculars and alarm clocks, bunches of keys, a woman's oval brooch with a porcelain painting, a lorgnette, a golden pince-nez, a monocle, shaving utensils, a cigar cutter, cufflinks, and a wedding ring. There were various cameras and camera accessories and watches of all kinds. Someone even found a dental bridge with an artificial tooth attached. Some of the *Hindenburg*'s crew were allowed to search the wreck for their own belongings. Remarkably, Eduard Boëtius, the navigator who had noticed the zeppelin was consistently tail-heavy during the landing, managed to find his missing cufflink, a family heirloom. Someone else located the bust of President Paul von Hindenburg, which had stood at the top of the stairwell as passengers ascended to A deck and was entirely undamaged. Scattered around the remains of the mess area were teapots, coffeepots, sugar bowls, and a cream pitcher, as well as a box of silverware—the real silverware—that had indeed survived the wreck. Of the 17,609 pieces of mail that were on board, only about 360 items could be saved and forwarded on to their intended recipients.

In the hours after the disaster, the surviving victims of the *Hindenburg* had been rushed to local New Jersey hospitals. Passengers had been sent to Point Pleasant Hospital and Royal Pines Clinic, while several crew members were recovering at Fitkin Memorial Hospital. The largest number went to Paul Kimball Hospital in nearby Lakewood, New Jersey, which was better equipped to receive some of the worst burn victims.

That afternoon, the outgoing German ambassador, Hans Luther, had an important duty to carry out before he returned to Germany. He drove from Washington to Paul Kimball Hospital to visit with those who had been badly wounded and to apologize to the American victims on behalf of the German state.

The small, bespectacled Luther, a public official of the old guard who had served as a chancellor of Germany during the Weimar Republic and later as finance minister and head of the Reichsbank during the banking and currency crises, had tears in his eyes as he went from room to room visiting the wounded. By the time he reached Philip Mangone, he was crying, even though Mangone himself was trying to make light of his misfortune. The fashion designer's eyes were swollen shut and his skin was the color of saffron. His family was with him, including his young granddaughter, who had been briefed, "Granddaddy looks a little funny . . . but if he asks you how he looks, tell him fine."

Instead, the little girl had blurted out, "You look awful, Grandpa," which had made him laugh.

"Thank God, somebody'll tell the truth," Mangone had cracked back.

After visiting with the wounded Americans, Luther paid a call on one of his countrymen. Captain Lehmann had also been taken to Paul Kimball Hospital, and when he had first arrived, he seemed better off than many others, including Captain Pruss, who was miserably burned across his head and face. Lehmann had had a number of visitors earlier that day and was supposed to have been moved to New York City along with Pruss, Captain Sammt, and radio officer Willy Speck for specialist treatment. A wealthy former passenger, William B. Leeds, the heir to a tin fortune, had previously befriended Pruss and arranged for their transfer to a burn center. But in the afternoon, Lehmann's condition quickly turned. It seemed that his internal injuries, perhaps from smoke inhalation, were far worse than doctors initially realized.

While Pruss, Sammt, and Speck were taken to New York covered with yellow, cast-like wrappings around their heads so that only their eyes were visible and moving, Lehmann lay, mummy-like, in his bed at Paul Kimball. His longtime friend Charles Rosendahl kept vigil at his side. Lehmann was clear-eyed and stoic as he realized both his life and his life's work were nearing a mutual terminus. With his remaining strength, he and Rosendahl puzzled over potential causes of the fire, each one leading to a dead end. Not even the lightning he had suspected was the culprit as he sat in the infirmary with Leonhard Adelt made sense in the light of day. "But of course," he said to Rosendahl, "regardless of the cause, the next ship must use helium." As his strength faded, he concluded solemnly to Rosendahl, "It must have been an infernal machine." Lehmann said it, Rosendahl observed, "with an air of finality, as if to summarize his judgment of the case, not with rancor but as if sick at heart that humanity could be so cruel." In its final hours, his mind could accept no other answer.

When the ambassador entered the room, it was late afternoon. By then, Lehmann was ashen faced. "*Herr Kapitän,*" Luther greeted the famous aviator lying before him swaddled in bandages. He looked nothing like the man so recognizable by his pipe, bow tie, and impish smile. "You are one of the bravest men I have seen in all Germany," the ambassador told him. "You will live—for we need men like you."

Lehmann's lips were cracked and caked with blood. He could not speak, but he summoned the energy to muster a smile and lift one of his burned and bandaged hands in appreciation. Gently, the two men shook hands in parting. Then Luther left him in peace. He could see there was little hope for the great captain. When the ambassador walked out of the room, tears were again streaming from his eyes.

An hour later, at 6:42 p.m., just five weeks after the death of his two-year-old son, Ernst Lehmann died, leaving his widow to mourn both husband and son alone.

While Lehmann was by far the most famous airshipman who had died on the *Hindenburg*, he was but one of many of his comrades. Twenty-two members of the crew perished in the inferno. Eight of the seventeen engine mechanics had been killed, as well as two of the three riggers. Two cooks were dead, two elevator men, a helmsman, an engineering officer, an electrician, and two radio officers, including Speck, who died twelve hours after Lehmann, despite his transfer to specialist care. Also among the dead were Max Schulze, the bar steward, and Emilie

Imhof, the stewardess making her first flight. If they had joined Wilhelm Balla as he went upstairs to watch the landing, perhaps they would have survived.

When Emilie Imhof's death was confirmed to German authorities, local police were sent to inventory her possessions. What the forty-three-year-old stewardess left behind was minimal. Each item was listed separately in her estate—a list that ran barely one and a half pages. One toothbrush, one box of matches, two bars of soap, one book. One dark blue suit, one white blouse, one green blouse, one pink blouse, one gray coat. One pair of oatmeal socks, one linen and one leather handbag, three white petticoats, three pajama sets, four dress collars, five coat hangers, thirteen handkerchiefs. In the spirit of thoroughness, they even listed her handful of underthings. It was, of course, a tragedy, but very neatly dealt with, especially for a woman who left little worldly impression on the state in either life or death.

Lehmann's death would be widely grieved, and the *Hindenburg* victims broadly lamented, but most of those who died, especially from the crew, passed on to the next life with little to say from the grave that would allow them to be mourned for their individual humanity.

At 11:45 a.m., Chicagoland listeners who turned their dials to WLS to hear the market reports and general news headlines were in for a surprise. "Ladies and gentlemen," an announcer began, "in place of the program originally scheduled for this period, we present now the most unique broadcast we have ever presented. An actual eyewitness description of the disaster at Lakehurst, New Jersey, last night. The destruction of the giant airship *Hindenburg*. In keeping with the policy of the National Broadcasting Company," the announcer explained, the audience would, of course, expect to hear live coverage. However, on this one occasion, circumstances required something different.

History unfolded before listeners' ears as they heard recorded content on the airwaves for the first time. Any concerns about listeners doubting its legitimacy or feeling a sense of detachment from a recorded broadcast were quickly dispelled. WLS aired the entire recording, all forty-two minutes of it, cutting into its precious lunchtime *Dinnerbell Program*. Midwesterners sat at rapt attention listening to Morrison's calm and artful description of the zeppelin's arrival quickly punctuated by his cry of "Oh, the humanity!" which lodged in listeners' minds as if they had been standing beside him in the misting rain.

At 2:30 p.m. Eastern Daylight Time, NBC's national ban on recorded content was temporarily lifted. Instead of soprano Dorothy Dreslin, listeners across the country heard the most dramatic excerpts of Morrison's recording. So gripping was the tragedy unfolding on the airwaves that the public demanded that the station air it again in prime time, which it agreed to do that same evening. WLS listeners, too, clamored for an encore, which WLS gave them in condensed form the following evening at 9:30.

From coast to coast, Morrison's words filled families' living rooms, albeit with his voice projecting in a more tenor register than his actual baritone, due to the slight problem with the recording speed. The repeat broadcasts of Herb Morrison's voice, combined with the newsreel footage from Pathé, Fox Movietone, Paramount, and Universal, seared the sounds and images of the disaster into the minds of Americans across the country, quickly making the *Hindenburg* disaster more familiar to them than their own memories.

When WLS aired their broadcast at midday on May 7, Morrison and Nehlsen, still somewhat in a state of shock, had not yet had time to go home, even for a shower and a shave. Instead, they spent most of that morning and afternoon having their pictures taken in a semidisheveled state after two days of travel, still smelling of singed wool, as colleagues and admirers pumped their hands in congratulations. When pressed on what the ordeal had been like as he stood watching the *Hindenburg* go down in a blaze, Morrison gave all credit to his sound engineer for what they had unexpectedly but miraculously achieved. "The whole night was like a horrible nightmare," he said. "If it hadn't been for Charlie, I would have broken down completely." But for his quick thinking when the explosive percussion had knocked the arm of the needle off the disc, there would have been no recording at all. Charlie Nehlsen had been "calm through it all and kept me on my course," Morrison lauded. "He was the real hero!"

When Nehlsen was pressed about it in turn, he simply shook his head and replied that anyone wanting to know about it should "ask Herb. He saw the whole thing. All I did was stick to my post and record his work."

CHAPTER 32

Chicago, Illinois, USA: May 10, 1937

Mildred Dolan passed the night of May 6 in the agony of uncertainty. She had spent hours on the phone calling anyone who might know something about her husband's whereabouts, if he was alive, and if he had even been on the *Hindenburg*'s passenger manifest at all. By midnight, she was exhausted and tried to sleep, still tormented by the lack of any clear information. The certainty she both desired and dreaded came the next day when a New Jersey priest called the Dolan home to tell Mildred that Bert's body had been found and identified by the passport in his pocket. It seemed that a piece of the burning wreck had fallen on him. The priest had personally given her husband his last rites. If it was any solace to Mildred, he had been clutching a rosary in his hand when he died.

His body arrived home on Saturday, May 8, less than forty-eight hours after the disaster. His brother-in-law went to identify him, and any last chance that there was some mix-up, that the entire situation was a mistake and Bert was halfway across the ocean on a steamer, disappeared. Never would Mildred see the cashmere coat he had selected in London, the one he had been so certain she would like. The last kisses he would give his wife and children would be on their pictures.

The next day, Mother's Day, Mildred sat down at the dining room table with her children. She looked at her twelve-year-old son, Bud—Burtis J. Dolan Jr.—and told him to sit at the head of the table. He was the man of the house now.

Letters of condolence began to arrive, especially from Bert's friends at the Edgewater Golf Club. The board of directors wrote on behalf of the entire membership to express their "deep and sincere sympathy." One took the time to write individually. Chick Evans, the champion golfer and one of Bert's close friends, had read the news of his death in the papers. "By a strange chance I had that day been thinking of the time we all talked together on the practice course at Edgewater. It seems but yesterday, and I cannot realize that he is gone," Evans wrote. "His death is a great grief to me, and I beg you and the children to accept my deepest sympathy."

On Monday, May 10, the Lelong company took out a small space in the *Chicago Tribune* for an announcement bordered in black: "In silent sorrow and respect for [Burtis J.] Dolan, vice-president of Lucien Lelong, Inc., victim of the *Hindenburg* disaster, our offices will remain closed, Monday, May 10, 1937." It was the day of his funeral, the first for any of the *Hindenburg* victims.

At the Dolan family's neighborhood parish, Saint Mary of the Lake, Major Burtis J. Dolan, veteran of the Great War, was given a military funeral, his coffin passing under an arch of crossed swords as it entered the stone edifice. The Reverend Thomas Mackin, Mildred's cousin, who had married the young lovers fifteen years earlier after their long courtship, said the requiem. When the family left the church, the Associated Press snapped a photograph of Mildred, black veil covering her face, with her children behind her.

Later that day, the family made its way north to the Calvary Cemetery on Lake Michigan. As the sound of taps played and American Legion companies fired a volley in salute, Bert Dolan was laid to rest alongside his brother, Leslie, buried in the family plot just five months earlier. The American flag that draped his coffin was removed and folded in ceremonial fashion and presented to his widow as waves gently lapped against the shore.

Of all the letters Mildred received in the days and weeks that followed, the most tragic was Bert's own. It had been tucked into his pocket along with his pocket watch and passport and found on his body after he died. The envelope was singed in the upper left-hand corner, but his notation of "Strictly Personal" on the envelope addressed to Mr. and Mrs. B. J. Dolan, care of his office in the Pittsfield Building, was entirely clear, as were all but a handful of the words he had scrawled on stationery from his hotel in Paris. His letter read like a premonition, part of God's larger plan that neither he nor Mildred could explain, which made it all the more heartbreaking. In it, she read of his encounter with Nelson in the South of France, and of how quickly his ticket had been booked, and of how he had hoped the trip might lead to some publicity for Lelong. Really, this last piece was just Bert talking himself into a plan he did not actually desire but could not turn down out of pride and worry over embarrassing himself in front of his friend. Throughout, the weight of Bert's feeling of guilt over having broken his promise to his wife rang through.

Above all, what his words conveyed was the limitless love he felt for his family. In his final two paragraphs, he left his wife with a message of parting so sweetly poignant that no father and husband could have written final words more sincerely from the heart:

> *So there is the story, angel, and if the Lord may call me, I wanted you to have my explanation. Until your letter came I had no fear at all because it did not seem to me you would think it foolish.*
>
> *If you could but know my lonesomeness these four months and my heartache for you you would understand how I could get into such a pickle. I have been so tired of it all—but striving to do so well that it would all be easier for you. I have done well and please God we will benefit by it.*
>
> *All my love forever sweet for you all,*
> *Bert*

Mildred was always foremost in his mind, and if they were to be parted, Bert had made sure that she would receive one last message from him before he left her in this world, a message she could carry with her until they were reunited in the next.

Famed airship captain
Hugo Eckener in 1924.

Captain Ernst Lehmann in his Deutsche Zeppelin-Reederei uniform and smoking his signature pipe.

Left to right: German ambassador Hans Luther, President Franklin D. Roosevelt, Hugo Eckener, and Ernst Lehmann during a congratulatory visit to the White House following the first transatlantic flight of the *Hindenburg* in May 1936.

William L. Shirer, Universal Service Berlin correspondent, ca. 1930s.

Bill and Tess Shirer on a winter holiday in Europe, ca. 1930s.

Partially inflated gas cells hang from the frame of the *Hindenburg* during construction in the Luftschiffbau Zeppelin hangar in Friedrichshafen.

With the *Hindenburg*'s frame and outer cover largely complete, gas cells have begun to be permanently attached throughout the body of the airship.

The mostly completed frame of the *Hindenburg* during construction.

Workers on forty-five-meter ladders brush "dope," a paint- and glue-like substance mixed with aluminum powder, on the canvas cover of the *Hindenburg*. Dope helped to make the cover taut and to deflect harmful sun rays that could damage the delicate gas cells inside.

Workers prepare lettering that will be applied to the outside cover of the newly named zeppelin in a vibrant shade of vermillion. The Nazis believed this angular script lettering, a typeface called Fraktur, to be authentically German in style. Each letter on the *Hindenburg* was written in lower case, as heavy Fraktur capitals were difficult to read at a distance.

The enormous scale of the *Hindenburg*'s tail and requisite swastika standard of Hitler's Third Reich.

The damaged tail fin of the *Hindenburg* after it smashed into the ground while its crew removed it from its hangar in high winds at the insistence of Reich Minister of Propaganda Joseph Goebbels. Goebbels was intent on using the *Hindenburg* and *Graf Zeppelin* to support propaganda efforts around the rigged March 1936 plebiscite and parliamentary election.

The *Hindenburg* and *Graf Zeppelin* fly over Berlin's iconic Brandenburg Gate in March 1936. As part of a publicity stunt, votes were cast on board the zeppelins while flying over the Rhineland, which returned unanimous support for Hitler's aggressive maneuver that violated the Treaty of Versailles.

The Reich Committee for Tourism commissioned commercial artist Jupp Wiertz to design a poster to attract tourists from North and South America to Germany in 1936 as part of a broader effort by the Third Reich to provide foreigners with a positive impression of the country. Germany's steamship line Norddeutscher Lloyd, its growing Deutsche Lufthansa airline, and, of course, the brand-new *Hindenburg* feature prominently against a collage of New York's skyline, Rio de Janeiro's Sugarloaf Mountain, and the Brandenburg Gate.

The impressive scale of the *Hindenburg* is fully appreciated when anchored to its mooring mast in the middle of the landing field at the Naval Air Station in Lakehurst, New Jersey, in 1936.

Burtis "Bert" J. Dolan, ca. 1930s.

Margaret Mather's passport photo, ca. 1914.

Mildred Dolan with her three oldest children, Burtis Jr. (2), Mildred (1), and Mary Alice (4), in 1927.

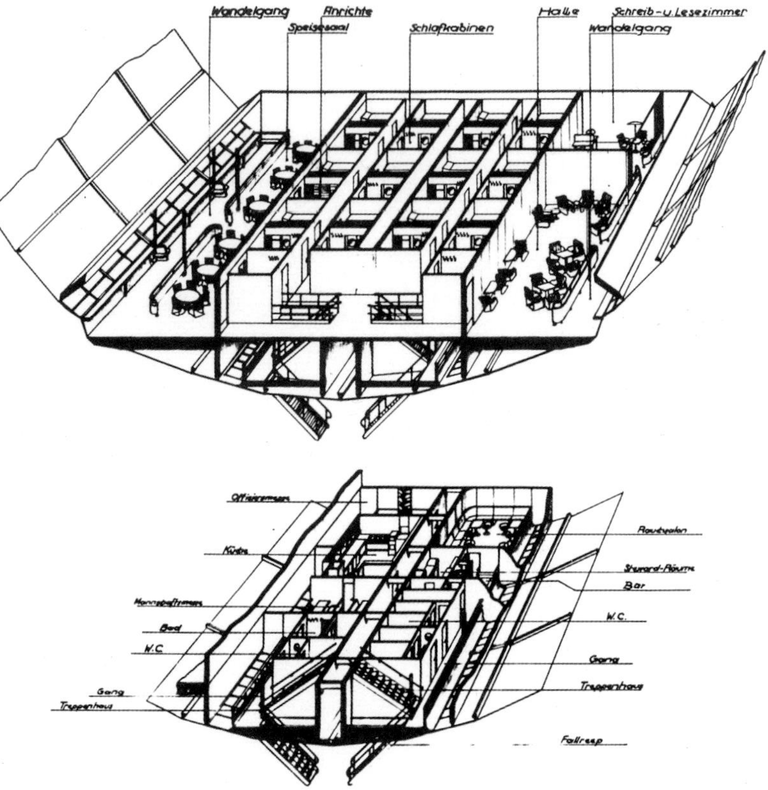

This cross section details the layout of the passenger areas of the *Hindenburg*. The larger A deck holds the dining room, lounge, and writing room, with passenger cabins in the middle. Below, the B deck features the bar, smoking lounge, restrooms, steward's cabin, passenger shower, kitchen, and crew's mess. Additional passenger cabins were added later.

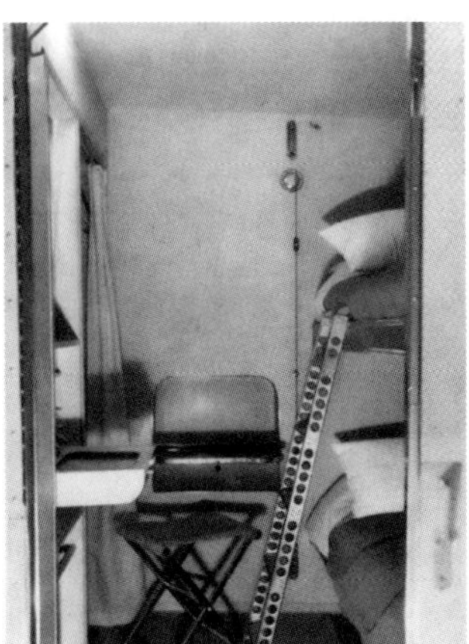

Left: Like sleeping berths on luxurious trains, the *Hindenburg*'s double-occupancy accommodations maximized efficiency and lightweight materials in their design.

Right: The smoking lounge, with Otto Arpke's illustrations of the history of aviation, was situated next to the bar on B deck behind an air-lock door.

The portside dining room, adorned with Otto Arpke's illustrations of scenes from a zeppelin flight to South America painted on silk to minimize weight, could be arranged as pictured, or with the tables combined to form one long, communal table where guests dined as a group. Beside the dining room, the long promenade with its sloping plexiglass windows offered stunning views of oceans, icebergs, and passing ships below.

Captain Max Pruss, commander of the *Hindenburg*'s final journey, shown here in the control gondola.

The starboard passenger lounge provided guests with a chic, modern space in which to relax and enjoy the company of fellow travelers. Its stylish design included lightweight aluminum furniture and a mural depicting some of history's great voyages across sea and sky.

Off-duty crew members—left to right: engine mechanics August Deutschle and Adolf Fischer and stewards Wilhelm Balla and Eugen Nunnenmacher—enjoy their leisure time with a female friend.

A teenage Joseph "Benny" Spah, performing under the name "Ben Dova," in a publicity shot for his *Kautschuk Gymnastiker* (rubber gymnastics) routine.

Gertrud and Leonhard Adelt with their son, Christian, at the beach, 1940.

Benny Spah as a young, daredevil aviator.

Benny Spah testing parachutes for seventy-five dollars.

Benny Spah strikes a casual pose atop his swaying lamppost in a publicity shot for his "Convivial Inebriate" routine, with his wife, Vera, a fellow performer, brandishing a policeman's baton below.

Herbert Morrison in his hometown of Scottdale, Pennsylvania, as Scoutmaster of Troop 2 in the late 1920s. Morrison scraped together as much money as he could from odd jobs like serving as a Boy Scouts fencing instructor to pay for flight lessons in hopes of someday earning a pilot's license.

To promote its exclusive connecting service between Lakehurst, Newark, and destinations beyond, American Airlines produced these baggage tags that depicted its new fleet of DC-3s as the sleek, glamorous, and modern American answer to Germany's wildly popular zeppelins. The baggage tag's designer subtly removed the *Hindenburg*'s controversial insignia, instead including a red dot on its tail.

The *Hindenburg* over New York City's skyline on May 6, 1937, just hours before tragedy struck, as captured by a press plane flying alongside.

The iconic image of the *Hindenburg* disaster as captured by photojournalist Sam Shere of Hearst's International News Photo. Shere would later say he had no time to put his Speed Graphic camera up to his eye and instead "literally 'shot' from the hip." A version of this photo would later be used as the cover art for Led Zeppelin's debut album in 1969.

Amateur photographer Arthur Cofod Jr. captured this image of a mushroom cloud of burning hydrogen hovering above the falling wreck of the *Hindenburg*, almost as if a spectral twin of the doomed zeppelin is hanging overhead.

Associated Press photographer Murray Becker captured the moment the *Hindenburg*'s stern section collapses into the ground as tongues of fire shoot through the nose and members of the landing crew sprint away from the hellscape.

U.S. Navy sailors from the Lakehurst Naval Air Station rush to help passengers and crew escape the blaze. One silhouetted survivor runs from the flames (right). Just moments after ignition, all that is left is its duralumin frame.

The Spah family (left to right: Richard, Vera, Marilyn, Benny, and Gilbert) reunited in hangar number 1 at Lakehurst Naval Air Station after the *Hindenburg* disaster. Benny's remarkable athleticism no doubt helped him survive a multistory fall with only a broken ankle.

German American passenger Moritz Feibusch's passport salvaged from the *Hindenburg*'s wreckage. Feibusch had built a highly successful business in San Francisco and was in the process of bringing his extensive family to the United States in the face of mounting hostility toward Jews in Germany.

The skeleton of the *Hindenburg* lies charred on the ground in the middle of the sandy landing field, with hangar number 1 in the distance.

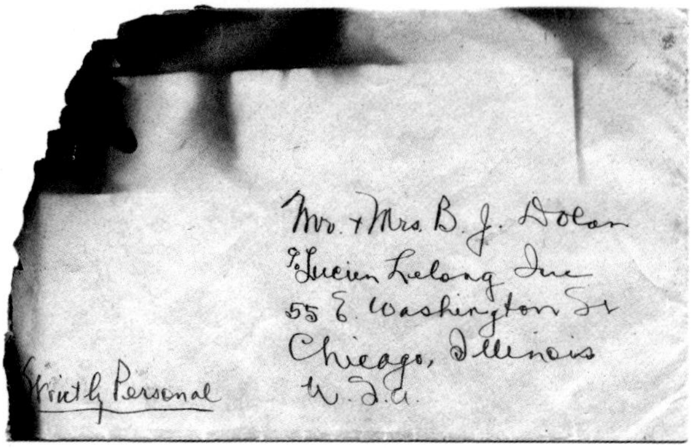

The envelope for Bert Dolan's unmailed letter, his notation marking it "Strictly Personal" visible despite the scorching.

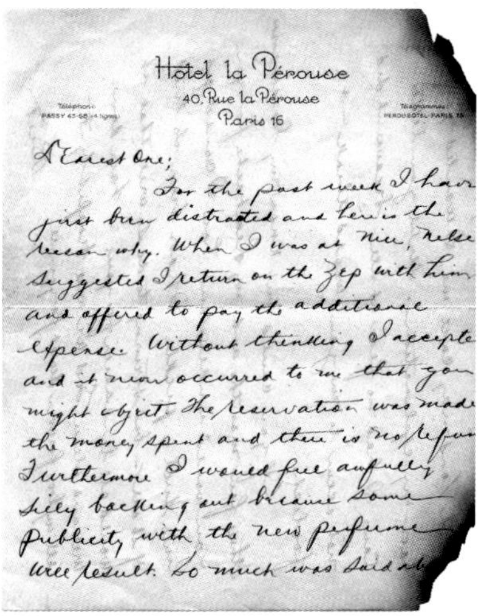

Hotel la Pérouse
40, Rue la Pérouse
Paris 16

Dearest One;

For the past week I have just been distracted and here is the reason why. When I was at Nice, Nelson suggested I return on the Zep with him and offered to pay the additional expense. Without thinking I accepted and it never occurred to me that you might object. The reservation was made the money spent and there is no refund. Furthermore I would feel awfully silly backing out because some publicity with the new perfume will result. So much was said ab

Bert Dolan's unmailed letter to his wife, Mildred, which survived the crash and was found on his person after he died. In his tragically poignant letter, he writes of breaking his promise to her that he would not fly, an ominous premonition of all that followed.

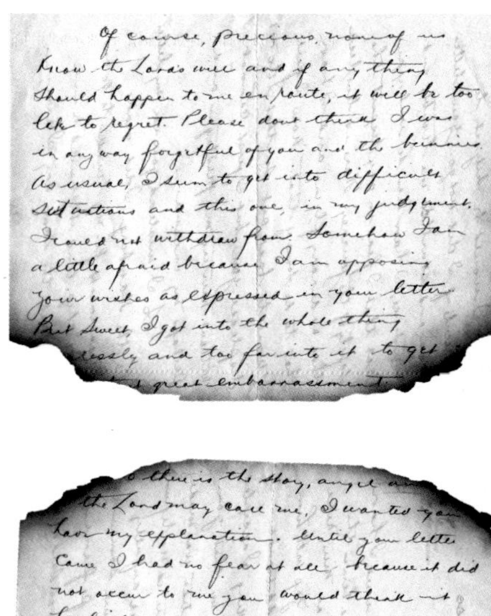

Of course, precious, none of us know the Lord's will and if anything should happen to me en route, it will be too late to regret. Please don't think I was in any way forgetful of you and the bunnies. As usual, I seem to get into difficult situations and this one, in my judgement, I could not withdraw from. Somehow I am a little afraid because I am opposing your wishes as expressed in your letter. But Sweet, I got into the whole thing lessly and too far into it to get great embarrassment

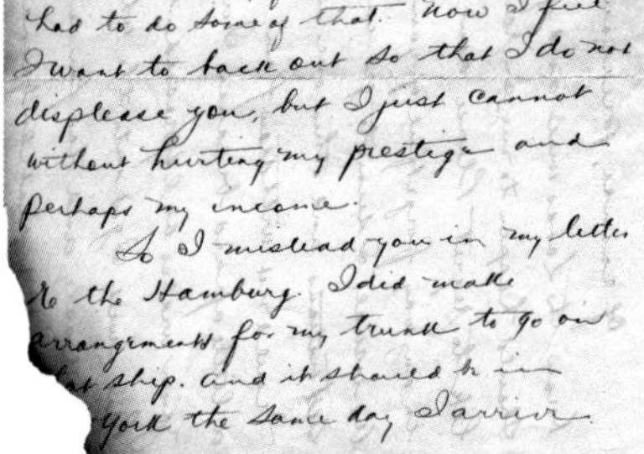

I would be subject to ridicule if I did not go. Your letter me and startled me terribly and ever since, I have been so unhappy. Not that I fear in any respect the safety of the journey. There is less risk than ordinary flying and I have had to do some of that. Now I feel I want to back out so that I do not displease you, but I just cannot without hurting my prestige and perhaps my income.

So I mislead you in my letter to the Hamburg. I did make arrangements for my trunk to go on at ship. And it should be in York the same day I arrive.

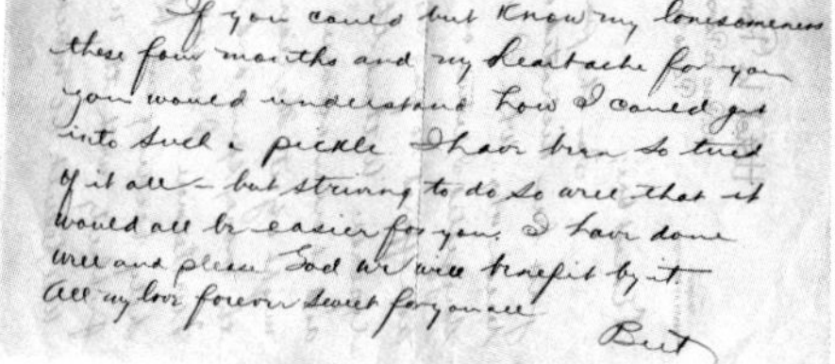

o there is the story, angel and the Lord may call me, I wanted you have my explanation. Until your letter came I had no fear at all because it did not occur to me you would think it foolish.

If you could but know my lonesomeness these four months and my heartache for you you would understand how I could get into such a pickle. I have been so tired of it all — but striving to do so well that it would all be easier for you. I have done well and please God we will benefit by it. All my love forever sweet for you and

Bert

Members of German American societies, clad in attire mirroring paramilitary groups in Germany, parade with arms raised in a Nazi salute past swastika-covered coffins of *Hindenburg* victims on the Hamburg-America Line pier in New York City, May 11, 1937.

Chief Steward Heinrich Kubis stands with a fatherly hand on cabin boy Werner Franz's shoulder at Lakehurst Naval Air Station several days after the disaster.

Surviving crew members, freshly attired in new suits, return home to Germany on the steamer *Europa*. Young Werner Franz stands in the middle with the *Europa*'s captain behind him in uniform. Chief Steward Heinrich Kubis is fourth from left, while Wilhelm Balla is third from right.

On May 23, 1937, six members of the *Hindenburg* crew are laid to rest in Friedrichshafen in a funeral ceremony filled with Nazi Party flourishes.

Nelson Morris and his wife, Blanche, returning to France in July 1937 following the *Hindenburg* disaster. Nelson wears gloves to protect the burned skin on his hands.

Gertrud and Leonhard Adelt join Benny and Vera Spah for a screening of Benny's *Hindenburg* footage during the performer's return trip to Germany, autumn 1937.

CHAPTER 33

New York and New Jersey, USA: Early to Mid-May 1937

In his Tudor house in Douglaston, New York, Benny Spah was inundated with telegrams and letters pouring into his mailbox from across the United States and Europe as his many family members, friends, and admirers wished him well in his recovery. Performers he had worked with sent their regards, including Joe Jackson's son, who wrote that the last few days had been "the worst days of my life" after learning that Benny Spah had been on the *Hindenburg* in no small part due to his father: "Gee Ben—God was good. He spared you for your wife & kiddies and my Dad for me." Benny also had a telegram from his old partner, Bernt, with whom he first came to America, as well as a letter from someone he did not know named Benjamin Dover, who had read about him in the newspaper and wondered if there might be any familial connection or particular reason that Joseph Spah had selected "Ben Dover" as his original stage name. Just two days after the disaster, Benny began receiving requests to come and speak to students and local clubs. He even had a letter from a most unusual source: "The writer of these lines is the travel agent from whom you bought your airline ticket in Munich. . . . Best wishes for a speedy recovery," the letter read. Apparently, the man felt compelled to contact him out of a sense of guilt over his small part in putting him in harm's way.

Relatives in Germany wrote asking what had happened to his luggage, including the oil paintings he had purchased abroad, as well as "faithful Ulla." Benny had certainly been thinking about what he had lost, Ulla in particular. The zeppelin company's American office had asked each passenger to submit a list of belongings lost in the fire, including their value. In his list, Benny included a typewriter, a silk bathrobe and pajamas, slippers, exposed film, one portrait oil painting, two landscape oil paintings, a box of children's toys, a tobacco pouch and pipe, a leather picture case, a wristwatch, a pocket compass, a toilet set, an English raincoat in the pocket of which had been his passport, a fountain pen, a pocketbook, binoculars, a Bell & Howell camera, and a "German Police Dog . . . two years old," which he had purchased for $250. The total for his lost items came to $912.00, with poor Ulla by far the most expensive thing on his list.

Benny had promised his children that Ulla had jumped to safety, and he was determined to find a new dog to replace the poor beast, so as not to upset them more than they already were. In the days following the disaster, they jumped whenever they heard loud noises, even though loud noises had never bothered them before. Benny knew some performer friends who were looking to sell a puppy, but it was a smaller dog of an entirely different breed. He hoped the children were young enough that they would not notice, but when Benny brought the dog home, four-year-old Gilbert piped up, "I thought you said it was a big dog." Thinking quickly, Benny told his son that Ulla had shrunk in the heat. She would soon return to normal size.

Several days later, Vera was looking through the newspaper when she noticed an article with pictures of lost items that had been found in the *Hindenburg* wreckage. In the picture was a Bell & Howell camera together with its case, as well as a pair of binoculars. She showed it to Benny. He could not believe it. Those were his binoculars and his camera, the one he had used to film his family on the ground and then to smash the plexiglass window. He contacted DZR's American office, which confirmed that the camera was in the custody of the Philadelphia customs authorities. A short time later, Benny drove to Philadelphia to retrieve his things. The binoculars and camera were scratched, some of the black paint had come off, and the leather camera case smelled distinctly of smoke. When he got home, he opened the camera. Reason suggested the highly flammable roll of cellulose nitrate film would have burned or melted, but when he looked inside, the film was still intact, in pristine condition. And when he fed it into his projector, black-and-white images of the ghostlike shadow of the *Hindenburg* swimming on the ocean's surface sprang to life.

Though the German expert delegation would not reach New Jersey until May 13, the Department of Commerce wasted no time commencing the investigation. The vast majority of people on the list of nearly one hundred witnesses they wanted to interview were *Hindenburg* crew and Naval Air Station personnel, though there were a handful of other experts and civilian witnesses, including two women, one the wife of a Lakehurst officer and the other a spectator. Curiously, though not badly injured and each just an hour's drive away, neither Margaret Mather nor Gertrud and Leonhard Adelt were on the list.

To field as wide an array of evidence as possible, the investigation committee also sent questionnaires and a simple diagram of the airship to several hundred eyewitnesses, asking them to indicate where they believed the fire began and the vantage from which they first observed it, and to describe the color and the sound of the flames. What the Board of Inquiry had not requested, however, were unsolicited tips from the general public, nor did the general public limit themselves to merely sending tips to South Trimble and the Bureau of Air Commerce, the Commerce Department's relevant subsection, which was responsible for the hearings. From May 7, the day immediately following the disaster, conspiracy theories began to run rampant. So-called tips flooded into the department, to Commander Rosendahl and the navy, to Ambassador Luther and the German consulate in New York, as well as to Dr. Eckener, New York Senator Royal Copeland, President Roosevelt, and especially the FBI. While the prevailing public reaction in the United States was undoubtedly one of great sadness accompanied by a reaffirmation of confidence in air travel and future scientific progress, there was a shadow sentiment lurking alongside this optimism deep within the recesses of certain individuals' minds and souls. Usually, this sentiment was kept at bay and remained hidden from view, but when such impulses find fertile ground, they emerge from a Pandora's box and can be shoved back in only with the greatest strain.

Some of the "tips" were the typical absurdities, each more ridiculous than the last. These included theories of curses, time bombs, and disgruntled inventors, a plotline that could have been lifted directly from the film that the *Yale Daily News* had panned. Multiple individuals suggested a gunman had leaned out the window of a circling airplane and fired a bullet that made the enormous zeppelin crash. Another suggested a cabal of photographers had conspired to create an accident for the sake of selling sensational photographs. Someone named E. O. Bagley Jr. from Little Rock, Arkansas, intimated that Captain Lehmann was jealous that Pruss had taken over his command and was depressed since the death of his son. He urged investigators to pursue the theory that Lehmann was out for revenge with a possible desire to collect insurance money. On the insurance theme, the American president of a group called the "PlanetAryans" wrote suggesting that a Nazi agent—a femme fatale—had planted a device inside the *Hindenburg* because the German government was short on cash and needed to collect insurance money.

Then there was the usual communist folderol. A man named Hans Omenitsch told the Commerce Department he had seen a secret code scattered throughout New York City newspapers "operated by an invisible super government," no doubt controlled by the Reds. (The FBI was already aware of this man "on account of his numerous suggestions which he had offered in connection with the Lindbergh kidnapping case.")

Far more unsettling than the communist conspiracy theories were the many letters laced with antisemitism. Some letters were relatively tame, one, in fact, almost tragically romantic despite its prejudice. The writer theorized that an ill passenger on board had tried to commit suicide but while attempting to shoot himself had missed and blown up the ship accidentally. It sounded like a typical crank letter, except for the fact that the author of the letter, Josephine Mair, specifically told the German consulate that she was motivated to write because the "friendship of both countries which are to me mother and fatherland, is to me personally just as holy as the love to my race—ARYAN."

Many letters were far more vicious in their hatred of Jews. Some authors of these vituperative "tips" were self-identified German Americans or appeared to be of German descent, but by no means were all obviously Germanic. These provided alarming insight into the widespread antisemitism that had permeated American society. One person wrote to the FBI that the *Hindenburg* disaster had been an "act of Jewish sabotage, inspired by the Talmud," the foundational text of Jewish law. Another man, named Tom Fagan, wrote to Rosendahl that he had "heard it was a Jewish deed." He claimed to have seen two men in an expensive car who were "dark" and "typical Jewish looking" talking to a poorly dressed man with a rifle that he tried to conceal under an overcoat. Fagan had supposedly heard them say, "Hide it quick," as "evidently they were waiting for the airship." A man named August Schütze wrote to Ambassador Luther that he had seen a picture in the *Detroit Times* of a Jewish father and son who were supposed to fly to Europe for the coronation of King George VI. He was surprised they would want to fly on an airship with a swastika on it. The only explanation he could come up with was that their planned trip was part of a Jewish conspiracy that involved a time bomb meant to have gone off on the return trip to Germany but for the hours-long delay in landing. He closed his letter, "With German Greetings: Heil Hitler!"

Meanwhile, "an American friend of Germany" wrote to Dr. Eckener that "some communist or disgruntled jew" had fired a rifle from a rooftop on Greenwich Street as the *Hindenburg* was passing over New York City, which had resulted in the fire. (The writer made no effort to explain the delayed onset of effects of such a bullet supposedly fired many hours before the ultimate disaster.) The bullet-fired-from-a-rooftop theory apparently had some traction. "You should send for . . . the half jew, half wop Mayor La Guardia in your *Hindenburg* examination," another person wrote to Senator Copeland, suggesting that La Guardia had wanted to prevent German boxer Max Schmeling, who was not even traveling on the zeppelin and was already in New York City, from fighting American boxing champion James J. Braddock. This person believed three shots had been fired from a building near the Battery by a "hireling of anti-nazis" who had been "paid by the jews." The writer concluded, "It wont be long now, Senator, before Americans start massacring kikes just as other nations have done. They are no good sons of bitches and have been so for ages."

Also popular was a ludicrous version of the "crazy inventor" theory, but with a distinctly anti-Semitic flavor. "Mr. X. Y. Z." claimed that a disgruntled "mad Genius" photographer who was a German Jewish refugee had shot down the *Hindenburg* with a bullet from a camera he had invented, which had more firepower than a machine gun. This tipster wished to remain anonymous and requested that any follow-up questions be addressed to him in the *New York Times* personal column.

There were not one but two such anti-Semitic "shooting photographer" letters. Perhaps the most rabidly delusional, invective-laden, and trope-filled rubbish came from an Ernst Goerner, who wrote to Ambassador Luther about a photographer who shot not film but an incendiary bullet from behind the cloak of an old-fashioned camera:

> *The Jews, as you already know, are a cunning and foxy breed, and resort to any device to accomplish their operations of terror upon the unsuspecting. What more advantageous a position could be taken for such a fiendish deed than that of hiding behind the cloak of a PHOTOGRAPHER—WHO SHOOTS. . . . You well know the Jews' weakness of showing off, capitalizing on the sufferings of others. Their love for seeing their names and faces on the front page of the press . . . A Jew always, in his desire to make a show of himself, always betrays himself, this to me is a very marked case of guilt. . . . I am sending several copies of this paper to Germany with my deepest sympathy for a much misunderstood country, the way of which has been paved with great Jewish money power, influence and highly paid propagandists, but with all this there is going on a slow awakening to facts—I have not lost faith in true Americanism.*

The FBI estimated that a full 20 percent of the *Hindenburg*-related correspondence it received—one in five pieces—blamed the tragic accident on Jews who had supposedly brought down the *Hindenburg* with various preposterous methods of sabotage. The Commerce Department Board of Inquiry and the FBI determined that such tips "failed to reflect any information of value upon which an investigation by the Bureau might be reasonably warranted in connection with any possible sabotage or other Federal violations."

Instead, the Board of Inquiry focused its time and efforts on the testimony and observations of the most knowledgeable eyewitnesses and experts in the field of lighter-than-air aviation and quickly got to work. Still, once these heinously appalling conspiracy theories had caught fire, it would be difficult to stamp out the sparks that seemed to blow on the wind across the country, burning brightly in the minds of those who, for reasons of insidious resentment, desperately wanted to believe them.

CHAPTER 34

New York, New York, and Atlantic City, New Jersey, USA: May 10–11, 1937

On May 10, the investigation officially got underway in Lakehurst. Commander Charles Rosendahl began the proceedings by leading the Commerce Department's Board of Inquiry out to the crash site so that they could see it with their own eyes. The charred remains of the *Hindenburg* lay still, the silhouette of its form seared black into the ground like an eight-hundred-foot shadow cast permanently from above. As they approached the wreck, they saw a slight boy arguing with a guard. At first glance, he might have looked like a local scamp hunting for a souvenir, but it was, in fact, the *Hindenburg*'s cabin boy, Werner Franz, who was searching what was left of the officers' mess for anything he could recognize. He had a small piece of something in his hand, and the guard was trying to make him put it back.

Rosendahl intervened and took a look at the item in the boy's hand. It was just a scrap of metal, charred and of no value to anyone. He settled the quarrel by allowing Franz to keep the worthless fragment if the memento meant so much to him and sent him on his way.

A small piece of the airship of dreams apparently did have some emotional value to the young boy desperately trying to bring order back to his world so far from home. For the last few days, he had been looked after by the family of Captain Anton Heinen, a veteran German airship commander who had moved to the United States fifteen years earlier to advise and train U.S. Navy airshipmen and now served as the Naval Air Station's primary captain. At least the Heinens spoke his language, and they did their best to serve as a surrogate family on what were surely the worst days of Franz's life.

The cabin boy was soon given a second balm to help ease his pain. Five days after the crash, on May 11, he finally got his wish to see New York City from the ground. Since the disaster, Franz had been wearing borrowed clothes, but now he needed something proper of his own. Along with ten fellow crew members who were relatively uninjured but whose uniforms were mostly scorched and tattered, Franz and his mates were sent on a bus into the city in the loaned uniforms of American marines to buy new clothing at Wanamaker's department store on Broadway on the zeppelin company's dime. A few hours later, dressed in new blue suits, Franz, Balla, and the others strolled up New York's famous street and ate lunch in a skyscraper, but neither the spiffy new outfits nor the chance to live like the kings of New York for an afternoon made any of them happy. That evening, they would be attending the funeral of twenty-eight of those who had died on the *Hindenburg*, including twenty-two of the crew and their beloved Captain Lehmann.

At 6:00 p.m. at the Hamburg-America Line's pier 86 at West Forty-Sixth Street and the Hudson River, ten thousand people gathered to say farewell to the dead, who would begin their final journey home to Germany on the SS *Hamburg* at midnight. The vast baggage hall along the thousand-foot pier had been transformed into a cavernous, church-like space. Green cedar boughs hid the pillars supporting the pier, along which lay twenty-eight identical tin coffins in a single row, each covered with the flag of the victim's national origin lying over a black shroud. The coffin of the Swedish passenger who had perished, Birger Brinck, was draped in the gold Nordic cross set against a field of blue, while Moritz Feibusch's coffin, ultimately bound for San Francisco, bore the Stars and Stripes of his adopted homeland. Stretching out down the pier, the remaining twenty-six were adorned with the flag of the Third Reich, the black and red punctuating the somber atmosphere. Above the coffins similarly hung the victims' national flags fluttering from the beams of the hall's canopy-like roof, while brown-shirted representatives of German American clubs and organizations formed an honor guard behind them. It was as if the German victims were already back in the fatherland. In fact, the ceremony along the Hudson River honoring the *Hindenburg*'s fallen was not the only one taking place in New York City that day. At the Yorkville Casino on East Eighty-Sixth Street, a neighborhood home to a sizable German population, another thousand people gathered at a memorial hosted by Fritz Kuhn's German American Bund, where, in the dimly lit hall, over one hundred members of the league's most dedicated members lined the center aisle for a tribute to the dead.

For two hours, mourners came to the pier to say goodbye. Many were from German societies and raised their right arms in the Nazi salute as they filed past the coffins. Soon each coffin was covered in a sea of flowers and wreaths practically spilling to the floor. None had more flowers than that of Captain Lehmann, who lay beside Birger Brinck in a place of honor in the middle of the row of the dead. Moritz Feibusch lay farther down. Whether or not the mourners who had gathered realized he was Jewish was unclear, but no doubt some would not have been pleased to have a German American Jew honored alongside their Aryan brethren.

Directly across from and facing Lehmann's coffin stood the speaker's stand, draped in a swastika and with an American flag flying overhead. At the podium, Reverend Paul Schulte, a man known as the "Flying Priest" who had flown aboard the *Hindenburg* on its first flight to the United States in 1936 and had said the world's first airborne Mass, offered a prayer to begin the ceremony. Five hundred crew members from the *Hamburg* had come to pay their respects. Franz, Balla, and the surviving crew from the *Hindenburg* who were well enough to attend sat solemn-faced in their new blue suits, white shirts, and matching ties in the first two rows of chairs that had been assembled for important guests. Though the memorial service was taking place in New York City, Mayor La Guardia had chosen not to attend. He sent the deputy police commissioner and six New York City police officers in his stead. Representatives from the

American, Swedish, and German governments also sat in the audience, while a U.S. Navy blimp, the *G-1*, which had been docked inside hangar number 1 along with the USS *Los Angeles* while the disaster unfolded, circled overhead in a tribute offered by the American lighter-than-air community.

The *Hamburg*'s band provided musical accompaniment for the ceremony. As the last echoes of Handel's "Largo" receded through the great hall, Ambassador Hans Luther took the speaker's stand. In English, he extended thanks from the German government for the "overwhelming sympathy . . . that we received in the hour of our great tragedy." Then, switching to German, Luther continued, relating a short story of an American woman who had told him, "'Believe me, these dead have not died in vain.'" She, like many others, was determined not to allow a dreadful accident to set back progress and innovation. "Let us hope," he continued, "that this tragic occurrence will give a new impetus to the common labor of mankind." As Luther left the stage, a rousing round of the German national anthem, "Deutschland über Alles," rang out through the cavernous hall as the honor guard dipped their red-and-black flags and raised their right arms in the Nazi salute. The crowd followed this with the "Horst Wessel Song," the Nazi Party anthem created by Joseph Goebbels after the death of a young SA "storm trooper" who had been killed by communists and was immediately made a martyr by Hitler's master of propaganda.

When the singing finally stopped, Commander Rosendahl, representing the United States, took to the platform. "From the ashes of the *Hindenburg* will arise much more efficient and much greater airships," he stated emphatically, before making a somewhat pointed remark implying that had Germany been allowed to fill its airship with helium, the deadly accident never would have occurred. "These men," he said, "were sacrificed to one weakness over which they had no control. Now, we have become so aware of that weakness that it will not happen again." Lighter-than-air flight would prevail, he was sure of it, in no small part thanks to his German counterparts. He had only the utmost respect for those men, as well as for the "people of the Fatherland for announcing their determination to carry on and make the airship a better carrier." When Rosendahl closed, the band began again, this time offering a rendition of the "Star-Spangled Banner" as he left the stage.

After remarks from the Swedish consul general and a speech by *Hamburg*'s captain, who would see the *Hindenburg* victims safely home, a young boy and girl from the represented German societies carried forward a ceremonial wreath. They laid it on the coffin of Captain Lehmann in one last tribute to the crew and their leader who had given their lives in service to Germany and to the spirit of adventure through which man would finally conquer the skies.

In Atlantic City, Gertrud Adelt sat in a cool, dark cinema and watched as a newsreel flickered on the screen in front of her. Over the last few days, footage of the giant fireball falling from the sky had played all across the country. In packed theaters on Broadway, women had reportedly fainted at the sight of silhouetted figures falling through the air and of survivors being led away from the crash whose clothes had been burned off and who were blackened beyond recognition.

Gertrud did not need to see what she had already lived through. She was here for something more somber in its simplicity. As the newsreel ran, images flashed across the screen showing thousands of people crushed together waiting their turn to enter the Hamburg-America pier to pay their final respects to the victims of the *Hindenburg.* The camera lingered for a moment on one coffin piled with more flowers than all the rest: Captain Lehmann. Her husband's friend, his coauthor, his fellow dreamer in the clouds, was gone. When Leonhard heard the news of Lehmann's death the day after the disaster, he could not believe that Lehmann had died simply from his wounds. Gertrud's husband was convinced his friend had succumbed "just as much to the emotional devastation" of "seeing his life's work destroyed" as he had to the physical injuries he had sustained from the smoke and flames.

Leonhard, too, had had to face a cruel reality in the days since the disaster, beyond simply recovering from his injuries, which were a good deal worse than he had realized. He had ultimately gone to a hospital for his burns and smoke inhalation and would need to recuperate for some time. With the loss of the *Hindenburg*, any idea of making a Hollywood film about zeppelins was now gone, and with it went the prospect of perhaps remaining in America with his wife and son. That dream would have to wait until Germany finished its new airship, the *LZ-130*, meant to have been the sister ship of the *Hindenburg*.

Most important, with Lehmann gone, it would now fall to Leonhard to see that his friend's final words made their way into print on American shores, so that the ideals in which he had believed all his life would live on in his death. The book was finished, but Leonhard would add one last chapter to bring the story of Ernst Lehmann's final journey to its conclusion, ending, as Leonhard believed, not in "defeat and destruction, but victory of the idea" that Lehmann "served faithfully to the end."

CHAPTER 35

Chicago, Illinois, to Lakehurst, New Jersey, USA: May 13–28, 1937

As the days passed, other, more cheerful news from around the world replaced the *Hindenburg* disaster on the front pages of newspapers across America. On May 8, War Admiral, a small but feisty Thoroughbred with a sleek brown coat, won the Kentucky Derby in resounding fashion in a wire-to-wire victory for the first leg of the year's Triple Crown races. And on May 12, King George VI and his wife, Queen Elizabeth, were officially crowned in Westminster Abbey. Even the monarchy was embracing the modern age, as the coronation was the first to be captured on motion picture film and broadcast on the radio.

Even with these welcome distractions, the tragedy remained top of mind for many Americans, including First Lady Eleanor Roosevelt, who had learned of the terrible accident while changing airplanes in Chicago on her way home to Hyde Park from Seattle. Four days after the crash, in her syndicated My Day column, to which millions of Americans turned six days a week, she addressed the disaster and its resonance with the human psyche in a reassuring and optimistic tone. "Not long ago," she began, "some one asked me why I liked to fly. From his point of view the only reason any one would want to fly would be to save time." Of course, there was beauty in looking down at the world from above, but there was so much more to it:

Even more than the beauty of sunrise or of sunset there is a fascination which I think every aviator must feel in conquering a new element. At the bottom of all study and invention lies that constant effort on the part of man to control his surroundings. It is really I imagine the instinct which has pushed man from the beginning gradually upward to a greater and greater effort to dominate the world.

In all of these efforts men give their lives but each loss brings something new to the sum total of knowledge which advances mankind as a whole. . . . Therein lies the greatness of man. Fear is never allowed to dominate that desire for greater knowledge and as long as mankind retains that spirit we will move forward.

Aviation may have had a temporary setback, but to think such a setback would become permanent in a field that was rapidly charging forward ran contrary to human instinct. And for other areas of innovation, the disaster was perhaps a necessary spark in the engines of progress.

In Chicago, plaudits poured in for Herbert Morrison and Charlie Nehlsen after their recording was broadcast on the radio. In recognition of "this most wonderful of all reporting jobs under the most terrific strain ever endured by a broadcaster," *Radio Guide*, a national weekly publication, presented both Herbert Morrison and Charlie Nehlsen with special "medals of merit" in a personal ceremony. Having featured Morrison in its February issue of *Stand By*, *Prairie Farmer*'s radio magazine prepared a cover feature on Charlie Nehlsen, complete with a slightly bemused headshot and a full biography of his early tribulations breaking into the radio industry. Their boss, WLS president and *Prairie Farmer* owner Burridge D. Butler, even presented both of them with gold watches in front of a full complement of onlookers from the company.

There was, however, one small oversight amid the fanfare. As Morrison had technically made the recording on his day off, WLS never saw fit to pay him for capturing the most remarkable event to date in broadcast history.

After ten days of accolades, the disaster was still heavy on Morrison's mind. On May 16, he sat down to respond to the questionnaire and diagram that the Department of Commerce investigation committee had mailed to him. Pondering those desperate moments he had described, he handwrote a full letter in response, recounting what he had witnessed from his unique vantage. From outside the information office where his equipment was shielded from the rain, he had had a view of the whole port side and part of the belly of the airship as it slowly sailed toward the mooring mast. He wrote that the zeppelin was "approaching us for normal landing—light rain. Ship nose down, two ropes on ground, neighborhood of one minute, two at the most." From where he was standing, it appeared that perhaps one of the motors had sputtered. He thought it possible the blaze had resulted from an engine backfire, though of course he could not be sure. "The flame traveled back a few feet, then ignited some other gas or substance traveling up and over the stabilizer and elevators seeming to ignite the gas in the tail interior," he explained. "The flame had changed from a reddish yellow to a sickening light yellow, typical of burning hydrogen. The contact of the flame with the inner gas caused the very tail tip to blow out like a skyrocket," as captured in Sam Shere's remarkable photograph. "My testimony can be backed up by my statements on electrical transcription from the time of the first flame until 9:10 P.M. . . . I did not stop talking until after the whole ship had been consumed and the flames limited to the burning of the oil reserve." He had forty-two minutes of firsthand testimony, a continuous record of the landing and crash, supplemented by several later interviews and colorful descriptions, to which they were welcome to listen.

"I was careful (purposely very careful)," he closed, "not to state in the records what I knew caused the burning of the *Hindenburg*. Realizing that we had the only sound recording apparatus on the base—we were extremely careful to get authentic information recorded. . . . My officers at West Point always told us to make sure we were right—excuses were never accepted."

Morrison's theory that a backfiring engine had emitted a spark that ignited the hydrogen gas was one of several that the Board of Inquiry was already exploring as the hearings got underway in Lakehurst. The board had assembled in a bright, windowed room in hangar number 1, partitioned from the vast space only by a twelve-foot wall. With its lack of ceiling and odd assortment of unmatched furniture, including a makeshift table of sawhorses and plywood for the Germans, who had arrived on May 14, the room looked a bit like the set in a middle school drama. The large American flag hanging on the wall behind the investigators was the only element lending official imprimatur to the proceedings.

Though the room itself was filled with a hodgepodge of odds and ends, the people who had gathered to investigate represented the world's most brilliant minds in lighter-than-air aviation. The Americans were led by South Trimble, Major R. W. Schroeder, assistant director of the Bureau of Air Commerce, and Dennis Mulligan, chief of the Regulation and Enforcement Division of the Bureau of Air Commerce, plus a team of six technical advisers, including Commander Rosendahl. They were joined by the German Commission, including Dr. Eckener, Dr. Dürr, Colonel Breithaupt of the Reich Ministry of Aviation, Drs. Guenther Bock and Walter Hoffmann of the Experimental Institute for Aviation, and Dr. Max Dieckmann of the College of Aeronautics in Munich. If they could not solve the mystery of what had destroyed the *Hindenburg*, there was likely no one on earth who could.

While an engine malfunction was possible, their primary focus was on atmospheric effects that might have caused a spark, such as static electricity or unusual forms of lightning. Both the American board and the German experts considered a deliberate act like sabotage a possible but remote and unlikely explanation. The German government had similarly continued to back away from suggestions of sabotage. As Hermann Göring told Hearst reporter Karl von Wiegand in a telephone interview on May 8, "Though sabotage"—the very idea of which he found "repellent"—"cannot be excluded 100 per cent, it is my personal conviction, based on such information as I have up to now, that the appalling disaster to our

Hindenburg, which shocked and stunned all Germany but did not dismay us, was an accident, what Americans call an 'act of God.' . . . Until other evidence is adduced, I lean to the belief that a spark of static electricity or an electric discharge from the clouds might have caused the tragedy.

"Of course," Göring continued with a pointed remark directed toward his American readers, "had the *Hindenburg* been filled with helium, instead of hydrogen, nothing whatever would have happened."

The Board of Inquiry considered a vast array of evidence and expertise. They examined newsreel footage from the news services that had been on the airfield that day, as well as photographs from both professionals and amateurs. They consulted with the NYPD Bomb Squad and Bureau of Explosives, who could find nothing conclusive in the wreckage. The board interviewed experts on engine propellers, who found nothing amiss, as well as meteorologists and other "men of science," including a Johns Hopkins University professor specializing in the field of electricity. They even spoke with a local coroner named Raymond Taylor who had been called to the scene. Though it was not a particularly helpful question in getting to the bottom of the fire's source, the board asked him whether it was "part of your duties to record the names of those that were injured."

"No," he replied dryly, "I am only interested as coroner in the dead ones."

From the very similarly named Lieutenant Raymond F. Tyler of the U.S. Navy, who was in charge of the ground crew and had particular expertise in hydrogen, the board confirmed the *Hindenburg* had dropped its mooring ropes at 7:21 p.m. All seemed normal, though the airship was definitely tail-heavy, even after dropping ballast aft. Tyler noted that when the mooring ropes hit the ground from about two hundred feet in the air, they emitted a cloud of dust, indicating that they were definitely dry, as the ground was too wet to have produced a puff of dirt on impact. The board asked him whether "any static charge [could] be dissipated through lines dropped in this case." No, he responded. He believed that dry ropes were "definitely non-conductors of electricity," though "if a line had been wet, then it might have been possible."

Lieutenant Benjamin May, who was stationed on top of the mooring mast and responsible for securing the bow of the airship, thought the *Hin-*

denburg's approach had been a bit fast, even for a high landing, and also noted that while the airship's crew had dropped "quite a bit of ballast" from the tail, it still appeared heavy as it was approaching. He, too, observed the cloud of dust when the mooring ropes hit the ground, and it was not until several minutes later that he heard a crack—perhaps the metal structure breaking—and looked up to see flames streaking out like long streamers. They were bright yellow at first but became increasingly red as the fire grew. When pressed on whether he observed anything unusual from the motors, he recalled there was a bit of exhaust smoke that quickly wafted away, but this was not abnormal when changing the throttle, which the Germans tended to do more aggressively than Americans.

Witness after witness repeated these same observations: The *Hindenburg* had made a high, fast landing, the dry ropes produced a cloud of dust when they hit the ground, and the airship was noticeably out of trim. It was possible the heaviness in the tail was due to the weight added by crew members moving into their assigned landing positions in the tail, or simply because of the rain that had collected on the skin as it passed through a shower twenty minutes before landing, which Captain Anton Wittemann noted could have added three to four tons of weight to the airship. Nothing with the engines seemed amiss. When the hydrogen gas was valved for the last time, the airship still had good forward speed and thus ventilation to clear the gas away into the surrounding air. Nothing seemed irregular to anyone until the muffled detonation followed by the flames, which many witnesses agreed occurred somewhere between three and four minutes after the crew dropped the mooring ropes. A yeoman from the Naval Air Station had kept a log of events that evening that confirmed the timing.

Curiously, one Lakehurst civilian engineer noted that the flame did not shoot out directly. To him, "it seemed first as if the fire was under the cover and was trying to get out." Meanwhile, a navy boatswain's mate thought that the *Hindenburg*'s cover seemed to "flutter" two or three seconds before a "ball of flame" erupted.

On May 13, with the assistance of several interpreters, the board interviewed a group of *Hindenburg* stewards and cooks who were well enough to testify. From their positions within the airship, they could not have seen the flames until the zeppelin was truly ablaze, so they had even less of an understanding of what had gone wrong than the men on the ground. The unblemished steward Max Henneberg saw not the flame itself but a "shine from the flame" through the windows of the portside dining room, and the sound of the explosion brought him back to the report of heavy guns from the Great War. Meanwhile, steward Fritz Deeg's clearest memories were not of the fire and the crash itself but of what had occurred once he leaped to the ground. After he jumped, he turned around and caught the little Doehner boys as their mother dangled them out the window, while another steward, Eugen Nunnenmacher, caught their sister, Irene. Deeg had then made the heroic decision to go back into the fire with Captain Ziegler and navigators Eduard Boëtius and Christian Nielsen to help a German woman, Elsa Ernst, to safety from the area of the dining room.

Aside from the strong headwinds, the crew reported nothing unusual about the voyage. The board asked Henneburg, Deeg, and steward Severin Klein if they had seen airplanes flying alongside the airship, following up on some of the quack "tips" about a gunman firing an incendiary bullet from the sky. They recalled seeing press planes around New York City, but there was absolutely nothing unusual about newspapers sending cameramen up to photograph a zeppelin in flight. It happened all the time. The board also inquired about any onboard equipment malfunctions, such as short-circuiting electronics. A cook, Alfred Groetzinger, testified that the electric stoves and kitchen equipment were in perfect order.

When it came time to swear in young Werner Franz for his testimony, the board realized they had a small problem. Captain Walter Ziegler, who had accompanied him to the hearing, informed the board that under German law, Franz was unable to be sworn in for a legal proceeding, as he was under fifteen.

"Does he believe in God?" South Trimble asked.

Ziegler answered for the boy in the affirmative. That was good enough for Trimble, and the scrawny boy, who looked a bit pale and dazed by the whole affair, took the stand. In the high-pitched voice of youth, he repeated the story of his astonishing, waterlogged escape from the *Hindenburg*, but aside from his remarkable survival, the cabin boy had nothing of use to share. He was just a child who barely knew how the airship operated.

Trimble wrapped up Franz's interview with a friendly tone. "The Board desires to congratulate you upon your miraculous escape from death in the *Hindenburg* accident," he told the boy from the middle of the table in front of the American flag. "You possess great courage and fortitude. You have impressed everyone you have come in contact with, with your friendliness and manliness, and you take back with you our best wishes." The boy's pallid face perked up in a smile as the translator conveyed Trimble's words in German.

As the hearings continued, other potentially obvious explanations were discarded. Heinrich Kubis confirmed no visitors had been allowed on board in the hours before takeoff, nor had anyone lit any matches or lighters that might have inadvertently caused the blaze. The crew had properly collected all flammable materials, which had not yet been returned to the passengers by the time of the fire. Nor had any of the passengers touring the *Hindenburg*, all of whom either he or Dr. Rudiger personally escorted, been allowed farther aft into the envelope than normal. He did not raise Benny Spah's unauthorized visits to his dog in the freight room. Apparently, these were not sufficiently concerning to warrant mention. Also quickly eliminated were any discernible issues with gas-valving procedures. Hans Freund, one of the riggers responsible for gas cell maintenance, Chief Engineer Rudolf Sauter, and Watch Officer Heinrich Bauer testified that on one trip to South America in 1936, a gas valve had gotten stuck slightly open, but it easily closed when Freund pulled on the valve. Nothing of the kind had happened this trip.

The board then turned to more scientific technicalities. A U.S. Navy meteorological expert believed it was possible a static discharge could have caused the fire, as the stormy atmospheric conditions had likely created a steep potential gradient, where the voltages of the air and the ground become very different and seek to equalize through a lightning discharge. However, while certainly a *possible* cause of the fire, he did not believe it *probable*, especially as modern airships were carefully bonded: All metallic parts were continuously connected to minimize differences in electrical potential and the risk of electrostatic discharge. Similarly, a physicist testified that something having to do with a large potential gradient and the landing ropes serving as a conductor was the "*least improbable* occurrence" out of various proposed "unlikely occurrence[s]." However, the crew had no way to measure an airship's electrical charge, nor to dissipate a large charge as long as the airship was not connected with the ground. As for bolts of lightning from storm clouds, no witnesses on either the zeppelin or the ground saw any during the landing. The last time the crew observed lightning was when they turned back toward Lakehurst far down the New Jersey coastline just after 7:00 p.m.

After ten days of testimony, there was still no smoking gun—literal or metaphorical. And despite Dr. Eckener's initial, sleep-deprived supposition that sabotage could have been at play, throughout the dozens of witness interviews, not once did anyone called to the stand suggest they had even the slightest suspicion of a deliberate act that had set off the blaze.

Aside from questions about airplanes flying alongside the *Hindenburg*, the only time sabotage was affirmatively raised on the record over the first ten days of the inquiry was after witness interviews had concluded the evening of May 18 and a handful of the American and German investigators met privately in Commander Rosendahl's quarters. At the end of that night's discussion, Rosendahl brought up one theory that remained unaddressed. If someone were to place an "infernal machine"—like a time bomb—inside the zeppelin, he believed the logical place would be in a shaft in the framework or between gas cells. As no unauthorized person had accessed the *Hindenburg* before departure, only someone on board could have placed a bomb. Having served for years with the highly trained and disciplined zeppelin officers and crew, he could not bring himself to believe in an inside job. If anyone had committed an act of sabotage, it must have been a passenger, and the only one who had acted in a suspicious manner was, as he put it, the "man who fed his dogs," Benny Spah. How Rosendahl even knew about Spah going back to the freight room unattended was unclear, likely from visiting his German friends in the hospital in the days since the disaster, but he certainly had nothing remotely resembling proof.

Perhaps, in searching for an explanation he could tolerate, he wanted to find it odd that Spah had claimed, "My dog will not eat unless I see him" (never mind the fact that the dog was a "she"), so as to not have to face the idea that there could be a fatal flaw in the technology to which he, like Eckener, Lehmann, Pruss, and so many others, had dedicated his career. Even if Rosendahl thought this was suspicious, none of the other investigators seemed to, at least not enough to put it on the record. And though Benny Spah was relatively nearby in Douglaston, Long Island, they did not call him to testify.

Doctor," South Trimble stated after swearing in Dr. Eckener on the makeshift witness stand in the hearing room in the late morning of May 22, "if you have any statement or observation that you would like to make, we would be very happy to receive it."

Eckener had indeed prepared remarks, and even though he had not seen the disaster himself, everyone gathered in the room listened intently as the world's greatest expert in lighter-than-air aviation offered his opinion on the cause of the tragedy. After pondering the various testimony he had heard that week, it had become clear to him that the disaster must have occurred due to an unlikely interaction between mechanical design and atmospheric conditions.

Sitting tall but stooped, and dressed in a double-breasted suit the same shade of "Prussian" gray as his closely cropped goatee, he began speaking in German to best express himself. American DZR representative Willy von Meister translated on his behalf. "If at this phase of the investigation I make any statement," he began humbly, "it is not because I have formed a very definite conclusion as to what may have happened, but only because a certain possibility might be brought to light. . . . As matters stand, there is not one possibility, but two which might be inter-connected." These, he emphasized as he clutched a cigar and fiddled with his spectacles, were "remote possibilities" and therefore unlikely to occur coincidentally, but once accepted, they formed the only logical through line that could explain what witnesses had observed and the destruction that ensued.

From the testimony of multiple witnesses who described the fire as originating in the upper part of the stern section and glowing along the airship's axis until the spark erupted into a blaze, Eckener had to make an essential assumption. Some not insignificant amount of hydrogen must have escaped from the gas cells and freely collected in the aft section of the airship. How the leak had occurred he would postulate momentarily, but first he had to address three potential sources of ignition. First was the unlikely possibility of "ball lightning," a rare, "incalculable and moody" natural phenomenon described over centuries as a luminescent orb that drifts and dances near the ground during a thunderstorm. Ball lightning was not properly understood by scientists and observers' descriptions seemed to belong to the realm of folklore, but its dance-like behavior in no way resembled the slowly building glow followed by a great surge of fire that witnesses had observed. Nor did the initial glow behave like Saint Elmo's fire, which creates a corona effect and had been observed on airships during the Great War. Eckener could also dismiss suggestions that engine sparks or exhaust ignited the blaze. The zeppelin team had previously conducted experiments in Germany showing that diesel exhaust, typically 250 degrees centigrade, could not reach hydrogen's ignition temperature, which was twice as hot. Even if sparks had flown to the top of the airship, they would have cooled considerably over a distance of at least fifty-five meters. "Therefore," Eckener explained confidently, there "only remains in my opinion the third possibility of the cause of ignition, that the gas, which, according to our assumption in this case, must have been present in the [aft] top part of the ship, was ignited either by lightning or by a static spark."

As expert witnesses had established, a significant potential gradient existed at Lakehurst on that fateful night thanks to the first thunderstorm that passed, followed by a smaller front that produced a lighter, more mist-like rain. The temperature had cooled substantially as the front rolled through, and the wind blew from the northwest. With such an unstable potential gradient, there was also a high likelihood that the charges between ground and sky would jump to equalize in the form of a static spark. "As we know," Eckener continued, "the ignition took place approximately three to four minutes after the dropping of the trail ropes, but for this there is a very simple explanation. The landing line was very dry, and therefore a poor conductor," as earlier witnesses had testified. At the moment the dry ropes hit the ground, the *Hindenburg* carried the charge of the air surrounding it. However, "slowly, the landing lines became damp by the light drizzle that was still observed at the time. Therefore, it is believable and possible that the potential between the ship and ground was slowly equalized" as the contact between the wet rope and the ground allowed the ground's charge to travel up the rope and thus give the entire airship the same charge as the ground. After this potential between the ground and the airship equalized as the *Hindenburg* hovered above the field, he theorized, the now-significant "potential gradient between the ship and the overlying air masses was sufficient to generate these static sparks" jumping between the zeppelin and the air. It was essentially like lightning hitting a flagpole in a storm as the current of electrons from the positively charged air flowed toward the highest point carrying the negative charge of the ground.

Now, this source of ignition was necessary but not sufficient to explain the fire. Without ignition meeting fuel, such a flow of static electricity would be harmless. As witnesses explained, it was nearly impossible to believe that a valve had become stuck without someone noticing, nor was it likely that valved gas could have accumulated in the well-ventilated chimney design that carried hydrogen up and away out of the airship. "I therefore can only assume that by a process still unexplained to myself, a leak must have occurred in one of the [aft] gas cells," Eckener concluded. Many reliable witnesses observed that the airship was tail-heavy. The cumulative effect of the dropped ballast water, gas valved in the bow of the airship, and weight redistribution as six men moved to the bow from the stern amounted to at least seventy thousand kilograms of trimming effect. This, combined with elevator controls that aerodynamically trimmed the ship as it came in to land, should have more than resolved the imbalance. The fact that it did not told Eckener that "the ship was very badly out of trim" in its final minutes.

A navy boatswain's mate had made a "remarkable observation" during a prior hearing that the outer cover of the airship seemed to have a "peculiar flutter" near where the fire broke out. His description only confirmed Eckener's assumption that a gas cell had developed a leak. He believed that this leak could only have formed in the final minutes during the landing approach while the crew was making many dynamic adjustments, or else they certainly would have noticed it earlier, when there were fewer changing variables. To Eckener, there was really only one explanation for this sudden gas leak: "The ship proceeded in a sharp turn to approach for its landing. That generates extremely high tension in the [aft] part of the ship, and especially in the center sections . . . which are braced by shear wires." As the sharp turn produced this higher-than-normal tension, he explained, "I can imagine that one of these shear wires parted and caused a rent in a gas cell. . . . Gas escaped from the torn cell upwards and filled up the space between the outer cover and the cells in the rear part of the ship, and then this quantity of gas . . . was ignited by a static spark" as the air around the *Hindenburg* tried to equalize with the charge of the ground. Initially, the small amount of gas that seeped out and sparked burned slowly in the enclosed space between the cell and the outer cover, but as it burned away the material of the gas cell, more and more gas escaped, thus producing the flutter, until it reached such a volume that when a large enough concentration of highly flammable hydrogen met the flame, it exploded the gas cell entirely. Once the first cell exploded, dispersing heat and flames in every direction, the chain reaction across all the hydrogen cells was unstoppable. The likelihood of all these factors occurring under such exact and ultimately dangerous conditions was remote, and yet it was the only scientific explanation for such a catastrophic result that made sense to Eckener.

The board allowed Eckener to speak, uninterrupted, for an hour as he laid out his theory, going into great detail regarding each step in his analysis. After he finished his prepared remarks, South Trimble called a brief recess. When they returned to the hearing room, Trimble had several questions. He did not doubt anything that Eckener had explained. Instead, for the sake of thoroughness, the board chairman asked the esteemed airship veteran whether there were any other theoretical possibilities they should consider, hinting at sabotage as an unlikely but as yet unaddressed issue. "As far as I know," Eckener responded, "there are no clues that such has been the case. . . . If one would like to give weight to reports that have from time to time appeared in the press, that is intimations, one might think that somebody had shot at the ship." They were welcome to use their imaginations, but there was no evidence to suggest sabotage. Nor would sabotage attempts like shooting at the *Hindenburg* necessarily have brought the airship down. In fact, during a 1930 *Graf Zeppelin* flight to Moscow, a nervous sentry had shot at the airship as it passed overhead. The bullet had hit a shear wire, which in turn punctured a gas cell as it tore away from the frame. The crew had not noticed the puncture at first, but eventually the gas seepage registered as the tail became increasingly heavy, so they slowed their speed and let a crew member down the outside of the airship on a rope to repair it. In half an hour, he had patched the cell and they proceeded on their journey. Eckener added that there was similarly no evidence that an "infernal machine" had been installed. A time bomb would have caused a single, immediate explosion rather than the slow burn followed by an explosion that witnesses had observed.

When Trimble and the other board members were finally satisfied, they concluded the session by asking whether there was anything else Eckener wished to add at the present time.

"I do not know of anything further now," he replied, "but you may rest assured that everything or anything that may come to my attention, I will be glad and anxious to communicate, because I am so much concerned in clearing up the reasons for this accident."

And with that, the board recessed for the weekend.

Though Eckener did not have evidence to prove his theory, the old principle of parsimony suggested that when weighing multiple explanations for a cause, the simplest explanation that connected all the pieces was correct. The logical progression that Eckener described brought all the factors that witnesses had observed into harmony without straying into significant hypothetical leaps, like dramatic notions of saboteurs planting bombs on airships. Nefarious plots worked well in motion pictures and evening radio dramas, but when trying to provide grieving families with answers surrounding the deaths of their loved ones, such intrigues were best left to the creative minds in Southern California.

There was, in a way, an irony to all that Eckener had described. The last disaster that had captured the public imagination in this manner had been the sinking of the *Titanic* before the war. The *Titanic*, a behemoth of a palace floating on the high seas, had been felled by a monstrous iceberg over a prolonged agony of hours, the sense of scale in a clash of titans only adding to the dramatic tragedy. Man had created a seemingly indestructible conveyance made of iron and steel, and only a colossus of ice lurking beneath the surface of man's consciousness had managed to put humans back in their place. But if Eckener was correct, the infinitely more delicate *Hindenburg*, a ship of the sky that was the opposite of the *Titanic* in every way save its comparable size, had met its fate on an entirely different path. It was not nature's largest, most solid obstacles that spelled the end for the *Hindenburg*, but rather subatomic charges invisible even under a microscope. These subatomic charges wreaked their unseen havoc not over freezing, anguish-filled hours but in a matter of flaming seconds. Nature proved it still had a few tricks remaining up its sleeve.

CHAPTER 36

New York, New York, USA: May 28, 1937

At the end of the day on May 26, having heard and seen all they could in Lakehurst, Trimble's investigators packed up the hearing room and drove to New York, leaving the cleanup crew to salvage whatever could be recovered from the crash site. Soon, all that would be left behind was scarred earth in the shape of the *Hindenburg*'s blackened silhouette.

Over the course of twenty-one days, the Board of Inquiry interviewed ninety-nine witnesses and experts, concluding with a handful of officers and passengers who remained hospitalized. On May 28, Captain Sammt recounted the *Hindenburg*'s final landing maneuvers from his New York City hospital bed, confirming what his fellow officers had already shared. Captain Pruss, still lingering with one foot in the anteroom of heaven, was much too poorly to be interviewed. His face was disfigured, his nose and ears almost entirely burned away. The backs of Pruss's hands, Sammt observed, were "charred to the bone." But somehow, thanks to transplants and days inside an oxygen tent, it seemed that Pruss would live.

After making their hospital rounds, the Board of Inquiry and German experts had one final interview to conduct. It was unlikely to deliver the certainty they sought to conclude their investigation, but at least they could rest assured they had done everything they could.

In the late afternoon of May 28, Nelson Morris arrived, black hair smooth as ever, at New York's Governor Clinton Hotel, opposite Penn Station, where the board had established another temporary committee room. Nelson's hands and wrists were still damaged from breaking red-hot duralumin girders, but they were well on the mend thanks to his sister's expert care. In all other ways, he was still himself, aside from the acute pain of losing his friend of twenty years. It was a feeling that no doubt would remain with him for the rest of his life.

"Give us your name and address," South Trimble began for the last time, getting the formalities out of the way.

"Nelson Morris, 18300 Leffertt Street, Homewood, Illinois."

"Were you a passenger on the *Hindenburg* on May 6, 1937, when the *Hindenburg* accident occurred?"

"That is correct."

"Will you please give us a description of what you saw, what you heard, what you did and what you felt in connection with the ship's approach to the mooring mast on that day?"

Nelson interrupted Trimble's standard flow of questions for a moment. "I will go back a little, if I may." He remembered details of the flight path and the weather that he wanted to share in hopes that it would help. Nelson described their journey, when exactly they saw the rain with lightning in the distance, and the precise time they had turned toward the airfield for their final approach, which he had noted on his watch was 7:08 p.m. He had, of course, synchronized his watch with the airship's clock. Rather than crowd around the portside windows of the dining room, he explained, "I and a companion, Major Dolan, remained in the writing room on the starboard side of the ship, on the upper deck. The two front landing ropes had been dropped. The first one was well taken care of by the crew, and the crew had just started to get hold and handle the second one. . . . The altimeter in the lounge showed 300 meters, but that is too high, because I understand the landing ropes were only 400 feet." He liked the science and precision that went into understanding how it all worked, and little details stood out, now seared into his memory. Perhaps they would assist in the investigation, perhaps not.

Then, he continued, came the explosion, which, "from where we stood, was not at all loud. It sounded in the writing lounge just as a regular service rifle would sound 15 to 20 feet from here. . . . Almost immediately the tail of the ship dropped. . . . We clung to a post to keep from sliding on account of the incline. . . . It took, in my opinion, a remarkably long time for the ship to fall." In his estimation, it was a little over a minute, if that. In reality, it was only half that amount of time, but those terrifying seconds seemed to stretch out in slow motion.

"Was the explosion the first indication that you received of anything wrong with the ship?" Trimble asked.

"It was absolutely the first indication of anything wrong," Nelson stated definitively. "I traveled twice on the *Graf Zeppelin* under Commander Dr. Eckener and the landings were somewhat different, but I would not say they were wrong. . . . The approach to the landing field was very much more [rapid] . . . In this case the ship swung off to the right of the mooring mast, and that, although I think it had nothing to do with the explosion, was probably an error."

"Colonel," Trimble continued, deferring to Nelson's rank in the National Guard, "when you spoke of being in the starboard side . . . how did you get out?"

"Major Dolan and I jumped through the forward window of the starboard writing lounge," he explained. They had landed amid some girders.

"How did you get through them?" Trimble asked.

"The most remarkable thing that I know in my life," Nelson recalled with wonder. "I took metal rods an inch thick in my hands and I broke them. They broke like paper."

Trimble then asked about the rain, which Nelson noted was very slight, "almost infinitesimal." The cloud ceiling was high, which he felt was typical for that time of night, and there was lightning in the distance.

"Have you had any experience in the actual operation of lighter-than-air ships or made any study of their operation?" Trimble inquired, perhaps surprised by Nelson's technical knowledge and recall, which was rather more specific than any of the other passengers'.

Nelson described his previous two trips (leaving out the detail of having raced his uncle back to Chicago), and remembered with pleasure how Eckener had let him have "the run of the whole ship. . . . Because I was a heavier than air pilot, I was very much interested in everything." However, he admitted, that was nine years ago, and even as a pilot, his experience was not extensive. "I took out a French pilot's license," he explained. "I should have taken out an American one. I made enough hours over here to take out one, and on the day for my final examination the weather was bad and the examiner could not get into town; something happened, and I forgot about it. . . . I never did pass the American examination." Still, he had read quite a bit about airships over the years.

Trimble continued with questions about the function of the motors, the atmospheric conditions, and the final movements of the airship, which Nelson recounted with precise technical detail. As for whether any passengers appeared suspicious, the answer was no, though, he recalled, "one passenger was drunk the whole trip." Clearly, William Leuchtenberg's squiffy state had not just made an impression on Margaret Mather.

When the board had heard all it needed from Nelson, it was time to bring the proceedings to their conclusion. Trimble thanked him for his time.

"We are very grateful to you for coming down here this afternoon and we want to congratulate you on your remarkable escape. However," the attorney added, "I cannot help but telling you at this time that in our visits to several hospitals both passengers and crew have told us of the wonderful work you have done since the accident in visiting them and mak[ing] their lives more comfortable."

He had not advertised it, nor had any journalists caught wind of his actions, but since the night of the disaster, Nelson had spent considerable time working in the background to ensure that those who had survived had everything they needed and received the best care. Though perhaps something of the international playboy the press liked to make him out to be, what with his French wives, high-profile divorce, and Clark Gable good looks, Nelson Morris was fundamentally a kind and generous man and had been his entire life. It was this generosity that had brought Bert Dolan into his life in the first place, and it was the reason he had cajoled his friend into traveling with him on the *Hindenburg* while in France—both because it would be more enjoyable to travel with a friend and because, after years of friendship, he likely knew how much it meant to Bert to spend every day he could in the company of his family. Nelson did not have any children, and he might have been cavalier in his own marriages, but he appreciated that Bert's wife and children meant the world to him. And now it was his fault that Bert was lost to them forever.

There was nothing more Nelson could do for Bert now aside from ensure that Mildred received the portions of the partnership to which Bert was entitled (and perhaps a bit more, though none of Bert's children could later say for sure what, if anything, Nelson Morris had arranged financially). Nelson might have taken pride in being able to impress the board with his technical knowledge of aviation, but when it came to his generosity, that remained private.

Adding no detail to extrapolate upon what Trimble had said and looking for no praise, Nelson simply replied, "Thank you, sir. That is the least I can do. And I hope to take the next trip on the new dirigible."

And with that, the hearings concluded and the board adjourned, albeit with fewer conclusions than they might have liked.

CHAPTER 37

Across Germany: May 15–22, 1937

Four days after the swastika-draped service along the Hudson River, thirteen members of the *Hindenburg* crew who were well enough to travel boarded another Hamburg-America Line steamer, the SS *Europa*, to make their way home. Their tourist-class tickets had been paid for by the zeppelin company, just like the suits they had worn to the memorial service. Werner Franz also had a new coat and a new trunk, though there was little in it aside from a box of chocolates some Americans he did not know had sent him to wish him well. Before the crew bade the city goodbye, Franz had fulfilled his one wish for his voyage to the New World—he had seen a film at Radio City.

On the *Europa*, the surviving crew of the *Hindenburg* were akin to celebrities and were trotted out in their new suits to pose for a photograph with the ship's captain. Otherwise, the crossing was smooth and unremarkable until they docked at Bremerhaven on May 22. There, an enormous crowd and a crush of reporters had come to greet them, along with Captain von Schiller, who had long since returned to Germany with the now-grounded *Graf Zeppelin*. Von Schiller helped to guide the young cabin boy through the crowd, a reassuring hand resting on his shoulder. With a belted trench coat and fedora, Franz looked like a miniature version of his older colleagues. As he disembarked on home soil, he smiled, realizing the date. It was his fifteenth birthday.

In the two weeks since the tragedy, the mood in Germany was beginning to shift from stunned grief to an almost defiant pride in their fallen heroes. Two days after the disaster, a Frankfurt newspaper described how boys in the Hitler Youth not much younger than Werner Franz himself had gone to school "sad and gloomy-faced" and "aged from the experience" of losing the airship. For boys like those who had clamored across the airfield the night the *Hindenburg* had departed Frankfurt for the last time, there was almost a "personification" with the zeppelin and how it projected the triumphant image of their nation, and in a sense their own selves, to the broader world.

Ever since Göring announced that Germany would press on posthaste with the *LZ-130*, donations to finance the construction of the *Hindenburg*'s replacement had continued to pour in both from across Germany and from abroad. A week after the disaster, the *Reichsminister* of the interior had to send out a directive asking people to stop sending money, as the airship was insured. Perhaps Reich leadership thought the donations suggested the regime was too poor or too cheap to pay for the new zeppelin itself. Money that the government had already received went toward a planned memorial for the *Hindenburg* dead and to a home for retired airmen.

For the zeppelin community in Friedrichshafen, the tragedy remained acute. The company prepared a special edition of its employee magazine with the biographies of "*die toten Kameraden*"—the dead comrades—and a compilation of condolence messages from leaders in Germany and around the world, including Hitler, Göring, Goebbels, King George VI, and President Roosevelt. However, the leadership in Berlin, specifically Göring, was quickly driving the narrative out of the hands of those mourning the loss of family and friends and into the service of the nation. Göring began to recast the deceased airmen as national martyrs who had given their lives for a great patriotic cause, rather than humble company men who had simply died in a tragic accident. To the zeppelin community itself, Göring promptly sent a message marshaling this change in tone. "When an inexplicable fate has hit us so hard," he rallied, "we are the last ones to allow ourselves to become faint-hearted. The strong show their strength in times of need. . . . Working together, we men of German aviation want to show the world that, despite everything, [Count] Zeppelin's idea and entrepreneurial spirit have stood the test of time, and that airship traffic between nations is today an indispensable work of peace." Newspapers quickly reflected this theme of martyrdom that Göring directed. Publications ranging from the Nazi Party daily, *Völkischer Beobachter*, to the SS weekly, *Das Schwarze Korps*, described the fallen crew members as "soldiers" of aviation.

Meanwhile, Göring did not neglect a little tender nurturing of the close-knit airship community in the United States. Technological collaboration and shared experience in the skies over the last decade had forged a genuine bond across the ocean, and leaders in American aviation, like Commander Rosendahl, would be crucial in driving public support for helium sales to Germany, which were essential if the Germans were to complete the *LZ-130*. Several weeks after the disaster, Commander Rosendahl's wife, Jean, received a note on official *Reichsminister der Luftfahrt* letterhead, complete with an embossed eagle carrying a swastika in its talons, from Göring himself. He wrote how "deeply moved" he was by the assistance and support she had personally shown the German passengers and crew: "You have taken care of my compatriots with infinite kindness and love. . . . Be assured that your self-sacrificing work and care will be felt with indelible gratitude not only by the passengers and crew directly affected by it. Far beyond that, the entire German *Volk* will always be sincerely grateful to you for the outstanding help you have given to its people." He enclosed a picture of himself, which he described as a "small token of my gratitude."

If Göring had hoped that pity for those killed at Lakehurst would result in a groundswell of American compassion toward his nation, especially after ten thousand mourners appeared at the New York service, he was to be sorely disappointed. There was indeed American sympathy for those who had been killed and some increased support for helium sales to Germany for the new airship, but it did not silence growing criticism of the Nazi regime.

On the morning of May 20, as the *Hindenburg* survivors were sailing toward Germany, Ambassador Dodd opened his morning newspapers over breakfast in Berlin to find the German press in the throes of "violent attacks" against one of the most respected men in his home city of Chicago. Two days earlier, at a seminary on Chicago's North Side just five miles south of the Dolan family's home, Cardinal George Mundelein, the archbishop of Chicago, had made a stirring speech at an otherwise unremarkable quarterly diocesan conference. If an American Catholic priest was making the newspapers for political speeches, it was usually Father Charles Coughlin criticizing Roosevelt on his radio program or through his political action group, the National Union for Social Justice, his words increasingly laced with antisemitism.

This, however, was quite different. In front of five hundred Catholic clergymen, Mundelein had, in no uncertain terms, excoriated the Nazi regime's recent efforts to eradicate Catholicism in Germany on the grounds that Catholics could not be loyal Nazis if their allegiance was split between the fatherland and the Vatican, as Hitler believed. Mundelein criticized Nazi show trials of monks, friars, and priests accused of financial corruption. Even worse, though Mundelein did not call out such accusations by name, Goebbels had claimed that some one thousand Catholic clergy awaited trial on sexual offenses. While a handful of those might have been rightly accused, most had been slandered with trumped-up charges of homosexuality and pedophilia. Meanwhile, the December 1936 State Youth Law had effectively eliminated all Catholic youth organizations. In Mundelein's opinion, the Catholic schools responsible for millions of German children's education were the next public target, though the regime had already been quietly undermining them for some time. In the historically Catholic city of Munich, some 84 percent of children had been enrolled in parochial schools as recently as 1934. Just three years later, the government had closed so many that this percentage had dropped to single digits.

In the face of relative silence from the international community, Mundelein was incensed. "If we show no interest in this matter now, if we shrug our shoulders and mutter, well, maybe there is some truth in it, or it is not our fight . . . well, when our turn comes, we too will be fighting alone," he argued. "How is it that a nation of 60,000,000 people, intelligent people will submit in fear and servitude to an alien, an Austrian paperhanger, and a poor one at that I am told, and a few associates like Goebbels and Göring who dictate every move of the people's lives?" he demanded, deriding one of Hitler's pejoratively rumored former occupations as a tradesman who hung wallpaper in people's homes.

Mundelein was not wrong, Dodd reflected just three days before the state funeral for the *Hindenburg* victims, which he planned to attend. In fact, just a few years earlier, such a funeral would have been a highly religious affair in a country that both had deep Catholic roots and was the birthplace of the Protestant Reformation. Now, as Dodd wrote in his diary, "the German system prohibits all opposition and criticism," including from religion. The Nazi Party would "have only one church," a sort of neo-pagan Christianity where the real focus of worship was the state. The new system had been at work for "only about three years but the people seem to have surrendered to an amazing extent" as the German military was restored to its former glory and workers were happily employed in factories producing all the materiel necessary to wage war. As Dodd's friend Bill Shirer had observed, given the restored sense of pride the Germans felt, few seemed to be losing sleep over their diminished right to the freedom of worship.

Later that morning, during a meeting with Hjalmar Schacht, *Reichsminister* for economics and head of the Reichsbank, Dodd raised the issue of Mundelein's speech, about which the brand-new German ambassador to the United States, Hans-Heinrich Dieckhoff, had officially complained in Washington. "Yes, Catholics, Jews, and teachers suffer in Germany," Schacht admitted. "It is the effect of the revolution like that of France in 1789." For the foreseeable future, nothing was going to stop it.

Dodd left the meeting utterly convinced that, save a momentary swell of sympathy for the German people following the tragedy in Lakehurst, there was no meaningful "prospect of improving German-American relations, no chance at all." If Schacht's words were to be taken at face value, the ambassador thought as he returned to his office to cable Washington, it could only mean that "the Hitler system [was] permanent."

On May 21, the SS *Hamburg* arrived at the port of Cuxhaven bearing the coffins of five German passengers and twenty-one of the deceased crew. As it entered the mouth of the Elbe River where it meets the North Sea, the steamer raised the DZR standard to half-mast, its red field with black diagonal cross joined at the center by an eagle carrying a globe. Alongside it hung the German and American flags in a mourning posture, as stipulated in a five-page document from the Reich Ministry of Aviation, which had mandated every detail of the funeral procession, including the precise attire for attendees representing the military: service uniform, high boots, large metal belt buckle, peaked cap, gray gloves, and sword. As instructed, a Luftwaffe company and military band lined up at attention on the lower landing area of the pier. They raised their arms in a silent salute as the ship nosed into dock. There was to be no shouting or waving. It was an entirely solemn affair. The normal, fare-paying passengers and their luggage were let off first. Then Captain von Schiller boarded the ship, followed by pallbearers from DZR and an additional twenty men from the Luftwaffe to assist. Von Schiller was to serve as a special pallbearer for Captain Lehmann in the funeral procession. Lehmann's coffin had not joined the others on the *Hamburg*, as it had been held back in New York to wait for Mrs. Lehmann. Two days after the *Hamburg* set sail, Mrs. Lehmann had boarded the *Europa* with her husband's body and the surviving crew members for the return trip to Germany. To make up for the delay, the Luftwaffe had then sent a plane to meet the *Europa* in Cherbourg to transport Mrs. Lehmann to Cuxhaven with her husband's remains in time for the service.

Just like the hall at the Hamburg-America pier in New York, this one had been decorated with flags and flowers, all paid for by the Ministry of Aviation. Once again, the coffins were arranged in a row, still draped in Nazi flags, as another swastika fluttered above the speaker's stand. The hall was packed with the families of the deceased, government representatives, and longtime members of the zeppelin company, like Knut Eckener, who stood in for his father. Notably, neither Hitler nor Göring had come, dispatching Dr. Hans Lammers, head of the Reich Chancellery, and General Erhard Milch from the Luftwaffe in their stead. Hitler generously sent a wreath to express his sympathies.

Alongside the mourners were members of the press, including journalists, photographers, newsreel cameramen, and radio broadcasters, all of whom had been carefully coordinated in conjunction with the Ministry of Propaganda, which helped to orchestrate the whole affair. The soft sounds of Beethoven's *Eroica*, or "Heroic" symphony, drifted through the hall, followed by speeches from several approved members of the Protestant clergy, who had been selected in consultation with local party officials. Then a chorus broke into Martin Luther's "Ein feste Burg ist unser Gott," the same hymn that the band had played at the Frankfurt zeppelin field just over two weeks earlier as onlookers serenaded the *Hindenburg*'s final farewell.

The end of the hymn concluded any religious elements of the service, minimal though they were. General Milch then took to the speaker's stand to offer his tribute on behalf of the führer. From beneath the swastika, the moonfaced Milch addressed the room. "With pride and appreciation," he stated, "the führer and the people have looked back over the last few years on the great achievements of our Zeppelin airships, which . . . brought honor to the German name, German manpower, and German technology throughout the world." To those who had died, he proclaimed with martial nationalism, "German aviation and the entire German people will never forget you!" There was nothing personal about the ceremony, nothing individual. The humanity was already gone, replaced by myth.

After the ceremony in Cuxhaven, the twenty-six coffins of the deceased were placed on trains bound for their respective hometowns. But not all of the dead were to have their final rest just yet. Always eager to capitalize on tragedy and turn it into martyrdom, state leadership planned even grander, more public funerals for those bound for Friedrichshafen and Frankfurt.

On Sunday, May 23, in an otherwise quiet corner of the Friedrichshafen cemetery looking down over the Bodensee, six of the *Hindenburg* crew were buried together before an honor guard. A beautiful display of spring flowers had been woven into some two hundred wreaths sent as tokens of love from far and wide. There was one from Göring, still putting on his best show of embracing the airshipmen as part of his brotherhood of the air, and another from the deputy führer, Rudolf Hess. The most personal touch was an arrangement sent by friends of the deceased from the Goodyear Zeppelin company, all the way in Akron, Ohio.

On the very same day in Frankfurt, the regime pulled out all the stops. In front of a full complement of German officials and foreign representatives from the United States, Italy, Britain, and France, the *Gauleiter*, or regional head of the province encompassing Frankfurt, put on a lavish display to lay five of the crew to rest in the Frankfurt main cemetery: chief radio officer Willy Speck, radio operator Franz Eichelmann, cook's assistant Fritz Flackus, electrician Ernst Schlapp, and, of course, Captain Ernst Lehmann. Ambassador Dodd, representing the United States, looked on as uniformed storm troopers in their brown shirts, the black-clad SS, and tens of thousands of Hitler Youth accompanied the swastika-draped coffins in a parade to the cemetery. The parade contingent was so large that regular civilians were pushed to the rear or off the streets entirely as the procession wound its way to the burial grounds in the north of the city. Once again, the führer was conspicuously absent.

Between the cemetery's chapel and a shady plot on the quiet northern boundary that had been set aside for an impressive cenotaph yet to come, the black- and brownshirts handed off their precious charges to an honor guard of Luftwaffe to ferry the dead the final four hundred meters to their place of rest. There, before crosses marked with each man's name under a canopy of dense green, it was not a Catholic priest or Protestant pastor but rather the *Gauleiter* who made the final remarks. Dodd listened carefully, noting the absence of any "reference to God or any possible salvation of souls except that contained in the ancient pagan belief," that the heroic dead had now, as the *Gauleiter* said, "passed on to Valhalla and to the eternity of the history of the German people."

At last, the swastika flags were removed and ceremonially folded, and the five coffins were lowered into the ground. When the burial was complete, a volley sounded as troops fired a gun salute as if at a military funeral. A moment later, the gathered masses looked up as the sound of engines droned in the sky. A squadron of Luftwaffe planes flew over the crowd in a final flourish, or rather, as a final nail in those coffins of the men whose lives had marked the beginning and the end of the age of airships and had now, unwillingly, ceded the supremacy of the skies.

1938

CHAPTER 38

Vienna, Austria: March 1938

For a man who had declared he would "never make a broadcaster" after that fraught night reporting live on the German reaction to the *Hindenburg* disaster, it must have come as a surprise to Bill Shirer that less than a year later, he was aching to get back on the air. Even more surprising was that just four months after that night, he was no longer in Germany.

In August 1937, William Randolph Hearst consolidated Universal Service into his other newswire, International News Service (INS), and suddenly, Shirer found himself with no job and his first baby on the way. When the cable arrived telling him he had been laid off, he had gone out for an evening walk along the Spree to clear his head and formulate some sort of plan. But by the time he returned to his office, fate had intervened. Another wire that he had overlooked had arrived just ten minutes before the harsh blow from New York. It was from a man he did not know but who was about to change his life.

"Will you have dinner with me at the Adlon Friday night?" the message read, signed, "Murrow, Columbia Broadcasting."

Shirer did not know this Edward R. Murrow fellow, but "dimly" remembered a friend had given him Murrow's card while in London earlier that summer and told him Murrow was connected with CBS. Murrow had wanted to meet Shirer, though Shirer had no idea why and had not been in London long enough to find out. If CBS wanted him to do more special radio reports, surely that would have come on the heels of his *Hindenburg* broadcast back in May, not months later. Puzzled but curious, and rather short on other options, Shirer wired back, "Delighted."

When the appointed evening came, Shirer's puzzlement only grew. He walked into the Hotel Adlon in his customary rumpled gray flannel jacket and pants to meet his dinner companion, only to find himself rather taken aback. Murrow was dark and handsome with tidy black hair, dark eyes, and a suit that looked like it came straight from Savile Row. "Just what you would expect from radio," Shirer thought. Surely the man was just here to "pump" him for a scoop for a broadcast from Berlin, or something like that. But when Murrow started speaking, it was clear there was something unexpected behind this Hollywood facade.

After casual chitchat over martinis, the waiter presented their dinner menus and Murrow got down to business. "I've got something on my mind," he said bluntly. Radio, he believed, offered all sorts of exciting possibilities, but it was falling well short of its potential. Murrow was not a journalist himself but rather the director of "talks," or educational programming, for CBS in Europe. He was looking to hire an experienced foreign correspondent to help him open a proper CBS European bureau. Ultimately, his plan was for CBS to become a legitimate news organization. "Are you interested?" he asked.

For a man imminently without income, the answer could only be, "Well, yes."

The more Shirer thought about it, the more energized he became at the prospect of this "new dimension" for reporting the news. With "instantaneous transmission," it was possible for an American sitting in his living room to actually hear events halfway across the world, from the pope's Easter blessing to Hitler "haranguing [his] storm troopers," which, Shirer thought, might tell Americans "more than all the written descriptions a newspaper reporter could devise."

Other reporters, however, thought he was crazy. He was a legitimate journalist. Making the switch to radio would be wasting both his talents and his time on a format so clearly centered around entertainment. "In two or three years, Bill," Frederick Birchall, a Pulitzer Prize–winning journalist from *The New York Times*, told him, "I'll wager you'll be wanting to get back to newspaper work." Perhaps, Shirer thought, but as no newspaper was offering him another job at present, he did not have much choice.

Nor did he really have a choice about leaving Berlin. Amid the chaos of that *Hindenburg* broadcast, Claire Trask had told him that the Nazis typically did not censor radio programming. In the months since, Nazi control over the medium had tightened. Now, in order to broadcast properly, Shirer and Murrow would have to establish the new CBS continental European bureau in a neutral country. They decided on Austria and Tess's home city of Vienna. Shirer was not exactly sad to leave Germany. Berlin would certainly continue to drive the events of the day, but both he and Tess had heightened concerns about raising a child in a "great land in evil ferment," as he called it.

Since the summer, the pace of alarming events had heightened. In June, after Ambassador Dodd's repeated efforts to secure a reprieve, the Nazis executed twenty-one-year-old American citizen Helmut Hirsch on the grounds of conspiracy to commit high treason. Less than two weeks later, they arrested five Protestant pastors, including one Shirer knew personally. In August, the regime expelled Shirer's friend Norman Ebbutt, Berlin correspondent of the London *Times*. Fifty fellow correspondents, including Shirer, saw Ebbutt off at the train station in a show of solidarity, despite the platform being full of Gestapo agents who took down their names and photographed them. Shirer's last assignment as a newspaper reporter had been an urgent request from United Press to cover the annual September Nuremburg Rally, where the führer attacked Jews as "inferior through and through." After three years in the heart of the Third Reich, it was time to leave.

"To sum up these three years," Shirer wrote, "personally, they have not been unhappy ones, though the shadow of Nazi fanaticism, sadism, persecution, regimentation, terror, brutality, suppression, militarism, and preparation for war has hung over all our lives, like a dark brooding cloud that never clears." After all the stories he and his colleagues had filed, he still felt there was "little understanding of the Third Reich, what it *is*, what it is up to, where it is going, either at home or elsewhere abroad." The landscape he and other journalists had painted for Americans was perhaps too complex and "uncoordinated . . . leaving the canvas as confusing and meaningless as an early Picasso."

Germany was a land of contradictions. Unless one actually lived there, it was difficult to understand its dialectics. Yes, Germany was poor. Its currency seemed perpetually in crisis. Food was short. Clothes were increasingly made of wood pulp. But what those back home could not understand was that what Germany lacked in raw materials it made up for in "aggressiveness of spirit, ruthless state planning . . . and the building up of a mighty military machine." How many times had he told foreign visitors, these "visiting firemen from London, Paris, and New York," as he pejoratively called them, that the "Nazi goal is domination!" and how many times had they laughed? Hitler was not even trying to hide it. It was all right there in *Mein Kampf*, which had sold millions of copies in Germany by 1938. And yet there remained a layer of haze obscuring the eyes of the outside world. Even something as simple as reading this bible of the new regime was more complicated than it appeared. There was no decent, unabridged English, or even French, translation of Hitler's manifesto, nor had Hitler authorized any foreign translations.

"I leave Germany in this autumn of 1937 with the words of a Nazi marching song still dinning in my ears," Shirer wrote in his diary as he closed both his trunks and a consequential chapter of his life to set off for Vienna with Tess:

> *"Today we own Germany,*
> *Tomorrow the whole world."*

Unfortunately, neither Vienna nor the CBS job was quite what Shirer had optimistically expected. Compared with his last stint in the Austrian capital, five years earlier, the city felt extremely poor. There were beggars on nearly every corner, and amid the economic turmoil an undercurrent of Nazism had taken hold. Shirer also noted that while Vienna had always had high levels of antisemitism, such views were meeting sympathetic ears among a quiet but growing choir supporting the Nazis.

Despite the social and political foment, it was choirs—real ones—that were taking up the bulk of his time. Both Murrow and Shirer viewed their role within CBS as one on a new frontier of proper radio journalism where Shirer could use his expertise and contacts to comment on world affairs, but by February, Shirer had yet to do any actual reporting on the radio. Instead, CBS continually dispatched him on assignments for "Columbia's American School of the Air," broadcasting children's choir performances and other wholesome cultural diversions from Brussels, Budapest, and the Baltics. Back in November, he had briefly covered a conference about Japan's war in China, where he had been allowed to put *other* reporters on the radio, but CBS did not permit him to report himself. If he could chase down his own stories, Shirer thought, even if they were more cultural in nature, that would be a step in the right direction.

Whether due to subconscious instinct or calculated strategy as he tried to carve out the role he desired, he decided to turn once again to the subject that had given him some of his biggest breaks: aviation. The new zeppelin, the *LZ-130*, soon to be rechristened the *Graf Zeppelin II*, was nearing completion. Men were working overtime to stay on schedule so that the *LZ-130* could begin operating in June. If Shirer could somehow finagle his way onto its maiden passenger flight and do a live broadcast during the voyage, that would be something halfway between what CBS envisioned for radio entertainment and where he and Murrow wanted the field to go. And thanks to the still-unfolding helium controversy between the United States and Germany, it might allow him to delve back into the drama of international relations.

After he consulted with New York, CBS seemed keen, so Shirer took the matter directly to the key man himself. "Dear Dr. Eckener: You may remember me from the days when I was with the Hearst Newspapers in Berlin with von Wiegand," he wrote, recalling the lunch with Eckener, Ambassador Dodd, Karl von Wiegand, and others now nearly two years earlier, just before Eckener had been about to depart on the *Hindenburg*'s first voyage to the United States. "We are interested in broadcasting from the new zeppelin when it makes its first trip to America. My New York Office is already in touch with yours there. I should like to come to Germany and talk the matter over with you. Could you kindly let me know when it would be convenient?"

Two days later, Eckener's office in Friedrichshafen wrote back: "In Dr. Eckener's absence from here we beg to acknowledge with many thanks [the] receipt of your kind letter. . . . Dr. Eckener will probably be back at Friedrichshafen not before the second half of February. We shall submit him your letter upon his return and shall give you further information as soon as it will be possible for Dr. Eckener to see you here and to talk the respective matter over with you." While it was not discouraging, Shirer had been hoping for something more definitive. Murrow tried to work the idea from a different angle. "If I don't make any progress on the Zeppelin question when I go to Berlin," he wrote to Shirer a few days later, "perhaps you could go down and have another go at them."

The tricky thing was that even if Shirer and Murrow could track down Eckener and secure his permission to broadcast from the new airship, there was no guarantee that there would be any passenger voyages for the *LZ-130* at all. It had been two years and one disaster since Shirer first met Eckener, and the airship veteran seemed little closer to obtaining the precious helium on which the future of the entire zeppelin program relied. In the immediate aftermath of the terrible accident at Lakehurst, there was an initial wave of American public support for approving helium sales to Germany. In late May, just weeks after the disaster, President Roosevelt appointed a cabinet committee to study the matter, particularly whether they could obtain a guarantee that Germany would not use helium for military purposes. At the same time, Eckener met with Harold Ickes, Roosevelt's secretary of the interior, who was responsible for strategic natural resources. The enigmatic Ickes merely assured Eckener that the committee's report had been sent to Congress for consideration.

In September, Eckener received word of the breakthrough for which he had been waiting. Congress passed a new Helium Act, which finally allowed strategic helium reserves to be opened to commercial and scientific use and sold as an export to nonhostile governments. Under the 1937 statute, export was permitted on the "joint recommendation of all the members of the National Munitions Control Board and the Secretary of the Interior." Germany promptly applied for eighteen million cubic feet of helium, enough for eighteen transatlantic round trips of the *LZ-130*, which the National Munitions Control Board approved in November. In

January 1938, the Germans sent a freighter to collect it from the port of Houston, but final approval still required Ickes's signature, which he refused to provide.

There was a bit of a catch to this new statute. Though the United States could now legally export helium, the 1937 Helium Act did not "permit accumulations of helium in quantities of military importance in any foreign country," and Ickes was not convinced that selling this much helium to Germany followed the letter of the law.

The secretary of the interior was known to be a bit of a tough nut. A self-described "curmudgeon," Ickes was one of the more peculiar characters in Roosevelt's cabinet, not least because he was a Republican who had been named to the Democrat's cabinet to appeal to moderate voters. An enthusiastic horticulturalist, Ickes had secured one of the first American patents on a flower for a hybrid variety of dahlia that he grew in the garden of the Tudor-style mansion he had built in Winnetka, Illinois. His precise and exacting nature extended from his garden to his home. Dwight Perkins, a noted Chicago architect and the head of the firm hired to design Ickes's house, discovered this the hard way after a sometimes-weekly barrage of complaints from Ickes landed in his mailbox. Particularly upsetting to Ickes was the depth of shelf corners in the linen closet and pantry. How could they be kept clean, he questioned, when they ran back so far they were "of no use except as dust collectors"? It was an issue, Ickes told Perkins, in which it seemed only "proper to take the head of the firm in my confidence."

Applying this same scrutiny to the language of the statute, Ickes concluded that the issue did not turn on whether a country might use the helium for a military *purpose* but rather whether it had military *importance*, regardless of what the country planned to do with it. Arguments that zeppelins were outdated for aerial warfare compared with increasingly sophisticated airplanes were somewhat beside the point. They could still be used for training exercises, scouting, and espionage overflights. There were even provisions in the 1937 United States government's naval bill for a new American airship. Most important, if Hitler had to promise helium would not be used for military purposes, did that not inherently imply that helium had military value?

Perhaps Ickes was not entirely wrong to withhold his approval, at least temporarily, as it did appear that something was brewing in Germany and Austria, though initial reports were a bit hazy. On February 13, Shirer learned that Hitler had commenced a secret meeting with the Austrian chancellor, Kurt Schuschnigg, in the führer's mountain retreat in Berchtesgaden, but reporters had yet to learn what the meeting involved. Between planning his cultural broadcasts for CBS and tracking down Eckener, Shirer had pitched a radio story to the higher-ups in New York about this mysterious meeting, but they did not bite.

Meanwhile, CBS was sending him to cover yet another children's choir in Sofia, Bulgaria, even though his baby was due any day. Just as he was preparing to leave, the news from Berchtesgaden finally broke. Under the threat of invasion by the German army, Hitler had forced Schuschnigg to appoint several Nazis to the Austrian cabinet, legalize the Austrian Nazi Party, release and grant amnesty to any and all Nazis in Austrian prisons, and agree to conduct joint foreign policy, military, and economic programs with Germany. Once again, rather than realize the magnitude of this huge step Germany had just taken in undermining Austria's sovereignty, Britain and France hardly reacted. "Well, there you are," Shirer wrote to his friend Edgar Mowrer of the *Chicago Daily News*, who had been forced out of Berlin by the Nazi regime five years earlier. "So long, Austria; And Czecho. And Europe. And decency."

On February 26, Shirer stepped off the train from Sofia to find his friend Ed Taylor from the *Chicago Tribune* waiting for him at the Vienna station. "Congratulations!" Taylor said through a forced smile. Shirer was a father. The baby, a girl, had arrived early that morning, but he could tell that something was wrong.

"And Tess?" he asked hesitantly.

"She's had a bit of a hard time, I'm afraid," Taylor replied. "Caesarean. But she's better now." They jumped in a taxi and raced to the hospital.

When Shirer arrived, he found his beautiful baby girl healthy and "full of beans," but Tess was weak and exhausted. While Shirer was in Sofia, Tess had gone into labor and struggled through contractions for two full days until the doctor, a Jewish man working at a Catholic hospital, had insisted on a caesarean, likely saving her life. Once the danger of the baby's delivery had passed, another developed. Phlebitis set in in one of Tess's legs, which threatened to cripple or even kill her. To make matters worse, a palpable aura of tense uncertainty had settled across Vienna to the point it was affecting hospital operations. The staff seemed muddled. No one was quite sure how to treat Tess, aside from applying leeches to her legs to try to improve blood flow.

Despite the building crisis within his family and across Austria, on March 8, with Tess still in the hospital, CBS sent Shirer to Ljubljana to broadcast a concert by coal miners' children. Three days later, he again returned to Vienna and emerged from the train to discover another surprise. Two planes flying overhead were dropping political leaflets, littering the streets. As he got into a taxi, Shirer asked the driver what was going on.

"Plebiscite," the driver responded tersely.

"What plebiscite?" Shirer asked.

"The one Schuschnigg ordered." The driver did not elaborate further.

Shirer hurried back to the hospital to sit with Tess, who remained critically ill. After sitting together a few hours, Tess fell asleep, so Shirer dashed out to the city center to see what he could learn about this plebiscite, which Chancellor Schuschnigg hoped would return a resounding call for Austria's continued sovereign independence.

That afternoon, tension crackled across Vienna. At Café Schwarzenberg, where his journalist friends liked to meet and trade information, Shirer heard that an emboldened band of Austrian Nazis had smashed windows near Stephansplatz, in the heart of the city. Just before 4:00 p.m., he was making his way to the subway station at Karlsplatz to head back to the hospital when a crowd of a thousand people, many of them wearing Nazi armbands, got in his way. One lone policeman was trying to contain the group, apparently successfully. While perhaps meant to be menacing, the situation seemed quite comical. "If that's all the guts the Nazis have," Shirer mused, "Schuschnigg *will* win, hands down."

But when he again left the hospital at the end of visiting hours that evening, he found a completely different situation well underway outside. Something big was brewing, far bigger than any story he could devise about Eckener's new airship, which very well might be finished. If the Americans thought the chaotic and unruly scene unfolding on Viennese streets was an imminent precursor to war, Eckener could say goodbye to any hope of helium.

Emerging from the station at Karlsplatz once again, Shirer found himself "swept along in a shouting, hysterical Nazi mob." He was instantly chilled by the expressions on their faces. He had seen these faces before at Nuremberg party conferences and especially at the Reichstag meeting that March morning after the remilitarization of the Rhineland almost exactly two years earlier: "fanatical eyes, the gaping mouths, the hysteria," he observed. "And now they were shouting like Holy Rollers: *'Sieg Heil! Sieg Heil! Sieg Heil! Heil Hitler! Heil Hitler! Heil Hitler!'*"

"The plebiscite!" a middle-aged woman shouted to him. "Called off!"

Schuschnigg had succumbed to Hitler's pressure. The German army would soon be marching in. This was the end of Austria as Shirer knew it.

That night, an almost tearful Schuschnigg went on the radio to address the Austrian people. "We have yielded to force since we are not prepared even in this terrible situation to shed blood," he explained. "We have decided to order the troops to offer no resistance."

Shirer had to reach Murrow. This was too big a story to miss, no matter what New York said. He was the only American broadcaster in Vienna, and if CBS did not act fast, it was going to miss the scoop. NBC's Max Jordan, who was based in Basel and whom NBC *did* increasingly allow to report his own stories on air, would be there within hours. But Murrow was in Warsaw on another cultural assignment and did not answer at the number he had left.

Shirer was supposed to broadcast one of his usual cultural programs from Vienna that night, so he went back downtown to the Austrian broadcasting office as crowds sang Nazi songs and threw bricks through Jewish shop windows, all while policemen stood lounging "good-naturedly" with new swastika armbands. One storm trooper in particular caught his notice. The man smelled distinctly of mothballs. His uniform had clearly been tucked away in the closet, ready and waiting for some time. Along the way, Shirer stopped back in at the coffeehouse to catch up on what he had missed, only to find a group of foreign correspondents crowded together in shock. A man with a familiar face strutted by. It was Shirer's former assistant from when he had worked in Vienna five years earlier with the *Chicago Tribune*, a man who was half Austrian and half American and had presented himself as anti-Nazi.

"Well, *meine Damen und Herren* . . . it was about time," he sneered as he reached for his lapel, unpinned a hidden swastika button, and replaced it proudly right side up in his buttonhole.

Just before his appointed 5:00 p.m. New York—11:00 p.m. Vienna—broadcast time, Shirer arrived at the studio, but men in gray uniforms with bayonets stopped him from entering. When they finally allowed him to pass, he found young men in SA and SS uniforms with revolvers swarming through the halls. One of the new men in charge informed him he would not be broadcasting that night and had him escorted from the building. Shirer had no choice but to return home.

At 3:00 a.m., as Shirer sat up in his apartment, unable to sleep, Murrow finally called.

"Fly to London, why don't you?" he suggested. "You can get there by tomorrow evening and give the first uncensored eyewitness account." Murrow would make his way back to Vienna to cover any new developments and also keep an eye on Tess. Shirer shot off a line to his wife to explain to her that he had to go and quickly called three other local correspondents to arrange backup for the Vienna office while he was away. He was unable to get anyone on the phone.

When Shirer left for the airport early in the morning, Vienna was unrecognizable. Swastika flags flew from nearly every home. "Where did they get them so fast?" he thought, gaping, as he passed. At the airport, every flight was booked, nearly all the seats bought by Viennese Jews. Shirer "offered fantastic sums" to several people for their seats on a flight to London. Understandably, they refused. Finally, he managed to get on a flight to Berlin, where no one wanted to go that morning, and from there to London via Amsterdam, finally arriving at the CBS London bureau in the late afternoon with a hastily scrawled script he had written on the plane after clearing the German border. Murrow had evidently fixed everything with New York, as the London office was ready and waiting. An actual invasion of a neutral country was apparently what it took to convince CBS to allow him to broadcast his own eyewitness reporting on the air.

At 11:30 p.m. London time, just as families were sitting down for dinner on the Eastern Seaboard of the United States, the CBS announcer in New York City began an introduction. Shirer stepped up to the microphone in the broadcast booth. The first time he had broadcast, he had been a nervous wreck in front of the microphone. This time, he had had practically no sleep for two days and was simultaneously too agitated and too exhausted to be afraid as the studio counted down the seconds to airtime.

"A little more than twenty-four hours ago, Nazi troops passed over the border into Austria," the announcer read out. "At the time of the invasion yesterday, William L. Shirer, Columbia's Central European director, was in Vienna. This afternoon he flew to London to bring you an uncensored, eyewitness account of the move. . . . We take you now to London."

AFTER

CHAPTER 39

Frankfurt, Germany

At the entrance to the Frankfurt Hauptfriedhof, the city's main cemetery, a cloistered mourning hall made of yellowed stone stands in the sunshine at the base of a cobbled circular drive. Across from its covered veranda is a caretaker's cottage picturesquely adorned in climbing white flowers and slate-blue shutters perfectly matching weathered copper trim. Though just off a busy thoroughfare with a tram stop outside the main gate, there is an omnipresent hushed aura surrounding everything within the cemetery grounds. From the circular drive, a footpath extends down a sloping lawn to the edge of a forest, where it suddenly disappears into a wall of trees covered in mossy abundance. Even at high noon on a warm day in May, only dim rays of sunlight filter through the canopy above, making for an eerie atmosphere akin to a Brothers Grimm fairy tale. It is strange to find such a density of leaves and underbrush in the middle of the city. Birds are so well disguised in the foliage it is nearly impossible to identify the source of their disembodied cries.

Following the path to a clearing along the northernmost edge of the cemetery, a large and unexpected monument comes into view. It is the cenotaph marking the graves of seven of the *Hindenburg* crew, the five initially buried in the public funeral over which the region's *Gauleiter* presided and two more who later joined them, having died in the hospital from their wounds. The cenotaph stands at odds with the lichenous nature around it. Tall and rectangular, its design falls somewhere between a brutalist and an art deco aesthetic. On its face, two figures meant to evoke the masculine ideal are chiseled into the stone, each looking out to a point far in the distance. Just as the elements woven into the 1936 Olympic Games were meant to hearken back to a classical Greco-Roman heritage, here, too, is that attempt to bridge Nazi Germany to the legacy of supposed Aryan superiority its leaders were desperate to embrace.

And yet such serious efforts by the regime to rewrite history could not help but be undermined by the surroundings. Just over the shoulder of these two male forms, not eight hundred feet away, is a small path bordered by an ivy-covered wall. This is the border between the Hauptfriedhof and the Neuer Jüdischer Friedhof, the New Jewish Cemetery, which opened in 1929. Though by the end of the 1930s, the Jewish population of Frankfurt was considerably smaller than it had been just a decade earlier as German Jews fled in the face of mass arrests, the cemetery remained a focal point for the community. In 1939, Frankfurt's Jews added a wall as a memorial in the middle of their cemetery, which was built out of stones from synagogues destroyed in the pogrom of November 1938. On this night, known as Kristallnacht, or the Night of Broken Glass, Hitler's foot soldiers smashed thousands of Jewish storefronts and houses of worship in coordinated fashion and arrested thirty thousand Jews, many of whom were sent to concentration camps. Surprisingly, the cemetery itself remained untouched. A survivor of the Nazis' destructive violence, it became part of a quiet yet lasting symbol of Jewish strength, with the community's gaze bearing down on the backs of the nearby stone men standing haughtily at attention.

Beneath the two mighty men on the cenotaph, there is a smaller, rectangular pedestal far less ostentatious than its upper half. Here, a simple line drawing of an airship is etched into the stone. Its elegant minimalism stands at odds with the detailed features of the stone men's physicality. Its imagery is perhaps a better representation of the vision of the men whose resting place it marks. Below the etching of the airship, the name *Hindenburg* is similarly carved. After the victims' funeral in late May 1937, it took more than a year for this cenotaph to make its way to the grave site, as DZR objected to the original design that had been proposed. How different this final version was from the original was not publicly shared, but perhaps the jarring juxtaposition of the cenotaph's two styles represented some sort of compromise.

Around the three remaining sides of the rectangular base are the names of the men for whom this cenotaph was constructed to mark their final place of rest: Chief Radio Officer Willy Speck, his fellow radioman Franz Eichelmann, bar steward Max Schulze, cook's assistant Fritz Flackus, electrician Ernst Schlapp, and helmsman Alfred Bernhardt. Alongside their names is that of Ernst Lehmann, their beloved captain. But Lehmann is not there.

Sometime after his burial, Lehmann's wife arranged for his remains to be removed from the state memorial at the Frankfurt Hauptfriedhof and reinterred in the small Bavarian market town of Grassau, three hundred miles to the south in the foothills of the Austrian Tyrolean Alps. It was there that they had buried their boy, Otto Luv, and Mrs. Lehmann wanted father and son to be reunited. Though he had devoted his life to zeppelins, in his death, she tried to ensure that his soul would belong neither to the state nor to his beloved enterprise. Instead, it should belong to his family, short though their time together on earth might have been.

While Lehmann's wife had physically taken him away from this place, it was impossible to remove him entirely from the tragic legacy of the zeppelins, both their political co-option and their demise, to which he would always be inextricably linked. His name is inerasably etched into this stone, and his tacit cooperation in life, like that of millions of other Germans, allowed the party to ensure that his memory belonged to them.

Tragic in an altogether different way is his name's attachment to a future that almost was. Tucked away in the woods beyond the Frankfurt airport is the tiny hamlet of Zeppelinheim, the prefabricated company town that had been created for the men of DZR in a more optimistic time. Running perpendicular to Doktor-Eckener-Platz and parallel to Flughafenstrasse and Kapitän-von-Schiller-Strasse, the proudly designated Kapitän-Lehmann-Strasse forms the backbone of this little enclave. On the street named for him are a town hall and a kindergarten, beside which runs a little footpath honoring the *Hindenburg*'s cabin boy, Werner-Franz-Weg, leading to the school's door. Perhaps Lehmann's own little boy might have attended this school, had both father and son lived to see its completion.

As the days passed following the *Hindenburg*'s downfall, fewer and fewer of Lehmann's former crewmates remained in Zeppelinheim, replaced instead by workers of all varieties as the country moved on from airships. The brand-new house specially built for Lehmann and his family was quickly carved up into smaller apartments to make room for more families who came to work in the trades powering Germany's industrial war machine. Before long, Zeppelinheim itself was swallowed up by the larger town of Neu-Isenberg, its name and independent status becoming a relic of the fleeting era to which it had belonged, the roar of jet engines just beyond the trees evidence of the town's anachronistic existence. To borrow a prescient line from Leonhard Adelt, written in his book *Der Flieger* back in 1913: "The melody of the new age was in the air above us, the song of the future roared with faith . . . of a different kind and a different form than everything that had existed before."

The zeppelins and the men who flew them began their journey as the melody of a new age, a melody of hope and progress. This melody was soon overtaken by a parallel tune in a minor key, initially upbeat and pleasant, but one that soon overwhelmed its predecessor such that it was impossible to separate this darker rendition from what had come before. To paraphrase Leonhard, a parable of liberation, once realized, can quickly become a parable of new bonds, until it is redeemed by liberation realized once more.

The zeppelin was meant to be the symbol of a new age, until it became irredeemably overshadowed by evil. Instead, it became a symbol of the complexity of man; man, who is, whether in the realm of the measurable or the moral, always striving but so often failing to reach up and touch the sky. And though, once tainted, some things can never be resurrected from the past to mean what they did once upon a time, man's ingenuity ensures there will always be something new waiting to take its own place, as yet uncorrupted and full of the promise of tomorrow.

EPILOGUE

In Friedrichshafen today, it is easy to imagine a world where airships still reign supreme. This historic airship capital is an almost whimsical city, where the snowcapped peaks of Switzerland and Austria reflect off the surface of the Bodensee. Nestled between vineyards in the nearby hills and the sparkling water, one feels removed from both the heavy Bavarian trappings of Munich and the brutalism and counterculture of postwar Berlin.

Here, one can see how Eckener and his men may have felt beyond the grip of Nazi power in Germany's far-off capital as they worked on their beloved airships in this little city of dreams. In a park along the lakeside promenade, there is a fountain, in the center of which a cherub stands on a globe proudly displaying his city's legacy. He gently holds a model of one of Count Zeppelin's early airships, longer and narrower than the later, elliptical *Graf Zeppelin* and *Hindenburg* but every bit as fantastic as its descendants. In the center of the city there is a children's play structure in the shape of a zeppelin, shiny and chrome with a chariot underneath akin to Jules Verne's imaginary airship *Albatross*. Eckenerstrasse runs through town. Up the street, there is a sweet shop selling zeppelin-shaped chocolates.

Most striking of all is the Zeppelin Museum, built inside the old Friedrichshafen ferry terminal and adorned with art deco flourishes. The museum houses a full-scale cross section of portions of the *Hindenburg*'s main passenger spaces, reconstructed as true to the original airship as possible. Light aluminum furniture fills the lounge and a replica of Otto Apke's map of the world adorns the wall, the routes of historic ships of both sea and sky traced across the oceans.

Above the central staircase of the museum, another, smaller model of the *Hindenburg* hangs from the ceiling, but here, something is notably missing. There are no black swastikas on its tail fins. While the zeppelin program long predated the Nazi regime, the *Hindenburg* bore the symbol of the Third Reich for its entire operational life. Perhaps this model is meant to represent the *Hindenburg* in its purest, ideal form as the zeppelin crews might have preferred to remember it, severed from the time in which it flew so that it may remain a ship of dreams.

The legacy of the last great airship is elusive, not just in Germany but around the world. It is an iconic event that everyone knows but almost no one can place. For some, it evokes the idea of the *Titanic* of the skies, but unlike this sister disaster, few can confidently say where or when it occurred and most are shocked to learn that anyone survived. Similarly, Herb Morrison's cry of "Oh, the humanity!" is a famous yet orphaned phrase. It is familiar and yet disassociated from context.

The *Hindenburg* disaster belongs to what one might consider the lost years of the mid-1930s. It lies between the depths of the Great Depression and the inevitable march toward war. Little else is discussed in between. Within this consequential yet underappreciated decade, 1937 itself is perhaps the most forgotten year. The years just before and after contain what we think of as the signposts in a chapter of a history textbook about the prelude to World War II in Europe. Hitler seized the chancellorship in 1933. He purged challengers to his power during the Night of the Long Knives in 1934. The Nuremburg Race Laws gave Jews a lesser legal status than their non-Jewish neighbors in 1935. Germany remilitarized the Rhineland in violation of the Treaty of Versailles in 1936. The fateful year of 1938 is full of the hallmark events found on any classroom's World War II timeline, from the Anschluss of Austria in March to the Sudeten crisis later that spring, when Hitler threatened to forcefully reunite ethnic Germans in a (natural resource–rich) region just over the Czechoslovakian border with their "true" homeland. On September 30, 1938, in the city of

Munich, British Prime Minister Neville Chamberlain agreed to give Hitler the Sudetenland, promising it would secure "peace for our time." This quickly derided policy of appeasement proved to do just the opposite. Just weeks later, on the night of November 9 and 10, was Kristallnacht. And, of course, on September 1, 1939, the world descended into war as Germany invaded Poland.

By contrast, 1937 has no such marquee event to which we peg our memories. In Germany, it was a year filled with industrial consolidation and political planning, currency controls, party rallies, and the passage of laws that further restricted civil liberties. None of these actions created the types of banner headlines that came before and after. But of course, it is in the quiet moments that authoritarianism slowly tightens its grip. Each small measure is digested by the average person with mild concern but without too much upset to daily life, until the cumulative effects have fundamentally changed the fabric of society.

However, for all the clouds that hang over the decade, there is also an oft-overlooked current running through those middle years of the 1930s that felt especially hopeful. Exciting technological advancements that would soon change the lives of everyday people gave the impression that a brighter tomorrow was on the horizon. The 1933 Chicago World's Fair, for example, steeped in streamlined modern and art deco aesthetics, was titled "A Century of Progress." Some forty million visitors from around the world saw a happier, almost utopian future unfurling before them. Visitors experienced innovations like electric dishwashers, air-conditioning, a Chevrolet production line, and, of course, a *Graf Zeppelin* flyover with Hugo Eckener at the controls. Those fairgoers might be surprised to learn that today we look back at the 1930s and see a time so shrouded in fear.

The *Hindenburg* disaster represents a crossroads between the 1930s' two competing paths that would inevitably come head-to-head. The German zeppelins began as a character in the hopeful story of the 1930s, a gleaming technological marvel soaring high above, where, as Ernst Lehmann said, "the heavens curved off into infinity." On an airborne ship of dreams, one could leave behind earthly problems like unemployment, inflation, and anxieties over rearmament, even if just for a few hours or a few days. One could even imagine that once mankind was connected by the skies, such tribulations would recede into history. All too soon, however, the zeppelins became consumed by the second, darker story of the 1930s, and the ship of dreams with the power to connect the world became yet another propaganda tool powering the Nazi machine. Such cooption came relatively easily. Some, like Eckener, offered a degree of resistance at first before quietly acquiescing, but for most people in Germany, like Ernst Lehmann, self-interest won out. This was not so much outright self-interest in an immediate sense, as for those who joined the Nazi Party seeking power and favors, but rather the self-interested pursuit of one's own chimeric dreams, which could come to fruition only with the resources the Nazis could provide. But a pact with the devil rarely comes without great cost to the human being, as individuals too often become faceless statistics co-opted by an authoritarian state to suit its own purposes. Never were there more appropriate words to sum up this slice of time than "Oh, the humanity!"

Despite the best efforts of airships' greatest champions, who struggled to keep their dream alive in the face of the gathering storm, the golden age of airships ended on May 6, 1937. The horrific sounds and images of the *Hindenburg* disaster that were seared into the public imagination ultimately proved insurmountable, especially when paired with Germany's increasing bellicosity.

As a September 1937 DZR report stated, in the United States, "the very strong feeling of distrust" regarding "Germany's foreign policy intentions caused many to have reservations" about selling helium to Germany, which was essential if the zeppelin program had any chance at a future. As months passed, more Americans became wary of selling this precious natural resource to the German state. By the spring of 1938, Secretary Ickes was receiving a steady stream of letters encouraging him not to authorize helium exports for a new German zeppelin. Hugo Eckener returned to Washington in May 1938 to press his case one more time. The new *LZ-130* was nearly ready, save the all-important gas to fill it. While President Roosevelt argued that they could sell the helium with a "guarantee from Hitler that it would not be used for military purposes," Ickes pushed back. "Who would take Hitler's word?"

Eckener's time with Ickes was brief. When he returned to Germany and shared the details of this meeting with the DZR board of directors, the board wrote Ickes off entirely, suggesting that the secretary of the interior was "unpopular" and "an oddball." Ickes would not have cared. Germany's Anschluss of Austria just two months earlier had only solidified his broader concerns about the future, not just about zeppelins but also for Europe, the United States, and the wider world. While many in the United States thought Americans should stay out of European disputes, Ickes was not convinced. "My theory," he wrote in his diary, "is that if the democratic theory of government is fighting for its life, we will have to fight for it sooner or later, and if we put it off too long, watching other democratic governments succumb to fascism, we will be forced to fight in the most disadvantageous circumstances." Ickes never did approve the helium delivery. If the Germans wanted to proceed, they would have no choice but to use hydrogen once more.

On September 14, 1938, the day after riots in Czechoslovakia prompted British Prime Minister Neville Chamberlain to contact Hitler and request a meeting in Munich to avert war, the *LZ-130* took off on her maiden voyage. Hugo Eckener, who by then had stopped publicly resisting the regime and thus was allowed to carry on with his zeppelin work, symbolically christened the new airship with a bottle of liquid air and aspirational words about the new zeppelin "carry[ing] forth the honor of German technology to all the world as a symbol of unshakeable German will." He ended his remarks with "*Sieg Heil!*" He was determined to stick with the zeppelins through what he hoped would be short-term unpleasantness so that he might lead them once more in whatever future came after the Nazi regime. Outfitted with various radio antennae and flying under the auspices of the Luftwaffe Department of Signals, the *LZ-130* made thirty flights in total, including along the British coastline. The crew, commanded by Captain Albert Sammt, were not informed of the purpose of their flights, but Luftwaffe personnel on board used the airship for electronic surveillance to listen to British military radio traffic and spy on the British radar system. Ickes had been right all along.

The *LZ-130* made its last flight on August 20, 1939, less than two weeks before the outbreak of World War II. On March 1, 1940, Hermann Göring visited the zeppelin hub in Frankfurt with a full entourage to survey the state of the German airship program. After listening to DZR employees' impassioned advocacy for airships' future, Göring posed with the husk of the *LZ-130*, which had been stripped for parts, and said, "Na, that thing's for the birds! . . . One match and the whole contraption will go up in flames!" Less than a month later, Göring ordered both the *Graf Zeppelin* and the *LZ-130*, or *Graf Zeppelin II*, to be scrapped. Finally, on May 6, 1940, the third anniversary of the *Hindenburg* disaster, the airship hangars in Frankfurt were set with charges and blown up by Göring's Luftwaffe.

The Nazis also seized the zeppelin works in Friedrichshafen. In September 1941, scientists responsible for developing long-range rockets, including Wernher von Braun (later one of the chief scientists behind American ballistic missile development and NASA's Apollo program after his controversial postwar relocation to the United States), traveled to Friedrichshafen in search of new facilities that could produce parts for the weapons they were building. After a meeting with Eckener and Luftschiffbau Zeppelin management, the company agreed to subcontract. From July 22, 1943, to September 29, 1944, Friedrichshafen served as an armament facility. A total of 1,202 Dachau concentration camp prisoners were brought in as laborers and were forced to construct components of V-2 long-range ballistic missiles. Germany fired these missiles on Allied cities like London and Antwerp, the very same cities on which zeppelins had dropped bombs in crude air raids thirty years earlier.

By the end of the war, the zeppelin company essentially ceased to exist. As Allied forces led postwar reconciliation and denazification efforts in Germany, Hugo Eckener found himself charged with Nazi collaboration in 1948 for his role as the head of the zeppelin company and its associated wartime activity, nominal though his position was by then. Though he was fined 100,000 marks and lost his civil privileges, he was ultimately "rehabilitated" and restored to both his professional and full civic standing. Soon after, in 1949, he wrote a memoir about his life's work and attempted to reengage with old partners, like Goodyear, in hopes of reviving interest in airships, but by then, airplanes had so far outpaced their lighter-than-air counterparts that no project ever came to fruition. Disappointed at having failed to resurrect the industry to which he had dedicated his life, Hugo Eckener lived out his days in Friedrichshafen surrounded by family and old friends and colleagues from the zeppelin glory days. He passed away in 1954 at the age of eighty-six.

As the zeppelin company's founding charter stated, if the company ceased to function, its residual assets would pass to the City of Friedrichshafen for charitable purposes. In 1947, Friedrichshafen officially launched the Zeppelin Foundation, with assets administered by the city for special communal social, cultural, and scientific purposes. At least some of these assets were used to help care for former crew members and their families in their twilight years. This fraternal support was meaningful to the old airshipmen, particularly after the war. For a time in the 1950s, there was even a *Zeppelin-Post* newsletter, "the purpose and task" of which, it explained in its first issue in 1952, "should be to revive and promote the feeling of camaraderie that connects the old Zeppeliners," which was "something that we Germans desperately need today. . . . We can still draw from this memory a certain sense of happiness in a world that is today so evil and confused and so poor in happiness." It was important, the newsletter stated, to discuss the pride they should feel for the history of which they were part—a history that long predated the corruption of the zeppelins as the Reich's propaganda playthings.

For the old zeppeliners, there was certainly much of which to be proud. While jet-engine airplanes soon roared into the skies, in certain crucial respects, zeppelins had accomplished what it took their heavier-than-air cousins decades to achieve. Pan Am flew its first commercial transpacific passenger flight in October 1936, island-hopping between San Francisco and Manila, but it was not until 1939 that the airline began commercial transatlantic passenger service with the Boeing 314 *Yankee Clipper* flying boat, which had to refuel in the Azores. Commercial landplanes could not reach continental Europe from the United States until 1945, and not without stopping in Newfoundland and Shannon, Ireland. The first nonstop, scheduled transatlantic passenger jet flight occurred in 1958 when a British Overseas Aircraft Corporation de Havilland Comet 4 began service between New York and London. Though it took a mere seven hours, compared with two and a half days in a zeppelin, it was essentially the same journey achieved by the British airship *R.34* all the way back in 1919.

While the *Hindenburg* disaster ended commercial airship travel, airships did not completely disappear from the skies. Until 1962, the U.S. Navy used small, helium-filled airships to accompany military convoys and conduct aerial reconnaissance across the Atlantic, Pacific, and Mediterranean. During World War II, fleets of airships escorted some 89,000 surface ships on over 55,000 flights. According to the United States Naval Institute, not a single vessel escorted by an airship was destroyed by enemy submarines.

In 1993, with investment from the endowment funded by the original zeppelin company, a new airship concern, ZLT Zeppelin Luftschifftechnik GmbH, was founded in Friedrichshafen to develop a new generation of airships. The resulting Zeppelin NTs (for *neue Technologie*) are a class of semirigid carbon-fiber airships, combining elements of both blimps and rigid airships, which are considerably smaller than the old zeppelins and are, most important, filled with helium. In 2011, Goodyear resumed its historical partnership with the zeppelin company and ordered three Zeppelin NT airships to serve in its fleet of Goodyear Blimps (though they are not technically blimps in the true, nonrigid sense). At premier sporting and cultural events across America, fans of the Goodyear Blimp can still look up with delight and see these Zeppelin NTs floating across the skies. In Friedrichshafen, tourists can even take sightseeing rides on Zeppelin NTs and fly over the Bodensee, just as in the days of Count Zeppelin.

Today, airships continue to delight and inspire. Their enduring legacy can be found across music and film, from the English rock band Led Zeppelin to the 1975 film *Hindenburg*, starring George C. Scott and Anne Bancroft, to Steven Spielberg's 1989 classic, *Indiana Jones and the Last Crusade*, in which Harrison Ford and Sean Connery make a remarkable escape from the Nazis who are tailing them by jumping into an airplane hooked onto a zeppelin and flying away. Perhaps it is the air of romantic tragedy inherent to the story of airships that continues to capture the imagination. The zeppelin, floating silently and gracefully in its silver glory, was outdated almost from the moment of inception, and yet it may have actually been ahead of its time.

The first golden age of airships may have passed, but perhaps we are at the dawn of a second. Since the Cold War, scientists have tried to imagine a genuine future for airships—including in the colonization of outer space—but only recently have they found a realistic role that airships might play in the modern world. Today's airship start-ups, like Google founder Sergey Brin's Lighter than Air Research, see airships as a green-energy answer to both long-distance cargo transportation and humanitarian disaster relief in remote locations. However, these modern projects, the prototypes for which are far larger than Goodyear Blimps, run into the same issue as their predecessors: the availability of helium.

Helium in liquid form is a vital cooling agent in modern scientific equipment, from the CERN Large Hadron Collider to MRI scanners to semiconductor and electric vehicle battery manufacturing. No existing technology can extract helium from the atmosphere or manufacture it artificially, and helium-rich gas deposits are found in only a few places on earth, including the United States, Qatar, Algeria, and Russia. Geopolitical strife easily upsets these supply chains, and in 2024, the United States sold its federal helium reserve stockpile near Amarillo, Texas, ironically to a German gas company, thus introducing more market uncertainty. Once again, that leaves hydrogen as the only reliably available lifting gas. Though scientific advances have made hydrogen far safer, lingering memories of the *Hindenburg* disaster, nicknamed "*Hindenburg* Syndrome" among today's airship entrepreneurs, would likely scare off investors, not least because scientists were long unable to definitively state what caused the accident in 1937. A 2021 experiment at the California Institute of Technology, however, may have finally put speculation and conspiracy theories to rest.

In conjunction with the PBS television program *NOVA*, Konstantinos Giapis, a professor of chemical engineering, conducted a series of experiments on a mock-up of the *Hindenburg*'s frame and cover in which he replicated the conditions of the zeppelin's landing that rainy night in May 1937. Focusing on the basics of Eckener's explanation for the disaster, that a high-intensity static spark created the deadly explosion, Giapis charged the model with an electrical voltage mimicking the atmospheric charge of the stormy conditions at Lakehurst. He then grounded the frame to replicate the effect of the landing ropes hitting the ground. This produced no spark. After misting salt water over the cover material to simulate the light rain falling on an airship cover coated in a salty residue from its transatlantic journey, Giapis reran the experiment. With the presence of the salt, significant audible and visible sparks instantly jumped and cracked across the model.

But this alone did not explain why it took four minutes from the time the landing ropes hit the ground for the deadly spark to occur. Eckener had assumed it had something to do with the fact that the mooring ropes were initially dry and thus supposedly not conductive when they first made contact, but that four minutes in the misting rain had made the material wet enough to become conductive. Giapis discovered that manila hemp rope, the kind used on the *Hindenburg*, is actually somewhat conductive when dry, so the fatal spark should have occurred right away. He also noted that before the model was grounded, the cover had a positive charge, as Eckener had posited all those years ago. However, when Giapis's "mooring ropes" touched ground, electrons from the ground moved up the ropes and gave the *frame* of the model an increasingly negative charge. The cover, which was completely separated from the metal frame by nonconductive types of twine and wooden dowels, a design the zeppelin engineers had thought was safer, retained its positive charge. As a result, the frame must have tried to equalize by pulling additional positive charge out of the surrounding atmosphere, but that charge could not move beyond the *Hindenburg*'s cover and on to the frame due to the twine and dowels. Thus, the cover developed an even *greater* charge differential.

Giapis realized the *Hindenburg* had essentially become an enormous capacitor. A capacitor is a device almost like a storage tank for electrons, which accumulates electric charges on two conductive surfaces that are close together but separated from each other with an insulating material that is such a poor conductor that electrons cannot flow through it. As a result, a significant voltage or potential difference builds up on each side over time, so that one side of the conductor becomes negative and one side positive. As the negatively charged electrons on one side are attracted to the abundance of positively charged protons that remain on the other side, like the opposite poles on a magnet, an electrical field develops because electrons are unable to jump across due to the insulating material in between. There is nowhere for them to go, unless another pathway develops. If another pathway is present, electrons on one side will move through this new pathway to the positively charged side until the charges equalize. Capacitors are used on circuit boards to even out electrical current in appliances like toasters or lamps to minimize interruptions in the flow of energy by providing alternate pathways, such as a wire, through which electrons that have built up can freely flow. This stops lamps from flickering and toasters from surging. However, an alternate pathway does not have to be a wire. It can be any conductive material, or even a stream of highly conductive gas, such as hydrogen, that encompasses both sides of the capacitor. By contrast, helium would not provide a pathway, as helium is a very poor conductor due to its chemical structure.

Building up a charge on a capacitor takes time. The greater the size of the capacitor, the more time it will take to accumulate a large voltage differential. On a capacitor as large as the *Hindenburg*, it would take approximately four minutes to fully charge. Though Giapis did not theorize how the hydrogen leak in the gas cell had formed, he realized that anywhere the frame and skin were in very close proximity, which they were in hundreds of spots across the airship, any one of those spots would have been acting as a capacitor. The potential difference between them was so great that if an alternate pathway developed, any of them could have created a spark as electrons flowed from one side to the other. It just so happened that at one of those hundreds of points there was indeed a hydrogen leak that formed an alternative pathway between the frame and the skin. This allowed the electrons to equalize, creating a spark that ignited the highly flammable hydrogen. Though all of this occurred at the subatomic level, invisible to the naked eye, it led to disastrous consequences.

After more than eighty years, the mystery of the *Hindenburg* disaster was solved thanks to a technically precise explanation rooted in basic chemistry and physics. It required no great imaginative leaps, like far-fetched sabotage plots, merely the leap of an electron from the negatively charged aluminum frame to the positively charged skin covering the airship. The principle of parsimony, where the simplest answer connecting all the pieces is the correct one, wins out. Though Hugo Eckener did not live long enough to see his general theory of the disaster confirmed, in the metaphysical world, perhaps he can finally rest in peace.

While the *Hindenburg* disaster is a story both of microscopic scientific principles and of sweeping systemic forces on a global scale, most important, it is a story about regular people whose lives were altered in an instant, perhaps by fate, but also by chance. Their legacies are forever intertwined, but their stories are individual, and they deserve to be remembered not just for their part in thirty-four ghastly seconds that shocked the world but also for their individual humanity, which existed before and after that moment frozen in time.

As renowned author and University of Chicago English professor Norman Maclean wrote in *Young Men and Fire*, a haunting tale of fifteen young smoke jumpers in Montana sent to fight the 1949 Mann Gulch forest fire, "I find in trying to record the tragedy of a good many characters . . . that a few remained distant from me and anonymous. . . . Only some came close to me and asked me to visit their crosses." Such is the nature of writing history, particularly a story such as this. When one begins to tell a story about a group of people, certain characters quickly announce their presence, reaching out from the past through what they have left behind. Others, meanwhile, seem content to let their personal histories lie undisturbed. Some may think it is the historian's role to choose the protagonists to carry a story, akin to that of a screenwriter or director. Instead, the decision of who carries the narrative is up to the people who lived it, long gone though they may be. Sometimes the protagonists are those you expect because of how they lived—more colorfully, more actively, more publicly than others—where an extensive trail of records follows in their wake. Other times they sneak up on you, working their way into your mind, heart, and words in unanticipated ways. Most maddeningly intriguing are those who announce themselves for a fleeting, palpable instant. They are satisfied to share their role in a moment in time, but then they retreat into privacy when the moment has passed, leaving the historian envious of the novelist and frustratedly unable to give them the send-off they deserve.

It is unsurprising that the Adelts, both writers, left behind clear voices for posterity to hear. As he recuperated in his hospital bed after the disaster, Leonhard Adelt dictated his memories of the *Hindenburg* and of Captain Lehmann, which were soon published in *Reader's Digest* and in the American edition of Lehmann's book, which was published posthumously. Gertrud chose to pen her thoughts for a German paper over a decade later. "When I remember the Zeppelin trip from Frankfurt to Lakehurst . . . before the dramatic reality of the end," she wrote about that fateful day, "the trip itself recedes into a kind of dream state from which images emerge in fragments, seemingly torn out of their context and yet inextricably linked to the beginning and end." For the Adelts, the trip on the *Hindenburg* belonged to what must have seemed like an idyllic fantasy before the world went up in flames. Upon reflection, it also must have felt like a harbinger of what fate cruelly had in store.

In June 1937, Gertrud and Leonhard returned to Germany by steamship and were finally reunited with their baby son, Christian. That autumn, they had an unexpected reunion with a fellow survivor of the *Hindenburg*, Benny Spah, who had returned to Germany for another vaudeville tour, this time with his entire family and their new dog, Ulla II. Initially, German authorities tried to shut down public interest in the tragedy while the investigation proceeded, but once the case was closed, there were "no longer any objections regarding mentions and accounts of events relating to the last flight and the accident." Alongside his tour, Benny was invited to showcase and lecture on the home movies he had taken during the voyage on his camera that had miraculously survived. In Berlin, Düsseldorf, and Essen, audiences saw his footage of the *Hindenburg*'s last departure from Frankfurt, its shadow racing impressively across ocean and icebergs, as well as the face of the beloved Captain Lehmann and Lakehurst's cheering crowds waving at the airship during its final minutes.

Gertrud and Leonhard attended one of Benny's film screenings. After the feature, the Spah family chatted with the Adelts and the two couples even took a picture together. Benny and Vera looked full of vim and vigor, smiling broadly while he posed with the projector. Beside them, Leonhard, bald, bespectacled, and benign, appeared to have fully recovered, while Gertrud, in a dark dress with a starched white collar, perched on the arm of her husband's chair and stared directly and expressionlessly into the camera. No doubt this special screening and reunion did not recall the fondest memories. Before they parted, Leonhard gave Benny a special gift—inscribed copies of two of his books, *Der Ozeanflug* (The ocean flight) and *Auf Luftpatrouille und Weltfahrt* (On air patrol and world tour), the German edition of the memoir he had penned with Captain Lehmann. In the second book, he left an inscription. "To Ben Dova," he wrote in German, "the companion in misfortune on the ill-fated voyage on the *LZ 'Hindenburg,'* on the happy reunion with his wife and children. Best wishes, Leonhard Adelt." Benny would keep the books for the rest of his life, but the two men would not meet again.

The Adelts were neither vocal supporters of the Nazi regime nor staunch opponents. Like most Germans, they fell somewhere in the middle, concerned mostly with their own family and security in an increasingly overwhelming situation but, like millions of others, implicated to some degree in what followed by their acquiescence through silence and passivity. Perhaps their situation was best characterized by an anecdote Gertrud passed on to her grandson, Ulrich. One day, Gertrud and her son, Christian, then about four or five and beginning to comprehend the world around him, were in a public square where the radio was broadcasting one of Hitler's ranting speeches. "Who is that terrible person speaking on the radio?" Christian asked his mother. Gertrud had to quickly shush him.

When war broke out, Leonhard was in his late fifties and too old to be drafted into service, so he was able to spend the next few years writing. He initially continued to write about airships to carry forward the momentum the *Hindenburg* disaster had brought him, but his subsequent works reflected the modern war posture of German aviation. Together, Gertrud and Leonhard published *Sturz in den Sieg: Das Wunder der Ju 88* (Falling into victory: The miracle of the Ju 88), about the remarkable Junkers Ju 88 bomber, one of the most versatile airplanes Germany ever produced, which saw action from the outbreak of war in Poland in 1939 through to the Eastern Front in 1945.

Sometime during this period, Gertrud and Leonhard also decided to leave Berlin and return to Dresden. Under cover of night on February 13, 1945, hundreds of Allied bombers droned in the skies above their historic city, dropping 200,000 incendiaries over a period of fifteen minutes. A second attack followed three hours later. By the next morning, thousands of fires across the city could be seen one hundred miles away. In the midst of the blaze were Gertrud and Leonhard. According to their grandson, though he could not be entirely sure of the details, when their house caught fire, Gertrud, Leonhard, and Christian ran safely outside, only for Leonhard to turn around and run back inside to rescue a manuscript he was determined to save. Leonhard had run through fire once, but this time, the flames caught up with him. Burning pieces of the house fell on top of him, and while neighbors managed to pull him out alive, he died of his injuries a week later at the age of sixty-three.

After the war, Gertrud spoke little about those days, or of Leonhard. In the war's immediate aftermath, she supported herself and her son by knitting dolls until she could get a job as a writer again, which she eventually did with *Film und Frau* magazine. Later, she contributed articles and book reviews to postwar newspapers like *Die Welt* and *Hamburger Abendblatt*. But tragedy seemed to follow Gertrud. In 1982, Christian, her only son, disappeared. The family believe he died in India, though his final days are a mystery. For the rest of her life, Gertrud remained proper, tidy, and intellectually curious. She took long walks every Saturday, sometimes going as much as twenty kilometers, usually while wearing a beret or other clothes too stylish for such a long jaunt. As her grandson remembered, she remained strong-willed, proud, and independent to the end. Above all, she never stopped to dwell on the cruelties of life and was content to leave tragedy in the past.

Throughout Benny Spah's life, he had little interest in speaking with adults about the *Hindenburg* disaster. He always preferred speaking with children, especially the students in his own children's and grandchildren's classes. They asked much better questions.

As soon as Benny's ankle healed, he was right back out in front of his audience performing his lamppost routine. Other acts soon followed, with bigger props and better tricks. He performed with a full bar balanced on his top hat. He even eventually put the old lamppost act on ice. Through it all, Vera was right by his side. Unsurprisingly, his children followed him into the family business of entertainment, each one more coordinated than the last. His son Gilbert became a renowned juggler, while Richard was a skater and later a key grip for Lucasfilm. Benny's two daughters, Marilyn and Evelyn (born in 1940), were talented skaters. For a time, he and Evelyn toured with a double-act version of his lamppost routine on ice. Throughout his life, Benny could always be found with camera in hand, taking home movies of his family. His family still has the camera and binoculars he had on the *Hindenburg*, and almost ninety years later, the leather camera case still smells faintly of smoke.

In later years, Benny agreed to sit for public interviews in conjunction with the highly fictionalized 1975 *Hindenburg* film starring George C. Scott, where he was portrayed by Robert Clary. He later joined Herb Morrison for a joint television interview in 1985. But his real starring turn came in 1976 in the film *Marathon Man*, starring Dustin Hoffman and Laurence Olivier, where he was cast in the role of Olivier's brother, who dies in a fiery car crash at the beginning of the movie. Perhaps he lent his real-life experience to the role.

Benny and his family always chose to look back at May 6, 1937, with gallows humor. His daughter Marilyn, just two years old when she saw the *Hindenburg* go up in flames, is now in her nineties. Still an avid runner, Marilyn says that whenever she has a bad hair day, she calls it "*Hindenburg* hair," just like in the photograph of her family sitting reunited on the couch in Lakehurst, her hair covered in ash and soot and sticking out every which way.

In 1986, after a lifetime of daring feats, Benny Spah died peacefully at the age of eighty-one. Toward the end of his life, he and Vera moved to Manassas, Virginia, to live with Marilyn. Nearby, there was an old country road where he liked to take drives. Marilyn's daughter, Jane, thought the rolling hills dotted with trees reminded him of his boyhood home in Alsace. Today, Marilyn still has one of Benny's lampposts. It sits in pieces in traveling cases in a shed in her sweeping Virginia backyard. On an overcast Sunday in May 2024, four generations of Benny's family happened to be together at Marilyn's house, and they took the old lamppost out of the traveling cases and put it back together. After enduring hundreds of performances, it could still stand freely. Rickety and dusty as it was, one of Benny's great-grandsons could not resist climbing up to the top.

When Werner Franz returned home to Frankfurt in May 1937, he was greeted at the train station by friends, neighbors, and many people he did not even know. For some time after his return, strangers would show up at his family's apartment out of curiosity. Franz's story had turned him into a minor national celebrity. Later that year, a book was published called *Kabinenjunge Werner Franz vom Luftschiff "Hindenburg"* (Cabin boy Werner Franz from the airship "*Hindenburg*") by W. E. Freiherr von Medem, supposedly written after the author's chance encounter with Franz on the island of Rügen, where Franz was recuperating in a convalescent home after his ordeal. Through a series of walks, von Medem says, Franz told him his story, which the author was compelled to share so that the nation's youth could learn the story of the brave cabin boy. How much of a role Franz had in writing it is unknown, nor is it clear if he and his family received compensation for his story, but Nazi Germany never let a good tragedy go to waste.

Franz's period of celebrity was short-lived. By the time the war broke out, he was sixteen. He served in the Luftwaffe as a radio operator and instructor. When it was over, he married a woman named Annerose, worked for the postal service repairing precision machines, and took up skating as a hobby. Franz was such a talented skater that he became a figure skating and roller-skating coach. One of his pupils, Marika Kilius, went on to become a two-time Olympic silver medalist in pairs figure skating in 1960 and 1964.

In 2012, the Navy Lakehurst Historical Society invited Werner Franz, then nearly ninety years old, to come from Germany to New Jersey to take part in a special seventy-fifth-anniversary commemoration of the *Hindenburg* disaster, along with eighty-three-year-old Werner Doehner, who had been eight years old on the zeppelin's last flight. Unfortunately, health problems prevented them both from attending, but after the event, admirers sent letters and photographs. Werner Franz and Werner Doehner sent letters and photographs to their new pen pals in return. Even after seventy-five years, Franz still had that same bright-eyed curiosity as he did when he was fourteen. Two years later, Werner Franz died at ninety-two. In 2019, Werner Doehner passed away at the age of ninety. They were the last living survivors of the *Hindenburg* disaster.

Remarkably, Captain Max Pruss recovered from his injuries thanks to months of skin grafts, a prosthetic nose, and facial reconstruction, first in New York and then at home in Germany. Though his reconstructed face would always have a swollen, waxen appearance, he returned to relatively full health. Along with his son, Klaus, and Commander Rosendahl, Pruss advocated for airships for the rest of his life. He was hopeful in 1956 when the first blimp returned to Germany, though of course he did not live long enough to see Zeppelins NTs flying in the sky.

The idea that the *Hindenburg* disaster was caused by a mechanical failure, due to either error or chance, was too much for Max Pruss to accept, especially as his men had been killed on his watch. By late 1937, as he wrote to friends, he was convinced that the *Hindenburg* had been felled by sabotage. Initially, he believed the zeppelin was brought down by an incendiary bullet, though he later changed his mind and thought an infernal machine designed to strike back against the Third Reich was to blame. By the time he was interviewed by Columbia University shortly before his death in 1960, he had somewhat softened, stating, "It may be sabotage; it may be electricity, lightning, nobody knows." He was still convinced sabotage was most likely. However, he continued, "If the sabotage was from the inside or otherwise, it's very difficult to say." Remarkably, in the interview, Pruss never addressed his pain, either the physical pain he had endured or that of losing his men. To him, flying in a zeppelin would only ever be associated with the wonder and joy of flying over land and sea in a manner with which no airplane could ever compare.

With only minor injuries, Nelson Morris quickly regained his health and returned to France with his wife, Blanche, just as he had planned. He remained an officer in the Illinois National Guard throughout World War II, though he did not see active duty. Blanche returned to the stage to raise funds for the French Relief Fund in 1940 and again for British relief efforts in 1941. Otherwise, the Morrises lived quietly as committed philanthropists. Nelson's sister Muriel, meanwhile, married Joseph Buttinger and continued her resistance activity. After the Anschluss, Muriel and her family fled to Paris before moving to the United States just before the fall of France in 1939. She later wrote about her experiences in a memoir called *Code Name "Mary."*

Though the exact nature of Nelson Morris's support for the Dolan family following Bert's death on the *Hindenburg* remained private between Nelson and Mildred, Bert's widow raised her children and lived out her life in comfort in their family home. As time passed, children in the neighborhood came to know their house as the one where the father had died on the *Hindenburg*. The Dolan family, each descendant just as friendly, outgoing, and gregarious as Bert himself, still has the precious letter Bert wrote to Mildred. It is tucked away for safekeeping in memory of the man who was gone all too soon.

On October 6, 1955, Nelson Morris was disembarking from the ocean liner *Liberté* in New York after several months at his home in France when he collapsed from a heart attack. He passed away at the age of sixty-three. Cherishing his time in uniform until the end, especially his role as Colonel Morris of the Illinois National Guard, he was buried in Arlington National Cemetery.

The *Hindenburg* passenger who reached out from the past to make her story known perhaps more vividly and more colorfully than all the rest was Margaret Mather. But just as quickly as she announced herself, she retreated back into the maddening privacy of obscurity and anonymity. In November 1937, the same month Leonhard Adelt published his account of the disaster in *Reader's Digest*, Margaret published an almost dreamlike description of the last voyage of the *Hindenburg* in *Harper's Monthly*. After so eloquently writing this detailed, ethereal account of her voyage and escape from disaster, Margaret returned to her quiet life. Following an extended visit with her brother and niece in Princeton, she returned to Rome. Unfortunately, after that, no more is heard from her, not even whether she stayed in Rome during the war, or if she chose to return to New Jersey for the duration. However, it is clear that after so many years abroad, she considered Rome her home. It was there that she passed away in 1969 at the age of ninety-one. Perhaps someday she will surprise us with words and memories that are as yet undiscovered.

Though little is known to date about Margaret Mather's life during the war, several of her American traveling companions made notable contributions to the war effort. Philip Mangone, the Italian American designer known for his chic women's suits, put his creative talents toward helping women in uniform. He designed the uniform coat and suit for the U.S. Women's Army Corps—the WAC—a force of 150,000 women serving in auxiliary roles throughout World War II.

Yale graduate Peter Belin was one of the only *Hindenburg* passengers to serve on active duty during the war, given his comparative youth. In 1938, he married Mary Cootes, a talented tennis player who competed at Wimbledon in 1938 (and who later played recreationally with CIA Director Allen Dulles), and returned to Berlin as private secretary to Admiral H. B. Wilson. In 1939, he joined the U.S. Naval Reserve while working for Pan

Am. He was called to active duty in January 1941, where he served in Naval Intelligence, working for the chief of naval operations in Washington, DC. In 1945, he was dispatched to London as the American embassy's naval attaché. He remained on active duty for the rest of his career, serving with the Sixth Fleet in Europe and Africa and as aide to the commander in chief of the Atlantic Fleet and at Supreme Headquarters Allied Powers Europe in Belgium. Always unassuming, Belin spoke little about his experience on the *Hindenburg*, including with his sons, one of whom learned details about his father's miraculous survival only after discovering papers in his family's basement archives in 2011. An avid pilot, skier, and tennis player throughout his life, Peter Belin died in 1982 at the age of sixty-nine. Years later, his family shared the photographs he had taken on board the *Hindenburg*, as well as the map on which he had charted its last voyage, with the Smithsonian Museums in Washington, DC. Belin's map is the closest thing to a logbook to have survived the inferno.

While few people today are familiar with the events of the *Hindenburg* disaster at any level of detail, even fewer realize its impact on modern media. Today, we think nothing of the most sensational breaking news headlines and their accompanying footage being played over and over again, but until Herbert Morrison's recorded broadcast went out on the air, the news had never been broadcast in that way. As proof of its historic nature, in January 1938, Herbert Morrison and Charlie Nehlsen's recording on those four green discs so carefully transported from Lakehurst to Chicago were sent to the National Archives in Washington, DC, where they remain preserved to this day.

While Morrison's *Hindenburg* broadcast broke down the ban on recorded content on the radio, wholesale industry change did not occur immediately, nor did the bias against recordings collapse overnight. It took until September 3, 1939, for NBC to allow another recording to be broadcast on air, this time when Neville Chamberlain declared war on Germany after Hitler refused to accept an ultimatum to withdraw troops from Poland. NBC rebroadcast Chamberlain's announcement every hour on the hour until noon that day, so that all Americans across all time zones had an opportunity to hear the declaration of war.

It also took a war for radio to become cemented in American culture as the news medium that people like Herb Morrison, Bill Shirer, and Ed Murrow envisioned. "This crisis has done one thing for us," Shirer reflected about the upheaval he witnessed the night Nazi Germany annexed Austria. "I think radio talks by Ed and me are now established. Birth of the 'radio foreign correspondent,' so to speak." After Shirer's first broadcast from London after Austria fell to the Nazis, CBS asked him to do another broadcast the next night, this time including live reports from all the major capitals of Europe—London, Berlin, Vienna, Paris, and Rome. It was to be a "European round-up," the first of its kind, covering breaking political developments on the Continent. Shirer had only eight hours late on a Sunday to organize reporters with access to shortwave transmitters to connect to New York. Miraculously, he and Murrow pulled it off, and the roundup style of reporting, which would instantly become one of the most important and lasting formats of broadcast journalism, was born. Shirer became one of the world's first true radio correspondents as one of "Murrow's boys," who scattered across Europe to send the war into Americans' living rooms. Murrow himself became a household name thanks to his wartime broadcasts from London, especially during the Blitz, which he opened each night with his signature introduction, "This is London."

There was one other unanticipated and rather odd impact the *Hindenburg* broadcast had on the history of radio and media. In October 1938, a young playwright named Orson Welles adapted H. G. Wells's novel *The War of the Worlds* for a Halloween episode of the radio series *Mercury Theatre on the Air*. In his adaptation, the story opens with a panicked radio announcer describing a sudden Martian attack on suburban New Jersey. Welles and the actor playing the announcer studied Morrison's *Hindenburg* broadcast for their show, and the ultimate performance sounded so realistic that some who tuned in late and missed the sponsorship announcements thought it was either an actual news report about a Martian attack or a German hoax. Some half dozen people even wrote to Welles to say they had fled their homes in terror.

Though Herbert Morrison helped to usher in the golden age of radio with broadcasting practices that embraced the creativity and technological innovation he had imagined, he did not seek out opportunities to become one of the war's famous voices. In 1939, he left WLS for a much larger station in New York affiliated with one of NBC's competitors, Mutual Broadcasting, but soon after the United States was attacked at Pearl Harbor in December 1941, Morrison left radio and entered the U.S. Army Air Corps in 1942. Seventeen years after leaving West Point, he became a captain and assistant post operations officer at Tinker Field in Oklahoma, finally fulfilling what was perhaps his original boyhood dream back in Scottdale, Pennsylvania.

While Morrison's colleague Charlie Nehlsen remained with WLS until he retired in the late 1960s, after the war, Morrison returned to broadcasting in Pittsburgh and eventually moved back to his hometown of Scottdale. At forty-three and still handsome, he finally shed his bachelor status and married a local woman named Mary Jane Kelly. In the 1950s, he left radio for television, becoming news director of a Pittsburgh television channel. He also ran for Congress as an Eisenhower Republican in 1954, 1956, and 1958, but lost each time to a Democratic incumbent. Morrison continued to fly and experiment with machines throughout his life. He even built his own electric lawnmower, which neighbors would see him use to tend to his yard. Toward the end of his career, he served as a consultant for the 1975 *Hindenburg* Hollywood film and helped to establish the radio and television news program at West Virginia University. Herbert Morrison retired to West Virginia, where he passed away in 1989 at age eighty-three, after forty-six years in broadcasting.

While Morrison embraced a quieter existence after the greatest conflict in human history finally came to an end, the rest of Bill Shirer's life would be defined by the war. He had reported on some of the most important breaking developments as Europe descended into war: the Sudeten crisis, the Munich Agreement, Germany's invasion of Poland, its blitzkrieg across Europe in the opening months of the war, and the fall of France. When he left Europe for CBS in New York in 1940, he smuggled out his notes and diaries. In 1941, he published *Berlin Diary*, an instant bestseller, based on his records from his years in the maelstrom of prewar Berlin. Though published as a diary, it is best read as a memoir rather than a day-by-day, contemporaneous account of life in Hitler's Germany.

After welcoming a second daughter, Linda, in 1945, Shirer returned to Germany to report on the Nuremburg Trials. In 1947, after almost a decade of groundbreaking collaboration with Murrow, the two men had a falling-out, the details of which were never entirely clear. Shirer left CBS, and for the next few years, times were tough. He was outspoken in his liberal views and was blacklisted after being smeared as sympathetic to communism in the 1950s. After a difficult decade that left him essentially broke, a friend and journal editor encouraged him to write a history of World War II based on his personal experience and reporting. In 1960, Shirer published *The Rise and Fall of the Third Reich*, a comprehensive story of a world gone up in flames. It was a first-of-its-kind history of the Second World War, and, though not an academic work, it set the standard for hundreds of histories of World War II that followed. His epic account of what he had witnessed received the 1961 National Book Award and sold millions of copies.

Unfortunately, professional success is never a guarantee of personal happiness. After nearly forty years of marriage, the beginning of which was forged by the crucible of the early days of the war, Bill and Tess divorced in 1970. Bill remarried, divorced, married again, and retired to Lenox, Massachusetts, where he continued to write and publish histories and memoirs. After a lifetime shaped by those years of turmoil, Bill Shirer passed away in 1993 at the age of eighty-nine. *The Rise and Fall of the Third Reich* remains one of the bestselling history books of all time.

Today, almost everyone who witnessed the events of May 1937 is gone. In Lakehurst, the physical signs of that fateful day have grown fainter and more elusive with the passage of time. The zeppelin's charred remains have long since been swept away; the ground once scarred by burning diesel fuel bleached by the sun and healed by the rain. Still, the legacy of the *Hindenburg* disaster, its horrors but especially its humanity, remains quietly present among a small community united by those thirty-four seconds that changed the fates of so many.

Every five years, on milestone anniversaries, what is today known as Joint Base McGuire-Dix-Lakehurst opens its gates to welcome those whose lives were touched by that day, as well as anyone else who wishes to join them in remembrance. In 2012, on the seventy-fifth anniversary of the tragedy, two hundred people, including soldiers, sailors, and airmen stationed at the base, gathered to lay wreaths in memory of the individuals who died on that historic May evening, with taps playing solemnly in the background. Joining the service that day were the grandson of Max Pruss, the granddaughter of Bert Dolan, and Robert Buchanan, a teenage member of the Lakehurst civilian ground crew in 1937, who was by then ninety-two. During the service, Bert's granddaughter Mary Alice recalled, people kept coming up to shake her hand, eager to meet Bert's descendant, even though she had never known him.

Lakehurst remains an active military base where servicemen from the army, navy, and air force train for modern operations. Over the years, the base has grown and changed as it has adapted to meet new challenges in times of war and peace, but amid that change, one will still find much of the old airship field as it was ninety years ago. It remains a windswept expanse surrounded by a forest, and though the building outside of which Herbert Morrison made his broadcast is long gone, the enormous hangar number 1 still looms in the distance. The navy has found a new purpose for this structure that unites ships and sky. Inside is a full-scale model of one third of the deck of an aircraft carrier, where carrier crews practice using the arresting gear apparatus that grabs landing fighter jets and brings them to a halt. The hangar does, however, still hold one lone airship, the USS *Los Angeles*, stored in pieces, perhaps to be reassembled someday.

Half a mile from the hangar, in the middle of the dusty airship field, the foundations of the old mooring mast also remain. Nearby, there are large, flat stones arranged on the ground in the shape of an airship, which are surrounded by a linked chain lying in the sand. In the center of the stones is a plaque, dedicated in 1987 on the *Hindenburg* disaster's fiftieth anniversary, which marks the site as a historic landmark.

Other than this simple memorial, the vast field remains unadorned, save a weather vane in the shape of an airship planted just beside it. The weather vane is simple and two-dimensional, standing tall and alone as it blows in the wind on the alluvial plane. On a sunny day, it casts a shadow upon the ground in the shape of the airship in miniature. As the sun moves across the sky, the weather vane's shadow circles the post like the ghost of a memory in which the *Hindenburg* lies not broken on the ground but somewhere up above as the sky's once and future king.

ACKNOWLEDGMENTS

Every book has a unique origin, but this one is perhaps a bit more unexpected than most. At Christmastime in 2021, my family and I were sitting in the living room chatting around the tree after watching one of our favorite classics, *A Christmas Story*, for the hundredth time. In the movie, as Ralphie is opening the infamous pink bunny outfit from Aunt Clara, his little brother, Randy, exclaims, "Wow! A zeppelin!" after discovering an airship toy under the tree.

"It's crazy to think that people used to fly on those," my own aviation-enthusiast younger brother, Oliver, announced. "Can you imagine what it was like to look up and see one flying overhead? It must have felt like science fiction." After a moment, he added. "Catherine, you should write a book about the *Hindenburg* disaster."

A few short years later, here we are. . . .

Writing is far less solitary than people might assume, and I am so fortunate to have many wonderful people in my corner. First and foremost, I cannot say thank you enough to express my appreciation to the families of the individuals who are the heart, soul, and humanity of this story. To the family of Joseph "Benny" Spah, especially Benny's remarkable daughter Marilyn Spah Kelly, an eyewitness to the disaster, and granddaughter Jane Kelly: Thank you for welcoming me into your home and for all the incredible stories, letters, photographs, artifacts—and even a demonstration with one of Benny's lampposts—that you shared with me with your hallmark effervescent kindness. You are both absolute treasures. To the grandchildren of Burtis J. Dolan, Patrick Dolan and especially the phenomenal Mary Alice Dolan Noone, thank you from the bottom of my heart for allowing me to read and share Bert's heartbreaking letter, for digging through countless boxes on the hunt for photographs and family records, and for spending a truly unforgettable day with me at Lakehurst. I cannot thank you enough for all of it. Thank you to Leonhard and Gertrud Adelt's grandson, Professor Ulrich Adelt, for your ready willingness to fill in many details of your family's fascinating history that has so enriched this story. And to the family of William L. Shirer—his daughter Linda Shirer Rae and his granddaughter Deirdre van Dyk—thank you for sharing your treasured memories of both Bill and Tess that brought to life those captivatingly terrifying years they witnessed in Berlin, as well as so many family photographs. I am forever grateful to all of you for your friendship, for welcoming me into your lives, and for sharing a piece of your families' extraordinary stories. Thanks also to the friends, relatives, neighbors, and colleagues of those in this story who kindly sat for interviews, including John Douglas, Marc Fisher, Michael Pallasch, Gerald Rafshoon, Frederick Rom, David Sanger, and Christian Williams.

Enormous gratitude goes to Philipp Heuermann. From a conversation at the Kong in Harvard Square (of all places) to a research trip to the Zeppelin Museum in Friedrichshafen three years later and beyond, thank you for being such a generous friend, tour guide across Germany, cultural interpreter, and expert translator. Special thanks to Paulina Llano Ruiz for your friendship and patience through it all. You both have added so much to this entire journey.

Many wonderful archives, archivists, experts, and historic sites across Europe and the United States held the keys to this story. Thanks in particular to Barbara Waibel and Christine Buecher at the Zeppelin Museum in Friedrichshafen; Gerhard Keiper and Ralf Engel at the Bundesarchiv in Lichterfelde and Koblenz; Harlene Hansen at Coe College; Cheryl Ganz at the Smithsonian Institution; the Zeppelin Museum in Zeppelinheim; the United States Military Academy at West Point; Wichita State University; the Franklin D. Roosevelt Presidential Library and Museum; the Staats- und Universitätsbibliothek Hamburg; the Musée de l'Air et de l'Espace at Le Bourget; the University of Texas at Dallas; Meagan McChesney at the Winnetka Historical Society; Tom Zwierzelewski at the Scottdale Historical Society; the Winnetka and Glencoe Public Libraries; Georgetown University Library; Mary Ryan at Evermay in Washington,

DC; Sabina Held at the Hotel Adlon in Berlin; Ben-Oliver Matias and the Manila Yacht Club; and Jessica Brady in Chicago. Special thanks to Izzy Craig for her excellent research assistance at Coe College. Two outstanding blogs provided a trove of information related to zeppelins and the *Hindenburg* disaster: Dan Grossman's Airships.net and Patrick Russell's *Faces of the Hindenburg*. One individual truly went above and beyond: James Warrick, 87th Air Base Wing and Joint Base Historian at Joint Base McGuire-Dix-Lakehurst, who not only answered a million questions but was so generous to spend a most memorable Saturday showing me all around the site where tragedy unfolded nearly ninety years ago. Thank you for your time, enthusiasm, friendship, historical materials, and invaluable expertise.

Friends and family far and near have made this process such a joy. First and foremost, enormous thanks to Robyn and David Grossberg, who enthusiastically joined me, James Warrick, and Bert Dolan's granddaughter Mary Alice at Lakehurst, and for the warmest welcome to your beautiful home in Philadelphia. Thank you for signing up for this journey, and so much more. You are the ultimate airship crew, the kindest, most generous friends, and I am so lucky to have you as my bonus aunt and uncle.

I am extraordinarily lucky to have some of the best extended family a girl could ever find. To my aunt and uncle Alanna and Rick Lanman, thank you for all your boundless love and support for so many years in so many ways. In this particular instance, thank you, Rick, for also serving as a scientific consultant. Your remarkable patience, humor, and detailed explanations were essential to helping me understand not only the complex science behind this moment in history but also so many other aspects of life. To my uncle Randy Hall, always so kind and thoughtful, thank you for allowing me to call upon your expertise as a chemist to elucidate the movement of subatomic particles as they swirled around this story. For this, and so much more, I am so grateful to have you all in my life.

Countless wonderful friends have supported me as this book came together and have made so many unique contributions. To name just a few, thank you to Miranda Burt, Susanne Clever, Ann Compton, Gioia Diliberto, Hayley Drozd, Omer Duru, Boris Feldman and my colleagues at Freshfields, Noah Feldman, Admiral Michael Franken, Jack Goldsmith,

William Greenlaw, Erica Hackett, Roger Hickey, Stephanie Hochschild of the Book Stall in Winnetka, Bashir Idris, Lena Klenk, Mia Kovacevic, Adam Lam, Caroline McLendon, Martha Minow, David Motadel, Joel Nelson, Matt O'Leary, Evan and Oscie Thomas, Hale Thomas, Evan Vlahandreas, Chris Vogt, Quirin von Blomberg, Shelley Wanger, Kurt Weiler, the Tuesday/Thursday Boeing UF crew, and Madison Graham's all-star team at Starbucks in Winnetka.

A special thank-you in particular to Jim Gordon for all you do, big and small, that means so much in the ways that matter most. You are the very best.

I am so fortunate to have an outstanding team behind me at CAA. A million thanks go to the incomparable Molly Atlas and Binky Urban. In particular, Molly, thank you for your wise and generous counsel at every step, and for believing in me and this story from the beginning. Thank you also to the fantastic John Ash and the foreign rights team in London.

I am doubly fortunate to work with a terrific editor and incredible champion for this story at Viking, Emily Wunderlich, who saw the potential for this project from page one. It has been such a joy working with you. Alongside Emily are her equally exceptional Viking colleagues: Brian Tart, Andrea Schulz, Kate Stark, Kristina Fazzalaro, Emily Fishman, Mary Stone, Morgan Fenton, Tess Espinoza, Alicia Cooper, Bridget Gilleran, Hilary Roberts, Kym Surridge, and Carlos Zayas-Pons. Thanks also to my outstanding team at Atlantic Books in the UK: Shoaib Rokadiya, Kate Straker, and Felice McKeown. It is such a pleasure to work with each and every member of this phenomenal team.

Most important, as always, thank you to my family. Not everyone is lucky enough to have the world's best and most honest editing team, brilliant conversationalists, and a "kitchen cabinet" full of advisers right within their own family. To my brother, Oliver, without whom this book never would have existed, thank you for your generosity of spirit, endless curiosity, sense of humor, and invaluable perspective that brought this book to life from its earliest days as just the glimmer of an idea and whose keen eye and enormous heart helped to hone the humanity within. To my sister, Bunny, who was with me on every page of every draft, thank you for your unparalleled and painstaking editorial guidance, for always pushing me to write to the best level, and for your trademark wit and wisdom that makes each day so much brighter. I am so grateful for the hours, emotion, and tremendous dedication you have poured into this with me every step of the way, line by line (not to mention your culinary masterpieces that helped bring this to the finale). You two are my very best friends and always will be. And finally, to my mom, the greatest on earth. How can one possibly capture all that a mother is, especially in all the irreplaceable, unseen ways each and every day? Among those innumerable qualities I could never adequately express, you brought the joy of wonderful stories into our lives, which opened our worlds and made our imaginations come alive. No matter how old I am, you will always be the person I can't wait to talk to—to share an idea or a chuckle at any hour of the day, to work through a challenge or read through chapter after chapter (and hopefully a zinger or two). The love you have always shown each of us has given us the confidence to go anywhere and do anything, because at the end of the day, we knew we could always come home. I love you all.

AVIATION TERMINOLOGY

(Adapted from "Airship Terminology," Harold K. Dick Papers, box 8, folder 7, Wichita State University)

Airship: A vehicle supported by air, usually referring to a lighter-than-air vehicle (e.g., hot air balloon, blimp, zeppelin).

Lighter-Than-Air Craft: A vehicle made buoyant using a gas that is lighter than the surrounding air (e.g., hydrogen, helium).

Heavier-Than-Air Craft: A non-buoyant vehicle that that achieves flight with aerodynamic lift created by airflow over a wing (e.g., kite, glider, airplane).

Free Balloon: A gas-inflated balloon without directional control capabilities (e.g., hot-air balloon).

Dirigible: Any lighter-than-air craft with directional control capabilities (e.g., blimp, zeppelin).

Nonrigid Airship (Blimp): An airship whose shape is maintained by internal air pressure, usually inflated ballonets (e.g., earlier models of the Goodyear Blimp).

Semirigid Airship: A nonrigid airship with the additional structural support of a longitudinal keel to partially carry the load e.g., *Norge* [*N-1*].

Rigid Airship: An airship that uses a rigid structural frame to maintain its shape (e.g., *Hindenburg* [*LZ-129*], *Graf Zeppelin* [*LZ-127*], USS Los *Angeles* [*LZ-126*], USS *Akron* [*ZRS-4*], and USS *Macon* [*ZRS-5*]).

Zeppelin: A rigid airship using the basic structure and design developed by Count Zeppelin; the airships designed by Luftschiffbau Zeppelin (e.g., *Hindenburg* [*LZ-129*], *Graf Zeppelin* [*LZ-127*], USS *Los Angeles* [*LZ-126*].

NOTES

Chapter 1

3 **Crimson tapestries from:** William L. Shirer, *Berlin Diary: The Journal of a Foreign Correspondent, 1934–1941,* rev. ed. (Alfred A. Knopf, 1941; Bonanza Books, 1984), April (undated) 1936, 60. Citations refer to the Bonanza edition. Cross-referenced with Ambassador Dodd's diary, it is clear this occurred on April 16. Interior and exterior design elements of Tiergartenstrasse 27a are from Erik Larson, *In the Garden of Beasts: Love, Terror and an American Family in Hitler's Berlin* (Crown, 2011), 85–86.

3 **Since moving to Berlin:** For more on the American ambassador's residence as a haven for subversive discourse, see, e.g., Prince Louis Ferdinand, *The Rebel Prince: Memoirs of Prince Louis Ferdinand of Prussia* (Henry Regnery, 1952), 253: "Many an evening I was the only guest at the Dodd table. When the servants were out of sight we opened our hearts. 'If you don't try to be more careful with your talk, Prince Louis,' the professor [Ambassador Dodd] used to warn me, 'they will hang you one of these days. I'll come to your funeral all right, but that won't do you much good, I am afraid,' he added with a sad smile." Also cited in Larson, *In the Garden of Beasts*, 87–88.

4 **There was little Shirer could:** William L. Shirer, *20th Century Journey,* vol. 2, *The Nightmare Years: 1930–1940* (Little, Brown, 1984), 52–53.

4 **Still, for a young man:** William L. Shirer, *20th Century Journey,* vol. 1, *The Start: 1904–1930* (Simon & Schuster, 1976), 24.

4 **Alongside Shirer, those:** William E. Dodd Jr. and Martha Dodd, eds., *Ambassador Dodd's Diary, 1933–38* (Harcourt, Brace, 1941), April 16, 1936, 333.

4 **"Hitler has the earmarks":** Karl von Wiegand, "Hitler Styled Mussolini of Teuton Crisis," *New York American*, November 12, 1922. See also Andrew Nagorski, *Hitlerland: American Eyewitnesses to the Nazi Rise to Power* (Simon & Schuster, 2013), 21–22.

4 **The man at the helm:** "Dr. Hugo Eckener und die deutsche Luftschiffahrt," Hamburg-America Line News Service, August 10, 1934, box 4, folder 4, Clara Adams Papers, Special Collections and Archives Division, History of Aviation Archives, University of Texas at Dallas; Henry Cord Meyer, *Airshipmen, Businessmen, and Politics: 1890–1940* (Smithsonian Institution Press, 1991), 122, 135. Count Zeppelin is often credited with hiring Eckener directly. In his memoir, Eckener describes a visit from Zeppelin as the beginning of his relationship with Deutsche Luftschiffahrts-Aktiengesellschaft

(DELAG), the predecessor company to Luftschiffbau Zeppelin. See Hugo Eckener, *My Zeppelins* (Arno Press: 1980), 12–14. However, Henry Cord Meyer, an expert on the leaders of the German airship program, credits Alfred Colsman with hiring Eckener. See also John Duggan and Henry Cord Meyer, *Airships in International Affairs, 1890–1940* (Palgrave, 2001), 54.

5 **"[attain] a moral":** Eckener, *My Zeppelins*, 157.

5 **In a world not far:** Shirer, *20th Century Journey,* vol. 1, 64.

5 **During its voyage:** "The First Airship Flight Around the World," *National Geographic 57, no. 6* (June 1930), courtesy of Musée de l'Air et de l'Espace, Le Bourget.

5 **Though the U.S. stock:** Meyer, *Airshipmen, Businessmen, and Politics,* 199; Duggan and Meyer, *Airships in International Affairs,* 4–5.

6 **In the last two years:** U.S. Department of Commerce, Bureau of the Census, Mortality Statistics 1935: Thirty-Sixth Annual Report (U.S. Government Printing Office, 1937), 17.

6 **After proving zeppelins':** The *LZ-128*, designed after the *LZ-127 Graf Zeppelin* and intended to be of similar size, existed only on paper. The plans were scrapped in favor of the much larger *LZ-129 Hindenburg,* thus the skip in numbering. For more on Hearst bankrolling the 1929 round-the-world flight, see Ricky W. Law, *Transnational Nazism: Ideology and Culture in German-Japanese Relations, 1919–1936* (Cambridge University Press, 2019), 43.

6 **May 6, 1936, would mark:** Film footage depicting interior shots of Hindenburg and Ernst A. Lehmann interview, May 20, 1936, courtesy of the 87th Air Base Wing Historian.

7 **The trouble had started:** Duggan and Meyer, *Airships in International Affairs,* 180–81. Eckener had also previously refused to allow Heinrich Brüning, chancellor from 1930 to 1932, to use the airship for political campaigning.

7 **DANGER FOR HITLER?:** Duggan and Meyer, *Airships in International Affairs,* 180–81.

7 **Still, it was best:** Frederick Oechsner, "Six-Day Campaign Opens for Hitler Who Runs Alone," *Oshkosh (WI) Northwestern* (syndicated article), August 14, 1934. In Michael McCarthy's *The Hidden Hindenburg: The Untold Story of the Tragedy, the Nazi Secrets, and the Quest to Rule the Skies* (Lyons Press, 2020), 51–52, McCarthy strongly emphasizes this three-minute address in arguing that Eckener was more complicit in supporting the regime than past scholars have suggested; however, as time has revealed, not all of the key speakers who participated in this public campaign ardently supported Hitler. One key speaker was 1928 and 1932 Olympic middle-distance runner Otto Peltzer, who, just a year later, was persecuted by the regime for homosexuality. Despite having joined the party, likely for self-preservation, he was ultimately arrested and sent to a concentration camp at Mauthausen in 1941, where he remained until liberation in 1945.

7 **"2 or 3 men":** William Shirer, Original Diary (Black Notebook), April 16, 1936, William L. Shirer Papers, Coe College, Cedar Rapids, IA (WLSP).

7 **"nothing but contempt":** Shirer, *Berlin Diary,* April (undated) 1936, 60.

8 **However, to make such:** Richard J. Evans, "Coercion and Consent in Nazi Germany," *British Academy Review,* no. 10 (2007): 26–27.

8 **the "wildest rumors":** Shirer, *Berlin Diary*, March 6, 1936, 48.

8 **to "seek freedom":** William Shirer to Arthur Shirer, April 2, 1937, Correspondence: Correspondence by Date, folder: 1936, WLSP; Shirer, *20th Century Journey*, vol. 1, 77–78.

8 **His contact had:** Shirer, *Berlin Diary*, March 6, 1936, 48–49. Figure from Joseph David Connors, "Paul Reynaud and French National Defense, 1933–1939" (PhD diss., Loyola University Chicago, 1977), 17n9.

8 **And yet, on March 7:** The *Reichstag* had been using the Kroll Opera House for its meetings since February 1933, one month after Hitler became chancellor, after an arson attack that burned down the *Reichstag* building. The Nazis blamed the fire on communists and persuaded German President Paul von Hindenburg to pass the *Reichstag* Fire Decree to suspend many civil liberties and allowed the Nazis to further consolidate power.

8 **"hysterical 'parliamentary' mob":** Shirer, *Berlin Diary*, March 7, 1936, 52–53.

9 **Shortly after arriving in Berlin:** The 1934 Nazi Party rally was one of Shirer's earliest assignments in Berlin. In the original notes he kept from 1934 and 1935, which form the basis for what became *Berlin Diary*, Shirer could see how the party primed the crowd with "mystic ritual" so that by the time Hitler began to speak, the gatherings of provincial men and boys, looking like "hams and sausages" in their black and brown uniforms, went mad for the führer. Shirer's original notes show how impressed he was with the effectiveness of these rallies and speeches, and that he came away feeling that Hitler had made a justifiable case for why Germany felt aggrieved but did ultimately desire peace. By the time he published *Berlin Diary* in 1941, he had scaled back his original assessment, which read as naively impressed with Hitler, to a more moderate, sober tone with the focus more on Hitler's impact on Germans than on himself. See, e.g., Shirer, Original Diary, December 1934, and May 22, 1935.

9 **"Now, more than ever":** Shirer, *Berlin Diary*, March 7, 1936, 53.

9 **When the crowd finally:** Shirer, *Berlin Diary*, March 7, 1936, 53.

9 **"swung the army":** Shirer, Original Diary, December 1934.

9 **Shirer spotted him nervously:** Shirer, *Berlin Diary*, March 7, 1936, 54.

9 **"Hitler has got away":** Shirer, *Berlin Diary*, March 8, 1936, 55.

10 **"request[ed]" that a number:** Eckener, *My Zeppelins*, 150–51.

10 **As Shirer quickly:** Shirer, *Berlin Diary*, March 29, 1936, 60.

10 **"in bad taste":** Eckener, *My Zeppelins*, 150–51.

10 **Hitler had reportedly:** Dodd and Dodd, *Ambassador Dodd's Diary*, 333.

10 **was also "howling mad":** Shirer, *Berlin Diary*, March 29, 1936, 60.

10 **Goebbels found a temporary:** Eckener, *My Zeppelins*, 150.

10 **Lehmann had captained:** Ernst A. Lehmann, *Zeppelin: The Story of Lighter-Than-Air Craft*, rev. ed. (Fonthill, 2015), 52–53. See also Ernst A. Lehmann, in collaboration with Leonhard Adelt, *Zeppelin: The Story of Lighter-Than-Air Craft* (Longmans, Green, 1937).

10 **The forty-nine-year-old veteran:** Alan Sutton, "Publisher's Preface," in Lehmann, *Zeppelin*, 10; Lehmann, *Zeppelin*, 292.

10 **As the zeppelin captain explained:** Shirer, *Berlin Diary*, April (undated) 1937, 60; Eckener, *My Zeppelins*, 151.

11 **American papers were even:** "Eckener Will Lose Honor of a Street Name; Berlin Suburb Orders Change to 'Adolf Hitler,'" *New York Times*, April 23, 1936; Rolf Italiaander, *Ein Deutscher namens Eckener* (Verlag Friedr. Stadler Konstanz, 1981), 335. Another article claims the street was renamed Zehlendorferdamm for the Zehlendorf neighborhood of Berlin, where it was located. "Eckener Still in Disgrace," *Times*, April 25, 1936, R 4902/6247, Deutsches Auslandswissenschaftliches Institut, Bundesarchiv, Berlin-Lichterfelde.

11 **On the day of the referendum:** In his memoir, Captain Albert Sammt discusses the enormous pressure the crew felt to continue with the propaganda flight even after the damage was sustained. Albert Sammt, *Mein Leben für den Zeppelin* (Verlag Pestalozzi Kinderdorf Wahlwies, 1980), 137–38; Eckener, *My Zeppelins*, 150; Die Aufzeichnungen des Luftschiffstewards Wilhelm Balla, 40–41, LZ 129, Besatzungs-Mitglieder Alphabetisch (BMA) I, Zeppelin Museum, Friedrichshafen. Pieces of paint from the damaged fin are on display at the Zeppelin Museum.

11 **While this debacle:** Shirer, *Berlin Diary*, March 29, 1936, 59.

11 **"marvel of German engineering":** Shirer, *Berlin Diary*, March 29, 1936, 60.

11 **"liberty, equality and peace":** Dodd and Dodd, *Ambassador Dodd's Diary*, March 28, 1936, 326.

11 **"gracefully" over Shirer's office:** Shirer, *Berlin Diary*, March 29, 1936, 60.

11 **Hitler must have been pleased:** William L. Shirer, *The Rise and Fall of the Third Reich* (Simon & Schuster, 1960), 294.

12 **"Goebbels hung up":** Shirer, *Berlin Diary*, April (undated) 1936, 60.

12 **"next time we have":** Shirer, Original Diary, April 16, 1936.

12 **"The sheep!" Shirer thought:** Shirer, Original Diary, April 16, 1936.

12 **As Eckener explained:** Dodd and Dodd, *Ambassador Dodd's Diary*, 333; Eckener, *My Zeppelins,* 162–6l; "Eckener Command Unaffected in Row," *New York Times*, April 16, 1936.

12 **"like a wicked fairy":** Eckener, *My Zeppelins*, 161.

13 **Even if Germany:** Helium Act of 1925, 50 U.S.C. § 161; Martin L. Levitt, "The Development and Politicization of the American Helium Industry, 1917–1940," *Historical Studies in the Physical and Biological Sciences* 30, no. 2 (2000). Initially, the U.S. Navy wanted to reserve the scarce supply of helium for its own experiments in lighter-than-air aviation, but later, national security concerns took root and the emphasis shifted toward thwarting potentially hostile nations' ability to advance their own aviation technology. Additionally, from the very beginning Count von Zeppelin had envisioned military uses for zeppelins, which he had even discussed with von Wiegand in an interview way back in 1915. Meyer, *Airshipmen, Businessmen, and Politics*, 34, 40, 42, 50–51.

13 **The German zeppelin men:** Eckener discusses their study of past airship accidents resulting in fire, after which they concluded most accidents were due to the use of highly flammable petrol to power engines, which had caught fire, rather than the hydrogen itself having caught fire. Luftschiffbau Zeppelin believed they had made zep-

pelins considerably safer, particularly by switching to diesel-powered engines, as diesel has a much higher flash point and thus requires much higher temperatures before it becomes combustible. Eckener, *My Zeppelins*, 174–75.

14 **described as "distinctly curious":** Franklin D. Roosevelt, diary entry, August 17, 1918, Franklin D. Roosevelt Presidential Library and Museum, cited in "Found in the Archives," *Forward with Roosevelt* (blog), January 5, 2012, fdr.blogs.archives.gov/2012/01/05/found-in-the-archives-24.

14 **The experience had left:** Roosevelt and his partners had even signed contracts with German airship designer Johann Schütte, a rival of Count Zeppelin and Eckener, to build airships. Papers relevant to Roosevelt's company, the American Investment Corporation, are held at the FDR Presidential Library in the Franklin D. Roosevelt Papers, Papers Pertaining to Family, Business and Personal Affairs, 1882–1945, box 7–8.

14 **Roosevelt was "horrified":** Duggan and Meyer, *Airships in International Affairs,* 78–79. See also Frank Freidel, *Franklin D. Roosevelt: The Ordeal,* vol. 2 (Little, Brown, 1954), 149. This incident occurred just days before FDR became paralyzed and was diagnosed with polio.

14 **"Well are you bringing":** Shirer, Original Diary, April 16, 1936. A similar version of this quip appears in Dodd and Dodd, *Ambassador Dodd's Diary*, 333.

14 **Dodd was a career:** Shirer, Original Diary, May 22, 1935, and April 16, 1936.

15 **"awkward" and "indiscreet":** Shirer, Original Diary, May 22, 1935, and April 16, 1936.

15 **After an uncomfortable:** Dodd and Dodd, *Ambassador Dodd's Diary*, 333.

15 **"there would be no flight":** Dodd and Dodd, *Ambassador Dodd's Diary*, 333.

Chapter 2

19 **Like his longtime superior:** Ernst A. Lehmann, *Zeppelin: The Story of Lighter-Than-Air Craft*, rev. ed. (Fonthill, 2015), 309–10.

19 **"hunter trailing a wolf":** Lehmann, *Zeppelin*, 81–82.

20 **Even before these leadership:** Charles E. Rosendahl, "Preface to the 1937 Edition," in Lehmann, *Zeppelin*, 20; film footage depicting interior shots of Hindenburg and Ernst A. Lehmann interview, May 20, 1936, courtesy of the 87th Air Base Wing Historian.

20 **It was so popular:** Leonhard Adelt, "Trauer und Zuversicht," in Ernst A. Lehmann, *Auf Luftpatrouille und Weltfahrt* (Schmidt & Günther, 1937), 400; Leonhard Adelt to Friderike Zweig, June 8, 1937, courtesy of Ulrich Adelt; David Turner, "Eine nahe Ferne: Die Briefe Stefan Zweigs an Leonhard Adelt als Ausdruck einer von ihren literarischen Anfängen geprägten Freundschaft," in *Studia austriaca II*, vol. 2, ed. Fausto Cercignani (University of Milan, 1993), 85. Longmans, Green & Co.'s parent company was British, but it has had a New York office since the 1880s.

20 **As with the ten:** Lehmann, *Zeppelin*, 313.

20 **Despite this move:** Liste über ausgegebene Fahrscheine, LS "HINDENBURG" Frankfurt–Lakehurst, 3 Mai 1. Nordamerikafahrt 1937, LZA 17/0567, Zeppelin Museum, Friedrichshafen.

20 **Yes, tickets were expensive:** Lehmann, *Zeppelin*, 24, 241.

21 **"progressive vision . . . wandering far":** Rosendahl, "Preface to the 1937 Edition," in Lehmann, *Zeppelin*, 21.

21 **"a true artist":** Hans von Schiller, *Zeppelinbuch* (Bibliographisches Institut, 1938), 207.

21 **As he wrote in his memoir:** Lehmann, *Zeppelin*, 23; W. E. von Medem, *Kabinenjunge Werner Franz vom Luftschiff "Hindenburg"* (Franz Schneider Verlag, 1938), 45; *Airship Voyages Made Easy* (Deutsche Zeppelin-Reederei, 1937, reprinted 1976), 12.

21 **But to Ernst Lehmann:** Lehmann, *Zeppelin*, 224–25; Max Geisenheyner, *E. A. Lehmann, Zeppelin-Kapitän* (Societäts-Verlag 1937), 133.

22 **Their zeppelins were given:** Albert Sammt, *Mein Leben für den Zeppelin* (Verlag Pestalozzi Kinderdorf Wahlwies, 1980), 57–58.

22 **Under the new agreement:** Under this agreement, the newly formed Goodyear-Zeppelin Corporation would receive North American and German rights to each company's respective patents. Luftschiffbau Zeppelin would also receive 10 percent of Goodyear-Zeppelin's stock. The two companies agreed to an exchange of personnel, with German engineers going to Akron to teach airship engineering while American engineers were seconded to Friedrichshafen. Harold G. Dick and Douglas H. Robinson, *The Golden Age of the Great Passenger Airships: Graf Zeppelin & Hindenburg* (Smithsonian Institution Press, 1985), 20–24; Hangar No. 1 National Historic Landmark Package: John D. McDermott, Hangar No. 1, Lakehurst Naval Air Station, New Jersey, National Survey of Historic Sites and Buildings, Special Report, U.S. Department of the Interior, National Park Service, 4, Registry of National Historic and Natural Landmarks, Report of Biennial Visit to Hangar No. 1, Lakehurst Naval Air Station, January 28 1972, courtesy of 87th Air Base Wing Historian. Lehmann had spent some time in Akron himself after delivering the *LZ-126* (USS *Los Angeles*).

22 **"such shouting and hurrahing":** Lehmann, *Zeppelin*, 220.

22 **as a "brilliant feat":** Lehmann, *Zeppelin*, 221, 222.

22 **"rehabilitated herself in the eyes":** Lehmann, *Zeppelin*, 222.

23 **"spontaneous enthusiasm" wherever they went:** Lehmann, *Zeppelin*, 247.

23 **When the silver giant:** Ricky W. Law, *Transnational Nazism: Ideology and Culture in German-Japanese Relations, 1919–1936* (Cambridge University Press, 2019), 31, 37. Law ascribes much of Japan's embrace of Germany during this period to an admiration for Germany's strong sense of national character and widespread coverage and reporting of German cultural, political, scientific, and economic developments in Japanese newspapers. During the Winter Olympics of 1936 in Garmisch-Partenkirchen, American journalists were even instructed to use German athletic and technical terms in their coverage for Japanese news outlets, as those were the terms Japanese audiences understood and preferred. James R. Young to INS Correspondents, December 23, 1935, Correspondence by Date—1936, William L. Shirer Papers, Coe College, Cedar Rapids, IA (WLSP).

23 **"bridge of sympathy":** Lehmann, *Zeppelin*, 266.

23 **"The heart of all Germany":** Lehmann, *Zeppelin*, 253–54; see also 224–25; Geisenheyner, *E. A. Lehmann*, 133.

23 **Whenever it appeared:** Lehmann, *Zeppelin*, 304.

23 **Across the country, zeppelin-themed:** A collection of historical zeppelin-themed merchandise and knickknacks are on display at the Zeppelin Museum.

24 **In 1926, the Italian:** On May 9, 1926, Richard Byrd and Floyd Bennett attempted a flight to the North Pole in a Fokker trimotor monoplane. They claimed they had reached the North Pole and were hailed as heroes; however, later calculations suggested that they could not have reached the North Pole at the speed they claimed to have flown in the number of hours they were in the air. The *Norge* did reach the North Pole three days later, which most aviation and exploration scholars today accept as the first flight to have reached the North Pole.

24 **"Of what other means":** Lehmann, *Zeppelin*, 41.

24 **The Weimar government:** Lehmann, *Zeppelin*, 292; also see Geisenheyner, *E. A. Lehmann*, 58–59.

25 **In March 1935:** Geschäftsbericht der Deutschen Zeppelin Reederei/Friedrichshafen für das Kalenderjahr 1935, 2, LZA 17/652, Zeppelin Museum, Friedrichshafen; main exhibit, Zeppelin Museum, Friedrichshafen. As the museum explains, since 1919, passenger flights had been jointly operated by Luftschiffbau Zeppelin and the Hamburg-America Line (HAPAG), which had replaced Deutsche Luftschiffahrts-Aktiengesellschaft (DELAG), the original zeppelin airline under Count Zeppelin, as the operating and booking entity by the time the *LZ-120 Bodensee* began operating. HAPAG continued to serve as booking agent.

25 **"empire of Adolf Hitler":** Geschäftsbericht der Deutschen Zeppelin Reederei/Friedrichshafen für das Kalenderjahr 1935, 1, LZA 17/652.

25 **The industry to which Lehmann:** Lehmann, *Zeppelin*, 292.

25 **"importance of Zeppelin airships":** Geschäftsbericht der Deutschen Zeppelin Reederei/Friedrichshafen für das Kalenderjahr 1935, 1, LZA 17/652.

25 **"the German airship, the heritage":** Deutsche Zeppelin-Reederei G.m.b.H. Berlin–Friedrichshafen, RZ 206/32997, Politisches Archiv des Auswärtiges Amts, Bundesarchiv, Berlin-Lichterfelde.

25 **"highways of the air":** Deutsche Zeppelin-Reederei G.m.b.H. Berlin–Friedrichshafen.

25 **"Eckener's flying sausages":** "Für Panik war keine Zeit," *Spiegel-Gesprach*, 21/2000, 128, LZ 129, BMA I, Zeppelin Museum, Friedrichshafen. See another derivative at "Reich Undaunted by Loss of Big Zep, Rushing Another," *Gazette and Daily* (York, PA), May 8, 1937, courtesy of 87th Air Base Wing Historian.

26 **Between 1933 and April 1937:** R. J. Overy, "German Air Strength 1933 to 1938: A Note," *Historical Journal* 27, no. 2 (1984): 469. Bombers include traditional bombers, dive-bombers, and auxiliary bombers, which could double as transport aircraft. Göring also consolidated the German aviation industry, starting in 1933 with airplane manufacturer Hugo Junkers, who was forced to transfer both the majority interest in his company and his patents to the Reich Ministry of Aviation. Junkers Aircraft, "Company History," n.d., junkersaircraft.com/en/history; Richard Evans, *The Third Reich in Power* (Penguin, 2005), 351.

26 **That very week:** Evans, *The Third Reich in Power*, 640.

26 **"even by express order":** NSDAP to Hans von Schiller, January 8, 1937, LZ 129, BMA III, Zeppelin Museum, Friedrichshafen. See also Hans von Schiller to NSDAP, December 9, 1936, LZ 129, BMA III, Zeppelin Museum, Friedrichshafen; and internal NSDAP record December 12, 1936, LZ 129, BMA III, Zeppelin Museum, Friedrichshafen.

26 **Some, like navigator:** "Für Panik war keine Zeit," *Spiegel-Gesprach*, 21/2000, 125, LZ 129, BMA I, Zeppelin Museum, Friedrichshafen.

26 **Two of Lehmann's longtime colleagues:** Viola Pruss, "Dreams in Flames: The Airship Hindenburg and Its Captain, My Great-Grandfather," CBC News, May 23, 2017, cbc.ca/news/canada/new-brunswick/hindenburg-pruss-max-crash-anniversary-1.4099243; Guillaume de Syon, *Zeppelin!: Germany and the Airship, 1900–1939* (Johns Hopkins University Press, 2007), 182.

27 **They generally did not:** Sammt, *Mein Leben*, 136–38.

27 **The one vocal:** Harold G. Dick Memoir, 25, box 7, FF 7; Harold G. Dick, "A Yankee's Five Years in Hitlers Pre-War Nazi Germany," 6, box 8, FF 3, Harold G. Dick Papers, Wichita State University.

27 **"smelly old fish":** Eugen Bentele, *The Story of a Zeppelin Mechanic: My Flights 1931–1938* (Wolfgang Meighörner-Schardt, 1992), 62.

27 **The swastika had been:** John Duggan and Henry Meyer, *Airships in International Affairs, 1890–1940* (Palgrave, 2001), 199.

27 **Even the Zeppelinfeld:** "The Nazi Party Rally Grounds," Dokumentationszentrum Reichsparteitagsgelände Museen der Stadt Nürnberg, museums.nuernberg.de/documentation-center/the-site/the-nazi-party-rally-grounds; Richard Overy, *The Dictators: Hitler's Germany, Stalin's Russia* (W. W. Norton, 2004), 386.

27 **Gone were the days:** Bentele, *Story of a Zeppelin Mechanic*, 17.

27 **"endless forest of foundries":** Lehmann, *Zeppelin*, 303; see also page 241.

27 **two more *Hindenburg*-class airships:** Harold G. Dick, Memoir, 85, FF 7, box 7, Harold G. Dick Papers, Wichita State University.

28 **DZR was also discussing:** Besprechungsergebnis der Sitzung vom 20. November 1936, 4, RZ 206/32997, Politisches Archiv des Auswärtiges Amts, Bundesarchiv, Berlin-Lichterfelde.

28 **To prove the *Hindenburg*'s:** "18 Trips for Hindenburg," *New York Times*, March 6, 1937.

Chapter 3

29 **"fatiguing monotony," as one visitor:** Harold M. Mayer and Richard C. Wade, *Chicago: Growth of a Metropolis* (University of Chicago Press, 1969), 3, 35.

29 **Over just six years:** Mayer and Wade, *Chicago*, 35, 44.

29 **By the time Chicago hosted:** Thomas Dyja, *The Third Coast: When Chicago Built the American Dream* (Penguin Books, 2013), xxi–xxii; Scott W. Berg, *The Burning of the World: The Great Chicago Fire and the War for a City's Soul* (Pantheon Books, 2023), xi.

30 **Engineers sometimes lifted:** "At the Tremont" and "One, Two, Three and Up She Goes!" *Chicago Daily Tribune*, February 26, 1861, loc.gov/resource/sn84031490/1861-02-26/ed-1/?st=pdf. Patrons included, in one case, a governor and a senator.

30 **In response, engineers devised:** For an innovative public history of Chicago's great industrial feats, see Geoffrey Baer, "How Chicago Reversed Its River: An Animated History," WTTW, interactive.wttw.com/chicago-river-tour/how-chicago-reversed-river-animated.

30 **The Great Chicago Fire of 1871:** Mayer and Wade, *Chicago*, 117; Berg, *Burning of the World*, ix.

30 **"Here . . . was power":** Louis Sullivan, *The Autobiography of an Idea* (Press of the American Institute of Architects, 1924), 196–97.

30 **In 1863 alone, all the hogs:** Mayer and Wade, *Chicago*, 48.

31 **Hair became brushes:** William Cronon, *Nature's Metropolis: Chicago and the Great West* (W. W. Norton, 1991), 252–53.

31 **For four decades:** Dominic Pacyga, *Chicago: A Biography* (University of Chicago Press, 2009), 317.

31 **"such a power":** Charles Edward Russell, *The Greatest Trust in the World* (Ridgeway-Thayer, 1905), 20.

31 **"attracted by new technology":** Muriel Gardiner, *Code Name "Mary"* (Yale University Press, 1983), 79.

31 **Nelson was born:** Ann Durkin Keating, ed., *Chicago Neighborhoods and Suburbs* (University of Chicago Press, 2008), 256; Mayer and Wade, *Chicago*, 45. Though well within range of the stench of the yards on a hot summer day, the South Side was considered the best part of Chicago because it did not require passage over either the north or the west branches of the Chicago River to reach downtown. This was a luxury in an era when bridges were either routinely swept away or took so long to turn when raised for passing boats that a quarter mile of traffic would build up in the time it took for them to close.

31 **"castlelike house of brown granite":** Gardiner, *Code Name "Mary,"* 8.

31 **During these voyages:** Gardiner, *Code Name "Mary,"* 9, 11.

32 **Their parents came:** Gardiner, *Code Name "Mary,"* 8–9.

32 **The erstwhile Moritz Beisinger:** Ira Nelson Morris, *Heritage from My Father: An Autobiography* (privately published, 1947), 3–4; Gardiner, *Code Name "Mary,"* 7–8; Walter Roth, "Nelson Morris and 'the Yards,'" *Chicago Jewish History* 32, no. 2 (Spring 2008), chicagojewishhistory.org/pdf/2008/CJH_2_2008-web.pdf; "The Union Stockyards: 'A Story of American Capitalism,'" Chicago Stories, WTTW, interactive.wttw.com/chicago-stories/union-stockyards/the-union-stockyards-a-story-of-american-capitalism.

32 **Less than ten years:** James R. Grossman, Ann Durkin Keating, and Janice L. Reiff, eds., *Encyclopedia of Chicago* (University of Chicago Press, 2004), 935. $11 million in approximately 1870 would be roughly $275 million in 2025. $100 million in 1907 would be approximately $3.4 billion today.

32 **Swift and his engineers:** Cronon, *Nature's Metropolis*, 233–34. Swift's innovation was to place ice at both ends of the railcar so that air blowing across the meat was uniformly chilled.

32 **Swift also recognized:** Cronon, *Nature's Metropolis*, 237.

33 **He took over the company:** Gardiner, *Code Name "Mary,"* 14–15.

33 **At the time of Edward's death:** Morris & Company advertisements in *Sunday Star* (Washington, DC), April 9, 1922, 13, available at Chronicling America: American Historical Newspapers, Library of Congress, chroniclingamerica.loc.gov/lccn/sn83045462/1922-04-09/ed-1/seq-45; *Ladies' Home Journal*, May 1923, 110; "Ed. Morris Dead; Left $40,000,000," *New York Times*, November 3, 1913.

33 **While his sisters:** Gardiner, *Code Name "Mary,"* 8, 14–15.

33 **In 1923, they negotiated:** "Packers Complete $550,000,000 Merger," *New York Times*, March 28, 1923.

33 **"a person of rare kindness":** Gardiner, *Code Name "Mary,"* 9, 11.

33 **One such investment:** "Nelson Swift Morris," *New York Times*, October 7, 1955. Lucien Lelong was a mentor to Christian Dior, who worked for Lelong between 1942 and 1947 before opening his own house. Lelong was also president of La Chambre Syndicale de la Couture from 1937 through World War II and was responsible for negotiating for French couture maisons to remain in business during the Nazi occupation, effectively saving the French couture industry.

34 **In 1917, almost exactly:** "Nelson Morris Is Put in Class 1A of Draft," *New York Times*, March 30, 1918; "Nelson Morris Off to Camp," *New York Times*, May 26, 1918; "Morris Gets Out of Army," *New York Times*, June 8, 1918; "Morris in Camp Again," *New York Times*, June 13, 1918; Nelson Morris Testimony, May 28, 1937, RG 197, box 8, National Archives and Records Administration (NARA), College Park, MD; Gardiner, *Code Name "Mary,"* 12; Nelson Morris Passport Application, May 1924, available at familysearch.org.

34 **"people flying through the air":** Morris, *Heritage from My Father*, 254.

34 **He decided to join them:** Nelson Morris did not return home from service in France until August 1919. Nelson Morris Passport Application, May 1924, available at familysearch.org.

35 **In 1783 the Montgolfiers invented:** Simon Schama, *Citizens* (Alfred A. Knopf, 1989), 123.

35 **A few weeks later:** Schama, *Citizens*, 126; this demonstration was again carried out in front of the king, as well as American diplomat and amateur scientist Benjamin Franklin, who had just signed the Treaty of Paris, officially ending the Revolutionary War with Britain. Ten days later in the Jardin des Tuileries, inventor Jacques Charles and two other brothers, Anne-Jean and Nicolas-Louis Robert, demonstrated the world's first crewed flight of a hydrogen-filled balloon.

35 **As a young officer:** Alexander Rose, *Empires of the Sky: Zeppelins, Airplanes, and Two Men's Epic Duel to Rule the World* (Random House, 2020), 7–11.

35 **"destined to erase":** Henry Cord Meyer, *Airshipmen, Businessmen, and Politics: 1890–1940* (Smithsonian Institution Press, 1991), 34.

36 **"splendid instruments of war":** Meyer, *Airshipmen, Businessmen, and Politics*, 42.

36 **"assur[ing] her military":** Meyer, *Airshipmen, Businessmen, and Politics*, 34.

36 **Nelson Morris was among:** Nelson Morris Testimony, May 28, 1937, RG 197, box 8, NARA. Nelson Morris was publicly known to many as "Colonel Morris," see, e.g., "Three

Chicagoans Among Survivors of Zeppelin Blast," *Daily Times* (Davenport, IA), May 7, 1937.

37 **Nelson had twice flown:** Nelson Morris Testimony, May 28, 1937, RG 197, box 8, NARA.

37 **"squad" of reporters:** "Zeppelin Wins Him Bet," *New York Times*, August 8, 1929.

37 **Deciding he was possessed:** "Woes of the Meatpacking Heirs with Their Pretty Actress Wives," *Independent Record* (Helena, MT), February 1, 1931; Société d'Histoire du Vésinet, "Jeanne Aubert, une étoile des années folles," histoire-vesinet.org/nelsonmorris.htm.

37 **She had worked hard:** "Story of an Artificial Flower Girl," *Brooklyn Daily Eagle*, March 26, 1933.

38 **She fled to Paris:** "Woes of the Meatpacking Heirs"; "Wife Sues Nelson Morris," *New York Times*, November 26, 1929; "Fixes $200 a Month as Morris Alimony," *New York Times*, March 7, 1930; "Protests Employing Wife," *New York Times*, January 8, 1930.

38 **"The world is a wheel":** Bookplate of Nelson Swift Morris, 1907 (approx.), Museum of Fine Arts, Boston.

38 **Finally accepting that Jeanne:** "Philanthropist, Former Actress Blanche Morris," *Chicago Tribune*, September 14, 1983; "Nelson Morris Reweds," *New York Times*, October 30, 1933.

38 **They had sailed:** "Philanthropist, Former Actress"; "Nelson Morris Reweds"; see also property listings for 18000 Perth Avenue, Homewood, IL. During the Hindenburg investigation, Morris gives his address as 18300 Leffertt Street, Homewood, IL. At some point between 1937 and 1955 when the home was sold, the street and lots appear to have been renamed and renumbered.

38 **While in Paris:** Gardiner, *Code Name "Mary,"* 79.

39 **Blanche, however, was less:** Gardiner, *Code Name "Mary,"* 79.

39 **Besides, shortly after:** Burtis Dolan to Mildred Dolan, undated 1937, Dolan Family Papers, courtesy of Mary Alice Dolan Noone.

39 **Bert had been in London:** Burtis Dolan to Mildred Dolan, February 6, 1937, and Burtis Dolan to Mildred Dolan, February 17, 1937, Dolan Family Papers.

39 **Why not, Nelson:** Burtis Dolan to Mildred Dolan, undated 1937.

40 **Bert was a successful:** "Burtis Dolan's Hindenburg Passenger Ticket," *Fire & Ice: Hindenburg and Titanic*, Smithsonian National Postal Museum, postalmuseum.si.edu/exhibition/fire-ice-hindenburg-and-titanic-exhibition-fire-ice-rarities/burtis-dolans-hindenburg#:~:text=The%20ticket%2C%20%232398%2C%20was,%24450%20during%20the%20Great%20Depression; Eugen Bentele, *The Story of a Zeppelin Mechanic: My Flights 1931–1938* (Wolfgang Meighörner-Schardt, 1992), 24.

40 **Nelson would cover:** "Burtis Dolan's Hindenburg Passenger Ticket"; Patrick Dolan, interview with the author, January 4, 2024; Mary Alice Dolan Noone, interview with the author, February 16, 2024.

40 **If Bert flew:** Patrick Dolan, interview with the author; Mary Alice Dolan Noone, interview with the author; Dennis R. Kromm, "Homecoming," in *Compex: Combined Philatelic Exhibition of Chicagoland, Incorporated, Commemorating the 50th Anniversary of the Last Flight of the Hindenburg* (May 1987), 55.

40 **They would arrange:** Liste über ausgegebene Fahrscheine, LS "HINDENBURG" Frankfurt-Lakehurst, 3 Mai 1. Nordamerikafahrt 1937, LZA 17/0567, Zeppelin Museum, Friedrichshafen; Burtis Dolan to Mildred Dolan, undated 1937.

Chapter 4

41 **"stretch out to prodigious":** Mark Twain, "The Chicago of Europe," *Chicago Daily Tribune*, April 3, 1892, republished in Peter Kaminsky, ed., *The Chicago of Europe: And Other Tales of Foreign Travel* (Sterling, 2009), 192.

41 **"cold, misty, and ugly":** William L. Shirer to John Gunther, November 26, 1934, box 5, Correspondence 1927–1937, John Gunther Papers, University of Chicago.

41 **As Berliners began:** William L. Shirer, *20th Century Journey*, vol. 2, *The Nightmare Years: 1930–1940* (Little, Brown, 1984), 266.

42 **Over the last few weeks:** William L. Shirer, *Berlin Diary: The Journal of a Foreign Correspondent, 1934–1941*, rev. ed. (Alfred A. Knopf, 1941; Bonanza Books, 1984), April 8, 1937, 70–71. Citations refer to the Bonanza edition.

42 **springtime "Hitler surprise":** Shirer, *Berlin Diary*, April 8, 1937, 70.

42 **Shirer was skeptical:** Shirer, *20th Century Journey*, vol. 2, 265.

42 **"nerves of the German":** Shirer, *Berlin Diary*, April 8, 1937, 70.

43 **"so-called period of surprises":** Adolf Hitler, "On National Socialism and World Relations," January 30, 1937, German Propaganda Archive, Calvin University, Grand Rapids, MI.

43 **"sickening adulation from all":** Shirer, *Berlin Diary*, April 20, 1937, 71.

43 **"more and more like a Caesar":** Shirer, *Berlin Diary*, April 20, 1937, 71.

43 **How easy it would:** Shirer, *Berlin Diary*, September 6, 1934, 21.

43 **"No figure in postwar":** William L. Shirer, Adolf Hitler Obituary, 1935, Obituaries, series 1, Willliam L. Shirer Papers, Coe College, Cedar Rapids, IA (WLSP).

43 **It was the DZR press:** Shirer, *Berlin Diary*, May 7, 1937, 72.

44 **Shirer had sent letters:** Josie Shirer to William L. Shirer, May 16, 1936, Correspondence by Date, 1935 [misfiled]; Verne Marshall, "Current Comment," *Cedar Rapids Gazette*, May (undated) 1936; Verne Marshall to William L. Shirer, May 13, 1936, Correspondence by Date, 1936, WLSP. Verne Marshall, who won a Pulitzer Prize in 1936 for investigating local corruption in state government, became a notorious isolationist crusader by the early 1940s.

44 **Americans were obsessed:** William L. Shirer, Original Diary (Black Notebook), September 18, 1935, WLSP.

44 **He had written a popular:** William L. Shirer, "Newest Zeppelin to Provide 2-Day Crossing of Atlantic," *Morning Post* (Camden, NJ), February 17, 1936; William L. Shirer, "New German Airship Faces Problems of Profit, Schedules," *Morning Post*, February 18, 1936; William L. Shirer, "Passengers' Comfort Stressed in Design of Super-Zeppelin," *Morning Post*, February 19, 1936; William L. Shirer, "Second 'Super-Zep' Planned if Trips of LZ-129 Prove Success," *Morning Post*, February 20, 1936.

44 **chance of writing a follow-up:** William L. Shirer to Hermann Köhl, undated 1935, Correspondence by Date, 1935, WLSP.
44 **"bloody, hysterical land":** William L. Shirer to John Gunther, January 4, 1936, box 5, Correspondence 1927–1937, John Gunther Papers, University of Chicago. Shirer was last in the United States in September 1935. Shirer, *Berlin Diary*, September 9, 1935, 42.
44 **"impossible" for him to leave:** Shirer, *Berlin Diary*, May 7, 1937, 72.
44 **Enticing as the offer:** Shirer, *20th Century Journey*, vol. 2, 266.
44 **"where almost anything":** Verne Marshall, "Current Comment," *Cedar Rapids Gazette*, May (undated) 1936, Correspondence by Date, 1936, WLSP.
44 **no choice but to tell:** Shirer, *20th Century Journey*, vol. 2, 266; Shirer, *Berlin Diary*, May 7, 1937, 72.
44 **If Shirer could not:** Shirer, *Berlin Diary*, May 7, 1937, 72.
44 **She was both artistic:** William L. Shirer to John Gunther, "Sunday" 1934, box 5, Correspondence, 1927–1937 P–S, John Gunther Papers, University of Chicago; Dierdre van Dyk, interview with the author, January 13, 2024; Linda Shirer Rae, interview with the author, December 20, 2023; Inga Shirer, Theresa Stiberitz Shirer Biography, General Files, folder: "Theresa Stiberitz Shirer Biography 2010," WLSP.
45 **"brilliant mind" of this young woman:** William Shirer to John Shirer, October 4, 1930, Correspondence, A–Z, folder: "Theresa Stiberitz 1930–1932," WLSP.
45 **After six years:** van Dyk, interview with the author.
45 **The prior February:** Shirer, *20th Century Journey*, vol. 2, 266.
45 **Alongside her many:** van Dyk, interview with the author; Shirer Rae, interview with the author; Christian Williams, interview with the author, October 12, 2023; Inga Shirer, Theresa Stiberitz Shirer Biography.
46 **They had been looking forward:** Shirer, *Berlin Diary*, April 14, 1937, 71.
46 **raised an "awful howl":** Shirer, *Berlin Diary*, April 14, 1937, 71.
46 **Shirer could not honestly:** Shirer, *Berlin Diary*, May 7, 1937, 72.
46 **Thanks to the time:** Shirer, "Newest Zeppelin."
46 **The postwar German zeppelins:** Shirer, "Second 'Super-Zep' Planned."
46 **"as safe as anything":** Shirer, "Newest Zeppelin."
46 **Perhaps the source:** Shirer, *20th Century Journey*, vol. 2, 267.
47 **"virtually is no danger of fire":** Shirer, "Newest Zeppelin."
47 **Unfortunately, when Eckener arrived:** Shirer, *20th Century Journey*, vol. 2, 267.
47 **Shirer articulated none:** Shirer, *20th Century Journey*, vol. 2, 266–67; Shirer, *Berlin Diary*, May 7, 1937, 72.
47 **Coincidentally, the Shirers had leased:** Shirer, *Berlin Diary*, June 3, 1935, 39–40.
47 **"curry Nazi favor":** Shirer, *Berlin Diary*, June 3, 1935, 40.
47 **More likely his termination:** Shirer, *Berlin Diary*, June 3, 1935, 40.
47 **"politely declined" the offer:** Shirer, *Berlin Diary*, May 7, 1937, 72.
47 **Then he hung up the receiver:** Shirer, *20th Century Journey*, vol. 2, 266.

Chapter 5

48 **During the war, he had served:** Burtis John Dolan, Draft Registration Card, 1917, available at familysearch.org; *The Book of the 332nd F. A.* (Stanley J. Low, 1920), 49.

48 **"denied the Great":** *Book of the 332nd F. A.*, 49.

48 **"greatest destructive force":** *Book of the 332nd F. A.*, 37–39.

49 **Thus far, it seemed:** Richard Overy, *The Dictators: Hitler's Germany, Stalin's Russia* (W. W. Norton, 2004), 260.

49 **Just before Christmas:** Mary Alice Dolan Noone, interview with the author, February 16, 2024; Obituaries, *Chicago Tribune*, December 25, 1936.

49 **The day after Christmas:** Obituaries, *Chicago Tribune.*

49 **Three weeks later:** Dennis R. Kromm, "Homecoming," in *Compex: Combined Philatelic Exhibition of Chicagoland, Incorporated, Commemorating the 50th Anniversary of the Last Flight of the Hindenburg* (May 1987), 54.

49 **The designer began a perfume:** Susan Teichman, "Ting-a-Ling, the Perfume Bottle That Sings," Cooper Hewitt Museum, June 3, 2018, cooperhewitt.org/2018/06/03/ting-a-ling-the-perfume-bottle-that-sings; Rachel Elspeth Gross, "Lucien Lelong: Christian Dior's Mentor Before the New Look," *Forbes*, February 22, 2024, forbes.com/sites/rachelelspethgross/2024/02/16/lucien-lelong-christian-diors-mentor-before-the-new-look; Kromm, "Homecoming," 54. Like many designers, Lelong did not sew, sketch, or drape fabric and instead hired a stable of designers to execute his vision. His protégés included Christian Dior, Pierre Balmain, and Hubert de Givenchy.

49 **Harmonizing the various operations:** Burtis Dolan to Mildred Dolan, February 6, 1937, Dolan Family Papers; Burtis Dolan to Mildred Dolan, February 17, 1937, Dolan Family Papers; Kromm, "Homecoming," 54.

49 **"gloomy as ever":** Burtis Dolan to Mildred Dolan, February 6, 1937.

50 **After three weeks in London:** Burtis Dolan to Mildred Dolan, February 6, 1937.

50 **had "temperamental" personalities:** Burtis Dolan to Mildred Dolan, February 17, 1937.

50 **"like[d] Lelong better":** Burtis Dolan to Mildred Dolan, February 17, 1937.

50 **"They are moving too slow":** Burtis Dolan to Mildred Dolan, February 17, 1937.

51 **visit a "smart shop":** Burtis Dolan to Mildred Dolan, February 6, 1937.

51 **"everyone talks English":** Burtis Dolan to Mildred Dolan, February 17, 1937.

51 **In Chicago, the Irish found:** "Letter from James Brooks to the Canal Commissioners Concerning Irish Rioters," February 22, 1838, document 11, "The Illinois and Michigan Canal, 1827–1911," A Selection of Documents from the Illinois State Archives.

51 **Like many in the growing:** "Fraternities Pledge New Members for Coming Year," *Daily Illini*, October 14, 1911; DePaul *Minerval* Graduation 1919, 92; DePaul *Minerval* February 1919, 290; Patrick Dolan, interview with the author, January 4, 2024.

52 **He landed in the banking:** Charles H. Slocum to Burtis J. Dolan Jr., February 7, 1979, Dolan Family Papers.

52 **Though only a compact:** Dolan, interview with the author; Noone, interview with the author; Kromm, "Homecoming," 53; Jimmy Corcoran, "The Roundup," *Chicago Daily News*, undated Dolan Family Papers.

52 **As an adult, he added:** Dolan, interview with the author; Chick Evans to Mildred Dolan, May 17, 1937, Dolan Family Papers.

52 **Bert was soon promoted:** Charles H. Slocum to Burtis J. Dolan Jr., February 7, 1979, Dolan Family Papers.

52 **After the interruption:** "Miss Mildred Philbin to Wed Army Major," *Chicago Tribune*, February 10, 1922; "Three Chicagoans Among Survivors of Zeppelin Blast," *Daily Times* (Davenport, IA), May 7, 1937.

52 **Meanwhile, Bert briefly:** Kromm, "Homecoming," 54.

52 **Working with Nelson:** Michael Pallasch, interview with the author, September 27, 2023.

52 **It had also allowed:** Pallasch, interview with the author.

53 **He loved it so much:** Hutchinson Street District, Chicago Landmark Designation Report, September 8, 1975, archive.org/stream/CityOfChicagoLandmarkDesignationReports/HutchinsonSt.District_djvu.txt; Pallasch, interview with the author.

53 **When Mildred embraced him:** Kromm, "Homecoming," 54.

53 **She also made him promise:** Dolan, interview with the author; Noone, interview with the author.

53 **They had met in 1913:** Kromm, "Homecoming," 53; Dolan, interview with the author; Noone, interview with the author; "Lakeview Avenue Row House District," Landmark Designation Report, September 1, 2016, 7–8, chicago.gov/content/dam/city/depts/zlup/Historic_Preservation/Publications/Lakeview_Ave_Row_House_Dist.pdf.

54 **"This man has been doting":** Noone, interview with the author.

54 **He had put up pictures:** Burtis Dolan to Mildred Dolan, February 17, 1937.

54 **lovingly called "the Bunnies":** Burtis Dolan to Mildred Dolan, February 6, 1937.

54 **"sure wish[ed] you all":** Burtis Dolan to Mildred Dolan, February 17, 1937.

55 **Uncharacteristically, he put off:** Burtis Dolan to Mildred Dolan, undated 1937, Dolan Family Papers.

55 **"Dearest One," he wrote:** Burtis Dolan to Mildred Dolan, undated 1937.

Chapter 6

56 **Its cotton canvas skin:** Main exhibit, Zeppelin Museum, Friedrichshafen.

56 **She had flown over:** Frank Jewett Mather Sr., "A Private Life," 1835–1929, TMs, with autograph corrections, pp. 1–75, undated, 129, series 1, Frank Jewett Mather Papers, C0025, Manuscripts Division, Department of Special Collections, Princeton University Library.

57 **"seasick wretch" like her:** Margaret Mather, "I Was on the Hindenburg," *Harper's Monthly*, November 1937.

57 **It was departing:** Margaret Mather, "I Was on the Hindenburg."

57 **She and her seven siblings:** Frank Jewett Mather Sr., "A Private Life," 117–22; *Dictionary of Art Historians*, "Mather, Frank Jewett, Jr.," arthistorians.info/matherf; S. Lane Faison Jr., "Frank J. Mather, Jr., 1868–1953," *College Art Journal* 13, no. 3 (1954).

58 **"Mussolini is certainly":** Frank Jewett Mather Sr., "A Private Life," 147.

59 **"I hope," he wrote:** Frank Jewett Mather Sr., "A Private Life," 148–49.

59 **"young green leaves":** Margaret Mather, "I Was on the Hindenburg."

60 **People milled about among:** Hotel Frankfurter Hof Pamphlet, 1930s.

60 **"silent tension" that languished:** Gertrud Stolte-Adelt, "Mein Sturz aus dem brennenden Luftschiff: Erinnerungen an eine tragische Atlantikfahrt," *Hamburger Abendblatt*, August 27, 1949.

60 **"We sit here together":** Stolte-Adelt, "Mein Sturz."

61 **There was a successful:** "Yale Man Leaps from Hindenburg," *Yale Daily News*, May 7, 1937.

61 **Perhaps most excited:** Martin Feibusch and Cheryl Ganz, "*Hindenburg* Crash Cover Forgeries and Passenger Moritz Feibusch," *Zeppelin Collector*, July 1998, 54.

61 **Margaret soon understood:** Margaret Mather, "I Was on the Hindenburg."

61 **warning: "*Sehr wichtig*!":** Cigarette bag, LZ 2016/009.004, Zeppelin Museum, Friedrichshafen.

61 **These little bags:** Willy von Meister to Ernst Lehmann, January 10, 1937, LZA 17/196, Zeppelin Museum, Friedrichshafen.

62 **"existing air-navigation laws":** *Airship Voyages Made Easy* (Deutsche Zeppelin-Reederei, 1937, reprinted 1976), 9.

62 **Flying over France:** Die Aufzeichnungen des Luftschiffstewards Wilhelm Balla, LZ 129, BMA I, Zeppelin Museum, Friedrichshafen; "Hindenburg Sets New Trans-Atlantic Record," *Tribune* (Manila), May 10, 1936.

62 **employees' search "courteous":** Margaret Mather, "I Was on the Hindenburg." Weight limitations stipulated in *Airship Voyages Made Easy*, 1937, 5–6.

62 **that April, DZR had also:** Einladung zum Richtfest der Zeppelin-Siedlung am Freitag, den 2. April 1937, LZ 129, BMA I, Zeppelin Museum, Friedrichshafen.

63 **As the evening's departure:** Douglas H. Robinson, "You Don't Fly in an Airship, You Go Voyaging," in *LZ 129 "Hindenburg,"* Famous Aircraft Series (Arco, 1964).

63 **It was incredible that:** Ernst A. Lehmann, *Zeppelin: The Story of Lighter-Than-Air Craft*, rev. ed. (Fonthill, 2015), 292.

64 **The hydrogen that filled:** Lehmann, *Zeppelin*, 304. Several years later, IG Farben would become infamous for producing another hydrogen gas mixed with cyanide (prussic acid), the basis for a chemical called Zyklon B, the toxic gas used to murder over a million Jews in concentration camps during World War II.

64 **He had served as commanding:** Figures combined from Lehmann, *Zeppelin*, 311, and Dan Grossman, "Max Pruss," Airships.net, n.d., airships.net/airship-people/captain-max-pruss.

64 **Though Pruss had a soldierly:** W. E. von Medem, *Kabinenjunge Werner Franz vom Luftschiff "Hindenburg"* (Franz Schneider Verlag, 1938), 22.

64 **touch of the elevator man:** Robinson, "You Don't Fly," quoting Hans von Schiller, *Zeppelinbuch*, 51.

65 **As the quickest way:** Lehmann, *Zeppelin*, 308.

65 **On its next round-trip journey:** Charles E. Rosendahl, "The Last Flight," in Lehmann, *Zeppelin*, 325; "U.S. Shows Supremacy in Men, Women's Dash Events at Olympics," *Des Moines Tribune*, August 10, 1936.

65 **Freight sometimes included:** Lehmann, *Zeppelin*, 308.

65 **In 1936, the *Hindenburg* had carried:** Robinson, "You Don't Fly."

65 **DZR did, however, draw:** Lehmann, *Zeppelin*, 308.

65 **If a New York subway:** Douglas H. Robinson, "Life in the Belly of Leviathan," in *LZ 129 "Hindenburg."*

65 **Inside the engine gondolas:** Robinson, "You Don't Fly"; Douglas H. Robinson, "Airship Diesels," in *LZ 129 "Hindenburg."*

66 **In the kitchen beside:** Robinson, "Life in the Belly."

66 **The kitchen was connected:** "Auszug aus einem Bericht des Herren Direktor Wronsky," March 30–April 10, 1936, LZA 17/197, Zeppelin Museum, Friedrichshafen.

66 **Max Schulze, perhaps the most:** Robinson, "Life in the Belly."

66 **Despite its central place:** *Hindenburg* drink menu, LZ 2016/009.004, Zeppelin Museum, Friedrichshafen.

67 **led by a chief steward:** Nachweis über die Zeit vom Tag der Schulentlassung bis zum Eintritt bei der Deutsche Zeppelin Reederei, February 12, 1938, LZ 129, BMA II, Zeppelin Museum, Friedrichshafen.

67 **Some also thought it:** Helmut Kreuzer, *Stewardess: 60 Jahre Traumberuf über den Wolken*, LZ 129, BMA II, Zeppelin Museum, Friedrichshafen.

67 **One of the younger stewards:** Die Aufzeichnungen des Luftschiffstewards; von Medem, *Kabinenjunge Werner Franz*, 14, 19–20, 24, 29, 39, 41, 45–46.

68 **At seven o'clock, Margaret:** Margaret Mather, "I Was on the Hindenburg"; Stolte-Adelt, "Mein Sturz."

68 **As they wound:** Stolte-Adelt, "Mein Sturz."

68 **The moment the airfield:** Margaret Mather, "I Was on the Hindenburg."

68 **In between were the Olympic rings:** As it hovered above the stadium, it had appeared to bow to the audience below, an act achieved by using the elevators to change the weight distribution of the ship, supplemented by crew members running fore to add more weight to the nose. Interview with *Hindenburg* navigator Eduard Böetius, "Für Panik war keine Zeit," *Der Spiegel*, May 21, 2000, LZ 129, BMA I, Zeppelin Museum, Friedrichshafen.

69 **The enthusiastic crowd:** Margaret Mather, "I Was on the Hindenburg."

69 **As Margaret was ushered:** Margaret Mather, "I Was on the Hindenburg."

69 **While the passengers finished:** Smithsonian National Postal Museum, "The Hindenburg Disaster," *Fire & Ice: Hindenburg and Titanic*, postalmuseum.si.edu/exhibition/fire-ice-hindenburg-and-titanic-exhibition/the-hindenburg-disaster#:~:text=Departing%20Germany%20for%20the%20last,boxed%20marking%20on%20the%20mail.&text=When%20Hindenburg%20met%20tragedy%20May,of%20mail%20burned%20to%20ashes.

70 **A batch of letters:** Smithsonian National Postal Museum, "The Hindenburg Disaster"; "Hindenburg Last Flight Cologne 'Dropped' Cover," Alexander Historical

Auctions, alexautographs.com/auction-lot/hindenburg-last-flight-cologne-dropped-cover_86F4BC298D.

70 **They entered on B deck:** Robinson, "Life in the Belly."

70 **She slid open:** Assorted photographs, Zeppelin Museum, Friedrichshafen; Dan Grossman, "The Hindenburg's Interior: Passenger Decks," Airships.net, n.d., airships.net/hindenburg/interiors; Robinson, "Life in the Belly."

71 **There was scarcely time:** Margaret Mather, "I Was on the Hindenburg"; Robinson, "Life in the Belly."

71 **At that instant:** Stolte-Adelt, "Mein Sturz"; Leonhard Adelt, "Trauer und Zuversicht," in Ernst A. Lehmann, *Auf Luftpatrouille und Weltfahrt* (Schmidt & Günther, 1937), 404.

71 **For a second time:** Margaret Mather, "I Was on the Hindenburg."

72 **"indescribable feeling of lightness":** Margaret Mather, "I Was on the Hindenburg."

Chapter 7

73 **For Gertrud Adelt:** Gertrud Stolte-Adelt, "Mein Sturz aus dem brennenden Luftschiff: Erinnerungen an eine tragische Atlantikfahrt," *Hamburger Abendblatt*, August 27, 1949.

73 **"reced[ed] into a kind":** Stolte-Adelt, "Mein Sturz."

73 **They were both journalists:** Liste über ausgegebene Fahrscheine LS "HINDENBURG" Frankfurt-Lakehurst, 3, Mail 1, Nordamerikafahrt 1937, LZA 17/567, Zeppelin Museum, Friedrichshafen.

73 **Not only did Lehmann:** Leonhard Adelt to Friderike Zweig, June 8, 1937, courtesy of Ulrich Adelt; David Turner, "Eine nahe Ferne. Die Briefe Stefan Zweigs an Leonhard Adelt als Ausdruck einer von ihren literarischen Anfängen geprägten Freundschaft," in *Studia austriaca II*, ed. Fausto Cercignani, vol. 2 (University of Milan, 1993), 85.

74 **Two of his brothers:** Leonhard Adelt, "Trauer und Zuversicht," in Ernst A. Lehmann, *Auf Luftpatrouille und Weltfahrt* (Schmidt & Günther, 1937), 400–401; Stolte-Adelt, "Mein Sturz."

74 **Gertrud had met Leonhard:** Turner, "Eine nahe Ferne," 67, 75.

74 **Always proper and tidy:** Ulrich Adelt, interview with the author, October 19, 2023.

74 **"the editor, Dr. Gertrud":** Adelt, "Trauer und Zuversicht," 400.

74 **She was proud:** Adelt, interview with the author.

74 **of a supposedly higher standard:** Gertrud Stolte-Adelt, "Wegbilder der Barockzeit im Münsterland: Ein Beitrag zur Geschichte der volkstümlichen Plastik Westfalens," in *Lebensräume der Kunst*, ed. Martin Wackernagel, Heft 4 (Karl Busch Verlag, 1936), 7.

75 **This was filled:** Film footage depicting interior shots of *Hindenburg* and Ernst A. Lehmann interview, May 20, 1936, courtesy of the 87th Air Base Wing Historian.

75 **Pound for pound:** Clara Adams, Description of Hindenburg Flight, 1936, box 2, folder 11, Clara Adams Papers, University of Texas Dallas Archives.

75 **"Since I learned":** Leonhard Adelt, *Der Flieger: Ein Buch aus unsern Tagen* (Literarische Anstalt Rütten & Loening, 1913), 40.

75 **Even Leonhard's bookplates:** Turner, "Eine nahe Ferne," 84.

75 **Gertrud leaned over:** Stolte-Adelt, "Mein Sturz."

76 **"In the cabin . . . there was hardly":** Hermann Hesse, *Die Kunst des Müßiggangs: Kurze Prosa aus dem Nachlaß* (Suhrkamp Taschenbuch Verlag, 1973), 199.

76 **"The world ran beneath":** Adelt, *Der Flieger*, 102–3.

76 **A succession of villages:** Margaret Mather, "I Was on the Hindenburg," *Harper's Monthly*, November 1937.

76 **Beyond the rows:** Adelt, "Trauer und Zuversicht," 401.

76 **something fluttered from the zeppelin:** "Hindenburg Last Flight Cologne 'Dropped' Cover," Alexander Historical Auctions, alexautographs.com/auction-lot/hindenburg-last-flight-cologne-dropped-cover_86F4BC298D; Smithsonian National Postal Museum, "Object Spotlight: Hindenburg Postcard Signed by Douglas Fairbanks," postalmuseum.si.edu/collections/object-spotlight/hindenburg-postcard-signed-by-douglas-fairbanks; Smithsonian National Postal Museum, "Hindenburg's Post Room," *Fire & Ice: Hindenburg and Titanic*, postalmuseum.si.edu/exhibition/fire-ice-hindenburg-and-titanic-exhibition-mail-ships/hindenburgs-post-room.

77 **After clearing the three-mile:** *Airship Voyages Made Easy* (Deutsche Zeppelin-Reederei, 1937, reprinted 1976), 9.

77 **As the clock struck ten:** Mather, "I Was on the Hindenburg."

77 **Gertrud and the others:** Standortmeldungen von L.S. Hindenburg auf seiner letzten Fahrt nach USA, LZA 17/567, Zeppelin Museum, Friedrichshafen.

77 **Typically, the passengers:** George Grant, "Notes on a Voyage of the AIRSHIP 'HINDENBURG' Under the Command of Captain Pruss," May 6, 1937, National Archives and Records Administration at College Park (NARA), available online at Patrick Russell, "George Grant," *Faces of the Hindenburg* (blog), January 21, 2009, facesofthehindenburg.blogspot.com/2009/01/george-grant.html; Clara Adams, Description of Hindenburg Flight, 1936, box 2, folder 11, Clara Adams Papers, University of Texas Dallas Archives.

77 **The stewards had arranged:** Mather, "I Was on the Hindenburg."

77 **Meanwhile, John Pannes:** Aktennotiz, February 4, 1937, LZA 17/196, Zeppelin Museum, Friedrichshafen.

77 **Like the Adelts:** Liste über ausgegebene Fahrscheine.

77 **Typically, Captain Lehmann:** Mather, "I Was on the Hindenburg"; Stolte-Adelt, "Mein Sturz"; von Medem, *Kabinenjunge Werner Franz*, 86.

78 **Whether it was difficult:** Mather, "I Was on the Hindenburg."

78 **"dapper, polished, suave":** Rosendahl, "Preface to the 1937 Edition," in Ernst A. Lehmann, *Zeppelin: The Story of Lighter-Than-Air Craft*, rev. ed. (Fonthill, 2015), 20.

78 **Lehmann wore his hair:** Assorted photographs, Zeppelin Museum, Friedrichshafen; Mather, "I Was on the Hindenburg."

78 **At last, Captain Pruss:** Mather, "I Was on the Hindenburg."

78 **Each place setting was anchored:** Main exhibit, Zeppelin-Museum Zeppelinheim; main exhibit, Zeppelin Museum, Friedrichshafen; Douglas H. Robinson, "Life in the Belly of Leviathan," in *LZ 129 "Hindenburg,"* Famous Aircraft Series (Arco, 1964).

79 **The only curious factor:** Nicole Jankowski, "When the Hindenburg Was the Height of Luxe In-Flight Dining," NPR, May 19, 2017, npr.org/sections/thesalt/2017/05/19/528508054/photos-when-the-hindenburg-was-the-height-of-luxe-in-flight-dining.

79 **By the end of every flight:** Eugen Nunnenmacher, "Im Luftschiff über Länder und Meere," 1936, LZ 129, BMA II, Zeppelin Museum, Friedrichshafen; Robinson, "Life in the Belly."

79 **In addition to the many:** Robinson, "Life in the Belly."

80 **On airships predating:** Harold G. Dick and Douglas H. Robinson, *The Golden Age of the Great Passenger Airships: Graf Zeppelin & Hindenburg* (Smithsonian Institution Press, 1985), 61, 67, 134; Museum Guide, Zeppelin-Museum Zeppelinheim.

80 **During the monthslong legal saga:** "Edward Is So Excited He Forgets Part of Luggage in Speed to Board Train," *Battle Creek Moon-Journal* (Battle Creek, MI), May 3, 1937; "Duke Leaves Austria for Betrothed After Word of Court Order," *Springfield News-Sun* (Springfield, OH); "The Camera Overseas: Schiaparelli Clothes," May 3, 1937, *Life*, May 17, 1937, 64, box 14, NARA.

81 **"Why must politics":** "Villagers Give Serenade for Duke on Lake," *Washington Herald* (Washington, DC), May 3, 1937.

81 **It was vital:** Charles E. Rosendahl, "The Last Flight," in Lehmann, *Zeppelin*, 325; Charles E. Rosendahl, *What About the Airship? The Challenges to the United States* (Charles Scribner's Sons, 1938), 4.

81 **While the passengers were enjoying:** Mather, "I Was on the Hindenburg"; Leonhard Adelt, "The Last Trip of the Hindenburg," *Reader's Digest*, November 1937; Standortmeldungen von L. S. Hindenburg auf seiner letzten Fahrt nach USA, LZA 17/567, Zeppelin Museum, Friedrichshafen.

81 **As dinner concluded:** Mather, "I Was on the Hindenburg."

81 **Despite the storm:** John Parris Jr. (United Press), "Survivor Describes Jump from Blazing Hindenburg," *Pittsburgh Press*, May 8, 1937.

81 **"quiet, swaying step":** Stolte-Adelt, "Mein Sturz."

82 **Normally, he liked to take:** Marilyn Spah Kelly and Jane Kelly, interview with the author, May 5, 1937.

82 **He was supposed to have:** Joseph Spah receipt for telegram on board the *Hindenburg*, May 3, 1937, Spah Family Papers, courtesy of the Spah family; Victoria Spah, *The Spah Family: Home Movies*, 2006; Marilyn Spah Kelly and Jane Kelly, interview with the author.

82 **"there was any chance":** Parris, "Survivor Describes Jump."

82 **Lehmann was well aware:** Lehmann, *Zeppelin*, 203.

82 **"almost impossible to conceive":** Lehmann, *Zeppelin*, 235, 293.

82 **It certainly could:** Lehmann, *Zeppelin*, 150; Max Pruss, New York Times Oral History Program, Columbia University Oral History Collection, part IV, 17–18.

82 **"from all directions":** Lehmann, *Zeppelin*, 148–50.

83 **Rather than provide:** Joseph Spah, interview in *Survival!*, produced by Sherman Grinberg, hosted by James Whitmore, 1964, Spah Family Papers; Parris, "Survivor Describes Jump."

83 **"barely glimpse" before crossing:** Adelt, "Last Trip of the Hindenburg."
83 **miss something "irretrievable":** Stolte-Adelt, "Mein Sturz."
83 **"calm, moonlit night":** Adelt, "Last Trip of the Hindenburg."
83 **The startled barks:** W. B. Courtney, "Sky Cruise," *Collier's*, May 8, 1937, box 14, NARA.
83 **"hand out the window":** Stolte-Adelt, "Mein Sturz."

Chapter 8

84 **His nocturnal hours:** Die Aufzeichnungen des Luftschiffstewards Wilhelm Balla, LZ 129, BMA I, Zeppelin Museum, Friedrichshafen.
84 **On a clear night:** Eugen Bentele, *The Story of a Zeppelin Mechanic: My Flights 1931–1938* (Wolfgang Meighörner-Schardt, 1992), 31.
84 **"devote [him]self entirely":** Ernst A. Lehmann, *Zeppelin: The Story of Lighter-Than-Air Craft*, rev. ed. (Fonthill, 2015), 24.
85 **"three favorite companions":** Hans von Schiller, *Zeppelinbuch* (Bibliographisches Institut, 1938), 207.
85 **It was an aluminum:** Douglas H. Robinson, "Life in the Belly of Leviathan," in *LZ 129 "Hindenburg,"* Famous Aircraft Series (Arco, 1964).
85 **After dinner, Lehmann:** Charles A. Rosendahl, "Preface to the 1937 Edition," in Lehmann, *Zeppelin*, 20; Charles E. Rosendahl, *What About the Airship? The Challenges to the United States* (Charles Scribner's Sons, 1938), 54; assorted photographs, Zeppelin Museum, Friedrichshafen.
85 **his "seaman's piano":** Lehmann, *Zeppelin*, 265. See also Rosendahl, "Preface to the 1937 Edition," 20.
85 **But his favorite:** Bentele, *Story of a Zeppelin Mechanic*, 64.
85 **became "an organ":** von Schiller, *Zeppelinbuch*, 207; Lehmann, *Zeppelin*, 265.
85 **Sometimes, when the young:** Bentele, *Story of a Zeppelin Mechanic*, 64.
85 **had been so keen:** Die Aufzeichnungen des Luftschiffstewards Wilhelm Balla, LZ 129, BMA I, Zeppelin Museum, Friedrichshafen.
86 **he had come upon Captain Lehmann:** Die Aufzeichnungen des Luftschiffstewards.
86 **Over the winter, the piano:** Dennis R. Kromm, "Homecoming," in *Compex: Combined Philatelic Exhibition of Chicagoland, Incorporated, Commemorating the 50th Anniversary of the Last Flight of the Hindenburg* (May 1987), 55.
86 **"almost the most":** Ernst Lehmann to landlady, September 7, 1934, LZ 129, BMA II, Zeppelin Museum, Friedrichshafen.
86 **In June 1934:** Ernst Lehmann to landlady, March 6, 1934, LZ 129 BMA II, Zeppelin Museum, Friedrichshafen; Lehmann to landlady, September 7, 1934; Rosendahl, "Preface to the 1937 Edition," 20.
87 **Soon afterward, his stepdaughter:** Ernst Lehmann to landlady, December 14, 1936, LZ 129, BMA II, Zeppelin Museum, Friedrichshafen.
87 **Best and most surprising:** Max Geisenheyner, *E. A. Lehmann, Zeppelin-Kapitän* (Societäts-Verlag 1937), 105.
87 **In the beautiful:** Geisenheyner, *E. A. Lehmann*, 37.

87 **Little Otto became:** Lehmann to landlady, December 14, 1936; Geisenheyner, *E. A. Lehmann*, 75–76.

87 **The growing success:** Lehmann to landlady, December 14, 1936.

87 **"Zeppelinheim" was tucked:** Original layout of Zeppelinheim featured in Zeppelin-Museum Zeppelinheim; main exhibit, Zeppelin Museum, Friedrichshafen; Zeppelin—Siedlung—Haustyp 3 E—Baubeschreibung, LZ 129, BMA I, Zeppelin Museum, Friedrichshafen.

87 **with a "bleeding heart":** Lehmann to landlady, December 14, 1936. See also Geisenheyner, *E. A. Lehmann*, 71.

88 **Then, at Easter:** von Schiller, *Zeppelinbuch*, 198; Geisenheyner, *E. A. Lehmann*, 78–79. Geisenheyner suggests the boy developed the flu, and while he initially recovered, he had to have an urgent ear operation and died shortly thereafter.

88 **The Adelts' one-year-old:** Ulrich Adelt, interview with the author, October 19, 2023.

88 **Meanwhile, Lehmann, whose life:** Geisenheyner, *E. A. Lehmann*, 83–84.

88 **"We are all":** Leonhard Adelt, *Der Flieger: Ein Buch aus unsern Tagen* (Literarische Anstalt Rütten & Loening, 1913), 62.

89 **the "blue Atlantic":** Lehmann, *Zeppelin*, 24.

Chapter 9

90 **Before Bill Shirer:** William Shirer, *Hindenburg* Dispatch, May 6, 1937, Journalist-Correspondent, Cables, Dispatches, Mail Stories, folder: Cables, Reports, 1936, 1937, 1939, William L. Shirer Papers, Coe College, Cedar Rapids, IA (WLSP).

90 **"for a time gripped":** William Shirer, "Review of the Year 1936," December 31, 1936, Journalist-Correspondent, Cables, Dispatches, Mail Stories, folder Mail Stories (with Notes) 1935–1938, WLSP.

90 **With nothing else:** William L. Shirer, *Berlin Diary: The Journal of a Foreign Correspondent, 1934–1941,* rev. ed. (Bonanza Books, 1984), May 3, 1937, 71.

Chapter 10

92 **The paper was just one:** In 1925, there were 6,435 weekly newspapers in circulation, as well as 2,116 daily newspapers. Weekly publications reached nearly sixteen million people. Alexander J. Field, "Newspapers and Periodicals: Number and Circulation by Type, 1850–1967," in *Historical Statistics of the United States*, ed. Susan B. Carter, Millennial ed., vol. 4 (Cambridge University Press, 2006), 1055, cited in University of Illinois Urbana-Champaign, "English 200P: Introduction to Literature and Culture," University Library LibGuides, guides.library.illinois.edu/adventures/industry.

92 **Midwestern publications proudly:** Field, "Newspapers and Periodicals."

92 **The *Chicago Tribune* was second:** "Sunday Tribune Circulation Now in Excess of 1,050,000," *Chicago Daily Tribune*, March 18, 1936, available at Michigan State University Library Archive, archive.lib.msu.edu/DMC/tribune/trib03181936/trib03181936018.pdf.

92 **"devoted to western agriculture":** See, e.g., *Prairie Farmer* 6, no. 1 (January 1846).

92 **Instead, the navy persuaded:** In creating RCA, General Electric entered a patent-sharing trust with Westinghouse Electric, AT&T, and the United Fruit Company, which owned a number of essential patents from its control over communications networks where it operated across Latin America. RCA president and later chairman David Sarnoff was a Russian Jewish immigrant with minimal formal education who had started his career as a teenage Marconi operator and claimed in a highly exaggerated tale to have been the Marconi operator in New York City who stayed by his transmitter for three straight days receiving messages confirming the fates of *Titanic* passengers. See, e.g., Louise M. Benjamin, *The NBC Advisory Council and Radio Programming, 1926–1945* (Southern Illinois Press, 2009), 3; and Michele Hilmes, "NBC and the Network Idea: Defining the 'American System,'" in *NBC: America's Network*, ed. Michele Hilmes (University of California Press, 2007), 10.

93 **In the meantime, hundreds:** Initially, NBC was split into two stations: NBC-Red, which ran on AT&T telephone lines and provided popular entertainment, and NBC-Blue, operating on Western Union telegraph connections and focusing on nonsponsored public service, cultural, and educational programs. By 1935, NBC had simplified the model and paid affiliates to take a slate of both sponsored and nonsponsored content. For additional background, see Hilmes, "NBC and the Network Idea," 5–23; Ralph Engelman, *Public Radio and Television in America: A Political History* (Sage Publications, 1996); Jim Cox, *American Radio Networks: A History* (McFarland, 2009); Christopher H. Sterling and John Michael Kitross, *Stay Tuned: A History of American Broadcasting*, 3rd ed. (Lawrence Erlbaum Associates, 2002).

93 **By 1937, 74 percent:** Hilmes, "NBC and the Network Idea," 5.

93 **While the neighborhood around:** Scott Childers, *Images of America: Chicago's WLS Radio* (Arcadia, 2008), 8.

93 **Innovative owner Burridge D. Butler:** Benjamin, *NBC Advisory Council*, 31, 35.

94 **WLS hired up-and-coming:** Childers, *Images of America*, 27, 31.

94 **"greatest single radio service":** Advertisement included in Childers, *Images of America*, 23.

94 **His first experience with radio:** Scottdale Historical Society, "Whispers of the Past—Herb Morrison and the Hindenburg," posted May 12, 2022, by Whispers of the Past, YouTube, youtube.com/watch?v=7Gs3DteAjDs&t=15s; Official Register of the Officers and Cadets, United States Military Academy, for 1925, courtesy of United States Military Academy, West Point, New York.

95 **Morrison worked various jobs:** "Around the Dial," *Stand By*, February 13, 1937, 13.

95 **The station did not need:** Scottdale Historical Society, "Whispers of the Past."

95 **From there Morrison followed:** "Around the Dial," 13.

95 **This had been NBC's official:** Michael McCarthy, "Crash of the *Hindenburg* (Herbert Morrison, reporting) (May 6, 1937)," Library of Congress, loc.gov/static/programs/national-recording-preservation-board/documents/Hindenburg.pdf.

95 **Stations were also concerned:** Brian Williams, host, *We Interrupt This Broadcast*, podcast, season 1, episode 1, "The Hindenburg Explosion—'Oh, the Humanity!'—(May 6, 1937)," July 20, 2021.

95 **Frequencies were not unlimited:** Marvin R. Bensman, "Regulation of Broadcasting by the Department of Commerce, 1921–1927," in *American Broadcasting: A Source Book on the History of Radio and Television*, ed. Lawrence W. Lichty and Malachi C. Topping (Hastings House, 1975), 550, quoting Secretary Herbert Hoover to Commissioner Carson, August 5, 1922, RG 40, National Archives and Records Administration at College Park; also see Hilmes, "NBC and the Network Idea," 11.

96 **In exchange for better:** Bensman, "Regulation of Broadcasting," 550–51, quoting *Hearings Before the Committee on Interstate Commerce*, U.S. Senate, 71st Cong., 1st Sess., May 24, 1929, 1071.

96 **Ultimately, this licensing scheme:** Bensman, "Regulation of Broadcasting," 553.

96 **In the early years:** Museum of Magnetic Sound Recording, "Manufacturer Profiles: Presto Recording Corporation," museumofmagneticsoundrecording.org/Manufacturers Presto.html.

96 **Starting in 1935:** "NBC Radio Broadcasts," The National Broadcasting Company at the Library of Congress, Library of Congress Research Guides, guides.loc.gov/nbc /radio-collections/broadcasts.

96 **In Morrison's opinion:** Herbert Morrison and Joseph Spah, interview in *Catastrophe: No Safe Place*, directed by Dan Gingold (Alan Landsburg Productions, 1980); Scottdale Historical Society, "Whispers of the Past"; Jesse Chapman, "Hindenburg Coverage Part of Movie," *Roanoke Times*, December 21, 1975; Carole Kass, "Hindenburg Crash Film Recalls Newsman's Feat in Recording," *Richmond (VA) Times-Dispatch*, December 14, 1975; Jim Marrs, "Hindenburg Tragedy Broadcaster Optimistic: A Dirigible in Your Future," *Fort Worth Star-Telegram*, December 26, 1975; "Announcer Recalls Tragedy," *Record Searchlight* (Redding, CA), May 9, 1987; Williams, *We Interrupt This Broadcast*, "The Hindenburg Explosion."

97 **In large part, credit:** "Around the Dial," *Stand By*, February 13, 1937, 13; "WLS Daily Programs," *Stand By*, February 13, 1937, 18.

97 **From Pittsburgh to southern:** "Radio on Duty at the Flood," *Stand By*, February 13, 1937; Bob Strickley, "79 Years Ago the 1937 Flood Crests at 79.9 Feet," *Cincinnati Enquirer*, January 26, 2016; NOAA National Weather Service, "1937 Ohio River Record Flood," weather.gov/iln/1937OhioRiverFlood#:~:text=The%201937%20flood%20 remains%20the,the%20Mississippi%20at%20Cairo%2C%20IL; Christopher Havern, "The Long Blue Line: Ohio River, 1937—Coast Guard's Largest Flood Response 85 Years Ago!," United States Coast Guard, July 29, 2022, mycg.uscg.mil/News/Article /3102189/the-long-blue-line-ohio-river-1937coast-guards-largest-flood-response-85 -years; excerpt from David Welky, *The Thousand Year Flood: The Ohio-Mississippi Disaster of 1937* (University of Chicago Press, 2011), available at press.uchicago.edu/books /excerpt/2012/welky_thousand-year.html.

98 **"You have no idea":** Jack Holden, "Ad Lib!," *Stand By*, February 13, 1937, 4.

98 **Motivated somewhat by:** Robert J. Serling, *Eagle: The Story of American Airlines* (St. Martin's, 1985), 93, 97–100; "Around the Dial," 13; Sterling and Kitross, *Stay Tuned*, 195.

98 **One person was so moved:** "Thank You!," *Stand By*, February 13, 1937, 5; "Herb Morrison and the Hindenburg."

99 **Since his days in Scottdale:** "Around the Dial," 13.

99 **unmarried "available bachelor":** Holden, "Ad Lib!," 4; Around the Dial," 13.

99 **However, if you asked:** Charles Nehlsen to John Toland, June 27, 1956, and July 14, 1956, box 99, folder 2, John Toland Papers, Manuscript Division, Library of Congress, Washington, DC.

99 **The fatal-accident rate:** U.S. Department of Commerce, Bureau of the Census, Mortality Statistics 1935: 36th Annual Report, 17, cdc.gov/nchs/data/vsushistorical/mortstatsh_1935.pdf.

100 **For non-carrier-operated flights:** United States Census Bureau, "Historical Statistics of the United States, 1789–1945," Series K 265-273—Air Transport—Accidents: 1927–1945, 225, census.gov/library/publications/1949/compendia/hist_stats_1789-1945.html.

100 **The DC-3's sleek design:** Serling, *Eagle*, 99–100.

100 **"Say! These new":** Serling, *Eagle*, 102–3.

101 **On its first arrival:** Serling, *Eagle*, 103.

101 **The Lakehurst Naval Air Station:** "Lakehurst Set for Handling of Hindenburg," *Springfield (MA) Daily Republican*, May 4, 1937.

101 **The Presto Recording Corporation:** "Announcer Recalls Tragedy," *Record Searchlight* (Redding, CA), May 9, 1987; "Herb Morrison and the Hindenburg"; Nehlsen to Toland, June 27, 1956, and July 14, 1956.

101 **Once Morrison and American:** "Under Fire!," *Stand By*, May 15, 1937, 2; Herbert Morrison, Hindenburg broadcast, May 6, 1937.

102 **Morrison even secured permission:** Williams, *We Interrupt This Broadcast*, "The Hindenburg Explosion."

102 **But when he presented:** In various interviews later in life, Morrison spoke about how the station was reluctant to let him make the broadcast. See, e.g. Michael Capuzzo, "'Oh, the Humanity of It All!,'" *Philadelphia Inquirer*, May 6, 1987; Williams, *We Interrupt This Broadcast,* "The Hindenburg Explosion."

102 **It likely also did not help:** See examples of coverage of the *Hindenburg*'s 1936 flights in Midwestern and Western newspapers: William C. Utley, "Transatlantic Air Service Begins," *Weekly Graphic* (Kirksville, MO), May 22, 1936; "Hindenburg Zeppelin Has Good Start on Transocean Hop to U.S.," *Daily Missoulian*, May 7, 1936; "Tail Wind Aid to Hindenburg," *Waco Times-Herald*, May 13, 1936; "New Takeoff Method Used by Hindenburg," *Richmond (IN) Item*, May 21, 1936.

102 **But it would be a real:** Chapman, "Hindenburg Coverage Part of Movie."

102 **What if, Morrison suggested:** As noted in "Herb Morrison and the Hindenburg."

103 **On the morning of May 4:** See, e.g., the AP's syndicated article "Zeppelin Hindenburg Off for United States," *Winston-Salem Journal*, May 4, 1937, and the UP's similar announcement, "Hindenburg on Way to America," *Berkshire Eagle* (Pittsfield, MA), May 4, 1937.

Chapter 11

104 **Though rotating shifts:** W. E. von Medem, *Kabinenjunge Werner Franz vom Luftschiff "Hindenburg"* (Franz Schneider Verlag, 1938), 55.

104 **The overnight crew:** Die Aufzeichnungen des Luftschiffstewards Wilhelm Balla, LZ 129, BMA I, Zeppelin Museum, Friedrichshafen; main exhibit, Zeppelin Museum, Friedrichshafen.

104 **The roughly dozen:** Harold G. Dick and Douglas H. Robinson, *The Golden Age of the Great Passenger Airships: Graf Zeppelin & Hindenburg* (Smithsonian Institution Press, 1985), 97.

104 **Balla had taken Franz:** Die Aufzeichnungen des Luftschiffstewards.

104 **"wash off the equator":** von Medem, *Kabinenjunge Werner Franz*, 67–68; Fragen (Werner Franz) LZ 129, BMA I, Zeppelin Museum, Friedrichshafen. The illustration of the certificate is included in Ernst A. Lehmann, *Zeppelin: The Story of Lighter-Than-Air Craft*, rev. ed. (Fonthill, 2015), 306.

105 **Werner Franz's days:** von Medem, *Kabinenjunge Werner Franz*, 21, 29, 45, 53, 55, 59; Fragen (Werner Franz).

105 **The twelve officers' bunks:** Dick and Robinson, *Golden Age*, 97.

106 **Back in the early 1920s:** Emilie Imhof, Ausstellung "Die Schwestern des Ikarus—Frau und Flug," June–September 2004, LZ 129, BMA II, complied from LZA 6/341, LZA 16/339, BMA II, Zeppelin Museum, Friedrichshafen; "The Feminine Touch," *The Aeroplane*, October 7, 1936, 460, LZ 129, BMA II, Zeppelin Museum, Friedrichshafen.

106 **After taking a quick:** von Medem, *Kabinenjunge Werner Franz*, 55; Fragen (Werner Franz).

107 **The crew accessed:** A scale replica of the control gondola is available inside the historic Hangar No.1 at Joint Base McGuire-Dix-Lakehurst, tour and information courtesy of 87th Air Base Wing Historian James Warrick. See also Dick and Robinson, *Golden Age*, 89–90.

107 **Unfortunately, that morning:** Margaret Mather, "I Was on the Hindenburg," *Harper's Monthly*, November 1937; Leonhard Adelt, "The Last Trip of the Hindenburg," *Reader's Digest*, November 1937.

107 **While Franz was sleeping:** Standortmeldungen von L.S. Hindenburg auf seiner letzen Fahrt nach USA, LZ 17/0567, Zeppelin Museum, Friedrichshafen.

Chapter 12

109 **It was really rather:** South Trimble to J. Edgar Hoover from South Trimble, July 1, 1937, FBI Hindenburg Case Files; Joseph Spah baggage receipt, Spah Family Papers; Joseph Spah list of lost belongings, Spah Family Papers; German family members to Joseph Spah, May 7, 1937, Spah Family Papers; Walter Ziegler Testimony, May 20, 1937 RG 197, box 8, National Archives and Records Administration at College Park.

109 **The dog, Ulla:** John Toland Interview with Mrs. Joseph Spah in Queens, "Evening, Nov. 25," box 99, folder 1, John Toland Papers, Manuscript Division, Library of Con-

gress, Washington, DC; Marilyn Spah Kelly and Jane Kelly, interview with the author, May 5, 2024; Victoria Spah, *The Spah Family: Home Movies* (self-published, 2006); Joseph Spah ID cards, Joseph Spah contract for dog, and Joseph Spah list of lost belongings, Spah Family Papers.

109 **He had purchased Ulla:** John Toland Interview with Mrs. Joseph Spah; Marilyn Spah Kelly and Jane Kelly, interview with the author; Spah, *Spah Family.* Various newspaper clippings have Joseph Spah performing across the UK from September 1936 through March 1937 before moving on to Germany. See, e.g. "Theaters, Cinemas, and Entertainments," *Evening Chronicle* (Newcastle, UK), September 18, 1936; and "Lucienne Boyer's Variety Debut," *Daily Telegraph,* March 9, 1937.

109 **They wanted to publicize:** Joseph Spah, interview in *Survival!,* produced by Sherman Grinberg, hosted by James Whitmore, 1964, Spah Family Papers.

109 **his "new pal":** Vera Spah to Joseph Spah, April 18, 1937; Joseph Spah list of lost belongings, Spah Family Papers. $250 in 1937 is about $5,000 in 2025.

110 **"getting so thrilled":** Vera Spah to Joseph Spah, April 18, 1937.

110 **had contacted him in Munich:** "In 'Hindenburg' Disaster," *Performer,* May 13, 1937; John Toland Interview with Mrs. Joseph Spah; Marilyn Spah Kelly and Jane Kelly, interview with the author; Spah, *Spah Family.*

110 **trick bicycle rider Joe Jackson:** Jackson was a natural comedian and practical joker. He lived on Greenwood Lake in New York, where he had a boat on which he would take his guests that was designed to partially fill up with water, and a collapsible outhouse whose walls he would pull down on unsuspecting visitors at the most inopportune moment. Marilyn Spah Kelly and Jane Kelly, interview with the author; Spah, *Spah Family.*

110 **he discovered that *Hindenburg* tickets:** Liste über ausgegebene Fahrscheine LS "HINDENBURG" Frankfurt-Lakehurst, 3 Mai, 1 Nordamerikafahrt 1937, Zeppelin Museum, Friedrichshafen; letter from Hamburg-America Agent, May 8, 1937, Spah Family Papers. It is possible Radio City producer Leon Leonidoff covered the cost of the booking. Jack O'Brien, "The Voice of Broadway," Spah Family Papers.

110 **"Oh, wait until":** Marilyn Spah Kelly and Jane Kelly, interview with the author; Spah, *Spah Family*; John Toland Interview with Mrs. Joseph Spah.

110 **In the meantime, Jackson:** Joe Jackson Jr. to Joseph Spah, May 7, 1937, Spah Family Papers.

110 **Perhaps, Benny thought:** Marilyn Spah Kelly and Jane Kelly, interview with the author; Spah, *Spah Family*; John Toland Interview with Mrs. Joseph Spah.

110 **"aerial journey into":** Die Aufzeichnungen des Luftschiffstewards Wilhelm Balla, LZ 129, BMA I, Zeppelin Museum, Friedrichshafen.

111 **In his act, he dressed:** Marilyn Spah Kelly and Jane Kelly, interview with the author; Spah, *Spah Family.*

111 **In 1932, his agent:** Marilyn Spah Kelly and Jane Kelly, interview with the author; Spah, *Spah Family.* A short video of Spah's Chanin Building performance can be found online at youtube.com/watch?v=jg9gh9P4TT0, courtesy of Victoria Spah.

112 **Everywhere he went:** Marilyn Spah Kelly and Jane Kelly, interview with the author.

112 **Benny was born:** Marilyn Spah Kelly and Jane Kelly, interview with the author; "Actor Dives into Lake; Calls Doc," *The Billboard*, June 26, 1926, Joseph Spah scrapbook, Spah Family Papers.

112 **For several hundred years:** German nationalist imperialist politician and writer Heinrich von Treitschke suggested, "We Germans, who know Germany and France, know better what is good for Alsace than the unhappy people themselves who through their French associations have lived in ignorance of the new Germany." Adolf Hausrath, "Treitschke: A Study of His Life and Work," foreword to *Treitschke: His Doctrine of German Destiny and of International Relations* (G. P. Putnam's Sons, 1914).

113 **Benny was the fourth:** Marilyn Spah Kelly and Jane Kelly, interview with the author.

113 **When Benny was eight:** Spah, *Spah Family*.

113 **By eleven, he was still:** "Falling to the Stage," *New York Times*, December 17, 1939, reproduced in Spah, *Spah Family*.

113 **At fourteen, he briefly:** Spah, *Spah Family*.

113 **His contract was supposed:** Joseph Spah tailor's apprentice contract, Spah Family Papers.

113 **Benny and a fellow:** "Falling to the Stage."

114 **By the time he was sixteen:** Joseph Späh United States of America Declaration of Intention, Form 2203, U.S. Department of Labor, Naturalization Service, January 9, 1925, Spah Family Papers.

114 **He found himself genuinely perplexed:** Marilyn Spah Kelly and Jane Kelly, interview with the author.

114 **He also had remarkable:** Vertrag für Truppenmitglieder, Spah Family Papers.

114 **Initially, his English:** William Bloeth, "Ben Dova Gets High but Stays on Ground," *New York World-Telegram*, undated, Spah Family Papers.

114 **Benny and Bernt:** Spah, *Spah Family*.

114 **"It is my bona fide intention":** Joseph Späh United States of America Declaration of Intention.

114 **He enjoyed amateur:** Marilyn Spah Kelly and Jane Kelly, interview with the author.

115 **Shortly after he arrived:** Spah, *Spah Family*.

115 **Within a year, he had:** Joseph Spah U.S. Volunteer Air Service Notification of Enlistment Acceptance, Spah Family Papers.

115 **Before he met Vera:** Spah, *Spah Family*; Marilyn Spah Kelly and Jane Kelly, interview with the author.

115 **Benny had also survived:** Bloeth, "Ben Dova Gets High"; John Toland Interview with Mrs. Joseph Spah; Marilyn Spah Kelly and Jane Kelly, interview with the author.

115 **Though he would always retain:** Spah, *Spah Family*; Marilyn Spah Kelly and Jane Kelly, interview with the author.

116 **"Herr Ben Dova!":** Letter to Joseph Spah, Düsseldorf, May 2, 1934, Spah Family Papers.

116 **Inside, there were no symbols:** Officer's uniform, Zeppelin-Museum, Zeppelinheim.

116 **In fact, Benny quite liked:** Marilyn Spah Kelly and Jane Kelly, interview with the author; Spah, *Spah Family*.

116 **Benny had run into Lehmann:** John Toland, "Terror in the Twilight," *Saturday Evening Post*, December 8, 1956; Joseph Spah to Hans Hörmann, November 1, 1976; Otto Edenharter to Joseph Spah, July 31, 1937, Spah Family Papers.

116 **in his private life:** Marilyn Spah Kelly and Jane Kelly, interview with the author.

117 **something of a "flying jinx":** Bloeth, "Ben Dova Gets High." Jonah was the biblical prophet who fled by ship from God's command to preach in the city of Nineveh. As the story went, as punishment for Jonah's disobedience, God sent a storm that tormented Jonah's ship until the sailors tossed him overboard, where he was famously swallowed by a whale.

117 **"You don't need to worry":** John Toland Interview with Mrs. Joseph Spah.

Chapter 13

118 **Lehmann had transported:** Ernst A. Lehmann, *Zeppelin: The Story of Lighter-Than-Air Craft*, rev. ed. (Fonthill, 2015), 308.

118 **the silent film actor:** Smithsonian National Postal Museum, "Object Spotlight: Hindenburg Postcard Signed by Douglas Fairbanks," postalmuseum.si.edu/collections/object-spotlight/hindenburg-postcard-signed-by-douglas-fairbanks; Die Aufzeichnungen des Luftschiffstewards Wilhelm Balla, LZ 129, BMA I, Zeppelin Museum, Friedrichshafen.

119 **"accustomed to the unusual":** Lehmann, *Zeppelin*, 241.

119 **"What was a miracle":** Lehmann, *Zeppelin*, 291.

119 **"In developing aviation":** Charles A. Lindbergh, *The Spirit of St. Louis* (Charles Scribner's Sons, 1953), 288–89.

119 **Only an airman knew:** Lehmann, *Zeppelin*, 156.

119 **"benumbing" and "monstrous":** Lehmann, *Zeppelin*, 265.

119 **So uncharted was their route:** "The First Airship Flight Around the World," *National Geographic* 57, no. 6 (June 1930), courtesy of Musée de l'Air et de l'Espace, Le Bourget; Vortrag von Luftschiffkapitän Heinrich Bauer (1937) in Frankfurt/Main (in abgeänderter Form später und auch in anderen Städten) "Luftschiff marsch!," LZ 129, BMA I, Zeppelin Museum, Friedrichshafen.

119 **it was a "refreshing":** Lehmann, *Zeppelin*, 265–66.

119 **"the prophetic vision":** *Airship Voyages Made Easy* (Deutsche Zeppelin-Reederei, 1937, reprinted 1976), 3.

120 **It had been aggressively:** Mr. Tustain, Report: The Zeppelin Transport COY, May 4, 1937, LZA 17/196, Zeppelin Museum, Friedrichshafen; Bericht über den Besuch einiger Agenturen in Paris, April 13–16, 1937, Besuchsbericht, Rom, March 23, 1937, Besuchsbericht, Genua, March 22, 1937, Bericht des Herren H. M. Wronsky über seine Reisen ach U.S.A., August 5, 1936, LZA 17/197, Zeppelin Museum, Friedrichshafen; Tätigkeitsbericht der Werbestelle für das Jahr 1936 und 1937, June 4, 1937, LZA 17/567, Zeppelin Museum, Friedrichshafen.

120 **So far, he had neglected:** George Grant, "Notes on a Voyage of the AIRSHIP 'HINDENBURG' Under the Command of Captain Pruss," May 6, 1937, National Archives

and Records Administration at College Park, available online at Patrick Russell, "George Grant," *Faces of the Hindenburg* (blog), January 21, 2009, facesofthehindenburg.blogspot.com/2009/01/george-grant.html.

120 **for these "little guests":** Hinrich Schröder to DZR, September 25, 1936, LZ 129, BMA II, Zeppelin Museum, Friedrichshafen.

121 **DZR's biggest effort:** Willy von Meister to Ernst Lehmann, January 10, 1937, 7, LZA 17/196, Zeppelin Museum, Friedrichshafen.

121 **"Our century has been called":** Lehmann, *Zeppelin*, 209.

121 **They included Wall Street:** $1 billion in 1937 is approximately $22 billion in 2025. At the conclusion of the flight, each guest was given a souvenir ashtray adorned with a glass airship filled with Esso diesel fuel. Esso (the trading name of Standard Oil of New Jersey, with "Esso" being the S and O of "Standard Oil" pronounced phonetically) supplied the engine fuel and the hydrogen and cosponsored the trip. Dan Grossman, "Hindenburg 'Millionaires Flight,'" Airships.net, n.d., airships.net/hindenburg/flight-schedule/millionaire-flight.

121 **It was only May:** Es waren reserviert, bezw. gebucht per 6. Mai 1937, Nordamerika, LZA 17/567, Zeppelin Museum, Friedrichshafen.

121 **Belin was related:** Ian Shapira, "A Family's Hidden History Is Revealed After the Sale of Their Grand Georgetown Estate," *Washington Post*, October 15, 2011; State Department Office of the Historian, "Ferdinand Lammot Belin (1881–1961)," history.state.gov/departmenthistory/people/belin-ferdinand-lammot; "Peter Belin Is Saved by Leap from Zeppelin," *Evening News* (Harrisburg, PA), May 7, 1937; "F. Lammot Belin Dies," *Washington Evening Star*, July 7, 1961; "Ferdinand Lammot Belin Dies," *Tribune* (Scranton, PA), July 7, 1961; "Yale Man Leaps from Hindenburg," *Yale Daily News*, May 7, 1937; Waverly Community House Archives, Special Collections, "Community Member Feature: F. Lammot 'Peter' Belin Jr.," September 19, 2016, wcharchives.wordpress.com/2016/09/19/community-member-feature-f-lammot-peter-belin-jr; "Waverly Community House to Host 50th Anniversary Celebration of Belin Arts Scholarship," *Times-Tribune*, (Scranton, PA), October 5, 2014; "Mary Cootes Is Engaged to Peter Belin," *Tribune* (Scranton, PA), December 5, 1938.

122 **Checking the airship's coordinates:** Willy von Meister to Ernst Lehmann, January 10, 1937, 12, LZA 17/196, Zeppelin Museum, Friedrichshafen; *Airship Voyages Made Easy* (Deutsche Zeppelin-Reederei, 1937, reprinted 1976), 12; Hindenburg Route Map belonging to Peter Belin, *Fire & Ice: Hindenburg and Titanic*, Smithsonian National Postal Museum, postalmuseum.si.edu/exhibition/fire-ice-hindenburg-and-titanic/exhibition#1.

122 **Feibusch was a German:** Martin Feibusch and Cheryl Ganz, "*Hindenburg* Crash Cover Forgeries and Passenger Moritz Feibusch," *Zeppelin Collector*, July 1998, 51–54; Moritz and Mignonne Feibusch Passports (1928, 1935), Landsturmstein Card (1906), and Quarantine Receipts from Moritz Feibusch and the Hindenburg, Magnes Collection of Jewish Art and Life, UC Berkeley; "The Original Nacional M. & F. Company of San Francisco Paid the Following for December 8, 1914," *L'Italia* (San Francisco),

December 19, 1914; "Man Known Here Among Victims of Burned Zep," *Oroville (CA) Mercury Register*, May 8, 1937; "Herr Hitler's £2,500 Gift," *Evening Standard* (London), May 7, 1937; "Feibusch Will to Be Probated," *San Francisco Examiner*, May 11, 1937.

123 **"*Souvenir de mon ascension*":** Feibusch and Ganz, "*Hindenburg* Crash Cover Forgeries," 51.

123 **Once again he had:** Feibusch and Ganz, "*Hindenburg* Crash Cover Forgeries," 51–54.

123 **Philip Mangone, for example:** "Philip Mangone, Couturier, Dead," *New York Times*, December 8, 1937.

123 **he had been booked to travel:** Sid Moody, "The Hindenburg Crash," *Morning Call* (Allentown, PA), May 6, 1962; Erik Larson, *Dead Wake* (Crown, 2015), 95.

124 **His booking on:** Elizabeth Henney, "Philip Mangone Insists Suits Make Any Woman Look 10 Years Younger," *Miami Herald*, January 1, 1951; Moody, "Hindenburg Crash."

124 **Von Meister, a tall:** "F.W. von Meister, 74, Airship Industry Pioneer," *Baltimore Sun*, July 8, 1978; Henry Cord Meyer, *Airshipmen, Businessmen, and Politics: 1890–1940* (Smithsonian Institution Press, 1991), 195–96; Leila von Meister, *Gathered Yesterdays* (Geoffrey Bles, 1963), 86.

124 **"Americans should not":** Willy von Meister to Ernst Lehmann, January 10, 1937, 5, LZA 17/196, Zeppelin Museum, Friedrichshafen.

124 **Menus and news:** von Meister to Lehmann, January 10, 1937, 7; Anregungen Rosendahl und von Meister für Unterhaltung der Passagiere an Board und Verbesserungen, November 19, 1936, LZA 196, Zeppelin Museum, Friedrichshafen.

124 **Von Meister also emphasized:** von Meister to Lehmann, January 10, 1937, 6–7.

125 **"It is very easy to imagine":** von Meister to Lehmann, January 10, 1937, 7–8.

125 **Passengers had complained:** Auszug aus einem Berich des Herrn Direktor Wronsky, March 30–April 10, 1936, LZA 17/197, Zeppelin Museum, Friedrichshafen; Grant, "Notes on a Voyage." Former passenger Clara Adams held the opposite opinion: "Passengers quickly became blasé and comported themselves within a few hours from the start exactly as though they were on shipboard at sea—even to putting their shoes outside cabin doors at night for shines and donning evening dress for dinner. But in my opinion the trip was too short that one should waste valuable time dressing up for dinner in elaborate style. The vast majority agreed that it was 'sensible' to remain simple in one's attire and that it was a lack of sportsmanship to appear in lacy evening gowns or stiff tuxedos." Descriptions of Hindenburg Flight, 1936, box 2, folder 11, Clara Adams Papers, UT Dallas Archives.

125 **"The kitchen," von Meister instructed:** von Meister to Lehmann, January 10, 1937, 9.

126 **"one felt like a boy":** "Payfarer," "Without a Roll to Rio," *The Aeroplane* (Le Bourget), April 1936.

126 **"drink less himself":** von Meister to Lehmann, January 10, 1937, 11.

126 **"according to American custom":** von Meister to Lehmann, January 10, 1937, 8.

126 **"these things don't cost much":** von Meister to Lehmann, January 10, 1937, 10–11.

126 **"only be of use":** von Meister to Lehmann, January 10, 1937, 10.

127 **"we are dealing with":** von Meister to Lehmann, January 10, 1937, 10.

127 **"Will men fly":** Charles A. Lindbergh, *The Spirit of St. Louis* (Charles Scribner's Sons, 1953), 288–89.

127 **"The fight to conquer":** Lehmann, *Zeppelin*, 321.

Chapter 14

128 **His ever-industrious friend:** Burtis Dolan to Miss Thompson, May 5, 1937, available in Dennis R. Kromm, "Homecoming," in *Compex: Combined Philatelic Exhibition of Chicagoland, Incorporated, Commemorating the 50th Anniversary of the Last Flight of the Hindenburg* (May 1987), 56; Burtis Dolan to William Miller, May 5, 1937, available at "Hindenburg's Post Room," *Fire & Ice: Hindenburg and Titanic*, Smithsonian National Postal Museum, postalmuseum.si.edu/exhibition/fire-ice-hindenburg-and-titanic-exhibition-mail-ships/hindenburgs-post-room.

128 **The two men set off:** Nelson Morris Testimony, May 28, 1937, RG 197, box 8, National Archives and Records Administration at College Park (NARA).

128 **Back then, Eckener:** Nelson Morris Testimony.

128 **This time, none:** George Grant Testimony, May 28, 1937, RG 197, box 8, NARA.

129 **After beginning his career:** Nachweis über die Zeit vom Tag der Schulentlassung bis zum Eintritt bei der Deutsche Zeppelin Reederei, February 12, 1938, LZ 129, BMA II, Zeppelin Museum, Friedrichshafen.

129 **By a quirk of design:** Harold G. Dick and Douglas H. Robinson, *The Golden Age of the Great Passenger Airships: Graf Zeppelin & Hindenburg* (Smithsonian Institution Press, 1985), 97.

129 **Their pots, pans:** Assorted photographs, LZF 129 series, Zeppelin Museum, Friedrichshafen.

129 **"It is false to imagine":** Ernst A. Lehmann, *Zeppelin: The Story of Lighter-Than-Air Craft*, rev. ed. (Fonthill, 2015), 314.

129 **Had their journey spanned:** See, e.g., Burtis Dolan to Mildred Dolan, February 6, 1937, Dolan Family Papers; Patrick Dolan, interview with the author, January 4, 2025; and Mary Alice Dolan Noone, interview with the author, February 16, 2024.

130 **The two friends were standing:** Dick and Robinson, *Golden Age*, 85, 91; Lehmann, *Zeppelin*, 234.

130 **Looking up, passengers:** Dan Grossman, "Myths About the Hindenburg Crash," Airships.net, n.d., airships.net/hindenburg/disaster/myths.

130 **Notably, the cover:** *NOVA*, season 48, episode 8, "Hindenburg: The New Evidence," written by Rushmore DeNooyer, directed by Kirk Wolfinger, aired May 19, 2021, on PBS.

130 **the *Graf Zeppelin* was caught:** Hans von Schiller, "Hoch über dem Meer stieg Knut Eckener aus," *Südkurier*, January 19, 1968, LZ 129, BMA I, Zeppelin Museum, Friedrichshafen.

131 **One had to be sure-footed:** Eugen Nunnenmacher, "Im Luftschiff über Länder und Meere," 1936, BMA II, Zeppelin Museum, Friedrichshafen.

131 **In the keel area:** Douglas H. Robinson, "You Don't Fly in an Airship, You Go Voyaging," in *LZ 129 "Hindenburg,"* Famous Aircraft Series (Arco, 1964).

131 **The most interesting cargo:** Emil Stoeckle Testimony, May 14, 1937, RG 197, box 7, NARA; Eugene Schauble Testimony, May 19, 1937, RG 197, box 7, NARA; Hugo Eckener, *My Zeppelins* (Arno Press: 1980), 174–75.

131 **"baby whales swimming":** Lehmann, *Zeppelin*, 230. An example of the engine catwalk is found at Zeppelin-Museum, Zeppelinheim.

131 **The engines each weighed:** Douglas H. Robinson, "Airship Diesels," in *LZ 129 "Hindenburg"*; Dick and Robinson, *Golden Age*, 85.

131 **Telephone lines ran:** Dick and Robinson, *Golden Age*, 90.

132 **Here, the catwalks:** Max Pruss, Columbia University Oral History Collection, 11–12; Hans Freund Testimony, May 17, 1937, RG 197, box 7, NARA. Some, like historian John Toland, have suggested that the axial walkway was covered with rubber and that the riggers working among the gas cells were required to wear asbestos coveralls so as not to conduct any static electricity, but this was not true.

132 **"giant mushrooms in a prehistoric":** Lehmann, *Zeppelin*, 68.

132 **There was so much gas:** Lehmann, *Zeppelin*, 230.

132 **In the last decade, American engineers:** "The Zeppelin L.Z. 129—'Hindenburg,'" *Aeroplane* (Le Bourget), April 29, 1936, 525; Dick and Robinson, *Golden Age*, 93; Lehmann, *Zeppelin*, 68.

132 **The filmstoff was somewhat:** Photograph, LZF 129/0608, Zeppelin Museum, Friedrichshafen.

132 **While zeppelins often flew:** Hugo Eckener, "Brief Instructions and Practical Hints for Piloting Zeppelin Airships for the Flight Personnel of the 'DELAG,'" 1919, reprinted in Robinson, *LZ 129 "Hindenburg"*; Robinson, "You Don't Fly"; Douglas H. Robinson, "There Were Giants in Those Days," in *LZ 129 "Hindenburg"*; Dick and Robinson, *Golden Age*, 65–66; Lehmann, *Zeppelin*, 239.

133 **Luftschiffbau Zeppelin had experimented:** Harold G. Dick, "The Use of Hydrogen in the Hindenburg," box 7, FF 7, Harold G. Dick Papers, Wichita State University; Dick and Robinson, *Golden Age*, 98–99.

133 **Their eventual, proposed solution:** Robinson, "There Were Giants"; Robinson, "You Don't Fly"; W. B. Courtney, "Sky Cruise," *Colliers*, May 8, 1937, 45, RG 197, box 14, NARA; Dick and Robinson, *Golden Age*, 93.

134 **"That is really no inducement":** Henry Cord Meyer, *Airshipmen, Businessmen, and Politics: 1890–1940* (Smithsonian Institution Press, 1991), 202.

134 **Second, for a transportation system:** Besprechungsergebnis der Sitzung vom 20. November 1936, 6, RZ 206/32997, Politisches Archiv des Auswärtiges Amts, Bundesarchiv, Berlin-Lichterfelde; Dick and Robinson, *Golden Age*, 100–101.

134 **In the event the Americans:** Dick and Robinson, *Golden Age*, 101; Margaret Mather, "I Was on the Hindenburg," *Harper's Monthly*, November 1937.

135 **"experience indicates that the":** Eckener, "Brief Instructions and Practical Hints."

136 **At 4:00 a.m. on December 22:** For more about the Morris & Company fire, see Becky Schlickerman, "100 Years Since Fire Raged in the Yards: Relatives, Historians Remember Chicago's 'Forgotten Tragedy,'" *Chicago Tribune*, December 21, 2010; Firefighter Record, ILFODD: Firefighter Memorial, Illinois Fire Service Institute, fsi.illinois.edu

/content/library/IFLODD/search/firefighter_detail.cfm?ff_id=324; Adam Groves, "Union Stockyards Fire, Chicago: December 22, 1910," Illinois Fire Service Institute (IFSI), Significant Fires and Emergencies in Illinois History, University of Illinois Urbana-Champaign; "Nelson Morris and Company Fire, Firemen Spraying over a Collapsed Wall on Fire," photograph DN-0056330, Chicago History Museum.

136 **Twenty-seven years later:** The Chicago Union Stockyards fire is the fourth-greatest loss of firefighters in U.S. history, with the largest being 9/11 (343 firefighters).

136 **"The whole thing always seems":** Walter Dornberger, *V-2* (Viking Press, 1954), 66, also quoted in Robinson, "There Were Giants." Hitler also told famous German boxer Max Schmeling that he had no interest in flying in a zeppelin despite having no qualms about airplanes. "Reich Undaunted by Loss of Big Zep, Rushing Another," *Gazette and Daily* (York, PA), May 8, 1937, courtesy of 87th Air Base Wing Historian.

137 **"I couldn't think":** Bella Fromm, *Blood and Banquets: A Berlin Social Diary* (Birch Lane Press, 1991), 219.

137 **Initially, they suggested:** Der Reichsminister der Luftfahrt, B I 3 Nr. 2004/35, Namensgebung des "LZ 129," July 6, 1935, R 43II/697b, Reichskanzlei, Bundesarchiv, Koblenz.

137 **for "linguistic reasons":** Der Reichsminister der Luftfahrt, B I 3 Nr. 2004/35, Der Staatssekretär und Chef der Reichskanzlei, Rk. 5679.35, Namensgebung des "LZ 129," July 16, 1935, R 43II/697b, Reichskanzlei, Bundesarchiv, Koblenz.

137 **The name was painted:** The name was set nine months before the airship was finished; however, it was not actually painted on the silver skin until three weeks after its first flight in March 1936, which was perhaps one additional source prompting the false rumors around the supposed naming controversy. Dan Grossman, "Happy Birthday, Hindenburg!—March 4, 1936," March 4, 2017, Airships.net, airships.net/blog/hindenburg-flight-march-4-1936. To apply the name *Hindenburg* to the airship, DZR commissioned Georg Wagner, an expert in scripts and typefaces, to design the unique script that would appear on its starboard side. The script's visual impression had to be instantly recognizable and evoke both its own and the airship's integral place in German culture, so Wagner decided on a custom version of the angular, historical Fraktur lettering deemed the official font of the Nazi regime for its supposed Germanic authenticity. In actuality, Fraktur, a calligraphy-like font where every stroke comprising each letter is clearly articulated, is much more difficult to read than a more modern, flowing font like Antiqua, which the Nazi regime adopted in 1941 after reversing course and banning Fraktur. After testing the lettering's visual effects by hanging the proposed design on the door of the hangar in Friedrichshafen, Wagner made some adjustments to improve long-distance identification, including increasing the spacing between letters. When the name was finally added to the airship's silver skin, it was fifty feet long and nearly nine feet high. Wagner was pleased with his contribution to the airship and the global recognition of Germanic writing and hoped that the *Hindenburg*'s example would "set the tone for all possible ways of advertising German cultural assets." Georg Wagner, "Deutsche Schrift in der Deutschen Luft- und Seefahrt," *Die zeitgemäße Schrift Studienhefte für Schrift u. Formgestaltung 1936*, July 1936, 49–54, Shelfmark 4 Graph. 506 e-1936/37, Bayerische Staatsbibliothek, Munich.

138 **Her anatomy classes:** Muriel Gardiner, *Code Name "Mary"* (Yale University Press, 1983), 43–44.

138 **Muriel had thought:** Gardiner, *Code Name "Mary,"* 45.

138 **Though she had a three-year-old:** Gardiner details her resistance work in chapter 2 of her memoir, *Code Name "Mary,"* 46–87. One of the people she hid was Kim Philby, a British intelligence officer later revealed to be a notorious double agent for the USSR, 51–53. Also see Katya Cengel, "The American Heiress Who Risked Everything to Resist the Nazis," *Smithsonian Magazine*, March 2023.

139 **She was hardly:** Gardiner, *Code Name "Mary,"* 10–11.

Chapter 15

140 **"The foreign correspondents":** William L. Shirer to Bob Pell, February 23, 1935, Correspondence, Correspondence by Date, folder 1935, William L. Shirer Papers, Coe College, Cedar Rapids, IA (WLSP).

140 **When Shirer and Young:** William L. Shirer, *Berlin Diary: The Journal of a Foreign Correspondent, 1934–1941,* rev. ed. (Bonanza Books, 1984), May 3, 1937, 71.

140 **"handsome into middle age":** Thomas Jones, *A Diary with Letters: 1931–1950* (Oxford University Press, 1954), 514–15. Lothian also considered himself a man of high Christian morals, particularly after having converted to Christian Science with his dear friend Nancy Astor.

140 **Though not presently active:** Margaret MacMillan, *Paris 1919: Six Months That Changed the World* (Random House, 2002), 42.

141 **"Oh, Göring asked":** Shirer, *Berlin Diary*, May 3, 1937, 71–72.

141 **Lothian also planned:** Frank McDonough, *The Hitler Years: Triumph, 1933–1939* (St. Martin's Press), 238. Lothian published this article in *The Nineteenth Century and After*, May 1937.

141 **"probably the most intelligent":** Shirer, *Berlin Diary*, May 3, 1937, 72.

141 **Ambassador Dodd, who would be seeing:** William E. Dodd Jr. and Martha Dodd, eds., *Ambassador Dodd's Diary, 1933–38* (Harcourt, Brace, 1941), May 6, 1937, 406–7.

141 **"a most especially undisciplined":** Jan Masaryk to John Gunther, January 14, 1937, box 34, Correspondence, series II, John Gunther Papers, University of Chicago.

142 **As he was drafting:** Albin Krebs, "John Gunther Dead; Wrote 'Inside' Books," *New York Times*, May 30, 1970.

142 **Nazis were simply "gangsters":** John Gunther, "After the Dollfuss Murder," Vienna, August 2, 1934, box 5, folder 8: Inside Europe, series I, John Gunther Papers, University of Chicago.

142 **"Tess's brother is a 19":** William L. Shirer to John Gunther, "Sunday" (undated) 1934, Correspondence, 1927-1937 P–S, box 5, series II, John Gunther Papers, University of Chicago.

142 **The rising Nazi threat:** Shirer, *Berlin Diary*, August 26, 1934, 14.

143 **"I was pretty heartbroken":** John Gunther to Hal O'Flaherty, June 3, 1933, Chicago Daily News 1933, box 5, series II, John Gunter Papers, University of Chicago.

143 **"more diversified report":** Hal O'Flaherty to John Gunther, September 16, 1933, Chicago Daily News 1933, box 5, series II, John Gunther Papers, University of Chicago.

143 **"hooked-cross boys":** William L. Shirer to Bob Pell, February 23, 1935, Correspondence, Correspondence by Date, folder 1935, WLSP.

144 **The *Volkswagen* (or "people's car"):** Allison C. Meier, "An Affordable Radio Brought Nazi Propaganda Home," *JSTOR Daily*, August 20, 2018, daily.jstor.org/an-affordable-radio-brought-nazi-propaganda-home.

144 **"Those who do not possess":** William L. Shirer, "German Conscription: Celebration on Heldengedenktag in Opera," March 18, 1935, Journalist-Correspondent, Cables, Dispatches, Mail Stories, folder Mail Stories (with Notes) 1935–1938, WLSP.

144 **"report at first hand":** William L. Shirer, *20th Century Journey*, vol. 1, *The Start: 1904–1930* (Simon & Schuster, 1976), 321.

144 **"where are we to belong":** George Weller to William L. Shirer, October 17, 1935, Correspondence, Correspondence by Date, folder 1935, WLSP.

145 **The news made up:** Erik Barnouw, *A History of Broadcasting in the United States,* vol. 2, *The Golden Web: 1933 to 1945* (Oxford University Press, 1968), 17; George H. Douglas, *The Early Days of Radio Broadcasting* (McFarland, 1987), 98, 103, 111–12; Brian Williams, host, *We Interrupt This Broadcast*, podcast, season 1, episode 1, "The Hindenburg Explosion—'Oh, the Humanity!'—(May 6, 1937)," July 20, 2021.

145 **Occasionally, stations would broadcast:** Christopher H. Sterling and John Michael Kitross, *Stay Tuned: A History of American Broadcasting*, 3rd ed. (Lawrence Erlbaum Associates, 2002), 87; Brian Williams, host, *We Interrupt This Broadcast*, podcast, season 2, episode 1, "The War of the Worlds: The Original 'Deepfake' of 1938," October 27, 2021.

145 **Some, like consumer goods:** Hilmes, "NBC and the Network Idea" in Hilmes (ed.), *NBC: America's Network*, 17–18; Barnouw, *A History of Broadcasting in the United States*, vol. 2, 17. By the mid-1930s, large companies were increasingly producing radio entertainment programs in their own in-house creative studios.

146 **"Say YES to Hitler":** Albert Sammt, *Mein Leben für den Zeppelin* (Verlag Pestalozzi Kinderdorf Wahlwies, 1980), 136–38.

146 **Germany produced no cotton:** Raymond C. Ahl, "The Nazi-Soviet Pact: Its Effects upon the German War Economy" (master's thesis, Marquette University, 1966), marquette.edu/library/theses/already_uploaded_to_IR/ahl_r_1966.pdf.

146 **"As its official name":** William L. Shirer, Four Year Plan article series, fourth article, Journalist-Correspondent, Cables, Dispatches, Mail Stories, folder Four Year Plan 1936, WLSP; Shirer, *Berlin Diary*, September 27, 1937, 85.

146 **"I say then":** William L. Shirer to Bob Pell, February 23, 1935, Correspondence, Correspondence by Date, folder 1935, WLSP.

147 **"I don't believe":** Jan Masaryk to John Gunther, January 14, 1937, box 34, Correspondence, series II, John Gunther Papers, University of Chicago. After the war, Jan Masaryk returned to Czechoslovakia. He was found dead in his pajamas in the courtyard of the Czech Foreign Ministry, which Communist leadership claimed was the re-

sult of a suicide; however, there has long been speculation he was murdered at the Communist government's behest by defenestration.

147 **"eternal law of life":** Shirer, *20th Century Journey,* vol. 1, 126.

147 **Shirer's father, the grandson:** Shirer, *20th Century Journey*, vol. 1, 80–81, 91–93.

147 **"Throughout the world there is":** "The World Citizen," Coe College—Seward Shirer, 1893 Interstate Oratorical Contest at Ohio State University, General Files, folder: "Shirer, Seward Smith - 1913," WLSP.

148 **"outdoing themselves to create":** Shirer, *Berlin Diary*, July 27, 1936, and August 16, 1936, 64–65.

148 **"pulled down all":** Shirer, *Berlin Diary*, January 23, 1936, 44–46.

148 **to "enlighten" them:** Shirer, *Berlin Diary*, February 1936, 47.

148 **"American correspondents were unfair":** Shirer, *Berlin Diary*, August 16, 1936, 65–66. Ralph Barnes would go on to become the first American journalist killed during World War II when a plane on which he and three others were traveling crashed in Yugoslavia en route to cover Mussolini's invasion of Greece.

149 **"temptation of scientific power":** Charles A. Lindbergh, *Of Flight and Life* (Charles Scribner's Sons, 1948), 18–19.

149 **"spoke out somewhat":** Shirer, *Berlin Diary*, July 23, 1936, 63.

149 **Just over a year earlier:** Shirer, *Berlin Diary*, March 18, 1935, 35.

149 **showed "no enthusiasm":** Shirer, *Berlin Diary*, July 23, 1936, 64.

150 **so "favourably impressed":** Shirer, *Berlin Diary*, July 23, 1936, 64.

150 **such a "shining beginning":** Shirer, *20th Century Journey,* vol. 1, 344.

150 **instead of covering lofty:** Shirer, *20th Century Journey,* vol. 1, 322–23, 330–31. The French Open tennis tournament, now known as Roland-Garros, became known as such only after Stade Roland Garros, named in honor of the famous World War I French aviator, was constructed in 1928.

150 **his "cannon-ball" serve:** Shirer, *20th Century Journey,* vol. 1, 330.

151 **Shirer had been keen:** Shirer, *20th Century Journey,* vol. 1, 110.

151 **"half-dozen sputtering":** Shirer, *20th Century Journey,* vol. 1, 110.

151 **In early May 1927:** Shirer, *20th Century Journey,* vol. 1, 325–26.

151 **On May 20:** Shirer, *20th Century Journey,* vol. 1, 330–31. See also Charles A. Lindbergh, *The Spirit of St. Louis* (Charles Scribner's Sons, 1953), 188; and Charles A. Lindbergh, "*We*" (G. P. Putnam's Sons, 1927), 216.

152 **"Every motor vehicle":** Shirer, *20th Century Journey,* vol. 1, 333–34.

152 **utter "bedlam" broke out:** Shirer, *20th Century Journey,* vol. 1, 335–37. See also Lindbergh, *Spirit of St. Louis*, 495–97; and Lindbergh, "*We,*" 224–26.

152 **By 4:00 a.m., Shirer:** Shirer, *20th Century Journey,* vol. 1, 339; Henry Wales, "Flies Atlantic Alone; 33 Hours 29 Minutes," *Chicago Tribune*, May 22, 1927. Unfortunately for Shirer, the article went out solely under Wales's byline.

153 **"Not bad . . . In fact":** Shirer, *20th Century Journey,* vol. 1, 339.

153 **"remained simple and modest":** Shirer, *20th Century Journey,* vol. 1, 340.

153 **four million people attended:** Alexander Rose, *Empires of the Sky: Zeppelins, Airplanes, and Two Men's Epic Duel to Rule the World* (Random House, 2020), 260–61.

153 **Souvenir seekers ransacked:** Bruce L. Larson, "Lindbergh's Return to Minnesota, 1927," *Minnesota History* 42, no. 4 (Winter 1970), 141–52.
153 **The U.S. Patent Office:** Jenifer Van Vleck, *Empire of the Air: Aviation and the American Ascendancy* (Harvard University Press, 2013), 52.
153 **There were, of course:** Lindbergh Display, Smithsonian National Air and Space Museum, Steven F. Udvar-Hazy Center.
153 **By the end of his:** Rose, *Empires of the Sky*, 261.
153 **"never seen a man":** Shirer, *20th Century Journey*, vol. 1, 340.
153 **"one authentic hero":** Shirer, *20th Century Journey*, vol. 1, 342–43.
154 **"bestow upon his countrymen":** Shirer, *20th Century Journey*, vol. 1, 342, quoting Kenneth S. Davis, *The Hero: Charles A. Lindbergh and the American Dream* (Doubleday, 1959), 10.
154 **"shockingly admiring of a mindless":** Shirer, *20th Century Journey*, vol. 1, 343.
154 **"Is aviation too arrogant?":** Lindbergh, *Spirit of St. Louis*, 288.

Chapter 16

155 **"charming" pearl-gray cabin:** Margaret Mather, "I Was on the Hindenburg," *Harper's Monthly*, November 1937.
156 **"most anxious to save":** Frank Jewett Mather Sr., "A Private Life," 1835–1929, TMs, with autograph corrections, pp. 1–75, undated, 98–99, series 1, Frank Jewett Mather Papers, C0025, Manuscripts Division, Department of Special Collections, Princeton University Library.
156 **"devot[ed] herself with untiring":** Frank Jewett Mather Sr., "Private Life," 60.
156 **He had witnessed marvelous:** Frank Jewett Mather Sr., "Private Life," 6–7.
156 **In his "wildest dreams":** Frank Jewett Mather Sr., "Private Life," 150.
157 **"The aeroplanes and dirigibles":** Frank Jewett Mather Sr., "Private Life," 6.
157 **Much like Margaret:** Frank Jewett Mather Sr., "Private Life," 99, 110a, 129.
157 **In 1853, when Samuel:** Frank J. Mather, "A Clipper Ship and Her Commander," *Atlantic Monthly*, November 1904, 649–50.
157 **This new navigational:** Under Maury's tenure, the Depot of Charts and Instruments was renamed the United States Naval Observatory.
157 **"longest way round":** Frank J. Mather, "Clipper Ship," 650.
158 **"seriously delayed by calms":** Frank J. Mather, "Clipper Ship," 651–52.
158 **They reached Melbourne:** Frank J. Mather, "Clipper Ship," 652.
159 **"soft colors, showing the history":** Margaret Mather, "I Was on the Hindenburg."
159 **The same winds:** Arthur Brisbane, "Today," *San Francisco Examiner*, March 12, 1936.
159 **"It would strike me with no":** Frank Jewett Mather Sr., "Private Life," 150.
160 **German scientists announced:** "Long-Distance Television Inaugurated in Germany," *Pittsburgh Post-Gazette*, March 2, 1936.
160 **"My quarrel with the Germans":** Frank Jewett Mather Sr., "Private Life," 72.

161 **"I know that there are those":** Frank Jewett Mather Sr., "Private Life," 76–77.

161 **"I hope Germany":** Frank Jewett Mather Sr., "Private Life," 148–49.

Chapter 17

162 **"lay like molten silver":** Gertrud Stolte-Adelt, "Mein Sturz aus dem brennenden Luftschiff: Erinnerungen an eine tragische Atlantikfahrt," *Hamburger Abendblatt*, August 27, 1949.

162 **Leonhard, on the other hand:** Leonhard Adelt, "The Last Trip of the Hindenburg," *Reader's Digest*, November 1937.

162 **With the return:** Stolte-Adelt, "Mein Sturz."

163 **Letter writers could:** Douglas H. Robinson, "Life in the Belly of Leviathan," in *LZ 129 "Hindenburg,"* Famous Aircraft Series (Arco, 1964).

163 **That day, Zabel stamped:** Joseph Spah to Hans Hörmann, November 1, 1976, Spah Family Papers.

163 **Bert Dolan would soon:** Dennis R. Kromm, "Homecoming," in *Compex: Combined Philatelic Exhibition of Chicagoland, Incorporated, Commemorating the 50th Anniversary of the Last Flight of the Hindenburg* (May 1987), 56; Burtis Dolan to William Miller, "Hindenburg's Post Room," *Fire & Ice: Hindenburg and Titanic,* Smithsonian National Postal Museum, postalmuseum.si.edu/exhibition/fire-ice-hindenburg-and-titanic-exhibition-mail-ships/hindenburgs-post-room.

163 **If either of those radios:** Dan Grossman, "Crew Areas and Keel," Airships.net, n.d., airships.net/hindenburg/interiors/crew-areas-keel.

163 **Willy Speck was a longtime:** "Die toten Kameraden: Oberfunkinspektor Willy Speck," *Werkzeitschrift der Zeppelin-Betriebe*, June 1, 1937, 100, Zeppelin Museum, Friedrichshafen.

163 **game of "Indians":** Stolte-Adelt, "Mein Sturz." In the acknowledgments in Michael Mooney's *The Hindenburg* (Dodd, Mead, 1972), he mentions this incident, which he reports was similarly remembered by Heinrich Kubis. However, one of the captains, Heinrich Bauer, did not recall this having happened. As Kubis and Speck served together far longer than Kubis and Bauer, and the story so clearly stood out to Gertrud Adelt among all the details she could have included in her piece in the *Hamburger Abendblatt*, it seems more likely to be true.

164 **"Our whole generation":** Stefan Zweig to Victor Fleischer, November 21, 1931, quoted in Arturo Larcati, "Eine Jugend in Wien: Alberto Stringas Freundschaft mit Stefan Zweig," in *Stefan Zweig: Positionen der Moderne*, ed. Martina Wörgötter, Schriftenreihe des Stefan Zweig Centre Salzburg (Königshausen & Neumann, 2017), 173, available at stefan-zweig-zentrum.at/fileadmin/content/images/publikationen/weitere-publikationen/Eine_Jugend_in_Wien._Alberto_Stringas_Freundschaft_mit_Stefan_Zweig_2017.pdf.

165 **At seventeen, he published:** Ulrich Adelt, interview with the author, October 19, 2023.

165 **A few years later, he moved:** David Turner, "Eine nahe Ferne. Die Briefe Stefan Zweigs an Leonhard Adelt als Ausdruck einer von ihren literarischen Anfängen geprägten Freundschaft," in *Studia austriaca II*, ed. Fausto Cercignani, vol. 2 (University of Milan, 1993), 85.

165 **By 1909, Zweig had firmly:** Leonhard Adelt to Richard Dehmel, January 31, 1906, Dehmel Papers, Staats- und Universitätsbibliothek, Hamburg (SUB); Leonhard Adelt to Richard Dehmel, October 30, 1906, Dehmel Papers, SUB.

165 **called his friend a "fantasist":** Turner, "Eine nahe Ferne," 86.

166 **"After you once pinned":** Turner, "Eine nahe Ferne," 86–87.

166 **"So does the airship":** Leonhard Adelt, *Der Flieger: Ein Buch aus unsern Tagen* (Literarische Anstalt Rütten & Loening, 1913), 109.

166 **"The airship," Leonhard wrote:** Adelt, *Der Flieger*, 109.

167 **"It is quite as impossible":** H. S. Maxim, "Aërial Navigation: The Power Required," *Century Magazine* 42, no. 6 (October 1891): 829, gwern.net/doc/technology/1891-maxim.pdf.

167 **Leonhard had wanted to build:** Lexikon Westfälischer Autorinnen und Autoren, "Leonhard Adelt," n.d., lexikon-westfaelischer-autorinnen-und-autoren.de/autoren/adelt-leonhard/#erwahnungen_in.

167 **The very same year:** Lexikon Westfälischer Autorinnen und Autoren, "Leonhard Adelt."

167 **When the war broke out:** Turner, "Eine nahe Ferne," 69, 85.

167 **"swindlers and profiteers":** Turner, "Eine nahe Ferne," 69.

167 **"never much more":** Leonhard Adelt to Stefan Zweig, December 4, 1930, series I, subseries A, Letters to Stefan Zweig, SC001.01.1, box 1.1, Shelfmark SZ-AP1/B-1.1, Stefan Zweig Collection, Daniel A. Reed Library, State University of New York at Fredonia.

168 **Leonhard had since moved:** One of Leonhard Adelt's postwar employers, *Berliner Tageblatt* (see, e.g., Leonhard Adelt to Richard Dehmel, July 13, 1920, Dehmel Papers, SUB), was threatened with closure by the Nazis in 1933 but ultimately remained in business after removing its Jewish editor in chief. The Nazis finally shut down the paper in 1939.

168 **He still had not:** Turner, "Eine nahe Ferne," 85; Leonhard Adelt to Friderike Zweig, June 8, 1937, courtesy of Ulrich Adelt.

Chapter 18

169 **When the appointed lunch hour:** Margaret Mather, "I Was on the Hindenburg," *Harper's Monthly*, November 1937.

170 **Marie Kleemann, was just:** "Andover Woman's Mother Tells of Hindenburg Explosion," *Andover Townsman*, May 14, 1937; "Hindenburg Passenger on Train for Boston," *Boston Globe*, May 7, 1937; Nat A. Barrows, "Woman Cannot Recall Escape," *Boston Globe*, May 8, 1937; "Mother Safe in Zepp Disaster," *Andover Townsman*, May 7, 1937.

170 **While women made up:** Alice Rogers Hager, "More Women Take to Air," *New York Times*, July 11, 1937.

171 **"I cannot tell you":** Lady Grace Hay Drummond-Hay to Clara Adams, May 8, 1936, available at Dan Grossman, "Lady Grace Drummond-Hay," Airships.net, n.d., airships .net/airship-people/lady-grace-drummond-hay.

171 **"'Hurtling across the skies'":** Anne Morrow Lindbergh, *North to the Orient* (Harcourt, Brace, 1935), 12–13.

172 **"Which country," she wondered:** Mather, "I Was on the Hindenburg."

172 **"how much [she] was enjoying":** Mather, "I Was on the Hindenburg."

172 **"merry young man":** Mather, "I Was on the Hindenburg."

173 **"dim, airy vault":** Gertrud Stolte-Adelt, "Mein Sturz aus dem brennenden Luftschiff: Erinnerungen an eine tragische Atlantikfahrt," *Hamburger Abendblatt*, August 27, 1949.

173 **"Oh," he remarked:** Stolte-Adelt, "Mein Sturz."

Chapter 19

174 **Since he was apparently:** Michael Capuzzo, "'Oh, the Humanity of It All!,'" *Philadelphia Inquirer*, May 6, 1987.

174 **"OK," his editor:** Capuzzo, "'Oh, the Humanity.'"

175 **WLS was allowing Morrison:** "Announcer Recalls Tragedy," *Record Searchlight* (Redding, CA), May 9, 1987.

Chapter 20

176 **In the late afternoon of May 5:** Heinrich Bauer Testimony, May 25, 1937, RG 197 Box 8, NARA.

176 **Passengers looking out:** Charles E. Rosendahl, "The Last Flight," in Ernst A. Lehmann, *Zeppelin: The Story of Lighter-Than-Air Craft*, rev. ed. (Fonthill, 2015), 326; George Grant, "Notes on a Voyage of the AIRSHIP 'HINDENBURG' under the Command of Captain Pruss," May 6, 1937, National Archives and Records Administration at College Park, available online at Patrick Russell, "George Grant," *Faces of the Hindenburg* (blog), January 21, 2009, facesofthehindenburg.blogspot.com/2009 /01/george-grant.html.

176 **Typically, the zeppelin:** Hindenburg Route Map belonging to Peter Belin, *Fire & Ice: Hindenburg and Titanic,* Smithsonian National Postal Museum, postalmuseum.si.edu /exhibition/fire-ice-hindenburg-and-titanic/exhibition#1; Standortmeldungen von L.S. Hindenburg auf seiner letzten Fahrt nach USA, LZA 17/567, Zeppelin Museum, Friedrichshafen; Gertrud Stolte-Adelt, "Mein Sturz aus dem brennenden Luftschiff: Erinnerungen an eine tragische Atlantikfahrt," *Hamburger Abendblatt*, August 27, 1949.

176 **Margaret Mather had been relaxing:** Margaret Mather, "I Was on the Hindenburg," *Harper's Monthly*, November 1937.

177 **Around five o'clock:** Standortmeldungen von L.S. Hindenburg; Leonhard Adelt, "The Last Trip of the Hindenburg," *Reader's Digest*, November 1937.

177 **The passengers crowded around:** Joseph Spah's personal film footage, May 5, 1937, Spah Family Films.

177 **Benny had been using:** Joseph Spah's personal film footage, May 5, 1937, Spah Family Films and Papers; Joseph Spah, interview in *Survival!,* produced by Sherman Grinberg, hosted by James Whitmore, 1964, Spah Family Papers.

177 **Even the cabin boy:** W. E. von Medem, *Kabinenjunge Werner Franz vom Luftschiff "Hindenburg"* (Franz Schneider Verlag, 1938), 82.

177 **Captain Pruss ordered:** Adelt, "Last Trip of the Hindenburg."

178 **"fantastic" giant formations:** George Hirschfeld, "Ich nahm mir felt vor, nicht den Kopf zu verlieren," *Bremer Zeitung,* May 21, 1937.

178 **like "swimming castles":** "Andover Woman's Mother Tells of Hindenburg Explosion," *Andover Townsman,* May 14, 1937.

178 **"white against the stone-gray sea":** Mather, "I Was on the Hindenburg."

178 **"[rise] from the depths":** Stolte-Adelt, "Mein Sturz."

178 **"magic marble statue[s]":** Adelt, "Last Trip of the Hindenburg."

178 **"a monument of sparkling":** Adelt, "Last Trip of the Hindenburg."

178 **"Rainbows sprang from everywhere":** Mather, "I Was on the Hindenburg."

178 **"pools of vivid green":** Mather, "I Was on the Hindenburg."

178 **"*Titanic* fell victim":** Stolte-Adelt, "Mein Sturz."

179 **Peter Belin's father:** Ian Shapira, "A Family's Hidden History Is Revealed After the Sale of Their Grand Georgetown Estate," *Washington Post,* October 15, 2011.

179 **As Philip Mangone:** Sid Moody, "The Hindenburg Crash," *Morning Call* (Allentown, PA), May 6, 1962; Erik Larson, *Dead Wake* (Crown, 2015), 95.

179 **"How dangerous it must":** Spah, interview in *Survival.* See also Joseph Spah, interview in *Catastrophe: No Safe Place,* directed by Dan Gingold (Alan Landsburg Productions, 1980).

179 **Though he had only a high school:** Marilyn Spah Kelly and Jane Kelly, interview with the author, May 5, 2024.

179 **On his travels:** Kelly and Kelly, interview with the author; Joseph Spah book collection, Spah Family Papers.

179 **"ashamed" that he had not:** Joseph Spah to Vera Spah, January 26, 1936, Spah Family Papers.

180 **After quietly lingering:** Joseph Spah's personal film footage.

180 **"ramming the iceberg":** Spah, interview in *Survival.* See also, Spah interview in *Catastrophe!.*

Chapter 21

181 **Herb Morrison and his sound engineer:** Scottdale Historical Society, "Whispers of the Past—Herb Morrison and the Hindenburg," posted May 12, 2022, by Whispers of the Past, YouTube, youtube.com/watch?v=7Gs3DteAjDs&t=15s; Herbert Morrison, *Hindenburg* broadcast, May 6, 1937; 1936 American Airlines Timetable, available at timetableimages.com/ttimages/aa/aa35/aa35-3.jpg; 1937 American Airlines Timetable, available at timetableimages.com/ttimages/complete/aa37/aa37-3.jpg; "Under Fire!" *Stand By,* May 15, 1937, 2.

182 **"anxious to see":** Scottdale Historical Society, "Whispers of the Past."

182 **Native Chicagoan Charlie Nehlsen:** Charles Nehlsen to John Toland, July 14, 1956, box 99, folder 2, John Toland Papers, Manuscript Division, Library of Congress, Washington, DC; "Twenty Years in Radio," *Stand By*, June 12, 1937, 7.

182 **"not much of a mixer":** Charles Nehlsen to John Toland.

182 **He had been with:** "Twenty Years in Radio."

183 **In 1927, there were:** Historical Statistics of the United States, 1789–1945, series K, 239–73, 224–25.

183 **In 1926, the U.S. Congress:** Alexander Rose, *Empires of the Sky: Zeppelins, Airplanes, and Two Men's Epic Duel to Rule the World* (Random House, 2020), 250; John H. Frederick, *Commercial Air Transportation* (Richard D. Irwin, 1947), 8–9; Smithsonian National Air and Space Museum, "Air Mail and the Birth of Commercial Aviation," December 9, 2021, airandspace.si.edu/stories/editorial/air-mail-and-birth-commercial-aviation.

183 **philanthropist Daniel Guggenheim:** Marilyn Bender and Selig Altschul, *The Chosen Instrument: Pan Am, Juan Trippe; The Rise and Fall of an American Entrepreneur* (Simon & Schuster, 1982), 80; Rose, *Empires of the Sky*, 251–52, 260–63; Bruce L. Larson, "Lindbergh's Return to Minnesota, 1927," *Minnesota History* 42, no. 4 (Winter 1970): 152; Reginald M. Cleveland, "What Is the Future of Aviation?," *Scientific American*, October 1929, 313. Lindbergh relied on instrument navigation as he flew across the ocean with zero forward visibility in the *Spirit of St. Louis*, as the fuel tanks were positioned directly in front of the cockpit to maximize the aircraft's range. The flurry of innovation in the late 1920s was also evident in the insurance market. In 1926, only one company had been willing to offer fledgling airlines insurance. By 1929, life insurance companies stopped restricting coverage or charging additional premiums for fare-paying passengers. With the insurance market's green light, private capital poured in as investors feared missing out on the biggest breakthrough since the invention of the automobile. So rabid was the zeal for investing in aviation stocks that one publicly traded railroad, the Seaboard Air Line, was mistaken for a commercial airline by investors too impatient to buy a piece of a rapidly rising market to bother to do any research at all. Of course, that changed when the market crashed that October, with many overnight millionaires suffering an abrupt reversal in fortune. See Rose, *Empires of the Sky*, 250; Alexander Klemin, "American Passenger Air Transport," *Scientific American*, October 1929, 361; Cleveland, "What Is the Future of Aviation?," 315; and T. A. Heppenheimer, *Turbulent Skies: The History of Commercial Aviation* (John Wiley & Sons, 1995), 22.

184 **Recognizing that short-term:** Smithsonian National Air and Space Museum, "Air Mail and the Birth of Commercial Aviation."

184 **Just that February:** Robert J. Serling, *Eagle: The Story of American Airlines* (St. Martin's, 1985), 105.

184 **"fly around the world":** "Why Dodge the Question: Afraid to Fly?," *Evening Star* (Washington, DC), April 19, 1937, available at chroniclingamerica.loc.gov/lccn/sn83045462/1937-04-19/ed-1/seq-20.

185 **"fly wives free":** Serling, *Eagle*, 109. For an example of a genuine wife who flew for

free, see Diary of Caroline Harnsberger, February 12, 1935, Winnetka Historical Society, Winnetka, IL.

185 **"Why dodge the question":** "Why Dodge the Question."

186 **"Now . . . FLY TO EUROPE":** 1936 American Airlines and DZR Timetable, 1937 American Airlines and DZR Timetable, and American Airlines baggage label, available at Dan Grossman, "American Airlines and the Hindenburg," Airships.net, February 18, 2017, airships.net/blog/american-airlines-hindenburg, and Dan Grossman, "Oh the Humanity: Herbert Morrison and the Hindenburg," Airshps.net, n.d., airships.net/hindenburg/disaster/oh-the-humanity-herbert-morrison-and-the-hindenburg.

187 **"any film in which":** Memorandum by the Chief of the Division of Western Affairs, James Clement Dunn, Washington, April 19, 1937 [document 292], Foreign Relations of the United States (FRUS), Diplomatic Papers, 1937, vol. II. The German consul general in Los Angeles, Georg Gyssling, who wrote the letter, had represented Germany in the 1932 Winter Olympics at Lake Placid. Crashes and injuries sidelined other members of the German team, and despite having no bobsled experience at all, Gyssling, then working in the New York consulate, was called up. See "D. Georg Gyssling," Olympics.com, n.d., olympics.com/en/athletes/d-georg-gyssling. In a 2017 book, Steven Ross reveals that Gyssling, a German nationalist at heart, disliked Hitler and the Nazi Party and passed classified information to American intelligence officers prior to World War II. Steven Ross, *Hitler in Los Angeles: How Jews Foiled Nazi Plots Against Hollywood and America* (Bloomsbury, 2017).

188 **"punishment for a similar crime":** Memorandum by the Special Assistant to the Secretary of State (James Clement Dunn), Washington, April 26, 1937 [document 295], FRUS, Diplomatic Papers, 1937, vol. II.

189 **Bund members occasionally turned up:** Harold G. Dick and Douglas H. Robinson, *The Golden Age of the Great Passenger Airships: Graf Zeppelin & Hindenburg* (Smithsonian Institution Press, 1985), 135.

189 **"chamber of horrors":** "Religious Center at Fair Proposed," *New York Times*, March 4, 1937. For more on this episode, see David M. Esposito and Jackie R. Esposito, "LaGuardia and the Nazis, 1933–1938," *American Jewish History* 78, no. 1 (September 1988): 38–53.

189 **"perverted maniac" seeking to:** "Ask Roosevelt Aid for German Jews," *New York Times*, June 6, 1933.

190 **"crimes against civilization":** "Nazis 'Convicted' of World 'Crime' by 20,000 in Rally," *New York Times*, March 8, 1934; "The 'Verdict' Found Against Hitlerism," *New York Times*, March 8, 1934; "LaGuardia Sees a Reign of Brute Force with a Revival of Pre-War Militarism," *New York Times*, March 8, 1934.

190 **Hull, who had been:** William E. Dodd Jr. and Martha Dodd, eds., *Ambassador Dodd's Diary, 1933–38* (Harcourt, Brace, 1941), March 6, 1937, 390; Esposito and Esposito, "LaGuardia and the Nazis," 45–46; Memorandum by the Chief of the Division of Western European Affairs (Dunn) to the Secretary of State, March 4, 1937 [document 271], FRUS, Diplomatic Papers, 1937, vol. II.

190 **the "Nazi press":** Ambassador in Germany (Dodd) to the Secretary of State, March 8, 1937 [document 272] FRUS, Diplomatic Papers, 1937, vol. II.

190 **"What would you say":** Harold L. Ickes, *The Secret Diary of Harold L. Ickes,* vol. 2, *The Inside Struggle, 1936–1939* (Simon & Schuster, 1954), March 6, 1937, 89–91. Several days after Roosevelt died in April 1945, La Guardia reflected on the incident during a radio talk at New York's city hall: "I called at the White House soon afterward to keep an appointment made before I made the remark. . . . The press and many persons thought I went there to be reprimanded because the German Ambassador had lodged a protest on behalf of his Government. The President smiled as I entered his office. Then he extended his right arm and said, 'Heil, Fiorello!' I snapped to attention, extended my right arm and replied, 'Heil Franklin!' And that's all that was ever said about it. Incidentally, it was the only time I ever addressed the President as Franklin. I always called him 'Chief' or 'Mr. Roosevelt.'" "Mayor Tells of Reaction to His 'Insult' to Hitler," *New York Times,* April 16, 1945. The same week as the La Guardia affair, Roosevelt also took umbrage at a separate incident when Democratic Senator Millard Tydings of Maryland made a speech implying that Hitler and Mussolini were undermining American democratic institutions in the face of a feeble Roosevelt administration's failure to condemn Hitler's oppression of German Jews. Tydings had also introduced a resolution calling for such a condemnation in January 1934, but the resolution never made it past the Senate Foreign Relations Committee. "Tydings Asks Plea to Reich on Jews," *New York Times,* January 9, 1934; Stephen H. Norwood, "Legitimating Nazism: Harvard University and the Hitler Regime, 1933–1937," *American Jewish History* 92, no. 2 (June 2004): 193.

191 **"uncovering possible infractions":** Ambassador in Germany (Dodd) to the Secretary of State, April 26, 1937 [document 238], FRUS, Diplomatic Papers, 1937, vol. II.

191 **"The suppression of":** Ambassador in Germany (Dodd) to the Secretary of State, April 29, 1937 [document 239], FRUS, Diplomatic Papers, 1937, vol. II.

Chapter 22

192 **silk walls charmingly decorated:** Douglas H. Robinson, "Life in the Belly of Leviathan," in *LZ 129 "Hindenburg,"* Famous Aircraft Series (Arco, 1964).

192 **While Bert Dolan addressed:** Burtis Dolan to Miss Thompson, May 5, 1937, available in Dennis R. Kromm, "Homecoming," in *Compex: Combined Philatelic Exhibition of Chicagoland, Incorporated, Commemorating the 50th Anniversary of the Last Flight of the Hindenburg* (May 1987), 56; Martin Feibusch and Cheryl Ganz, "*Hindenburg* Crash Cover Forgeries and Passenger Moritz Feibusch," *Zeppelin Collector,* July 1998, 51.

193 **"Greetings on the maiden":** In *The Hindenburg,* Michael Mooney claims that passenger William Leuchtenberg said this to Feibusch, though he errs in saying Feibusch bought the cards from one of the stewards on the airship. He could not have done so, as they were personalized designs, so there are doubts over the accuracy of this account. Michael Mooney, *The Hindenburg* (Dodd, Mead, 1972), 196. On the other hand, in *Who Destroyed the Hindenburg?* A. A. Hoehling writes that Heinrich Kubis said this to

Feibusch, and the surrounding details supporting this anecdote are accurate. A. A. Hoehling, *Who Destroyed the Hindenburg?* (Little, Brown, 1962), 70.

193 **Nelson had cabled:** Kromm, "Homecoming," 57.

193 **He had also addressed:** Mary Alice Dolan Noone, interview with the author, February 16, 2024.

193 **"Dearest one," Bert had begun:** Burtis Dolan to Mildred Dolan, undated 1937, Dolan Family Papers.

Chapter 23

196 **"slept like a child":** Margaret Mather, "I Was on the Hindenburg," *Harper's Monthly*, November 1937.

196 **The stewards stripped:** Leonhard Adelt, "The Last Trip of the Hindenburg," *Reader's Digest*, November 1937.

196 **Normally, if the zeppelin landed:** Narrative of Events Immediately Preceding and Following the Destruction of the Airship Hindenburg, May 19, 1937, Lakehurst Naval Air Station, courtesy of 87th Air Base Wing Historian.

196 **had an extra spring:** Joseph Spah, interview in *Survival!,* produced by Sherman Grinberg, hosted by James Whitmore, 1964, Spah Family Papers.

197 **Wearing a pinstripe suit:** Assorted photographs, Spah Family Papers; Fritz Deeg Testimony, May 13, RG 197, box 7, National Archives and Records Administration at College Park (NARA).

197 **As the passengers tidied:** Adelt, "Last Trip of the Hindenburg."

197 **DZR had been trying:** Harold G. Dick and Douglas H. Robinson, *The Golden Age of the Great Passenger Airships: Graf Zeppelin & Hindenburg* (Smithsonian Institution Press, 1985), 145; Bericht des Herrn H. M. Wronsky über seine Reisen ach U.S.A. am 5 August 1936, and Auszug aus einem Bericht des Herren Direktor Wronsky, March 30–April 10, 1936, LZA 17/197, Zeppelin Museum, Friedrichshafen; Willy von Meister to Ernst Lehmann, January 10, 1937, LZA 17/196, Zeppelin Museum, Friedrichshafen.

197 **Benny Spah had observed:** Victoria Spah, *The Spah Family: Home Movies* (self-published, 2006).

198 **That spring, *the Hindenburg*:** Dick and Robinson, *Golden Age*, 142–44.

198 **After breakfast, Margaret:** Mather, "I Was on the Hindenburg."

198 **In front of the city:** Heinrich Bauer Testimony, May 25, 1937, RG 197, box 8, NARA; Mather, "I Was on the Hindenburg."

198 **"great elation" washed over her:** Mather, "I Was on the Hindenburg."

199 **"all conversations stopped":** Gertrud Stolte-Adelt, "Mein Sturz aus dem brennenden Luftschiff: Erinnerungen an eine tragische Atlantikfahrt," *Hamburger Abendblatt*, August 27, 1949.

199 **Leonhard assumed that she:** Leonhard Adelt, "Trauer und Zuversicht," in Ernst A. Lehmann, *Auf Luftpatrouille und Weltfahrt* (Schmidt & Günther, 1937), 401.

199 **"Sorry I can't let":** "Andover Woman's Mother Tells of Hindenburg Explosion," *Andover Townsman*, May 14, 1937.

199 **Her son-in-law was coming:** "Andover Woman's Mother."

199 **The *Hindenburg* was meant:** Charles E. Rosendahl, "The Last Flight," in Ernst A. Lehmann, *Zeppelin: The Story of Lighter-Than-Air Craft*, rev. ed. (Fonthill, 2015), 326.

199 **From the research:** Herbert Morrison, *Hindenburg* broadcast, May 6, 1937.

200 **Morrison and Nehlsen had rested:** Morrison, *Hindenburg* broadcast; Charles Nehlsen to John Toland, June 27, 1956, box 99, folder 2, John Toland Papers, Manuscript Division, Library of Congress (LOC).

200 **With only sixty-three:** Morrison, Hindenburg broadcast.

200 **On August 25, 1927:** C. E. Rosendahl, "U.S.S. 'Los Angeles,'" *United States Naval Institute Proceedings* 57, no. 340 (June 1931), usni.org/magazines/proceedings/1931/june/uss-los-angeles; "NH 845668 Los Angeles (ZR-3)," Naval History and Heritage Command, history.navy.mil/our-collections/photography/numerical-list-of-images/nhhc-series/nh-series/NH-84000/NH-84568.html.

201 **"The story is told":** "Lakehurst Secret Out," *Freehold Transcript & Monmouth Inquirer*, December 10, 1915.

201 **After the Russian Revolution:** James Warrick, 87th Air Base Wing Historian, interview with the author, June 8, 2024. A Russian Orthodox church and cemetery can be found on the road to Lakehurst today.

201 **prelude to a "great event":** Morrison, *Hindenburg* broadcast.

201 **Charlie Nehlsen, an amateur:** *Radio Guide*, week ending May 29, 1937, 12.

201 **There were almost one hundred:** Narrative of Events; Frank Ward Oral History, Smithsonian National Postal Museum, March 20, 2012; John Toland Interview with Calvin Keck, November 30, Lakehurst, box 99, folder 1, John Toland Papers, LOC; Dennis R. Kromm, "Homecoming," in *Compex: Combined Philatelic Exhibition of Chicagoland, Incorporated, Commemorating the 50th Anniversary of the Last Flight of the Hindenburg* (May 1987), 57.

201 **Off in the distance towered:** William F. Althoff, *USS* Los Angeles*: The Navy's Venerable Airship and Aviation Technology* (Potomac Books, 2005), 196.

201 **In fact, the hangar:** Warrick, interview with the author. This microclimate phenomenon still occurs at the historic airship hangar at Moffett Field in California. Nicolas Rivero, "Why These Startups Think Zeppelins Could Be the Future of Air Travel," *Washington Post*, May 15, 2025.

202 **Clouds hung over:** Morrison, *Hindenburg* broadcast.

202 **Vendors had set up:** John Toland interview with Philip Mangone and Katherine Mangone Lusty, November 23, New York, box 99, folder 1, Toland Papers, LOC.

202 **There were mothers:** Fred Rom, interview with the author, April 9, 2024.

202 **The zeppelin arrivals:** Die Aufzeichnungen des Luftschiffstewards Wilhelm Balla, LZ 129, BMA I, Zeppelin Museum, Friedrichshafen.

202 **With the forecast:** Charles Nehlsen to John Toland, June 27, 1956, box 99, folder 2, Toland Papers, LOC; Brian Williams, host, *We Interrupt This Broadcast*, podcast, season 1, episode 1, "The Hindenburg Explosion—'Oh, the Humanity!'—(May 6, 1937)," July 20, 2021.

203 **As expected, Morrison:** John Toland Interview with Murray Becker, undated, box

99, folder 1, Toland Papers, LOC; John Toland Interview with Harry Kroh, November 26, box 99, folder 1, Toland Papers, LOC; Herb Rau to John Toland, January 2, box 99, folder 2, Toland Papers, LOC.

203 **Murray Becker, a twenty-eight-year-old:** John Toland Interview with Murray Becker.

203 **With nothing to do:** John Toland Interview with Millie Brown, November 30, Lakehurst, box 99, folder 1, Toland Papers, LOC.

203 **One of the hardened:** Scottdale Historical Society, "Whispers of the Past—Herb Morrison and the Hindenburg," posted May 12, 2022, by Whispers of the Past, YouTube, youtube.com/watch?v=7Gs3DteAjDs&t=15s.

203 **As the clock struck 3:00 p.m.:** Narrative of Events.

203 **"swam into view":** Mather, "I Was on the Hindenburg."

204 **the pointed inlet of Little Neck:** Spah, interview in *Survival!*.

204 **Hamburg-America Line's public relations:** Hamburg-America Line–North German Lloyd News Service, "Hindenburg Here on First Flight of the Season," for release May 6, 1937, available at Alexander Historical Auctions, alexautographs.com/auction-lot/hindenburg-arrival-notice-and-passenger-list-from_CC146EDB2A.

204 **The stewards served:** Mather, "I Was on the Hindenburg."

204 **flew over Ebbets Field:** John Toland, *Ships in the Sky* (Frederick Muller, 1957), 222; Baseball Reference, "Pittsburgh Pirates vs Brooklyn Dodgers Box Score, May 6, 1937," baseball-reference.com/boxes/BRO/BRO193705060.shtml.

204 **The last communication:** Narrative of Events.

205 **Zeppelins were capable:** Hugo Eckener, "Brief Instructions and Practical Hints for Piloting Zeppelin Airships for the Flight Personnel of the 'DELAG,'" 1919, reprinted in Douglas H. Robinson, *LZ 129 "Hindenburg,"* Famous Aircraft Series (Arco, 1964).

205 **As Pruss swooped:** Mather, "I Was on the Hindenburg"; W. E. von Medem, *Kabinenjunge Werner Franz vom Luftschiff "Hindenburg"* (Franz Schneider Verlag, 1938), 81–82, 87.

205 **"sidewalks were swarming":** von Medem, *Kabinenjunge Werner Franz*, 83.

206 **"with its steely":** Isaac Goldberg, *George Gershwin: A Study in American Music* (F. Ungar, 1958), 139.

206 **As the airship reached:** Adelt, "Last Trip of the Hindenburg."

206 **resemble glinting "needles":** Stolte-Adelt, "Mein Sturz."

206 **"a board full of nails":** Adelt, "Last Trip of the Hindenburg"; Susanne Droste, "Lakehurst 1937: Stationen einer Fahrt ins Unglück," *Ansifter,* October 2001, LZ 129, BMA III, Zeppelin Museum, Friedrichshafen.

206 **Down below on the famous:** Adelt, "Last Trip of the Hindenburg."

206 **In 1930, as construction:** Rebecca Maksel, "Docking on the Empire State Building," *Smithsonian Magazine*, April 1, 2013; Christopher Gray, "Not Just a Perch for King Kong," *New York Times*, September 23, 2010. William Shirer saw the zeppelin mast on the Empire State Building during a trip home in September 1935. Seeing the Empire State Building on a moonlit night, he remarked that the skyscraper was "not impressive. It lacked lighted windows up its mountainous sides to convey its staggering height. Its illuminated Zeppelin mast was just a column of light hanging in the sky, without a base, with little connection with the street." William L. Shirer, Original Diary (Black

Notebook), September 18, 1935, Willliam L. Shirer Papers, Coe College, Cedar Rapids, IA.

207 **"voice of the ports":** Stolte-Adelt, "Mein Sturz"; Mather, "I Was on the Hindenburg"; Die Aufzeichnungen des Luftschiffstewards.

207 **young Werner Franz:** von Medem, *Kabinenjunge Werner Franz*, 83.

207 **"The viaducts and highways":** Adelt, "Last Trip of the Hindenburg."

207 **Finally, after about:** Adelt, "Last Trip of the Hindenburg"; Mather, "I Was on the Hindenburg"; David Sanger, interview with the author, December 11, 2024. One of the boys playing basketball was *New York Times* national security correspondent David Sanger's father, Kenneth E. Sanger, who would grow up to found WQXR, New York's first classical radio station, which had a broadcasting antenna on the Empire State Building. Ironically, David Sanger's first big assignment as a journalist was covering the *Challenger* disaster.

Chapter 24

208 **The road to Lakehurst was packed:** Die Aufzeichnungen des Luftschiffstewards Wilhelm Balla, LZ 129, BMA I, Zeppelin Museum, Friedrichshafen.

208 **"Conditions still unsettled":** Narrative of Events Immediately Preceding and Following the Destruction of the Airship Hindenburg, May 19, 1937, Lakehurst Naval Air Station, courtesy of 87th Air Base Wing Historian.

208 **"not necessary to execute":** Hugo Eckener, "Brief Instructions and Practical Hints for Piloting Zeppelin Airships for the Flight Personnel of the 'DELAG,'" 1919, reprinted in Douglas H. Robinson, *LZ 129 "Hindenburg,"* Famous Aircraft Series (Arco, 1964).

208 **and a "flying mooring":** Rosendahl Testimony, May 26, 1937, RG 197, box 8, National Archives and Records Administration at College Park (NARA); 1936 *Hindenburg* archival footage, Pathétone, courtesy of 87th Air Base Wing Historian; "The Zeppelin L.Z. 129—"Hindenburg" (translation of introduction by Hugo Eckener for the *Journal of the Society of German Engineers*), *The Aeroplane* (Le Bourget), April 29, 1936, 525.

209 **"The captain and crew":** *Hindenburg* disaster article, May 6, 1937, Journalist-Correspondent, Cables, Dispatches, Mail Stories, folder: Cables, Reports, 1936, 1937, 1939, William L. Shirer Papers, Coe College, Cedar Rapids, IA.

209 **Down below, Werner Franz:** W. E. von Medem, *Kabinenjunge Werner Franz vom Luftschiff "Hindenburg"* (Franz Schneider Verlag, 1938), 87.

209 **"It must have been bad weather":** von Medem, *Kabinenjunge Werner Franz*, 86.

209 **"a pack of hungry wolves":** Leonhard Adelt, "The Last Trip of the Hindenburg," *Reader's Digest*, November 1937.

209 **"line of thunderstorms":** Gertrud Stolte-Adelt, "Mein Sturz aus dem brennenden Luftschiff: Erinnerungen an eine tragische Atlantikfahrt," *Hamburger Abendblatt*, August 27, 1949.

210 **With lunch now hours:** Eugen Nunnenmacher Testimony, May 13, 1937, RG 197, box 8, NARA; Stolte-Adelt, "Mein Sturz"; Margaret Mather, "I Was on the Hindenburg," *Harper's Monthly*, November 1937.

210 **offered his tray to Margaret:** Mather, "I Was on the Hindenburg."

210 **"black and ominous" clouds:** Mather, "I Was on the Hindenburg"; Albert Sammt Testimony, May 28, 1937, RG 197, box 8, NARA; Max Zabel Testimony, May 19, 1937, RG 197, box 8, NARA.

210 **"Not at all dangerous":** Mather, "I Was on the Hindenburg."

210 **Once, in November 1935:** Ernst A. Lehmann, *Zeppelin: The Story of Lighter-Than-Air Craft*, rev. ed. (Fonthill, 2015), 30–31, 38. Lehmann believed it to be the longest flight, but Douglas Robinson contests this, saying that the *Dixmude* set the record in 1923 (118 hours, 41 minutes). Douglas Robinson, *Giants in the Sky* (University of Washington Press, 1973), 281, 346.

210 **"foolish with happiness":** Mather, "I Was on the Hindenburg."

211 **"How d'you do, everyone?":** Herbert Morrison, *Hindenburg* broadcast, May 6, 1937; Charles Nehlsen to John Toland, July 14, 1956, box 99, folder 2, John Toland Papers, Manuscript Division, Library of Congress, Washington, DC (LOC).

211 **"We both flew down":** Morrison, *Hindenburg* broadcast.

212 **approach to the mooring mast:** Nehlsen to Toland, July 14, 1956; Morrison, *Hindenburg* broadcast, May 6, 1937.

212 **"Now, we've been":** Harold N. Schenck, home movie footage, featured in *NOVA*, season 48, episode 9, "Hindenburg: The New Evidence," written by Rushmore DeNooyer, directed by Kirk Wolfinger, aired May 19, 2021, on PBS.

212 **"I'm going to step":** Morrison, *Hindenburg* broadcast.

213 **"Recommend landing now":** Narrative of Events.

213 **"with lowered nose":** Adelt, "The Last Trip of the Hindenburg"; Albert Sammt Testimony.

213 **"encroaching darkness of the evening":** Stolte-Adelt, "Mein Sturz."

213 **Nearby, stewards were:** Eugen Nunnenmacher Testimony; Heinrich Kubis Testimony, May 14, 1937, RG 197, box 7, NARA.

213 **settled the last:** Smithsonian National Postal Museum, "Ferdinand Lammot 'Peter' Belin," *Fire & Ice: Hindenburg and Titanic*, postalmuseum.si.edu/exhibition/fire-ice-hindenburg-and-titanic-exhibition-survivors/ferdinand-lammot-%E2%80%9Cpeter%E2%80%9D-belin-jr; Cheryl R. Ganz and Daniel Piazza, *Fire & Ice: Hindenburg and Titanic* (Smithsonian National Postal Museum, 2012), 26, repository.si.edu/bitstream/handle/10088/21719/npm_ganz_and_piazza_hindenburg_2012.pdf?sequence=1&isAllowed=y.

213 **"AIR TRAVEL has certainly":** George Grant, "Notes on a Voyage of the AIRSHIP 'HINDENBURG' under the Command of Captain Pruss," May 6, 1937, NARA, available online at Patrick Russell, "George Grant," *Faces of the Hindenburg* (blog), January 21, 2009, facesofthehindenburg.blogspot.com/2009/01/george-grant.html.

214 **Downstairs on B deck:** von Medem, *Kabinenjunge Werner Franz*, 88; Die Aufzeichnungen des Luftschiffstewards; "Andover Woman's Mother Tells of Hindenburg Explosion," *Andover Townsman*, May 14, 1937.

214 **Balla joined the group:** Die Aufzeichnungen des Luftschiffstewards; Matilda Doehner to John Toland, box 99, folder 1, Toland Papers, LOC.

214 **Nearby, Benny Spah:** Joseph Spah to Department of Commerce Board of Inquiry, May 29, 1937, FBI Hindenburg Case Files; John Parris Jr. (United Press), "Survivor Describes Jump from Blazing Hindenburg," *Pittsburgh Press*, May 8, 1937.

214 **Benny put his camera's:** Joseph Spah, personal film footage, May 6, 1937, Spah Family Films.

214 **new blue Ford station wagon:** John Toland, draft of *Ships in the Sky*, box 99, folder 1, 25, Toland Papers, LOC; Marilyn Spah Kelly and Jane Kelly, interview with the author, May 5, 2024.

215 **Earlier that afternoon:** Mather, "I Was on the Hindenburg."

215 **It was that glorious:** Though Yale's status as having invented the Frisbee is disputed, Frisbie pie tins were certainly thrown on the Yale campus in the 1930s. Nora Wessel, "Local Pie Tin First Frisbee, Legend Holds," *Yale Daily News*, November 5, 2007, yaledailynews.com/blog/2007/11/05/local-pie-tin-first-frisbee-legend-holds.

215 **his cousin Gaspard d'Andelot Belin:** Masthead, *Yale Daily News*, May 7, 1937.

215 **Emma Pannes told Margaret:** Mather, "I Was on the Hindenburg."

215 **The roll of film:** Smithsonian National Postal Museum, "Ferdinand Lammot 'Peter' Belin"; Ganz and Piazza, *Fire & Ice*.

215 **Down in the throngs:** John Toland, notes for *Ships in the Sky*, box 99, folder 1, Toland Papers, LOC.

215 **Margaret felt the airship:** Mather, "I Was on the Hindenburg."

215 **It was now 7:15 p.m.:** Narrative of Events.

215 **The conditions were right:** Charles Rosendahl Testimony.

215 **With Pruss manning the engines:** Albert Sammt Testimony.

216 **With the zeppelin out beyond:** Albert Sammt Testimony; Eduard Boetius Testimony, May 19, 1937, RG 197, box 7, NARA; Heinrich Bauer Testimony, May 19, 1937, RG 197, boxes 7–8, NARA.

216 **As they dropped:** Joseph Kirkman Testimony, May 21, 1937, RG 197, box 8, NARA.

216 **Still, they were somewhat:** Albert Sammt Testimony; Eduard Boetius Testimony; Heinrich Bauer Testimony.

216 **Now they were practically:** Albert Sammt Testimony.

216 **Manila hemp landing ropes:** Adelt, "The Last Trip of the Hindenburg"; Leonhard Adelt, *Der Flieger: Ein Buch aus unsern Tagen* (Literarische Anstalt Rütten & Loening, 1913), 105.

217 **hit the ground with a thud:** Raymond F. Tyler Testimony, May 12, 1937, RG 197, box 7, NARA; Lt. Benjamin May Testimony, May 12, 1937, RG 197, box 7, NARA.

217 **going to miss the 8:00 p.m.:** 1937 American Airlines schedule, timetableimages.com/ttimages/complete/aa37/aa37.pdf.

217 **Looking down, they saw:** Nelson Morris Testimony, May 28, 1937, RG 197, box 8, NARA; Parris, "Survivor Describes Jump"; *NOVA*, "Hindenburg: The New Evidence."

217 **Nelson was a bit surprised:** Nelson Morris Testimony; Narrative of Events.

217 **the bubble in the inclinometer:** Eduard Boetius Testimony; Albert Sammt Testimony.

217 **"Well, here it comes":** Morrison, *Hindenburg* broadcast.

218 **There was an older woman:** Herbert Morrison, interview in *Catastrophe: No Safe Place,* directed by Dan Gingold (Alan Landsburg Productions, 1980).
218 **"the moment we have waited":** Morrison, Hindenburg broadcast.
219 **Pruss had commanded:** Dan Grossman, "Max Pruss," Airships.net, n.d., airships.net/airship-people/captain-max-pruss.
219 **"acted as the chief":** Morrison, *Hindenburg* broadcast.

Chapter 25

220 **washed in a "remarkable stillness":** Leonhard Adelt, "The Last Trip of the Hindenburg," *Reader's Digest*, November 1937.
220 **"faint little bang":** Stolte-Adelt, "Mein Sturz aus dem brennenden Luftschiff: Erinnerungen an eine tragische Atlantikfahrt," *Hamburger Abendblatt*, August 27, 1949.
220 **"no louder than":** Adelt, "Last Trip of the Hindenburg."
220 **Depending on where:** See, e.g., George Hirschfeld, "Ich nahm mir felt vor, nicht den Kopf zu verlieren," *Bremer Zeitung*, May 21, 1937.
220 **To Nelson Morris:** Nelson Morris Testimony, May 28, 1937, RG 197, box 8, National Archives and Records Administration at College Park (NARA).
220 **"dull muffled sound":** Margaret Mather, "I Was on the Hindenburg," *Harper's Monthly*, November 1937.
221 **felt a "dull thud":** W. E. von Medem, *Kabinenjunge Werner Franz vom Luftschiff "Hindenburg"* (Franz Schneider Verlag, 1938), 88.
221 **"What could that be?":** Albert Sammt, *Mein Leben für den Zeppelin* (Verlag Pestalozzi Kinderdorf Wahlwies, 1980), 141.
221 **Nearby, one of the other:** Anton Wittemann Testimony, May 20, 1937, RG 197, box 8, NARA.
221 **Sammt looked out:** Sammt, *Mein Leben*, 141.
221 **"delicate rose glow":** Adelt, "Last Trip of the Hindenburg."
221 **had "risen steeply":** Stolte-Adelt, "Mein Sturz."
221 **"hurled a distance":** Mather, "I Was on the Hindenburg."
222 **"thrown together like":** Die Aufzeichnungen des Luftschiffstewards Wilhelm Balla, LZ 129, BMA I, Zeppelin Museum, Friedrichshafen.
222 **Somehow, in the writing:** Nelson Morris Testimony, May 28, 1937, RG 197, box 8, NARA.
222 **"bloomed" in a "yellow-red glow":** Stolte-Adelt, "Mein Sturz."
222 **"It burst into flames and it's falling!":** Herbert Morrison, *Hindenburg* broadcast, May 6, 1937; Harold N. Schenck, home movie footage, featured in *NOVA*, season 48, episode 9, "Hindenburg: The New Evidence," written by Rushmore DeNooyer, directed by Kirk Wolfinger, aired May 19, 2021, on PBS.
222 **To some on the ground:** Joseph Kirkman Testimony, May 21, 1937, RG 197, box 8, NARA.
222 **"Watch it, watch it":** Morrison, *Hindenburg* broadcast; Schenck, home movie footage.

223 **The thud of sound:** Charles Nehlsen to John Toland, June 27, 1956, box 99, folder 2, John Toland Papers, Manuscript Division, Library of Congress, Washington, DC (LOC).

223 **In those seconds:** Various newsreel footage of the *Hindenburg* disaster, see, for example, the Library of Congress National Film Registry, also available online: Pathé, youtu.be/fURATK5Yt30?si=IGVJu-9jOwBXNVVx; Movietonc, youtu.be/rWeO1q0gHJE?si=6UU_lJeirolbLeIK; Universal, wikipedia.org/wiki/File:1937-05-10_Special_Release_-_Zeppelin_Explodes_Scores_Dead.ogv; Murray Becker, Associated Press photographs, May 6, 1937.

223 **Morrison stared in horror:** Herbert Morrison to Investigation Board, May 16, 1937, RG 197, box 1, NARA.

223 **"terrific swish like compressed air":** Morrison to Investigation Board, May 16, 1937.

224 **While the fire:** Charles E. Rosendahl, *What About the Airship? The Challenges to the United States* (Charles Scribner's Sons, 1938), 6; various newsreel footage of the *Hindenburg* disaster; Becker, Associated Press photographs; Schenck, home movie footage.

224 **Fireworks seemed to explode:** Charles L. Harwood Testimony, May 17, 1937, NARA.

224 **"It's crashing—and it's crashing":** Morrison, Hindenburg broadcast.

224 **With all the gas:** Morrison to Investigation Board, May 16, 1937; Schenck, home movie footage.

224 **"it's falling on the mooring":** Morrison, *Hindenburg* broadcast, May 6, 1937.

225 **The rest of the zeppelin's:** Various newsreel footage of the *Hindenburg* disaster.

225 **And as the nose:** Charles E. Rosendahl, "The Last Flight," in Ernst A. Lehmann, *Zeppelin: The Story of Lighter-Than-Air Craft*, rev. ed. (Fonthill, 2015), 326; Rosendahl, *What About the Airship?*, 7.

225 **The air feeding the flames:** Scottdale Historical Society, "Whispers of the Past—Herb Morrison and the Hindenburg," posted May 12, 2022, by Whispers of the Past, YouTube, youtube.com/watch?v=7Gs3DteAjDs&t=15s; Jesse Chapman, "Hindenburg Coverage Part of Movie," *Roanoke Times*, December 12, 1975; various newsreel footage of the *Hindenburg* disaster.

226 **"I—I can't talk":** Morrison, *Hindenburg* broadcast.

226 **Now her knees gave out:** Emmett Weaver, "Hindenburg Tragedy Reporter Reminisces," *Birmingham Post-Herald*, December 12, 1975; Herbert Morrison, interview in *Catastrophe,* directed by Dan Gingold (Alan Landsburg Productions, 1980); Scottdale Historical Society, "Whispers of the Past."

226 **"Lady, I'm sorry":** Morrison, *Hindenburg* broadcast.

226 **"Honestly, I can hardly":** Morrison, *Hindenburg* broadcast.

Chapter 26

227 **"Come on, Mr. Pannes":** John Toland, notes for *Ships in the Sky*, box 99, folder 1, Library of Congress, Washington, DC.

228 **it was every man:** Die Aufzeichnungen des Luftschiffstewards Wilhelm Balla, LZ 129, BMA I, Zeppelin Museum, Friedrichshafen; Toland, notes for *Ships in the Sky*.

228 **Benny Spah never actually:** Joseph Spah to Department of Commerce Board of Inquiry, May 29, 1937, FBI Hindenburg Case Files.

228 **Taking it off:** Marilyn Spah Kelly and Jane Kelly, interview with the author, May 5, 2024; Hubert Griggs, "Melbourne Mom Can't Forget Hindenburg Disaster Terror," *Orlando Sentinel*, May 6, 1977; James L. Kilgallen (International News Service), "'God Saved Me' Said Philip Mangone as He Described the Explosion of the Hindenburg," *Daily Reporter* (Greenfield, IN), March 25, 1957.

228 **Benny knew he had to:** John Parris Jr. (United Press), "Survivor Describes Jump from Blazing Hindenburg," *Pittsburgh Press*, May 8, 1937; Joseph Spah, interview in in *Survival!,* produced by Sherman Grinberg, hosted by James Whitmore, 1964, Spah Family Papers.

228 **As he dangled:** Judi Hasson, "Man Who Escaped from Hindenburg," *St. Louis Post-Dispatch*, January 8, 1976.

228 **"Quickly the end":** Gertrud Stolte-Adelt, "Mein Sturz aus dem brennenden Luftschiff: Erinnerungen an eine tragische Atlantikfahrt," *Hamburger Abendblatt*, August 27, 1949.

228 **"reality ceased with one":** Leonhard Adelt, "The Last Trip of the Hindenburg," *Reader's Digest*, November 1937.

229 **still on their feet:** Nelson Morris Testimony, May 28, 1937, RG 179, box 8, National Archives and Records Administration at College Park (NARA).

229 **Bert somehow managed:** Dennis R. Kromm, "Homecoming," in *Compex: Combined Philatelic Exhibition of Chicagoland, Incorporated, Commemorating the 50th Anniversary of the Last Flight of the Hindenburg* (May 1987), 58.

229 **"*Es ist das Ende!*":** Margaret Mather, "I Was on the Hindenburg," *Harper's Monthly*, November 1937.

229 **For reasons known only:** William Leuchtenberg Testimony, May 28, 1937, RG 197, box 8, NARA.

230 **"No!" Captain Sammt shouted:** Albert Sammt, *Mein Leben für den Zeppelin* (Verlag Pestalozzi Kinderdorf Wahlwies, 1980), 141.

230 **Sammt and Pruss had just:** Walter Ziegler Testimony, May 20, 1937, RG 197, box 8, NARA; Max Pruss, Columbia University Oral History Collection, 16.

230 **"Everybody outside," Lehmann commanded:** Anton Wittemann Testimony, May 20, 1937, RG 197, box 8, NARA.

230 **It was still about a five-meter:** Sammt, *Mein Leben*, 141.

230 **Franz found himself completely alone:** W. E. von Medem, *Kabinenjunge Werner Franz vom Luftschiff "Hindenburg"* (Franz Schneider Verlag, 1938), 88–93; Werner Franz Testimony, May 13, 1937, RG 197, box 8, NARA.

231 **"*Ich bin der* cabin-boy":** von Medem, *Kabinenjunge Werner Franz*, 97–98.

232 **When he finally:** Parris, "Survivor Describes Jump"; Spah, interview in in *Survival!*; "'I Was Blown into the U.S.,' 'Cracks' Acrobat Survivor," *Times Union* (Albany, NY), May 7, 1937; Marilyn Muse, "'Grandpa' Survived Hindenburg Fire," *Potomac News*, January 16, 1976; Kelly and Kelly, interview with the author.

232 **Neither Leonhard nor:** Adelt, "Last Trip of the Hindenburg"; Stolte-Adelt, "Mein Sturz."

232 **"impenetrable darkness of black oil":** Adelt, "Last Trip of the Hindenburg."

233 **"tired, dead tired":** Stolte-Adelt, "Mein Sturz."

233 **"running again like a mechanical":** Adelt, "Last Trip of the Hindenburg."

233 **"guided by a steward":** Leonhard Adelt, "Trauer und Zuversicht," in Ernst A. Lehmann, *Auf Luftpatrouille und Weltfahrt* (Schmidt & Günther, 1937), 403.

233 **"smoldering black skeleton":** Stolte-Adelt, "Mein Sturz."

233 **Nelson Morris hit the ground:** Nelson Morris Testimony; Kromm, "Homecoming," 58; Patrick Dolan, interview with the author, January 4, 2024.

234 **"Come out, lady!":** Mather, "I Was on the Hindenburg."

234 **While a group:** "Andover Woman's Mother Tells of Hindenburg Explosion," *Andover Townsman*, May 14, 1937; photograph of Marie Kleemann, available at Patrick Russell, "Marie Kleemann," *Faces of the Hindenburg* (blog), December 15, 2008, facesofthe hindenburg.blogspot.com/2008/12/marie-kleemann.html.

Chapter 27

236 **An emergency call:** Narrative of Events Immediately Preceding and Following the Destruction of the Airship Hindenburg, May 19, 1937, Lakehurst Naval Air Station, courtesy of 87th Air Base Wing Historian; William F. Althoff, *USS Los Angeles: The Navy's Venerable Airship and Aviation Technology* (Potomac Books, 2005), 196.

236 **American Airlines also dispatched:** Herbert Morrison, Hindenburg broadcast, May 6, 1937.

236 **"Charlie, this is terrible":** Morrison, Hindenburg broadcast.

236 **Nehlsen told him to "relax":** Charles Nehlsen to John Toland, July 14, 1956, box 99, folder 2, John Toland Papers, Manuscript Division, Library of Congress, Washington, DC (LOC).

237 **"Philip Mangone," he told Morrison:** Morrison, *Hindenburg* broadcast.

237 **Mangone was terribly burned:** John Toland Interview with Philip Mangone and Katherine Mangone Lusty, November 23, undated (1950s), New York, box 99, folder 1, Toland Papers, LOC.

237 **"rat in a trap":** Elizabeth Toomey (United Press), "Survivor Recalls Actions at Hindenburg Disaster," *Austin Statesman*, May 8, 1952.

237 **"scrap[ing] a hole":** James L. Kilgallen (International News Service), "'God Saved Me' Said Philip Mangone as He Described the Explosion of the Hindenburg," *Daily Reporter* (Greenfield, IN), March 25, 1957; John Toland Interview with Philip Mangone and Katherine Mangone Lusty.

237 **Morrison did not press him:** Morrison, *Hindenburg* broadcast; John Toland, *Ships in the Sky* (Frederick Muller, 1957), 246; Emmett Weaver, "Hindenburg Tragedy Reporter Reminisces," *Birmingham Post-Herald*, December 13, 1975.

238 **the man said "Spay":** Morrison, *Hindenburg* broadcast.

238 **Others' backs were black:** Markus Reiter, "Erinnerungen an die Hölle von Lakehurst," LZ 129, BMA III, Zeppelin Museum, Friedrichshafen.
238 **By the time Morrison:** Morrison, *Hindenburg* broadcast.
238 **While Morrison was out:** Charles Nehlsen to John Toland, June 27, 1956, box 99, folder 2, Toland Papers, LOC.
238 **"It sounds like Spay":** Morrison, *Hindenburg* broadcast.
239 **Peter Belin had jumped:** John Toland, notes for *Ships in the Sky*, box 99, folder 1, Toland Papers, LOC; "Yale Man Leaps from Hindenburg," *Yale Daily News*, May 7, 1937.
239 **"insensate" with grief:** John Toland, notes for *Ships in the Sky*, box 99, folder 1, Toland Papers, LOC.
239 **Belin was eager:** John Toland, notes for *Ships in the Sky*; "Yale Man Leaps from Hindenburg."
239 **The May 7 paper:** Advertisements, *Yale Daily News*, May 7, 1937.
240 **"not to mention His majesty":** "Flickers," *Yale Daily News*, May 7, 1937.
240 **"It's all sheer nonsense!":** *The Girl from Scotland Yard*, directed by Robert G. Vignola (Paramount, 1937).
240 **"Thank God, you are safe":** Margaret Mather, "I Was on the Hindenburg," *Harper's Monthly*, November 1937; George Grant Testimony, May 28, 1937, RG 197, box 8, National Archives and Records Administration at College Park.
240 **There was a steward wandering:** Morrison, *Hindenburg* broadcast; Nehlsen to Toland, June 27, 1956.
240 **Meanwhile, a public relations:** John Toland Interview with William Craig, November 18, undated (1950s), New Jersey, box 99, folder 1, Toland Papers, LOC.
241 **"Can't do it":** Mather, "I Was on the Hindenburg."
241 **"always looked alert":** Mather, "I Was on the Hindenburg."
242 **"Even in the midst":** Mather, "I Was on the Hindenburg."
242 **"demon-like urge of self-destruction":** Leonhard Adelt, "The Last Trip of the Hindenburg," *Reader's Digest*, November 1937.
243 **"There is no more":** Gertrud Stolte-Adelt, "Mein Sturz aus dem brennenden Luftschiff: Erinnerungen an eine tragische Atlantikfahrt," *Hamburger Abendblatt*, August 27, 1949.
243 **"disturbed ant heap":** Adelt, "Last Trip of the Hindenburg."
243 **"young nurses dressed":** Stolte-Adelt, "Mein Sturz."
243 **"morphine syringe the size of":** Adelt, "Last Trip of the Hindenburg."
243 **Gertrud sat in a wicker:** Stolte-Adelt, "Mein Sturz"; Adelt, "Last Trip of the Hindenburg."
243 **"which only God":** Stolte-Adelt, "Mein Sturz."
243 **He was sitting hunched:** Adelt, "Last Trip of the Hindenburg."
243 **"What caused it?":** Adelt, "Last Trip of the Hindenburg"; Leonhard Adelt, "Trauer und Zuversicht," in Ernst A. Lehmann, *Auf Luftpatrouille und Weltfahrt* (Schmidt & Günther, 1937), 405.
243 **"no longer contain":** Adelt, "Last Trip of the Hindenburg."

243 **"Only the flying poseur":** Leonhard Adelt, *Der Flieger: Ein Buch aus unsern Tagen* (Literarische Anstalt Rütten & Loening, 1913), 181, 184.

244 **"writhing in their pain":** Die Aufzeichnungen des Luftschiffstewards Wilhelm Balla, LZ 129, BMA I, Zeppelin Museum, Friedrichshafen.

244 **"Pruss, is it you?":** Albert Sammt, *Mein Leben für den Zeppelin* (Verlag Pestalozzi Kinderdorf Wahlwies, 1980), 141–42.

244 **Pruss looked much worse:** Die Aufzeichnungen des Luftschiffstewards.

244 **Balla limped over:** Die Aufzeichnungen des Luftschiffstewards; W. E. von Medem, *Kabinenjunge Werner Franz vom Luftschiff "Hindenburg"* (Franz Schneider Verlag, 1938), 98.

245 **"Mrs. Spah, please come":** Marilyn Spah Kelly and Jane Kelly, joint interview with the author, May 5, 2024.

245 **"Journey's end," he said:** John Parris Jr. (United Press), "Survivor Describes Jump from Blazing Hindenburg," *Pittsburgh Press*, May 8, 1937; Kelly and Kelly, interview with the author; John Douglas, interview with the author, April 21, 2024.

245 **He even still had:** Joseph Spah wallet items, Spah Family Papers.

245 **Someone found a couch:** Kelly and Kelly, interview with the author; Spah family photo, Spah Family Papers.

246 **"Ulla jumped out":** Victoria Spah, *The Spah Family: Home Movies* (self-published, 2006).

246 **"Oh those poor kids":** "Dirigible Passenger Tells How He Jumped to Safety," *Washington Herald*, May 7, 1937.

246 **In downtown Chicago:** Dennis R. Kromm, "Homecoming," in *Compex: Combined Philatelic Exhibition of Chicagoland, Incorporated, Commemorating the 50th Anniversary of the Last Flight of the Hindenburg* (May 1987), 57. Broadcast historian Dr. Michael Biel of Morehead State University explains that NBC broadcast bulletins from both the Red and Blue Networks at 7:45 p.m. EDT, from 9:07 to 9:11 p.m. EDT, and from 9:15 to 9:21 p.m. EDT. Biel's old-time radio newsletter is reproduced at Michael Biel, "The Hindenburg Broadcast," jeff560.tripod.com/hindenburg.html. Biel's further commentary is available at Brian Williams, host, *We Interrupt This Broadcast,* podcast, season 1, episode 1, "The Hindenburg Explosion—'Oh, the Humanity!'—(May 6, 1937)," July 20, 2021.

247 **"Brace yourself, Mildred":** Kromm, "Homecoming," 58; Patrick Dolan, interview with the author, January 4, 2024; Mary Alice Dolan Noone, interview with the author, February 16, 2024.

Chapter 28

248 **"crashed, caught on fire":** William L. Shirer, *20th Century Journey,* vol. 2, *The Nightmare Years: 1930–1940* (Little, Brown, 1984), 267; William L. Shirer, *Berlin Diary: The Journal of a Foreign Correspondent, 1934–1941,* rev. ed. (Bonanza Books, 1984), May 7, 1937, 72.

248 **Before he could even:** Shirer, *20th Century Journey*; Shirer, *Berlin Diary.*

249 **"I cannot imagine [what]":** Shirer, *Hindenburg Dispatch*, May 6, 1937, Journalist-Correspondent, Cables, Dispatches, Mail Stories, folder: Cables, Reports, 1936, 1937, 1939, William L. Shirer Papers, Coe College, Cedar Rapids, IA.

249 **Unsurprisingly, no one else:** Shirer, *20th Century Journey*, vol. 2, 267.

249 **"Seven years of flying":** "Second 'Super-Zep' Planned If Trips of LZ-129 Prove Success," *Morning Post* (Camden, NJ), February 20, 1936.

249 **As he lay there:** Shirer, *Berlin Diary*, May 7, 1937, 72.

Chapter 29

250 **Herb Morrison tried:** Herbert Morrison, *Hindenburg* broadcast, May 6, 1937.

250 **Security had tightened:** Charles Nehlsen to John Toland, June 27, 1956, box 99, folder 2, John Toland Papers, Manuscript Division, Library of Congress, Washington, DC (LOC).

250 **Morrison had to wait:** Nehlsen to Toland, June 27, 1956.

250 **O'Loughlin had been:** John Toland, notes for *Ships in the Sky*, box 99, folder 1, Toland Papers, LOC.

251 **Morrison had also spoken:** Morrison, *Hindenburg* broadcast.

251 **At 8:21 p.m.:** Narrative of Events Immediately Preceding and Following the Destruction of the Airship Hindenburg, May 19, 1937, Lakehurst Naval Air Station, courtesy of 87th Air Base Wing Historian.

251 **"toasted to ashes":** Toland, notes for *Ships in the Sky*.

252 **"blown the tops":** Morrison, *Hindenburg* broadcast.

252 **All night, American Airlines:** Morrison, *Hindenburg* broadcast.

252 **forty-two minutes of commentary:** Herbert Morrison to Investigation Board, May 16, 1937, RG 197, box 1, National Archives and Records Administration at College Park.

252 **It was after 9:00 p.m.:** See, e.g., A. A. Schechter, *I Live On Air* (Frederick A. Stokes, 1941), 259–63; Broadcast historian Dr. Michael Biel notes the arrival of mobile units that night in his newsletter, reproduced at Michael Biel, "The Hindenburg Broadcast," jeff560.tripod.com/hindenburg.html.

252 **Morrison had approached:** Brian Williams, host, *We Interrupt This Broadcast*, podcast, season 1, episode 1, "The Hindenburg Explosion—'Oh, the Humanity!'—(May 6, 1937)," July 20, 2021.

253 **In the three short:** John Dunning, *On the Air: The Encyclopedia of Old-Time Radio* (Oxford University Press, 1998), 434–36.

253 **"hustled to knock":** Nehlsen to Toland, June 27, 1956.

253 **Morrison took on:** "Under Fire!," *Stand By*, May 15, 1937, 15; Nehlsen to Toland, June 27, 1956.

253 **Nearby, photographer Murray Becker:** John Toland interview with Murray Becker, December 1, AP Offices; John Toland, notes for *Ships in the Sky*, box 99, folder 1, Toland Papers, LOC; "Murray Becker, Photographer Who Shot Hindenburg Blaze," *New York Times*, March 20, 1986. The AP's wire service commenced in 1935. Sending a photo on the wire was then a revolutionary technology. For more, see Nicole Meir, "90

Years Since AP Wirephoto Revolutionized News Technology," Associated Press, January 8, 2025, ap.org/the-definitive-source/behind-the-news/90-years-since-ap-wirephoto-revolutionized-news-technology.

254 **a few hours to kill:** The 1937 American Airlines schedule lists this flight at 1:00 a.m. However, both Charles Nehlsen and a contemporaneous news article have it taking off at 2:00 a.m. It likely took off late that night given the circumstances. Nehlsen to Toland, June 27, 1956; "Bystander Heard Four Explosions," *Buffalo Evening News,* May 7, 1937.

254 **The pilots, Johnny Deater:** "Bystander Heard Four Explosions."

254 **Nehlsen hung back:** Nehlsen to Toland, June 27, 1956; Scottdale Historical Society, "Whispers of the Past—Herb Morrison and the Hindenburg," posted May 12, 2022, by Whispers of the Past, YouTube, youtube.com/watch?v=7Gs3DteAjDs&t=15s; "Childs Restaurant Founder Is Dead," *New York Times,* March 18, 1925; Williams, *We Interrupt This Broadcast,* "The Hindenburg Explosion."

254 **As they left New Jersey:** Scottdale Historical Society, "Whispers of the Past."

255 **Just before 4:00 a.m.:** Nehlsen to Toland, June 27, 1956; "Bystander Heard Four Explosions."

255 **"It was probably":** "Bystander Heard Four Explosions."

256 **"with numbed senses":** Gertrud Stolte-Adelt, "Mein Sturz aus dem brennenden Luftschiff: Erinnerungen an eine tragische Atlantikfahrt," *Hamburger Abendblatt,* August 27, 1949; Ulrich Adelt, correspondence with the author, October 22, 2023.

256 **Now his hands:** Photograph of Nelson Morris, available at Patrick Russell, "Nelson Morris," *Faces of the Hindenburg* (blog), January 8, 2009, facesofthehindenburg.blogspot.com/search/label/Nelson%20Morris.

256 **Margaret Mather still:** Margaret Mather, "I Was on the Hindenburg," *Harper's Monthly,* November 1937; "Mather, Margaret," Passenger List Index Cards, 1883–1948, Philadelphia, available at familysearch.org.

257 **"Do you know":** Mather, "I Was on the Hindenburg."

257 **After receiving treatment:** W. S. Deveraux to J. Edgar Hoover, May 19, 1937, FBI Hindenburg Case Files.

257 **It was typically:** "'I Was Blown Into the U.S.,' 'Cracks' Acrobat Survivor," *Times Union* (Albany, NY), May 7, 1937; Toland, notes for *Ships in the Sky.*

258 **When they finally arrived:** Marilyn Spah Kelly and Jane Kelly, interview with the author, May 5, 2024.

258 **His ankle, now in a cast:** Photograph, Spah Family Papers.

258 **"I was literally blown":** "'I Was Blown Into the U.S.'"

258 **"I do think I am":** Joseph Spah, May 7, 1937, interview in *Survival!,* produced by Sherman Grinberg, hosted by James Whitmore, 1964, Spah Family Papers.

258 **"I haven't lost faith":** John Parris Jr. (United Press), "Survivor Describes Jump from Blazing Hindenburg," *Pittsburgh Press,* May 8, 1937.

258 **When the plane carrying:** Nehlsen to Toland, June 27, 1956.

259 **recording needle had punctured:** Scottdale Historical Society, "Whispers of the Past."

259 **He had, unfortunately, set:** The broadcast played at the correct speed, with an accurate sound of Herb Morrison's voice, is available at "Memories of the Hindenburg Crash, 70 Years Later," NPR, May 6, 2007, npr.org/transcripts/10033397?storyId=10033397?storyId=10033397; Scottdale Historical Society, "Whispers of the Past."

Chapter 30

260 **feeling decidedly "ill-tempered":** William L. Shirer, *Berlin Diary: The Journal of a Foreign Correspondent, 1934–1941,* rev. ed. (Bonanza Books, 1984), May 7, 1937, 72.

260 **Before Shirer even:** William L. Shirer, *20th Century Journey,* vol. 2, *The Nightmare Years: 1930–1940* (Little Brown, 1984), 267.

260 **Above all, New York:** For example, *The New York Times* and the *Chicago Tribune* both used Murray Becker's photo of fire shooting from the nose of the *Hindenburg* as it crashed into the ground at a forty-five-degree angle as the image on the front pages of their May 7, 1937, papers. The *Los Angeles Times* and *St. Lous Post-Dispatch* used Sam Shere's photo of the tail exploding with the mooring mast in the foreground. These are just four of thousands of papers that published these two images on May 7, 1937.

261 **He had managed to snap:** National Museum of American History, "Hindenburg Airship in Flames, Partially on the Ground," americanhistory.si.edu/collections/object/nmah_1320100.

261 **Shere had photographed:** Mary O'Donnell Hulme, "Sam Shere," International Center of Photography, icp.org/browse/archive/constituents/sam-shere?all/all/all/all/0. Sam Shere's picture won the 1937 Editor and Publisher Award for best news picture of the year. This is the image that would later become even more famous as the album art for the band Led Zeppelin's debut album.

261 **"never broadcast in [his] life":** Shirer, *Berlin Diary,* May 7, 1937, 72.

261 **"very idea of talking":** Shirer, *20th Century Journey,* vol. 2, 267.

261 **As he set about:** Shirer, *Berlin Diary,* May 7, 1937, 72.

261 **NEW YORK WELCOMES:** William L. Shirer, *Hindenburg* Dispatch, May 6, 1937, Journalist-Correspondent, Cables, Dispatches, Mail Stories, folder: Cables, Reports, 1936, 1937, 1939, William L. Shirer Papers, Coe College, Cedar Rapids, IA (WLSP).

262 **President Roosevelt was on:** M. H. McIntyre to Franklin D. Roosevelt, May 6, 1937, PPF 3829: Hindenburg (Zeppelin), Franklin D. Roosevelt Presidential Library and Museum.

262 **"you and the German":** Pare Lorentz Center at the FDR Presidential Library, "May 1937: U.S. and World Events Plus Additional Resources," Franklin D. Roosevelt Day by Day, fdrlibrary.marist.edu/daybyday/event/may-1937-2. See also Pare Lorentz Center at the FDR Presidential Library, "May 7th, 1937: Transcript," Franklin D. Roosevelt Day by Day, fdrlibrary.marist.edu/daybyday/daylog/may-7th-1937.

262 **"your excellency sincerely":** United Press, "Hitler Thanks Mr. Roosevelt," *Pittsburgh Press,* May 8, 1937; "Anteilnahme in der ganzen Welt," *Werkzeitschrift der Zeppelin-Betriebe,* June 1, 1937, 86, Zeppelin Museum, Friedrichshafen.

262 **"I am deeply shocked":** King George VI to Adolf Hitler, May 8, 1937, reproduced in "From the Archive, 8 May 1937, Hindenburg Airship Disaster Leaves 33 Dead," *Guardian*, May 8, 2012, theguardian.com/theguardian/2012/may/08/archive-1937-hindenburg-disaster.

262 **Similar messages arrived:** "Anteilnahme in der ganzen Welt," 86–87.

262 **Hitler himself had just:** Jochen von Lang, notes for *Stern*, 3, LZ 2016/009.006, Zeppelin Museum, Friedrichshafen.

262 **"stunned by the news":** "Hitler Awoken in Middle of Night with News of Hindenburg Disaster," *United Press*, May 7, 1937, upi.com/Archives/1937/05/07/Hitler-awoken-in-middle-of-night-with-news-of-Hindenburg-disaster/2313810415298.

262 **Shirer's sources had told:** Shirer, *Hindenburg* Dispatch; "Kundgebung des Führers," *Werkzeitschrift der Zeppelin-Betriebe*, June 1, 1937, 83, Zeppelin Museum, Friedrichshafen. Thirty thousand reichsmarks is roughly the equivalent of $12,000 in 1937, or $265,000 in 2025.

262 **Germans were so attached:** Shirer, *Hindenburg* Dispatch.

263 **tracked down Eckener:** Hugo Eckener, *My Zeppelins* (Arno Press, 1980), 167.

263 **The reporter's call:** Harold G. Dick from Goodyear Zeppelin, seconded to Friedrichshafen, recalled, "About four o'clock in the morning I had received the news about the Hindenburg casualty but it seemed like a bad dream until morning when there was no question about its reality." Harold G. Dick Memoir, 35, box 7, FF 7, Harold G. Dick Papers, Wichita State University.

263 **In 1844, Edgar Allan Poe:** Dwight Thomas and David K. Jackson, eds., *The Poe Log: A Documentary Life of Edgar Allan Poe, 1809–1949* (G. K. Hall, 1987), 457–60.

263 **Eckener wanted to leave:** Eckener, *My Zeppelins*, 166, 168–69; Hugo Eckener to Johanna Eckener, May 12, 1937, reprinted in Rolf Italiaander, *Ein Deutscher namens Eckener* (Verlag Friedr. Stadler Konstanz, 1981), 357; Hugo Eckener, "Ausklang der Erlebnisse und Erinnerungen von Dr Hugo Eckener," *Hamburger Abendblatt*, August 27, 1949; Henry Cord Meyer, *Airshipmen, Businessmen, and Politics: 1890–1940* (Smithsonian Institution Press, 1991), 214.

263 **"could only conclude":** Eckener, *My Zeppelins*, 168. Colonel Joachim Breithaupt, who had been sent by the Reich Ministry of Aviation to mind Eckener, was himself a World War I zeppelin captain.

263 **"I do not want to believe":** Shirer, *Hindenburg* Dispatch.

263 **"The only thing which":** Shirer, *Hindenburg* Dispatch.

264 **"never thought much":** Hugo Eckener to Johanna Eckener, May 12, 1937, 357; Eckener, *My Zeppelins*, 168.

264 **"on political grounds":** Eckener, *My Zeppelins*, 168; Hugo Eckener to Johanna Eckener, May 12, 1937, 357; Hugo Eckener, "Ausklang der Erlebnisse und Erinnerungen von Dr Hugo Eckener."

264 **Sabotage necessarily implied:** Harold G. Dick, "Questions That Have Yet to Be Answered," box 8, FF 3, Harold G. Dick Papers, Wichita State University.

264 **zeppelin "most unpleasant":** Eckener, *My Zeppelins*, 168.

264 **When von Schiller's radio:** Hans von Schiller, *Zeppelinbuch* (Bibliographisches Institut,

1938), 201–2, 210; Karl Vey, "Michael Max Pruss, Luftschiff-Kapitän," LZ 129, BMA III, Zeppelin Museum, Friedrichshafen.

264 **From his calls:** Shirer, *Hindenburg* Dispatch; Hugo Eckener to Johanna Eckener, May 12, 1937, 358–59; Charles E. Rosendahl, *What About the Airship? The Challenges to the United States* (Charles Scribner's Sons, 1938), 13.

265 **As Shirer finished:** Shirer, *Berlin Diary*, May 7, 1937, 73.

265 **The men who had perished:** Photograph, LZF 183/0132, Zeppelin Museum, Friedrichshafen.

266 **"Here in Berlin":** Shirer, *Hindenburg* Dispatch.

266 **That evening, Shirer arrived:** Shirer, *Berlin Diary*, May 7, 1937, 73; Shirer, *20th Century Journey*, vol. 2, 268.

267 **"What a lot of nerve-wracking":** Shirer, *20th Century Journey*, vol. 2, 268.

267 **"voice skipped up":** Shirer, *Berlin Diary*, May 7, 1937, 73.

267 **exhausted and "limp":** Shirer, *20th Century Journey*, vol. 2, 268; Shirer, *Berlin Diary*, May 7, 1937, 73.

267 **"Fear I will never":** Shirer, *Berlin Diary*, May 7, 1937, 73.

Chapter 31

268 **In New Haven:** "Yale Man Leaps from Hindenburg," *Yale Daily News*, May 7, 1937.

268 **Though his name:** Rolf Italiaander, *Ein Deutscher namens Eckener* (Verlag Friedr. Stadler Konstanz, 1981), 353–54.

269 **"*Gott im Himmel!*":** Associated Press, "Luck Alone Saves Max Schmeling from Being Aboard Liner This Trip," *Boston Globe*, May 7, 1937; Italiaander, *Ein Deutscher namens Eckener*, 353–54. Schmeling did not end up fighting Braddock, who canceled the bout to defend his heavyweight title, instead choosing to fight rising star Joe Louis in Chicago for a much larger purse and over the American public's concerns about Schmeling's ties to Hitler. According to Frank McDonough, Schmeling supported Hitler but was not a Nazi Party member, and his New York manager, Joe Jacobs, was Jewish. Frank McDonough, *The Hitler Years: Triumph, 1933–1938* (St. Martin's Press, 2019).

269 **circulated a correct roster:** See, e.g., "Dead or Not Accounted For," "Official List of Survivors," and "Hindenburg's Passenger List," *Chattanooga Daily Times*, May 7, 1937.

269 **With Clifford Osbun:** "3 Chicagoans Saved, 1 Missing in Zep Disaster," *Chicago Daily Tribune*, May 7, 1937.

269 **Around 11:00 a.m.:** Narrative of Events Immediately Preceding and Following the Destruction of the Airship Hindenburg, May 19, 1937, Lakehurst Naval Air Station, courtesy of 87th Air Base Wing Historian.

269 **For nearly four hours:** Russell B. Porter, "Rosendahl Is Mystified by the Hindenburg Fire; Advised Captain to Land," *New York Times*, May 11, 1937.

269 **the fires were out:** Narrative of Events.

269 **Still, that did not stop:** 87th Air Base Wing Historian James Warrick, interview with the author, June 8, 2024.

270 **They came from as far:** Fred Rom, interview with the author, April 9, 2024.

270 **They found binoculars:** Liste von der "Hindenburg" Katastrophe geretteten Gegenstaende, deren Eigentuemer noch nicht festgestellt ist, LZ 129, BMA I, Zeppelin Museum, Friedrichshafen; Liste der nicht identifizierten Sachen, LZ 129, BMA I, Zeppelin Museum, Friedrichshafen; American Zeppelin Transport Inc., "Complete List of Articles Which Were Salvaged from the Airship 'Hindenburg' the Owners of Which Have Not Yet Been Determined," July 30, 1937, Spah Family Papers.

270 **Remarkably, Eduard Boëtius:** "Für Panik war keine Zeit," *Spiegel-Gesprach*, 123–24, LZ 129, BMA I, Zeppelin Museum, Friedrichshafen.

270 **Someone else located:** W. E. von Medem, *Kabinenjunge Werner Franz vom Luftschiff "Hindenburg"* (Franz Schneider Verlag, 1938), 100.

270 **Scattered around the remains:** "Hindenburg" Bergungsmaterial verschifft an die Deutsche Zeppelin-Reederei, Frankfurt am Main, July 17, 1937, LZA 17/562, Zeppelin Museum, Friedrichshafen.

270 **Of the 17,609:** Manfred Bauer (translated by John Duggan), "Hindenburg Crash Mail from the Collection of Luftschiffkapitän Heinrich Bauer," 2005, LZ 129, BMA I, Zeppelin Museum, Friedrichshafen; Smithsonian National Postal Museum, "Mail Ships," *Fire & Ice: Hindenburg and Titanic*, postalmuseum.si.edu/exhibition/fire-ice-hindenburg-and-titanic-exhibition/mail-ships.

270 **Passengers had been sent:** "List of the Hindenburg Survivors and Missing," *Times Union* (Albany, NY), May 7, 1937.

270 **That afternoon, the outgoing:** Ambassador Luther paid a farewell visit to President Roosevelt on April 22, 1937. Ambassador in the United States to the Foreign Ministry, April 26, 1937, document no. 338, *Documents on German Foreign Policy, 1918–1945*, series C (1933–1937), vol. 6, *The Third Reich: First Phase (November 1, 1936–November 14, 1937)* (U.S. Government Printing Office, 1983).

271 **By the time he reached:** John Toland Interview with Philip Mangone and Katherine Mangone Lusty, November 23, New York, box 99, folder 1, John Toland Papers, Manuscript Division, Library of Congress, Washington, DC (LOC).

271 **"Granddaddy looks a little":** John Toland Interview with Philip Mangone and Katherine Mangone Lusty.

271 **Lehmann had had a number:** United Press, "Injuries Fatal to War Hero," *Pittsburgh Press*, May 8, 1937; Max Pruss, Columbia University Oral History Collection, 16–17; "William B. Leeds, Sportsman, Dead," *New York Times*, January 3, 1972.

272 **"regardless of the cause":** Charles E. Rosendahl, *What About the Airship? The Challenges to the United States* (Charles Scribner's Sons, 1938), 27–28.

272 ***"Herr Kapitän,"* Luther greeted:** United Press, "Injuries Fatal to War Hero."

272 **Lehmann's lips were cracked:** United Press, "Injuries Fatal to War Hero"; Leonhard Adelt, "Trauer und Zuversicht," in Ernst A. Lehmann, *Auf Luftpatrouille und Weltfahrt* (Schmidt & Günther, 1937), 405.

272 **An hour later:** Narrative of Events.

273 **When Emilie Imhof's death:** Verzeichnis über den Nachlass der Frau Emilie Imhof, May 28, 1937, LZ 129, BMA II, Zeppelin Museum, Friedrichshafen.

273 **At 11:45 a.m., Chicagoland:** *Radio Guide*, Week Ending May 8, 1937, 42. *Radio Guide* lists both the CST and CDT times, but WLS remained on CST for its programming schedule. See "Program Changes in Effect April 25," *Stand By*, April 24, 1937, 5.
273 **"in place of the program":** Original WLS introduction featured in Brian Williams, host, *We Interrupt This Broadcast*, podcast, season 1, episode 1, "The Hindenburg Explosion—'Oh, the Humanity!'—(May 6, 1937)," July 20, 2021.
274 **WLS aired the entire:** *Radio Guide*, Week Ending May 8, 1937, 42; Charles Nehlsen to John Toland, June 27, 1956, box 99, folder 1, Toland Papers, LOC.
274 **At 2:30 p.m. Eastern Daylight Time:** "Under Fire!" *Stand By*, May 15, 1937, 2; *Radio Guide*, Week Ending May 8, 1937, 42. Specifically, this was the NBC-Red Network.
274 **"The whole night":** "Under Fire!"

Chapter 32

276 **She had spent hours:** Dennis R. Kromm, "Homecoming," in *Compex: Combined Philatelic Exhibition of Chicagoland, Incorporated, Commemorating the 50th Anniversary of the Last Flight of the Hindenburg* (May 1987), 58.
276 **His body arrived home:** Kromm, "Homecoming," 58.
276 **She looked at her:** Mary Alice Dolan Noone, interview with the author, February 16, 2024.
277 **"deep and sincere sympathy":** Edgewater Golf Club Board of Directors to Mildred Dolan, May 9, 1937, Dolan Family Papers.
277 **"By a strange chance":** Chick Evans to Mildred Dolan, May 17, 1937, Dolan Family Papers.
277 **"In silent sorrow":** Announcement, *Chicago Tribune*, May 10, 1937.
277 **It was the day of:** Kromm, "Homecoming," 58–59; "Rites for Zep Victim," *New York Daily News*, May 11, 1937.
277 **The Reverend Thomas Mackin:** "Funeral Held for Victim of Hindenburg Disaster," *Chicago Tribune*, May 11, 1937.
277 **When the family left:** "Rites for Zep Victim."
277 **the family made its way:** "Funeral Held for Victim"; Kromm, "Homecoming," 58–59; Burtis Dolan, Obituaries, *Chicago Tribune*, December 25, 1936.
278 **"*Until your letter came*":** Burtis Dolan to Mildred Dolan, undated 1937, Dolan Family Papers.

Chapter 33

279 **"worst days of my life":** Joe Jackson Jr. to Joseph Spah, May 7, 1937, Spah Family Papers.
279 **Benny also had a telegram:** Bernt to Joseph Spah, May 20, 1937, Spah Family Papers; Benjamin Dover to Joseph Spah, May 7, 1937, Spah Family Papers.

279 **Just two days after:** George Mozely to Joseph Spah, May 8, 1937, Spah Family Papers; John N. Connoly to Joseph Spah, May 18, 1937, Spah Family Papers.

279 **"The writer of these lines":** Munich ticket agent to Joseph Spah, May 8, 1937, Spah Family Papers.

280 **"faithful Ulla":** Handwritten letter from Spah family members, Munich, May 7, 1936 (misdated), Spah Family Papers.

280 **In his list:** List of lost belongings, Spah Family Papers.

280 **In the days following:** William Bloeth, "Ben Dova Gets High but Stays on Ground," *New York World-Telegram,* undated.

280 **"I thought you said":** Victoria Spah, *The Spah Family: Home Movies* (self-published, 2006).

280 **Vera was looking through:** Marilyn Spah Kelly and Jane Kelly, interview with the author, May 5, 2024.

280 **He contacted DZR's:** American Zeppelin Transport, Inc., to Joseph Spah, May 19, 1937, Spah Family Papers.

280 **The binoculars and camera:** Kelly and Kelly, interview with the author.

281 **list of nearly one hundred:** Alphabetical List of Witnesses to the Hindenburg Accident, RG 197, box 7, National Archives and Records Administration at College Park (NARA). Leonhard sent a handwritten letter to investigators about his last interaction with Lehmann on May 30, 1937. The letter, stored in the National Archives, is also reproduced in Michael McCarthy, *The Hidden Hindenburg: The Untold Story of the Tragedy, the Nazi Secrets, and the Quest to Rule the Skies* (Lyons Press, 2020), 249.

281 **To field as wide:** The collection of collected diagrams and witness responses to questionnaires is located in RG 197, box 1 (General Records), NARA.

281 **So-called tips:** A large collection of these "tips" can be found in RG 197, box 3 (Miscellaneous Correspondence), NARA, and in the FBI Hindenburg Case Files.

282 **Multiple individuals suggested:** See, e.g., Joseph Dermoutz to German Consulate, May 12, 1937, RG 197, box 3, NARA; K. W. Beck to Hugo Eckener, May 27, 1937, RG 197, box 3, NARA.

282 **Another suggested a cabal:** Redacted name to Col. Harold E. Hartney, May 11, 1937, FBI Hindenburg Case Files.

282 **Someone named E. O. Bagley:** E. O. Bagley Jr., undated, RG 197, box 3, NARA.

282 **On the insurance theme:** American President of PlanetAryans to Dr. Fred Fagg Jr., Bureau of Air Commerce, RG 197, box 3, NARA.

282 **"operated by an invisible":** Hans Omenitsch to Joseph B. Weaver, May 15, 1936 (misdated), FBI Hindenburg Case Files; "Destruction of Airship 'Hindenburg'" (report), June 17, 1937, FBI Hindenburg Case Files.

282 **"on account of his numerous":** "Destruction of Airship 'Hindenburg.'"

283 **"the love to my race":** Josephine Mair to German Consul General, May 10, 1937, RG 197, box 3, NARA. Another woman, named Gertrude, declared in her letter that a Jewish girl named Henrietta Sommers, who lived in New Jersey, supposedly "swore vengeance" on the *Hindenburg* and prophesized, "That ship shall burn in mid-air and all aboard her shall perish." Gertrude to German Consul General, May 10, 1937, RG 197, box 3, NARA.

283 **"act of Jewish sabotage":** Redacted name to Col. Harold E. Hartney, May 9, 1937, FBI Hindenburg Case Files.

283 **"heard it was a Jewish":** Tom Fagan to Charles Rosendahl, May 23, 1937, RG 197, box 3, NARA.

283 **"With German Greetings":** August Schütze to Amb. Hans Luther, May 7, 1937, RG 197, box 3, NARA.

283 **"some communist or disgruntled jew":** An American friend of Germany to Hugo Eckener, May 13, 1937, RG 197, box 3, NARA.

283 **"You should send for":** Redacted name to Senator Royal Copeland, May 7, 1937, FBI Hindenburg Case Files.

284 **disgruntled "mad Genius":** Mr. X.Y.Z., undated, RG 197, box 3, NARA.

284 **"*The Jews, as you*":** Ernst Goerner to Amb. Hans Luther, undated, RG 197, box 3, NARA.

284 **The FBI estimated:** "Destruction of Airship 'Hindenburg.'"

285 **"failed to reflect":** "Destruction of Airship 'Hindenburg.'"

Chapter 34

286 **On May 10:** DIARY: Investigation by the Department of Commerce of the Accident to Airship HINDENBURG, RG 197, box 1, National Archives and Records Administration at College Park (NARA).

286 **they saw a slight boy:** "Boy's Miraculous Escape from Hindenburg Is Told," *New York Times*, May 11, 1937.

286 **For the last few days:** W. E. von Medem, *Kabinenjunge Werner Franz vom Luftschiff "Hindenburg"* (Franz Schneider Verlag, 1938), 103–5; Die Aufzeichnungen des Luftschiffstewards Wilhelm Balla, LZ 129, BMA I, Zeppelin Museum, Friedrichshafen; Charles E. Rosendahl, "The Last Flight," in Ernst A. Lehmann, *Zeppelin: The Story of Lighter-Than-Air Craft*, rev. ed. (Fonthill, 2015), 335.

287 **At 6:00 p.m.:** Die Aufzeichnungen des Luftschiffstewards; "Funeral Services Today," *New York Times*, May 11, 1937, "3 Countries Honor Hindenburg Dead," *New York Times*, May 12, 1937; photograph, LZF 129/0729, Zeppelin Museum, Friedrichshafen; photograph, courtesy of 87th Air Base Wing Historian; photograph, "Funeral Service for the Victims of the 'Hindenburg' Catastrophe in the Halls of the Norddeutscher Lloyd (North German Lloyd) in New York, Organized by the German Colony," Alamy, May 11, 1937, alamy.com/funeral-service-for-the-victims-of-the-hindenburg-catastrophe-in-the-halls-of-the-norddeutscher-lloyd-north-german-lloyd-in-new-york-organized-by-the-german-colony-image360302900.html and alamy.com/funeral-service-for-the-victims-of-the-hindenburg-catastrophe-in-the-halls-of-the-norddeutscher-lloyd-north-german-lloyd-in-new-york-organized-by-the-german-colony-image360302899.html. Today, pier 86 is home to the *USS Intrepid*.

288 **At the Yorkville Casino:** "3 Countries Honor Hindenburg Dead."

288 **For two hours:** "10,000 at Services for Zeppelin Dead on Steamship Pier," *Universal* newsreel, May 12, 1937, available at criticalpast.com/video/65675051407_caskets

_Nazi-flags_German-ship-Hamburg_United-States-officers; "3 Countries Honor Hindenburg Dead"; Associated Press, "Throng Honors Alien Victims of Zepp Crash," *Kennebec Journal* (Augusta, ME), May 12, 1937.

288 **Directly across from and facing:** "3 Countries Honor Hindenburg Dead"; "10,000 at Services"; von Medem, *Kabinenjunge Werner Franz,* 104–5.

289 **"overwhelming sympathy . . . that we received":** "3 Countries Honor Hindenburg Dead"; "Funeral Service for the Victims."

289 **"From the ashes of the *Hindenburg*":** "3 Countries Honor Hindenburg Dead."

290 **In Atlantic City:** Gertrud Stolte-Adelt, "Mein Sturz aus dem brennenden Luftschiff: Erinnerungen an eine tragische Atlantikfahrt," *Hamburger Abendblatt,* August 27, 1949; "Many Women Swoon at Movies of Crash," *Pittsburgh Press,* May 8, 1937; "Disaster Films Booked by Theaters," *Pottstown (PA) Mercury,* May 8, 1937.

290 **As the newsreel:** Stolte-Adelt, "Mein Sturz"; "10,000 at Services."

290 **"just as much":** Leonhard Adelt, "Trauer und Zuversicht," in Ernst A. Lehmann, *Auf Luftpatrouille und Weltfahrt* (Schmidt & Günther, 1937), 399.

291 **With the loss of the *Hindenburg*:** Leonhard Adelt to Friderike Zweig, June 7, 1937, courtesy of Ulrich Adelt.

291 **"defeat and destruction":** Adelt, "Trauer und Zuversicht," 406.

Chapter 35

292 **Even with these:** Pare Lorentz Center at the FDR Presidential Library, "May 1937: U.S. and World Events Plus Additional Resources," Franklin D. Roosevelt Day by Day, fdrlibrary.marist.edu/daybyday/event/may-1937-2.

293 **"*Even more than*":** Eleanor Roosevelt, My Day, May 10, 1937, The Eleanor Roosevelt Papers Digital Edition (2017), George Washington University.

293 **"this most wonderful":** "Special Medal of Merit," *Radio Guide,* Week Ending May 22, 1937; "Heroes and a Heroine," *Stand By,* June 12, 1937, 10.

293 **Having featured Morrison:** "Twenty Years in Radio," *Stand By,* June 12, 1937, 7.

293 **Their boss, WLS president:** "Heroes and a Heroine," *Stand By,* June 12, 1937, 10.

294 **As Morrison had technically:** Scottdale Historical Society, "Whispers of the Past—Herb Morrison and the Hindenburg," posted May 12, 2022, by Whispers of the Past, YouTube, youtube.com/watch?v=7Gs3DteAjDs&t=15s.

294 **"approaching us for normal":** Herbert Morrison to Investigation Board, May 16, 1937, RG 197, box 1, National Archives and Records Administration at College Park (NARA).

295 **The board had assembled:** R. W. Knight, Department of Commerce Bureau of Air Commerce Safety and Planning Division, Report No. 11, "The Hindenburg Accident: A Comparative Digest of the German and American Reports of the Hindenburg Accident," August 1938, RG 197, box 12, NARA; Investigation Opening Remarks for May 14, 1937, RG 197, box 7, NARA; "Eckener to Sail for Inquiry Here," *New York Times,* May 8, 1937.

295 **While an engine malfunction:** DIARY: Investigation by the Department of Commerce of the Accident to Airship HINDENBURG, RG 197, box 1, NARA.

295 **"Though sabotage"—the very idea:** Karl H. von Wiegand, "Goring Calls Blast Accident," *Buffalo News,* May 8, 1937.

296 **They consulted with:** DIARY: Investigation by the Department of Commerce.

296 **The board interviewed experts:** DIARY: Investigation by the Department of Commerce; Frank W. Caldwell Testimony, May 19, 1937, RG 197, box 7, NARA.

296 **"part of your duties":** Raymond Taylor Testimony, May 24, 1937, RG 197, box 8, NARA.

296 **"any static charge":** Raymond F. Tyler Testimony, May 12, 1937, RG 197, box 7, NARA.

297 **"quite a bit of ballast":** Lt. Benjamin May Testimony, May 12, 1937, RG 197, box 7, NARA.

297 **Witness after witness repeated:** Lt. William Alexander Buckley Testimony, May 12, 1937; Lt. Richard S. Andrews Testimony, May 12, 1937; Chief Boatswain's Mate Frederick Joseph Tobin Testimony, May 12, 1937; Chief Boatswain's Mate Willie Mac Bishop Testimony, May 12, 1937; Heinrich Bauer Testimony, May 19, 1937; Captain Anton Wittemann Testimony, May 20, 1937; Walter Ziegler Testimony, May 20, 1937; Kurt Schoenherr Testimony, May 20, 1937; George A. Werner Testimony, May 20, 1937; John Francis Leonhard Testimony, May 21, 1937, Commander Jesse L. Kenworthy Testimony, May 21, 1937; J. Peter Quille Testimony, May 21, 1937; Lester K. Coleman Testimony, May 21, 1937; George Daniel Ream Testimony, May 24, 1937; and August Deutschle Testimony, May 25, 1937, all in RG 197, boxes 7–8, NARA.

297 **A yeoman from:** Arthur Harold Eaton Testimony, May 21, 1937, RG 197, box 8, NARA.

297 **"it seemed first":** George A. Werner Testimony, May 20, 1937, RG 197, box 8, NARA.

297 **seemed to "flutter":** R. H. Ward Testimony, May 21, 1937, RG 197, box 8, NARA.

297 **On May 13:** The interpreters included the enormously tall head of the American side of DZR operations, Willy von Meister, Benjamin Schnitzer of the Goodyear Zeppelin Company of Akron, Ohio, Captain Anton Heinen, and Karl Loerky from the German consulate.

298 **"shine from the flame":** Max Henneberg Testimony, May 13, 1937, RG 197, box 7, NARA.

298 **Meanwhile, steward Fritz:** Fritz Deeg Testimony, May 13, 1937; Severin Klein Testimony, May 13, 1937; Eugen Nunnenmacher Testimony, May 13, 1937; Christian Nielsen Testimony, May 19, 1937; and Eduard Boetius Testimony, May 19, 1937, all in RG 197, box 8, NARA.

298 **A cook, Alfred Groetzinger:** Alfred Fritz Groetzinger Testimony, May 13, 1937, RG 197, box 7, NARA.

298 **"Does he believe":** Werner Franz Testimony, May 13, 1937, RG 197, box 7, NARA; "Hindenburg Mess Boy Commended After Describing Leap from Air," *Chattanooga Daily Times,* May 14, 1937.

299 **Heinrich Kubis confirmed:** Heinrich Kubis Testimony, May 13, 1937, RG 197, box 7, NARA.

299 **Also quickly eliminated:** Hans Freund Testimony, May 17, 1937; Rudolph Sauter Testimony, May 18, 1937; and Heinrich Bauer Testimony, May 19, 1937, all in RG 197, box 7, NARA.

299 **A U.S. Navy meteorological expert:** Francis W. Reichelderfer Testimony, May 17, 1937, RG 197, box 7, NARA.

300 **"*least improbable* occurrence":** Francis B. Silsbee Testimony, May 24, 1937, RG 197, box 8, NARA. Emphasis added.

300 **However, the crew:** Anton Wittemann Testimony, May 20, 1937, RG 197, box 8, NARA.

300 **"man who fed":** DIARY: Investigation by the Department of Commerce. Rosendahl did continue with this theory and presented it to the FBI the next morning. Though not investigating officially, the Department of Commerce and the navy had included the FBI in the Lakehurst proceedings as observers. "The innuendo of the entire matter," the FBI agent wrote in a postmeeting memorandum, "is that this acrobat could have climbed out on the motor gondola, removed the cover on the exhaust pipe of the motor, and allowed the flames to set fire to the fabric and explode the hydrogen." The basis for Rosendahl's suspicion came from rumors he had heard from Captain Lehmann and others about DZR having received a warning about someone wanting to sabotage the airships, though such warnings occurred regularly. While logged with the German embassy, they never amounted to anything. The FBI placed some degree of "surveillance" on Benny Spah, though this was limited to consultations with the Passport Division regarding his citizenship, inquiries with the State Department, IRS, Treasury, and Immigration and Naturalization Service, and a review of Spah's letter in response to the Board of Inquiry's request for witnesses to share their observations of the disaster. Unfortunately, the contents of the FBI's full report on Spah, sent from J. Edgar Hoover to South Trimble, are entirely redacted. Ultimately, the FBI dropped the investigation. See "Memorandum for Mr. Tolson," May 8, 1937; W. S. Deveraux to J. Edgar Hoover, May 19, 1937; "Destruction of Airship 'Hindenburg'" (report), June 17, 1937; P. E. Foxworth, "Memorandum for Mr. Tamm," May 19, 1937; W. S. Deveraux to J. Edgar Hoover, May 19, 1937; Joseph Spah to Department of Commerce Board of Inquiry, May 29, 1937; and J. Edgar Hoover to South Trimble Jr., June 24, 1937, all in the FBI Hindenburg Case Files.

301 **"Doctor," South Trimble:** Hugo Eckener Testimony, May 22, 1937, RG 197, box 8, NARA.

301 **Sitting tall but stooped:** "Eckener Attributes Fire to Static Spark," *Dayton Daily News* (special to the *New York Herald-Tribune* and the *Dayton Daily News*), May 23, 1937.

301 **"If at this phase":** Hugo Eckener Testimony; United Press, "Eckener has Atmospheric Spark Theory," *Oregon Daily Journal*, May 23, 1937.

302 **"Therefore," Eckener explained:** Hugo Eckener Testimony.

302 **"As we know":** Hugo Eckener Testimony.

Chapter 36

307 **interviewed ninety-nine witnesses:** Alphabetical List of Witnesses to the Hindenburg Accident, RG 197, box 8, National Archives and Records Administration at College Park (NARA).

307 **On May 28:** Captain Albert Sammt Testimony, May 28, 1937, RG 197, box 8, NARA; DIARY: Investigation by the Department of Commerce of the Accident to Airship HINDENBURG, RG 197, box 1, NARA.

307 **"charred to the bone":** Albert Sammt, *Mein Leben für den Zeppelin* (Verlag Pestalozzi Kinderdorf Wahlwies, 1980), 146.

308 **"Give us your name":** Nelson Morris Testimony, May 28, 1937, RG 197, box 8, NARA.

311 **There was nothing more:** Dennis R. Kromm, "Homecoming," in *Compex: Combined Philatelic Exhibition of Chicagoland, Incorporated, Commemorating the 50th Anniversary of the Last Flight of the Hindenburg* (May 1987), 59; Patrick Dolan, interview with the author, January 4, 2024; Mary Alice Dolan Noone, interview with the author, February 16, 2024.

311 **"Thank you, sir":** Nelson Morris Testimony.

311 **the hearings concluded:** DIARY: Investigation by the Department of Commerce.

Chapter 37

312 **after the swastika-draped service:** Photograph, ZM 1996/197.2, Zeppelin Museum, Friedrichshafen; Die Aufzeichnungen des Luftschiffstewards Wilhelm Balla, LZ 129, BMA I, Zeppelin Museum, Friedrichshafen.

312 **Their tourist-class tickets:** W. E. von Medem, *Kabinenjunge Werner Franz vom Luftschiff "Hindenburg"* (Franz Schneider Verlag, 1938), 105–6.

312 **akin to celebrities:** Photograph, ZM 1996/197.2; Die Aufzeichnungen des Luftschiffstewards Wilhelm Balla; Wilhelm Balla, "Das Luftschiff brennt und stürtz ab," *Photographica Cabinett: Das Magazin für Sammler*, July 2000, 20–21, LZ 129, BMA I, all in Zeppelin Museum, Friedrichshafen.

312 **There, an enormous crowd:** Die Aufzeichnungen des Luftschiffstewards; von Medem, *Kabinenjunge Werner Franz*, 105–6, 108 (photograph).

313 **"sad and gloomy-faced":** Guillaume de Syon, *Zeppelin!: Germany and the Airship, 1900–1939* (Johns Hopkins University Press, 2007), 196, quoting *Frankfurter Zeitung*, May 8, 1937.

313 **A week after:** Der Reichs und Preussische Minister des Innern, V W 6339/11.5/a/37, Schnellbrief, May 13, 1937, R 43II/697b, Reichskanzlei, Bundesarchiv, Koblenz.

313 **Money that the government:** De Syon, *Zeppelin!*, 197.

313 **The company prepared:** "Die toten Kameraden," *Werkzeitschrift der Zeppelin-Betriebe*, June 1, 1937, 96–100, Zeppelin Museum, Friedrichshafen.

313 **"When an inexplicable fate":** "Göring an die Männer der deutschen Luftfahrt," *Werkzeitschrift der Zeppelin-Betriebe*, June 1, 1937, 82, Zeppelin Museum, Friedrichshafen. During this period, *Der Welt-Spiegel*, the weekend supplement to the *Berliner*

Tageblatt, wrote about the helium issue in a surprisingly well-rounded manner, citing the U.S. monopoly on helium but the indisputable fact that helium was more expensive and considerably less buoyant, thus making a new airship far less economical. *Der Welt-Spiegel*, May 23, 1937, 4, available from Staatsbibliothek zu Berlin.

314 **Publications ranging from:** *Völkischer Beobachter*, May 8, 1937; *Das Schwarze Korps*, May 27, 1937; both quoted in de Syon, *Zeppelin!*, 196.

314 **how "deeply moved":** Herman Göring to Jean Rosendahl, June 1937, box 76, folder 2, Charles Rosendahl Papers, University of Texas at Dallas Archives.

315 **"violent attacks" against:** William E. Dodd Jr. and Martha Dodd, eds., *Ambassador Dodd's Diary, 1933–38* (Harcourt, Brace, 1941), May 20, 1937, 409.

315 **In front of five hundred:** Two months earlier, the pope had written an encyclical titled "Mit brennender Sorge" (With deep anxiety) criticizing the German Reich for violating its 1933 concordat with the Holy See intended to guarantee the rights of the Catholic Church in Germany in exchange for the church refraining from involvement in German politics. Following increasingly anti-Catholic actions, the pope authorized the papal encyclical, which was smuggled into Germany, published in German, and read aloud in Catholic churches across the country on Palm Sunday. See, e.g., "Condolences," *Baltimore Sun*, May 8, 1937; Cardinal George Mundelein Speech, May 18, 1937, available as an appendix to Thomas M. Keefe, "The Mundelein Affair: A Reappraisal," *Records of the American Catholic Historical Society of Philadelphia* 89, no. 1 (1978): 79–84; and Richard Evans, *The Third Reich in Power* (Penguin, 2005), 235–39, 242–46.

315 **"If we show no interest":** Cardinal George Mundelein Speech.

316 **"the German system":** Dodd and Dodd, *Ambassador Dodd's Diary*, May 20, 1937, 409.

316 **As Dodd's friend:** William L. Shirer, *Rise and Fall of the Third Reich* (Simon & Schuster, 1960), 240.

316 **"Yes, Catholics, Jews":** Dodd and Dodd, *Ambassador Dodd's Diary*, May 20, 1937, 410.

317 **As it entered the mouth:** Verlauf der Trauerfeier für die beim Untergang des Luftschiffes "Hindenburg" ums Leben gekommenen Mitglieder der Besatzung und Fahrgäste, May 13, 1937, LZ 2019/007, Zeppelin Museum, Friedrichshafen; Wilhelm Balla clippings, undated, LZ 129, BMA I, Zeppelin Museum, Friedrichshafen; "Heimkehr der Toten von LZ 'Hindenburg,'" *Werkzeitschrift der Zeppelin-Betriebe*, June 1, 1937, 89–90, Zeppelin Museum, Friedrichshafen; May 13, 1937; Hugo Eckener to Johanna Eckener, May 12, 1937 reprinted in Rolf Italiaander, *Ein Deutscher namens Eckener* (Verlag Friedr. Stadler Konstanz, 1981), 357–58.

317 **Just like the hall:** Verlauf der Trauerfeier; "Heimkehr der Toten," 89–90.

318 **"With pride and appreciation":** "Die Staatliche Trauerfeier," *Werkzeitschrift der Zeppelin-Betriebe*, June 1, 1937, 90, Zeppelin Museum, Friedrichshafen.

319 **A beautiful display:** "Beisetzung von sechs Besatzungsmitgliedern in Friedrichshafen," *Werkzeitschrift der Zeppelin-Betriebe*, June 1, 1937, 91–92, Zeppelin Museum, Friedrichshafen; photograph, MS 99-01, box 12, FF 6, Harold G. Dick Papers, Wichita State University.

319 **In front of a full:** Helmsman Alfred Bernhardt and bar steward Max Schulze, who died in the hospital, would later join them.

319 **Ambassador Dodd, representing:** Dodd and Dodd, *Ambassador Dodd's Diary*, May 29, 1937, 411–12; "Trauerfeier in Frankfurt am Main," *Werkzeitschrift der Zeppelin-Betriebe*, June 1, 1937, 95–96; Jochen Lang, notes for *Stern*, 3, LZ 2016/009.006, Zeppelin Museum, Friedrichshafen.

319 **Between the cemetery's chapel:** "Trauerfeier in Frankfurt am Main," *Werkzeitschrift der Zeppelin-Betriebe*, June 1, 1937, 95–96; Dodd and Dodd, *Ambassador Dodd's Diary*, May 29, 1937, 411–12; Wilhelm Balla clippings, undated, LZ 129, BMA I, Zeppelin Museum, Friedrichshafen.

319 **"reference to God":** Dodd and Dodd, *Ambassador Dodd's Diary*, May 29, 1937, 412.

319 **"passed on to Valhalla":** "Trauerfeier in Frankfurt am Main."

319 **When the burial:** Dodd and Dodd, *Ambassador Dodd's Diary*, May 29, 1937, 412.

Chapter 38

323 **"Will you have dinner":** Wiliam L. Shirer, *Berlin Diary: The Journal of a Foreign Correspondent, 1934–1941,* rev. ed. (Bonanza Books, 1984), August (undated) 1937, 78–79.

323 **Murrow had wanted:** William L. Shirer, *20th Century Journey,* vol. 2, *The Nightmare Years: 1930–1940* (Little Brown, 1984), 273.

324 **wired back, "Delighted":** Shirer, *Berlin Diary*, August (undated) 1937, 79.

324 **"Just what you would expect":** Shirer, *Berlin Diary*, August 20, 1937, 80; Shirer, *20th Century Journey,* vol. 2, 274–76.

324 **this "new dimension":** Shirer, *20th Century Journey,* vol. 2, 281.

324 **"In two or three":** Shirer, *20th Century Journey,* vol. 2, 280–81.

325 **"great land in evil ferment":** Shirer, *Berlin Diary*, September 27, 1937, 84.

325 **In June, after:** Shirer, *Berlin Diary*, September 27, June 4, 1937, 74.

325 **arrested five Protestant pastors:** Shirer, *Berlin Diary*, June 15, 1937, 76.

325 **In August, the regime:** Shirer, *Berlin Diary*, August 16, 1937, 78.

325 **"inferior through and through":** Adolf Hitler, Nuremburg speech, September 1937, quoted in Richard Evans, *The Third Reich in Power* (Penguin, 2005), 575.

325 **"To sum up these three":** Shirer, *Berlin Diary*, September 27, 1937, 83.

326 **"aggressiveness of spirit":** Shirer, *Berlin Diary*, 84–86. The first comprehensive translations of *Mein Kampf* did not appear until the next year, and only with resistance from the Nazis.

326 **"I leave Germany":** Shirer, *Berlin Diary*, 87.

326 **Compared with his last:** Shirer, *Berlin Diary*, December 25, 1937, 90.

327 **Both Murrow and Shirer:** Shirer, *20th Century Journey*, vol. 2, 288. See, e.g., William L. Shirer to Baron Wimpffen, January 19, 1938, and William L. Shirer to Dr. von Reding, February 12, 1938, both in Correspondence, Correspondence by Date, folder: 1938, William L. Shirer Papers, Coe College, Cedar Rapids, IA (WLSP).

327 **Back in November:** Shirer, *Berlin Diary*, November 11, 1937, 89.

327 **Men were working overtime:** Harold G. Dick to Willy von Meister, January 21, 1938, box 3, FF 5, Harold G. Dick Papers, Wichita State University; "Transport: Helium to Germany," *Time*, January 17, 1938.

327 **"Dear Dr. Eckener":** William L. Shirer to Dr. Hugo Eckener, February 3, 1938, Correspondence, Correspondence by Date, folder: 1938, WLSP.

328 **"In Dr. Eckener's absence":** H. Bühler to Shirer, February 5, 1938, Correspondence, Correspondence by Date, folder: 1938, WLSP; Eckener was in Berlin at the time and returned to Friedrichshafen by at least February 15, 1938. Harold G. Dick to Willy von Meister, January 21, 1938, and Harold G. Dick to Willy von Meister, February 15, 1938, both in box 3, FF 5, Harold G. Dick Papers, Wichita State University.

328 **"If I don't make any":** Edward R. Murrow to William L. Shirer, February 14, 1938, Correspondence, Correspondence by Date, folder: 1938, WLSP.

328 **initial wave of American:** Karl Anstein to Harold G. Dick, June 10, 1937, box 3, FF 5, Harold G. Dick Papers, Wichita State University.

328 **appointed a cabinet committee:** Harold L. Ickes, *The Secret Diary of Harold L. Ickes, vol. 2, The Inside Struggle, 1936–1939* (Simon & Schuster, 1954), June 17, 1937, 146–47.

328 **"joint recommendation of all":** Helium Act of 1937, Pub. L. No. 75-411, 50 Stat. 885 (1937), S. 1567, Sect. "Post World War I." In the House, the bill met with strong anti-Nazi sentiment and passed by the narrowest of margins. Karl Arnstein to Harold G. Dick, September 14, 1937, box 3, FF 3, Harold G. Dick Papers, Wichita State University.

328 **Germany promptly applied:** "Transport: Helium to Germany," *Time*, January 17, 1938; Wheeler M. Sears, *Helium: The Disappearing Element* (Springer International, 2015), 111; Willy von Meister to Harold G. Dick, February 4, 1938, box 3, FF 5, Harold G. Dick Papers, Wichita State University.

329 **"permit accumulations of helium":** Helium Act of 1937, S. 1567, Sect. "Post World War I." Congress was amenable to selling helium for commercial use in part because production at the Amarillo Helium Plant had greatly exceeded production estimates and demand was down, as the navy had ended its rigid-airship program in 1935.

329 **An enthusiastic horticulturalist:** "New Secretary of Interior Ickes Has Been a Dahlia Enthusiast for Years," *Bulletin of the American Dahlia Society*, April 1933, 5–7.

329 **"of no use":** Harold Ickes to Dwight H. Perkins, January 10, 1916, Harold Ickes Papers, Winnetka Historical Society.

329 **Applying this same:** Ickes, *Secret Diary*, vol. 2, May 12, 1938, 393; Karl Arnstein to Harold G. Dick, May 20, 1937, box 3 FF 3, Harold G. Dick Papers, Wichita State University.

330 **Hitler had commenced:** William L. Shirer to Edward R. Murrow, February 1[?], 1938, Correspondence, Correspondence by Date, folder: 1938, WLSP.

330 **Meanwhile, CBS was sending:** Shirer, *Berlin Diary*, February 22, 1938, 93; Evans, *Third Reich in Power*, 649–50.

330 **"So long, Austria":** William L. Shirer to Edgar Mowrer, February 16, 1938, Correspondence, Correspondence by Date, folder: 1938, WLSP.

330 **"Congratulations!" Taylor said:** Shirer, *Berlin Diary*, February 26, 1938, 93–94.

331 **While Shirer was in Sofia:** William L. Shirer to Frank Gervasi, February 28, 1938, Correspondence, Correspondence by Date, folder: 1938, WLSP; William L. Shirer to Mrs. Packard, March 3, 1938, Correspondence, Correspondence by Date, folder: 1938, WLSP; William L. Shirer to Arno Walter Dosch-Fleurot, April 26, 1938, Correspondence, Correspondence by Date, folder: 1939 (misfiled), WLSP; Shirer, *20th Century Journey*, vol. 2, 292–93.

331 **Despite the building crisis:** Shirer, *Berlin Diary*, March 10, 1938, 95.

331 **"Plebiscite," the driver responded:** Shirer, *Berlin Diary*, March 11–12, 1938, 96.

331 **"If that's all the guts":** Shirer, *Berlin Diary*, March 11–12, 1938, 97.

332 **"swept along in a shouting":** Shirer, *Berlin Diary*, March 11–12, 1938, 97–98.

332 **"We have yielded":** Shirer, *Berlin Diary*, March 11–12, 1938, 99.

332 **He was the only American:** Shirer, *Berlin Diary*, March 11–12, 1938, 95, 100–101.

333 **"Well, *meine Damen*":** Shirer, *Berlin Diary*, March 11–12, 1938, 101.

333 **"Fly to London":** Shirer, *Berlin Diary*, March 11–12, 1938, 102.

333 **Murrow would make:** Shirer, *20th Century Journey*, vol. 2, 308.

333 **Shirer shot off:** William L. Shirer to Paul White, April 28, 1938, Correspondence, Correspondence by Date, folder: 1939 (misfiled), WLSP. As he later explained to his boss, who criticized him for leaving his post briefly unattended while Murrow was en route, the first person he tried was sobbing hysterically, the second had been arrested that night, and the third, he later learned, was hiding and was preparing to make a run for the Swiss border before the German army arrived.

333 **"Where did they get":** Shirer, *Berlin Diary*, March 11–12, 1938, 103.

334 **"A little more than":** Shirer, *20th Century Journey*, vol. 2, 303. When Shirer returned to Vienna, he found Tess in a dire condition. The hospital, like Vienna, was in chaos. An X-ray revealed that an instrument had been left inside her during the caesarean section and was causing sepsis. No one could find the doctor who had performed the operation. As he was Jewish, he had gone into hiding following the Anschluss, fearing for his life. Shirer somehow managed to track him down, and he agreed to operate on Tess to remove the instrument, but only in a convent clinic in Wienerwald in the middle of the night. The operation was successful, and six weeks after entering the hospital, Tess finally came home. Amid the upheaval, the Shirers had forgotten to name their daughter. They decided on Eileen Inge, though neither was pleased that when her birth certificate was issued, it listed her place of birth as "Vienna, Germany." Linda Shirer Rae, interview with the author, December 20, 2023; Deirdre van Dyk, interview with the author, January 13, 2024; Shirer, *20th Century Journey*, vol. 2, 319.

Chapter 39

338 **In 1939, Frankfurt's Jews:** New Jewish Cemetery, "Vielfalt der Moderne: Architektur und Kunst 1900 bis 1935," vielfaltdermoderne.de/en/new-jewish-cemetery.

338 **After the victims' funeral:** Niederschrift über die Sitzung des Aufsichtsrates und der Bilanzkommission der Deutschen Zeppelin-Reederei G.m.b.H. June 17, 1938. See also longer draft of notes from same meeting, LZA 17/665, Zeppelin Museum, Friedrichshafen.

339 **Sometime after his burial:** Michael McCarthy, *The Hidden Hindenburg: The Untold Story of the Tragedy, the Nazi Secrets, and the Quest to Rule the Skies* (Lyons Press, 2020), 243–44.

340 **The brand-new house:** Betr.: Siedlung Zeppelinheim, September 27, 1937, LZA 17/566, Zeppelin Museum, Friedrichshafen.

340 **"The melody of the new":** Leonhard Adelt, *Der Flieger: Ein Buch aus unsern Tagen* (Literarische Anstalt Rütten & Loening, 1913), 113.

340 **To paraphrase Leonhard:** Leonhard Adelt, *Der Herr der Luft: Flieger- und Luftfahrergeschichten* (Georg Miller, 1914), VIII.

Epilogue

343 **"the heavens curved off":** Ernst A. Lehmann, *Zeppelin: The Story of Lighter-Than-Air Craft*, rev. ed. (Fonthill, 2015), 24.

344 **Despite the best efforts:** DZR to the Reichsminister of Aviation, "Betr. Probe- und Erprobungsfahrten des LZ 130 mit Wasserstoff," July 9, 1938, LZA 17/665, Zeppelin Museum, Friedrichshafen. DZR had begun trial flights of the LZ-130 in June 1938.

344 **"the very strong feeling":** Schreiben der American Zeppelin Transport Inc. an Deutsche Zeppelin-Reederei v. 16 Sept. 1937 betr.: HELIUM, LZA 17/567, Zeppelin Museum, Friedrichshafen.

344 **By the spring of 1938:** Harold L. Ickes, *The Secret Diary of Harold L. Ickes*, vol. 2, *The Inside Struggle, 1936–1939* (Simon & Schuster, 1954), May 1, 1938, 385; Tom A. Knowles to Harold G. Dick, April 9, 1938, box 3, FF 5, Harold G. Dick Papers, Wichita State University.

344 **"guarantee from Hitler":** Ickes, *Secret Diary*, vol. 2, May 1, 1938, 392–93.

344 **Eckener's time with:** Ickes, *Secret Diary*, vol. 2, May 1, 1938, 391–93.

345 **"unpopular" and "an oddball":** Niederschrift über die Sitzung des Aufsichtsrates und der Bilanzkommission der Deutschen Zeppelin-Reederei G.m.b.H., June 17, 1938, LZA 17/665, Zeppelin Museum, Friedrichshafen.

345 **"My theory," he wrote:** Ickes, *Secret Diary*, vol. 2, May 1, 1938, 382.

345 **Hugo Eckener, who by then:** Harold G. Dick and Douglas H. Robinson, *The Golden Age of the Great Passenger Airships: Graf Zeppelin & Hindenburg* (Smithsonian Institution Press, 1985), 168.

345 **"carry[ing] forth the honor":** John Duggan and Henry Meyer, *Airships in International Affairs, 1890–1940* (Palgrave, 2001), 220–21.

345 **Outfitted with various:** Duggan and Meyer, *Airships in International Affairs*, 221, 226–27; Rolf Italiaander, *Ein Deutscher namens Eckener* (Verlag Friedr. Stadler Konstanz, 1981), 373, quoting John M. Carroll, *The Electronic War* (Berlin, 1967); main exhibit, Zeppelin Museum, Friedrichshafen; Lehmann, *Zeppelin*, 44n, 351.

346 **"Na, that thing's":** Henry Cord Meyer, *Airshipmen, Businessmen, and Politics: 1890–1940* (Smithsonian Institution Press, 1991), 228.

346 **Less than a month:** Italiaander, *Ein Deutscher namens Eckener*, 374–75. Ironically, the officer in charge of seeing that the order was carried out was Ernst Udet, who had

conducted the hook-on experiments and personally admired the zeppelins. Udet committed suicide in November 1941 in part due to a fraught relationship with the Nazi Party, particularly Hermann Göring and Erhard Milch.

346 **Finally, on May 6:** Dick and Robinson, *Golden Age*, 171; Main exhibit, Zeppelin Museum.

346 **In September 1941:** Michael Neufeld, *The Rocket and the Reich: Peenemünde and the Coming of the Ballistic Missile Era* (Free Press, 1995), 143.

346 **A total of 1,202:** Main exhibit, Zeppelin Museum; Duggan and Meyer, *Airships in International Affairs*, 240.

346 **As Allied forces led:** Guillaume de Syon, *Zeppelin!: Germany and the Airship, 1900–1939* (Johns Hopkins University Press, 2007), 207.

347 **founding charter stated:** Main exhibit, Zeppelin Museum.

347 **At least some:** Karl Beuerle to Herr Österle, April 12, 1962, thanking the Zeppelin Foundation for its Easter gift and asking for assistance with expenses for prosthetic leg for his wife; Luftschiffbau Zeppelin GmbH to Karl Beuerle, November 15, 1966, wishing him a happy eightieth birthday; Xaver Maier to Herr Sauter, January 10, 1992, thanking Luftschiffbau Zeppelin GmbH for an eightieth-birthday gift basket, all in LZ 129, BMA I–II, Zeppelin Museum, Friedrichshafen.

347 **"the purpose and task":** *Zeppelin-Post*, no. 1, January 1952, LZ 129, BMA I, Zeppelin Museum, Friedrichshafen.

348 **Until 1962, the U.S. Navy:** Main exhibit, Zeppelin Museum; Naval History and Heritage Command, "Airships & Dirigibles," August 23, 2024, history.navy.mil/browse-by-topic/exploration-and-innovation/airships-dirigibles.html.

348 **During World War II:** Lt. Col. Robert H. Rankin, "Goodbye to the Gas Bags," *United States Naval Institute Proceedings* 87, no. 10 (October 1961). As Norman Polmar points out in his October 2021 article "Blimps Versus U-Boats" for the U.S. Naval Institute's *Naval History*, these ships were also escorted by surface ships in their convoys, so the blimps were not solely responsible. Hangar No. 1 National Historic Landmark Package: McDermott, Hangar No. 1, Lakehurst Naval Air Station, New Jersey, National Survey of Historic Sites and Buildings, Special Report, U.S. Department of the Interior, National Park Service, 4, Registry of National Historic and Natural Landmarks, Report of Biennial Visit to Hangar No. 1, Lakehurst Naval Air Station, January 28, 1972, courtesy of 87th Air Base Wing Historian.

348 **In 1993, with investment:** Goodyear, goodyear.com/en_US/blimp/information/inside-the-blimp.html; Goodyear Blimp 100th Anniversary 2025 Media Kit, next.frame.io/share/f1d6aee6-716d-4d7c-a2b7-0a348d9f127c/view/4e0f6488-7a38-4690-9edc-bf7842f5d1cf; Lewis Page, "Goodyear Blimps to Be Replaced by German Zeppelins," *Register*, May 4, 2011.

348 **In Friedrichshafen, tourists:** Zeppelin NT, "The Special Experience at the Bodensee," n.d., zeppelinflug.de/en/zeppelin-flights. In a gesture to history, the tourism arm of the modern zeppelin company even operates under the legal name Deutsche Zeppelin-Reederei GmbH, a new "DZR."

348 **Their enduring legacy:** Led Zeppelin's name has several possible origin stories. The most famous suggests it was a name inspired by a remark by The Who's John Entwistle

and Keith Moon, who were considering making a supergroup with members of a band called the Yardbirds in the late 1960s. One of them supposedly said that if such a group ever came together, it would have "gone down like a lead balloon." Riffing on the joke, the word *zeppelin* was swapped in for *balloon* and *lead* changed to *led* to avoid confusion over pronunciation. Another version suggests Jimmy Page, who wore trinkets on his clothes, had a small zeppelin trinket made of lead, an intriguing juxtaposition of light versus heavy and an aura of something explosive. Zeppelins have also inspired English- and German-language musicals. The *Hindenburg* has lent its name to everything from recording software for journalists to a now-defunct American investment research firm specializing in activist short-selling called Hindenburg Research, which looked for companies running into "man-made, totally avoidable disasters."

349 **Since the Cold War:** In the 1970s, Soviet engineer Sergey Viktorovich Zhitomirskiy imagined a space colony in the atmosphere of Venus, which has gravitational and pressure characteristics similar to Earth's, where floating cities based on zeppelin designs, fancifully named the "Floating Islands of Venus," would circle the planet. In 2014, NASA studied a High-Altitude Venus Operational Concept (HAVOC), which proposed crewed Venus missions in a zeppelin-like airship.

349 **Today's airship start-ups:** LTA Research, "Explore Pathfinder 1," ltaresearch.com/technology; Nicolas Rivero, "Why These Startups Think Zeppelins Could Be the Future of Air Travel," *Washington Post*, May 15, 2025; Mark Piesing, "Pathfinder 1: The Airship That Could Usher In a New Age," BBC, February 1, 2025; Darren Ore, "The Electric Airship Revolution Is Almost Here. Are We Ready?," *Popular Mechanics*, August 2, 2023. Brin's company, Lighter Than Air Research, has constructed a four-hundred-foot-long prototype, *Pathfinder 1*, a rigid proof-of-concept electric dirigible developed in part at Goodyear's historic Akron Airdock. When it made its first untethered test flight at NASA's Moffett Field in California in October 2024, it was the first true dirigible to take flight since the *LZ-130* in August 1939.

349 **Geopolitical strife easily:** Callum Baines, "The World Keeps Running Out of Helium. There Is Now a Race to Prepare for the Next Shortage," BBC, April 1, 2025.

349 **nicknamed "*Hindenburg* Syndrome":** Ore, "Electric Airship Revolution." One airship start-up, H2 Clipper Inc., still intends to use hydrogen.

349 **In conjunction with the PBS:** For a full explanation of Giapis's experiments, see *NOVA*, season 48, episode 9, "Hindenburg: The New Evidence," written by Rushmore DeNooyer, directed by Kirk Wolfinger, aired May 19, 2021, on PBS; Emily Velasco, "History's Mysteries: Caltech Professor Helps Solve Hindenburg Disaster," *Caltech News*, May 17, 2021.

353 **As he recuperated:** Leonhard Adelt to Friderike Zweig, June 7, 1937, courtesy of Ulrich Adelt.

353 **"When I remember":** Gertrud Stolte-Adelt, "Mein Sturz aus dem brennenden Luftschiff: Erinnerungen an eine tragische Atlantikfahrt," *Hamburger Abendblatt*, August 27, 1949.

353 **In June 1937, Gertrud:** Leonhard Adelt to Friderike Zweig, June 8, 1937, courtesy of Ulrich Adelt.

353 **That autumn, they had:** Marilyn Spah Kelly and Jane Kelly, interview with the author, May 5, 2024. Benny left the dog to be trained while he toured with his show, and thus for the rest of her life, Ulla II responded only to German commands.

353 **"no longer any objections":** Eine Frühvorstellung im Apollo mit dem Film "Die letzte Fahrt des LZ 129 'Hindenburg' von Frankfurt am Main nach Lakehurst," December 3, 1937; letter to Director Lutz, December 4, 1937, Spah Family Papers.

354 **Gertrud and Leonhard attended:** Photograph, Spah Family Papers.

354 **"To Ben Dova":** Inscription in *Auf Luftpatrouille und Weltfahrt*, Spah Family Papers.

354 **"Who is that terrible":** Ulrich Adelt, interview with the author, October 19, 2023.

354 **He initially continued:** Adelt, interview with the author.

355 **Under cover of night:** Marshall De Bruhl, *Firestorm: Allied Power and the Destruction of Dresden* (Random House, 2006), 208–11; Antony Beevor, *The Second World War* (Little, Brown, 2012), 716–17.

355 **According to their grandson:** Adelt, interview with the author; Dr. Gertrud Stolte-Adelt, "Heir to a Friendship," in *Liber Amicorum: Friderike Maria Zweig, in Honor of Her Seventieth Birthday, December 4, 1952*, ed. Harry Zohn (Dahl, 1952), 11.

355 **Gertrud spoke little:** Adelt, interview with the author.

355 **Throughout Benny Spah's life:** Kelly and Kelly, interview with the author. At some point after the *Hindenburg* disaster, whether on his return from Germany in late 1937 or on one of his subsequent trips, Benny Spah also had a reunion with George Grant. They must have discussed the oil paintings Benny had been bringing home from Germany and had lost to the fire. During their visit, Benny admired an oil painting Grant had collected depicting a man playing a mandolin. As a token of their unique connection as survivors of the *Hindenburg*, Grant gave Benny the painting, which Benny's son Richard proudly displays in his home to this day. Jane Kelly, correspondence with the author, July 17–24, 2025; John Toland Interview with Mrs. Joseph Spah in Queens, "Evening, Nov. 25," box 99, folder 1, John Toland Papers, Manuscript Division, Library of Congress, Washington, DC (LOC).

356 **calls it "*Hindenburg* hair":** Kelly and Kelly, interview with the author.

356 **he and Vera moved:** Kelly and Kelly, interview with the author.

357 **When Werner Franz returned:** W. E. von Medem, *Kabinenjunge Werner Franz vom Luftschiff "Hindenburg"* (Franz Schneider Verlag, 1938), 106.

357 **Later that year:** von Medem, *Kabinenjunge Werner Franz*, 9–10. Von Medem was a newspaper editor and later a Nazi Party and SA member, and a regional commissioner in Nazi-occupied Latvia during World War II.

357 **He served in the Luftwaffe:** Bruce Weber, "Werner Franz, Survivor of the Hindenburg's Crew, Dies at 92," *New York Times*, August 29, 2014; Matt Schudel, "Werner Franz, One of the Last Survivors of the 1937 Hindenburg Crash, Dies at 92," *Washington Post*, August 30, 2014.

358 **In 2012, the Navy:** JD Watson, "2 Living Survivors of Hindenburg Disaster on 75th Anniversary," *Patch* (Darien, CT), May 6, 2012.

358 **Remarkably, Captain Max Pruss:** Viola Pruss, "Dreams in Flames: The Airship Hindenburg and Its Captain, My Great-Grandfather," CBC, May 23, 2017.

358 **Along with his son:** Klaus Pruss to John Toland, January 16, 1956, February 24, 1956, June 4, 1956, and July 12, 1956, box 99, folder 2, Toland Papers, LOC.

358 **By late 1937:** Max Pruss to Oberstleutnant Breihaupt, September 22, 1937; Max Pruss to Leni Kirchmeier, October 8, 1937; Max Pruss to Albrecht Hiller, December 16, 1937; and Max Pruss to Henry Tegtmeier, December 16, 1937, all in LZ 2016/009.004, Zeppelin Museum, Friedrichshafen.

358 **Initially, he believed:** Klaus Pruss to Jochen von Lang, February 18, 1927, LZ 2016/009.005, Zeppelin Museum, Friedrichshafen.

358 **"It may be sabotage":** Max Pruss, Columbia University Oral History Collection, 17–18.

359 **Remarkably, in the interview:** Viola Pruss, "Finding Max—Podcast Trailer," *The Hook*, CBC New Brunswick, May 4, 2018.

359 **To him, flying:** Max Pruss, Columbia University Oral History Collection, 19.

359 **Though the exact nature:** Patrick Dolan, interview with the author, January 4, 2024; Mary Alice Dolan Noone, interview with the author, February 16, 2024; Michael Pallasch, interview with the author, September 27, 2023.

359 **On October 6, 1955:** "Nelson Morris Dies in N.Y. as He Leaves Ship," *Chicago Tribune*, October 7, 1955; "Nelson Swift Morris," *New York Times*, October 7, 1955; "Philanthropist, Former Actress Blanche Morris," *Chicago Tribune*, 1983.

360 **He designed the uniform coat:** "Philip Mangone, Couturier, Dead," *New York Times*, December 8, 1957.

360 **In 1938, he married:** Naval History Division, "Captain Peter Belin, U.S. Navy," Navy—Biographies Branch, 0I-450, August 29, 1956, history.navy.mil/content/dam/nhhc/research/library/research-guides/modernbios/b/belin-peter_Redacted.pdf; "Peter Belin, 69," *Washington Post*, January 27, 1982; Ian Shapira, "A Family's Hidden History Is Revealed After Sale of Their Grand Georgetown Estate," *Washington Post*, October 15, 2011.

361 **It took until September 3:** William L. Shirer, *Berlin Diary: The Journal of a Foreign Correspondent, 1934–1941,* rev. ed. (Bonanza Books, 1984), September 3, 1939, 200; Brian Williams, host, *We Interrupt This Broadcast*, podcast, season 1, episode 1, "The Hindenburg Explosion—'Oh, the Humanity!'—(May 6, 1937)," July 20, 2021.

362 **"This crisis has done one":** Shirer, *Berlin Diary*, April 12, 1938, 112.

362 **After Shirer's first broadcast:** Shirer, *Berlin Diary*, March 14, 1938, 104–7.

362 **In October 1938:** A. Brad Schwartz, *Broadcast Hysteria: Orson Welles's* War of the Worlds *and the Art of Fake News* (Hill & Wang, 2015), 14, 50, 61, 75, 82; A. Brad Schwartz, interview on Brian Williams, host, *We Interrupt This Broadcast*, podcast, season 2, episode 1, "The War of the Worlds: The Original 'Deepfake' of 1938," October 27, 2021; Diary of Caroline Harnsberger, October 30, 1938, Winnetka Historical Society.

363 **In 1939, he left WLS:** Scottdale Historical Society, "Whispers of the Past—Herb Morrison and the Hindenburg," posted May 12, 2022, by Whispers of the Past, YouTube, youtube.com/watch?v=7Gs3DteAjDs&t=15s; Scott Childers, *Images of America: Chicago's WLS* (Arcadia, 2008), 40.

364 **When he left Europe:** For publication, Shirer did make some revisions to his early notes, including expanding entries based on his memories where his notes were sparse, editing his style for a narrative through line, and, perhaps most notably, modifying a 1935 entry covering Hitler's May 22, 1935, "peace" speech, whose sincerity Shirer, in his early and inexperienced days in Berlin, had been more willing to believe in than he would have been just a few years later. Though certainly never sympathetic to Nazism, in his later memoir, *Twentieth Century Journey*, he addressed his early naivete, which by 1941 he had certainly recognized and was too embarrassed to publish. William L. Shirer, *20th Century Journey*, vol. 2, *The Nightmare Years: 1930–1940* (Little, Brown, 1984), 222. For more on Shirer's *Berlin Diary* in context, see Michael Strobl, "Writings of History: Authenticity and Self-Censorship in William L. Shirer's *Berlin Diary*," *German Life and Letters* 66, no. 3 (June 17, 2013).

365 **In 2012, on the seventy-fifth:** Dan Grossman, "Hindenburg Memorial Service at Lakehurst," Airships.net, May 9, 2012, airships.net/blog/hindenburg-memorial-service-lakehurst.

365 **During the service:** Noone, interview with the author.

SELECTED BIBLIOGRAPHY

Archives, Libraries, Museums, and Private Collections

Adelt Family Papers (courtesy of Ulrich Adelt)

Bayerische Staatsbibliothek (Munich)

Bundesarchiv (Berlin-Lichterfelde)

NS 15: Der Beauftragte des Führers für die Überwachung der gesamten geistigen und weltanschaulichen Schulung und Erziehung der NSDAP

R 43-II: Reichskanzlei

R 4902: Deutsches Auslandswissenschaftliches Institut

R 8034: Reichslandbund-Pressearchiv, Personalia

RZ 206: Politisches Archiv des Auswärtiges Amts, Länderabteilung II, II F—Luft

RZ 211: Politisches Archiv des Auswärtiges Amts, Politische Abteilung, Pol. I Luft

ZSG 101: Sammlung Brammer zur Pressepolitik des NS-Staates

Bundesarchiv (Koblenz)

ZSG 117: Presseausschnittsammlung Hauptarchiv der NSDAP

Calvin University (Grand Rapids, MI)

German Propaganda Archive

Chicago History Museum

Coe College (Cedar Rapids, IA)

William L. Shirer Papers

Columbia University

New York Times Oral History Program, Columbia University Oral History Collection (Max Pruss)

Cooper Hewitt Museum

Dokumentationszentrum Reichsparteitagsgelände Museen der Stadt Nürnberg (Nuremberg)

Dolan Family Papers (courtesy of the family of Burtis J. Dolan)

87th Air Base Wing Historian (Joint Base McGuire-Dix-Lakehurst, formerly Lakehurst Naval Air Station)

Evermay (Washington, DC)

Federal Bureau of Investigation (Washington, DC)

Hindenburg Case Files
Foreign Relations of the United States (1937)
Franklin D. Roosevelt Presidential Library & Museum
FDR: Family, Business & Personal Subject File: American Investigation Corp. Commercial Airship Operation
PPF 3829: Hindenburg (Zeppelin)
George Washington University
Eleanor Roosevelt Papers Project (My Day)
Illinois State Archives (Springfield, IL)
Library of Congress
American Institute of Aeronautics
William R. Dodd Papers
John Toland Papers
Magnes Collection of Jewish Art and Life, University of California, Berkeley
Moritz Feibusch Papers
Michigan State University Library Archives (East Lansing, MI)
Musée de l'Air et de l'Espace du Le Bourget
Museum of Fine Arts Boston
Museum of Magnetic Sound Recording (Austin, TX)
National Archives and Records Administration at College Park (College Park, MD)
RG 197: Records of the Civil Aeronautics Board, Records of the Bureau of Air Commerce, Records Relating to the *Hindenburg* Disaster
Newberry Library
Princeton University
Frank Jewett Mather Sr. Papers
Scottdale Historical Society (Scottdale, PA)
Smithsonian National Air and Space Museum
George Henry Mills Collection
Hindenburg Memorabilia Collection of Willy von Meister
Smithsonian National Postal Museum
Spah Family Papers (courtesy of the Spah family)
Staatsarchiv Hamburg
Staatsbibliothek zu Berlin
Staats- und Universitätsbibliothek Bremen
Staats- und Universitätsbibliothek Hamburg
Dehmel-Archiv
State University of New York at Fredonia, Daniel A. Reed Library
Stefan Zweig Collection
UCLA Film and Television Archive
United States Military Academy at West Point

University of Chicago
John Gunther Papers
University of Texas at Dallas
Clara Adams Papers
Douglas H. Robinson Papers
Charles E. Rosendahl Papers
Wichita State University
Harold G. Dick Papers
Winnetka Historical Society (Winnetka, IL)
Harold Ickes Papers
Caroline Harnsberger Papers
Zeppelin Museum, Friedrichshafen
LZ 129 Besatzungs-Mitglieder Alphabetisch I–III
LZ 129 John Duggan Research
LZ 1997 / 064.003
LZ 2006 / 001
LZ 2016 / 009.004-.006
LZ 2019 / 007
LZA 17 / 196
LZA 17 / 197
LZA 17 / 562
LZA 17 / 566
LZA 17/ 567
LZA 17 / 652
LZA 17 / 665
Zeppelin-Museum Zeppelinheim (Neu-Isenburg)

Author Interviews

Ulrich Adelt (October 19, 2023)
Patrick Dolan (January 4, 2024)
John Douglas (April 21, 2024)
Marc Fisher (December 5, 2023)
Marilyn Spah Kelly and Jane Kelly (May 5, 2024, and February 1, 2025)
Ben-Oliver Matias (February 25, 2024)
Mary Alice Dolan Noone (February 16, 2024)
Michael Pallasch (September 27, 2023)
Linda Shirer Rae (December 20, 2023)
Gerald Rafshoon (October 20, 2023)
Frederick Rom (April 9, 2024)

Mary Ryan (Evermay) (December 4, 2023)
David Sanger (December 11, 2024)
Deirdre van Dyk (January 13, 2024)
Christian Williams (October 12, 2023)

Published Primary Sources

Adelt, Leonhard. *Der Flieger: Ein Buch aus unsern Tagen*. Literarische Anstalt Rütten & Loening, 1913.

Adelt, Leonhard, ed. *Der Herr der Luft: Flieger- und Luftfahrgeschichten*. Georg Müller, 1914.

———. *Der Ozeanflug*. Reuss & Itta, Verlagsanstalt, 1917.

———. "The Last Trip of the Hindenburg." *Reader's Digest*, November 1937.

Airship Voyages Made Easy. Deutsche Zeppelin-Reederei, 1937, reprinted 1976.

Bentele, Eugen. *The Story of a Zeppelin Mechanic: My Flights 1931–1938*. Wolfgang Meighörner-Schardt, 1992.

Book of the 332nd F. A., The. Stanley J. Low, 1920.

Cleveland, Reginald M. "What Is the Future of Aviation?" *Scientific American*, October 1929.

Dobson, Alan P. *FDR and Civil Aviation: Flying Strong, Flying Free*. Palgrave MacMillan, 2011.

Documents on German Foreign Policy, 1918–1945. Series C (1933–1937). Vol. 6, *The Third Reich: First Phase (November 1, 1936–November 14, 1937)*. U.S. Government Printing Office, 1983.

Dodd, Martha. *Through Embassy Eyes*. Harcourt, Brace, 1939.

Dodd, William E. Jr., and Martha Dodd, eds. *Ambassador Dodd's Diary, 1933–38*. Harcourt, Brace, 1941.

Dornberger, Walter. *V-2*. Translated by James Cleugh and Geoffrey Halliday. Viking Press, 1954.

Eckener, Hugo. "Ausklang der Erlebnisse und Erinnerungen von Dr Hugo Eckener." *Hamburger Abendblatt*, August 27, 1949.

Eckener, Hugo. *My Zeppelins*. Translated by Douglas Robinson. Arno Press, 1980.

Francois-Poncet, André. *The Fateful Years: Memoirs of a French Ambassador in Berlin, 1931–1938*. V. Gollancz, 1949.

Fromm, Bella. *Blood and Banquets: A Berlin Social Diary*. Birch Lane Press, 1991.

Gantenbein, James Watson, ed. *Documentary Background of World War II, 1931–1941*. Columbia University Press, 1948.

Gardiner, Muriel. *Code Name "Mary."* Yale University Press, 1983.

Gunther, John. *Inside Europe*. Revised ed. Harper & Brothers, 1938.

Hesse, Hermann. *Die Kunst des Müßiggangs: Kurze Prosa aus dem Nachlaß*. Suhrkamp Taschenbuch Verlag, 1973.

Hirschfeld, George. "Ich nahm mir felt vor, nicht den Kopf zu verlieren." *Bremer Zeitung*, May 21, 1937.

Ickes, Harold L. *The Secret Diary of Harold L. Ickes*. Vol. 2, *The Inside Struggle, 1936–1939*. Simon & Schuster, 1954.

Jones, Thomas. *A Diary with Letters: 1931–1950*. Oxford University Press, 1954.

Klemin, Alexander. "American Passenger Air Transport." *Scientific American*, October 1929.

Lehmann, Ernst A. *Zeppelin: The Story of Lighter-Than-Air Craft*. 1937. Facsimile of the first edition. Fonthill, 2015.

Lehmann, Ernst A., and Leonhard Adelt. *Auf Luftpatrouille und Weltfahrt*. Schmidt & Günther, 1937.

———. *Zeppelin: The Story of Lighter-Than-Air Craft*, edited by Jay Dratler. Longmans, Green, 1937.

Lindbergh, Anne Morrow. *Listen! The Wind*. Harcourt, Brace, 1938.

———. *North to the Orient*. Harcourt, Brace, 1935.

Lindbergh, Charles A. *Of Flight and Life*. Charles Scribner's Sons, 1948.

———. *The Spirit of St. Louis*. Charles Scribner's Sons, 1953.

———. *The Wartime Journals of Charles A. Lindbergh*. Harcourt Brace, 1970.

———. *"We."* G. P. Putnam's Sons, 1927.

Lochner, Louis P. "Aboard the Airship Hindenburg: Louis P. Lochner's Diary of Its Maiden Flight to the United States." *Wisconsin Magazine of History* 49, no. 2 (Winter 1965–1966).

Louis Ferdinand, Prince of Prussia. *The Rebel Prince: Memoirs of Prince Louis Ferdinand of Prussia*. Henry Regnery, 1952.

Mather, Frank J. Sr. "A Clipper Ship and Her Commander." *Atlantic Monthly*, November 1904.

Mather, Margaret. "I Was on the Hindenburg." *Harper's Monthly*. November 1936.

Maxim, H. S. "Aerial Navigation: The Power Required." *Century Magazine* 42, no. 6 (October 1891).

Morris, Ira Nelson. *Heritage from My Father: An Autobiography*. Privately printed, 1947.

Mundelein, Cardinal George. Speech, May 18, 1937. Available as an appendix to Thomas M. Keefe, "The Mundelein Affair: A Reappraisal," *Records of the American Catholic Historical Society of Philadelphia* 89, no. 1 (1978): 79–82.

Murchie, Guy. *Song of the Sky*. Houghton Mifflin, 1945.

Rosendahl, C. E. *Up Ship!* Dodd, Mead, 1931.

———. "U.S.S. 'Los Angeles,'" *United States Naval Institute Proceedings* 57, no. 340 (June 1931).

———. *What About the Airship? The Challenges to the United States*. Charles Scribner's Sons, 1938.

Russell, Charles Edward. *The Greatest Trust in the World*. Ridgeway-Thayer, 1905.

Sammt, Albert. *Mein Leben für den Zeppelin*. Verlag Pestalozzi Kinderdorf Wahlwies, 1980.

Schechter, A. A. *I Live on Air*. Frederick A. Stokes, 1941.

Schmidt, Paul. *Hitler's Interpreter*. MacMillan, 1951.

Sevareid, Eric. *Not So Wild a Dream*. A. A. Knopf, 1946.

Shirer, William L. *20th Century Journey*. Vol. 1, *The Start, 1904–1930*. Simon & Schuster, 1976.

———. *20th Century Journey*. Vol. 2, *The Nightmare Years, 1930–1940*. Little, Brown, 1984.

———. *20th Century Journey*. Vol. 3, *A Native's Return, 1945–1988*. Little, Brown.

———. *Berlin Diary: The Journal of a Foreign Correspondent, 1934–1941*. Alfred A. Knopf, 1941.

———. *The Rise and Fall of the Third Reich*. Simon & Schuster, 1960.

Spah, Victoria. *The Spah Family: Home Movies* (companion guide to the DVD set). Self-published, 2006.

Stolte-Adelt, Gertrud. "Heir to a Friendship." In *Liber Amicorum: Friderike Maria Zweig, in Honor of Her Seventieth Birthday, December 4, 1952*, edited by Harry Zohn. Dahl, 1952.

———. "Mein Sturz aus dem brennenden Luftschiff: Erinnerungen an eine tragische Atlantikfahrt." *Hamburger Abdendblatt*, August 27, 1949.

———. "Wegbilder der Barockzeit im Münsterland: Ein Beitrag zur Geschichte der volkstümlichen Plastik Westfalens." In *Lebensräume der Kunst*, vol. 4, edited by Martin Wackernagel. Karl Busch Verlag, 1936.

Sullivan, Louis. *The Autobiography of an Idea*. Press of the American Institute of Architects, 1924.

Twain, Mark. "The Chicago of Europe." *Chicago Daily Tribune*, April 3, 1892. Republished in *The Chicago of Europe: And Other Tales of Foreign Travel*, edited by Peter Kaminsky. Sterling, 2009.

United States Census Bureau. "Historical Statistics of the United States, 1789–1945." June 1949. census.gov/library/publications/1949/compendia/hist_stats_1789-1945.html.

Verne, Jules. *Around the World in Eighty Days*. State University of New York Press, 2013. Originally published in English in 1873.

———. *Robur the Conqueror*. Translated by Alex Kirstukas. Wesleyan University Press, 2017. Originally published in English in 1887.

von Medem, W. E. *Kabinenjunge Werner Franz vom Luftschiff "Hindenburg."* Franz Schneider Verlag, 1938.

von Meister, Leila. *Gathered Yesterdays*. Geoffrey Bles, 1963.

von Schiller, Hans. *Zeppelinbuch*. Biblographisches Institut, 1938.

"Yale Man Leaps from Hindenburg." *Yale Daily News*, May 7, 1937.

Secondary Sources

Ahl, Raymond C. "The Nazi-Soviet Pact: Its Effects upon the German War Economy." Master's thesis, Marquette University, 1966.

Althoff, William F. *USS* Los Angeles*: The Navy's Venerable Airship and Aviation Technology*. Potomac Books, 2005.

Archbold, Rick. *Hindenburg: Reliving the Era of the Great Airships*. Madison Press Books, 1994.

Barnouw, Erik. *A History of Broadcasting in the United States*. Vol. 2, *The Golden Web: 1933 to 1945*. Oxford University Press, 1968.

Barth, Rüdiger, and Hauke Friederichs. *The Last Winter of the Weimar Republic: The Rise of the Third Reich*. Pegasus Books, 2020.

Beevor, Antony. *The Second World War*. Little, Brown, 2012.

Bender, Marilyn, and Selig Altschul. *The Chosen Instrument: Pan Am, Juan Trippe, the Rise and Fall of an American Entrepreneur*. Simon & Schuster, 1982.

Benjamin, Louise M. *The NBC Advisory Council and Radio Programming, 1926–1945*. Southern Illinois Press, 2009.

Bennett, Leon. *Churchill's War Against the Zeppelin 1914–18: Men, Machines and Tactics*. Helion, 2015.

Bensman, Marvin R. "Regulation of Broadcasting by the Department of Commerce, 1921–1927." In *American Broadcasting: A Source Book on the History of Radio and Television*, edited by Lawrence W. Lichty and Malachi C. Topping. Hastings House, 1975.

Berg, A. Scott. *Lindbergh*. Putnam, 1998.

Berg, Scott W. *The Burning of the World: The Great Chicago Fire and the War for a City's Soul*. Pantheon Books, 2023.

Bernstein, Mark, and Alex Lubertozzi. *World War II on the Air: Edward R. Murrow and the Broadcasts That Riveted a Nation*. Sourcebooks, 2003.

Bilstein, Roger E. *Flight in America: From the Wrights to the Astronauts*. 3rd ed. Johns Hopkins University Press, 2001.

Blum, Matthias, and Alan de Bromhead, "Rise and Fall in the Third Reich: Social Mobility and Nazi Membership." Queens University Centre for Economic History Working Paper Series, April 2017.

Bouverie, Tim. *Appeasement*. Tim Duggan Books, 2019.

Brendan, Piers. *The Dark Valley: A Panorama of the 1930s*. Alfred A. Knopf, 2000.

Boyd, Julia, and Angelika Patel. *A Village in the Third Reich: How Ordinary Lives Were Transformed by the Rise of Fascism*. Pegasus Books, 2023.

Childers, Scott. *Images of America: Chicago's WLS Radio*. Arcadia, 2008.

Cloud, Stanley. *The Murrow Boys: Pioneers on the Front Lines of Broadcast Journalism*. Houghton Mifflin, 1996.

Cohen, Deborah. *Last Call at the Hotel Imperial: The Reporters Who Took On a World at War.* Random House, 2022.

Connors, Joseph David. "Paul Reynaud and French National Defense, 1933–1939." PhD diss., Loyola University Chicago, 1977.

Cox, Jim. *American Radio Networks: A History.* McFarland. 2009.

Craig, Gordon Alexander. *The Diplomats: 1919–1939.* Princeton University Press, 1953.

Cronon, William. *Nature's Metropolis: Chicago and the Great West.* W. W. Norton, 1991.

Davies, R. E. G. *Airlines of the United States Since 1914.* Putnam, 1972.

Davis, Kenneth S. *The Hero: Charles A. Lindbergh and the American Dream.* Doubleday, 1959.

De Bruhl, Marshall. *Firestorm: Allied Power and the Destruction of Dresden.* Random House, 2006.

de Syon, Guillaume. *Zeppelin!: Germany and the Airship, 1900–1939.* Johns Hopkins University Press, 2002.

Dick, Harold G., and Douglas H. Robinson. *The Golden Age of the Great Passenger Airships: Graf Zeppelin & Hindenburg.* Smithsonian Institution Press, 1985.

Douglas, George H. *The Early Days of Radio Broadcasting.* McFarland, 1987.

Duggan, John, and Henry Cord Meyer. *Airships in International Affairs, 1890–1940.* Palgrave, 2001.

Dunning, John. *On the Air: The Encyclopedia of Old-Time Radio.* Oxford University Press, 1998.

Dyja, Thomas. *The Third Coast: When Chicago Built the American Dream.* Penguin Books, 2013.

Engelman, Ralph. *Public Radio and Television in America: A Political History.* Sage, 1996.

Esposito, David M., and Jackie R. Esposito. "LaGuardia and the Nazis, 1933–1938." *American Jewish History* 78, no. 1 (September 1988).

Evans, Richard. *The Third Reich in Power.* Penguin, 2005.

Evans, Richard J. "Coercion and Consent in Nazi Germany." *British Academy Review*, no. 10 (2007).

Feibusch, Martin, and Cheryl Ganz. "*Hindenburg* Crash Cover Forgeries and Passenger Moritz Feibusch." *Zeppelin Collector*, July 1998.

Field, Alexander J. "Newspapers and Periodicals: Number and Circulation by Type, 1850–1967." In *Historical Statistics of the United States.* Vol 4., *Economic Sectors*, edited by Susan B. Carter. Millennial ed. Cambridge University Press, 2006.

Frederick, John H. *Commercial Air Transportation.* Richard D. Irwin, 1947.

Ganz, Cheryl R., and Daniel Piazza. *Fire & Ice: Hindenburg and Titanic* (exhibit companion). Smithsonian National Postal Museum, 2012.

Geisenheyner, Max. *E. A. Lehmann, Zeppelin-Kapitän.* Societäts-Verlag, 1937.

Gellately, Robert. *The Oxford Illustrated History of the Third Reich.* Oxford University Press, 2019.

Gilbert, Martin. *Winston S. Churchill*. Vol. 4, *The Stricken World, 1917–1922*. Houghton Mifflin, 1975.

———. *Winston S. Churchill*. Vol. 5, *The Prophet of Truth, 1922–1939*. Houghton Mifflin, 1976.

Goldberg, Isaac. *George Gershwin: A Study in American Music*. F. Ungar, 1958.

Grossman, Dan, et al. *Zeppelin Hindenburg: An Illustrated History of LZ-129*. History Press, 2019.

Grossman, James R., Ann Durkin Keating, and Janice L. Reiff, eds. *Encyclopedia of Chicago*. University of Chicago Press, 2004.

Gwynne, S. C. *His Majesty's Airship: The Life and Tragic Death of the World's Largest Flying Machine*. Scribner, 2023.

Hausrath, Adolf. "Treitschke: A Study of His Life and Work." Foreword to *Treitschke: His Doctrine of German Destiny and of International Relations*. G. P. Putnam's Sons, 1914.

Head, Sydney W. *Broadcasting in America: A Survey of Television and Radio*. Houghton Mifflin, 1972.

Heppenheimer, T. A. *Turbulent Skies: The History of Commercial Aviation*. John Wiley & Sons, 1995.

Hilmes, Michele. "NBC and the Network Idea: Defining the 'American System.'" In *NBC: America's Network*, edited by Michele Hilmes. University of California Press, 2007.

Italiaander, Rolf. *Ein Deutscher namens Eckener*. Verlag Friedr. Stadler Konstanz, 1981.

———. *Hugo Eckener: Ein moderner Columbus*. Verlag Friedr. Stadler Konstanz, 1979.

Johnson, Nicholas. "Towers of Babel: The Chaos in Radio Spectrum Utilization and Allocation." *Law and Contemporary Problems* 34 (Summer 1969).

Keating, Ann Durkin, ed. *Chicago Neighborhoods and Suburbs: A Historical Guide*. University of Chicago Press, 2008.

Kershaw, Ian. *Hitler: 1889–1936, Hubris*. Allen Lane, 1998.

———. *Hitler: 1936–1945, Nemesis*. Allen Lane, 2000.

Kolm, Suzanne L. "'Who Says It's a Man's World?' Women's Work and Travel in the First Decades of Flight." In *The Airplane in American Culture*, edited by D. A. Pisano. University of Michigan Press, 2003.

Kromm, Dennis R. "Homecoming." In *Compex: Combined Philatelic Exhibition of Chicagoland, Incorporated, Commemorating the 50th Anniversary of the Last Flight of the Hindenburg*. May 1987.

Larcati, Arturo. "Eine Jugend in Wien: Alberto Stringas Freundschaft mit Stefan Zweig." In *Stefan Zweig: Positionen der Moderne*, edited by Martina Wörgötter. Schriftenreihe des Stefan Zweig Centre Salzburg. Könighausen & Neumann, 2017.

Large, David Clay. *Between Two Fires: Europe's Path in the 1930s*. Norton, 1990.

Larson, Bruce L. "Lindbergh's Return to Minnesota, 1927." *Minnesota Historical Society*, Winter 1970.

Larson, Erik. *Dead Wake: The Last Crossing of the Lusitania*. Crown, 2015.

———. *In the Garden of Beasts: Love, Terror and an American Family in Hitler's Berlin.* Crown, 2011.

Law, Ricky W. *Transnational Nazism: Ideology and Culture in German-Japanese Relations, 1919–1936.* Cambridge University Press, 2019.

Levitt, Martin L. "The Development and Politicization of the American Helium Industry, 1917–1940." *Historical Studies in the Physical and Biological Sciences* 30, no. 2 (2000).

Levy, Buddy. *Realm of Ice and Sky: Triumph, Tragedy, and History's Greatest Arctic Rescue.* St. Martin's Press, 2024.

Lewis, Tom. *Empire of the Air: The Men Who Made Radio.* Edward Burlingame Books, 1991.

MacMillan, Margaret. *Paris 1919: Six Months That Changed the World.* Random House, 2002.

Mayer, Harold M., and Richard C. Wade. *Chicago: Growth of a Metropolis.* University of Chicago Press, 1969.

McCarthy, Michael. *The Hidden Hindenburg: The Untold Story of the Tragedy, the Nazi Secrets, and the Quest to Rule the Skies.* Lyons Press, 2020.

McDonough, Frank. *The Hitler Years: Triumph, 1933–1939.* St. Martin's Press, 2019.

Meyer, Henry Cord. *Airshipmen, Businessmen, and Politics: 1890–1940.* Smithsonian Institution Press, 1991.

Nagorski, Andrew. *Hitlerland: American Eyewitnesses to the Nazi Rise to Power.* Simon & Schuster, 2013.

Neufeld, Michael. *The Rocket and the Reich: Peenemünde and the Coming of the Ballistic Missile Era.* Free Press, 1995.

Norwood, Stephen H. "Legitimating Nazism: Harvard University and the Hitler Regime, 1933–1937." *American Jewish History* 92, no. 2 (June 2004).

Pacyga, Dominic A. *Chicago: A Biography.* University of Chicago Press, 2009.

Overy, Richard J. "German Air Strength 1933 to 1938: A Note." *Historical Journal* 27, no. 2 (1984).

———. *The Dictators: Hitler's Germany, Stalin's Russia.* W. W. Norton, 2004.

Rankin, Robert H. "Goodbye to the Gas Bags." *United States Naval Institute Proceedings* 87, no. 10 (October 1961).

Robinson, Douglas. *Giants in the Sky: A History of Rigid Airships.* University of Washington Press, 1973.

Robinson, Douglas H. *LZ 129 "Hindenburg."* Famous Aircraft Series. Arco, 1964.

Ronald, Susan. *Hitler's Aristocrats: The Secret Power Players in Britain and America Who Supported the Nazis, 1923–1941.* St. Martin's Press, 2023.

Rose, Alexander. *Empires of the Sky.* Random House, 2020.

Ross, Steven. *Hitler in Los Angeles: How Jews Foiled Nazi Plots Against Hollywood and America.* Bloomsbury, 2017.

Roth, Walter. "Nelson Morris and 'The Yards.'" *Chicago Jewish History* 32, no. 2 (Spring 2008).

Schama, Simon. *Citizens*. Alfred A. Knopf, 1989.

Schroth, Raymond A. *The American Journey of Eric Sevareid*. Steerforth Press, 1995.

Schwartz, A. Brad. *Broadcast Hysteria: Orson Welles's War of the Worlds Broadcast and the Art of Fake News*. Hill & Wang, 2016.

Serling, Robert J. *Eagle: The Story of American Airlines*. St. Martin's Press, 1985.

Sontag, Raymond James. *A Broken World, 1919–1939*. Harper & Row, 1971.

Sterling, Christopher H., and John Michael Kitross. *Stay Tuned: A History of American Broadcasting*. 3rd ed. Lawrence Erlbaum Associates, 2002.

Strobl, Michael. "Writings of History: Authenticity and Self-Censorship in William L. Shirer's *Berlin Diary*," *German Life and Letters* 66, no. 3 (June 17, 2013).

Taylor, A. J. P. *The Origins of the Second World War*. Athenaeum, 1962.

Thomas, Dwight, and David K. Jackson, eds. *The Poe Log: A Documentary Life of Edgar Allan Poe, 1809–1949*. G. K. Hall, 1987.

Tittel, Lutz. *LZ 129 "Hindenburg."* Städisches Bodensee-Museum Friedrichshafen-Zeppelin-Abteilung, 1987.

Toland, John. *Ships in the Sky*. Frederick Muller, 1957.

———. "Terror in the Twilight." *Saturday Evening Post*, December 8, 1956.

———. *The Great Dirigibles: Their Triumphs & Disasters*. Dover, 1972.

Tooze, Adam. *The Wages of Destruction: The Making and Breaking of the Nazi Economy*. Viking, 2006.

Turner, David. "Eine nahe Ferne. Die Briefe Stefan Zweigs an Leonhard Adelt als Ausdruck einer von ihren literarischen Anfängen geprägten Freundschaft." In *Studia austriaca II*, vol. 2, edited by Fausto Cercignani. University of Milan, 1993.

Ullrich, Volker. *Germany 1923: Hyperinflation, Hitler's Putsch, and Democracy in Crisis*. Liveright, 2023.

———. *Hitler: Ascent: 1889–1939*. Alfred A. Knopf, 2016.

van der Linden, F. Robert. *Airlines and Air Mail: The Post Office and the Birth of the Commercial Aviation Industry*. University Press of Kentucky, 2002.

Van Vleck, Jenifer. *Empire of the Air: Aviation and the American Ascendancy*. Harvard University Press, 2013.

von der Goltz, Anna. *Hindenburg: Power, Myth, and the Rise of the Nazis*. Oxford University Press, 2009.

Welky, David. *The Thousand-Year Flood: The Ohio-Mississippi Disaster of 1937*. University of Chicago Press, 2011.

Wick, Steve. *William L. Shirer and the Rise and Fall of the Third Reich*. Palgrave Macmillan, 2011.

Radio Programs, TV Series, Podcasts, and Digital Resources

Gingold, Dan, dir. Joseph Spah and Herbert Morrison interviews in *Catastrophe*. Alan Landsburg Productions, 1980.

Grinberg, Sherman, prod. Joseph Spah interview in *Survival!*, hosted by James Whitmore, 1964. (Courtesy of the Spah family.)

Grossman, Dan. Airships.net: The Graf Zeppelin, Hindenburg, U.S. Navy Airships, and Other Dirigibles. airships.net.

Morrison, Herbert. "The Last Flight of the *Hindenburg*: Complete Original Radio News Broadcast as Witnessed by Herb Morrison" (May 7, 1937). A George Garabedian Production, Mark56 Records, 1974.

Russell, Patrick. *Faces of the Hindenburg*. facesofthehindenburg.blogspot.com.

Williams, Brian, host. *We Interrupt This Broadcast*, podcast. Season 1, episode 1, "The Hindenburg Explosion—'Oh, the Humanity!'—May 6, 1937," July 20, 2021.

Williams, Brian, host. *We Interrupt This Broadcast*, podcast. Season 2, episode 1, "The War of the Worlds: The Original 'Deepfake' of 1938," October 27, 2021.

Wolfinger, Kirk, dir. *NOVA*. Season 48, episode 9, "Hindenburg: The New Evidence." Aired May 19, 2021, on PBS.

CREDITS

Page 1, top left: Library of Congress Prints and Photographs Division, National Photo Company Collection, LC-DIG-npcc-12450

Page 1, top right; Page 2, top left; Page 3, all images; Page 4, center left and bottom right; Page 6, top; Page 7, center right; Page 8, top left; Page 15, bottom right; Page 16, top: ©Zeppelin Museum Friedrichshafen

Page 1, center right: Library of Congress Prints and Photographs Division, Harris & Ewing Collection, LC-DIG-hec-47233

Page 1, bottom left and right: Courtesy of the Shirer family

Page 2, center right and bottom left; Page 4, top left; Page 6, bottom left and right; Page 7, top and bottom left: Harold G. Dick Airships Collection, Wichita State University Libraries, Special Collections and University Archives

Page 5, top; Page 13, bottom: Courtesy of the 87th Air Base Wing Historian

Page 5, center left and bottom left; Page 14, all images: Family of Burtis J. Dolan

Page 5, bottom right: National Archives and Records Administration

Page 8, top right: Courtesy of Ulrich Adelt

Page 8, bottom left and right; Page 9, top left and center right; Page 13, top left; Page 16, bottom right: Courtesy of the Spah family

Page 9, bottom left: Courtesy of the Scottdale Historical Society

Page 10, top left: Courtesy of American Airlines

Page 10, center right; Page 12; Page 15, bottom left: AP Images

Page 10, bottom: Sam Shere, International News Photo (Pictorial Press Ltd/Alamy)

Page 11, top: Arthur Cofod Jr. (Everett Collection, Shutterstock)

Page 11, bottom right: Murray Becker/Associated Press (Everett Collection, Shutterstock)

Page 13, center right: The Magnes Collection of Jewish Art and Life at UC Berkeley

Page 15, top right: Everett Collection, Shutterstock

Page 16, center left: Bettmann (Getty Images)

INDEX